Tools and Techniques for Implementing International E-Trading Tactics for Competitive Advantage

Yurdagül Meral
İstanbul Medipol University, Turkey

A volume in the Advances in E-Business Research (AEBR) Book Series

IGI Global
DISSEMINATOR OF KNOWLEDGE

Published in the United States of America by
IGI Global
Business Science Reference (an imprint of IGI Global)
701 E. Chocolate Avenue
Hershey PA, USA 17033
Tel: 717-533-8845
Fax: 717-533-8661
E-mail: cust@igi-global.com
Web site: http://www.igi-global.com

Library of Congress Cataloging-in-Publication Data

Names: Meral, Yurdagul, 1961- editor.
Title: Tools and techniques for implementing international e-trading tactics for competitive advantage / Yurdagul Meral, editor.
Description: Hershey, PA : Business Science Reference, [2019]
Identifiers: LCCN 2019015721| ISBN 9781799800354 (hardcover) | ISBN 9781799800378 (ebook) | ISBN 9781799800361 (softcover)
Subjects: LCSH: Electronic commerce. | Strategic planning. | Personnel management.
Classification: LCC HF5548.32 .T66 2019 | DDC 658.8/72--dc23 LC record available at https://lccn.loc.gov/2019015721

This book is published in the IGI Global book series Advances in E-Business Research (AEBR) (ISSN: 1935-2700; eISSN: 1935-2719)

British Cataloguing in Publication Data
A Cataloguing in Publication record for this book is available from the British Library.

Advances in E-Business Research (AEBR) Book Series

In Lee
Western Illinois University, USA

ISSN:1935-2700
EISSN:1935-2719

Mission

Technology has played a vital role in the emergence of e-business and its applications incorporate strategies. These processes have aided in the use of electronic transactions via telecommunications networks for collaborating with business partners, buying and selling of goods and services, and customer service. Research in this field continues to develop into a wide range of topics, including marketing, psychology, information systems, accounting, economics, and computer science.

The **Advances in E-Business Research (AEBR) Book Series** provides multidisciplinary references for researchers and practitioners in this area. Instructors, researchers, and professionals interested in the most up-to-date research on the concepts, issues, applications, and trends in the e-business field will find this collection, or individual books, extremely useful. This collection contains the highest quality academic books that advance understanding of e-business and addresses the challenges faced by researchers and practitioners.

Coverage

- Semantic Web
- E-business strategies
- Outsourcing and e-business technologies
- Social Network
- Mobile Business Models
- E-business technology investment strategies
- E-business systems integration
- Virtual Collaboration
- Web 2.0
- Economics of e-business

IGI Global is currently accepting manuscripts for publication within this series. To submit a proposal for a volume in this series, please contact our Acquisition Editors at Acquisitions@igi-global.com or visit: http://www.igi-global.com/publish/.

The Advances in E-Business Research (AEBR) Book Series (ISSN 1935-2700) is published by IGI Global, 701 E. Chocolate Avenue, Hershey, PA 17033-1240, USA, www.igi-global.com. This series is composed of titles available for purchase individually; each title is edited to be contextually exclusive from any other title within the series. For pricing and ordering information please visit http://www.igi-global.com/book-series/advances-business-research/37144. Postmaster: Send all address changes to above address.

Titles in this Series

For a list of additional titles in this series, please visit:
https://www.igi-global.com/book-series/advances-business-research/37144

Business Transformations in the Era of Digitalization
Karim Mezghani (Al Imam Mohammad Ibn Saud Islamic University, Saudi Arabia & University of Sfax, Tunisia) and Wassim Aloulou (Al Imam Mohammad Ibn Saud Islamic University, Saudi Arabia & University of Sfax, Tunisia)
Business Science Reference • copyright 2019 • 360pp • H/C (ISBN: 9781522572626) • US $215.00 (our price)

E-Manufacturing and E-Service Strategies in Contemporary Organizations
Norman Gwangwava (Botswana International University of Science and Technology, Botswana) and Michael Mutingi (Namibia University of Science and Technology, Namibia)
Business Science Reference • copyright 2018 • 366pp • H/C (ISBN: 9781522536284) • US $205.00 (our price)

Multi-Sided Platforms (MSPs) and Sharing Strategies in the Digital Economy Emerging Research and Opportunities
Sergey Yablonsky (St. Petersburg University, Russia)
Business Science Reference • copyright 2018 • 192pp • H/C (ISBN: 9781522554578) • US $165.00 (our price)

Crowdfunding and Sustainable Urban Development in Emerging Economies
Umar G. Benna (Ahmadu Bello University, Nigeria) and Abubakar U. Benna (Durham University, UK)
Business Science Reference • copyright 2018 • 343pp • H/C (ISBN: 9781522539520) • US $205.00 (our price)

Improving E-Commerce Web Applications Through Business Intelligence Techniques
G. Sreedhar (Rashtriya Sanskrit Vidyapeetha (Deemed University), India)
Business Science Reference • copyright 2018 • 363pp • H/C (ISBN: 9781522536468) • US $225.00 (our price)

Optimizing Current Practices in E-Services and Mobile Applications
Mehdi Khosrow-Pour, D.B.A. (Information Resources Management Association, USA)
Business Science Reference • copyright 2018 • 366pp • H/C (ISBN: 9781522550266) • US $210.00 (our price)

Mobile Platforms, Design, and Apps for Social Commerce
Jean-Éric Pelet (ESCE International Business School, Paris, France)
Business Science Reference • copyright 2017 • 411pp • H/C (ISBN: 9781522524694) • US $215.00 (our price)

The Internet of Things in the Modern Business Environment
In Lee (Western Illinois University, USA)
Business Science Reference • copyright 2017 • 340pp • H/C (ISBN: 9781522521044) • US $205.00 (our price)

IGI Global
DISSEMINATOR OF KNOWLEDGE

701 East Chocolate Avenue, Hershey, PA 17033, USA
Tel: 717-533-8845 x100 • Fax: 717-533-8661
E-Mail: cust@igi-global.com • www.igi-global.com

Table of Contents

Detailed Table of Contents

The changes brought about by trends such as globalization, technological developments, and knowledge-based economy, and the speed of these changes are forcing the enterprises to create more innovative ways of doing business and business processes. This rapid change has also affected and altered human resources departments' way of business. In this chapter, the changes in human resources management functions and applications with the effect of technology during this time have been explained. In addition, the electronic human resources management process and its applications, which have been more important as a result of developed human resources technology, are examined and presented in this chapter.

The aim of the study is to measure the effectiveness of commercial banks in the agricultural financing in Turkey. For this purpose, 10 different criteria are identified based on five different SERVQUAL perspectives. Moreover, 10 different Turkish deposit banks traded on BIST are taken into consideration in the analysis process. Interval type-2 fuzzy DEMATEL (IT2 FDEMATEL) method is used to weight the dimensions and criteria. Also, deposit banks are ranked with interval type-2 fuzzy TOPSIS (IT2 FTOPSIS). The findings show that flexibility of needs, branch availability, and qualified personnel are the most important criteria for agricultural financing. Hence, it is recommended that banks design a system in which customers can access the banks in flexible times related to the agricultural financing. Another important recommendation is that banks open new branches near the agricultural regions so that farmers can reach the banking services easily. Furthermore, banks should also improve their personnel for agricultural issues with necessary trainings.

The purpose of this study is to search for the difference between traditional marketing and electronic marketing on tourism. The data is based on empirical researches and literature reviews. The study is based on descriptive analysis. An overview of this study indicates that hotels and mostly visitors prefer to use an online reservation system and online travel agencies. This study provides tourism suppliers with ways to use electronic marketing and communication with visitors. Also, tourism suppliers are able to prepare marketing strategies based on visitor choice to use while travel planning.

Electronic commerce (e-commerce) has started to become an important explanatory component of economic growth via innovations in information technology in recent years. Studies within this framework show that countries that invest more in e-commerce have reached higher growth rates. In this regard, this chapter has examined the relationship between e-commerce represented by two sub-components as fixed and mobile-cellular telephone subscriptions and economic growth for chosen countries (BRICS and Turkey) with 2000-2016 annual data by using Panel VAR, impulse response analysis, and variance decomposition. Results of the study show that economic growth and e-commerce are related. These results suggest that countries that want to increase their economic growth rate should focus on policies to increase e-commerce volume.

Internet technology can be used not only in commercial applications but also in the implementation and distribution of public services like education and health, making e-commerce essential not only for the business world but also for all of society. Thus, companies can take advantage of internet opportunities in order to develop their strategies in e-commerce environment, creating working groups by bringing together employees in different geographical locations with tools such as newsgroups, communication rooms, etc., benefiting from customer suggestions. Therefore, it is important to examine and analyze the companies that have commercial activities in e-commerce environments in terms of strategic management. From a strategic point of view, the aim of companies should be to increase their activities by influencing their existing customers and continuously gaining new customers within the e-commerce environment.

Technological advances and correspondingly the spreading usage of the Internet have significantly changed commerce, and also the concept of money has become more abstract. Customers with the help of the technological advances don't have the necessity of cash money, and consumers/firms tend towards alternative payment methods. At this point, electronic commerce (e-commerce) web sites have started to use block chaining payment methods. In this digital world, new payment technologies have started to spread far and wide thanks to fast improvements in payment technologies, and they offer different options in payment methods. Each electronic payment (e-payment) system has some advantages; however, each of them has some disadvantages as well. The aim of this study is to investigate the e-payment systems which are different from traditional payment methods.

Documentation plays a very important role in international trade. Information technology has changed practises in international trade as well. In this chapter, international rules of electronic presentation of documents under documentary credit are defined to guide importers and exporters. This will enable them to speed up transactions to conduct their business as per these rules. Paperback presentation and electronic presentation international rules differences are explained. Electronic presentation will help import export management to facilitate transactions which will increase international trade volume. It is recommended that electronic presentation will help them to speed up their transactions. In the long run, electronic presentation will be cheaper compared to paper presentation and much safer.

Today, the Internet has become a frequently-used tool in trading information, products, and services. Together with the transformations in the Internet, new media, and mobile technologies, the retail sector is also developing its service area. With the development of mobile technologies, retail giants determine the expectations and needs of their consumers in a good and fast way with artificial intelligence applications. This situation transforms it into purchasing behavior with the reflection of customer preferences on products and increasing personalization. One of the key issues in the mobile retail sector is to make the purchasing behavior permanent by ensuring the satisfaction of consumers. In the study, Getir application, a mobile marketing application was analyzed with focus group research technique performed on university students selected in accordance with certain criteria. As a result of the research, the availability, awareness, and satisfaction status of the participants on Getir application were revealed.

Electronic trade has a key role for today's companies with help of technology affecting marketing environment. The emergence of the Internet has led to huge changes in both the production and strategy channels and the consumer's purchasing process. Previous studies from different contexts examine electronic trade focusing on different aspects on concept. An integrative approach combining theory with cases can help to a better understanding of electronic trade and competitive markets. This study aims to examine electronic trading decision making with digital marketing approach. The study identifies a three-step marketing plan for competitive advantage about electronic trading. First step includes identifying standards, seasonalities, and anomalies related to market. Second step continues with further evaluation of market environment by including sentiment analysis and network analysis cases. Third step goes further with predicting cases by focusing on future. The study also contains solutions and recommendations, future research directions, and conclusion sections.

Electronic commerce and electronic business concepts are highly researched in recent management literature. Network economy has revealed e-commerce, a new trade route that is carried out over the interlinked computers and mobile devices. E-commerce is a method used by almost all businesses that are physically processing. Therefore, there should be a significant distinction between e-business and e-commerce. With the development of e-commerce, new ways of doing business have emerged. Thus, many e-commerce companies have emerged, traditional businesses have started trading in electronic networks, and new business models have begun to be created in digital environments. In order to understand how e-businesses make money, many business models have been studied. For this reason, the concept of business model in the new economy and the transformation of business models into e-business models are examined. In line with this, it is aimed in this chapter to examine e-businesses, to clarify e-business models, and to explain e-commerce types and e-business model types in detail, with examples.

This chapter was written to demonstrate the effect of consumer emotion on online purchasing behavior. According to the results obtained from 418 data, it was observed that both positive and negative emotions impacted online buying behavior. In this context, as the positive emotions of the online consumer increases, the frequency of purchases increases, but as the negative emotions of the online consumer increases, the frequency of purchases decreases. In addition, user interface quality, product information quality, service information quality, site awareness, security perception, information satisfaction, and relational benefit factors are factors that negatively affect consumers emotionally in purchasing online. On the other hand, only product information quality, user interface quality, and security perception factors positively affect emotions of online consumers.

In a digital transformation environment, most businesses shift towards e-business and encounter businesses and customer interaction on digital channels. Information Technology renders data access and processing more efficient, and use of customer data in decision making has become a focal interest area that attracts researchers. Customer data is a relevant subject for numerous studies in Data Mining. In this chapter, Association Rule Mining has been utilized to extract purchase behavior patterns with a multilevel approach. Basket data obtained from an online retailer was analyzed to discover purchase behaviors with a focus on category and brand attributes of products. Brands and categories purchased together frequently were discovered. Brand and category-wise association rules were also presented in the results. The analysis differs from the majority of prior analyses, by referring to the category and brand attributes in basket data. It could be noted that generalized rules obtained with this approach might prove useful in recommending new items of existing brands or categories.

Recent decades brought about astonishing technologies that affected organizations in several ways. With the latest developments, organizations earned the capabilities to carry out their functions more efficiently and rapidly. Having several tasks affecting both interior and exterior customers, human resources departments also benefited from these technological developments. Owing to the digital revolution, e-HR emerged as a new way of practicing HRM activities with the latest web-based and computer-based tools and applications. These applications eased the work of HR professionals and served them the opportunity to focus on their core work, namely strategic human resources activities rather than procedural paperwork of the department. With a holistic and integrative approach, this digital transformation in HRM has been dispersed among all services in human resources including recruitment, career management, training and development, performance management, and compensation.

E-commerce brings companies and customers together in an exchange market environment, beyond any physical, cultural, and legal boundaries, and on an unimaginable scale, which was considered to be technically impossible before. The companies' online facilities have been improved and become accessible to everyone through smart phones, tablets, etc. as the web pages and social networks started to direct individuals towards e-commerce. E-commerce not only raises economic concerns related to competition and pricing, but also reveals new social and environmental threats that can be quite widespread and viral. Several studies have been conducted to examine the transformation of traditional business models into e-businesses, the impact of e-commerce businesses on traditional business activities, or opportunities brought by technological innovations. For this reason, the effects of the competitive strategies will be explained in terms of ensuring sustainable competitive advantage within e-commerce companies.

The aim of this study is to evaluate the customer satisfaction for mobile applications in the Turkish banking industry. For this purpose, the last 500 customer comments of 24 different Turkish deposit banks' mobile applications are analyzed with data mining approach. In this process, the most frequent one keyword, two keywords and three keywords are identified, and the most important dimensions are classified into four different categories. Secondly, IT2 fuzzy DEMATEL methodology is considered to weight these dimensions. The findings show that operational and usability are the most important dimensions regarding the customer satisfaction in mobile applications. This situation explains that customers give importance to the quality and variability of the services given by the mobile applications. Hence, it is recommended that different services, such as credit card payment and money transferring should be provided in these applications by the banks. Another important point is that these applications should be designed effectively so that the customer can easily make their operations.

Preface

International trade in other words trade of goods and services between different countries has been affected from Internet like all other sectors. With the evolution of traditional international trade into electronic international trade, the tools and techniques have been changed as well. Internet has changed nearly everything in our lives as well as trading. Hence, electronic commerce (e-commerce) is defined by the European Union as selling goods and services over the Internet. Now a buyer can order products in a different country via internet, can pay online via Internet and the product will be shipped to be delivered from another country. Cross-border e-commerce, in other words, e-export and e-import, cover online international trade using Internet. It refers to the purchase and sale of products through online stores through national borders. In cross-border e-commerce, buyers and sellers do not reside in the same country, usually do not use the same currency, speak different languages and are subject to different jurisdictions.

This book consists of 15 chapters covering electronic trading from different aspects. Chapter 1 and Chapter 13 focus on digital human resources practices, web-based, computer-based tools and applications, covering human resources management changes with internet. Chapter 2 uses IT2 fuzzy decision-making model in e-banking industry and Chapter 15 uses Fuzzy Dematel model for evaluating customer satisfaction for mobile applications in banking sector as well.

Internet has changed service trade in our lives like tourism as well. Chapter 3 defines how life has changed in tourism sector, which is a very important aspect of international trade services and how Internet has changed traditional process to digital processes like online booking. Traditional payment system has been changed completely with electronic version of payments with internet now and the electronic payment systems are detailed with differences are given in Chapter 6 which is followed by Chapter 7 of which the electronic presentation of shipping documents in documentary payment system are explained.

Chapter 4 is the study about the relationship between economic growth and e-commerce, where Chapter 5 is examining effects of strategic management on e-commerce companies. Internet has changed marketing completely with mobile marketing, and with a study of an application in Turkey is detailed in Chapter 8, followed with Chapter 9 which is also about digital marketing approach with cases and e-trading decision making.

Chapter 10 explains the distinction between e-business and e-commerce, where purchasing behaviour and shopping behaviour is investigated in Chapter 11 and Chapter 12, and Chapter 14 examines e-commerce companies from the point of competitive strategies.

International trade is affected by using electronic media (Internet). Importers and exporters in the world market are found via Internet. It is faster, easier, and reliable to reach new markets via Internet if handled professionally and products and services in electronic environment can be marketed in the international market easily as well. International electronic trade in other words e-export and e-import can be defined shortly as international trade via Internet.

International trade itself being a very popular topic itself, with digital era has increased attention of different researchers and publishers, these publications generally focus on either technical aspects like site building, others cover digital marketing, digital advertising and consumer behaviour. However, electronic international trade, that is e-export and e-import cover all these aspects in addition covers not only goods, but covers services like tourism, e-human resources applications along with electronic documentation and electronic presentation and electronic payments, digital marketing, digital advertising as well. This book covering said different aspects of international electronic trade is believed to be interesting to all parties involved in international electronic trade as given below. Target Audience and potential users of this book are defined below.

- Researchers
- Academicians
- Exporters
- Importers
- Transporters
- Banks for International Payments
- International Logictics Companies
- International Digital Marketing Companies
- Policy Makers
- Government Officials
- Customs Officials
- Students in the concerned fields
- Members of Chambers of Commerce
- Top Managers of the Companies

It is believed that this book makes an important contribution to the related literature and will attract attentions of related parties involved in electronic international trade, in e-export and e-import of goods and services via Internet between two different countries.

Chapter 1
The Role of E-HRM Practices on Digital Era

Nurten Polat Dede
Istanbul Medipol University, Turkey

ABSTRACT

The changes brought about by trends such as globalization, technological developments, and knowledge-based economy, and the speed of these changes are forcing the enterprises to create more innovative ways of doing business and business processes. This rapid change has also affected and altered human resources departments' way of business. In this chapter, the changes in human resources management functions and applications with the effect of technology during this time have been explained. In addition, the electronic human resources management process and its applications, which have been more important as a result of developed human resources technology, are examined and presented in this chapter.

INTRODUCTION

The increasing competition with globalization in today's business world and the developments in communication technologies push the enterprises to develop effective working styles and to adapt rapidly to the changes. Changes in company strategies and business practices created by globalization, supply and demand situation of labor force, current labor force situation, developments in technology, HRM practices of competitors, economic developments, changes in legislation, changes in employee expectations, cost reduction expectations, mergers and acquisitions have created the need for the restructuring of HRM processes and it became necessary fort he HRM units to undertake more strategic HRM roles (Cook, 1999; Bondarouk & Ruel, 2009; Marler, 2009).

The changing roles of HR managers foresee a transition from the realization of traditional operational activities to the realization of long-term strategic activities. The HR managers are increasingly taking advantage of the expertise and opinions of the senior management in strategic decisions, providing support function instead of being excluded from the strategic decisions of the organization (Barney & Wright, 1998). On the other hand, the strategic and traditional roles of the HR manager cannot coexist.

DOI: 10.4018/978-1-7998-0035-4.ch001

For this reason, it is envisaged that traditional roles will be carried out by creating integrable HR service centers or by external sources (Ulrich, 1996; Caldwell, 2003).

As a result, the responsibilities of the HR manager are narrowed in scope; however, they have more strategic and higher responsibilities. In other words, it is important that the HR manager's main roles in the personnel management period are separated from the changing current roles; It is envisaged that the HR manager will be valued in a position closer to the top management and in a more strengthened position and will be able to identify and identify the organization with the strategy and the desired values (Legge, 1989; Ulrich, 1998).

The efforts to restructure the HRM processes to provide added value to the operational results have revealed restructuring efforts involving the inclusion of information technology in the processes (Iqbal, Ahmad, Raziq, & Borini, 2019). Accordingly, HR departments are focused on reducing the intensity of the transaction volume by using information technology.

In this process, information technologies and human resources management experts worked together to create software and systems that transfer human resources information and decision-making systems from personnel files to computers, and played an important role in implementing E-HRM applications by restructuring HRM processes (Hall & Moritz, 2003).

In the Human Resources Management (HRM) processes, computers and internet has made it possible for human resources departments to assume more strategic roles to contribute to the operational results. Recruitment, success assessment, in-house transfers, remuneration, work security, personnel affairs, training and development, performance measurements, rewarding and punishment management processes were transferred to electronic systems, and it was possible to manage these processes with a holistic approach. In addition, the bureaucracy in the management of the human resources processes in enterprises has been reduced and instead of the manual methods that are performed inadequately, with more efficient HRM processes time and cost savings have been ensured. This has made it easier for business managers and HR experts to spend more time concentrating on strategic issues than on routine jobs (Cook, 1999; Ulrich & Lake,1990; Snell, 1994).

In the following sections of the study, the concept, scope and importance of electronic human resources management, the characteristics of electronic human resources management, the role of electronic human resources in HRM processes, the important effects of human resources management departments in assuming more strategic roles, the advantages and disadvantages of electronic human resources management in terms of enterprises will be explained extensively.

THE CONCEPT AND CONCEPT OF ELECTRONIC HUMAN RESOURCES MANAGEMENT

The concept of E-HRM was first used in the late 1990s with the concept of e-commerce, which became widespread in order to carry out commercial transactions (Hall and Moritz, 2003). E-HRM is defined as the effective use of internet technology-based systems in designing and implementing the human resources strategies, policies and practices of the enterprise (Sylvester, Bamidele & Oluyemi, 2015). In other words, e-HRM can be defined as the transfer of human resources systems to the computer environment by using communication technologies. E-HRM concept, is expressed as the implementation of the human resources management systems via the Internet, intranet and networks, or directly through the use of these channels (Ruël, Bondarouk, & Looise, 2004).

The main aim of E-HRM is to create more favorable conditions for harmonizing the organizational strategies and objectives and HRM targets and strategies. When we look at the previous studies in this field, it is seen that the concept of E-HRM is expressed in the literature with different concepts and it is not agreed on a common concept. Examples include web-based HRM, human resource information system (HRIS), virtual HRM and business-to-employee (B2E) systems (Strohmeier, 2007). These concepts are close to each other but point to separate functions.

Virtual HRM refers to networks that mediate the delivery of human resources activities within the business and to external actors in a virtual environment, without individuals in the Human Resources (HR) departments. E-HRM refers to the implementation of human resources activities through the internet and human resources department and includes less advanced technological applications (Lepak & Snell, 1998). Web-Based HRM is a concept that emphasizes direct internet networks. E-HRM is integrated with internet networks as well as additional technologies such as systems like ERP, LOGO etc. (Ruël, Bondarouk & Looise, 2004).

The Human Resources Information System (HRIS), the sub-system of E-HRM, is a special form of information system established for the need of human resource management and is one of the first systems that can be seen as a form of Electronic Human Resource Management in an organization. It is expressed as a systematic procedure for collecting, storing, maintaining, receiving and verifying the data that an organization needs for human resources management (Venterink, 2017). The users of HRIS are mostly human resources department personnel. The HRMS system aims to improve the business processes of the human resources department and to achieve more efficient results in business processes. E-HRM is designed for the personnel who are outside the human resources department and the employees and managers of the organization. (Ruël et al., 2004). Briefly, E-HRM enables human resources applications to be used by organization employees without having any place and time limit outside the organization (Celep & Fındıklı, 2018).

Human resource information systems (HRMS) and e-HRM are different from each other. HRMS is mainly directed to the HR department itself. The users of these systems are HR professionals. This type of system aims to improve the processes within the HR department. Processes such as payment of wages, storage of employees' work contracts and registration of necessary files for web sites are covered by HRMS. The contribution of HRMS to the objectives of business units is indirect. With this feature, e-HRM refers to a technological structure. HRMS is not a technology on its own, but the integration of HR processes with information and communication technologies. From this point of view, e-HRM, web-based HRM and IT-based HRM practices can be considered as development and stages that facilitate the functioning of HRMIS (Ruël, Magalhães, & Chiemeke, 2011).

Finally, B2E deals with HR practices for internal actors of the organization, such as department managers and HR experts. The E-HRM includes practices that are open to all relevant actors, such as job applicants, HR consultants, other than the employees of the institution (Huang, Jin, &Yang, 2004).

E-HRM after the explanations of the differences between similar concepts frequently used in literature related to E-HRM; In particular, information technology can be defined as the application of at least two individual or more users to both network and support systems to enable them to perform HR activities on a shared platform (Stronhmeier & Piazza, 2011).

The inclusion of human resources information technologies in HRM processes and issues within the scope of traditional human resources management can be solved in a shorter time and with less effort in electronic environment. Quick access to the right data can be provided.

E-HRM PURPOSE

It is seen that most of the e-human resources management activities are carried to the web environment in order to provide effective and productive human resource applications for the employees and provide the information needed for the organization. Thanks to E-human resources management activities, it is at the forefront of features such as reducing stationery, saving time and reducing costs (Güler, 2006).

The strategic benefits of e-human resources for businesses are as follows (Ruël, Bondarouk, & Looise, 2004; Öğe, 2004; Güler, 2006; Nivlouei, 2014):

- Providing organizations with effective and efficient human resources applications and communicating the expected information about the organization.
- Providing the appropriate environment for human resources employees in order to create and implement strategic human resources service.
- Using motivators such as e-mails, greeting messages to make employees feel special and valuable through electronic systems to improve the motivation and talents of the employees within the organization.
- Increasing the quality of services offered.
- Increasing the communication within the organization with employees provides an increase in the possibility of producing and implementing new ideas.
- Reduce internal cost and administrative procedures.
- Employees share their ideas and suggestions with their colleagues in the organization, for example due to the use of internal blogs. Providing an increase in the information shared in the organization and creating a basis for human resources within the organization.
- Reducing the number of employees and human resources department employees in E-Human Resources, as it creates an alternative to meet the needs of the employees in the intranet.
- E-HR, human resource management in human resources development and support to members of the organization in the career planning process and to provide new opportunities.
- In this new model, we contribute to the separation of the organizational practices from the centralization in the classical understanding and to enable the creative and the subordinates to act together in accordance with the organisation's objectives.
- International organizations to manage those who work in different geographical locations using the same system in a universal way.
- Ensuring the institutionalization of enterprises at higher levels.
- Harmonizing the skills of employees within the organization in line with the needs of the organization and providing organizational flexibility.
- Designing the trainings to be given to the employees according to job descriptions and skill requirements of individuals.
- Ensure that more informed decisions are taken.
- Ensuring the active participation of employees in applications through EHRM and thus increasing employee satisfaction.
- Being able to focus on the issues that create value through e-HRM activities without depending on the location and time zone, without disrupting the routine work processes of the organization.
- Providing information about the important human resources events of the organization and the news in the organization.

- Minimization of response time for human resources applications.
- Establishing a flexible human resources model to adapt to the globalizing world and labor needs.

E-HRM STAGES

Nowadays, in the changing economy with technology, human resources management develops electronic solutions through some stages (LeTart, 1998). These stages are as given below:

Information Sharing: The first step of human resources is sharing information within the organization. The activities at this stage are the one-way transfer of information within the organization to the employee within the organization. Most commonly used applications in information sharing; The organizational chart of the organization, employee's job description and responsibilities, areas of activity, organizational history, organizational policies, organizational news and bulletins, employee lists and contact information.

Database Creation: It is a database that includes staff's information such as demographic information, working area and working hours, duties and responsibilities, date of employment, premium and salary increase, health records and retirement status.

Basic Human Resources Transactions: It is the activity of transferring the internal information to the electronic environment and updating the changes in full time. These activities include the renewal of personal information of the personnel and the transfer of changes such as new assignments of the personnel to the database.

Complex Human Resources Transactions: Analysis of the responsibilities of personnel, evaluation of data, investigation of compliance of business processes, classification of multidimensional operations and applications according to various variables within this scope.

Network-Based Human Resources Transactions: The staff and managers of the organization are provided with the opportunity to use human resources processes via computer without using paper or administrative support. When integrated with in-house networks and non-organizational networks, the scope of human resources management expands as well

With the rapid development of technology, Cloud-Based applications yıl applications have been used since 2010. With the transition to the cloud-based information system, there is an increase in the use of mobile applications and social media by organizations. For example, shifting the choice of potential elements to an electronic election field with the increasing use of social media (Johnson, Lukaszweski, & Stone, 2015).

The types of e-HRM applied by organizations are related to some factors. The examples of these factors are like organizations having technology experts who can apply and design information technology systems specific to the organization, having human resources specialists who can do special application and design in the organization, number of employees who have personal computers and the level of computer literacy of the employees within the organization (Hall & Moritz 2003).

Some organizations choose an evolutionary process from simple to complex E-HRM types, while some organizations prefer to switch to transformational E-HRM with sudden changes (Ruël, Bondarouk, & Looise, 2004).

In previous studies, E-HRM has been shown to be separated by three main categories (Rajalakshmi & Gomathi, 2016).

Operational E-HRM: It is the e-HRM application that performs administrative functions such as salary and payroll management. The most significant goal of operational e-HRM is to increase the efficiency and efficiency of human resources management with automation and supports.

Relational E-HRM: The function of the organizational process in the organization deals with organizational functions such as employment, staff performance management and training and development activities. Relational E-HRM aims to improve the relations of its stakeholders and service delivery. In addition, it aims to support the business process through training, employment and performance management.

Transformational E-HRM: Includes the strategic function of human resources. It aims to improve organizational support and strategy management of E-HRM such as information management and strategic redirection.

HUMAN RESOURCES MANAGEMENT PROCESSES AND ELECTRONIC APPLICATIONS

The functions carried out by E-HRM under this heading will be discussed in detail.

E-Organization Structure, Business Processes and Document Tracking

In the process of E-HRM, an enterprise-specific HRIS needs to be developed in order to carry out the organizational structure, business processes and the follow-up of the documentation. In MIS, all information about the organization should be defined first. This information should be defined in the organization's departments, tasks, employee titles, work places and positions, organizational chart, process flows, approval mechanisms, flows that may require documents. In addition, positions should be established for the organization based on these jobs defined to HRMS and the personnel with the position characteristics specified for the positions created should be indicated. All information required to be kept in HRIS should be kept historically. The organization chart of the organization should be formed in line with all these structures. Since all the hierarchical structures created will be kept on the historical basis in the system, the changes and developments within the organization over time are also open to analysis (Daud, 2010).

In line with the rules and procedures set out in the organization, there can be a definition of flow for each work process and document requirements for each phase.

E-Workforce Planning

The organizational prediction that aims to use the best available human resources of the organization and to determine the quality and quantity of human resources for the future is called 'Human Resource Planning' (Şimşek & Öge, 2011). These activities carried out under E-HRM are transferred to electronic environment. In the electronic applications developed, each classification shows the number of personnel required at each level of the work. All analyzes and evaluations, actions and plans made during the human resources planning process are kept electronically. In this way, human resources specialists can reach the required information at the required time, and the presence of existing plans in electronic environment facilitates their control at any time. In addition, these systems provide some benefits in the operational sense via the electronic operation. The work processes that require intensive work of human resources are made to be transferred to electronic environment faster (Emmerichs, Marcum, & Robber, 2004). The number of personnel, reserve and additional personnel that will be required can be determined and the calculations such as total work rate, labor turnover rate, continuity analysis are made more accurately and faster by means of computers, by the system. In addition to the calculations, the information and data obtained can be kept in electronic environment and it is also possible to see the periodic changes and the comparisons (Doğan, 2011).

E-Recruitment System

Nowadays, many companies prefer electronic hiring methods instead of traditional hiring methods due to their advantages such as cost, time and efficiency. In the traditional recruitment process, while interdependent chaining steps are followed, e-recruitment processes are simultaneous online processes. The relationship of the candidate pools with the internet applications of the enterprises has made the electronic recruitment activities more integrated. The benefits of integrated recruitment systems have been accepted and widely used by enterprises (Sylva & Mol, 2009). Electronic recruitment is the use of electronic tools which efficiently fill open positions within the company (Lee, 2005). Using corporate websites, companies can create unlimited job vacancies for the employees they need and create a candidate pool with low cost. The recruitment process decreased by 75% compared to previous periods and the costs decreased by 95% (Cappelli, 2001).

E-recruitment process stages (Lee, 2005):

- Definition of open positions.
- Notification and approval of job vacancies on career portals.
- Announcement of the job on the internet.
- Announcement of the need for open position to potential candidates in electronic environment.
- Enabling current announcements to be seen by job seekers.
- Job seekers evaluating themselves whether or not the position is suitable for them.
- The applicant's application via system who intends to apply for a job.
- The HRM department's evaluation of the pool in the virtual environment.
- Job interview by human resources authorities.
- Job offers and contracts.

Electronic hiring seems to be an effective process where some activities are performed simultaneously, compared to the traditional recruitment method. (Lee, 2005).

Business advertisements that companies announce through their corporate websites provide low cost for companies and provide easier access within job seekers (Körfez, 2008).

Companies can create a corporate resume pool in a single database by taking recruitment processes from different sources such as consultancy firms, career sites, other than corporate websites. The data such as interviews, examinations, interviews and evaluations with the candidates to be hired can be monitored historically. Companies are able to follow in-house evaluations via electronic media with features such as reporting and scoring according to the open position criteria on the candidate pools they create. The candidate pool can be taken into the register for further positions in the future. In electronic recruitment, collection of resume data in a virtual pool provides productivity with labor, time and cost savings (Barber, 2006).

The employees who want to apply to positions of which the companies hire through their websites should consider well whether they meet the criteria in the job description. If the processes carried out to save time, are not evaluated well, there is a risk of not selection the the appropriate candidate. If the appropriate employee is not selected, it is necessary to repeat these processes (Bonti & Cori, 2004).

Looking at the rapid change, it is estimated that electronic recruitment will be used more widely in the years to come and the competition will increase among the human resources sites. It is clear that e-recruitment seems to be an effective solution when it is taken into consideration that businesses want to provide the labor force that will provide them with added value in a short time (Körfez, 2008).

E-Personal Information, Payroll Accounts, Leaves and Exit Procedures System

Payroll and personnel transactions from the activities that form the basis of Human Resources Management have been transferred to the electronic environment within the scope of E-HRM. In this respect, firstly, each personnel defines personal registration numbers and all human resources processes related to the person are monitored with this number. Personal information of the personnel, education details, contact information, demographic details like date of birth etc, address information, work experiences, foreign language information, family and child information, driver's certificates, official institutions are included in the personal information of the records. In the same way, the demands of the personnel regarding the excuses, paid and unpaid leaves, and the right of permission are made through electronic information systems. However, in the classical permission management applications, all registries like including employee's leave of absence requests written by hand and other details were kept kept in the personnel files.

With the electronic application system, employees can easily follow their entitlements in electronic environment according to the labor law, and they can send their leave of absence like vacation requests to the system by entering the location and time information. It is easily seen on the electronic information system by the managers of the unit when they request for vacation leave etc, at what date they are allowed to use and how much unused permissions they have. Time and paper savings were ensured along with the electronic permission application, and the managers started to make their business plans more effective and the problems caused by keeping the employee's permit/vacation information in the personnel files were eliminated (Sylva & Mol, 2009; Allahverdi, 2006).

E-Job Evaluation and E-Remuneration System

With the development of human resources management information technologies, wage management and business valuation processes of enterprises have been transferred to the electronic environment. E-Pricing; it means collecting, storing, processing, analyzing and using the information and data required for the establishment of the compensation systems of the organization on electronic media. The electronic environment provides both time and cost advantages to businesses in collecting the data analysis data that form the basis of wage systems and other HRM systems. For example, if the business prefers to use the survey method as a business analysis, the questionnaires are easily delivered to all operating personnel and the employees' answers about the business information can be obtained more quickly. HRM departments can analyze and summarize the data they have obtained and finally prepare job descriptions for all positions in the enterprise.

Moreover, the e-remuneration system also facilitates the conversion of business analysis data into job evaluation points. The fee research information obtained from the web pages of different institutions and organizations can be easily integrated with the job evaluation points. Thus, these data are used to determine wage degrees and to create wage systems of companies (Dulebohn & Marler, 2005). HRM departments can design and manage wage systems efficiently and effectively using web-based software systems with e-pricing. HRM departments can provide more effective services and provide necessary information to employees in electronic environment.

The e-remuneration system allows businesses to process all kinds of fees faster. It can be solved without any problems in the system such as installment payments, personnel with special insurance, advance transactions as well as wage transactions. According to the legislation in force, information requested by social insurance institutions, tax offices, employment agencies or electronic forms are automatically generated by the system. All forms and reports are established in accordance with the standards set by the institutions. The data related to the salary payroll of the personnel can be obtained from the regional offices and mobile workers in a safe way via internet.

E-remuneration also offers advantages in terms of providing fair wages for employees in the same positions in business and other businesses. The benefits such as pension, insurance and health services provided to the personnel can be managed more effectively in electronic environment.

Through the use of information technologies, it is possible to identify the needs of employees by obtaining the opinions of the employees and to offer personalized, flexible side benefits to the employees. Personalized benefits increase employees' commitment to business and increase their motivation. One of the most important components of HRM practices, which is expressed as high commitment work practices, increases employee loyalty and performance, is the wage systems of firms.

E-Performance Management System

Performance management is a goal-oriented process to maximize the efficiency of organizational processes, employees, teams, and ultimately the organization. Each employee's efforts in performance management should focus on the achievement of strategic objectives. In recent years, performance management has become the biggest contributor to organizational effectiveness. An effective performance management system should be the responsibility of everyone in the organization, starting with the chairman of the executive committee; because an organization ignoring the performance system can not progress, can not develope. Performance evaluation is an official system for the examination and evaluation of task performance as an individual or as a team (Mondy & Mondy, 2012).

Developing information technologies enable performance management and evaluation applications to be realized in electronic environment. Thanks to electronic performance evaluation systems, all data on performance interviews, reconciliations, standards, objectives, performance problems and evaluation results are kept in electronic data centers, and it has provided time to human resources professionals in terms of accessing data and time. For the transparent and objective decision-making and implementation of the performance development process, both the employee and the manager should start with these data. The use of information technologies enables the performance evaluation system to ensure traceability, impartiality and continuity in a fast and easy way (Karcıoğlu & Öztürk, 2009).

Electronic Performance Management Systems (e-PMS) facilitate performance measurements by keeping records of certain data such as completed work quantities, error rates, time spent on tasks. E-PMS facilitates managers to give quick feedback to the employees. For example, in multi-assessments or 360-degree evaluations through intranet networks in enterprises, all assessors are asked to perform an online performance assessment of the person to be assessed by e-mail. Afterwards, the evaluation data are combined to provide feedback to the evaluated person and enable them to improve their performance (Stone, Stone-Romero, & Lukaszewski, 2003). E-performance is an application that is adapted to the needs of institutions and provides a fast and effective solution to the performance evaluation process. In this system, evaluations are made by keeping privacy and security in the foreground.

Electronic performance is an application that is adapted to the needs of the company and provides an effective and fast solution to the performance evaluation system. In this system, evaluations are made in a virtual environment by taking into consideration the security and confidentiality criteria.

Organizational performance with E-PMS improves employee loyalty and loyalty, increases efficiency, exceeds communication barriers, explains accountability and provides cost advantages. Explains employees' expectations, self-assessment opportunities clarify job responsibilities and contribute to performance improvement, clearly define career paths and improve job satisfaction. Administrators receive immediate feedback on performance and draw attention to the performances of individual employees. Furthermore, there is no need for performance contracts to be rewritten every year. Simply, it can be loaded from the previous period and can be edited (Celep, 2017).

E-Performance management systems enable employees to monitor their developmental levels and to make plans for the future as a result of their knowledge and skill levels, the current status of their work performance and their training. One of the important objectives of E-Performance management systems is the matching of individual and business competencies. The integration of system performance management systems with other HRM systems, it is possible to ensure that the appropriate job-suitable candidate to be placed, and that the development of the competencies of the employees according to the positions to be employed in the future is correctly planned and developed accordingly. In addition, the potential candidate or the current employee's competencies to determine the job, to ensure compliance with the job-person are faciliated. The competencies required for the job are divided into two as compulsory and optional, and the level of compliance of the individuals with the competencies can be determined and statistical comparison can be made. The business and job specific competency inventory can establish the measurement standards of these competencies, and the competence levels of the individual can be compared at the organizational and business level. Thus, the development process of the person is monitored and a competency-based performance evaluation, backup and career planning system is created. Competency data include competence, level of competence, time interval during which competence is achieved, the method where competence is obtained, and the next date to be evaluated (Ghazzawi & Accoumeh, 2014; Daud, 2010).

E-Training and Development

Training and development are initiatives and efforts to improve the current and future performance of employees within the organization by increasing their ability to work. Distance education is the realization of the educational function, which is one of the functions of human resources, independent of time and space. Electronic learning, which is a subset of distance education, consists of processes and applications that involve digital based and virtual spaces. With the support of e-learning information and communication technologies, educational content is realized by transferring the contents of the internet to the electronic media via multimedia tools such as internet, intranet and extranet as well as audio, videotape, interactive television broadcast and CD-ROM (Schank, 2002).

The main difference between distance education and electronic learning is learning through a web network. Electronic learning is the structure in which materials (video, audio, text, multimedia) are used together. These different materials, which are used, adopt being oriented towards employees whose learning styles change. The harmonious use of electronic learning with traditional education methods facilitates the development of the competencies of employees when effectively designed with the support of the right computer technologies (Yazıcı, 2004).

E-training and development activities can be provided at a lower cost than the traditional training and development practices (Schank, 2002). In addition, it improves the quality and effectiveness of training and by making training suitable for the job requirements, learning by applying and accessing information in a timely manner. In addition, personalized learning content increases the motivation of employees with the sense that employees are valued by their institutions and ensures the retention of talented individuals.

Although e-learning has so many benefits to enterprises and employees, staff who are accustomed to training in physical environment may be prejudiced against electronic education, they may experience adaptation problems. Despite such disadvantages, the benefits of electronic training and development cannot be ignored. It is seen that if the changing structure of education is planned well together with technological developments, visionary enterprises can not be indifferent to electronic learning (Aydın, 2016).

E-Career Management and Talent Management

Career is the advancement of an individual in any field of work, gaining experience and skills (Tunçer, 2012). Corporate career management refers to policies and practices that are deliberately designed by institutions to increase the career effectiveness of their employees (Seema & Sujatha, 2013). Career management is the development of the career plan of the people with the career development tools of the enterprise. The main goal of the career management of the company is to increase the productivity of the enterprise and to ensure the development and improvement of the employees in the business, and to plan and shape them in order to meet the needs of the qualified employees in the future (Atay, 2006). Nowadays, employees are analyzing their situation in their businesses and other businesses and making their own career plans. In this case, businesses are giving too much importance to career management.

E-HRM practices provide various tools for employees to manage their careers. Employees can obtain information about the internal and external job opportunities in the system they enter with their personal accounts and benefit from different training opportunities. In this way, E-HRM practices create an environment where employees can receive self-education to acquire new skills (Esen, 2011). Businesses can provide e-career services to their organization employees through their own corporate web pages, as well as other web sites created for the same purpose. The HR portals created by the enterprises benefit from the training and development opportunities for the employees to manage their career ladders, to obtain data for the job opportunities in and out of the company.

With e-career planning, businesses can reach the results of trainings, competencies, career goals and performance measurement obtained by their employees. In this direction, promotions can be made among the candidates who have the required competencies according to the labor force gap within the enterprise (Aydın, 2016).

The career planning model developed in electronic environment and the qualifications of the employees included in the career planning system are evaluated. As a result, the opportunities for promotion and progress within the enterprise are determined and the backup lists of the employees providing the necessary conditions are established (Dündar, 1995).

E-mentoring

E-mentoring method is a system in which the employees of the enterprise can be supported with their problems with their organization and career development. This method allows the interaction between the employee and the client to be realized over the Internet. Expert advisors can advise and support the employees in different positions, job changes, personal development and similar issues. For example, like the "Ask the employer" web site and similer web sites, are web sites where professional specialists in network-mentoring units answer questions and suggests about the career planning to the employees (Allahverdi, 2006).

E-Administrative and Support Services System

The electronic environment can also be created in a more advanced manner by using different human resources data. These reports are updated after each new information entry. For example; personnel attendance control systems control the employees' entry and exit. New employees are provided with identification numbers and personnel ID cards. In the event that the personnel cards are read to the card readers during the entry and exit, all data is collected through the terminals. After measuring the entry-exit movements of the employees of this program during the day, the payroll data which constitute the actual payroll are arranged according to the contract conditions. Statistics and analysis reports are then produced for all users. In many enterprises, electronic applications are widely used which contribute to the rapid execution of administrative and support services at lower costs.

E-Worker Health and Safety System

Companies are obliged to minimize the risk factors when dealing with the security and health conditions of the existing human resources. The company is trying to take precautions against health and security problems from human resources issues that cause job loss. Regular records should be kept on which approach to choose and use in all health and safety related activities (Robson, Clarke, Cullen, Bielecky, Severin, Bigelow, & Mahood, 2007).

It prepares reports for the management of occupational health and occupational safety from records such as monitoring occupational diseases with occupational health and safety systems of the enterprises, keeping records about injuries and occupational accidents. In addition to this, it is necessary to prepare the information of the employees who may be faced with the chemicals, the inventories and the distribution within the company. The safety training received by the employees is classified according to the type of education they receive.

Businesses can submit their legal documents that they are obliged to do by means of the internet, for example, by sending them electronically. Employees in the company can make examinations about occupational health and safety online and can give motivation to employees who have succeeded at the end of the exam. Employees can be asked online about their current safety importance in their workplace (Doğan, 2011).

E-Industry Relations

The organizational structure is changing the employer relations and the nature of the work in a way that information technologies will not be restored (Armstrong, 2011). Businesses provide their employees with dialogue with the opportunities offered by technology. The companies' surveys, communication contacts, recalls and solutions for problems can be applied on the internet.

The software is carried out in an electronic data-based manner in order to decide on the problems that may arise in industrial relations and to determine these problems in their managers. This software can be found in software that responds to issues such as laws without applying to a lawyer or consultant (Doğan, 2011).

Social and Cultural Services System

Different activities are carried out in order to increase the requests of the employees within the Company. Cultural activities and social responsibility projects are carried out with employees through internal communication departments. The company also supports hobbies for various employees. Activities, business greeting dinner, sports, picnics during the year, social responsibilities are carried out periodically. In addition to these, meetings are organized in order to support corporate internal communication within the institution, in order to provide information about magazines, spelling and information during the year. On the whole, all these activities are planned by the human resources department, and the personnel can be reported to the personnel by giving authority and responsibility. In terms of feedback, it is possible to answer the questions directed to the people in a virtual environment with the help of a survey conducted to the personnel (Bondarouk, Ruël & Kees Looise, 2011).

SOLUTIONS AND RECOMMENDATIONS

In human resources, it is believed that the use of electronic systems will increase productivity. In order to realize this idea, it is not enough to transfer the human resources fields of activity to the electronic environment. Companies also need to redesign human resource management practices and processes. The success of E-HRM practices requires a transparent environment in a constantly learning, renewed, open-to-development organizational culture, discipline and reward policies. Alignment of E-HRM and organizational culture is another important factor which determines success in this process. In the transformation of organizational culture, senior management, other department managers and HRM managers must cooperate.

FUTURE RESEARCH DIRECTIONS

The study aims to explain extensively the ways in which HRM applications can be used in HRM processes and contribute to the literature. In this study, it is tried to emphasize that the ultimate aim of the departments of human resources management is to develop applications that affect the financial performance of enterprises and to restructure the HRM processes in a way to achieve strategic results.

HRM departments that want to create added value for organizational outputs need to restructure HRM processes. It is stated in some studies that E-HRM applications increase the efficiency of HRM applications by increasing the quality of the employees (Iqbal, Ahmad, Raziq, & Borini, 2019; Ramezen et al., 2013; Wahyudi & Park, 2014). The quality of E-HRM applications is also stated to affect the quality and perception of HRM services. (Meijerink et al., 2016; Iqbal, Ahmad, Raziq, & Borini, 2019; Ruel & Kapp, 2012). In some studies, it is claimed that HRM practices lead to higher operating performance with e-HRM (Bondarouk and Ruel, 2006; Meijerink et al., 2016). On the other hand, Nivlouei (2014) defines as the labor force commitment, high competence, cost efficiency, and positive effects on institutionalization level.

The number of empirical studies investigating the effects of electronic human resources management on operational performance and results should be increased in the literature. In addition, it is recommended to increase the research studies of the relationships between the perceptions of company employees about the effectiveness of E-HRM practices and the perceptions of the quality of the services provided by HRM departments.

Besides, although the enterprises use significant budgets for E-HRM applications, the effect of business culture on the process of adaptation of E-HRM applications in enterprises should be investigated.

CONCLUSION

Through the increasing focus on transformational outcomes over the last decade, the role of the HR professional has evolved from an administrative character to a more strategic structure (Gardner, Lepak, & Bartol, 2003). Therefore, the strategic role of HRM in the changing role of an HR expert has become increasingly important (Ruël Bondarouk and Looise, 2004). E-HRM practices help organizations create a more effective and strategically focused HR function in organizations. It provides a fast and accurate interpretation of information technology-based data, thus providing a competitive advantage in aligning qualitative and quantitative data for human resources with business strategies (Lazazzara & Galanaki, 2018).

In addition, HRM has recently turned into a concentration on information sharing and strategic workforce analysis and has increasingly become an important contributor to organizational strategic management (Troshani & Jerram & Rao, 2011). E-HRM ensures compliance of IT tools with organizational objectives and strategies. Therefore, the main objective of E-HRM is to create conditions to balance the goals of the organization and HR objectives and strategies (Sadegh, Kohansal, & Haghshenas, 2016).

There is a need for the support of senior management for the use of electronic human resource management practices in organizations. The costs for the first establishment of electronic human resources management in the organization may be slightly higher. Senior management, who will accept these costs and encourage the use of electronic human resources management practices by managers and employees in the organization, will be able to increase the advantages to be achieved through the use of these practices.

The biggest problem in the implementation of E-HRM systems is the adaptation of E-HR management to the organization. When implementing the adaptation, the organization should work with an expert team and the HRM departments should train their employees in this field and take an active role in the process. In addition, E-HRM practices should be accepted and used correctly by all employees. It is not possible for an E-HRM system that is not properly used and implemented. It also has the disadvantages of not having a face-to-face communication because the system interacts in a virtual environment. Not having a face-to-face communication may in some cases reduce collaboration between employees.

Another important disadvantage of E-HRM applications is the safety of information. Businesses that do not take a high level of security measures may be at risk of cyber attack within or outside the organization (Gueutal, 2003).

The impacts of E-HRM and its employees on both organizational and employee performance will continue to be important in the future together with the ever-developing information technology.

REFERENCES

Allahverdi, M. (2006). *Elektronik İnsan Kaynakları Yönetimi ve Türkiye'deki Uygulamalarına Yönelik Bir Araştırma.* Konya: Selçuk Üniversitesi Sosyal Bilimler Enstitüsü Yüksek Lisans Tezi.

Armstrong, M. (2011). Armstrong's handbook of strategic human resource management. London, UK: Kogan Page Publishers.

Atay, Ş. (2006). *Kariyer Yönetiminin Örgütsel Bağlılığa Etkisi.* Afyon Kocatepe Üniversitesi, Sosyal Bilimler Enstitüsü, Yüksek Lisans Tezi, Afyon.

Aydın, K. (2016). *Elektronik İnsan Kaynakları Yönetimi Uygulamaları ve İnovasyon Performansı.* İstanbul, Turkey: Bahçeşehir Üniversitesi, Sosyal Bilimler Enstitüsü, Yüksek Lisans Tezi.

Barber, L. (2006). *E-recruitment Developments.* Brighton, MA: Institute for Employment Studies.

Barney, J. B., & Wright, P. M. (1998). On Becoming A Strategic Partner: The Role Of Human Resources İn Gaining Competitive Advantage. Human Resource Management: Published in Cooperation with the School of Business Administration, *The University of Michigan and in alliance with the Society of Human Resources Management, 37(1),* pp. 31-46.

Bondarouk, T., Ruël, H., & Kees Looise, J. (Eds.). (2011). Electronic HRM in theory and practice. Bingley, UK: Emerald Group Publishing Limited. doi:10.1108/S1877-6361(2011)8

Bondarouk, T. V., & Ruel, H. J. M. (2009). Electronic Human Resource Management: Challenges in the digital era. *International Journal of Human Resource Management, 20*(3), 505–514. doi:10.1080/09585190802707235

Bonti, M., & Cori, E. (2004). The Communication of Company Values and Internetland empirical evidence. In Information, Knowledge and Management: Re-assessing the Role of ICTs in Public and Private Organization.

Caldwell, R. (2003). The changing roles of personnel managers: Old ambiguities, new uncertainties. *Journal of Management Studies, 40*(4), 983–1004. doi:10.1111/1467-6486.00367

Cappelli, P. (2001). Making the most of on-line recruiting. *Harvard Business Review, 79*(3), 139–148. PMID:11246921

Celep, M. (2017). *Elektronik İnsan Kaynakları Uygulamalarının Örgütsel Çıktılar Üzerindeki Etkileri: Türkiye'de Yabancı İştirakli Sigorta Şirketlerinde Bir Araştırma*. İstanbul, Turkey: Bahçeşehir Üniversitesi Sosyal Bilimler Enstitüsü Yüksek Lisans Tezi.

Celep, M., & Fındıklı, M. A. (2018). Elektronik İnsan Kaynakları Uygulamalarının Örgütsel Çıktılar Üzerindeki Etkileri: Türkiye'de Yabancı İştirakli Sigorta Şirketlerinde Bir Araştırma. *Bilgi Ekonomisi ve Yönetimi Dergisi*, *13*(1), 63–77.

Cook, M. F. (1999). *Outsourcing Human Resources Functions: Strategies For Providing Enhanced HR Services At Lower Cost*. New York, NY: American Management Association.

Daud, K. İ. (2010). *İnsan Kaynakları Yönetim Süreçlerinde Bilgi Teknolojilerinin Kullanımı ve E-İK Uygulamaları*. İstanbul, Turkey: İstanbul Teknik Üniversitesi, Fen Bilimleri Enstitüsü, Yüksek Lisans Tezi.

Doğan, A. (2011).. . *Elektronik İnsan Kaynakları Yönetimi ve Fonksiyonları, İnternet Uygulamaları ve Yönetimi Dergisi*, *2*(2), 51–80.

Dulebohn, H., & Marler, J. H. (2005). E-Compensation: The Potential to Transform Practice? In *H. G. Gueutal, & D. L. Stone (Eds.), The Brave New World of eHR: Human Resources Management in the Digital Age* (pp. 166–189). San Francisco, CA: Jossey Bass.

Dündar, İ. G. (1995). *Stratejik İKY'de İK Bilgi Sistemleri'nden Yararlanılması ve Kariyer Yönetimi Sistemine İlişkin Bir Model Önerisi*. İstanbul, Turkey: İstanbul Üniversitesi, Sosyal Bilimler Enstitüsü, Yayınlanmamı Doktora Tezi.

Emmerichs, R. M., Marcum, C. Y., & Robbert, A. A. (2004). An operational process for workforce planning. Santa Monica, CA: Rand Corporation.

Esen, M. (2011). *Bireysel Ve Kurumsal Hazır oluşun Teknolojik Kabulüne Etkisi: Elektronik İnsan Kaynakları Yönetimi (E-İKY)*. Alanında Ampirik Bir Araştırma, Kocaeli Üniversitesi Sosyal Bilimler Enstitüsü, Doktora Tezi, Kocaeli.

Gardner, S. D., Lepak, D. P., & Bartol, K. M. (2003). Virtual HR: The Impact of Information Technology on the Human Resource Professional. *Journal of Vocational Behavior*, *63*(2), 159–179. doi:10.1016/S0001-8791(03)00039-3

Ghazzawi, K., & Accoumeh, A. (2014). Critical success factors of the e-recruitment system. *Journal of Human Resources Management and Labor Studies*, *2*(2), 159–170.

Gueutal, H. G. (2003). *The Brave New World of E-HR: Advances in Human Performance and Cognitive Engineering Research*. USA: Emerald Group Publishing Limited.

Güler, E. Ç. (2006). İşletmelerin E-İnsan Kaynakları Yönetimi ve E-İşe Alım Süreçlerindeki Gelişmeler. *Ege Akademik Bakış Dergisi*, *6*(1), 17–23.

Hall, M. L., & Moritz, S. (2003). The Impact of e-HR on the Human Resource Management Function. *Journal of Labor Research*, *14*(3), 365–379. doi:10.100712122-003-1001-6

Huang, J. H., Jin, B. H., & Yang, C. (2004). Satisfaction with Business-to-Employee Benefit Systems and Organizational Citizenship Behavior: An Examination of Gender Differences. *International Journal of Manpower*, *25*(2), 195–210. doi:10.1108/01437720410535990

Iqbal, N., Ahmad, M., Raziq, M. M., & Borini, F. M. (2019). Linking e-hrm practices and organizational outcomes: Empirical analysis of line manager's perception. *Revista Brasileira de Gestão de Negócios*, *21*(1), 48–69. doi:10.7819/rbgn.v21i1.3964

Johnson, R., Lukaszweski, K. M., & Stone, D. L. (2015). The Evolution of The Field of Human Resource Information Systems: Co-Evolution of Technology and HR Processes. *Communications of the Association for Information Systems*, *38*(28), 533–553.

Karcıoğlu, F., & Öztürk, Ü. (2009). İşletmelerde Performans Değerleme ile İnsan Kaynakları Bilgi Sistemleri (İKBS) Arasındaki İlişkisi-İstanbul İlinde Bir Araştırma. *Atatürk Üniversitesi Sosyal Bilimler Enstitüsü Dergisi*, *13*(1), 343–366.

Körfez, E. P. (2008). *Elektronik İse Alım ve Seçimin İnsan Kaynakları Yönetimi Açısından Yeri ve Önemi ve Bir Uygulama*. İstanbul, Turkey: Yıldız Teknik Üniversitesi, Sosyal Bilimler Enstitüsü, Yüksek Lisans Tezi.

Lazazzara, A., & Galanaki, E. (2018). E-HRM Adoption and Usage: A Cross-National Analysis of Enabling Factors. In C. Rossignoli, F. Virili, & S. Za (Eds.), *Digital, Technology and Organizational Change: Reshaping Technology, People, and Organizations Towards a Global Society*. Lecture Notes in Information Systems and Organisation. doi:10.1007/978-3-319-62051-0_11

Lee, I. (2005). The Evolution of E-Recruiting: A Concent Analysis of Fortune 100 Career Web Sites. *Journal of Electronic Commerce in Organizations*, *3*(3), 57–68. doi:10.4018/jeco.2005070104

Legge, K. (1989). Human resource management: a critical analysis. New perspectives on human resource management. In J. Storey (Ed.), New Perspectives on Human Resource Management. Abingdon, UK: Routledge, pp. 19-40.

Lepak, D. P., & Snell, S. A. (1998). Virtual HR: Strategic human resource management in the 21st century. *Human Resource Management Review*, *8*(3), 215–234. doi:10.1016/S1053-4822(98)90003-1

LeTart, J. F. (1998). Virtual HR, HR Magazine, p. 62.

Marler, J. H. (2009). Making human resources strategic by going to the Net: Reality or myth? *International Journal of Human Resource Management*, *20*(3), 515–527. doi:10.1080/09585190802707276

Mondy, R. W., & Mondy, J. B. (2012). *Human Resource Management*. London, UK: Pearson Education.

Nivlouei, F. B. (2014). Electronic Human Resource Management System: The Main Element in Capacitating Globalization Paradigm. *International Journal of Business and Social Science*, *5*(2), 147–159.

Öğe, S. (2004). *Elektronik İnsan Kaynakları Yönetimi (E-HRM)'nde İnsan Kaynakları Enformasyon Sistemi (HRIS)'nin Önemi ve Temel Kullanım Alanları. 3* (pp. 109–117). Ulusal Bilgi, Ekonomi ve Yönetim Kongresi.

Rajalakshmi, R., & Gomathi, S. (2016). A review on E-HRM: Electronic human resource management. *Indian Journal of Research, 5*(8).

Ramezen, M., Nazari, Y., & Ahmadi, M. M. (2013). The effect of electronic human resources management on quality of services provided by human resources in the insurance industry (case study: Iran Insurance Company in Khorramabad City). *Journal of Social Issues & Humanities, 1*(7), 223–232.

Robson, L. S., Clarke, J. A., Cullen, K., Bielecky, A., Severin, C., Bigelow, P. L., ... Mahood, Q. (2007). The effectiveness of occupational health and safety management system interventions: A systematic review. *Safety Science, 45*(3), 329–353. doi:10.1016/j.ssci.2006.07.003

Ruël, H., Bondarouk, T., & Looise, J. K. (2004). E-HRM: Innovation or Irritation. *Management Review, 15*(3), 364–381.

Ruël, H., Magalhães, R., & Chiemeke, C. C. (2011). Human Resource Information Systems: An Integrated Research Agenda. In Electronic HRM in Theory and Practice (pp. 21–39). Binkley, UK: Emerald Group Publishing Limited. doi:10.1108/S1877-6361(2011)0000008006

Ruël, H., & van der Kaap, H. (2012). E-HRM Usage and Value Creation: Does a Facilitating Context Matter? *Zeitschrift für Personalforschung, 26*(3), 260–281.

Ruel, H. J., Bondarouk, T. V., & Van der Velde, M. (2007). The contribution of e-HRM to HRM effectiveness. *Employee Relations, 29*(3), 280–291. doi:10.1108/01425450710741757

Sadegh, T., Kohansal, M. A., & Haghshenas, M. (2016). E-HRM: From acceptance to value cretion. *Journal of Information Technology Management, 27*(1), 18–27.

Schank, R. C. (2002). Designing world-class e-learning: How IBM, GE, Harvard Business School, and Columbia University are succeeding at e-learning.

Seema, A., & Sujatha, S. (2013). Conceptual work on career management strategies from an organization perspective. *International Journal of Management, IT and Engineering, 3*(7), 184.

Şimşek, M. Ş., & Öğe, H. S. (2011). İnsan Kaynakları Yönetimi, *Eğitim Akademi Yayınları*. Baskı, Yayınevi Sertifika, (14824).

Snell, N. (1994). Virtual HR: Meeting New World Realities. *Compensation and Benefits Review, 26*(12), 35–37. doi:10.1177/088636879402600606

Stone, D. L., Stone-Romero, E. F., & Lukaszewski, K. (2003). The functional and dysfunctional consequences of human resource information technology for organizations and their employees. In Advances in human performance and cognitive engineering research (pp. 37–68). Binkley, UK: Emerald Group Publishing Limited.

Strohmeier, S. (2007). Research in e-HRM: Review and Implications. *Human Resource Management Review, 17*(1), 19–37. doi:10.1016/j.hrmr.2006.11.002

Strohmeier, S., & Piazza, F. (2011). "Web Mining" as a Novel Approaching e-HRM Research. In Electronic HRM in Theory and Practice (pp. 41–53). Binkley, UK: Emerald Group Publishing Limited. doi:10.1108/S1877-6361(2011)0000008007

Sylva, H., & Mol, S. T. (2009). E-Recruitment: A study into applicant perceptions of an online application system. *International Journal of Selection and Assessment*, *17*(3), 311–323. doi:10.1111/j.1468-2389.2009.00473.x

Sylvester, E. O., Bamidele, A. D., & Oluyemi, O. S. (2015). Implementing E-HRM System in Developing Countries: Challenges and Prospects. *International Journal of Applied Information Systems*, *9*(8), 38–41. doi:10.5120/ijais2015451452

Troshani, I., Jerram, C., & Rao, S. (2011). Exploring the Public Sector Adoption of HRIS. *Industrial Management & Data Systems*, *111*(3), 470–488. doi:10.1108/02635571111118314

Tunçer, P. (2012). Değişen İnsan Kaynakları Yönetimi Anlayışında Kariyer Yönetimi. *Ondokuz Mayıs Üniversitesi Eğitim Fakültesi Dergisi, 31*(1).

Ulrich, D. (1996). Human resource champions: The next agenda for adding value and delivering results. Brighton, MA: Harvard Business Press.

Ulrich, D. (1998). A New Mandate For Human Resources. *Harvard Business Review*, *76*(1), 128. PMID:10176915

Ulrich, D. L. (1990). *Organizational Capability: Competing From the Inside/Out* (pp. 78–94). New York, NY: John Wiley & Sons.

Venterink, J. H. (2017). *Practical Future Developments in e-HRM, HR SSC's and Employee Involvement.* (Master thesis, University of Twente).

Wahyudi, E., & Park, S. M. (2014). Unveiling the value creation process of electronic human resource management: An indonesian case. *Public Personnel Management*, *43*(1), 83–117. doi:10.1177/0091026013517555

Yazıcı, S. (2004). *E-Öğrenme: İnsan Kaynakları Eğitiminde Stratejik Dönüşüm.* İstanbul, Turkey: Alfa Basım.

KEY TERMS AND DEFINITIONS

Electronic Human Resources Management (E-HRM): It means electronic human resources management system including practices that are open to all relevant actors, such as job applicants, HR consultants, other than the employees of the institution

Electronic Performance Management Systems (E-PMS): Electronic performance management system consists of partially e-HRM and HR information system. Via information technology integration of strategies, policies, practices and performance management process was enabled.

Electronic Recruitment Systems: To collect candidates with their characteristics in a pool in the electronic system and then to recruit personnel with related characteristics or information in this pool for the recruitment of vacant positions.

Electronic remuneration (E-remuneration): is a system that refers to the organization collecting, storing, processing, analyzing, using and distributing data and information related to the remuneration over the web system.

Employee Self Service (ESS): Employee Self-Service (ESS) is seen in the service tools. Employee self-service is a whole networked application that allow all managers and employees to create, record and correct personnel information about themselves

Human Resource Information Systems (HRMS): HRMS is mainly directed to the HR department itself. The users of these systems are HR professionals.

Intranet: Intranet is a person-specific or organizational specific state of the Internet. While anyone can access web sites on the Internet, only those who are authorized have to access the intranet created on the web. The authorized users require user name and a password to enter.

Chapter 2
SERVQUAL-Based Performance Analysis of Agricultural Financing in E-Banking Industry:
An Evaluation by IT2 Fuzzy Decision-Making Model

Serhat Yüksel
İstanbul Medipol University, Turkey

Hasan Dinçer
Istanbul Medipol University, Turkey

ABSTRACT

The aim of the study is to measure the effectiveness of commercial banks in the agricultural financing in Turkey. For this purpose, 10 different criteria are identified based on five different SERVQUAL perspectives. Moreover, 10 different Turkish deposit banks traded on BIST are taken into consideration in the analysis process. Interval type-2 fuzzy DEMATEL (IT2 FDEMATEL) method is used to weight the dimensions and criteria. Also, deposit banks are ranked with interval type-2 fuzzy TOPSIS (IT2 FTOPSIS). The findings show that flexibility of needs, branch availability, and qualified personnel are the most important criteria for agricultural financing. Hence, it is recommended that banks design a system in which customers can access the banks in flexible times related to the agricultural financing. Another important recommendation is that banks open new branches near the agricultural regions so that farmers can reach the banking services easily. Furthermore, banks should also improve their personnel for agricultural issues with necessary trainings.

DOI: 10.4018/978-1-7998-0035-4.ch002

INTRODUCTION

The agricultural sector meets the compulsory vital needs of people in the country. In other words, meeting the food needs of the country depends on the agricultural sector. In addition to this, the agricultural sector contributes to the unemployment rate by providing employment in the country. Moreover, with the help of the agricultural sector, raw material is provided to agriculture-based industry. Also, through the export of agricultural products, the agricultural sector has a positive effect on the current account balance of the country (Sagib et al., 2015).

In contrast, the agricultural sector faces some difficulties in terms of its structure. As an example, there is periodic income as the agricultural sector depends on climate. Costs are continuous, although manufacturers need long-term waiting to reach revenue. On the other hand, in today's world, the agricultural sector must be connected to modern agricultural machinery rather than physical power. In this way, it will be possible to increase the efficiency of agricultural production. Therefore, agricultural producers need to provide financial support to have modern agricultural machinery (Antón & Cattaneo, 2019).

Banks are the financial institutions that play key role in agricultural financing. They can provide appropriate financial products to the farmers according to their demands. In this framework, loans with flexible maturity can be given to the farmers. Another important point is that operational procedures can be minimized for these people so that they can take loans easily. Additionally, appropriate credit cards can be designed to satisfy the liquidity needs of the farmers. Furthermore, necessary branches and ATMs can be opened near to the agricultural regions (Cook et al., 2015).

Hence, performance analysis of the banks related to the agricultural financing should be made periodically since they play a key role for this industry. In this circumstance, the essential point is that appropriate methodology should be chosen for this performance measurement. Otherwise, incorrect results lead to ineffective strategies. Therefore, performance management method should consider many different factors at the same time in order to reach more effective results.

SERVQUAL is the methodology that is used to measure service quality of the companies. This method has mainly 5 different factors. All physical aspects of the company are taken into account in the "physical appearance". The "reliability" aspect of the SERVQUAL model deals with how much customers trust the company. On the other side, "response" considers the time of the service provided. In addition to the mentioned issues, the confidence level of the employees to the company is discussed in "assurance" dimension. Finally, in the "empathy", sensitivity of the companies to the customers is evaluated (Galeeva, 2016).

In this study, it is aimed to measure effectiveness of Turkish banks for agricultural finance. The theoretical approach to the study is based on the 5 main components of service quality according to the SERVQUAL measurement model. First, the direction and magnitude of the interaction between these key elements will be measured by IT2 FDEMATEL method. Subsequently, with the help of the IT2 FTOPSIS method, Turkish banks are evaluated according to the performance results.

The main novelty of this study is presenting criteria set for the performance measurement of the banks regarding agricultural finance. Another novelty in our study will be the comparative analysis of public, private and foreign banks on the financing of agriculture. Another originality in our study is the analysis of the Turkish banks' performance in the financing of agriculture by integrating IT2 FDEMATEL and the IT2 FTOPSIS methods.

This study consists of 4 different sections. In this part, the main reason of selecting this topic is defined. In the second section, the studies focused on agricultural financing are classified and the missing part is stated. The third section demonstrates the analysis made by IT2 FDEMATEL and the IT2 FTOPSIS methods. In the conclusion section, recommendations are explained to improve the effectiveness of the banks.

LITERATURE REVIEW

The subject of agricultural finance was evaluated for many different purposes in the literature. Many researchers defined the importance of government and cooperatives in agricultural finance. In this framework, Turvey (2017) tried to evaluate the agricultural finance in America. It is concluded that government plays a key role for agricultural loans. In this framework, it is defined that farm mortgages can be very beneficial for this purpose. Martin and Clapp (2015), Pokharel et al. (2019) and Ouma (2016) also concluded that government should take necessary actions in agriculture finance to provide sustainable growth. Abate et al. (2016) aimed to understand the impacts of the financial institutions on agricultural technology adoption in Ethiopia. It is concluded that access to the credit should be improved in order to increase technology adoption for the farmers. For this situation, financial cooperatives play a key role in the allocation of the loans. Additionally, Qi and Sun (2017) also made a study on the contribution of the effective finance on agricultural development of China. In this study, they defined the significance of credit cooperatives to increase agricultural production.

Some studies also underlined the importance of agricultural risk management and insurance. For example, Porth and Tan (2016) made a study related to the stability and growth of the agriculture sector. In this study, the vital role of the agriculture for the enhancement of the world food security is emphasized. Therefore, it is concluded that there should be an effective risk management in agricultural industry. Power (2016) also stated that short-term and long-term risks in agricultural production should be identified effectively to provide sustainability in agricultural development. Additionally, Ye et al. (2019) created the agricultural logistic park information platform to minimize high risks in agricultural financing. Woodard (2016), Antón and Cattaneo (2019), Adnan et al. (2018), and Severini et al. (2017) are other studies which stated the significance of effective risk management and insurance systems to develop agriculture industry.

The subject of Islamic agricultural finance was also examined by many researchers. In this context, Shafiai and Moi (2015) focused on the problems of the farmers in Malaysia. For this purpose, interviews and a questionnaire were conducted. They defined that Islamic finance method of agricultural product and loss sharing has an important positive effect on the solving the problems. Similar to this study, Saqib et al. (2015) stated that Qard-al-Hassan system of Islamic banking provides some opportunities to minimize problems in local agricultural financing. In addition to these studies, Obaidullah (2015) and Yahuza (2019) identified the benefits of other Islamic finance approaches, such as microfinance and Muzara'ah so as to have sustainable growth in agricultural finance. Elhiraika (2013), Adam and Ahmed (2005) and Bamakhramah (2005) are also other researchers which underlined the positive contribution of Islamic banking system on agriculture industry.

In a significant portion of the studies, banks have a positive effect on the agricultural sector. Shahbaz et al. (2011) examined the relationship between the financial sector and the agricultural sector in Pakistan. In this study, where Granger causality analysis is used, it is understood that financial development contributes to growth in agricultural sector. Similar to this study, Hye and Wizarat (2011) concluded that Pakistan's financial sector contributed to agricultural growth. Chisasa and Makina (2013) also analyzed the effect of bank loans on agricultural sector in South Africa. Regression analysis was performed in this study in order to reach this purpose. According to the results of the analysis, it is determined that bank loans have an increasing effect on agricultural production. Stein et al. (2016), Rahman et al. (2014), Barani et al. (2015) and Acha et al. (2017) stated that bank loans to the agriculture industry makes a contribution to the technological development. Similarly, Dawson et al. (2017), Vitiello et al. (2015), and Cook et al. (2015) also identified that banks have a positive and important contribution to the development of the agriculture sector.

When these studies in the literature are evaluated in general, it is observed that a significant part of the studies examined the role of banks in the agricultural sector. In addition, it is understood that some other studies provide some information about the financing of the agricultural sector and offer the best method of financing. As it can be seen, the missing part in the literature is that the banks have not been examined in order to be more efficient in the sector.

METHODOLOGY

IT2 Fuzzy Sets

IT2 fuzzy sets are mainly developed to minimize the uncertainty in IT1 fuzzy sets. Within this context, $\tilde{A}$ .gives information about type-2 fuzzy set and $\mu_{\tilde{A}(x,u)}$ .demonstrates type-2 membership function which can be between 0 and 1 (Mendel, 2017). Equation (1) indicates these issues (Dinçer et al., 2019 c,d,e; Yüksel et. al., 2019).

$$\tilde{A} = \left\{\left((x,u), \mu_{\tilde{A}(x,u)}\right) | \forall_x \in X, \forall_u \in J_x \subseteq [0,1]\right\} \text{ or } \tilde{A} = \int_{x\in X}\int_{u\in J_x} \mu_{\tilde{A}}(x,u) / (x,u) J_x \subseteq [0,1]. \tag{1}$$

The union of all x and u is represented by $\iint$. When $\mu_{\tilde{A}(x,u)}$ .equals to 1, IT2 fuzzy set is given as equation (2).

$$\tilde{A} = \int_{x\in X}\int_{u\in J_x} 1 / (x,u) J_x \subseteq [0,1]. \tag{2}$$

Also, $\tilde{A}_i^U$ .and $\tilde{A}_i^L$ .explain upper and lower trapezoidal membership functions as in the equation (3).

$$\tilde{A}_i = \left(\tilde{A}_i^U, \tilde{A}_i^L\right) = \left(\left(a_{i1}^U, a_{i2}^U, a_{i3}^U, a_{i4}^U; H_1\left(\tilde{A}_i^U\right), H_2\left(\tilde{A}_i^U\right)\right), \left(a_{i1}^L, a_{i2}^L, a_{i3}^L, a_{i4}^L; H_1\left(\tilde{A}_i^L\right), H_2\left(\tilde{A}_i^L\right)\right)\right). \tag{3}$$

$H_j\left(\tilde{A}_i^U\right)$ .and $H_j\left(\tilde{A}_i^L\right)$ .show the membership values whereas $a_{i1}^U \ldots a_{i4}^L$ .explain the reference values. Equations (4)-(8) explain the calculation process.

$$\tilde{A}_1 \oplus \tilde{A}_2 = \left(\tilde{A}_1^U, \tilde{A}_1^L\right) \oplus \left(\tilde{A}_2^U, \tilde{A}_2^L\right) = \\ \left(\left(a_{11}^U + a_{21}^U, a_{12}^U + a_{22}^U, a_{13}^U + a_{23}^U, a_{14}^U + a_{24}^U; \min\left(H_1\left(\tilde{A}_1^U\right), H_1\left(\tilde{A}_2^U\right)\right), \min\left(H_1\left(\tilde{A}_1^U\right), H_2\left(\tilde{A}_2^U\right)\right)\right), \right. \\ \left. \left(a_{11}^L + a_{21}^L, a_{12}^L + a_{22}^L, a_{13}^L + a_{23}^L, a_{14}^L + a_{24}^L; \min\left(H_1\left(\tilde{A}_1^L\right), H_1\left(\tilde{A}_2^L\right)\right), \min\left(H_1\left(\tilde{A}_1^L\right), H_2\left(\tilde{A}_2^L\right)\right)\right)\right) \tag{4}$$

$$\tilde{A}_1 \ominus \tilde{A}_2 = \left(\tilde{A}_1^U, \tilde{A}_1^L\right) \ominus \left(\tilde{A}_2^U, \tilde{A}_2^L\right) = \\ \left(\left(a_{11}^U - a_{21}^U, a_{12}^U - a_{22}^U, a_{13}^U - a_{23}^U, a_{14}^U - a_{24}^U; \min\left(H_1\left(\tilde{A}_1^U\right), H_1\left(\tilde{A}_2^U\right)\right), \min\left(H_1\left(\tilde{A}_1^U\right), H_2\left(\tilde{A}_2^U\right)\right)\right), \right. \\ \left. \left(a_{11}^L - a_{21}^L, a_{12}^L - a_{22}^L, a_{13}^L - a_{23}^L, a_{14}^L - a_{24}^L; \min\left(H_1\left(\tilde{A}_1^L\right), H_1\left(\tilde{A}_2^L\right)\right), \min\left(H_1\left(\tilde{A}_1^L\right), H_2\left(\tilde{A}_2^L\right)\right)\right)\right) \tag{5}$$

$$\tilde{A}_1 \otimes \tilde{A}_2 = \left(\tilde{A}_1^U, \tilde{A}_1^L\right) \otimes \left(\tilde{A}_2^U, \tilde{A}_2^L\right) = \\ \left(\left(a_{11}^U \times a_{21}^U, a_{12}^U \times a_{22}^U, a_{13}^U \times a_{23}^U, a_{14}^U \times a_{24}^U; \min\left(H_1\left(\tilde{A}_1^U\right), H_1\left(\tilde{A}_2^U\right)\right), \min\left(H_1\left(\tilde{A}_1^U\right), H_2\left(\tilde{A}_2^U\right)\right)\right), \right. \\ \left. \left(a_{11}^L \times a_{21}^L, a_{12}^L \times a_{22}^L, a_{13}^L \times a_{23}^L, a_{14}^L \times a_{24}^L; \min\left(H_1\left(\tilde{A}_1^L\right), H_1\left(\tilde{A}_2^L\right)\right), \min\left(H_1\left(\tilde{A}_1^L\right), H_2\left(\tilde{A}_2^L\right)\right)\right)\right) \tag{6}$$

$$k\tilde{A}_1 = \\ \left(k \times a_{11}^U, k \times a_{12}^U, k \times a_{13}^U, k \times a_{14}^U; H_1\left(\tilde{A}_1^U\right), H_2\left(\tilde{A}_1^U\right)\right), \left(k \times a_{11}^L, k \times a_{12}^L, k \times a_{13}^L, k \times a_{14}^L; H_1\left(\tilde{A}_1^L\right), H_2\left(\tilde{A}_1^L\right)\right) \tag{7}$$

$$\frac{\tilde{A}_1}{k} = \\ \left(\frac{1}{k} \times a_{11}^U, \frac{1}{k} \times a_{12}^U, \frac{1}{k} \times a_{13}^U, \frac{1}{k} \times a_{14}^U; H_1\left(\tilde{A}_1^U\right), H_2\left(\tilde{A}_1^U\right)\right), \left(\frac{1}{k} \times a_{11}^L, \frac{1}{k} \times a_{12}^L, \frac{1}{k} \times a_{13}^L, \frac{1}{k} \times a_{14}^L; H_1\left(\tilde{A}_1^L\right), H_2\left(\tilde{A}_1^L\right)\right) \tag{8}$$

IT2 FDEMATEL

DEMATEL explains the expression of "decision making trial and evaluation laboratory". With this approach, it is aimed to examine the interdependence among the factors. Another important benefit of DEMATEL model is that it can be possible to weight different items according to their significance (Abdullah & Zulkifli, 2015; Yüksel et al., 2017; Dinçer & Yüksel, 2018). Firstly, evaluations of decision makers are provided and converted into the interval fuzzy sets. Additionally, the second step includes the initial direct-relation fuzzy matrix by considering the evaluations collectively (Dinçer et al., 2018 a,b). After that, initial direct-relation fuzzy matrix $\tilde{Z}$ is calculated with the equations (9) and (10).

$$\tilde{Z}=\begin{bmatrix} 0 & \tilde{z}_{12} & \cdots & \cdots & \tilde{z}_{1n} \\ \tilde{z}_{21} & 0 & \cdots & \cdots & \tilde{z}_{2n} \\ \vdots & \vdots & \ddots & \cdots & \cdots \\ \vdots & \vdots & \vdots & \ddots & \vdots \\ \tilde{z}_{n1} & \tilde{z}_{n2} & \cdots & \cdots & 0 \end{bmatrix}. \tag{9}$$

$$\tilde{Z}=\frac{\tilde{Z}^1+\tilde{Z}^2+\tilde{Z}^3+\ldots\tilde{Z}^n}{n}. \tag{10}$$

In the next step, the normalization process is occurred with the equations (11)-(13).

$$\tilde{X}=\begin{bmatrix} \tilde{x}_{11} & \tilde{x}_{12} & \cdots & \cdots & \tilde{x}_{1n} \\ \tilde{x}_{21} & \tilde{x}_{22} & \cdots & \cdots & \tilde{x}_{2n} \\ \vdots & \vdots & \ddots & \cdots & \cdots \\ \vdots & \vdots & \vdots & \ddots & \vdots \\ \tilde{x}_{n1} & \tilde{x}_{n2} & \cdots & \cdots & \tilde{x}_{nn} \end{bmatrix} \tag{11}$$

$$\tilde{x}_{ij}=\frac{\tilde{z}_{ij}}{r}=\left(\left(\frac{Z_{a_{ij}}}{r},\frac{Z_{b_{ij}}}{r},\frac{Z_{c_{ij}}}{r},\frac{Z_{d_{ij}}}{r};H_1\left(z_{ij}^U\right),H_2\left(z_{ij}^U\right)\right),\left(\frac{Z_{e_{ij}}}{r},\frac{Z_{f_{ij}}}{r},\frac{Z_{g_{ij}}}{r},\frac{Z_{h_{ij}}}{r};H_1\left(z_{ij}^L\right),H_2\left(z_{ij}^L\right)\right)\right) \tag{12}$$

$$r=max\left(max_{1\leq i\leq n}\sum_{j=1}^{n}Z_{d_{ij}},max_{1\leq i\leq n}\sum_{j=1}^{n}Z_{d_{ij}}\right). \tag{13}$$

Total influence fuzzy matrix is generated in the fourth step by considering the equations (14)-(18).

$$X_a=\begin{bmatrix} 0 & a'_{12} & \cdots & \cdots & a'_{1n} \\ a'_{21} & 0 & \cdots & \cdots & a'_{2n} \\ \vdots & \vdots & \ddots & \cdots & \cdots \\ \vdots & \vdots & \vdots & \ddots & \vdots \\ a'_{n1} & a'_{n2} & \cdots & \cdots & 0 \end{bmatrix}, \ldots, X_h=\begin{bmatrix} 0 & h'_{12} & \cdots & \cdots & h'_{1n} \\ h'_{21} & 0 & \cdots & \cdots & h'_{2n} \\ \vdots & \vdots & \ddots & \cdots & \cdots \\ \vdots & \vdots & \vdots & \ddots & \vdots \\ h'_{n1} & h'_{n2} & \cdots & \cdots & 0 \end{bmatrix}. \tag{14}$$

$$\tilde{T}=\lim_{k\to\infty}\tilde{X}+\tilde{X}^2+\ldots+\tilde{X}^k. \tag{15}$$

$$\tilde{T} = \begin{bmatrix} \tilde{t}_{11} & \tilde{t}_{12} & \cdots & \cdots & \tilde{t}_{1n} \\ \tilde{t}_{21} & \tilde{t}_{22} & \cdots & \cdots & \tilde{t}_{2n} \\ \vdots & \vdots & \ddots & \cdots & \cdots \\ \vdots & \vdots & \vdots & \ddots & \vdots \\ \tilde{t}_{n1} & \tilde{t}_{n2} & \cdots & \cdots & \tilde{t}_{nn} \end{bmatrix}. \tag{16}$$

$$\tilde{t}_{ij} = \left(a''_{ij}, b''_{ij}, c''_{ij}, d''_{ij}; H_1\left(\tilde{t}_{ij}^{\,U}\right), H_2\left(\tilde{t}_{ij}^{\,U}\right)\right), \left(e''_{ij}, f''_{ij}, g''_{ij}, h''_{ij}; H_1\left(\tilde{t}_{ij}^{\,L}\right), H_2\left(\tilde{t}_{ij}^{\,L}\right)\right). \tag{17}$$

$$\left[a''_{ij}\right] = X_a \times \left(I - X_a\right)^{-1}, \ \ldots, \ \left[h''_{ij}\right] = X_h \times \left(I - X_h\right)^{-1}. \tag{18}$$

The next step is related to the calculation of the defuzzified total influence matrix with the help of the equations (19)-(22) are used.

$$Def_T = \frac{\dfrac{\left(u_U - l_U\right) + \left({}^{2}{}_U \times m_{1U} - l_U\right) + \left(\pm_U \times m_{2U} - l_U\right)}{4} + l_U + \left[\dfrac{\left(u_L - l_L\right) + \left({}^{2}{}_L \times m_{1L} - l_L\right) + \left(\pm_L \times m_{2L} - l_L\right)}{4} + l_L\right]}{2}. \tag{19}$$

$$Def_T = T = \left[t_{ij}\right]_{n\times n}, \ i, j = 1, 2, \ldots, n. \tag{20}$$

$$\tilde{D}_i^{def} = r = \left[\sum_{j=1}^{n} t_{ij}\right]_{n\times 1} = \left(r_i\right)_{n\times 1} = \left(r_1, \ldots, r_i, \ldots, r_n\right). \tag{21}$$

$$\tilde{R}_i^{def} = y = \left[\sum_{i=1}^{n} t_{ij}\right]'_{1\times n} = \left(y_j\right)'_{1\times n} = \left(y_1, \ldots, y_i, \ldots, y_n\right). \tag{22}$$

Moreover, the defuzzification is occurred by considering the values of $\left(\tilde{D}_i + \tilde{R}_i\right)^{def}$ .and $\left(\tilde{D}_i - \tilde{R}_i\right)^{def}$. In this circumstance, $\tilde{D}_i^{def}$ .explains the sum of all vector rows while $\tilde{R}_i^{def}$ .gives information about the sum of all vector columns. Thus, higher $\left(\tilde{D}_i + \tilde{R}_i\right)^{def}$ .shows that it is closer to the central point. Also, $\left(\tilde{D}_i - \tilde{R}_i\right)^{def}$ demonstrates the degree of the causality.

IT2 FTOPSIS

The word TOPSIS is obtained from the expression of "Technique for Order Preference by Similarity to Ideal Solution". The main aim of this method is to rank different factors by considering the positive (A^+).and negative (A^-) ideal solutions. In this context, the distance from this ideal solution is used to understand the best alternative. Also, the weighted values of the defuzzified matrix is shown as v_{ij}.(Wu et al., 2018; Dinçer et al., 2017). Equation (23) explains the details of this process.

$$A^+ = \max\left(v_1, v_2, v_3, \dots v_n\right),\ A^- = \min\left(v_1, v_2, v_3, \dots v_n\right). \tag{23}$$

The next step includes the calculation of D^+ and D^- with the help of the equations (24) and (25).

$$D_i^+ = \sqrt{\sum_{i=1}^{m} (v_i - A_i^+)^2}\ . \tag{24}$$

$$D_i^- = \sqrt{\sum_{i=1}^{m} (v_i - A_i^-)^2} \tag{25}$$

In the final step, the closeness coefficient (CC_i) is computed as in equation (26).

$$CC_i = \frac{D_i^-}{D_i^+ + D_i^-} \tag{26}$$

AN APPLICATION ON TURKISH BANKING SECTOR

In order to measure the effectiveness of the deposit banks in Turkey for agricultural loans, the criteria are selected based on SERVQUAL method. According to this measurement model, service quality has 5 main elements. All physical aspects of the company are taken into account in the "physical appearance". For this purpose, the physical features of the service area are included. In this respect, it is important to understand how much the building of the company affects customers visually.

The "reliability" aspect of the SERVQUAL model covers how much customers trust the company. In this context, issues such as how much the promises made by the workplace to customers and the accuracy of transactions with customers are discussed. On the other hand, the time of the service given is discussed in the "response" dimension. In this context, it is mentioned that company personnel are willing to help customers quickly.

In addition to the mentioned issues, the extent to which the employees of the company constitute a feeling of trust in customers is mentioned in the "confidence" dimension. Hence, the qualifications of the staff play an important role in this context. Finally, it is taken into consideration whether firms are sensitive to customers regarding "empathy". In this dimension, it is important whether the company understands the specific needs of the customers (Parasuraman et al., 1988).

SERVQUAL approach was frequently preferred in the literature by the researchers. Ali and Raza (2017), Kumar et al. (2018), Dinçer et al. (2019a) and Ahmed et al. (2017) used SERVQUAL approach in banking sector to improve customer satisfaction. On the other side, Rezaei et al. (2018) tried to make quality assessment of airline baggage handling systems with the help of this method. Similarly, Basfirinci and Mitra (2015) also measured service quality of the airline industry by using SERVQUAL method. Additionally, this approach was also used in many different industries, such as tourism (Stefano et al., 2015; Beheshtinia & Farzaneh Azad, 2017), education (Galeeva, 2016; Zakariah et al., 2016) and energy (Dinçer et al., 2019b). The criteria used in the analysis process are obtained according to the dimensions of SERVQUAL approach. The details of these criteria are shown on Table 1.

Flexibility of Needs (operating time) (C10) Daly and Gebremedhin (2015); Pradella (2015)

Table 1 gives information that 10 different criteria are defined based on 5 different perspectives of the balance scorecard approach. Regarding physical conditions, branch availability and qualified personnel give opportunity to provide better services to the farmers. In this framework, opening branches near to agricultural regions and employing personnel who are specialized in agricultural issues play a key role for this condition. Additionally, providing data and physical security has a positive influence on the confidence of the customers.

On the other hand, with respect to the responsiveness dimension, customer feedback should be taken into consideration by the banks. Similar to this condition, bank should also give fast response for any requests of the customers. Moreover, customer loyalty and brand equity are selected as criteria for reliability dimension. Furthermore, as for empathy perspective, customer expectations should be understood by the banks. In this context, a detailed survey can be made with the selected customers to learn their needs. Also, customer access to the banks in different times should be provided.

This study aims to determine the financing of agricultural activities of commercial banks in Turkey. In this context, all state, private and foreign deposit banks whose shares are traded in Istanbul Stock

Table 1. SERVQUAL-based Determinants of Agricultural Financing

Dimensions	Criteria	Literature
Physical Conditions (D1)	Branch Availability (C1)	Řepková (2015); Ohsato, and Takahashi (2015)
	Qualified Personnel (C2)	Monferrer-Tirado et al. (2016); Farah (2017)
Confidence (D2)	Data Security (C3)	Thota et al. (2017); Wang et al. (2016)
	Physical Security (C4)	Ammirato et al. (2019); Ryan (2017)
Responsiveness (D3)	Customer Feedback (C5)	Moliner-Tena et al. (2019); Bratawisnu et al. (2017)
	Speed of Response (C6)	Le Nguyen (2018); Loureiro and Sarmento (2017)
Reliability (D4)	Loyalty (C7)	Amin (2016); Kaura et al. (2015)
	Brand Equity (C8)	Altaf et al. (2017); Yoganathan et al. (2015)
Empathy (D5)	Customer Expectations (C9)	Paul et al. (2016); Amin (2016)
	Flexibility of Needs (operating time) (C10)	Daly and Gebremedhin (2015); Pradella (2015)

Exchange (BIST) are included in the scope of the review. The details of 10 deposit banks are given on Table 2.

In the analysis process, IT2 fuzzy logic is taken into consideration. Table 3 gives information about the linguistic scales and IT2 fuzzy numbers used in the evaluation process.

In this study, three different decision makers made evaluations. These people have at least 10-year experience in this area. Their linguistic evaluations for the criteria are given on Table 4.

After that, these dimensions and criteria are evaluated by IT2 FDEMATEL. In this context, defuzzification process is performed. In this context, defuzzified total relation matrix is calculated as in Table 5.

On the other side, the weighted results of the dimensions and criteria are presented on Table 6.

Table 6 explains that the dimension of the physical conditions (D1) has the highest importance. In addition, confidence (D2) and empathy (D5) are other significant dimensions. On the other side, reliability (D4) dimension has the lowest weight. While considering these results, it can be understood that the appearance of physical facilities of the banks plays a very key role in agricultural financing. Additionally, customers also give importance to trust to the banks and they prefer that their needs are understood by the banks in agricultural finance.

Table 2. Bank Alternatives for Agricultural Financing

Ownership	Banks
State-owned	Bank 1 (Alternative 1)
	Bank 2 (Alternative 2)
Private	Bank 3 (Alternative 3)
	Bank 4 (Alternative 4)
	Bank 5 (Alternative 5)
	Bank 6 (Alternative 6)
Foreign	Bank 7 (Alternative 7)
	Bank 8 (Alternative 8)
	Bank 9 (Alternative 9)
	Bank 10 (Alternative 10)

Table 3. Linguistic Scales and IT2 Fuzzy Numbers for the Evaluations

Alternative Evaluations	Criterion Evaluations	IT2 Fuzzy Numbers
Very Poor (VP)	Very low (VL)	((0,0,0,0.1;1,1), (0,0,0,0.05;0.9,0.9))
Poor (P)	Low (L)	((0,0.1,0.1,0.3;1,1), (0.05,0.1,0.1,0.2;0.9,0.9))
Medium Poor (MP)	Medium Low (ML)	((0.1,0.3,0.3,0.5;1,1), (0.2,0.3,0.3,0.4;0.9,0.9))
Fair (F)	Medium (M)	((0.3,0.5,0.5,0.7;1,1), (0.4,0.5,0.5,0.6;0.9,0.9))
Good (G)	Medium high (MH)	((0.5,0.7,0.7,0.9;1,1), (0.6,0.7,0.7,0.8;0.9,0.9))
Very Good (VG)	High (H)	((0.7,0.9,0.9,1;1,1), (0.8,0.9,0.9,0.95;0.9,0.9))
Best (B)	Very high (VH)	((0.9,1,1,1;1,1), (0.95,1,1,1;0.9,0.9))

Source: Adapted from Baykasoglu and Golcuk (2017); Dincer and Yuksel (2019)

Table 4. Linguistic evaluations for the criteria

	C1			C2			C3			C4			C5		
	DM1	DM2	DM3	DM1	DM2	DM3	DM1	DM2	DM3	DM1	DM2	DM3	DM1	DM2	DM3
C1	-	-	-	ML	L	L	MH	H	M	M	M	M	M	M	M
C2	VH	VH	VH	-	-	-	H	VH	H	M	ML	M	M	M	M
C3	MH	H	VH	M	M	M	-	-	-	M	MH	M	M	M	M
C4	MH	H	H	M	MH	MH	M	M	M	-	-	-	MH	H	M
C5	MH	MH	H	MH	M	M	M	M	ML	ML	ML	ML	-	-	-
C6	M	MH	H	M	M	MH	M	ML	ML	M	ML	ML	M	M	M
C7	ML	M	ML	M	MH	M	M	ML	M	M	M	M	ML	M	M
C8	M	MH	MH	ML	M	ML	M	M	M	M	M	M	ML	ML	M
C9	MH	M	ML	M	M	M	ML	M	M	M	ML	ML	M	M	M
C10	VH	VH	VH	M	M	MH	M	M	MH	M	M	MH	H	MH	H

	C6			C7			C8			C9			C10		
	DM1	DM2	DM3	DM1	DM2	DM3	DM1	DM2	DM3	DM1	DM2	DM3	DM1	DM2	DM3
C1	M	MH	M	ML	ML	M	ML	M	M	ML	M	M	ML	ML	L
C2	M	M	MH	ML	M	M	ML	M	M	M	M	M	M	MH	M
C3	M	MH	ML	M	MH	ML	M	M	M	M	MH	M	M	M	MH
C4	M	ML	M	M	M	M	M	M	M	MH	M	M	MH	M	M
C5	M	M	M	M	M	M	ML	M	M	M	M	M	MH	ML	M
C6	-	-	-	ML	M	M	ML	ML	ML	M	M	M	M	ML	ML
C7	ML	M	MH	-	-	-	MH	M	MH	M	M	M	MH	M	ML
C8	M	MH	M	M	M	M	-	-	-	ML	M	ML	M	M	ML
C9	M	M	M	ML	M	M	M	M	M	-	-	-	M	M	M
C10	H	H	VH	MH	M	MH	MH	H	VH	M	MH	MH	-	-	-

Table 5. Defuzzified Total Relation Matrix

	C1	C2	C3	C4	C5	C6	C7	C8	C9	C10
C1	0.13	0.12	0.18	0.15	0.16	0.17	0.13	0.15	0.15	0.12
C2	0.28	0.12	0.23	0.17	0.19	0.20	0.17	0.17	0.18	0.18
C3	0.26	0.17	0.13	0.18	0.18	0.19	0.17	0.18	0.18	0.18
C4	0.26	0.19	0.19	0.11	0.21	0.18	0.17	0.18	0.19	0.18
C5	0.23	0.17	0.17	0.14	0.11	0.18	0.16	0.16	0.17	0.16
C6	0.21	0.16	0.15	0.14	0.16	0.11	0.15	0.14	0.16	0.14
C7	0.19	0.17	0.16	0.16	0.16	0.18	0.10	0.18	0.17	0.16
C8	0.21	0.14	0.17	0.15	0.15	0.18	0.16	0.10	0.15	0.15
C9	0.20	0.16	0.16	0.14	0.17	0.17	0.15	0.16	0.11	0.15
C10	0.30	0.20	0.22	0.20	0.24	0.26	0.21	0.24	0.22	0.14

Table 6. Dimensions and Criteria Weights

Dimensions	Weights	Criteria	Weights
D1	0.210	C1	0.108
		C2	0.102
D2	0.203	C3	0.104
		C4	0.099
D3	0.195	C5	0.098
		C6	0.097
D4	0.187	C7	0.094
		C8	0.094
D5	0.204	C9	0.094
		C10	0.110

It is also concluded that flexibility of needs (C10) and branch availability (C1) are the most important criteria for the banks in agricultural finance. Furthermore, qualified personnel (C2) and data security (C3) are other significant items for the banks. However, it is also seen that loyalty (C7), brand equity (C8) and customer expectations (C9) have the lowest weights. It is seen that banks should mainly give importance to provide services to the customers in flexible times. In other words, if customer can access to the banks in different times related to the agricultural financing, this situation can increase the effectiveness of the banks in this area. Daly and Gebremedhin (2015) and Pradella (2015) also underlined the importance of the flexible working times for the banks so that the customers can get better services.

Additionally, it is also obvious that having necessary branches near to agricultural area has an important effect on the effectiveness of the banks regarding agricultural finance. In this circumstance, it is strongly recommended that banks should open enough number of branches to the strategic location where farmers can reach easily. For this purpose, firstly, a detailed analysis should be made by the banks to select the appropriate locations for the branches. In the literature, Řepková (2015) and Ohsato and Takahashi (2015) also identified that branch availability is a key item for the effectiveness of the banks. Another important point is that banks should improve their personnel for agricultural issues. Within this framework, necessary trainings should be given to these personnel in this context. Hence, it can be possible to give better services to the farmers so that the banks can be preferred more. Monferrer-Tirado et al. (2016) and Farah (2017) also concluded that banks should employ qualified personnel in different areas to increase their competitive powers. After examining criteria dimensions are also ranked with IT2 FTOPSIS. The linguistic evaluations of the decision makers for the alternatives are presented on Table 7.

In the next step, defuzzified decision matrix is developed and shown in Table 8.

In the final stage, 10 deposit banks are ranked according to effectiveness of the agricultural financing. Table 9 gives information about this ranking.

Table 9 demonstrates that state-owned banks (A1 and A2) are in the best position in the ranking. In addition to them, the third and fourth banks are foreign banks (A10 and A7). In spite of this situation, another foreign bank (A9) is on the last rank. This situation shows that state-owned banks in Turkey have better performance in comparison with others with respect to the agricultural finance. On the other side, there is not a strict priority between private and foreign banks for this situation. By considering these

Table 7. Linguistic Evaluations for the Alternatives

	Alternative 1			Alternative 2			Alternative 3			Alternative 4			Alternative 5		
	DM1	DM2	DM3	DM1	DM2	DM3	DM1	DM2	DM3	DM1	DM2	DM3	DM1	DM2	DM3
C1	VG	B	B	B	VG	G	VG	G	G	G	G	VG	G	VG	VG
C2	G	VG	VG	G	VG	M	VG	VG	G	VG	VG	B	VG	G	G
C3	VG	VG	B	VG	VG	B	VG	G	B	VG	VG	VG	VG	B	VG
C4	B	VG	B	B	VG	B	VG	VG	B	VG	VG	VG	B	B	VG
C5	B	B	VG	G	B	VG	B	VG	VG	VG	VG	G	VG	G	G
C6	B	VG	VG	B	VG	VG	VG	G	VG	VG	VG	VG	VG	VG	VG
C7	VG	B	VG	B	VG	VG	VG	G	VG	VG	VG	VG	VG	VG	G
C8	VG	B	B	B	VG	VG	VG	VG	VG	VG	G	VG	VG	VG	G
C9	B	B	VG	B	B	VG	G	G	VG	G	G	VG	G	VG	VG
C10	B	VG	VG	VG	VG	VG	VG	G	G	VG	G	M	G	G	VG
	Alternative 6			Alternative 7			Alternative 8			Alternative 9			Alternative 10		
	DM1	DM2	DM3	DM1	DM2	DM3	DM1	DM2	DM3	DM1	DM2	DM3	DM1	DM2	DM3
C1	VG	VG	G	B	VG	G	B	VG	G	G	VG	VG	M	VG	G
C2	G	M	G	VG	G	G	B	VG	G	VG	VG	G	VG	VG	VG
C3	B	VG	VG	VG	VG	VG	B	G	VG	VG	VG	VG	VG	VG	VG
C4	B	VG	B	VG	B	VG	B	VG	VG	VG	VG	VG	VG	B	VG
C5	VG	VG	VG	VG	G	VG	VG	G	VG	VGV	VG	G	VG	VG	G
C6	VG	G	VG	G	VG	VG	G	VG	VG	G	VG	VG	B	VG	VG
C7	VG	VG	G	VG	VG	G	G	VG	VG	G	VG	VG	G	VG	VG
C8	B	VG	VG	VG	VG	VG	VG	VG	VG	G	VG	VG	G	VG	VG
C9	B	VG	VG	G	VG	VG	G	VG	VG	VG	VG	VG	B	VG	VG
C10	G	M	G	VG	VG	G	G	M	G	G	VG	B	G	VG	B

Table 8. Defuzzified Decision Matrix

	A1	A2	A3	A4	A5	A6	A7	A8	A9	A10
C1	9.47	8.86	8.26	8.26	8.64	8.64	8.86	8.86	8.64	7.86
C2	8.64	7.86	8.64	9.25	8.26	7.47	8.26	8.86	8.64	9.03
C3	9.25	9.25	8.86	9.03	9.25	9.25	9.03	8.86	9.03	9.03
C4	9.47	9.47	9.25	9.03	9.47	9.47	9.25	9.25	9.03	9.25
C5	9.47	8.86	9.25	8.64	8.26	9.03	8.64	8.64	6.90	8.64
C6	9.25	9.25	8.64	9.03	9.03	8.64	8.64	8.64	8.64	9.25
C7	9.25	9.25	8.64	9.03	8.64	8.64	8.64	8.64	8.64	8.64
C8	9.47	9.25	9.03	8.64	8.64	9.25	9.03	9.03	8.64	8.64
C9	9.47	9.47	8.26	8.26	8.64	9.25	8.64	8.64	9.03	9.25
C10	9.25	9.03	8.26	7.86	8.26	7.47	8.64	7.47	8.86	8.86

Table 9. Ranking Results for the Alternatives

Ownership	Alternatives	D+	D-	Closeness Coefficient	Ranking
State-owned	Alternative 1	0.062	0.420	0.872	1
	Alternative 2	0.170	0.326	0.657	2
Private	Alternative 3	0.239	0.281	0.541	5
	Alternative 4	0.264	0.262	0.499	6
	Alternative 5	0.245	0.213	0.464	8
	Alternative 6	0.298	0.258	0.464	9
Foreign	Alternative 7	0.203	0.260	0.562	4
	Alternative 8	0.260	0.254	0.494	7
	Alternative 9	0.307	0.225	0.423	10
	Alternative 10	0.223	0.302	0.575	3

issues, it is defined that private and foreign banks should take some actions to improve their effectiveness related to agricultural finance. For this purpose, it is mainly recommended that they should open new branches near to agricultural regions and they employ people who are specialized in agricultural subjects.

SOLUTIONS AND RECOMMENDATIONS

IT2 FTOPSIS results also give information that state-owned banks in Turkey have better performance in comparison with others with respect to the agricultural finance. However, there is no priority between private and foreign banks for agricultural finance. Thus, it is recommended that especially private and foreign banks should open new branches near to agricultural regions and they employ people who are specialized in agricultural subjects. This situation improves agricultural production in the country.

FUTURE RESEARCH DIRECTIONS

In the future studies, new evaluations can be made with different approaches, such as hesitant fuzzy ANP and VIKOR. Therefore, it can be possible to make a comparison between different results. Another important point is that evaluation of the bank performance in agricultural finance can be made for European banking industry.

CONCLUSION

In this study, it is aimed to evaluate the effectiveness of Turkish banks for agricultural finance. In the first stage, 10 different criteria, which have an influence on this situation, are identified based on 5 different SERVQUAL perspectives. In addition to this issue, 10 different Turkish deposit banks traded on

BIST are selected as alternatives. The dimensions and criteria are weighted by using IT2 FDEMATEL approach. Moreover, these banks are ranked with IT2 FTOPSIS according to the performance results.

It is concluded that the physical condition is the most important dimension. In addition, confidence and empathy are other significant dimensions. It is also determined that flexibility of needs and branch availability are the most important criteria for the banks in agricultural finance. Moreover, qualified personnel (C2) and data security (C3) are other significant items for the banks. While considering these issues, it is recommended that banks should design a system in which customers can access to the banks in flexible times related to the agricultural financing.

Another important conclusion is that banks should open enough number of branches to the strategic location where farmers can reach easily. Hence, the farmers do not waste too much time to reach the banks in agricultural services. In this circumstance, banks should make a detailed analysis to select the appropriate locations for the branches. Parallel to this aspect, it is also recommended that banks should improve their personnel for agricultural issues with necessary trainings. This situation has a positive impact on the effectiveness of the banks regarding agricultural finance.

ACKNOWLEDGMENT

This study was supported by İstanbul Medipol University Scientific Research Project Commission (Project No: 2018/13).

REFERENCES

Abate, G. T., Rashid, S., Borzaga, C., & Getnet, K. (2016). Rural finance and agricultural technology adoption in Ethiopia: Does the institutional design of lending organizations matter? *World Development*, *84*, 235–253. doi:10.1016/j.worlddev.2016.03.003

Abdullah, L., & Zulkifli, N. (2015). Integration of fuzzy AHP and interval type-2 fuzzy DEMATEL: An application to human resource management. *Expert Systems with Applications*, *42*(9), 4397–4409. doi:10.1016/j.eswa.2015.01.021

Acha, I. A., Michael, E. I., & Essien, J. M. (2017). Nigeria's Investment Environment: Issues of Economic Growth and Development. *Expert Journal of Finance*, *5*, 1–11.

Adam, B. E., & Ahmed, S. B. (2005). On the experience of Islamic agricultural finance in Sudan: Challenges and sustainability. *Islamic Econ*, *18*, 63–65.

Adnan, K. M., Ying, L., Sarker, S. A., Hafeez, M., Razzaq, A., & Raza, M. H. (2018). Adoption of Contract Farming and Precautionary Savings to Manage the Catastrophic Risk of Maize Farming: Evidence from Bangladesh. *Sustainability*, *11*(1), 1–19. doi:10.3390u11010029

Ahmed, R. R., Vveinhardt, J., Štreimikienė, D., Ashraf, M., & Channar, Z. A. (2017). Modified SERVQUAL model and effects of customer attitude and technology on customer satisfaction in banking industry: Mediation, moderation and conditional process analysis. *Journal of Business Economics and Management*, *18*(5), 974–1004. doi:10.3846/16111699.2017.1368034

Ali, M., & Raza, S. A. (2017). Service quality perception and customer satisfaction in Islamic banks of Pakistan: The modified SERVQUAL model. *Total Quality Management & Business Excellence*, *28*(5-6), 559–577. doi:10.1080/14783363.2015.1100517

Altaf, M., Iqbal, N., Mohd. Mokhtar, S. S., & Sial, M. H. (2017). Managing consumer-based brand equity through brand experience in Islamic banking. *Journal of Islamic Marketing*, *8*(2), 218–242. doi:10.1108/JIMA-07-2015-0048

Amin, M. (2016). Internet banking service quality and its implication on e-customer satisfaction and e-customer loyalty. *International Journal of Bank Marketing*, *34*(3), 280–306. doi:10.1108/IJBM-10-2014-0139

Amin, M. (2016). Internet banking service quality and its implication on e-customer satisfaction and e-customer loyalty. *International Journal of Bank Marketing*, *34*(3), 280–306. doi:10.1108/IJBM-10-2014-0139

Ammirato, S., Sofo, F., Felicetti, A. M., & Raso, C. (2019). A methodology to support the adoption of IoT innovation and its application to the Italian bank branch security context. *European Journal of Innovation Management*, *22*(1), 146–174. doi:10.1108/EJIM-03-2018-0058

Antón, J., & Cattaneo, A. (2019). Agricultural Risk Management and Climate Change: What Role for Policy? *Global Challenges For Future Food And Agricultural Policies*, *1*, 281–306. doi:10.1142/9789813235403_0015

Bamakhramah, A. S. (2005). Book Review: On the Experience of Islamic Agricultural Finance in Sudan: Challenges and Sustainability. *Journal of King Abdulaziz University: Islamic Economics*, *18*(2).

Barani, N., Menhaj, M. H., Ramezanpoor, E., & Borazjani, M. A. (2015). Investigating the Impacts of Credits Granted by Agricultural Bank of Iran on Economic Conditions of Farmers in Hirmand Region. *International Journal of Agricultural Management and Development (IJAMAD)*, *5*(1047-2017-1604).

Basfirinci, C., & Mitra, A. (2015). A cross cultural investigation of airlines service quality through integration of Servqual and the Kano model. *Journal of Air Transport Management*, *42*, 239–248. doi:10.1016/j.jairtraman.2014.11.005

Baykasoğlu, A., & Gölcük, İ. (2017). Development of an interval type-2 fuzzy sets based hierarchical MADM model by combining DEMATEL and TOPSIS. *Expert Systems with Applications*, *70*, 37–51. doi:10.1016/j.eswa.2016.11.001

Beheshtinia, M. A., & Farzaneh Azad, M. (2017). A fuzzy QFD approach using SERVQUAL and Kano models under budget constraint for hotel services. *Total Quality Management & Business Excellence*, 1–23.

Bratawisnu, M. K., Giri, R. R. W., & Rinaldi, R. (2017, May). Association perception customer feedback with text network analysis in social media (case study on internet banking BRI, BCA, Mandiri in Indonesia). In *2017 5th International Conference on Information and Communication Technology (ICoIC7)* (pp. 1-6). IEEE.

Chisasa, J., & Makina, D. (2013). Bank credit and agricultural output in South Africa: A Cobb-Douglas empirical analysis. *The International Business & Economics Research Journal (Online)*, *12*(4), 387–398.

Cook, J., Oviatt, K., Main, D. S., Kaur, H., & Brett, J. (2015). Re-conceptualizing urban agriculture: An exploration of farming along the banks of the Yamuna River in Delhi, India. *Agriculture and Human Values, 32*(2), 265–279. doi:10.100710460-014-9545-z

Daly, A., & Gebremedhin, T. A. (2015). Can An "Indigenous Employment Program" Work? A Case Study of National Australia Bank. *Economic Papers: A journal of applied economics and policy, 34*(3), 128-138.

Dawson, S. K., Warton, D. I., Kingsford, R. T., Berney, P., Keith, D. A., & Catford, J. A. (2017). Plant traits of propagule banks and standing vegetation reveal flooding alleviates impacts of agriculture on wetland restoration. *Journal of Applied Ecology, 54*(6), 1907–1918. doi:10.1111/1365-2664.12922

Dinçer, H., Hacıoğlu, Ü., & Yüksel, S. (2017). A Strategic Approach to Global Financial Crisis in Banking Sector: A Critical Appraisal of Banking Strategies Using Fuzzy ANP and Fuzzy Topsis Methods. [IJSEM]. *International Journal of Sustainable Economies Management, 6*(1), 1–21. doi:10.4018/ijsem.2017010101

Dincer, H., Uzunkaya, S. S., & Yüksel, S. (2019d). An IT2-Based Hybrid Decision-Making Model Using Hesitant Fuzzy Linguistic Term Sets for Selecting the Development Plan of Financial Economics. *International Journal of Computational Intelligence Systems, 12*(2), 460–473. doi:10.2991/ijcis.d.190312.001

Dinçer, H., & Yüksel, S. (2018). Financial Sector-Based Analysis of the G20 Economies Using the Integrated Decision-Making Approach with DEMATEL and TOPSIS. In *Emerging Trends in Banking and Finance* (pp. 210–223). Cham, Switzerland: Springer. doi:10.1007/978-3-030-01784-2_13

Dincer, H., & Yuksel, S. (2019). IT2-Based Fuzzy Hybrid Decision Making Approach to Soft Computing. *IEEE Access: Practical Innovations, Open Solutions, 7*, 15932–15944. doi:10.1109/ACCESS.2019.2895359

Dinçer, H., Yuksel, S., & Bozaykut-Buk, T. (2018b). Evaluation of Financial and Economic Effects on Green Supply Chain Management With Multi-Criteria Decision-Making Approach: Evidence From Companies Listed in BIST. In Handbook of Research on Supply Chain Management for Sustainable Development (pp. 144–175). Hershey, PA: IGI Global. doi:10.4018/978-1-5225-5757-9.ch009

Dinçer, H., Yüksel, S., Korsakienė, R., Raišienė, A. G., & Bilan, Y. (2019c). IT2 Hybrid Decision-Making Approach to Performance Measurement of Internationalized Firms in the Baltic States. *Sustainability, 11*(1), 296. doi:10.3390u11010296

Dinçer, H., Yüksel, S., & Martínez, L. (2019a). Analysis of Balanced Scorecard-based SERVQUAL Criteria based on Hesitant Decision-making Approaches. *Computers & Industrial Engineering.*

Dinçer, H., Yüksel, S., & Martínez, L. (2019e). Interval type 2-based hybrid fuzzy evaluation of financial services in E7 economies with DEMATEL-ANP and MOORA methods. *Applied Soft Computing.*

Dinçer, H., Yüksel, S., & Pınarbaşı, F. (2019b). SERVQUAL-Based Evaluation of Service Quality of Energy Companies in Turkey: Strategic Policies for Sustainable Economic Development. In The Circular Economy and Its Implications on Sustainability and the Green Supply Chain (pp. 142-167). Hershey, PA: IGI Global.

Dinçer, H., Yüksel, S., & Şenel, S. (2018a). Analyzing the global risks for the financial crisis after the great depression using comparative hybrid hesitant fuzzy decision-making models: Policy recommendations for sustainable economic growth. *Sustainability, 10*(9), 3126. doi:10.3390u10093126

Ekwere, G. E., & Edem, I. D. (2014). Effects of agricultural credit facility on the agricultural production and rural development. *International Journal of Environment, 3*(2), 192–204. doi:10.3126/ije.v3i2.10529

Elhiraika, A. B. (2003). On the experience of Islamic agricultural finance in Sudan: challenges and sustainability. Jeddah, Saudi Arabia: Islamic Development Bank.

Farah, M. F. (2017). Consumers' switching motivations and intention in the case of bank mergers: A cross-cultural study. *International Journal of Bank Marketing, 35*(2), 254–274. doi:10.1108/IJBM-05-2016-0067

Galeeva, R. B. (2016). SERVQUAL application and adaptation for educational service quality assessments in Russian higher education. *Quality Assurance in Education, 24*(3), 329–348. doi:10.1108/QAE-06-2015-0024

Hye, Q., & Wizarat, S. (2011). Impact of financial liberalization on agricultural growth: A case study of Pakistan. *China Agricultural Economic Review, 3*(2), 191–209. doi:10.1108/17561371111131317

Kaura, V., Durga Prasad, C. S., & Sharma, S. (2015). Service quality, service convenience, price and fairness, customer loyalty, and the mediating role of customer satisfaction. *International Journal of Bank Marketing, 33*(4), 404–422. doi:10.1108/IJBM-04-2014-0048

Kumar, M., Sujit, K. S., & Charles, V. (2018). Deriving managerial implications through SERVQUAL gap elasticity in UAE banking. *International Journal of Quality & Reliability Management, 35*(4), 940–964. doi:10.1108/IJQRM-10-2016-0176

Le Nguyen, C. (2018). Preventing the use of financial institutions for money laundering and the implications for financial privacy. *Journal of money laundering control, 21*(1), 47-58.

Loureiro, S. M. C., & Sarmento, E. M. (2017, September). The Impact of Generation Y's Customer Experience on Emotions: Online Banking Sector. In *Conference on Creativity in Intelligent Technologies and Data Science* (pp. 616-639). Cham, Switzerland: Springer. 10.1007/978-3-319-65551-2_45

Martin, S. J., & Clapp, J. (2015). Finance for agriculture or agriculture for finance? *Journal of Agrarian Change, 15*(4), 549–559. doi:10.1111/joac.12110

Mendel, J. M. (2017). Type-2 fuzzy sets. In *Uncertain rule-based fuzzy systems* (pp. 259–306). Cham, Switzerland: Springer. doi:10.1007/978-3-319-51370-6_6

Moliner-Tena, M. A., Monferrer-Tirado, D., & Estrada-Guillén, M. (2019). Customer engagement, non-transactional behaviors and experience in services: A study in the bank sector. *International Journal of Bank Marketing, 37*(3), 730–754. doi:10.1108/IJBM-04-2018-0107

Monferrer-Tirado, D., Estrada-Guillén, M., Fandos-Roig, J. C., Moliner-Tena, M. Á., & Sanchez Garcia, J. (2016). Service quality in bank during an economic crisis. *International Journal of Bank Marketing, 34*(2), 235–259. doi:10.1108/IJBM-01-2015-0013

Obaidullah, M. (2015). Enhancing food security with Islamic microfinance: Insights from some recent experiments. *Agricultural Finance Review*, *75*(2), 142–168. doi:10.1108/AFR-11-2014-0033

Ohsato, S., & Takahashi, M. (2015). Management efficiency in Japanese regional banks: A network DEA. *Procedia: Social and Behavioral Sciences*, *172*, 511–518. doi:10.1016/j.sbspro.2015.01.394

Ouma, S. (2016). From financialization to operations of capital: Historicizing and disentangling the finance–farmland-nexus. *Geoforum*, *72*, 82–93. doi:10.1016/j.geoforum.2016.02.003

Parasuraman, A., Zeithaml, V. A., & Berry, L. L. (1988). Servqual: A multiple-item scale for measuring consumer perc. *Journal of Retailing*, *64*(1), 12.

Paul, J., Mittal, A., & Srivastav, G. (2016). Impact of service quality on customer satisfaction in private and public sector banks. *International Journal of Bank Marketing*, *34*(5), 606–622. doi:10.1108/IJBM-03-2015-0030

Pokharel, K. P., Regmi, M., Featherstone, A. M., & Archer, D. W. (2019). Examining the financial performance of agricultural cooperatives in the USA. *Agricultural Finance Review*, *79*(2), 271–282. doi:10.1108/AFR-11-2017-0103

Porth, L., & Tan, K. S. (2016). Introduction–2014 International Agricultural Risk, Finance, and Insurance Conference (IARFIC). *Agricultural Finance Review*, *76*(1). doi:10.1108/AFR-05-2016-0049

Power, G. J. (2016). Quantitative finance for agricultural commodities: Discussion and extension. *Agricultural Finance Review*, *76*(1), 27–41. doi:10.1108/AFR-02-2016-0013

Pradella, L. (2015). The working poor in Western Europe: Labour, poverty and global capitalism. *Comparative European Politics*, *13*(5), 596–613. doi:10.1057/cep.2015.17

Qi, T., & Sun, R. (2017, July). An empirical study on the contribution of agricultural policy finance to agricultural economic growth in China. In *2017 3rd International Conference on Economics, Social Science, Arts, Education and Management Engineering (ESSAEME 2017)*. Atlantis Press. 10.2991/essaeme-17.2017.22

Rahman, S., Hussain, A., & Taqi, M. (2014). Impact of agricultural credit on agricultural productivity in Pakistan: An empirical analysis. *International Journal of Advanced Research in Management and Social Sciences*, *3*(4), 125–139.

Řepková, I. (2015). Banking efficiency determinants in the Czech banking sector. *Procedia Economics and Finance*, *23*, 191–196. doi:10.1016/S2212-5671(15)00367-6

Rezaei, J., Kothadiya, O., Tavasszy, L., & Kroesen, M. (2018). Quality assessment of airline baggage handling systems using SERVQUAL and BWM. *Tourism Management*, *66*, 85–93. doi:10.1016/j.tourman.2017.11.009

Ryan, C. (2017). Gendering Palestinian dispossession: Evaluating land loss in the West bank. *Antipode*, *49*(2), 477–498. doi:10.1111/anti.12280

Saqib, L., Zafar, M. A., Khan, K., Roberts, K. W., & Zafar, A. M. (2015). Local agricultural financing and Islamic banks: Is Qard-al-Hassan a possible solution? *Journal of Islamic Accounting and Business Research*, *6*(1), 122–147. doi:10.1108/JIABR-04-2012-0018

Severini, S., Tantari, A., & Di Tommaso, G. (2017). Effect of agricultural policy on income and revenue risks in Italian farms: Implications for the use of risk management policies. *Agricultural Finance Review*, *77*(2), 295–311. doi:10.1108/AFR-07-2016-0067

Shafiai, M. H. M., & Moi, M. R. (2015). Financial problems among farmers in Malaysia: Islamic agricultural finance as a possible solution. *Asian Social Science*, *11*(4), 1.

Shahbaz, M., Shahbaz Shabbir, M., & Sabihuddin Butt, M. (2013). Effect of financial development on agricultural growth in Pakistan: New extensions from bounds test to level relationships and Granger causality tests. *International Journal of Social Economics*, *40*(8), 707–728. doi:10.1108/IJSE-01-2012-0002

Stefano, N. M., Casarotto Filho, N., Barichello, R., & Sohn, A. P. (2015). A fuzzy SERVQUAL based method for evaluated of service quality in the hotel industry. *Procedia CIRP*, *30*, 433–438. doi:10.1016/j.procir.2015.02.140

Stein, H., Maganga, F. P., Odgaard, R., Askew, K., & Cunningham, S. (2016). The formal divide: Customary rights and the allocation of credit to agriculture in Tanzania. *The Journal of Development Studies*, *52*(9), 1306–1319. doi:10.1080/00220388.2016.1146701

Thota, C., Manogaran, G., Lopez, D., & Vijayakumar, V. (2017). Big data security framework for distributed cloud data centers. In Cybersecurity breaches and issues surrounding online threat protection (pp. 288–310). Hershey, PA: IGI Global. doi:10.4018/978-1-5225-1941-6.ch012

Turvey, C. G. (2017). Historical developments in agricultural finance and the genesis of America's farm credit system. *Agricultural Finance Review*, *77*(1), 4–21. doi:10.1108/AFR-09-2016-0076

Vitiello, D., Grisso, J. A., Whiteside, K. L., & Fischman, R. (2015). From commodity surplus to food justice: Food banks and local agriculture in the United States. *Agriculture and Human Values*, *32*(3), 419–430. doi:10.100710460-014-9563-x

Wang, Y., Hahn, C., & Sutrave, K. (2016, February). Mobile payment security, threats, and challenges. In *2016 second international conference on mobile and secure services (MobiSecServ)* (pp. 1-5). IEEE. 10.1109/MOBISECSERV.2016.7440226

Woodard, J. (2016). Big data and Ag-Analytics: An open source, open data platform for agricultural & environmental finance, insurance, and risk. *Agricultural Finance Review*, *76*(1), 15–26. doi:10.1108/AFR-03-2016-0018

Wu, T., Liu, X., & Liu, F. (2018). An interval type-2 fuzzy TOPSIS model for large scale group decision making problems with social network information. *Information Sciences*, *432*, 392–410. doi:10.1016/j.ins.2017.12.006

Yahuza, B. S. (2019). Viability of Muzara'ah Contract on Agro-financing in Alleviating Rural Poverty in Kano State, Nigeria. *Al-Muzara'ah*, *6*(2), 91–102. doi:10.29244/jam.6.2.91-102

Ye, H., Hu, X., & Xie, M. (2019, February). Research on Supply Chain Finance Model based on Agricultural Logistics Park Information Platform. In *2018 International Symposium on Social Science and Management Innovation (SSMI 2018)*. Atlantis Press. 10.2991smi-18.2019.40

Yoganathan, D., Jebarajakirthy, C., & Thaichon, P. (2015). The influence of relationship marketing orientation on brand equity in banks. *Journal of Retailing and Consumer Services*, *26*, 14–22. doi:10.1016/j.jretconser.2015.05.006

Yüksel, S., Dinçer, H., & Emir, Ş. (2017). Comparing the performance of Turkish deposit banks by using DEMATEL, Grey Relational Analysis (GRA) and MOORA approaches. *World Journal of Applied Economics*, *3*(2), 26–47. doi:10.22440/wjae.3.2.2

Yüksel, S., Dinçer, H., & Meral, Y. (2019). Financial Analysis of International Energy Trade: A Strategic Outlook for EU-15. *Energies*, *12*(3), 431. doi:10.3390/en12030431

Zakariah, M. R., Zakariah, S., & Pyeman, J. (2016). IPA vs. SERVQUAL: Service quality measurement for higher education industry. In *Proceedings of the 1st AAGBS International Conference on Business Management 2014 (AiCoBM 2014)* (pp. 139-150). Singapore: Springer. 10.1007/978-981-287-426-9_12

KEY TERMS AND DEFINITIONS

DEMATEL: The decision-making trial and evaluation laboratory.
SERVQUAL: An approach to evaluate service quality of the companies.
TOPSIS: Technique for order preference by similarity to ideal solution.

Chapter 3
Effects of Internet on Tourism Marketing:
An Empirical Analysis About Online Tourism

Nihan Garipağaoğlu Uğur
İstanbul Medeniyet Üniversitesi, Turkey

ABSTRACT

The purpose of this study is to search for the difference between traditional marketing and electronic marketing on tourism. The data is based on empirical researches and literature reviews. The study is based on descriptive analysis. An overview of this study indicates that hotels and mostly visitors prefer to use an online reservation system and online travel agencies. This study provides tourism suppliers with ways to use electronic marketing and communication with visitors. Also, tourism suppliers are able to prepare marketing strategies based on visitor choice to use while travel planning.

INTRODUCTION

Tourism is the world's largest sector which has got new activities, destinations, markets and rapid changes with dynamic growth. People are traveling the world. Joining the tour packages, adventure experiences, cruises. During their trip, visitors and activities make economic and social impact on the local communities. First impression of tourism is people who visit places for sightseeing, visiting relatives or friends, take vacation and also participation in business trip or professional activity and need transportation for their vacation (Goeldner & Ritchie, 2009).

Tourism identified four perspectives:

- Tourist looking for experiences and satisfactions.
- Business people make profit by providing goods and services for tourism market.
- Government of the local community see tourism as a wealth factor for economy.

DOI: 10.4018/978-1-7998-0035-4.ch003

- Host community see tourism as an employment factor.

Tourism is the interaction among tourist, tourism suppliers, governments, host communities and environment (Goeldner & Ritchie, 2009). Tourism has heterogeneous structure with stakeholders than other industries (Le Roux, 2015). Technology has changed the customers purchasing habits with tourism products. Also customers endowed with technology to classify, customize and purchase tourism product. Additional that support tourism organizations to develop and distribute their services worldwide (Buhalis & Laws, 2008).

Definitions of Tourism

Definition by United Nations World Tourism Organization (UNWTO, 2019) is “Tourism is a social, cultural and economic phenomenon which entails the movement of people to countries or places outside their usual environment for personal or business/ professional purposes. These people called visitors and tourism has to do with their activities, some of which imply tourism expenditure”

Visitor who is taking a trip to outside of usual environment for any purpose and stay less than a year. Tourist or overnight visitor means is “trip includes overnight stay”. Excursionist or same-day visitor mean is visit a place but not stay overnight (UNWTO, 2019). Excursionist also called day-trippers because they stay less than twenty-four hours. Destinations and activities are influenced tourist choice and travel motivation. Such as natural resources and environment; the built environment that reflections of cultural and historical of host region; the infrastructure of tourism destination and also superstructure should respond to demands of visitors; information is the effective manner to present of tourism destination. (Goeldner & Ritchie, 2009).

Operating Sectors

The tourism sector is the gathering different productions units that provide “goods and services” demanded by visitors (UNWTO, 2019). Visitors defined the quality of services are created by employees and human factor that holds the level of quality in service business (Kandampully & Hu, 2007).

Transportation

Tourism and transportation are inseparably close to each other. There are different models of transportation which are air travel; road travel, railway, and cruises (Goeldner & Ritchie, 2009).

Accommodation

Providing accommodation for travelers is oldest commercial business. Dwelling-place and food service are huge important for tourism economy (Goeldner & Ritchie, 2009). Seven segments affect to customer satisfaction; reservations, check-in/check-out, room, food and beverage, services especially cleaning, facilities, cost and fees (Le Roux, 2015)

Figure 1. Operating sectors of tourism industry (Goeldner & Ritchie, 2009)

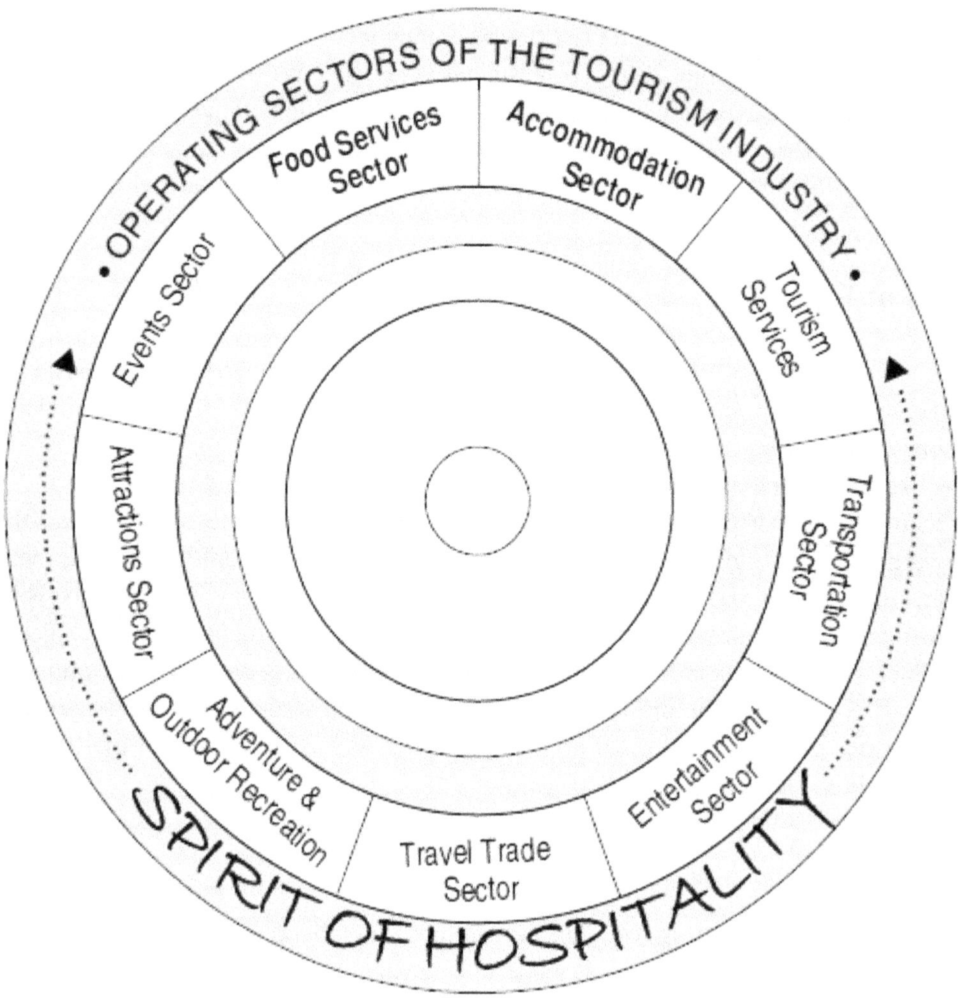

Food Service

Food service industry is a pretty old trade. Taverns and inns provided food and accommodations. Today restaurants, fast food services, vending, coffee shops, cafeterias provide food and atmosphere (Goeldner & Ritchie, 2009).

Meeting and Conventions

Meeting and conventions business is huge and needs more meeting planners, consultants and suppliers of goods. Domestic conferences provide source of business; also international conventions, conferences and congress are very attractive segment of tourism market (Goeldner & Ritchie, 2009).

Number of meetings per country 2017

Table 1. Worldwide ranking: number of meeting per country (ICCA, 2017)

RANK	COUNTRY	MEETINGS
1	USA	941
2	Germany	682
3	United Kingdom	592
4	Spain	564
5	Italy	515
6	France	506
7	Japan	414
8	China- P.R.	376
9	Canada	360
10	Netherland	307

Turkey is 49th country with 57 meeting and come after Uruguay in ranking list of worldwide meeting (ICCA, 2017).

Travel Agents

All travels need arrangements with variety of choices regarding accommodations and transportations. In addition to that destination, attractions and activities have an important role of holiday trip. Visitors may gather all information and make reservation by themselves or prefer to use travel agents for all arrangements. Travel agency is a middleman; bringing buyer and seller together as a broker. Travel agents is a specialist who saves client money and time. Internet has changed the commerce type. Internet provide to deal directly with customers and sellers. Using internet bring e- ticket system for airlines and online booking via online travel agencies (Goeldner & Ritchie, 2009).

Global Distribution System (GDS)

Global Distribution System is use for electronic travel reservation system which in use throughout the world such as Amadeus, Sabre, Galileo and Worlspan. Online travel is huge success for e-commerce. Travel distributions have new trends with GDS. Travel e-commerce, electronic ticketing, graphic seat selection are most important innovation. An expert of travel marketing organization provide assistance in planning and sales campaign, select market and research the target market, finds new markets and lead a sales and marketing program (Goeldner & Ritchie, 2009).

Internet and Electronic Commerce

Internet is a new channel of distribution that makes direct selling from supplier to customer. “E-commerce” refers to selling purchase via internet. Tourism related “goods and services” are also the kind of internet sales and online travel sales are increasingly growing (Goeldner & Ritchie, 2009).

The purpose of this study is to use internet in tourism industry and development of sales channels. Changing ways of sales are important to understand the new marketing trends.

MARKETING

Academically, marketing officially began early in twentieth century. Marketing is the conception of carry out the process of pricing, promotion and distributions of goods and services to customer satisfactions (Tetteh, 2017:8)

Traditional marketing is based on discover and satisfy of customer needs and wants. Marketing consultant communicate with customer such as face to face, via magazines or catalogues. Good and services create for customers need and want. "Marketing is the process of planning and executing the conception, pricing, promotion and distribution of ideas, goods and services to create exchange that satisfy individual and

organizational objectives." (Kotler, 2003). The marketing assignment is not to find just customer for the goods and services but to find the right good and services to suites the customer needs and wants (Kaaya, 2014) . Marketing is not only to getting right product to right target market but also provide it at the "right place", at the "right price", "right time", additionally that "right communications and promotion". Marketing process consist of: analyzing market opportunities, developing strategies, planning and managing the marketing effort (Londre, 2014).

Marketing Mix (4P) Theory

Marketing Mix is the decision, planning, and combination of how to set up individual tools to produce a desired response. This includes everything to influence or control the demand of a product. This describes as a combination of individual building blocks, for a specific goal (Zrener, 2015)

According to Philip Kotler's (2003) marketing mix, also known as 4P includes Product, Price, Place and Promotion. Four Ps determined how a service given, how a product is made, costs, distributed place and how promoted (Van Der Merwe, 2003).

Product

Product is the key of the customer needs and wants. There are different viewpoints of product for needs. Main point is what kind of functions that customer is looking for in the product. For that, it is necessary to studying the market in depth (Kotler, 2003).

Combination of goods and services including design, branding, featuring, quality, maintenance contracts, guarantee and return/replace policies (Londre, 2014). Customer value has five hierarchy levels for product: "core benefit, basic product, expected product, augmented product and potential product". Buying a product is self-benefit for customer. Basic product is produce for customer needs. Expected product is full fill the customer expectations. Augmented product is more than what customer expects. Potential product is might be wanted product. (Varfan, 2008).

Figure 2. The 4P's of marketing mix

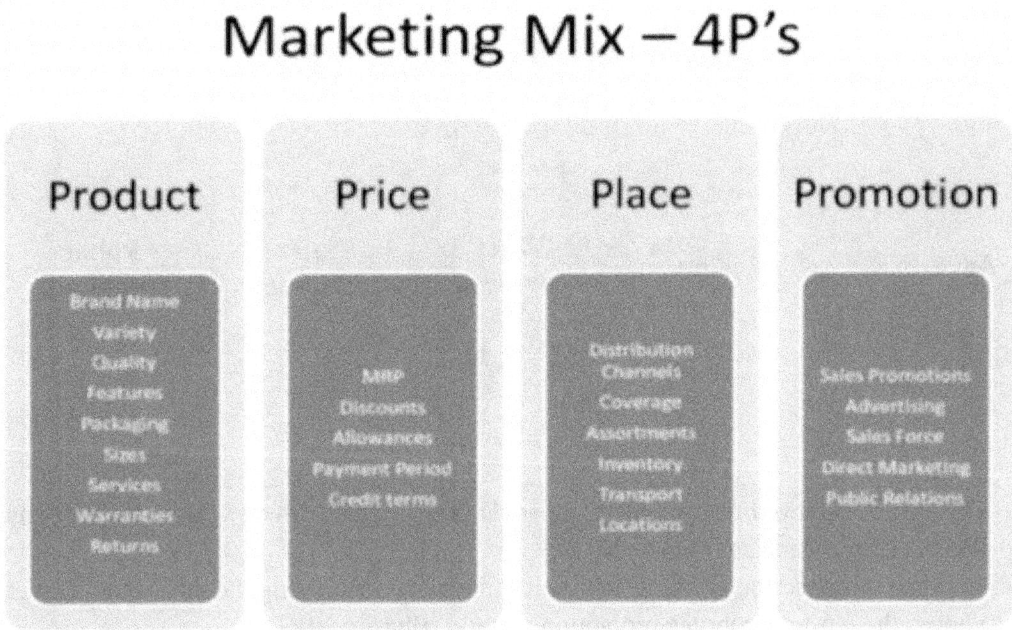

Price

How much money a customer willing to pay for product? This is all about pricing issue. Pricing also includes discounts, wholesale, promotional sale, payment periods, credit terms. All decisions about prices, depends on competitive environment, buyer perceptions and economic conditions (Londre, 2014). There are six steps for setting a price: Selection of product; Determination of market demand; Opinion of cost; Searching competitors' prices; Choosing of pricing method; Deciding final price (Varfan, 2008)

Place

The supplier firm's functions that make the product ready to use, choose trade and distribution channels, locations, inventory, transportation. The point is put on the market a product at the right place, right price, right time with right partner. It is important that develop an effective distribution plan, strategies and tactics (Londre, 2014). Place means in which location settled and also decision on distribution channels and transportation (Kotler, 2003)

Promotion

Promotion is mainly focus on company's targeted customers and communicate ways to them (Kotler, 2003). Communication means on which channels suitable for company and products, both for customers and employees. This can be both classic with print media, radio and television, as well as online via social media websites. The distribution policy determines the ways in which the product should be distributed. The essential part of the sales policy is to bridge the distance between production and purchase of the

Figure 3. Promotional Mix; https://www.marketing91.com/promotional-mix/

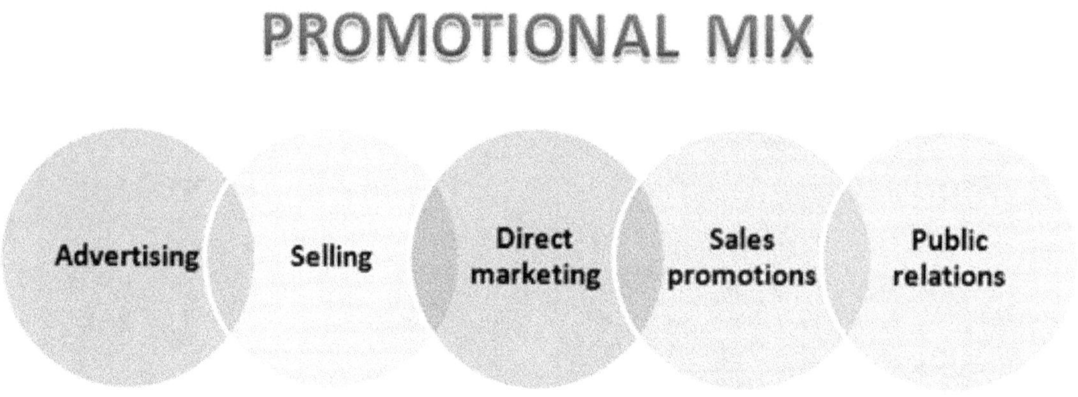

product. This can be achieved through the company's own website, directly on site or in tourism with the help of other travel agencies (Zrener, 2015).

A promotional mix described as achieve a goal and make profit during the manage to deliver a message that chosen the most appropriate promotion method (Bhasin, 2019)

Advertising

One of the main factor of marketing. It shows how the market perceives the company. It helps to carry message to potential customers and reach the far and wide area (Bhasin, 2019). Non personal or mass selling such as TV, radio, magazines, online, mobile or newspaper. Usually paid for advertising and use convincing essence about products (Londre, 2014).

Selling

Sales Force is the company's human power about offering solution for customer needs (Varfan, 2008). Personal selling is the one by one communication between buyers and sellers. Despite of expensive method, it still most successful as buyer-seller relationship (Bhasin, 2019).

Direct Marketing

Online, direct mail, database management, catalogs, telemarketing, database, face to face response for communicate with customers. Interactive or online marketing is a form that uses internet to deliver messages to customers. (Londre, 2014). Face to face marketing is using by companies where they send to their sales personal to potential buyers. Mailing use when company make an announcement or reminder for customers. Catalogs send to potential buyers for introduce products to the market. Telemarketing is another direct marketing way. Sales personals call potential buyers and gives information about products and deal about it (Varfan, 2008).

Sales Promotions

Promotion tools make value for the company such as speed up sales; incentive customer to buy. Includes discounts, money-refunds, frequency or loyalty programs, events, coupons, premiums and more (Londre, 2014). Promotions are major factor in marketing. Promotions attract the customers. This strategy usually uses for reach short term to make high gain. Promotion could be use in different types. Such as targeting new customers or rewarding loyal customers (Varfan, 2008).

Public Relations

Public relations (PR) enable to company to influence and manipulate the target market. Create positive image for company (Bhasin, 2019). Public relation works with various programs that designed to protect or promote a company's image (Londre, 2014).

In order to achieved promotional mix, company should have a look at the competitors because monitoring their promotions and events might provide a guidance to assist at the company's promotional mix. While establishing promotional mix, decide a few factors: determine the target market; objective about expectations about promotion mix; design the content of message; select promotional channel; determine of budget; choose promotional mix; measure the results of the program (Bhasin, 2019).

Social Media Marketing

Traditional marketing is defined as TV, radio, print media and internet advertising. In addition to advertisement, use public relation strategies and mailings. Thus, social media marketing is defined as promotion or selling goods and services on social media sites. Social media has growth with internet and following that smart phones, tablets, notebooks allow people to connect at everywhere (Cowden, 2014). Mass media is perceived hotchpotch, however alternative media channels are becoming more attractive to consumers. Despite of online and social media marketing seems to take attention of youngest, this does not mean that traditional marketing is totally end. Companies both use traditional marketing methods and new alternative marketing methods together (Barlow & Birkhahn, 2005).

Social media is a compound factor of promotion mix because it enables to companies directly contact with customers which is traditional sense and also enables customers talk to each other which is non-traditional sense (Mangold & Faulds, 2009). Social media marketing and e-WOM (electronic word of mouth) use with correct methods, it can be perfect way to get new customers (Trusov, Bucklin, & Pauwels, 2009). Internet has extended and provide more opportunities to companies in marketing. Company's website could have lots of attention and present the company in common media. Internet has become a powerful marketing tool (Varfan, 2008). Internet helps the companies to be able to target potential consumers and also helps the companies to find out customer needs (Kotler, 2003).

Internet marketing describes as "the application of the Internet and related digital technologies to achieve marketing objectives and support the modern marketing concept". Even internet marketing is dominant, traditional marketing is still valid and marketing mix are still relevant. Internet gives new opportunities to marketers (Chaffey, Chadwick, Johnston, & Mayer, 2000). Internet provides a chance to offering a product that please the customers' needs. Besides that enable the companies to give more information about company and essence of products (Varfan, 2008). When customers buy a product from internet, they can touch or try it. Therefore companies offer guarantee for products (Pui-Mun, 2002).

Figure 4. Internet Users In the World by Region – 2019 (Internet World Stats, 2019)

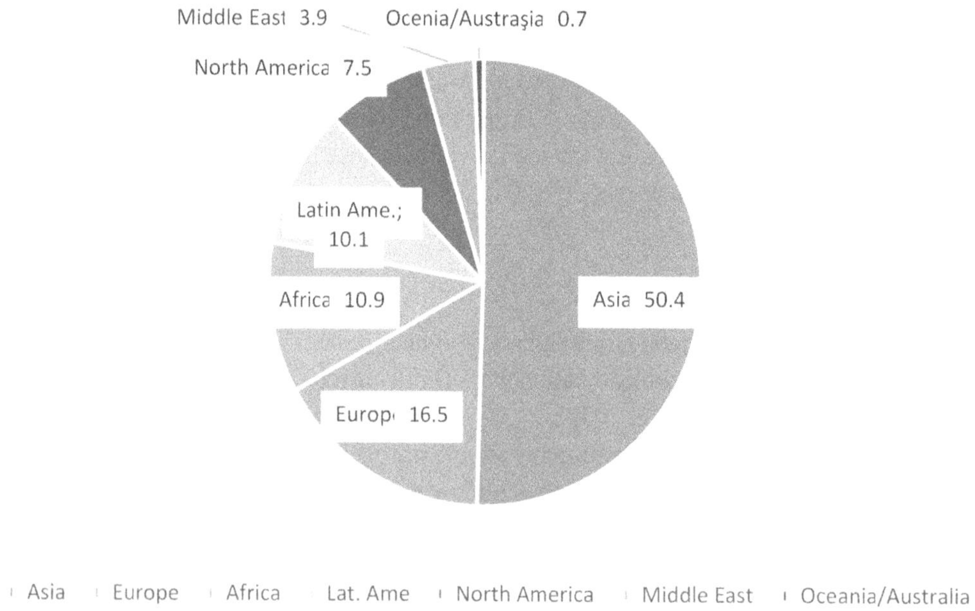

Price of product that sells on internet is very competitive because it is easy to compare price among others (Hagel & Armstrong, 1997). Companies expand from local market to international markets via internet. Internet also provide companies to make profit from new markets. Internet also use for promotional mix which are public relations, advertising, sales promotions and direct marketing by using mail and website (Chaffey et al., 2000).

TOURISM MARKETING

Tourism is combine of personalized goods and services. Tourism marketing is organized and interconnected with other service providers to satisfy the tourists. (Pillai, 2010).

Difference of Tourism Marketing

There are some differences between tourism marketing and manufacturer marketing (Kaaya, 2014).

İntangibility

Tourism distribution channels are similar manufacturing or agricultural industries. Their products reach the costumer through distributors and wholesaler. However tourism produce mostly services. Services are intangible. This means there is not physical product to touch (Goeldner & Ritchie, 2009). The major products of tourism and hospitality organizations like transport companies, hotels, travel agencies

Figure 5. Scale of Market entitles (Shostack, 1977)

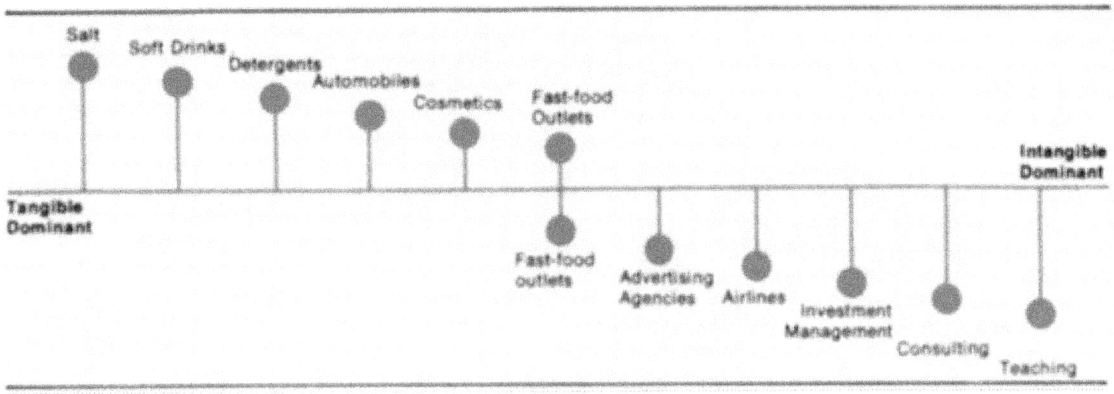

provide intangible services. Even they use tangible elements to provide but services are intangible and make value (Kusluvan, 2003).

Inseparability

Manufacturer goods produce first, then sell them to consumers. Even if not sold, it could stock. It can sell at another time. However service providers and customers should be together during the production. Production and consumption of services are same time and same place therefore customers' presence is necessary. In tourism and hospitality sector, employees and customers are usually face to face contact during services and that means a lot to customer satisfaction (Kusluvan, 2003).

Heterogeneity

Heterogeneity define is characteristic of services which have variations and discrepancy. Heterogeneity makes difficult to standardize the quality of services because from one service to another or even in same service can change day to day or customer to customer perception (BD Dictionary, 2019). Variability is involved with people. It deepens on customer perceptions, employees' attitudes, behaviors. Variability, inseparability and intangibility are characteristic of services and play huge role of quality and customer satisfaction (Kusluvan, 2003).

Marketing Mix (7P) in Tourism

Marketing mix 4P related with marketing; 7P related with service marketing (Market Research, 2019). Variability, inseparability and intangibility causes some difference in tourism marketing mix.

Tourism Product

Customers not only buy a tourism product but also buy the expectation of benefits. Customer perception of product benefits, adapting products to meet customer expectations are the process of find target market. Tourist visits defined as pack of tangible and intangible components at a destination. These

Figure 6. Marketing Mix 7P (Professional Academy,2019)

components are: attraction and environment of destination; accessibility to destination; facilities and services; images; price. These components mostly effective on customer motivation to choose (Middleton, Fyall, & Morgan, 2009).

Place for Tourism

Location or geographical environment create huge importance for tourism and hospitality sector (Pillai, 2010). Place means that the point of sale, and access customers to reach products via distribution channels. Travel agents are the one way to access tourism product. Internet provides alternative distribution channels for travel, accommodation and tourism products (Middleton et al., 2009).

Promotion for Tourism

Traditionally advertising attract attention and make impression on someone who watches TV or reads paper. Hopefully they remember this advertisement while visiting a travel agency. Instead of traditional advertisement, a website is consulted when a customer need information. Online searching provides customer information to the company (Middleton et al., 2009).

Price for Tourism

Pricing of services is harder than pricing of goods. Service provider not only charge for cost of goods but also calculate a price for ambiance and service (MSG, 2019). There different segment of customers. Marketers classified and located them with their price choices. While new tourism developments are planned, those segments are considered and feasible plans are required to identify the customers willing the pay price. Lots of people motivated with price (Middleton et al., 2009). Customers pay different prices for different tourism product. The price band of services represent the range of price that customer is willing to pay. Price indicate value to the customer. If there are competitors on the market, customers will demand elasticity for price. On the other hand, if there is lack of availability, there will be no elasticity on price (Saxena, 2008). Price changes by seasons, activities, exchange rates, facilities and services.

People

People are most important factor in tourism industry because service is providing for consumer. Also inseparable from employee providing in service industry (MSG, 2019). People in target market is require for exact types of goods and services. Therefore, company's employees are important in marketing because they deliver the services. Hire the right people to deliver services to customers is important for service quality and customer satisfaction (The Marketing Mix, 2019).

Process

The process of service providing is crucial. Same standard of service always requires (MSG, 2019). Usually service delivered in front of the customers and they present to how services delivered and what is paying for (Professional Academy, 2019).

Physical Evidence

Even tourism services are intangible, some physical elements included in service business (Professional Academy, 2019). Physical evidence refers how a product perceived for consumers (The Marketing Mix, 2019).

E MARKETING IN TOURISM

Tourism destination is a place where a visitor can stay overnight. Tourism destination provides set of goods and services; activities; experiences that make value about tourism. A destination combined with

Table 2. Marketing mix 7P & 7C (Kusluvan, Tourism Marketing Lecture Notes, 2019)

7P (SERVICE PROVIDER)	7C (CUSTOMER PERSPECTIVE)
Product	Customer needs and wants
Price	Cost to the customer
Place	Convenience
Promotion	Communication
People	Caring
Processes	Co-ordinated and complete
Physical Evidence	Comfort and cleanliness

different type of stakeholders and connect to other destinations. Marketing organization for a destination is contain various stakeholders, facilities and tourism sector partnership. A tourism product is contained different elements such as cultural, natural and man-made resources, facilities, attractions, services and activities around the destination. This is the destination marketing mix. "Tourism value chain" is the set of primary and supportive activities which are essential for performance of the tourism sector. Main activities are planning, product development, packaging, promotion, marketing, distribution, sales, services and operations on destination. Tourism destination's quality is the result of process. Involve in satisfaction of tourism product and services (UNWTO (CTC), 2019).

Tourism marketing process has been increased with electronic marketing methods (Machlouzarıdes, 2009) . Companies using E Marketing models provide achievement for strategic marketing objectives. Companies choose appropriate e marketing methods, they can increase to customers and business partners. (Philips, 2003).

Spreading the e marketing model for a company comprised of four steps (Osterwalder & Pigneur, 2002):

- Organization' good and services deliver a remarkable value to customers.
- The organization's network should be outlined. Should identify the partners, internal structure that make value for goods and services.
- Company should acknowledgment and specification of customers and channel structures shall distribute to service them.
- Company income model shall have specific techniques.

Organizational E Marketing Deployment Models

Organization whether sells a product or services to customers, other business or both of them, there are different ways to get marketplace and gain. Marketing business models are described how an organization goes about this process. Some marketing models use in physical world for long time that have been adopted on the internet. Such as "mail-order models", "advertising models", "free-trial models", "direct marketing models" and "subscription models". Others are native to internet and e-commerce (Encyclopedia.com, 2002 a)

Advertising Model

The advertising model means organization main business is distribution and advertising message to consumers (Hoffman & Novak, 2000)

Affiliate Model

The affiliate model means that provide for buyers to get direct link trough the product or services suppliers websites (Fiore, Shawn, & Foreword By Marciano, 2001).

Brokerage Model

The brokerage model sees organization to make easier transaction between buyer and seller (Law & Huang, 2008). Broker organization provide such transactions in "business to business" (B2B); "business to customer" (B2C); and "customer to customer" (C2C) markets. Broker organization usually gain commission on transactions; like paypal.com (Machlouzarıdes, 2009).

Community Model

The community model means make real communities for earning of common purpose (Kim, 2000). Community organization users loyalty that contribute the operations such as Wikipedia.com (Machlouzarıdes, 2009).

Infomediary Model

Information intermediaries model means collect and analysis of customer and products data. Infomediary organization gain commission for providing information about target market (Machlouzarıdes, 2009). The infomediary model is a major one which based on sharing information. Companies require user to register before access to website. Customer needs to register before downloading any data from website so company get contact information and be able to use this information to make sales calls (Encyclopedia.com, 2002 a)

Manufacturer Model

The manufacturer or direct model means that use information and communication technologies (ICT) to contact with customers directly (Stewart, 2002). Manufacturer model describe how an organization make revenue from their effort by detailing the ways service or product. Information is used for commercial activity. For example a third party organization such as distributor or online marketplace, enable transaction between companies or consumers (Encyclopedia.com, 2002 b)

Merchant Model

The merchant model means the sale and distribution of "goods and services" (Handfield & Nichols, 2002). The merchant model of e commerce is electronic storefront on the world wide web. It is an infor-

Table 3. Traditional travel and tourism organizations' models (Machlouzarıdes, 2009)

Organizational Model	Example Organization
Travel and Tourism Organizers	Travel Agent, Tour Operators
Transportation Providers	Airlines, Car Rental, Cruise, Railway etc.
Accommodation Providers	Hotels, Apart, Motels, Camping etc.
Food and Entertainment Providers	Restaurants, Bar, Recreation areas etc.
Tourism Product Management	National and Regional Tourism Organizations

mation technology base which capable of receiving and processing orders, provide security and safety, secrecy. Also legitimacy of transaction which means proof of payments. After that completing orders via delivery or shipping (Encyclopedia.com, 2002 c).

Subscription Model

The subscription model means, company charge fee to users for their services provided. Customer has to pay a price to access to a service or product (Wikipedia, 2019).

Utility Model

The utility model means, organization charge their customers for the services which they provide (Malhotra, 2000). Utility models based on the notion of mattered use. People pay for services as they are used. Such as micro payments for download, commission fees for transactions. Mobile devices become like personal assistance and use for payments (Encyclopedia.com, 2002 d).

E-Marketing Models in Tourism and Hospitality

Tourism and hospitality industry is so dynamic by its nature, require the e Marketing models to promote and distribute "goods and services" towards satisfying the customer needs (Machlouzarıdes, 2009).

Tourism researcher have underline the importance of the internet on tourism and hospitality. The internet provides a selling way to their products or services to potential travelers. Suppliers be able to control their servers to display information at electronic speed (Law, 2000). At the supplier's perspective, a website should have larger market share with lost cost and higher revenue. For a traveler, internet provide the communicate directly with tourism suppliers. Travelers have information about product or services at anytime, anywhere (Olmeda & Sheldon, 2002). Internet provide fast information at a low cost. Tourists can have wide, related information in real environment to assist their decision-making process. Tourism suppliers can understand each customer's needs and target each customer individually. By using internet marketing, suppliers sell their products and services directly to customers (Law, Leung, & Wong, 2004).

Tourism and hospitality organizations models were group into five categories:

Information and communication technologies (ICT) boost the traditional tourism and hospitality marketing model to improve e marketing models. Therefore, tourism and hospitality organizations achieved their strategic marketing objectives. (Rodríguez, 2008).

Figure 7. The Travel Value Chain (Offutt, 2013)

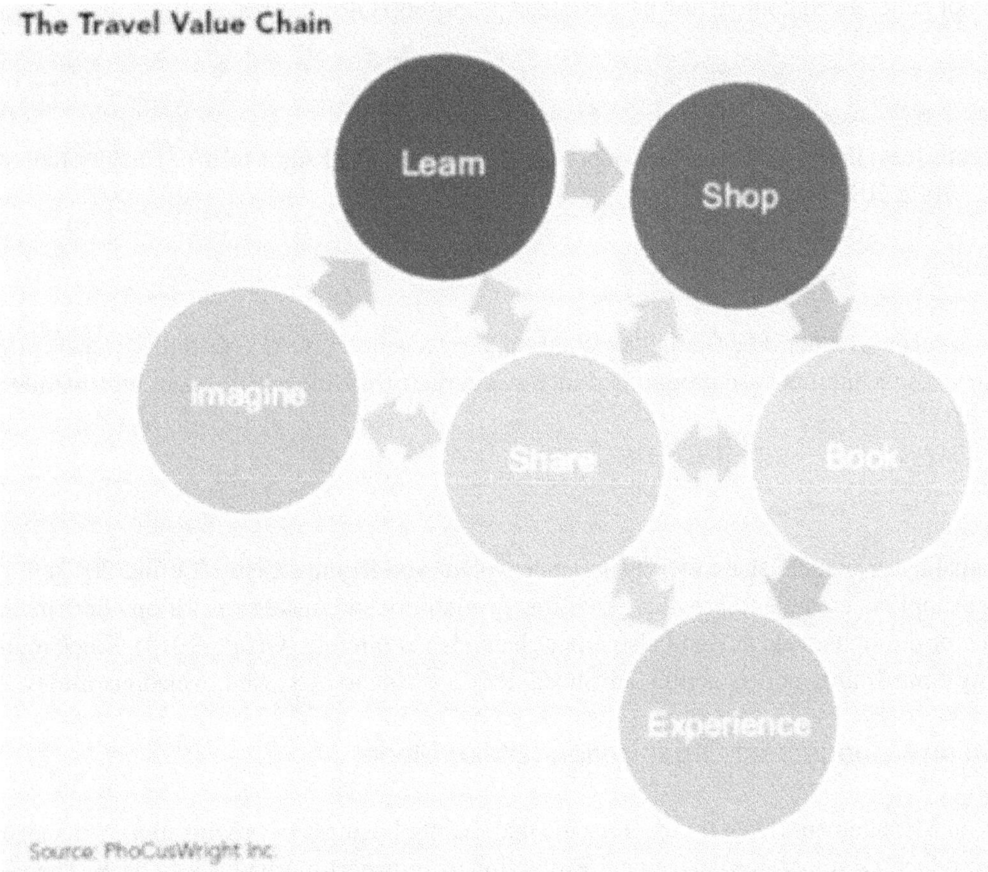

Imagine

Imagine contain of implicit and explicit preferences. Explicit preferences are obvious. Travelers' implicit preferences are based on their family or friends with similar interest. Travelers' restaurant searches or past reservations, can be good sign of preferences. Using preferences on social networks emphasize the social media's power. Consumer shopping profile is so important to selection (Offutt, 2013).

Learn

Travel tools collect the data of traveler's preferences and motivate to customer chose relevant organization. This leave enough time for planning and booking to customer. Online travel agencies (OTA's) have big advantage to learn about customer search parameters (Offutt, 2013).

Shop

Travelers can fine-set factors such as departure time, non-stop fly, discounts, hotels, transportation, activities and restaurants. Video play have big role to see destination, room and other activities. Customized offers and key references as travelers select places and others, they can shop. Each supplier offers a mixture of generalized content and personalized proposals (Offutt, 2013).

Book

Available airlines, hotels and other providers offer booking for all sight of trip. Loyalty redemption is offered. (Offutt, 2013).

Experience

Travelers's needs whether it be finding a restaurant, how to summon a taxi or traffic issues, provide via mobile devices or internet base programs. Since rising realty, travelers have exact information at sharp (Offutt, 2013)

Share

Internet enable travelers to share their experiences, plans and feelings easily (Offutt, 2013).

Travel suppliers are able to provide exact time availability and make reservation confirmation from direct sale or through an agency and also other channels via internet (Offutt, 2013). Since tourism and hospitality e marketing models getting advanced, they are able to classified (Machlouzarıdes, 2009).

Destination Management Organization (DMO) Model

Destination Management (DMO) model means that mainly business of organization is management of tourism product. Destination Management Professionals transport tourist back to back. Therefore they work with local destination management companies. Local destination management companies not only handle transportation but also provide local tours, venue, entertainment etc. By using local destination management company not only save time but also get better outcome (Schaumann, 2004). Digital economy is brutal, rapid and continuously grow. Destination Management organizations foresee and adapt to evolving market conditions. The key of achievement is to maintain a steady flow of information between destinations via internet (Liautaud & Hammond, 2000).

Low-Cost Airline Model

A low-cost carrier (LCC) also known as no-frills or budget airline. This airline types offer low fares and exclude many services. They usually have one passenger class, using secondary airports, one type of airplane, no reservation seats, internet booking only. Passengers make only a call to an airline or travel agency or get on the internet for booking to desired destination (Goeldner et al., 2009).

Online Travel Intermediary Model

Also known as online travel agency (OTA). Internet has changed the travel purchase habits and way of commerce. OTAs improved their sites about online booking and provide information for customers. "Global distribution system" (GDS is describe the electronic travel reservation system which use all around the world. OTAs offer suppliers with opportunities to distribute their goods and services at low cost and also provide customers to get information about tourism and travel options (Goeldner et al., 2009).

Travel Search Engine (TSE) Model

The TSE model means that an organizations focus on simplification on buying process for tourism products. This model helps the customer's search and select among the different tourism products (Machlouzarıdes, 2009).

As a result of that the internet is some degree of new marketing medium. It can use by everyone in tourism industry. Travel suppliers have promotional and distribution tool for their business and save cost via internet marketing (Goeldner et al., 2009).

Online Travel Agents (OTAs)

Information in tourism important because depending on the featuring of tourism product, visitors are usually live far from the destination where products or services delivered. Advertising use information to build positive image of destination and attract visitors. Information gives uniform message about tourism product (Kozak & Kozak, 2008). Consumers while planning a trip, they use travel agency or arranging the trip themselves (Le Roux, 2015). Traditional travel agent effort of creating catalogues that provide information to potential customers. It becomes more difficult for traditional travel agency to compete with online travel agency which offer online reservations easily. Customers prefer to online booking because there is potential in visualizing travel destination with 3D interactive tours. Researchers studied that virtual experiences make similar impressions as direct experiences. Visualization help customer during their decision-making process (Bogdanovych, Berger, Simoff, & Sierra, 2006).

According to O'Connor & Frew, (2002) "Information is acknowledged to be the lifeblood of tourism because without information, the customer's motivation and ability to travel is severely limited" Consumers are seeking out information to minimize the difference from their expectation to actual travel experiences. Traditional booking required customers to use first distribution channels to get information and then complete the transaction. Customer get information from brochure or guide book then make a reservation via travel agent. However, IT-based system let the customer get information and make reservation in same time. This process provides the consumer to keep time and money.

Kaynama & Black, (2008) studied that some companies in tourism industry concerning the impact of internet on travel agencies. Especially airlines, car rental companies and hotels bypassing travel agency and allow customer to make booking online directly (quoting Hibbard, 1998) but for some other travel agencies, internet is an opportunity to promote services to reach global market and selling services to customers online (quoting Lifsitz, 1998). Some travel agencies use the internet as a line to communicate with customers, for example sending or receiving e mail. This kind of agencies usually provide specialized travel services for niche markets and give personal attention. Another kind of travel agencies providing personal attention and at same time, allow customers to make reservation on website. At the other hand, online travel agencies (OTAs) offer tourism product only through online (Kaynama & Black, 2008).

Travel agency industry has been pioneer for electronic distribution and electronic marketing. Online travel agencies have been first commercial establishments on the internet among electronic distribution and air travel industry. Customers can make online reservation and ticketing because of electronic interaction between customer and travel agency. When a customer inquiry flight time, an OTA offer all

Figure 8. E commerce services in travel agencies (Quoting Kaynama & Black, 2008)

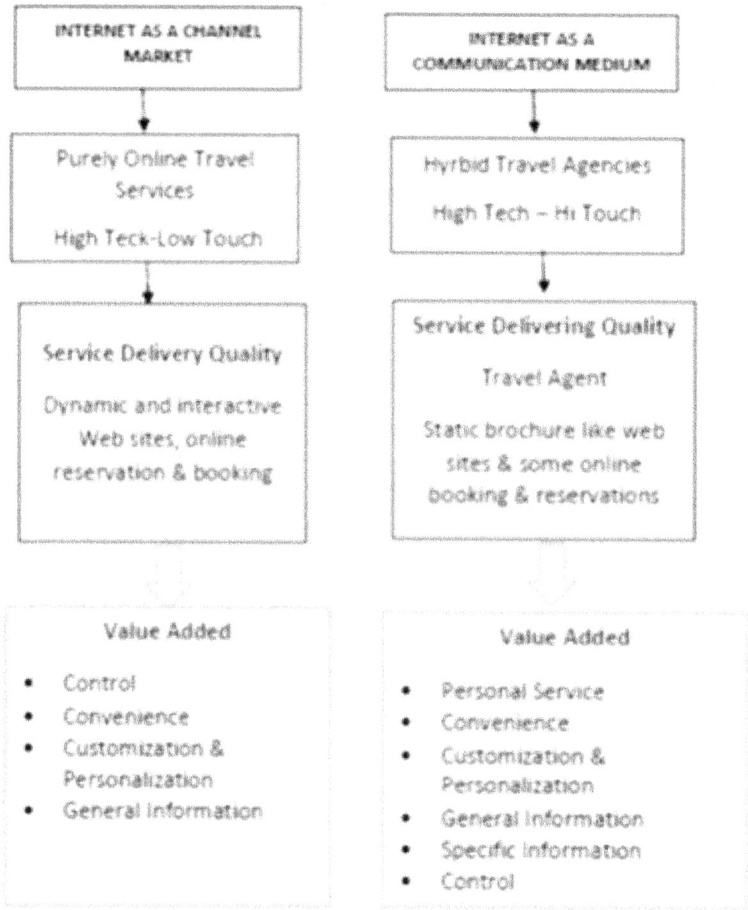

flights and prices which may be cheaper and OTA find connection ticket that may be necessary sometimes (Clemons, Hann, & Hitt, 1998)

There are some OTAs representing online travel agents, airlines, traditional agents and computerized reservation system OTAs provide a contact via World Wide Web (WWW) to allow customers to search and make reservation. When a customer finds suitable fare and available ticket or accommodation, book it by OTA. Operational process of an OTA is, first collect information from customer such as flight details, travel destination and dates. Than OTA takes this request and put them in to computerized reservation system (CRS) which searches for available products. After that present the options to customer. Finally, customer choose an option and buy it. After that OTA make real reservation via CRS and get commission from main seller. It is important to note that OTAs have to pay CRS a fee for each request but only earn commission if customer makes reservation (Clemons, Hitt, & Hann, 2002).

According to Inversini & Masiero, (2014) hotel managers always monitor OTAs, managing entity, pricing and occupancy (Quoted Toh, Raven, & DeKay, 2011). Hospitality managers fallow the social media to have communication channels with tourists. Guests pass their experiences to other potential visitors. Hotel managers realize that new trends of online sales provide benefits with competitors (Inversini & Masiero, 2014).

Word of Mouth (E-WOM)

Individuals can share their thoughts and opinions to internet users easily. Electronic word of mouth (e-WOM) have huge influence on travel decisions. Word of Mouth (WOM) communication among consumers, sharing their personal experiences with product or trip. This communications effect on consumers purchase decision. Especially within tourism services because service is intangible. Customers rely on word of mouth from experienced source. When a consumer is not familiar with service provider, word of mouth information is much important which is especially for travel related decision. Travel decision making process effected on e-WOM (Gretzel & Yoo, 2008).

Blogs, social networking, websites and online reviews let customers to share information, options and thoughts about goods and services. Web 2.0 allow online user to interaction. Online reviews considered as electronic version of WOM. In the travel industry, visitors published their experiences about goods and services. The published experiences include satisfaction level to help other travelers. Potential travelers get information about accommodation, transportation, restaurants, service quality (Filieri & McLeay, 2014).

Researchers found that consumers search hotels on more than one OTA. Also guests posted their similar comments to booking.com and TripAdvisor (Le Roux, 2015). Consumers need information about tourism product before making decision and get this information through media, TV, brochures, word of mouth or comments of web (Quoting Werthner & Ricci, 2004). Researchers notice that information sources have different type of classification. “Internal sources consist of personal experiences for specific or similar destinations”. External source of information gets from media; travel consultant; destination specific literature; family and friends. There is also relationship between culture and information search. Use of information source may have various types from one culture to another. Depend on the customer origin, use of information sources show variation (Kozak & Kozak, 2008).

E-Innovation

E-innovation describes to development of customer relationship to provide business benefits for long time on the internet that provide new services. Each company had found a way for their normal operations to get into the internet and allow their customers to use of website. The website updates frequently with news and ideas to attract customers back to the site. Links usually offer with tourist attractions and transportation companies. If customer needs extra information, dialogue occur in real time. Web sites, connecting worldwide markets through internet build long term relations with customers. Researchers suggest that there are three level of consumer impact provided by website: informational, transactional and relational levels (Martin, 2004).

Tourism Value Chain

Travel industry have various companies such as airlines, hotels, tour operators, transportation companies, travel agents and many more recreation companies which are provide services for tourist. Tourism also covered various of small to medium size networked companies (Evans, Stonehouse, & Campbel, 2012). Different type of companies provides services together in tourism industry which are hooked the each other. If one of them cannot served to customer, it effects on the other one. Tourism products and services have characteristics of "intangibility", "perishability" and "inseparability". This close-knit of tourism nature, plays big role of service quality. Therefore, various companies work together and add value to tourism product and services. Customers see and wish the tourism product as a perfect good and services. Hence, that requires handle from customer point of view. Tourism value chain is a whole with customer oriented and starts with customer order. Customers have different alternatives while arrange tourism product. Transportation between origin place and tourism destination is also an important for "tourism value chain" (Yılmaz & Bititci, 2006).

IMPACT OF ONLINE SOCIAL MEDIA

The impact of new technologies and Web 2.0 on tourism planning has been impressive. Social media has a big role on whole travel process. People use "social media" before travel, during the holiday and after the trip. They especially share their personal experiences and make influence other consumers' decision. Researchers studied that consumers always influenced by development in information communication technologies while search for tourism services. Customers search for online reviews, blogs, website to get online feedback for their travel related (Fotis, Buhalis, & Rossides, 2012).

Nature of the travel and tourism product has high risks and as a result need extensive information search (Sirakaya & Woodside, 2005). Researchers studied that consumers rely on other travelers' experiences. Online content perceives like recommendations provided by friends. Hence, social media has big role in travel planning. In additional that social media enable the customers share their activity on real time. Consumers also review and rating website. That online review posted impact on decision making process; reduce risk, assist to select accommodation (Fotis et al., 2012).

Visitor attraction at some place make them to decide for travel. Temptation of cheap air travel, attraction of destination, special promotion makes impact on consumers. Other attractions such as shopping, activities at destination, visiting relatives also effect on tourism decision process. Each destination has its own special appeal. Online marketing should manage effectively to get visitor attractions (Thomas, 2018). According the researchers, "social media in tourism" is still in beginning level. Some of the tourism marketing managers can leverage social media to develop consumer discussions and some others have offered strategies for social media marketing campaigns. Marketers use social media for increase the destination attraction and sell the tourism product. In the entertainment industry, social media id used and managed by sports and venue managers (Hudson, Roth, Madden, & Hudson, 2015)

According to Fotis et al. (2012), influence of travel blogs and traditional WOM is more trustable than blog posts (Quoting Mack, Blose, & Pan, 2008). Researcher notice that Social media user is perceived as more credible when posted from tourism agency then travel blogs. Social media usually used before the holiday. During the trip and after holiday usages limited. After holiday customers share memories on social media. Social media users interest in ravel related photos and these photos effect on travel plans for potential customers (Fotis et al., 2012).

Thomas, (2018) studied that one of the important tourist motivation factors is visiting an attractive destination when satisfied customer needs and wishes (quoting Leiper, 2004). Tourist motivation "push" them to the attraction. Destination attractive features "pull" the tourist.

Internet Marketing Performance

E-Commerce

E-Commerce define that all personal or commercial investment companies around the world that involve e-commerce because they exchange of information, goods and services online. Researchers studied that E-commerce is interaction between business to business (B2B) transactions which also need higher security because it is more complex. E-commerce between business to consumer (B2C) is transaction of products or services from company to individual customers. Shortage of technical skills, B2C transactions lower than expected. However researchers found that there are great demand for B2C e-commerce activities with mobile devices. Another e-commerce is business to business to consumer (B2B2C) such as airlines or hotels make deal with travel agency and then travel agency deal with customer and sell the ticket or make booking to hotel (Moustafa, 2011).

Mobile Commerce

E-commerce transactions handle in a wireless environment as mobile devices. According to several researchers the importance of e-commerce transactions in changing business process to speed and efficiency which effect on customer satisfaction and revenue. Tourism industry is one of the top sector in electronic marketplace. Mobile commerce has become popular between consumer and business organizations. Make reservation or buy a ticket is easier with m-commerce (Moustafa, 2011).

Difference between m-commerce and e-commerce is that m-commerce use wireless technologies. Mobile device provides to reach and accessibility for user. Individual can be accessible from anywhere at any time. Also mobile devices has addressability which means that consumer and marketers to send and receive messages wherever located (Standing, McManus, Standing, & Karjaluoto, 2007).

Researchers studied that tourism destination marketers may benefit from the use internet applications for distribute and share information with customers. Hence, attract the potential customers, improve the destination image and also increase the loyalty of customers (Moustafa, 2011).

CONCLUSION

This research a content traditional marketing and internet marketing which use online travel booking. Internet is the most common use for research travel data by consumers. Internet give an opportunity to access information easily and save money during reservation process. Social media has huge effect on tourism. Therefore, travel suppliers can use social media for their own benefit. Tourism suppliers could have information about customer needs and wishes via internet.

RECOMMENDATIONS

Companies focus on sales via OTAs, and social media. Marketers focus on sales strategies by internet. Using internet for commercials also require safety. Suppliers must provide security for their customers.

Table 4. Internet Marketing Performance Metrics by channel (Mariussen, 2012)

Channel	Metrics	Source
	Hits, requests, clicks, visitors, unique visitors, sessions, views, exposures, impressions, visits, click rate, click-through rates, inquiries, average time on page, duration time, frequency, depth, leads, traffic	Novak and Hoffman (1996)
Internet marketing	Net profit, ROI, customer life cycle, hits, visitors, page views, traffic, reach, acquisition, conversion, retention, loyalty, abandonment, attrition, churn, velocity, regency, frequency, monetary value, duration, stickiness, slipperiness, focus, "optimal site path", "cost per acquisition", "cost per conversion", yield, net yield, personalization index, "freshness factor", connect rate	Michopoulou and Buhalis (2008)
	Number of times a site is accessed, number of inquires	Benoy et al. (2001)
	Visits, leads, conversion, cost per lead	Wilson (2004)
	Hits, sessions, leads, sales cycle, revenue, sales, feedback	Sterne (1999)
	Revenue from advertising impressions	Trusov et al. (2010)
	Number of users joining the group, number of discussions, amount of comments, amount of positive or negative comments, total amount of customers attracted via social media, number of friend requests	Michaelidou et al. (2011)
Social media	Total fans, followers, authors, number of comments posted, advocates influence profile, rank of topics discussed, "positive vs. negative sentiment", retail locater results activity, leads to ecommerce partners, product brochure downloads, reach, quality of mentions, quality of authors, where on social media discussions take place, chatter topics, tone, sentiment, purchases, leads.	Murdough (2010)
	Interactions, word-of-mouth episodes, relationship types of people who interacted (strangers, best friends, friends, acquaintances, romantic partners, relatives, spouses, co-workers)	Walter (2006)
	Visitors' opinions, interactions, viewed webpages	Ioakimidis (2007)
	Navigation/organization, ease of use, usability, information, web content, usefulness of the site, fun, enjoyment, entertainment, delight, layout, presentation, web appearance, convenience	Trieblmaier and Pinterits (2009)
	Search engine visits, direct visits, referring site visits	Plaza (2011)
Websites	ROI, traffic, browser, operating system the customer came from, keywords, search engines they use, referring site, visit duration, pages they visit, returning customers, unique IP address of the user's computer, date and time of the request, conversion rate, page views, bounce rate, abandonment rate, cost per conversion	Ryan and Jones (2009)
	Site traffic, profitability, exposure, usability, accessibility, navigation, ease of use, price, trustworthiness, image, credibility, search ability, accuracy, information quality	Belanger et al. (2006)
	Visits, page views	Welling and White (2006)
	Time per session, number of page views, duration of page views, impressions, webpages by type (home page, purchase page)	Bucklin and Sismeiro (2009)
	Views, click-through rate, visits, ad impressions	Rowley (2004)
	Impressions, click-through, outcomes (e.g., inquires, purchases), exposure, unique visitors, brand attitude change, purchase intention, brand awareness, banner ad duration time	Shen (2002)
Banners	Click-through rate, interactivity, brand attitude, purchase intention, attitude towards the ad, clicks	Pharr (2004)
	Hits, page views, impressions	Krishnamurphy (2000)
	Clicks, click through, exposure, reach, frequency	Bucklin and Sismeiro, 2009
Search Engine Advertising	Advertisement cost, clicks, cost per impression, visits, purchases	Kumar and Kohli (2007)
Channel Online advertising	**Metrics** Reach, impressions, "total schedule cost", "frequency distribution", effective reach, continuity, media type budget allocation, "online purchase rate", click-through, visitor duration, unique visitors, hits, page views, cost per action/outcome	**Source** Cheong et al. (2010)
	Page views, click-through, reach, frequency, impressions, number of visitors, number of visits, number of pages, time spent, number of repeat visits	Dreze and Zufryden (1998)
Email	Click-through	Bucklin and Sismeiro (2009)

Also improve their web site regularly. Travel agencies, hotels and other travel suppliers can let their customer to share their photos and experiences in their web site.

FUTURE RESEARCH

This study based on literature research. At the future study, researchers can focus on perception of elder consumers to internet shopping, OTAs and social media.

REFERENCES

Barlow, A., & Birkhahn, T. (2005). Traditional Marketing Not Ready for the Junk Heap Just Yet. *PR News, 61*(43), 1.

Bhasin, H. (2019). *Marketing91.* Marketing Management. Promotional mix – What are the different types of promotions? Retrieved from https://www.marketing91.com/promotional-mix/adresinden alındı

Bogdanovych, A., Berger, H., Simoff, S., & Sierra, C. (2006). Travel agents vs. online booking: Tackling the shortcomings of nowadays online tourism portals. *Information and communication technologies in tourism 2006*, 418-428.

Buhalis, D., & Laws, E. (2008). Progress in information technology and tourism management: 20 years on and 10 years after the Internet - The state of eTourism research. *Tourism Management, 29*(4), 609–623. doi:10.1016/j.tourman.2008.01.005

Chaffey, D., Chadwick, F. E., Johnston, K., & Mayer, R. (2000). Internet Marketing: Strategy, Implementation and Practice. London, UK: Pearson Education Limited.

Clemons, E., Hann, I.-H., & Hitt, L. (1998). *The Nature of Competition in Electronic Markets: An Empirical Investigation of Online Travel Agent Offerings.* The Wharton School of the University of Pennsylvania.

Clemons, E. K., Hitt, L. M., & Hann, I.-H. (2002). Price dispersion and differentiation in online travel: An empirical investigation. *Management Science, 48*(4), 534–549. doi:10.1287/mnsc.48.4.534

Cowden, A. (2014). *Effect of Social Media Marketing on Traditional Marketing Campaigns in Young Icelandic Companies.* (Master thesis, Reykjavic University, Iceland).

Dictionary, B. D. (2019). *Heterogeneity.* BD Dictionary. Retrieved from http://www.businessdictionary.com/definition/heterogeneity.htmladresinden alındı

Encyclopedia.com. (2002a). *Infomediary Model.* Encyclopedia.com. Retrieved from https://www.encyclopedia.com/economics/encyclopedias-almanacs-transcripts-and-maps/infomediary-modeladresindenalındı

Encyclopedia.com. (2002b). *Manufacturer Model.* Encyclopedia.com. Retrieved from https://www.encyclopedia.com/economics/encyclopedias-almanacs-transcripts-and-maps/manufacturer-modeladresindenalındı

Encyclopedia.com. (2002c). *Merchant Model*. Encyclopedia.com. Retrieved from https://www.encyclopedia.com/economics/encyclopedias-almanacs-transcripts-and-maps/merchant-modeladresindenalındı

Encyclopedia.com. (2002d). *Utility Model*. Encyclopedia.com. Retrieved from https://www.encyclopedia.com/economics/encyclopedias-almanacs-transcripts-and-maps/utility-modeladresindenalındı

Evans, N., Stonehouse, G., & Campbel, D. (2012). *Strategic management for travel and tourism*. Abingdon, UK: Taylor & Francis. doi:10.4324/9780080498294

Filieri, R., & McLeay, F. (2014). E-WOM and accommodation: An analysis of the factors that influence travelers' adoption of information from online reviews. *Journal of Travel Research*, *53*(1), 44–57. doi:10.1177/0047287513481274

Fiore, F., Shawn, C., & Foreword By-Marciano, J. (2001). *Successful affiliate marketing for merchants*. Hoboken, NJ: Que Corp.

Fotis, J., Buhalis, D., & Rossides, N. (2012). Social media use and impact during the holiday travel planning process. Berlin, Germany: Springer-Verlag, 13-24.

Goeldner, C., & Ritchie, B. J. (2009). *Tourism Principles, Practices, Philosophies* (11th ed.). Hoboken, NJ: John Wiley & Sons.

Gretzel, U., & Yoo, K. (2008). Use and impact of online travel reviews. *Information and communication technologies in tourism*, 35-46.

Hagel, J., & Armstrong, A. (1997). *Net Gain - Expanding Markets through Virtual Communities*. Boston, MA: Harvard Business School Press.

Handfield, R., & Nichols, E. (2002). *Supply Chain Redesign: Transforming Supply Chains into Integrated Value Systems*. Upper Saddle River, NJ: Financial Times Prentice Hall.

Hibbard, J. (1998). Airlines, Online Agencies Battle for Customers–Enhancements to Web Sites Aimed at Getting More People to Book Travel Online. *Information Week*, 685 words.

Hoffman, D., & Novak, T. (2000). Advertising Pricing Models for the World Wide Web. *Internet Publishing and Beyond: The Economics of Digital Information and Intellectual Property MIT Press.*

Hudson, S., Roth, M., Madden, T., & Hudson, R. (2015). The effects of social media on emotions, brand relationship quality, and word of mouth: An empirical study of music festival attendees. *Tourism Management, 47*, 68-76.

ICCA. (2017). *ICCA Statistics Report Country & City Rankings Public Abstract*. International Congress and Convention Association.

Internet World Stats. (2019). *Internet World Stats*. Internet Users in the World by Region - March 2019. Retrieved from https://www.internetworldstats.com/stats.htmadresindenalındı

Inversini, A., & Masiero, L. (2014). Selling rooms online: The use of social media and online travel agents. *International Journal of Contemporary Hospitality Management*, *26*(2), 272–292. doi:10.1108/IJCHM-03-2013-0140

Kaaya, E. A. (2014). *Assesment Of Marketıng Strategıes Tour Operators Use For Marketıng And Promotıon Of Tanzanıa Tourısm Products: A Case Of Arusha Cıty. Open University Of Tanzania*. Yüksek Lisans Tezi.

Kandampully, J., & Hu, H. (2007). Do hoteliers need to manage image to retain loyal customers? *International Journal of Contemporary Hospitality Management, 19*(6), 435–443. doi:10.1108/09596110710775101

Kaynama, S., & Black, C. (2008). A Proposal to Assess the Service Quality of Online Travel Agencies: An Exploratory Study. *Journal of Professional Services Marketing, 21*(1), 63–88. doi:10.1300/J090v21n01_05

Kim, A. (2000). Community Building on the Web: Secret Strategies for Successful Online Communities. San Francisco, CA: Peachpit Press.

Kotler, P. (2003). *Marketing Management.* Upper Saddle River, NJ: Prentice Hall (11th edition).

Kozak, N., & Kozak, M. (2008). Information sources available to visitors: A segmentation analysis. *Tourism Review, 63*(4), 4–12. doi:10.1108/16605370810912173

Kusluvan, S. (2003). *Managing employee attitudes and behaviors in the tourism and hospitality industry.* Hauppage, NY: Nova.

Kusluvan, S. (2019). *Tourism Marketing Lecture Notes.* İstanbul, Turkey: İstanbul Medeniyet Üniversitesi.

Law, R., & Chen, F. (2000). Internet in Travel and tourism - Part I. *Journal of Travel & Tourism Marketing, 9*(4), 83–87. doi:10.1300/J073v09n04_05

Law, R., & Huang, T. (2008). Internet and Tourism-Part XII. *Journal of Travel & Tourism Marketing, 14*(2), 105–109. doi:10.1300/J073v14n02_06

Law, R., Leung, K., & Wong, J. (2004). The impact of the Internet on travel agencies. *International Journal of Contemporary Hospitality Management, 16*(2), 100–107. doi:10.1108/09596110410519982

Le Roux, I. (2015). The influence of online travel agent performance on customer satisfaction levels at a selected hotel. Nelson Mandela Metropolitan University. Yüksek Lisans Tezi.

Leiper, N. (2004). Tourism Management. London, UK: Pearson.

Liautaud, B., & Hammond, M. (2000). *E-Business Intelligence: Turning Information into Knowledge into Profit.* New York, NY: McGraw-Hill.

Lifsitz, R. (1998). Net As an Opportunity. *Travel Weekly, 57*(45), F6.

Londre, L. (2014). *Marketing, IMC, Advertising, Promotion, Media and More.* Los Angeles, CA: Londre Marketing Consultants.

Machlouzarıdes, H. (2009). *Improvıng The Deployment Model Of Modern Electronıc Marketıng Methods For The Cyprus Tourısm Organısatıon.* Doktora Tezi.

Mack, R., Blose, J., & Pan, B. (2008). Believe it or not: Credibility of blogs in tourism. *Journal of Vacation Marketing, 14*(2), 133–144. doi:10.1177/1356766707087521

Malhotra, Y. (2000). Knowledge Management for E-Business Performance: Advancing Information Strategy to 'Internet Time'. *Information Strategy, The Executives Journal, [Online] 16(4),* 5-16 .

Mangold, W., & Faulds, D. (2009). Social Media: The New Hybrid Element of The Promotion Mix. *Business Horizons, 52*(4), 357–365. doi:10.1016/j.bushor.2009.03.002

Marııssen, A. (2012). *A grounded theory of affiliate marketing performance measurement in the tourism and hospitality context.* (Doctoral thesis, Business School, Oxford Brookes University).

Martin, L. (2004). E-innovation: Internet impacts on small UK hospitality firms. *International Journal of Contemporary Hospitality Management, 16*(2), 82–90. doi:10.1108/09596110410519964

Middleton, V., Fyall, A., & Morgan, M. (2009). *Marketing in Travel and Tourism* (4th ed.). Oxford, UK: Butterworth-Heinemann.

Moustafa, M. (2011). *Evaluating the Potential of Mobile Technology in Tourism Destination Marketing.* (Doctoral dissertation, Cardiff Metropolitan University, UK).

MSG. (2019). *The 7 P's of Services Marketing.* Management Study Guide. Retrieved from https://www.managementstudyguide.com/seven-p-of-services-marketing.htmadresindenalındı

O'Connor, P., & Frew, A. J. (2002). The future of hotel electronic distribution: Expert and industry perspectives. *The Cornell Hotel and Restaurant Administration Quarterly, 43*(3), 33–45. doi:10.1016/S0010-8804(02)80016-7

Offutt, B. (2013). Travel Distribution 2018: A Look Ahead. *PhoCusWright's Analysis.* Retrieved from https://www.ithotelero.com/wp-content/uploads/2014/01/Analysis_TravelDistribution2018.pdf

Olmeda, I., & Sheldon, P. (2002). Data Mining Techniques and Applications for Tourism Internet Marketing. *Journal of Travel & Tourism Marketing, 11*(2-3), 1–20. doi:10.1300/J073v11n02_01

Osterwalder, A., & Pigneur, Y. (2002). *An e-Business Model Ontology for Modeling e-Business.* In *Proceedings of the 15th BLED Electronic Commerce Conference e-Reality: Constructing the e-Economy,* Slovenia.

Pender, L. (1999). *Marketing Management for Travel and Tourism.* Cheltenham, UK: Stanley Thornes.

Philips, P. (2003). E-Business Strategy. New York, NY: McGraw Hill Education.

Pillai, K. (2010). Seven Ps Spectrum of Marketing in Tourism. *Indian Journal of Tourism & Hospitality Management, 1*(2), 84–97.

Professional Academy. (2019). *MARKETING THEORIES – THE MARKETING MIX – FROM 4 PS TO 7 PS.* Retrieved from https://www.professionalacademy.com/blogs-and-advice/marketing-theories---the-marketing-mix---from-4-p-s-to-7-p-sadresindenalındı

Pui-Mun, L. (2002). Behavioral Model of Online Purchasers in E-Commerce Environment. *Electronic Commerce Research, 2*(1-2), 75–86.

Rodríguez, W. (2008). E-Business Method: A Cyclical-Model for Internet Commerce Development. *Journal of Internet Commerce, 2*(3), 87–98. doi:10.1300/J179v02n03_07

Saxena, R. (2008). *Marketing Management* (3rd ed.). New York. NY: Tata McGraw-Hill.

Schaumann, P. (2004). *The Guide to Successful Destination Management*. Hoboken, NJ: John Wiley & Sons.

Shostack, L. (1977). Breaking Free from Product Marketing. *Journal of Marketing*, *41*(2), 73–80. doi:10.1177/002224297704100219

Sirakaya, E., & Woodside, A. (2005). Building and testing theories of decision making by travellers. *Tourism Management*, *26*(6), 815–832. doi:10.1016/j.tourman.2004.05.004

Standing, C., McManus, P., Standing, S., & Karjaluoto, H. (2007). Searching for value in researching the adoption and use of m-services. [IJeC]. *International Journal of e-Collaboration*, *3*(3), 16–30. doi:10.4018/jec.2007070102

Stewart, A. (2002). A Model of Web Use in Direct and Online Marketing Strategy. *Electronic Markets*, *12*(4), 262–269. doi:10.1080/101967802762553521

Tetteh, V. A. (2017). *Marketing Decision - Making*. Salem Basın Ansiklopedisi.

The Marketing Mix. (2019). *Marketing Mix Definition of the 4P's and 7P's*. Retrieved from https://marketingmix.co.uk/adresindenalındı

Thomas, D. (2018). *Managing online communications andfeedback relating to the Welsh visitor attraction experience: apathy and inflexibility in tourism marketing practice?* (Doctor of Philosophy dissertation, University of Wales Trinity Saint David, UK).

Toh, R., Raven, P., & DeKay, F. (2011). Satış odaları: Oteller vs. üçüncü taraf web siteleri. *Cornell Hospitality Üç Aylık*, *52*(2), 181–189. doi:10.1177/1938965511400409

Trusov, M., Bucklin, R., & Pauwels, K. (2009). Effect of Word-of-Mouth Versus Traditional Marketing: Findings from an Internal Social Networking Site. *Journal of Marketing*, *73*(5), 90–102. doi:10.1509/jmkg.73.5.90

UNWTO. (2019). *Understanding Tourism: Basic Glossary*. United Nations World Tourism Organization. Retrieved from http://cf.cdn.unwto.org/sites/all/files/docpdf/glossaryenrev.pdfadresindenalındı

UNWTO. (CTC). (2019). *Definitions Committee on Tourism and Competitiveness (CTC)*. Available at http://cf.cdn.unwto.org/sites/all/files/pdf/unwto_tourism_definitions.pdfadresindenalındı

Van Der Merwe, M. C. (2003). *Marketing communication methods used by tour operators in Guateng*. (Research Dissertation, University of South Africa, South Africa).

Varfan, M. (2008). *Traditional Marketing vs. Internet Marketing A comparison*. (Bachelor thesis, Mälardalen University, Sweden).

Werthner, H., & Ricci, F. (2004). E-commerce and Tourism. *Communications of the ACM December, 47(12)*.

Wikipedia. (2019). *Subscription business model*. Retrieved from https://en.wikipedia.org/wiki/Subscription_business_modeladresindenalındı

Yılmaz, Y., & Bititci, U. (2006). Performance measurement in tourism: A value chain model. *International Journal of Contemporary Hospitality Management*, *18*(4), 341–349. doi:10.1108/09596110610665348

Zrener, C. (2015). *Ausarbeitung eines Marketingkonzeptes für Radissimo Radreisen mit regionalem Schwerpunkt in Hinblick auf Kommunikations- und Distributions politik*. (Faculty of Media, Bachelor Thesis).

KEY TERMS AND DEFINITIONS

B2B: Business to Business is Exchange of products, service or information between businesses on the internet.

B2B2C: Business to Business to Customer is an e-commerce among to businesses and consumer (B2C) for complete product or service transaction.

B2C: Business to Consumer means that selling products directly to consumers.

C2C: Customer to Customer means that customers can trade with each other.

CRS: Computerized Reservation System.

E-WOM: Electronic Word Of Mouth means that communication directed at consumers through internet.

GDS: Global Distribution System.

ICT: Information and Communication Technology.

LCC: Low Cost Airline.

OTA: Online Travel Agency.

WOM: Word of Mouth.

WWW: World Wide Web.

Chapter 4
An Empirical Study on the Relationship Between Economic Growth and E-Commerce

Asuman Koc Yurtkur
Bulent Ecevit University, Turkey

Bersu Bahtiyar
Bulent Ecevit University, Turkey

ABSTRACT

Electronic commerce (e-commerce) has started to become an important explanatory component of economic growth via innovations in information technology in recent years. Studies within this framework show that countries that invest more in e-commerce have reached higher growth rates. In this regard, this chapter has examined the relationship between e-commerce represented by two sub-components as fixed and mobile-cellular telephone subscriptions and economic growth for chosen countries (BRICS and Turkey) with 2000-2016 annual data by using Panel VAR, impulse response analysis, and variance decomposition. Results of the study show that economic growth and e-commerce are related. These results suggest that countries that want to increase their economic growth rate should focus on policies to increase e-commerce volume.

INTRODUCTION

Science, technology and innovation are like the arms of a triple helix. The rise of one of them depends on the rise of the others. In this sense, innovation policies and science and technology policies must be thgought as a whole and in most cases, innovation and science processes should be included in science and technology policies. When a new fact is mentioned in a country, this innovation should be supported by science and technology. When the scientific and technological developments in all over the world are examined, it is necessary to transform scince and technology to economic and social benefit as well as developing science and technology (Özsağır, 2013, p. 43). Therefore, the conversion of the

DOI: 10.4018/978-1-7998-0035-4.ch004

developments in science and technology into gain constitutes the essence of the matter. One of the most important examples of this is the developments in electronic commerce.

Computer age, also known as the third industrial revolution, is a product of technological developments. With the occurance of computers and internet at the end of 1980s, there was a revolution in both communication and trade in the global sense. By the beginning of the 21st century, a process where large capitals could be transferred across all over the world by means of a single button has become experienced. As a result of these revolutionary developments, there has been a significant economic growth on global scale and technology has been considered as the fuel of the economy (Conway, 2009, pp. 176-177).

As the developments in technology have become the driving force of global competition -especially developments in internet technology-, electronic commerce has become increasingly widespread all over the world. The developments in information technology have made international trade easier and the economies that can internalize this process have achieved significant growth dynamics. Countries such as China and India are leading the way in order to gain a superior growth trend by bringing new technologies in international trade (Conway, 2009, pp. 176-177). Since 1990s, it has been observed that businesses that adopt electronic commerce as a new business management style have positive developments in terms of productivity and employment. The rapid expansion of the internet has brought along important developments in terms of trade and competition not only from a national perspective but also internationally. Today, the developments in information and communication areas have made e-commerce an important concept for all markets and sectors and it is stated that although it has been based on a decade of history since electronic commerce has become publicly known, it has existed for thirty years.

Electronic commerce or e-commerce is known as an e-business defined as the transfer of goods and services through electronic communication in the light of technological developments (Tian & Stewart, 2008, p. 1). It is stated that e-commerce is related to internet economy and digital economy. With its scope, the usage of new information and communication technologies constitutes the focal point. The internet economy means that generating income of economic activity through goods and services related to internet (Da Costa, 2003). For this reason, e-commerce before the internet is not named as internet economy. Digital economy is based on digital technologies such as computers, software and digital networks, but all activities in the digital economy aren't e-commerce activities. For example, purchasing a computer material from a showcase vendor isn't an activity of e-commerce. So it is stated that e-commerce, internet economy and digital economy are related to each other but have different content.

Although electronic commerce doesn't have a single common definition, it is possible to encounter different definitions made from many different aspects. According to Wigand (1997), electronic commerce is the application of information and technology, until it reaches its goal throughout the value chain of the electronically conducted business process. According to Kalakota and Whinston (1997), electronic commerce is the process of implementing technologies for business transactions and automation of business processes, while Clarke (1999) defines e-commerce as the process of conducting the trade of goods and services through telecommunication-based equipments. This indicates that perspectives about e-commerce can arise in many aspects such as communication, business process, value system, online service and electronic processing. In this context, the definition of electronic commerce can be expanded to generate business value that that creates and uses new business opportunities at any time.

The narrowest definition of electronic commerce is that commercial transactions and payments are made to consumers through open networks such as the internet. Here only the goods and services that sold to consumers and payments made in return are included in the scope of this. There is no clearness about which transactions should be considered commercial if the inter-enterprise transactions are included in the definition. The broad definition of electronic commerce is; is to share the structured and unstructured business information among the producers, consumers, public institutions and other institutions via electronic instruments. Based on this definition, all transactions that do not have a direct commercial result but provide substructure are included in the scope of electronic commerce (Yumuşak, 2001, p. 3).

Electronic commerce is a form of trade that occurs along with the development of communication technologies and that complements and facilitates traditional trade. Electronic trade is, implementing of information and communication technologies from first to the last stage of the business processes by a company (Jentzsch & Miniotas, 1999, p. 435). Electronic commerce is about trading in an electronic environment where data that include text, sound and images are processed and transmitted electronically. This trade includes a variety of activities such as trade and delivery of goods and services, online delivery of digital content, electronic fund transfer, online sourcing, commercial auctions, public procurement (Commission of the European Communities, 1997, p. 2).

There are a number of features that must be present in electronic payment systems where payment of goods and services that subject to e-commerce are realized. Reliability is the most difficult and essential feature of a payment system. The basic criterion here is that, regardless of what form of payment is used, digital payment tools also fulfill the security requirements of a conventional payment instrument. In addition, the existence of integrity that states that all the economic agents who attended the payment transaction are authorized and rights-holder, is an important component. Functionality is the factor that means that payment systems should be technically sound. Anonymity of payment transactions, determining the scope of transaction costs, online control, ease of use, divisiveness, general acceptance and durability are the other factors that must be fulfilled fort he electronic payments systems (Berber, 2002, pp. 36-43). The existence of all these components plays an important role in the increasingly widespread usage of electronic commerce.

As a result of the developments in electronic commerce, many countries and global organizations are interested in this subject and studying on various aspects. World Trade Organization (WTO), Economic Cooperation and Labor Organization (OECD), United Nations Conference on Trade and Development (UNCTAD), World Bank (WB) and International Trade Center (ITC) is one of the leading global organizations and approach the term within the framework of their interests. Also, the national institutions of countries and international trade associations are closely examining this issue and trying to provide infrastructure opportunities for their members.

While E-commerce was a form of trade that was made through closed networks before the internet became widespread, it is made with open networks associated with the developments in technology and the spread of the internet. In this context, the classification of traditional and online e-commerce types is given in the table below:

Most common types of electronic commerce are classified into four categories: Business-to-Business (B2B), Business-to-Customer (B2C), Business-in-Business (B1B), Consumer-to-Consumer (C2C):

The most common form of electronic commerce is Business-to-Business (B2B) which means intercorporate and intercompany sales. The type of e-commerce which the buyer and seller trade in an interactive environment is defined as B2B. B2B e-commerce includes finance, purchasing, inventory management, sales, advertising, payment and delivery transactions, customer service and many other business activities (Söylemez, 2006, p. 11). Many industry experts agree that there is a huge B2B e-commerce potential in developing and underdeveloped countries. The purpose of the e-commerce model from business to the

Table 1. Comparison of Traditional Electronic Commerce and Internet Electronic Commerce

Traditional e-Commerce	Internet E-Commerce
Business to Business	Business to Consumers Business to Business Business to Public Administration User to User
Industry-Specific Closed Groups	Open market, Global Scale
Limited Participant	Unlimited Participants
Closed Networks	Open Networks
Known and Trusted Partners	Known and Unknown Partners
Networks Security	Security and Need for Approval
The Market is a Club	The Network is the Market

Source: Commission of the European Communities, 1997, "Communication from the Commission to the Council, The European Parliament, The Economic and Social Committee and the Committee of the Regions", Brussel, p.3.

business is to provide selling, using and sharing of products, services and information between companies by integration of automated systems into business units that make common actions.

Business-to-Customer (B2C) that is the most widely known type of e-commerce, is a virtual store that occurs with the development of web and wap technologies. B2C e-commerce brings close together sellers and buyers in the online marketplace for shopping. B2C e-commerce companies has a virtual shop for consumers that eliminates the need to physically see and touch the product to purchase goods and services. In the Business to Customer (B2C) e-commerce, products and services are provided to consumers through campaigns. The Business to Business (B2B) type e-commerce works by providing connections between suppliers, distributors and other business partners through electronic networks. Although the business to consumer (B2C) e-commerce is well known by the public, business to business (B2B) e-commerce is dominant of e-commerce in terms of income (Tian & Stewart, 2008, p. 1).

Business-in-Business (B1B) e-commerce is defined as trade within a company. Large companies can conduct commercial transactions between various business units in this way. For example, the information technology department of the company may shop with various business units in the field of information technology services. B1B e-commerce is primarily applicable to large enterprises. SMEs have a limited number of employees and opportunities to sustain Business-in-Business (B1B) information technology applications in a commercial manner.

Customer to customer (C2C) e-commerce is a technic that has just began and people sell their old stuff to random people. This process is a non-permanent commercial activity and is limited to the goods of the seller family. C2C includes a process in which two consumers get together through electronic instruments such as e-mail and make a deal about goods and services. However, it is difficult to obtain and evaluate accurate information and data about C2C (Jentzsch & Miniotas, 1999, pp. 438-439).

With the new developments in information technology, e-commerce applications have increased and started to become a form of trade which has completed and facilitated traditional trade. The e-commerce market is growing all over the world via increasing number of technology and internet users, and this situation offers significant economic-wide, financial and social gains especially to developing countries. Thus, developing countries have the opportunity to find themselves among the developed countries in the globalized competition market. The studies conducted in this context show that, the increasing e-commerce volume with the expansion of globalization and internet usage has a positive effect on the economic growth levels of the countries. In this regard, the aim of this study is to investigate the relationship between e-commerce -as a factor that gives more advantage to the countries which invest in it- and economic growth in Brazil, Russia, India, China, South Africa (BRICS) and Turkey covering the period 2000-2016. This study proceeds in the following manner. In first section, empirical literature about the relationship between economic growth and e-comerce was reviewed with some selected studies. The second section provides a description about econometric methodology and data that are used in the study. In third section presents empirical findings of econometric analysis and finally fourth section highlights the concluding remarks.

LITERATURE REVIEW

There is an increasing interest in studies investigating the relationship between e-commerce and economic growth, a topic that has become more popular with the widespread usage of the internet in the economic literature.

Morrison and Siegel (1997) studied the positive impact of e-commerce on productivity and economic performance. Among the findings of the study, it is concluded that the fact that information factors are originated from technology increases the return. effects of e-commerce will increase in the future periods. Tan and Ouyang (2002) examined the global and national factors affecting E-commerce in China. In this study, the size of the Chinese economy and population is mentioned and human resources and unemployment rates are given. It has been suggested that e-commerce is developing rapidly in China. Coşkun (2004) investigates the factors affecting the development of e-commerce and the barriers to e-commerce development among countries. In the research, graphical analysis was performed by means of data affecting e-commerce.

Gibbs and Kreamer (2010) examined factors such as technology resources, business compatibility, external pressures, firm size, financial resources that affect e-commerce by using Least Squares Method. Emprical results showed the most significant variable as technological sources. Le (2010) examined the China's e-commerce and economic development by using VAR model in 1999-2007 periods. Le found a positive relationship between e-commerce and economic development. The results also show that e-commerce values have increased in years and have a positive effect on the development of Chinese economy. Therefore, the increase in the support of the government and relevant departments on e-commerce, the positive effects of e-commerce will increase in the future periods. Similarly, Liu (2013) studied the effects of electronic commerce on macroeconomic performance of Chinese national economy by using time series analysis. The study suggested that e-commerce leads to economic development and contributes to economic globalization. The results demonstrate that, such as variables e-commerce, international bandwidth, number of internet users, number of online shoppers, online advertising, the number of web sites has a positive effect on GDP and the development of e-commerce also positively affects economic growth.

Elsoud (2014) examined the impact of electronic commerce on economic growth for Saudi Arabia covering period 2001-2013.This study which take into consideration the factors that affect the growth of Saudi Arabian economy, models economic growth by including variables such as labor, capital, public and private consumption expenditures as well as e-commerce indicators. In the analysis, it is concluded that, the size of the private sector, increase in exports, commercial transactions through the internet, the number of export transactions via internet and the increase in the number of credit cards positively affected the economic growth.

Wu (2014) analyzed the relationship between internet consumption(as an indicator of electronic commerce) and gross domestic product (GDP) and between internet consumption and traditional consumption, telecommunication industry and Express delivery industry for China in the 2006-2013 period with quarterly data. The results of study which were found by using multivariate VAR analysis and granger causality test following Toda-Yamamato approach suggest that internet consumption had a positive effect on gross domestic product. The study concluded that, the increase in internet consumption has an impact on the telecommunications, transportation and retail sector and there is bi-directional causality between Internet consumption and GDP, retail and telecommunications sectors.

Chunling (2015) investigated the relationship between e-commerce transaction volume and GDP in China through cointegration and causality tests. Empirical results suggest that there is no long-term stable co-integration relationship. However, according to the causality test results, e-commerce is the reason for GDP growth.

Çetinkaya (2016) investigated the positive and negative results and development of e-commerce applications. The growing size of the e-commerce market with the developing technology is also growing. Demirdögmez (2018) studied the development of e-commerce over the years in terms of Turkey, especially the momentum gained in the last ten years aims to develop. In this study, secondary data and the reports of both public and private companies, which are explained in terms of years and years, have been used.

METHODOLOGY AND EMPIRICAL RESULTS

The purpose of this study is to examine the relationship between e-commerce and economic growth for selected countries. On the basis of data availability, the countries included in model are Brazil, Russia, India, China, South Africa and Turkey and we use annual data covering the period 2000-2016. The variables are employeed in analysis that we investigate the relationship between e-commerce and economic growth and their sources are listed below in Table 2:

Stationary tests are considered as a prerequisite analysis to obtain unbiased, effective and consistent parameter estimators in time series and panel data analyzes. In this respect, it is important to examine the stability of the series over time before statistical analysis (Tatoğlu, 2013, p. 199). In case of working with non-stationary time series, a fake regression problem may be encountered and the results obtained obtain with regression analysis may not reflect the truth (Granger & Newbold, 1974, p. 9). We apply three different panel unit root tests, which are Levin Lin Chu (LLC), Im Peseran Shin (IPS) and Augmented Dickey Fuller (ADF), to test the stationarity of the variables. Table 3 shows the results of unit root tests that estimated for all selected variables with trend, without trend and none:

It can be seen from the results displayed in Table 3, null hypothesis (H0), which mean series are not stationary, are rejected with all of the three tests; so all the variables are found to be stationary at level. Hence, it is used the level values of all variables to estimate the panel VAR model. It is an important issue to decide appropriate lag-order in VAR estimation. There are different information criteria available for choosing a more parsimonious model, and we have applied the Schwarz (1978) information criterion (SC), the Akaike (1974) information criterion (AIC) and the Hannah-Quinn (1979) information criterion (HQC). Table 4 shows the VAR lag-length results:

Table 2. Variables and Sources

Notations	Variables	Description	Sources
Y	Economic Growth	Economic Growth Rate (annual %)	WDI
F	Fixed Telephone Users	Fixed Telephone Subscriptions per 100 Inhabitants	ITU
M	Mobile-Telephone Users	Mobile-cellular Telephone Subscriptions per 100 Inhabitants	ITU
P	Population	Population Growth Rate (annual %)	WDI

Table 3. Unit Root Tests

	LLC			IPS		ADF		
	Intercept	Trend and Intercept	None	Intercept	Trend and Intercept	Intercept	Trend and Intercept	None
y	-2.40689* (0.0080)	-3.69086* (0.0001)	-1.3827 (0.0834)	-1.11449 (0.1325)	-0.79446 (0.2135)	17.4912 (0.1320)	15.865 (0.2060)	17.4483 (0.1335)
f	0.52376 (0.6998)	-1.89510* (0.0290)	-3.01052* (0.0013)	1.18229 (0.8815)	0.12832 (0.5511)	8.71537 (0.7270)	15.0740 (0.2374)	23.5059 (0.0237)
m	-2.15933* (0.0154)	-4.1753 (0.3381)	0.14349 (0.5570)	0.23235 (0.5919)	0.14434 (0.5574)	9.95271 (0.6201)	11.0143 (0.5277)	4.74020 (0.9661)
p	-3.32599* (0.0004)	-9.25884* (0.0000)	-1.2366 (0.1081)	-3.65133* (0.0001)	-6.69658* (0.0000)	39.0760* (0.0001)	57.4206* (0.0000)	12.6715 (0.3974)

Note: * indicates the significance at 5% level. The values in the brackets represent probability.

According to the results reported in Table 4, appropriate lag-length is determined 5 by the Akaike information criterion, while the Schwarz and Hannah-Quinn information criterions decided 3 lag-length. Thus, on the basis of these results, Table 5 presents VAR model estimations tested by using 2 lag-length:

Impulse response functions investigate the direction of the response of an endogenous variable to a standard deviation shock occuring in another variable in the system. It is necessary to analyze impulse response functions and variance decomposition in an attempt to examine the source of the changes in the variables employeed in the analysis. In this context, the graphs below show the results of the impulse response functions for all countries:

Table 4. VAR Lag-Order Selection Results

Lag	AIC	SC	HQ
0	23.41026	23.53675	23.46062
1	11.82947	12.46188	12.08123
2	9.702157	10.84049*	10.15533
3	9.444068*	11.08833	10.09865*
4	9.493728	11.64391	10.34972
5	9.669580	12.32569	10.72699

Table 5. VAR Estimation Results

	Y	M	F	P
C	7.449653 (2.29702) [3.24319]	17.66488 (5.36545) [3.29234]	0.732823 (0.49546) [1.47907]	0.021233 (0.01598) [1.32912]
y(-1)	0.346877 (0.11412) [3.03967]	-0.037913 (0.26656) [-0.14223]	-0.033927 (0.02461) [-1.37834]	0.000562 (0.00079) [0.70783]
y(-2)	0.014934 (0.10981) [0.13601]	0.052263 (0.25649) [0.20376]	-0.004379 (0.02368) [-0.18491]	-0.001040 (0.00076) [-1.36206]
y(-3)	0.099473 (0.10379) [0.95840]	-0.337965 (0.24244) [-1.39403]	-0.009041 (0.02239) [-0.40385]	-1.19E-05 (0.00072) [-0.01648]
m(-1)	-0.105611 (0.05103) [-2.06951]	1.337748 (0.11920) [11.2225]	0.019024 (0.01101) [1.72824]	-0.001036 (0.00035) [-2.91851]
m(-2)	0.089418 (0.08665) [1.03193]	-0.346129 (0.20240) [-1.71009]	-0.027824 (0.01869) [-1.48867]	0.002226 (0.00060) [3.69289]
m(-3)	-0.033714 (0.05403) [-0.62397]	-0.103858 (0.12621) [-0.82291]	0.005610 (0.01165) [0.48140]	-0.001240 (0.00038) [-3.30098]
f(-1)	0.298623 (0.53315) [0.56011]	0.165693 (1.24534) [0.13305]	1.708714 (0.11500) [14.8585]	0.004024 (0.00371) [1.08523]
f(-2)	-0.554642 (0.92819) [-0.59755]	-1.360243 (2.16810) [-0.62739]	-0.708721 (0.20021) [-3.53991]	-0.010868 (0.00646) [-1.68353]
f(-3)	0.250026 (0.47999) [0.52090]	1.160735 (1.12117) [1.03528]	-0.019006 (0.10353) [-0.18357]	0.006755 (0.00334) [2.02343]
p(-1)	-1.117082 (12.9163) [-0.08649]	69.51760 (30.1704) [2.30417]	-1.661909 (2.78602) [-0.59652]	2.273742 (0.08983) [25.3111]
p(-2)	13.62657 (24.8064) [0.54932]	-102.8800 (57.9437) [-1.77552]	1.831521 (5.35069) [0.34230]	-1.828641 (0.17253) [-10.5992]
p(-3)	-13.50951 (13.4150) [-1.00705]	29.40591 (31.3352) [0.93843]	-0.408678 (2.89358) [-0.14124]	0.537820 (0.09330) [5.76441]
R^2	0.543253	0.977044	0.995843	0.998795

Note: The values in the brackets represent probability.

Figure 1 represents the response of economic growth to a standard deviation shocks that occurs in economic growth, fixed telephone subscriptions per 100 inhabitants, mobile-cellular telephone subscriptions per 100 inhabitants and population growth respectively for 10 period. The response of economic growth to one standard deviation shock in itself is positively and decreasingly. This major effect continues until the end of the last month. The impact of mobile-cellular telephone subscriptions on economic growth is negatively and decreasingly until the end of fourth period. Then this negative impact increases and it

Figure 1. Response of Economic Growth to Shocks

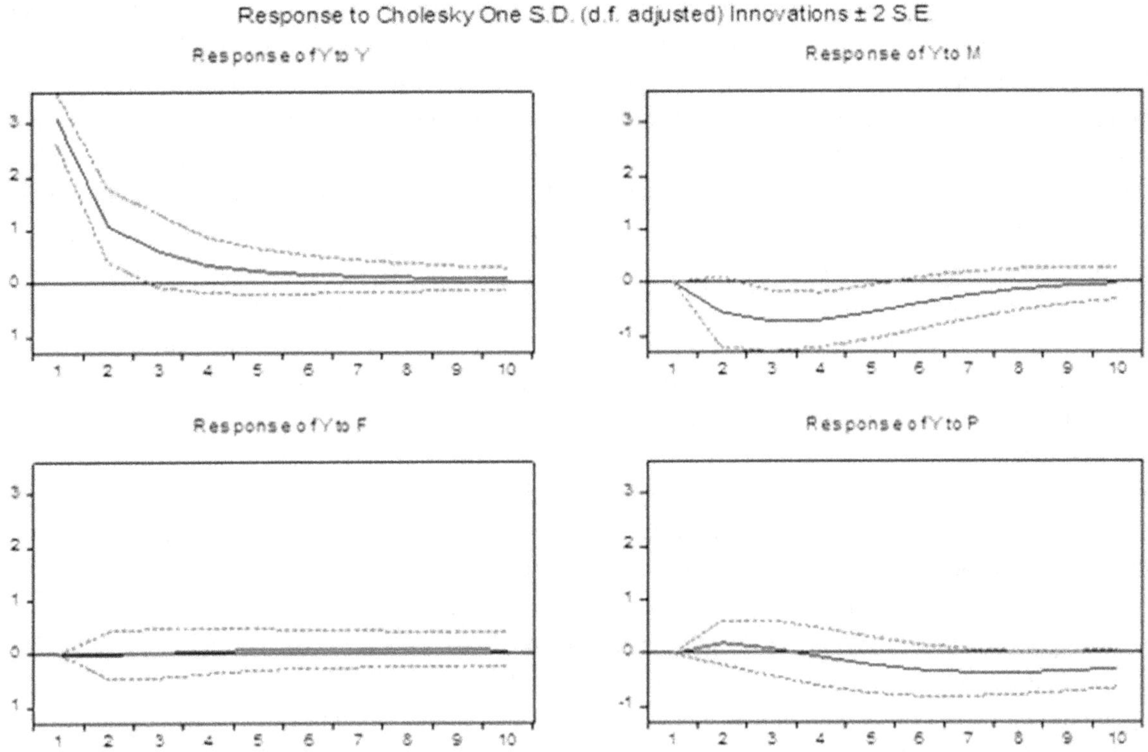

diseppears in the last period. The impact of fixed telephone subscriptions shocksis uncertain firstly. After that, a small positive effect seen at the end of the fourth period. And lastly, the response of economic growth to a population growth shock is in a positive way until the fourth period, and then it continues negatively and decreasingly.

Figure 2 shows the response of mobile-cellular telephone users to a standard deviation shocks that occurs in economic growth, fixed telephone subscriptions per 100 inhabitants, mobile-cellular telephone

Figure 2. Response of Mobile-cellular Telephone Subscriptions to Shocks

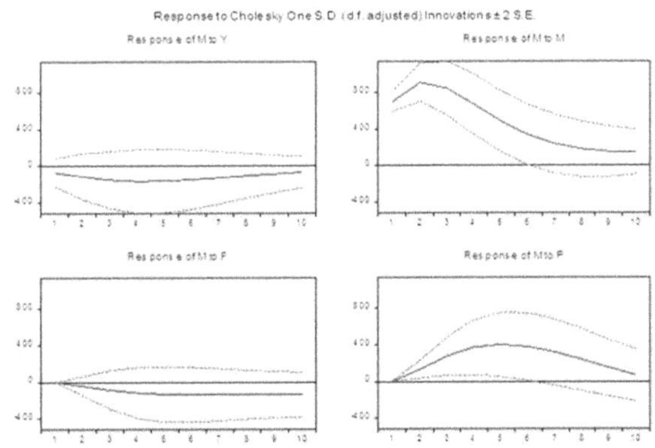

subscriptions per 100 inhabitants and population growth respectively. The impact of economic growth shock on mobile-cellular telephone subscriptions is negative during ten period. This negative impact decreases until the fifth period and increases between fifth and tenth periods. Mobile-cellular telephone subscriptions is affected from a shock in itself positively and increasingly before, then effect continues in a positive and decreasing way at the beginning of the second period. The impact of fixed telephone subscriptions negatively and decreasingly until fifth period. This decreasing affect lost in the beginning of fifth period. The impact of population growth shock on mobile-cellular telephone subscriptions is positively and increasingly until the fifth period and decreasingly between fifth and tenth periods.

Figure 3 represents the response of fixed telephone users to a standard deviation shocks that occurs in economic growth, fixed telephone subscriptions per 100 inhabitants, mobile-cellular telephone subscriptions per 100 inhabitants and population growth respectively. The economic growth shock has a very small positive effect on fixed telephone subscriptions until the third period. In the beginning of third period, this positive effect turns into negative until the end of the tenth period. The impact of fixed telephone subscriptions shock on mobile-cellular telephone subscriptions is positively during ten period. Fixed telephone subscriptions is affected from a shock in itself positively. And the effect of a shock in population growth is uncertain in the first two periods, then a small negative impact occurs and this impact continuse negatively and decreasingly.

Figure 4 displays the response of population growth to a standard deviation shocks that occurs in economic growth, fixed telephone subscriptions per 100 inhabitants, mobile-cellular telephone subscriptions per 100 inhabitants and population growth respectively. The impact of the economic growth shock on popuation growth is uncertain in first four periods and then a very small negative effect occurs in the beginning of fourth period. The response of population growth to mobile-cellular telephone subscriptions shock is negatively and decreasingly. In the sixth period this decreasing effect is lost. The response of population growth to fixed telephone subscriptions shock is uncertain until the end of second period. After that, it is observed that a a very small positive effect and this small effect continues until the end of tenth period. And lastly, the response of population growth to shock in itself is in a positive and incresing way until the sixth period, and then the increasing effect lost between seventh and tenth periods.

The variance decomposition informs about the impacts of the variables on rates of change, while impulse-response function analysis are related to the sign, duration and size of the change in variables. Variance decomposition shows that how much of the changes in dependent variable are derived from its

Figure 3. Response of Fixed Telephone Subscriptions to Shocks

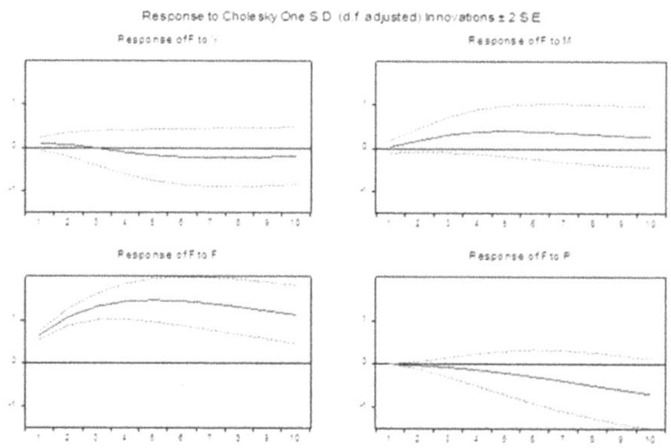

Figure 4. Response of Population Growth to Shocks

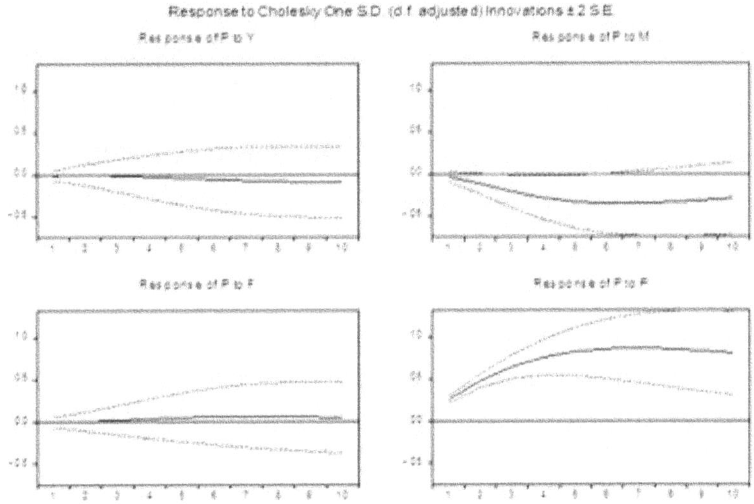

own shocks and shocks of the other variables. Accordingly, the tables below report the results of varince decomposition analysis of all the variables in the system:

Table 6 reports the results of variance decomposition tests for economic growth. According to reported results, the main source of the changes in economic growth is itself with 100% in first period. This impact decreases during ten periods. In the fifth period, change in the economic growth is explained by the change caused by itself with about 87%; while this impact is observed about 82% in tenth period. Results in the Table 6 show that, the second important variable to explain changes in the economic growth is mobile-cellular subscriptions as from second period. Mobile-cellular telephone subscriptions explains changes in economic growth with about 2.82% in the second term, but this effect gradually decreases until tenth period. In the tenth period, about 14% of the changes in economic growth stem from mobile-cellular telephone subscriptions and it is observed that population growth explains 5% of the changes in economic growth, while fixed telephone subscriptions explains about 0.34%. These results indicate that mobile-cellular telephone subscriptions is among the important sources of change in the economic growth.

The variance decomposition test results of mobile-cellular subscription variable that displayed in Table 7 show that changes in mobile-cellular subscriptions stem from the shocks that occurs in itself with about 99% and from changes in economic growth about 1% in first term. Fixed telephone subscriptions

Table 6. Variance Decomposition Results for Economic Growth

Period	y	m	f	p
1	100.0000	0.000000	0.000000	0.000000
2	96.85573	2.812826	0.000838	0.330603
3	92.57358	7.052375	0.006375	0.367673
4	88.93671	10.63186	0.036211	0.395228
5	86.40888	12.72645	0.091038	0.773626
10	81.03555	13.61033	0.349249	5.004870

Table 7. Variance Decomposition Results for Mobile-cellular Telephone Subscriptions

Period	y	M	f	P
1	1.018853	98.98115	0.000000	0.000000
2	1.345855	97.21609	0.140043	1.298009
3	1.937684	93.28793	0.450500	4.323883
4	2.534358	88.32791	0.864921	8.272814
5	3.040762	83.50672	1.319660	12.13285
10	4.065210	74.32569	3.561577	18.04752

and population growth don't affect mobile-cellular subscriptions changes. The explanation ratio of the changes in mobile-cellular subscriptions with its own dynamics decreased to 97% in the second period and reaches the long-run equilibrium value in the tenth period with about 74%. Results in the Table 7 indicate that, the second important variable to explain changes in mobile-cellular subscriptions is population growth as from second period. In the tenth term, the changes in mobile-cellular subscriptions stem from population growth with about 18%, from economic growth with about 4% and from fixed telephone subscriptions with about 3.56%. Hence, these results show that the most important varible to explain mobile-cellular telepone subscriptions among these variables is population growth.

The results of the variance decomposition tests for fixed telephone subscriptions have been presented in the Table 8. When the decomposition results in Table 8 are analyzed, the most important source of change in fixed telephone subscriptions is shocks that stem from itself with 97%.In the second period, this impact decrease to 96% and as of the last period, it reaches an equilibrium value of 85%. Secondary sources that explain fixed telephone subscriptions are population growth with about 8% and mobile-cellular telephone subscriptions with about 6% in the last term. Economic growth has a very small effect with about 1.5%.

Table 9 shows the results of variance decomposition results for population growth. According to results reported in Table 9, the main source of changes in population growth is itself with about 98% in first period. This impact decreases between first and last terms and reaches long term equilibrium about with 87%. Mobile-cellular telephone subscriptions is the second main factor that explain changes in population growth with 1% in first period and with 11% in last period. Economic growth and fixed telephone subscriptions have very small effect on population growth for chosen countries in chosen

Table 8. Variance Decomposition Results for Fixed Telephone Subscriptions

Period	y	M	f	P
1	1.938967	0.405512	97.65552	0.000000
2	0.931396	2.365056	96.62152	0.082025
3	0.440692	4.046717	95.27860	0.233990
4	0.438823	5.135631	93.94439	0.481157
5	0.658598	5.699230	92.75917	0.882999
10	1.463703	5.471754	85.59932	7.465224

Table 9. Variance Decomposition Results for Population Growth

Period	y	M	F	P
1	0.026870	1.001336	0.000429	98.97137
2	0.017629	3.976110	0.020786	95.98547
3	0.012399	6.872159	0.076461	93.03898
4	0.040582	9.097114	0.153822	90.70848
5	0.090613	10.60360	0.237183	89.06860
10	0.460698	11.95527	0.408399	87.17564

period. In respect of this, mobile-cellular telephone subscriptions is an important source ofexplaining the changes in population growth.

SOLUTIONS AND RECOMMENDATIONS

The borders between countries began to disappear with the globalization that accelerate since 1980 and many positive and negative innovations brought by this globalization process. These innovations brought about by globalization are among the important factors used in the economic literature to explain the differences in economic growth between countries. The results of the study show that economic growth and e-commerce are related in log-run and especially mobile-cellular telephone subscriptions is one of the important component that explains the changes in economic growth for BRICS countries and Turkey. These results suggest that countries that want to increase their economic growth rate should focus on policies to increase e-commerce volume. In this regard, it is very important to concentrate on innovations that enhance economic growth through e-commerce.

FUTURE RESEARCH DIRECTIONS

Technological developments that increase their speed gradually bring more innovation in terms of economic efficiency. As a matter of fact, with the development of e-commerce, economic efficiency and growth process started to be affected rapidly. This has led to the existence of e-commerce as an important factor affecting economic growth. It is obvious that the effects of e-commerce developments on the economic growth of the countries will increase in the future. For this reason, it is very important for countries to follow the developments in technology in economic growth processes and to take part in them. As the developments continue, it is thought that e-commerce is an important factor. In this respect, it is extremely necessary for the countries that are continuing e-commerce growth processes to give the necessary importance.

CONCLUSION

A large number of studies have aimed to explain the reasons of different growth rates among developed and developing countries in economic literature. Most commonly variables used in these studies are labour, physical and human capital, investments and technology. Recent studies show that, the increasing e-commerce volume with the expansion of globalization occurs in 1980s has a positive effect on the economic growth levels of the countries, likewise these common variables. In this context, this paper explores the relationship between economic growth-which is one of the common main problems of developed and developing countries-and e-commerce covering the period 2000-2016 by using panel VAR analysis. Based on the studies in the recent literature, we use the mobile-cellular telephone subsciptions and fixed telephone subscriptions as the indicators of e-commerce. The study investigates the impact of the shocks that occur in economic growth, mobile-cellular telephone subscriptions, fixed telephone subscriptions and population growth for the country group that involves Brazil, Russia, India, China, South Africa and Turkey.

Results suggest that the impact of the e-commerce on economic growth is statistically significant and the policies to increase volume of the e-commerce provide an important contribution to economic growth of countries. The results of the impulse response functions and variance decomposition analysis show that the impact of e-commerce may change for different indicators of e-commerce. Firstly, while the the impact of mobile-cellular telephone subscriptions on economic growth is negatively and decreasingly, then this negative impact increases and it diseppears. The impact of fixed telephone subscriptions shocks is uncertain firstly. After that, a small positive effect seen at the end.

According to the results of variance decomposition analysis, while most of the changes in economic growth stem from changes in itself, mobile-cellular telephone subscriptions, one of the determinants of e-commerce, is one of the important components explaining the changes in economic growth in our sample.

Consequently, it can be stated that there is a significant relationship between e-commerce and economic growth for chosen countries. Therefore, it is very important to implement appropriate e-commerce policies for increasing economic growth and it is recommended that countries who wish to provide sustainable economic growth allocate more resources to their e-commerce infratructure.

REFERENCES

Berber, L. K. (2002). *İnternet üzerinden yapılan işlemlerde elektronik para ve dijital imza*. Yetkin Yayınları.

Çetinkaya, Ş. (2016). E-ticaret uygulamalarının makro ekonomik göstergelere etkisi SWOT Analizi ve Türkiye'de e-ticaret gelişimi için bir eylem planı önerisi. *Yalova Üniversitesi Sosyal Bilimler Dergisi*, *6*(11), 235–256.

Chan, E., & Swatman, P. M. (1999, November). Electronic commerce: a component model. In *Proceedings of the 3rd Annual CollECTeR Conference on Electronic Commerce* (p. 1999).

Chunling, W. (2015). Research on economic growth and information exchange based on b2b e-commerce. *The Open Cybernetics & Systemics Journal*, *9*(1), 2065–2069. doi:10.2174/1874110X01509012065

Clarke, R. (1999). Electronic commerce definitions. Retrieved from http://www.anu.edu.au/people/Roger.Clarke/EC/ECDefns.html

Commission of the European Communities. (1997). *A European initiative in electronic commerce.* Brussels, Belgium.

Conway, E. (2009). *Gerçekten bilmeniz gereken 50 ekonomi fikri.* İstanbul, Turkey: Domingo Yayınevi.

Coşkun, N. (2004). Elektronik ticaretin gelişiminde temel dinamikler ve gelişimi önündeki engeller. Çukurova Üniversitesi Sosyal Bilimler Enstitüsü Dergisi, 13(2).

Da Costa, E. (2003). *Global e-commerce strategies for small businesses.* Cambridge, MA: MIT Press.

Elseoud, M. S. A. (2014). Electronic commerce and economic growth in Saudi Arabia. *International Journal of Economics, Commerce and Management*, *2*(5), 1–16.

Gibbs, J. L., & Kraemer, K. L. (2004). A cross-country ınvestigation of the determinants of scope of e-commerce use: An ınstitutional approach. *Electronic Markets*, *14*(2), 124–137. doi:10.1080/10196780410001675077

Granger, C. W. J., & Newbold, P. (1974). Spurious regressions in econometrics. *Journal of Econometrics*, *2*(2), 111–120. doi:10.1016/0304-4076(74)90034-7

Jentzsch, R., & Miniotas, A. (1999, December). The application of e-commerce to a sme. In *Proceedings 10th Australasian Conference on Information Systems* (pp. 435-448).

Kalakota, R., & Whinston, A. B. (1997). Electronic commerce: a manager's guide. Boston, MA: Addison-Wesley Publishing.

Kao, C. (1999). Spurious regression and residual-based tests for cointegration in panel data. *Journal of Econometrics*, *90*(1), 1–44. doi:10.1016/S0304-4076(98)00023-2

Le, X. (2010). Analysis of China's e-commerce and economic development by VAR model. *The Conference on Web Based Business Management*. pp. 621-624.

Liu, S. (2013, June). An empirical study on e-commerce's effects on economic growth. In *2013 Conference on Education Technology and Management Science (ICETMS 2013)*. Atlantis Press. 10.2991/icetms.2013.260

Morrison, C., & Siegel, D. (1997). External capital factors and ıncreasing returns in USA manufacturing. *The Review of Economics and Statistics*, *79*(4), 647–654. doi:10.1162/003465397557051

Özsağır, A. (2014). *Yenilik ekonomisi.* Seçkin Yayıncılık.

Pedroni, P. (1999). Critical values for cointegration tests in heterogeneous panels with multiple regressors. *Oxford Bulletin of Economics and Statistics*, *61*(S1), 653–678. doi:10.1111/1468-0084.61.s1.14

Pedroni, P. (2004). Panel cointegration: Asymptotic and finite sample properties of pooled time series tests with an application to the ppp hypothesis. *Econometric Theory*, (20), 597–625.

Tan, Z., & Ouyang, W. (2002). Global and national factors affecting e-commerce diffusion in China.

Tatoğlu, F. Y. (2013). *İleri panel veri analizi: stata uygulamalı*. İstanbul, Turkey: Beta Yayıncılık.

Tian, Y., & Stewart, C. (2008). History of e-commerce. In A. Becker (Ed.), Electronic Commerce: Concepts, Methodologies, Tools, and Applications: Concepts, Methodologies, Tools, and Applications. Hershey, PA: IGI Global. doi:10.4018/978-1-59904-943-4.ch001

Wigand, R. T. (1997). *Electronic commerce: definition, theory, and context. The Information Society. v13, n1*. January-March.

Wong, P. K. (2003). Global and national factors affecting e-commerce diffusion in Singapore. *The Information Society*, *19*(1), 19–32. doi:10.1080/01972240309471

Wu, Y. (2014). The ımpact of ınternet consumption on China's economic development.

Yumuşak, İ. G. (2001). Elektronik ticaretin gelişmekte olan ülkelere etkileri ve türkiye üzerine bir değerlendirme. (*Çevrimiçi http://128.118, 178.*)

KEY TERMS AND DEFINITIONS

B1B: Business in Business e-commerce is defined as trade within a company. Large companies can conduct commercial transactions between various business units in this way.

B2B: Business to Business e-commerce that includes finance, purchasing, inventory management, sales, advertising, payment and delivery transactions, customer service and many other business activities.

B2C: Business to Customer e-commerce that is the most widely known type of e-commerce, is a virtual store that occurs with the development of web and wap technologies.

C2C: Customer to Customer e-commerce is a technic that has just began and people sell their old stuff to random people.

E-COMMERCE: Electronic commerce which is a concept that has been started to be an important explanatory component of economic growth via innovations in information technology in recent years, is defined as the production, advertisement and distribution of goods and services through telecommunication networks and these developments in information technology enhance volume of e-commerce applications.

ITC: International Trade Center.

OECD: Economic Cooperation and Labor Organization.

UNCTAD: United Nations Conference on Trade and Development.

WB: World Bank.

WTO: World Trade Organization.

Chapter 5
Examination of the Extent and Effects of Strategic Management on E-Commerce Companies

Zafer Adiguzel
Istanbul Medipol University, Turkey

ABSTRACT

Internet technology can be used not only in commercial applications but also in the implementation and distribution of public services like education and health, making e-commerce essential not only for the business world but also for all of society. Thus, companies can take advantage of internet opportunities in order to develop their strategies in e-commerce environment, creating working groups by bringing together employees in different geographical locations with tools such as newsgroups, communication rooms, etc., benefiting from customer suggestions. Therefore, it is important to examine and analyze the companies that have commercial activities in e-commerce environments in terms of strategic management. From a strategic point of view, the aim of companies should be to increase their activities by influencing their existing customers and continuously gaining new customers within the e-commerce environment.

INTRODUCTION

E-commerce is about the purchase and sale of products, services, and information through computer networks and is a very important phenomenon for both companies and consumers. E-commerce provides marketing platforms for products, services and information, enables customer support before and after the sale, and builds commercial communication between organizations and customers through computer networks. Furthermore, e-commerce enables instant access to information, products and services all over the world. The organisations with strong internet infrastructure can offer 24/7 e-commerce options, which eliminate 'time problems' that limit the shopping experiences of consumers/customers.

Due to ever-increasing competition and constantly evolving market conditions, society has created the concept of a new economy. When we say new economy, we think of a situation where people's mental activities have adapted along with the formation of advanced technologies. This concept of a new economy

DOI: 10.4018/978-1-7998-0035-4.ch005

is also considered a creation of e-commerce organisations operating over the internet (Marangoz, 2014). Most importantly, e-commerce companies offer products and/or services in the internet environment to other regions, and they have to think fast and make swift strategic decisions in order to create value. In this new economic environment, the products and services of e-commerce companies depend on two different technologies (Marangoz, 2014):

- Information
- Communication

The tools of these technologies are computer software, telecommunications, and the internet. E-commerce companies benefit from the opportunities provided by the internet environment: keeping records and information on virtual platform, the ease of accessing information in an electronic environment any place and at any time without the need of another person.

Indeed, it is specifically because the Internet allows consumers to compare products/services according to their prices and quality before making decisions and purchase dependent on budgets and requirements that e-commerce companies must consider these factors before creating their strategy (Zwass, 2003). Internet technology offers access to information regardless of location and in the event of problems experienced by customers, the ability of e-commerce companies to use internet to reach information increases a company's responding to the needs of its customers (Dixon & Quinn 2004). In this way, customers value the service they received and remain as permanent customers. Thanks to ever-developing technology, the Internet provides an infrastructure for sharing data and enables the co-operation of employees. In terms of business strategies, there are two types of e-commerce companies: companies with no physical stores or those with physical stores (Erkan, 2012). At the same time, there are two types of operational dimensions within e-commerce: Narrow or Broad sense. A Narrow business strategy allows businesses to carry out their activities freely and offer their own products and services to consumers over web-based systems (Bozkurt, 2000). In the broad sense, an e-commerce business strategy is defined as the inclusion of special e-commerce systems in addition to the shopping experience of consumers/customers over the internet. In this article, the importance of e-commerce in terms of its advantages and disadvantages, as well as its effects on an organization will be examined within the framework of strategic management.

DEFINITION OF E-COMMERCE

E-commerce in the internet environment not only enables more efficient transactions, but also provides an opportunity for companies to take advantage of cost advantages and provide better service to customers. The internet provides opportunities to companies to reduce their costs while making it possible for most services to be carried out online (Lituchy & Rail, 2000). The rapid growth of the internet enables service and manufacturing companies to create a distribution channel at a low cost and to have easier access to global markets (O'Connor, 1999).

Nowadays, the quality of customer service can be evaluated according to the services companies offer through the Internet (Heung, 2003). With the emergence of the Internet and the continuous development of Internet technology, the search and purchase behaviour of consumers has changed significantly. The service and products of companies can be compared as there are many web portals publishing evaluations, therefore it leads companies to provide products and services that are customer-oriented. The most important privilege offered by e-commerce is that customers use the opportunities offered by technology with devices such as smart phones, tablets, laptops, etc. (it may even be possible to make purchases from smart wristwatches), and they can now receive service whenever and wherever they want (Chung & Law, 2003). Customers who are interested in technology can also select parts according to their requirements and likings and create the product themselves. The opportunities provided in the e-commerce environment change the shopping habits of the customers, allowing them to order over the internet, save time, and get the products delivered to their prepared location instead of visiting stores. In this way, customers enjoy and value the shopping experience more fully.

Law (2000) explains that the internet allows direct communication with customers and suppliers by eliminating barriers. In particular, the fact that customers give more importance to the quality of service has led companies to start offering more personalized services to their customers through their website (Lituchy & Rail, 2000). Due to the faster growth of the services sector, the use of traditional indirect distribution channels has decreased and more direct channels have developed (Williams & Palmer, 1999). As consumers & customers gain more internet experience, the probability of them getting used to electronic shopping rises (Card, Chen, & Cole, 2003). Companies that understand the importance of e-commerce see their web sites as a tool that brings 80-90% of business from around the world, with the internet being the most important primary marketing tool (Eimer, 2000).

Since 1995, with the increase in internet usage, e-commerce has become more widespread and gained importance in terms of competition between companies (Wymer, & Regan 2005). During the years that the Internet was not an option or was not widespread, the companies would offer their goods and services to markets using tools such as radio, newspaper, and television. In today's world, the wide use of the Internet gradually caused an increase in virtual markets, both in terms of the number of e-commerce businesses and the number of products & services offered to customers. In terms of business strategies, there are two types of e-commerce companies:

- Companies without physical stores
- Companies with physical stores (Erkan 2012).

Narrow e-commerce refers businesses that operate freely, offering their own products and services in web-based systems (Bozkurt, 2000). Whereas, broad e-commerce is described as shopping on the internet, which includes special electronic commerce systems. Specifically, companies should consider some important elements during their decision-making process, before starting their activities in the e-commerce environment:

- Electronic Funds Transfer (EFT)
- Electronic Banking, Electronic Data Interchange (EDI)
- Electronic Message Sending and Receiving etc.

Electronic Funds Transfer (EFT): The EFT system is used as a transfer of money between two banks. Today, thanks to the internet banking offered by banks, payments can be made via smart phones, tablets, and laptops at any time with EFT (Coşkun, 2004).

Electronic Data Interchange (EDI): EDI was first used in North America in the 1960s, and it is also called information exchange. The aim of the system is to reduce paper consumption, help commercial transactions between companies, and provide faster shipments (Sezgin, 2013).

Sending and Receiving Electronic Messages: From the 1970s until present, messages have been sent through the internet, and the most important tool for sending messages has been e-mail. One of the main objectives in the development of the e-mail system is to prevent the consumption of paper and to quickly communicate information (Çubukcu & Bayzan, 2013).

The New Economy: The concept of the new economy was created by businesses offering their products and services through their web pages (Marangoz, 2014). In particular, the new economy is a situation where people's' mental activities increase in pace with the development of advanced technology opportunities. Thus, the emergence of the new economy concept is to increase customer potential by reaching more consumers, while improving thinking and decision making.

In the new economy, products and services are based on two different technologies (Marangoz, 2014):

- Information (structured and formatted data)
- Communication (transfer of information from sender to recipient)

The tools needed to these two technologies are computer software, telecommunications, and the internet. One of the most obvious advantages that the Internet provides is advertisement for e-commerce companies that costs less if at all (Rogers, Bennett, & Grewal, 2007) . With the increasing number of social network users over the internet, e-commerce companies have started to display their ads on social networks primarily because smart phone users share information around their social networks, increasing ad visibility with their social media activities.

The Historical Development of E-Commerce

In 1950, the production of computers started with the advent of ARPANET, the name that represented a project between the army and university in 1969, and later became known as the Internet (Erkan, 2012). With the discovery of the Internet, people began to communicate more easily, and with the development of communication opportunities, this innovation led to the development of e-commerce (Zhu & Kraemer, 2002). And, through e-commerce, companies found new markets and started to increase their market share, starting with. the company that made the first sale over the Internet an American restaurant in central Texas. Starting in 1990, with widespread internet use, e-commerce was one of the most innovative concepts in today's world. Just a couple years later, in 1994, a Pizza Hut restaurant accepted its first order via their web page, followed by the establishment of some of the most important companies of e-commerce: Amazon.com in 1994, and Ebay.com in 1995 (Worzala et al., 2002).

Marketing and trade have been reshaped through the development of the Internet (Yeşil, 2008), but within the e-commerce world, there are differences between concepts of marketing and trade. Trade is limited to the exchange of a product between seller and buyer; however, marketing is about providing product information, promotion, and after-sales activities. The gains achieved in trade and marketing are two important concepts in terms of strategic management, and on the Internet, trades between the buyer and the seller mean more marketing. The traditional marketing is very costly and takes time to reach people; whereas, internet marketing can reach millions of people, if not billions, in seconds using an effective marketing method (Hart, Doherty, & Ellis-Chadwick, 2000). Internet marketing has many advantages compared to traditional marketing methods, including the necessity of face-to-face contact with customers in business relations, a key disadvantage in traditional marketing (Schibrowsky, Peltier, & Nill, 2007).

As a whole, the modern e-marketing methods are strategically important, as they are faster, less costly, and do not require face-to-face contact with customers. Therefore, when we look at the characteristics of the development of internet marketing (Figure 1), there are important elements of e-commerce environment.

Before the internet, some international brands were providing distant sales in a diverse ways.

Companies such as Oriflame and Avon were performing their marketing activities in traditional ways prior to e-commerce (Erkan 2012). Similarly, there were companies such as Shopping TV and Top Shop which carried out marketing activities with TV programs. Nowadays, these companies still continue their activities, showing the importance of e-commerce.

Scope of E-Commerce

Information technologies, communication, and similar concepts are parts of e-commerce (Yeşil, 2008). Each activity within the commercial sector has results on the internet that are seen as e-commerce. Businesses want to keep in close contact with their suppliers in order to respond to the expectations of their customers more efficiently. It is possible to look at e-commerce from two perspectives: the commercial and service vantage point. The commercial aspect of e-commerce depends on technology; whereas, the service aspect of e-commerce is related to providing information, payments and similar services over the internet (Forman, Goldfarb, & Greenstein, 2005). In short, e-commerce is the sale of goods and services, carrying out transactions such as insurance, distribution, etc. over the internet.

When we consider e-commerce in a broader sense, there are several issues listed below that companies should give attention to in terms of strategic management and customer satisfaction (Marangoz, 2014):

Figure 1. Characteristics of Internet Marketing

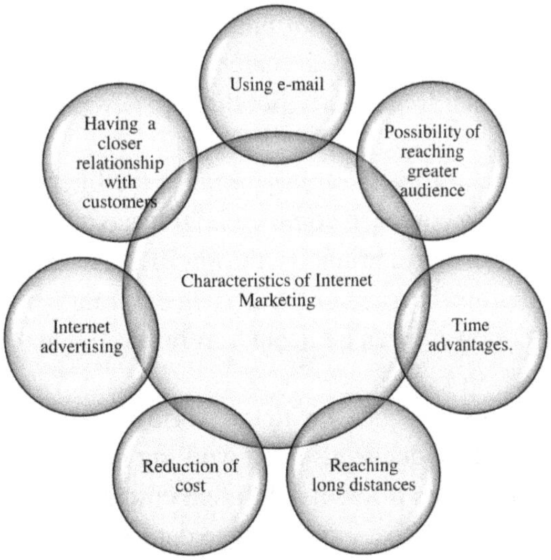

Scope of E-Commerce

- Production planning and production chain creation
- Electronic exchange of goods and services
- Bank operations in a virtual environment
- Electronic bank transactions and fund transfers
- Ordering
- Sending a bill of lading via the internet
- Customs clearance
- Public procurement on the internet
- E-mail related transactions
- E-share and stock market trading
- Transfer of intellectual property rights
- Making a deal
- Production planning
- Taxation on the internet
- Creating and transferring on-site information
- Marketing to consumers
- Keeping and monitoring of trade records
- Electronic signature and electronic notary

Scope of E-Commerce Summary

Carrying out business activities in the electronic environment is called e-commerce, which includes electronic processing and transmission of commercial transactions in text, audio, and video format. E-commerce includes all activities related to the design, production, promotion of products, commercial transactions and payments, as well as all types of activities through computer networks (King, Sen, & Xia, 2004). In summary, e-commerce covers all kinds of goods and services. In order to conduct e-commerce relations, it is necessary to have communication facilities with internet technology, and the most efficient and rapid development of the internet is definitely web pages where businesses with specialized e-commerce activities can be accessed using web search tools (Kaufmann, Cliquet, & Achabal, 2010).

Many IT companies continue their R & D activities through new e-commerce tools and environment, some of which are;

Electronic commerce has developed very rapidly because the Internet environment eliminates time and space limitations, providing low costs and commercial transactions that can be carried out by one or more people in an interactive platform. Additionally, the internet is more flexible than other e-commerce tools, resulting in the difficulties and barriers of the trading environment decreasing (Ene, 2002).

The important points of e-commerce can be listed as follows: (Dolanbay, 2000)

- E-commerce is the largest business gateway to the world.
- E-commerce may require radical decisions in all working methods.
- E-commerce addresses consumers through a different culture.
- In the e-commerce system, it is almost impossible to detect the mass of consumers and the market share in advance.

Figure 2. E-commerce Tools

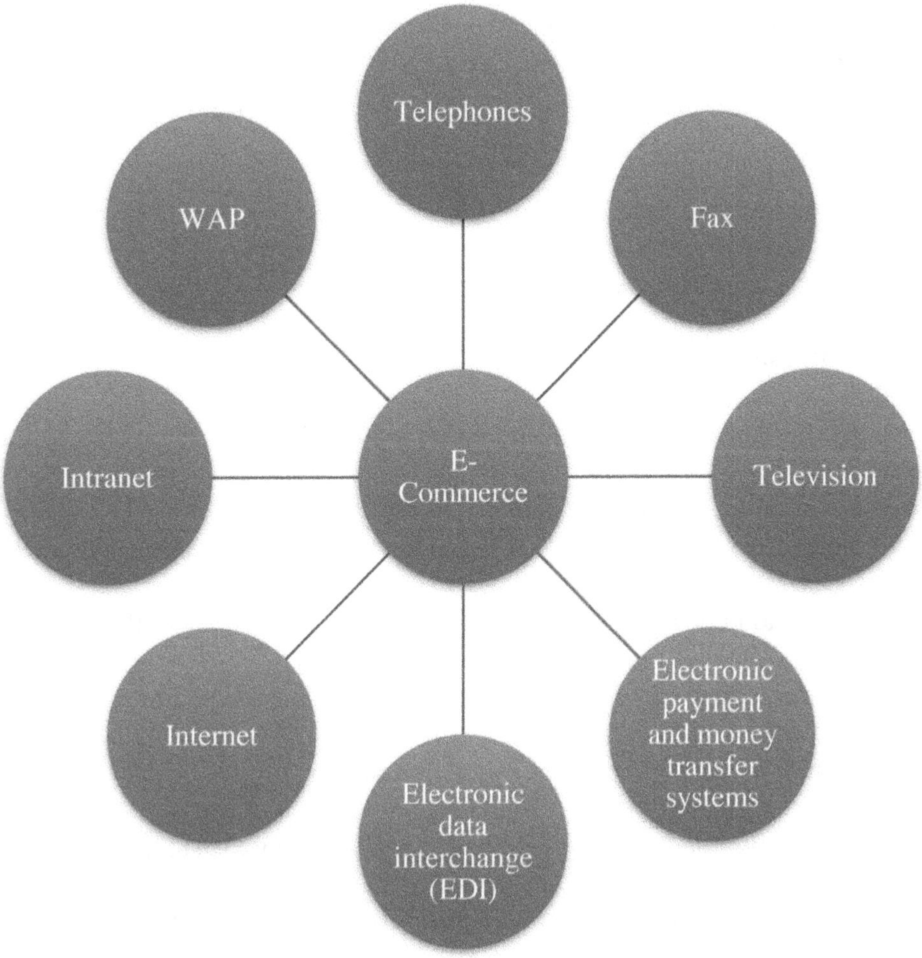

- The future position of the e-commerce business will be determined by planned services.
- E-commerce requires leaving the idea of regionalism.

E-commerce activity types can be examined according to their legal status (Arıkan, 1999).

Promotion activities on the market: The buyer and seller in the e-commerce environment without face-to-face contact;

- Sellers carry out market research, product planning, and advertising the product
- The buyer determines the best product by comparing them in an e-commerce environment.

Contractual activities: At the stage of contracting in an electronic environment;

- The buyer orders the product under the terms and conditions.

- The seller can start the transaction according to the order.

Communication between the two sides about logistics operations:

- E-commerce can provide systems that show the location of the product, transfer, and delivery processes.

Activities related to the payments:

- Payment and billing are among the activities of e-commerce in an electronic environment.

E-Commerce Standards

Some of the standards that e-commerce companies must follow (Canpolat, 2001; Çakırer, 2013):

- E-commerce companies should develop the Frequently Asked Questions (FAQ) section.
- E-commerce companies should inform their customers about the amount of existing products, delivery times, and estimated delays.
- The customer should be able to see the product stock information about the product he or she wants to buy.
- E-commerce companies should inform the customers regarding the return procedures before the purchase of the product.
- The customer must be able to see all the billing information of the company before purchasing the product.
- E-commerce companies should specify the warranty conditions for each product to their customers.
- Customers must be informed about after-sales support and services.
- E-commerce companies should put "search engines" on their websites which enable their customers to easily search for products or services.
- E-commerce companies should announce that the customer information is secure and will not be shared with third parties.
- E-commerce companies cannot request information unrelated to business transactions (such as race, religion, sect) without the consent of customers, and if they get this information with the consent of their customers, they should take preventive measures to keep it confidential
- E-commerce companies should take measures to prevent brand age and protect their logo against any abuse.
- E-commerce companies are responsible for the security of all information regarding payment, financial information, and buyer identity.
- E-commerce companies should correct the missing and/or wrong information as soon as possible.
- E-commerce companies should provide payment facilities (Credit Card, Debit Card, EFT/Money Transfer etc.) for the customer who want to buy the product.
- E-commerce companies should get the payment of the product either during the online sale or when the product is delivered.
- E-commerce companies should indicate when the customer will be charged for the purchase of the products on the last transaction page.

- E-commerce companies must notify the customer in advance of the delivery date of the product.
- E-commerce companies should notify the customers about the products they ordered by e-mail, fax, sms, or through web pages.
- E-commerce companies should ask the billing information of the customer.
- The customer should see the latest status of the product with internet-based reporting.
- E-commerce companies should insure the product against any damage that may occur during delivery.
- E-commerce companies should tell the customer how long it takes for the product to reach the customer.
- E-commerce companies should provide cargo information about the product by e-mail, fax or web page.
- E-commerce companies should provide customers the right to return the product in a pre-specified period and offer refunds as soon as possible.
- E-commerce companies should provide information about the return conditions and the refund policy regarding the product.
- E-commerce companies should provide information about the last return date with the refund conditions.
- The customer should easily be able to access the return conditions on the e-commerce company's website.
- E-commerce company's web page should display a link to customer services.
- E-commerce companies should review and respond to questions and complaints about products and/or services from customers.
- E-commerce companies should provide the customer with the opportunity to contact the manufacturer if they cannot solve the problem regarding the product and/or service.
- E-commerce companies should inform the customer after supplying a product that is not in stock.
- E-commerce companies should inform the customer if it cannot supply the requested product.
- E-commerce companies should inform customers about changes in the policies of the company.
- E-commerce companies should not collect specific information for themselves and third parties by taking advantage of the naivety and inexperience of children under 12 years of age without the direct knowledge and consent of parents.
- E-commerce Companies definitely should not take orders from children without the consent of parents (Canpolat, 2001; Çakırer, 2013).

E-Commerce According to Activities

E-commerce activities can be examined in sections, according to their activities both indirect and direct (Ene 2002).

Indirect Parties to E-Commerce; The main indirect parties of e-commerce are buyers, sellers, manufacturers, banks, brokers, insurance companies, transport companies, non-governmental organizations, universities, customs offices, Foreign Trade Offices, and information technology companies. Networks that the parties communicate with are multiple: the Internet, Intranet and an Extranet (Özbay & Akyazı, 2004).

Figure 3. E-commerce activities (Ene 2002)

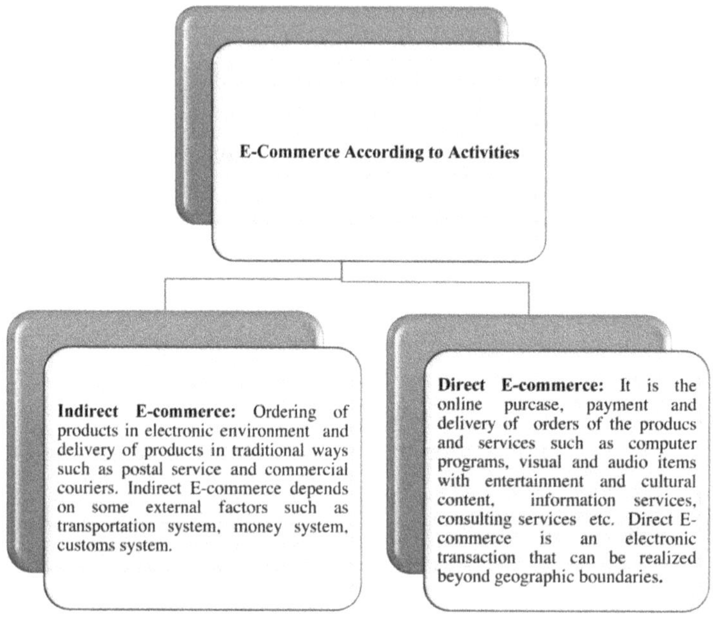

Effects and Benefits of E-Commerce

E-commerce has caused some economic and social changes (Arpacı & Uluçay 2012).

- Through e-commerce, economic impacts are increasing.
- Through e-commerce, competition is increasing among organisations.
- Through e-commerce, the overall costs of organisations are decreasing
- Through e-commerce, the decrease in costs is reflected in the prices of the products.
- Through e-commerce, product options are increasing.
- Through e-commerce, market power is transferred to the consumer.
- Through e-commerce, 24/7 continuous trading and shopping opportunities are offered.
- Through e-commerce, 'transparency' and 'openness' are becoming widespread.
- Through e-commerce, the importance of being geographically close to the market is disappearing.
- Through e-commerce, the efficiency of web-based marketing and online order is increasing.
- Through e-commerce, the market structure is changing.

E-commerce has different effects on companies, societies, and individuals. E-commerce companies are more adaptive to the conditions in the markets and to customer expectations, thereby gaining competitive advantages against other companies (Ngai & Wat, 2002). With e-commerce, business processes are shortened, daily work tracking takes shorter time frames, costs decrease, and productivity increases. Thanks to e-commerce, companies can increase their product options on their web pages, the quality of the products increase as the buyers have the opportunity to make comparisons, payments can be made quickly and with different methods, and the product can be delivered faster (Molla & Licker, 2005).

Furthermore, the entry of low-priced and high-quality products into the market leads to increased competition among manufacturers and reduces the cost of all business transactions. Thanks to e-commerce and the development of Internet technology this development starts from computers and goes up to the smart phones and smart wristwatches today, information provided to the customers about the products in the market from all over the world and new manufacturers are allowed to enter the world market (Wade & Nevo, 2005). It is almost impossible for us to imagine what technology will come up with in the next 10 years as it continues to develops. In fact, these developments push companies to make new strategic moves and to think with a technology-focused approach. E-commerce brings manufacturers and consumers together and eliminates commercial barriers and disadvantages: distance to the market, lack of information, and an inability to produce according to demand etc. If companies do not have any knowledge and experience in e-commerce, they are still able to use the Internet for the purpose of advertising or market research in the first stage (Becker, 2007). As they gain knowledge and experience, they can start to conduct more professional e-commerce activities. E-commerce is the best solution for companies that want to sell abroad but cannot open stores. Although the initial investment costs are high, it is still an economical alternative due to the fact that the company will have less expenses over time, in terms of location, sales services, and customer service.

The Effects of E-Commerce on Economic Life

E-commerce affects almost every field of economic life and causes great changes. However, some units of business life are more affected by this change.

Economic Life Activities Affected by E-Commerce

E-commerce activities that affect economic life (Korkmaz, 2002);

- Marketing, sales, and promotion
- Pre-sale and supply
- Financing and insurance
- Business transactions: order, delivery, and payment
- Service and maintenance
- Mutual product development and work
- Using public and private services
- Public transactions, taxes, customs etc.
- Delivery and logistics
- Public procurement
- Accounting
- Automated trading of electronic products
- Settlement of disputes.

Changes Brought by E-Commerce

Changes brought by e-commerce (Kepenek, 1999)

E-Commerce carries the marketplace from a physical place to a virtual platform. The latest reorganization of shopping activities and the maintenance of trade-related services will require the training of skilled manpower to carry out these functions.

E-Commerce has an accelerating and disseminating effect on trading and related transactions. In particular, the process of the transactions change depending on the developing technological infrastructure of the organisations.

E-Commerce increases the operating density of the economy as economic relations between businesses and consumers are reinforced by e-commerce, enabling businesses and consumers to operate on a world scale.

Businesses should be transparent towards their customers and suppliers. As a whole, the most beneficial aspect of e-commerce is that it is expected to strengthen competition, and the most disadvantageous aspect is the need to protect private information against possible attacks.

E-Commerce changes the relative importance of time since there is a principal that the economic activities are realized in a short period of time, thereby shortening the processing times.

Benefits of E-Commerce

E-commerce enables the commercial transactions & activities between the buyer and seller to be realized over the internet. Companies can engage in marketing activities about their products and/or services through the internet network, and can respond to requests and complaints from their customers, provide after-sales services, and thus, have the chance to collect significant data regarding customer satisfaction (Young, Clark, & McIntyre, 2006). The most important advantage of e-commerce is that it breaks down the traditional trade concepts and enables the buyers and sellers from all over the world to meet 24/7 (Hoffman & Novak, 2000). Thanks to the internet, companies can expand their customer portfolio by crossing borders. E-commerce is not only a matter of concern to companies, but it also concerns all consumers and customers who benefit from the opportunities and advantages of E-commerce (Gibbs & Kraemer, 2004). There are definitely positive changes through e-commerce (Afra, 2014):

- Through e-commerce, companies are growing beyond the borders and competition is increasing.
- E-commerce reduces the costs of companies.
- Through e-commerce, consumers have the opportunity to buy quality and cheap products at any time.
- E-commerce systems reduce companies' inventory costs.
- Through e-commerce, consumers have the chance to compare products and prices.
- E-commerce facilitates the planning of production, and therefore, the efficiency of production increases.
- E-commerce allows companies to provide efficient and effective customer service.
- E-commerce reduces the costs of sales, marketing, and distribution.
- Through e-commerce, companies can quickly and effectively adapt to the changes that will occur in the market as well as the introduction of products.
- Through e-commerce, trade is made easier and more efficacious.
- Through e-commerce, companies develop their commercial activities and become global, gathering more shares from international trade.

Effects of E-Commerce on Management

E-commerce has a positive effect on working areas of the companies and on the speed of communication with their customers (Korkmaz, 2002). Consumers and customers are able to make purchases in the e-commerce environment at any time for the products and/or services they want to buy. Buyers have the opportunity to make comparisons between products and/or services, while companies with intranet network have access to up-to-date promotional advertisements and prices for products and/or services (Porter & Michael; ilustraciones Gibbs, 2001). With the widespread use of the internet, it is possible to reach the requested information anywhere and at any time (Forman, 2005). With the increasing use of this opportunity, the e-commerce companies have developed online customer service operating from their web pages in order to provide better quality service to their customers (Kantarcı et al., 2017). The internet not only offers advantages to buyers, but also allows business people to access information about the production and sales numbers from web pages at any time (Luo, Hongxin, Zhao, & Du, 2005). It has become even more important for buyers and sellers to reach information comfortably, and in today's world, the companies with different locations can collect data from each location and create working groups with Internet technology. Data from different locations and working groups create a platform where new strategically ideas and opinions are generated.

STRATEGIC MANAGEMENT AND ITS ELEMENTS AS A CONCEPT

When examining the concept strategy, we see the term 'strategos', which Greek means 'General'. What is the strategy in literature? It is a question that does not have a mutual or clear answer. According to Mintzberg and colleagues, one of the famous strategy theorists, the concept of strategy refers to "army" and "governing" (Mintzberg et al., 2003). The reason behind Mintzberg's thinking is that the concept of "General" is related to both the army and the concept of governance. Naturally it was difficult to explain in a single concept. When we look at the concept of strategy in terms of business management, it is explained as the process that defines business goals and policies. However, since the concept of strategy includes very different ideas and opinions, it has been considered from different perspectives and different definitions in the literature.

According to Eren (2010), it has been defined as a selection of elective decisions on how to optimize the operations of an organisation that has an important effect on the organization and general objectives of the business, helping a business to find solutions to complex business situations. Ülgen and Mirze (2010) define strategy as the whole of result-oriented and dynamic decisions, which are taken with a visionary perspective by analyzing the competitors, in order to reach the objectives of the business. In short, it can be explained as leaders and managers who analyze the external environment of the business, bring the resources together, and organise them effectively to achieve the long term aims of the organisation.

Basic Elements of Strategic Management

Strategic management begins with the strategic consciousness of an organisation. The initiation of strategic consciousness starts when the managers think about the various strategies of competitors, how they can develop counter moves against these strategies, and how they can benefit from opportunities and threats in the competitive environment (Hitt, Ireland, & Hoskisson, 2012). From this perspective,

Figure 4. Basic Elements of Strategic Management

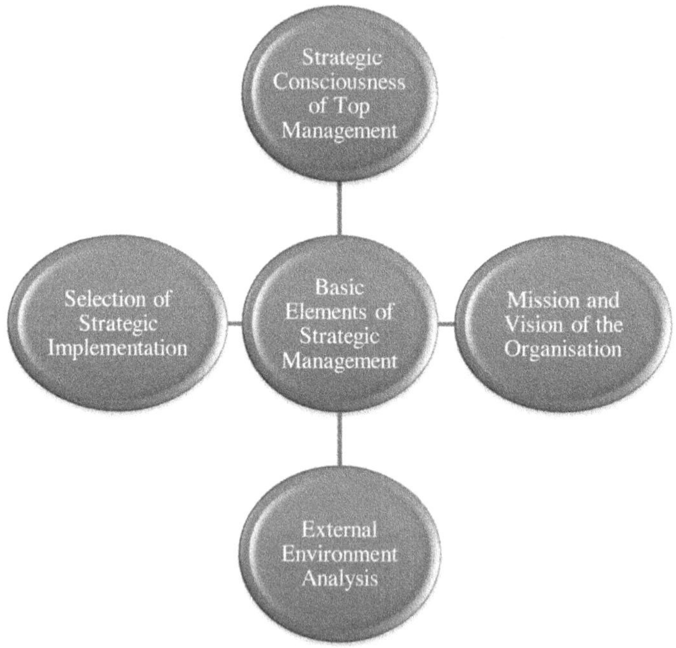

the basic elements of strategic management include important elements such as the mission and vision of the organisation, the strategic consciousness of top managers, strategic choices, and the analysis of the external environment.

If senior executives want to be successful architects and coordinators, they need to be global leaders with both intuitive and participatory aspects in analyzing and making decisions with the data they obtained (Dinçer, 2007).

Senior executives need to respond to two key questions in the strategic management process (Dinçer, 2007):

a) What is our type of business and what is the work being done?

This question is entirely related to the mission of the business and how the organisation defines itself. For this reason, organisations have to define their missions to society in a clear, understandable, and open manner.

b) Why are we doing this?

In order to define objectives, an organisation should answer the question of why it is carrying out the work. Companies wishing to operate in the field of e-commerce should strategically determine what they want to do, why they want to operate in this field, what their objectives are. After defining the mission, vision, goals and objectives, prospective e-commerce companies should be careful in terms of analysis, finding the right direction, determination of strategies, and the final steps of evaluation and implementation (Martin & Pénard, 2005). In terms of strategic management, e-commerce companies need to identify their vision. Today, vision is one of the most misunderstood and overused words. Vision means a picture shared by all employees about the organization's future; the place where the organization wants to be in the future its horizon. In other words, the vision is a cognitive design that combines the beliefs of how to reach a desired situation, how to be at a targeted place in the future (Güçlü, 2003).

In terms of strategic management, e-commerce companies need to analyze their external environment. If this analysis is not carried out, we cannot say that the life of the companies operating in the field of e-commerce will be very long because the changes and developments of the external environment are considered one of the most decisive elements of strategic management in terms of decision-making and implementation. The continuous changes in the environment and the long time horizon of strategic management increase the uncertainty and thus highlight the importance for the organisation (Mariz-Pérez & García-Álvarez, 2009). Therefore, for the decision-making mechanisms in strategic management, it is important for e-commerce companies to identify opportunities and threats through the analysis of the external environment. The external environment analysis is important for choosing the appropriate strategy for the success and development of the company in the long term (Üzün, 2000).

Types of Strategies

The selection of appropriate strategies is the most important phase of the strategic management process. However, prior to the selection, strategies should be defined and upper and lower strategies should be defined as well. We can classify strategies into two main categories (Ülgen & Mirze, 2010);

- Basic Strategies
- Strategies according to Management Levels.

Basic Strategies

Basic Strategies about the work and activities that organisations should or should not do in the future in order to sustain their lives and gain a competitive advantage (Porter 2008).

The first of the strategies is the **Growth Strategy** and refers to the numerical and qualitative development of organisations. The organisations can go further by building their existing assets and capabilities in order to improve their activities in the sector, thereby gaining more returns.

The second basic strategy is the **Downsizing Strategy** whereby organisations can withdraw from sectors where business is inefficient and focus on attracting more efficient areas: Organisations can consciously reduce some of their activities in order to generate more revenue.

The third basic strategy is **Stable Strategies**. Organisations can choose stable strategies if competition is very intense and if other strategies will not produce gains above average, or if there is no new opportunities in the market.

Finally, businesses can use any of the basic strategies simultaneously or consecutively. While implementing a stable strategy in one sector, it may turn to growth strategies in another sector. In such cases, the companies implement '**mixed strategies**'.

Strategy According to the Management Levels

It is also necessary to classify the strategies according to responsible management levels. Strategies can be classified into three groups according to management levels, the purpose of implementation, and perspectives (Ülgen & Mirze, 2010). Corporate Governance Strategies are related to the issues that senior executives of an organisation are constantly thinking and seeking solutions to, such as what business areas to operate, how to implement activities in order to survive in the long term, and how to increase value by having a competitive advantage in the future. Therefore, this strategy is about the main areas of activity within organisations, and how they should implement their activities.

Functional Strategies are prepared and implemented at the middle or lower management levels and are functional or departmental strategies, such as marketing, production, finance, human resources, research and development, etc. which are usually dealt with at the middle management levels (Ülgen & Mirze, 2010).

The Strategic Use of E-Commerce

The first thing that comes to mind about e-commerce is the strategic threats and opportunities in business life. At the beginning of the list of strategic issues lies communication formed with business partners, competitors, and potential customers. It can be said that e-commerce is a structure that provides a new and powerful information system and communication channel to consumers and organisations with the help of information and communication technologies. This allows buyers and sellers to come together in more efficient ways and to create new markets and opportunities for the re-organization of economic processes, personalization of products, re-definition of distribution approaches to products and services (Ada et al., 2008). The strategic use of the Internet is evident by the fact that there is now 24 hours of uninterrupted communication and an unlimited flow of information. Another important issue in the use of e-commerce is the innovative change in the supply chain that are mainly made by using electronic channels with digital and electronic products, forcing the restructuring of the traditional supply chain rules (Sadowski et al., 2002). One of the most important issues here is the savings on stock costs. The acceleration of orders and their provisions leads to a remarkable reduction in inventory. Reducing inventory costs, especially in times of crisis, eliminates a huge burden for organisations and transfers resources from stock costs to more efficient areas in organisations (Bozkurt, 2000).

The third important issue in the strategic use of e-commerce is the cost issue, which can be great opportunity but also an important threat. However, this cost is not the cost of investment, it is the cost of learning and managing the technological infrastructure. For companies, transitioning to e-commerce requires the right timing. The use of this infrastructure solely for the purpose of reducing commercial costs can create a lower optimization hazard (Porter, 2002).

The effect of e-commerce on the competitiveness of companies is very robust leading to reduced costs, the elimination of barriers to access the market, ability of customers and producers to reach information easily, and more conscious consumers and changes in consumer habits causing competition to intensify (Phan, 2003). This situation forces companies to restructure and review market strategies. In addition, the fact that small, medium-sized, and large enterprises have equal conditions in terms of market entry conditions makes competition more ruthless. This point is already the most important feature that distinguishes the internet from other technological innovations. The adaptation of all economic actors to the transformation created by the internet and information technology, the development of new technologies, and the fact that everyone can reach these opportunities through less expensive technology increases everybody's chance to have a place in the global market (İşler, 2008).

The Driving Force And Scope Of E-Commerce Strategies

In previous studies, different perspectives of trade strategies have been shown. For example, many researchers have explored the ways in which the internet offers strategic opportunities as opposed to traditional trade (Levenburg, 2005; Pavitt, 1997). Another important research group examined the possible economic effects of trade on the internet and how internet-based e-commerce can affect pricing and competition (Wood et al., 2005). Furthermore, in terms of opportunities created by e-commerce, an important feature discovered was the power shift towards the consumer and the effect of changing power structures in the supply chain (Priluck, 2001). As the volume of shopping in the e-commerce environment grows, the internet has the potential to change physical retail transactions (Burt & Sparks, 2003).

The adoption of the internet among companies engaged in trade has so far varied. Although some companies are relatively aggressive, there are some aims to provide a wide range of product portfolios, to exist in the e-commerce environment, and to develop websites accordingly (Dholakia & Kshetri, 2004). Some small-scale companies that did not adopt the e-commerce environment preferred to continue their traditional trading practices and faced leaving the market. As a matter of fact, trading companies have seen the internet as a channel for reaching larger markets and have begun to invest continuously in their infrastructure on the Internet, which broadens and significantly affects trade volumes.

Success Of E-Commerce Strategies

The success of e-commerce strategies comes from the fact that it adopts a customer oriented method. In other words, the strategies identified in the e-commerce environment aim to measure the attitudes and reactions of the buyers and sellers and their strategic position in terms of various elements (Doherty, Ellis-Chadwick, & Hart, 2003). These attitudes and reactions may even cause changes in the design of web pages in the e-commerce environments of companies (Cliquet et al., 2007). The ease of use, quality of the web pages, the loyalty of the customers and their intention to continue shopping online, the perception of consumers, and the interaction and shopping pleasure are current strategic issues (Wolfinbarger & Gilly, 2003). In their study, Goode and Harris (2007) state that consumers place importance on the reputation, reliability, site design, and security provided by e-commerce companies. There are a reasonable number of studies about the success and failure of e-commerce initiatives (Lunce et al., 2006), with an important empirical study on the success of e-commerce companies having been conducted by Zhuang and Lederer (2003). However, this study only focused on the benefits of e-commerce and was not able to answer exactly what the cause of success was.

E-Commerce Strategies

The e-commerce strategy is the adoption of long-term activities in order to achieve a competitive advantage in a changing environment through the structuring of resources and skill of the organization to meet the expectations of stakeholders (Johnson, Scholes, & Whittington, 2008). The E-commerce strategy is vital for companies and provides a framework for operational planning, enhancing organizational efficiency, and clarifying the direction of organizational activities. In addition, e-commerce helps companies to achieve long-term benefits (Chang, Jackson, & Grover, 2003).

For e-commerce strategies, companies should consider their internal environment, including strategic investment logic and internal coordination capability (McAfee & Brynjolfsson, 2008). For the implementation of e-commerce strategies, the external environment should be taken into account, including market environment, market position of the organization in the value chain, and customer participation (El Sawy, Malhotra, Gosain, & Young, 1999; Urban, Sultan, & Qualls, 2000; Venkatesan & Kumar, 2004). The business transactions, application principles, and corresponding strategies can be developed considering the business environment and product characteristics for various e-commerce activities (Lee & Whang, 2001; Chatterjee, Grewal, & Sambamurthy, 2002). In addition, companies should develop approaches to evaluate the stages of e-commerce development and the implementation of e-commerce strategies (Barua, Konana, Whinston, & Yin, 2004; Hackbarth & Kettinger, 2004). The development of e-commerce strategies and the implementation of E-commerce provide frameworks for managing organizational changes in this process (Grandon & Pearson, 2004). For the successful implementation of e-commerce strategies, important factors are the use of technology and adaptive changes in business processes and in organizational structures (Benjamin & Levinson, 1993).

The lack of knowledge in the implementation of the e-commerce strategy will limit the skills of organizations in e-commerce initiatives because insufficient organizational skills block the organizational transformation processes (Gilbert, 2005). In particular, traditional companies that are not involved in e-commerce should understand the importance of acquiring information to overcome such obstacles. In order to overcome the difficulties arising from insufficient organizational skills, a successful e-commerce strategy should be implemented (Johnson, 1988).

The rapid change and development of technology and internet has also begun to change the consumer understanding of shopping. Thanks to smart phones and smart watches of the future, consumers will be able to take advantage of time saving advantages of online shopping (Levy & Weitz, 2004). Reasons for the activity of companies to participate in e-commerce field are multiple:

- A constantly expanding e-commerce market,
- Having a widespread consumer network in the field of e-commerce,
- Having ubiquitous access without any boundaries through internet technology
- Change of consumer habits due to the Internet and technology,
- Expectations of Companies to increase their revenues as a result of e-commerce activities where they can offer online purchases on their web pages.

Companies not only offer online shopping on their web pages in terms of selling products and/or services in the e-commerce environment, but also aim to provide satisfaction and loyalty for customers who buy from the company (Tek & Orel, 2008). Because, unlike traditional shopping methods, a variety of products and services can be provided without physical shelf limitation.

The power, scope, and interaction created by the Internet is considered to provide customers with a unique opportunity to experience shopping in the e-commerce environment (Doherty & Ellis-Chadwick, 2006). In particular, e-commerce provides an extremely rich and flexible new trade channel by providing information over the internet, making customer communication easier, enabling market research activities, allowing the collection of data over the internet for more swift strategic decisions, and introducing products and services through social networks (Basu & Muylle, 2003).

From a strategic point of view, the Internet offers these opportunities to companies:

- Expansion of target markets
- Improving communication with customers
- Ensuring product diversity
- Ensuring cost efficiency
- Development of customer relations
- Offering personalized offers (Srinivasan et al., 2002).

Indeed, with the rapid growth of internet usage, there has been an increase in the volume of online shopping (Forsythe & Shi, 2003). In spite of the apparent commercial potential of the internet, many of the companies that did not have a visionary perspective and could not see that the future was technology-focused went bankrupt when the '.com' exploded in 2001. Although e-commerce provides sustainable growth for companies, technology-oriented companies that develop technological infrastructure have become dominant in their sector (Min & Wolfinbarger, 2005; Evanschitzky et al., 2004).

SOLUTIONS AND RECOMMENDATIONS

There are still a number of issues that continue to be explored for companies that have operations in the field of e-commerce. Many factors such as management support, competitive pressures and technical infrastructure continue to be strategically examined. There is too much variation between studies and therefore further studies are needed in this area in terms of identifying and adopting new strategic approaches in e-commerce. Especially, it should not be forgotten that there are differences between Western culture and Eastern culture. Valid strategic management theories may cause the emergence of new theories due to cultural differences and Strategic approaches in the field of e-commerce should take cultural differences into consideration (Venkatesan & Kumar, 2004). For example, Japan might be a technology giant, but many Japanese people still use classic mobile phones which were used before smart phones. In this case, can companies that want to operate in the field of e-commerce and develop strategies offer online shopping through smart phones? Can they implement effective strategies that need to be realized through smart phones in this country? It is important to remember that this situation consists entirely of cultural differences. In the early days of the e-commerce market, many companies made a strategic mistake lagging behind the leading companies by not creating a web page on the Internet. However, companies should also offer good and secure web pages on the Internet because when consumers & customers find the web page very simple they may think the company is not reliable or secure (Rao & Frazer, 2006). At the same time, consumers see complaint portals as important reference points showing how reliable and high quality the work of e-commerce companies is.

Within this framework, there are important determinants to be considered in terms of the success of e-commerce strategies:

- Identify different factors in the e-commerce strategies that can be implemented against competitors for the success of the organisation.
- Analyze whether the identified factors are appropriate to the organizational structure of the firm
- Examine the composition of the strategic success arising from the identified factors

- Evaluate the relationship between the scope of e-commerce strategy and its perceived success.

Opinions will always be needed regarding how e-commerce companies should approach strategy development. It is possible that today's strategies may not be valid tomorrow. When we want to criticize theoreticians in the field of strategic management, they want us to provide evidence, but the real evidence is that they forget the theories were examined in which country, in which market conditions, in which companies, in which sector. The general acceptance of a theory is determined by the extent to which it can be proven to be appropriate for every company, every sector, and every culture.

FUTURE RESEARCH DIRECTIONS

Although it is accepted that the determinants of the success of e-commerce strategies are cost and marketing, it is also strongly associated with resources. If e-commerce companies want to be successful, they should be able to distribute resources and skills to several internet transactions at the same time, and they should manage an efficient budget because the concerns over cost can have a negative impact on success. The underlying factor behind the success of e-commerce companies is the powerful management support and strategic adaptation to the e-commerce field. It is important to remember that there is a very strong and positive relationship between a visionary strategic perspective and e-commerce success. In e-commerce companies, managers must be aware of the slight differences between the determinants of success and the factors that influence the scope of a strategy. And, the management team must initiate strategic moves when they receive full organizational support in order to be successful in e-commerce. The scope and the success of e-commerce is related to a company's internet-oriented thinking, ability to carry out research activities for future use, and the steps to expand the number of users and carry out original activities.

Companies wishing to operate in the field of e-commerce should aim to benefit from sales but be cautious and adopt e-commerce models that actively involve the Web (internet) (Trice 2001). Furthermore, companies need to invest in the design, implementation, and advertising of a web site. This investment will vary according to the target audience and the organisation objectives. However, it is very important to provide a web site which generates the perception of a safe, quality, virtual environment. Investment in new technologies in the field of e-commerce will mean that the company can have more flexibility and better capacity against its competitors. The advantage of a web site is that it allows the realization of new developments and changes ahead of competitors, also forcing the organisation to rethink their business methods and processes. The most important benefit of e-commerce strategy is bringing a company ahead of competition and creating a positive impact on a firm's growth potential. Furthermore, the creation of a functional and useful web page is very important in the implementation phase. The length of time spent by consumers on the website is related to the user-friendliness and the product diversity of the web page.

CONCLUSION

From a strategic point of view, the key factors for success are the decisive steps of senior management (however, these decisive steps must definitely be future-oriented, and the data must be very well analyzed), the realization of strategic cohesion, and the distribution of company resources and capabilities. The internet is an important, highly dynamic and global phenomenon, therefore it is important for the companies to follow their competitors, identify their weaknesses and plan counter strategic steps. In order to determine the mutual and different driving forces of e-commerce companies, it is important to analyze many factors. For example, as mentioned before, to perform similar studies in various sectors and in various countries. It is not acceptable to put forward acceptable theory from a study conducted in only one country since the theory has meaning when it is accepted by everyone. Also, the determinants of an e-commerce strategy may be related to the direction of managerial orientation or the intensity of competition. For example, companies in weak competitive markets may need greater incentives and encouragement to invest in an e-commerce strategy when the return on investment is uncertain. E-commerce companies should strategically measure the intensity of competition accurately or take into account the adoption of a specific e-commerce strategy. Therefore, in e-commerce strategy, it is useful to collect additional data about cost and performance, as well as about other multi-channel strategies (e.g. mobile commerce, social use) (Ayanso & Yoogalingam, 2009).

E-commerce companies start their activities by establishing their own websites for both communication and sales purposes. Before starting this activity, however, they should consider the multivariate concepts, such as brand value, brand image, reputation, customer satisfaction, accessibility, quality, performance, etc., which are good indicators of whether a company will stay in the market. The purpose of communication is to reach the widest audience possible and provide information about products and services. When the success of communication reflects on sales, a company starts to actively compete and take a share in the market. Finally, the companies with strong customer service may have to adopt special e-commerce strategies. Companies will have an opportunity to make comparisons between customer behaviour on the company's web site and in the store. This comparison can be related to product perceptions, shopping experiences and customer service (Jarvenpaa & Todd, 1996), customer satisfaction (Cao, Gruca, & Klemz, 2003), and behavioural loyalty (Huang, 2011). This information makes it possible to develop strategies in the e-commerce field by analyzing the reasons for different customer behaviours.

REFERENCES

Ada, E., Ventura, K., Aracioglu, B., Savasci, I., & Kazancoglu, Y. (2008). KOBI'lerin Rekabet Gucu ve E-Ticarete Gecis Sureci: Bir Model Onerisi. *Ege Academic Review*, *8*(1), 53–68.

Afra, S. (2014). *Dijital Pazarın Odak Noktası eTicaret: Dünya'da Türkiye'nin Yeri, Mevcut Durum ve Geleceğe Yönelik Adımlar*. İstanbul, Turkey: TÜSİAD.

Arıkan, A. S. (1999). *Dünyada ve Türkiye'de Elektronik Ticaret Çalışmalarına Hukuki Bir Yaklaşım*. Ankara, Turkey: Yetkin Yayınları.

Arpacı, T., & Uluçay, U. (2012). Dünyada ve Türkiye'de E-Ticaret: Tüketicilerin İnternet Üzerinden Alışveriş Alışkanlıkları Üzerine Bir Uygulama.

Ayanso, A., & Yoogalingam, R. (2009). Profiling retail web site functionalities and conversion rates: A cluster analysis. *International Journal of Electronic Commerce*, *14*(1), 79–114. doi:10.2753/JEC1086-4415140103

Barua, A., Konana, P., Whinston, A. B., & Yin, F. (2004). An empirical investigation of net-enabled business value. *Management Information Systems Quarterly*, *28*(4), 585–620. doi:10.2307/25148656

Basu, A., & Muylle, S. (2003). Online support for commerce processes by web retailers. *Decision Support Systems*, *34*(4), 379–395. doi:10.1016/S0167-9236(02)00065-9

Becker, A. (Ed.). (2007). Electronic Commerce: Concepts, Methodologies, Tools, and Applications: Concepts, Methodologies, Tools, and Applications. Hershey, PA: IGI Global.

Benjamin, R. I., & Levinson, E. (1993). A framework for managing IT-enabled change. *Sloan Management Review*, *34*(4), 23–33.

Bozkurt, V. (2000). Elektronik Ticaret, stanbul: Alfa Basım Yayım Dağıtım Ltd.

Burt, S., & Sparks, L. (2003). E-commerce and the retail process: A review. *Journal of Retailing and Consumer Services*, *10*(5), 275–286. doi:10.1016/S0969-6989(02)00062-0

Çakırer, M. A. (2013). *Elektronik ticaret*. Ekin Basım Yayın Dağıtım.

Canpolat, Ö. (2001). *E-ticaret ve Türkiye'deki gelişmeler*. Sanayi ve Ticaret Bakanlığı.

Cao, Y., Gruca, T. S., & Klemz, B. R. (2003). Internet pricing, price satisfaction, and customer satisfaction. *International Journal of Electronic Commerce*, *8*(2), 31–50. doi:10.1080/10864415.2003.11044291

Card, J. A., Chen, C. Y., & Cole, S. T. (2003). Online travel products shopping: Differences between shoppers and nonshoppers. *Journal of Travel Research*, *42*(2), 133–139. doi:10.1177/0047287503257490

Chang, K. C., Jackson, J., & Grover, V. (2003). E-commerce and corporate strategy: An executive perspective. *Information & Management*, *40*(7), 663–675. doi:10.1016/S0378-7206(02)00095-2

Chatterjee, D., Grewal, R., & Sambamurthy, V. (2002). Shaping up for e-commerce: Institutional enablers of the organizational assimilation of web technologies. *Management Information Systems Quarterly*, *26*(2), 65–89. doi:10.2307/4132321

Chung, T., & Law, R. (2003). Developing a performance indicator of hotel websites. *International Journal of Hospitality Management*, *22*(1), 119–125. doi:10.1016/S0278-4319(02)00076-2

Cliquet, G., Hendrikse, G., Tuunanen, M., & Windsperger, J. (Eds.). (2007). Economics and management of networks: Franchising, strategic alliances, and cooperatives. Berlin, Germany: Springer Science & Business Media. doi:10.1007/978-3-7908-1758-4

Coşkun, A. G. D. N. (2004). Elektronik ticaretin gelişiminde temel dinamikler ve gelişimi önündeki engeller. Çukurova Üniversitesi Sosyal Bilimler Enstitüsü Dergisi, 13(2).

Çubukcu, A., & Bayzan, Ş. (2013). Türkiye'de dijital vatandaşlık algısı ve bu algıyı internetin bilinçli, güvenli ve etkin kullanımı ile artırma yöntemleri. *Middle Eastern & African Journal of Educational Research*, *5*, 148–174.

Delone, W. H., & Mclean, E. R. (2004). Measuring e-commerce success: Applying the DeLone & McLean information systems success model. *International Journal of Electronic Commerce*, *9*(1), 31–47. doi:10.1080/10864415.2004.11044317

Dholakia, R. R., & Kshetri, N. (2004). Factors impacting the adoption of the Internet among SMEs. *Small Business Economics*, *23*(4), 311–322. doi:10.1023/B:SBEJ.0000032036.90353.1f

Dinçer, Ö. (2007). *Stratejik Yönetim ve İşletme Politikası*. İstanbul, Turkey: Alfa Yayınları.

Dixon, H., & Quinn, B. (2004). Franchising and the Internet: An exploratory study of franchisor Web sites. *Internet Research*, *14*(4), 311–322. doi:10.1108/10662240410555324

Doherty, N., Ellis-Chadwick, F., & Hart, C. (2003). An analysis of the factors affecting the adoption of the Internet in the UK retail sector. *Journal of Business Research*, *56*(11), 887–897. doi:10.1016/S0148-2963(01)00275-2

Doherty, N. F., & Ellis-Chadwick, F. E. (2006). New perspectives in internet retailing: A review and strategic critique of the field. *International Journal of Retail & Distribution Management*, *34*(4/5), 411–428. doi:10.1108/09590550610660305

Dolanbay, C. (2000). E-Ticaret: Strateji ve Yöntemler. Meteksan Sistem Yayınları, 229-230.

Eimer, M. (2000). B&B internet marketing: The inside story. *Library Journal*, *125*(18), 150.

El Sawy, O. A., Malhotra, A., Gosain, S., & Young, K. M. (1999). IT-intensive value innovation in the electronic economy: Insights from Marshall Industries. *Management Information Systems Quarterly*, *23*(3), 305–335. doi:10.2307/249466

Ene, S. (2002). *Elektronik ticarette tüketicinin korunması ve bir uygulama*. Pusula Yayıncılık ve İletişim.

Eren, E. (2010). *Staretjik Yönetim ve İşletme Politikası*. İstanbul, Turkey: Beta Yayınevi.

Erkan, M. (2012). *E-ticaret çağı: profesyoneller için Türkiye'de ve dünyada e-ticaret*. Optimist Yayın Dağıtım.

Evanschitzky, H., Gopalkrishnan, R., Hesse, J., & Dieter, A. (2004). E-satisfaction: A re-examination. *Journal of Retailing*, *80*(3), 239–247. doi:10.1016/j.jretai.2004.08.002

Forman, C. (2005). The corporate digital divide: Determinants of Internet adoption. *Management Science*, *51*(4), 641–654. doi:10.1287/mnsc.1040.0343

Forman, C., Goldfarb, A., & Greenstein, S. (2005). How did location affect adoption of the commercial Internet? Global village vs. urban leadership. *Journal of Urban Economics*, *58*(3), 389–420. doi:10.1016/j.jue.2005.05.004

Forsythe, S. M., & Shi, B. (2003). Consumer patronage and risk perceptions in Internet shopping. *Journal of Business Research*, *56*(11), 867–875. doi:10.1016/S0148-2963(01)00273-9

Gibbs, J. L., & Kraemer, K. L. (2004). A cross-country investigation of the determinants of scope of e-commerce use: An institutional approach. *Electronic Markets*, *14*(2), 124–137. doi:10.1080/10196780410001675077

Gilbert, C. G. (2005). Unbundling the structure of inertia: Resource versus routine rigidity. *Academy of Management Journal*, *48*(5), 741–763. doi:10.5465/amj.2005.18803920

Goode, M. M., & Harris, L. C. (2007). Online behavioural intentions: An empirical investigation of antecedents and moderators. *European Journal of Marketing*, *41*(5/6), 512–536. doi:10.1108/03090560710737589

Grandon, E. E., & Pearson, J. M. (2004). Electronic commerce adoption: An empirical study of small and medium US businesses. *Information & Management*, *42*(1), 197–216. doi:10.1016/j.im.2003.12.010

Güçlü, N. (2003). Stratejik yönetim. Gazi Üniversitesi Gazi Eğitim Fakültesi Dergisi, 23(2).

Hackbarth, G., & Kettinger, W. J. (2004). Strategic aspirations for net-enabled business. *European Journal of Information Systems*, *13*(4), 273–285. doi:10.1057/palgrave.ejis.3000511

Hart, C., Doherty, N., & Ellis-Chadwick, F. (2000). Retailer adoption of the Internet–Implications for retail marketing. *European Journal of Marketing*, *34*(8), 954–974. doi:10.1108/03090560010331441

Heung, V. C. (2003). Barriers to implementing E-commerce in the travel industry: A practical perspective. *International Journal of Hospitality Management*, *22*(1), 111–118. doi:10.1016/S0278-4319(02)00075-0

Hitt, M. A., Ireland, R. D., & Hoskisson, R. E. (2012). Strategic management cases: competitiveness and globalization. Boston, MA: Cengage Learning.

Hoffman, D. L., & Novak, T. P. (2000). How to acquire customers on the web. *Harvard Business Review*, *78*(3), 179–188. PMID:11183979

Huang, C. Y. (2011). Excess loyalty in online retailing. *International Journal of Electronic Commerce*, *16*(2), 115–134. doi:10.2753/JEC1086-4415160206

İşler, D. B. (2008). Rekabetçi Avantaj Yaratma Çerçevesinde Kobi'lerde E-Ticaret ve E-Ticaretin Stratejik Kullanımı. Süleyman Demirel Üniversitesi İktisadi ve İdari Bilimler Fakültesi Dergisi, 13(3).

Jarvenpaa, S. L., & Todd, P. A. (1996). Consumer reactions to electronic shopping on the World Wide Web. *International Journal of Electronic Commerce*, *1*(2), 59–88. doi:10.1080/10864415.1996.11518283

Johnson, G. (1988). Rethinking incrementalism. *Strategic Management Journal*, *9*(1), 75–91. doi:10.1002mj.4250090107

Johnson, G., Scholes, K., & Whittington, R. (2008). Exploring corporate strategy: text & cases. London, UK: Pearson Education.

Kantarcı, Ö., Özalp, M., Sezginsoy, C., Özaşkınlı, O., & Cavlak, C. (2017). *Dijitalleşen dünyada ekonominin itici gücü: E-ticaret*. İstanbul, Turkey: TUSIAD Yayınları.

Kaufmann, P. J., Cliquet, G., & Achabal, D. D. (2010). Implementing multi-channel strategies: Issues and opportunities for franchise system websites. In *Proceedings of the 24th ISoF Conference*, Sydney, Australia.

Kepenek, Y. (1999). *Ekonomik Yönleriyle Elektronik Ticaret*. Ankara, Turkey: ODTÜ İktisat Bölümü ve Tekpol.

King, R. C., Sen, R., & Xia, M. (2004). Impact of web-based e-commerce on channel strategy in retailing. *International Journal of Electronic Commerce*, *8*(3), 103–130. doi:10.1080/10864415.2004.11044297

Korkmaz, N. (2002). *Sorularla internet ve e-ticaret rehberi*. İTO.

Law, R. (2000). Internet and travel and tourism marketing part I. *Journal of Travel & Tourism Marketing*, *9*(3), 65–71. doi:10.1300/J073v09n03_05

Lee, H. L., & Whang, S. (2001). Winning the last mile of e-commerce. *MIT Sloan Management Review*, *42*(4), 54–62.

Levenburg, N. M. (2005). Delivering customer value online: An analysis of practices, applications, and performance. *Journal of Retailing and Consumer Services*, *12*(5), 319–331. doi:10.1016/j.jretconser.2004.11.001

Levy, M., & Weitz, B. A. (2004). *Retailing Management*. New York, NY: McGraw Hill Irwin.

Lituchy, T. R., & Rail, A. (2000). Bed and breakfast, small inns, and the internet: The impact of technology on the globalization of small businesses. *Journal of International Marketing*, *8*(2), 77–86. doi:10.1509/jimk.8.2.86.19625

Lunce, S. E., Lunce, L. M., Kawai, Y., & Maniam, B. (2006). Success and failure of pure-play organizations: Webvan versus Peapod, a comparative analysis. *Industrial Management & Data Systems*, *106*(9), 1344–1358. doi:10.1108/02635570610712618

Luo, Y., Hongxin Zhao, J., & Du, J. (2005). The internationalization speed of e-commerce companies: An empirical analysis. *International Marketing Review*, *22*(6), 693–709. doi:10.1108/02651330510630294

Marangoz, M. (2014). İnternette Pazarlama, Beta yayınları.

Mariz-Pérez, R., & García-Álvarez, T. (2009). The Internationalization strategy of Spanish indigenous franchised chains: A resource-based view. *Journal of Small Business Management*, *47*(4), 514–530. doi:10.1111/j.1540-627X.2009.00281.x

Martin, L., & Pénard, T. (2005). Investing in a website: a top dog or a resource-based strategy for firms?.

McAfee, A., & Brynjolfsson, E. (2008). Investing in the IT that makes a competitive difference. *Harvard Business Review*, *86*(7/8), 98. PMID:18271321

Min, S., & Wolfinbarger, M. (2005). Market share, profit margin, and marketing efficiency of early movers, bricks and clicks, and specialists in e-commerce. *Journal of Business Research*, *58*(8), 1030–1039. doi:10.1016/j.jbusres.2004.02.005

Mintzberg, H., Ghoshal, S., Lampel, J., & Quinn, J. B. (2003). The strategy process: concepts, contexts, cases. London, UK: Pearson Education.

Molla, A., & Licker, P. S. (2005). Perceived e-readiness factors in e-commerce adoption: An empirical investigation in a developing country. *International Journal of Electronic Commerce*, *10*(1), 83–110. doi:10.1080/10864415.2005.11043963

Ngai, E. W., & Wat, F. K. T. (2002). A literature review and classification of electronic commerce research. *Information & Management*, *39*(5), 415–429. doi:10.1016/S0378-7206(01)00107-0

O'Connor, P. (1999). *Electronics information distribution in tourism and hospitality*. Oxford, UK: CAB International.

Özbay, S., & Akyazı, S. (2004). Elektronik ticaret: e-ticaret.

Pavitt, D. (1997). Retailing and the super high street: The future of the electronic home shopping industry. *International Journal of Retail & Distribution Management*, *25*(1), 38–43. doi:10.1108/09590559710156099

Phan, D. D. (2003). E-business development for competitive advantages: A case study. *Information & Management*, *40*(6), 581–590. doi:10.1016/S0378-7206(02)00089-7

Porter, M. E. (2001). *Michael; ilustraciones Gibbs*. Strategy and the Internet.

Porter, M. E. (2002). Strateji ve İnternet. Stratejide İlerlemeler (11-59). İstanbul, Turkey: MESS Yayınları.

Porter, M. E. (2008). *Competative Strategy. Çev. Gülen Ulubilgen*. İstanbul, Turkey: Sistem Yayıncılık.

Priluck, R. (2001). The impact of Priceline. com on the grocery industry. *International Journal of Retail & Distribution Management*, *29*(3), 127–134. doi:10.1108/09590550110385883

Rao, S., & Frazer, L. (2006). Australian franchisor websites: Moving towards network behaviour. *Journal of Theoretical and Applied Electronic Commerce Research*, *1*(1).

Rogers, J., Bennett, C., & Grewal, S. (2007). E-commerce for successful franchisors. *Franchising World*, *39*(8), 23.

Sadowski, B. M., Maitland, C., & van Dongen, J. (2002). Strategic use of the Internet by small-and medium-sized companies: An exploratory study. *Information Economics and Policy*, *14*(1), 75–93. doi:10.1016/S0167-6245(01)00054-3

Schibrowsky, J. A., Peltier, J. W., & Nill, A. (2007). The state of internet marketing research: A review of the literature and future research directions. *European Journal of Marketing*, *41*(7/8), 722–733. doi:10.1108/03090560710752366

Sezgin, A. G. (2013). Dünyada ve Türkiye de E-ticaret Sektörü. Türkiye İş bankası İktisadi Araştırmalar Bölümü.

Srinivasan, S. S., Anderson, R., & Ponnavolu, K. (2002). Customer loyalty in e-commerce: An exploration of its antecedents and consequences. *Journal of Retailing*, *78*(1), 41–50. doi:10.1016/S0022-4359(01)00065-3

Tek, O. B., & Orel, F. D. (2008). *Perakende Pazarlama Yönetimi*. İzmir, Turkey: Birleşik Matbaacılık.

Trice, M. B. (2001). Managing Internet Issues Within the Franchise System: A Legal Perspective. *Franchising World*, *33*(5), 37–38.

Ülgen, H., & Mirze, S. K. (2010). *İşletmelerde Stratejik Yönetim (5. Baskı)*. İstanbul, Turkey: Beta Basım Yayım Dağıtım.

Urban, G. L., Sultan, F., & Qualls, W. J. (2000). Placing trust at the center of your Internet strategy. *Sloan Management Review*, *42*(1), 39–48.

Üzün, C. (2000). *Stratejik Yönetim ve Halkla İlişkiler*. İzmir, Turkey: Eylül Yayınları.

Venkatesan, R., & Kumar, V. (2004). A customer lifetime value framework for customer selection and resource allocation strategy. *Journal of Marketing*, *68*(4), 106–125. doi:10.1509/jmkg.68.4.106.42728

Wade, M. R., & Nevo, S. (2005). Development and validation of a perceptual instrument to measure e-commerce performance. *International Journal of Electronic Commerce*, *10*(2), 123–146. doi:10.2753/JEC1086-4415100205

Williams, A. P., & Palmer, A. J. (1999). Tourism destination brands and electronic commerce: Towards synergy. *Journal of Vacation Marketing*, *5*(3), 263–275. doi:10.1177/135676679900500306

Wolfinbarger, M., & Gilly, M. C. (2003). eTailQ: Dimensionalizing, measuring and predicting etail quality. *Journal of Retailing*, *79*(3), 183–198. doi:10.1016/S0022-4359(03)00034-4

Wood, C. M., Alford, B. L., Jackson, R. W., & Gilley, O. W. (2005). Can retailers get higher prices for "end-of-life" inventory through online auctions? *Journal of Retailing*, *81*(3), 181–190. doi:10.1016/j.jretai.2005.07.001

Worzala, E. M., McCarthy, A. M., Dixon, T., & Marston, A. (2002). E-commerce and retail property in the UK and USA. *Journal of Property Investment & Finance*, *20*(2), 142–158. doi:10.1108/14635780210420034

Wymer, S. A., & Regan, E. A. (2005). Factors influencing e-commerce adoption and use by small and medium businesses. *Electronic Markets*, *15*(4), 438–453. doi:10.1080/10196780500303151

Yeşil, A. (2008). *E-ticaret-internet ortamında ticaret*. İstanbul, Turkey: Kum Saati Yayınları.

Young, J. A., Clark, P. W., & McIntyre, F. S. (2006). The web as an e-commerce medium: An exploratory study of consumer perceptions in a restaurant setting. *Journal of Marketing Channels*, *14*(1-2), 5–22. doi:10.1300/J049v14n01_02

Zhu, K., & Kraemer, K. L. (2002). E-commerce metrics for net-enhanced organizations: Assessing the value of e-commerce to firm performance in the manufacturing sector. *Information Systems Research*, *13*(3), 275–295. doi:10.1287/isre.13.3.275.82

Zhuang, Y., & Lederer, A. L. (2003). An instrument for measuring the business benefits of e-commerce retailing. *International Journal of Electronic Commerce*, *7*(3), 65–99. doi:10.1080/10864415.2003.11044274

Zwass, V. (2003). Electronic commerce and organizational innovation: Aspects and opportunities. *International Journal of Electronic Commerce*, *7*(3), 7–37. doi:10.1080/10864415.2003.11044273

Chapter 6
Electronic Payment Systems in Electronic Commerce

Rana Atabay Kuscu
https://orcid.org/0000-0001-9968-5983
Istanbul Medipol University, Turkey

Yasemin Cicekcisoy
Istanbul Halic University, Turkey

Umit Bozoklu
Istanbul Gedik University, Turkey

ABSTRACT

Technological advances and correspondingly the spreading usage of the Internet have significantly changed commerce, and also the concept of money has become more abstract. Customers with the help of the technological advances don't have the necessity of cash money, and consumers/firms tend towards alternative payment methods. At this point, electronic commerce (e-commerce) web sites have started to use block chaining payment methods. In this digital world, new payment technologies have started to spread far and wide thanks to fast improvements in payment technologies, and they offer different options in payment methods. Each electronic payment (e-payment) system has some advantages; however, each of them has some disadvantages as well. The aim of this study is to investigate the e-payment systems which are different from traditional payment methods.

INTRODUCTION

Almost 40 years ago, e-commerce started to come into our lives. As Miva (2011) suggests, e-commerce has allowed many new businesses to enter the online sector and it has still been growing with the advancements in science, new technologies and innovations. There are apparently two time periods for this sector: the first period from the 1960s to 1990s was based on Electronic Data Interchange (EDI)

DOI: 10.4018/978-1-7998-0035-4.ch006

and the second the period was after 1990s when e-commerce was fostered by the emergence of World-Wide-Web (Yang, 2017).

E-commerce is sure to be one of the most leading services which showed up as a result of the spread of the common Internet users all across the world. With the advancements in technology, the attempts to design mobile devices with a high internet speed as well as mobile technology have made it possible for users to utilize those devices and services like reading e-mails and Web browsing wherever they are and whenever they wish for performing e-commerce transactions.

Throughout centuries, payment systems have undergone a change in a radical way, which include coins, papers and data. The reason why payment systems have continually evolved is that the new technologies included in these systems provide convenience and efficiency at a high speed. The advancements in global electronic payments have changed the humans' point of view. In today's world, many different e-payment systems are being used internationally in a common way and provide security and economic transparency as well as easiness for processes. The users throughout the world provide great benefits vie this payment network. Payments are the basic factors of the economies. With the common adoption of e-payment systems, sale of goods and services has continually been increasing. E-payment has also ruled out the obstacles of immediate liquidity and credit. Today, there are many different e-payment opportunities provided by financial institutions for the customers. As an example, ATM machines, credit cards, debit cards, online banking and mobile banking are among these e-payment systems. E-payment systems are relatively cost-saving over traditional paper-based payments.

In addition to those (Read, 1989) arguing that the use of cash will be removed in the near future, and a non-cash economy is not very far away, there are also approaches suggesting the exact opposite of this argument (Harrop, 1989). Furthermore, many studies in the relevant literature reach a consensus that as economies grow and globalize, physical money will be replaced in shopping by e-payment methods in various forms due to the developments experienced on the internet and e-commerce and the importance of physical money will decline. Accordingly, the more common use of e-payment methods instead of physical money in today's and future's commercial forms is inevitable.

Today, more companies have started performing their company operations through e-commerce. In this way, the purchase of the goods and services produced in any part of the world by consumers depends on the healthy and secure functioning of millions of e-payment processes performed on the internet every day. In this context, the subject of e-payment and e-payment systems, which are among the basic elements of uninterrupted and healthy functioning of the process in the e-commerce-related process, is an area of research coming into the forefront recently with its various aspects.

Each electronic e-payment system has some advantages; however, each of them has some disadvantages as well. The aim of this study is to investigate the e-payment systems which are different from traditional payment methods. In this sense, this paper presents a comprehensive explanation that aims to provide raising awareness regarding the development of e-payment systems. For this purpose, firstly, the concept of e-commerce and secondly, e-payment methods will be addressed. Lastly, the facts regarding e-payments in e-commerce practices will be explained.

E-Commerce in the World

E-commerce has reached to significant levels in all countries, particularly in developed countries. Dues to the increase in internet use and thus, e-commerce, changes that could only be imagined in the past have become a part of daily lives and e-commerce has become a new competition space for businesses.

The main difference between e-commerce and other commercial activities is that customers have increased their purchasing power regardless of their location. E-commerce eliminates limitations for businesses and customers who need to wander markets and make purchases with certain limitations on locations. With online stores operating in the field of e-commerce, customers around the world can do shopping from their homes or businesses, compare prices of products or services they need, and access sellers' information without any limitations on location or time (Ersoy, 2002).

These characteristics made it inevitable for e-commerce to spread around the world. Additionally, commerce, production, marketing and advertisement applications reached a new dimension with e-commerce that makes collaborations and partnerships between businesses operating in different parts of the world easier. It is possible to suggest that there is a correlation between the increase in device penetration due to tablets and smartphones and the increase in the volume of e-commerce. Moreover, through mobile applications such as user interface designs that include current payment systems of e-commerce businesses, there is an increase on mobile device sales. With the increase on mobile penetration, it is expected that a certain population who has not participated in the process yet to be in the digital purchase process. This forces marketing plans to include all customer masses. These marketing plans should target accessing and influencing all users of devices that are connected to the Internet (Criteo, 2015).

According to data on e-commerce in the world from Turkish Industry and Business Association (TÜSİAD, 2017), it is seen that retail e-commerce has reached a trading volume of 1.6 trillion dollars in 2016 and that it is expected this growth rate will continue. Developing countries constituted 38% of e-commerce in 2012 while it's predicted as 63% for 2018. In 2020, it is expected that 64% of the total volume will consist of developing countries. Goldman Sachs, an investment bank, predicts a global trading volume of around 3 trillion dollars in 2020. Figure 1 present's data on e-commerce trading volumes around the world between 2012 and 2020. According to Figure 1, the volume of e-commerce in the world is 632 billion dollars in 2012 while the growth continued and reached 1.6 trillion dollars in 2016. While developing countries constitute 38% in 2012, this ratio increased to 59% and surpassed developed countries.

Figure 1. E-Commerce Volume in The World (Billions Dollars)
Source. TÜSİAD (2017). F:Forecasting

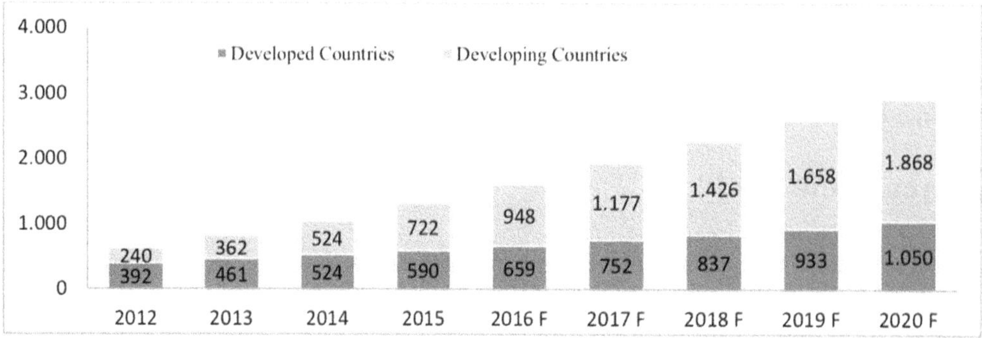

E-Commerce in Turkey

The concept of online shopping emerged in the early 1990s with the opening of e-commerce businesses. As a result of this process, the trading volume of purchases through e-commerce reached 1 trillion dollars and the interest in the new shopping sector increased. E-commerce has been growing in Turkey as well. However, this growth has not positioned Turkey as a competitor in the international arena. The reason for not being able to reach the e-commerce potential is prejudice by customers due to lack of knowledge on e-commerce and lack of technological, regulational and financial infrastructure required for e-commerce (TÜSİAD, 2014, 58). Additionally, it is observed that all indicators of e-commerce's growth potential such as number of internet users, penetration, smartphone usage, young population, etc. are at competitive level (TÜSİAD, 2017, 41).

Financial sector was the pioneer of e-commerce in Turkey. With a broader scope, the first application of internet marketing understanding was performed by Turkish Republic Central Bank (TCMB) in 1992 with electronic fund transfer between banks. Access to the Internet by large masses such as commercial organizations and households occurred in 1996. In parallel to the developments in the world since 1997, the concept of internet and commerce became popular in Turkey.

BCG has conducted a study to analyze countries' internet densities in three dimensions – providing opportunities (infrastructure development), - expenses (consumers' expenditure on e-commerce and digital advertisement), and participation (frequency of internet use by businesses, government, and consumers). According to this e-density report published in 2016, Turkey is listed after developed countries in the index order but shows a similar performance with developing countries. In the e-density index, it is seen that Turkey has an important potential with its performance in developing countries (TÜSİAD, 2017, 41).

The internet penetration which was 45% in 2012 has grown rapidly and by 2016 it reached to 58% internet penetration with 46.2 million users in Turkey. The estimation for 2020 in Turkey is 62 million internet users with a 76% Internet penetrations. As a result of an increase in internet use, Turkey is the 17th country that has the most internet users in the world with its population of 80 million and 46.2 million internet users and 58% internet penetration. Although when the ratios of Turkey are compared to the 90% penetration rate in developed countries are low, it is similar to developing countries. While the smartphone penetration of 6% in 2010 was below the world average of 9.6%, it reached 65% penetration with the increase in smart phones in the past six years and went above the world average by five points.

Smartphone penetration and the use of mobile internet have become one of the important channels to accelerate e-commerce. As of 2016 in Turkey, about 19% of e-commerce operations have been carried out by smartphones and tablets while it is estimated to reach 49% by 2021. Given the present level of 44% in the world, Turkey is likely to quickly take the lead in mobile commerce with the effect of its young population and higher smartphone penetration.

Results of a study conducted by Deloitte (2017) show that Turkey's position in e-commerce can be determined by comparing to developed and developing countries in order to evaluate the current situation more accurately. Figure 2 represents a comparison of Turkey's e-commerce structure with the e-commerce structure of developed and developing countries. According to Figure 2, the size of market share in retail is obtained by dividing total retail size by online retail size which gave a result of 4.1%. This ratio is 9.8% in developed countries and 4.8% in developing countries. When the ratios of purchases in the last month are evaluated, Turkey has the least purchase ratio in developed and developing countries listed in Table 1.

Table 1. E-Commerce 2017 Market Size

Country	Online Retail/ Total Retail (%)	Internet Penetration (%)	Mobile Broadband Penetration (%)	Online Shoppers (%)	Mobile Shoppers (%)	Per Capita Income PPP (S)	Population (Million)
UK	15,7	38,6	89,0	78	40	44,1K	66,0
USA	11,8	33,6	128,6	67	36	59,5	325,7
Germany	9,1	39,4	78,6	74	23	50,4	82,9
France	8,3	42,0	81,2	61	17	43,8	64,6

Source. Deloitte, etid, TÜBİSAD (2017).

When purchases made through mobile devices are examined, it is seen that Turkey has a higher ratio compared to countries such as France, Germany, Poland, Russia, and Brazil. Considering all the data, the fact that market share has not developed yet can be considered as a positive element towards ventures directed at e-commerce. Additionally, the level of purchases made through mobile devices being at the same level as developed countries is important in terms of ventures' e-commerce activities. However, fixed broadband and mobile broadband penetration which reflects Turkey's informatics infrastructure is below the ratios of developed and developing countries. This creates a disadvantage in e-commerce in terms of ventures.

Today, e-commerce activities are mostly done as B2C sales in Turkey. Practices around the world show that sales from business to business constitute a significant portion of e-commerce volume. In Turkey, it is seen that many organizations including big corporates moved transactions between their suppliers and distributors to the internet environment. An increase in the speed is expected over time. Due to e-commerce activities and the increase in gained income, many organizations own their own websites to not lose their customers and to access more customers. Many established brands opened their online stores and internet service providers rent online stores in virtual shopping platforms they created. These developments will result in an increase in the number of companies providing consultant services on e-commerce. Retail portion of the market has grown with an average of 33% annually since 2013 and increased from 7.3 billion TL to 22.9 billion TL in 2017. Only online retail commerce was 14.7 billion TL (Figure 2).

Although there has been a significant growth lately in Turkey, this growth was not sufficient to increase the retail share. In terms of infrastructural processes, Turkey is not different from other developing countries, and it precedes countries such as South Africa, India and China in terms of smartphone use and internet penetration. However, its total share in e-commerce retail is relatively smaller. In the retail e-commerce sector in which China reached the level of 17.1%, England 14.9% and USA 10.5%, Turkey has still room for improvement (Figure 3).

Figure 2. E-Commerce Volume in Turkey (Billions Dollars)
Source. TÜBİSAD (2017)

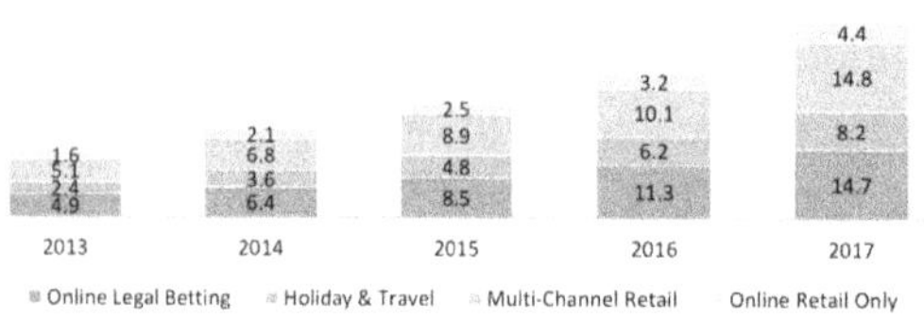

Figure 3. The Share of EC in Total Trade (2012-2016,%)
Source. TÜSİAD (2017)

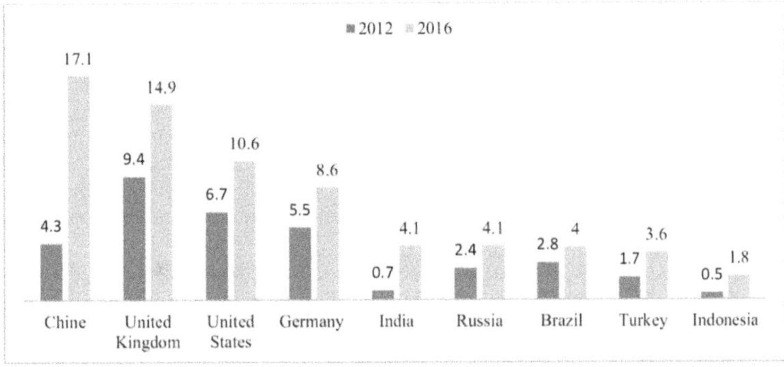

As in ''the E-Commerce in Turkey'' prepared by Twentify (2018), Turkey's expectation for five years between 2018 and 2022 is that this figure will be more than 9.6%, which is the estimated global growth. The expectation for Turkey's growth rate is 12%, which is more than the global growth rate. According to the survey in question, India is at the top of the list with 19.9% growth expectation.

Although Turkey is not different from other developing countries in terms of infrastructure, and that it precedes countries such as China, India, and South Africa in internet penetration and smartphone use, its share from total retail in e-commerce is relatively low. The share of 1.7% in e-commerce total retail in 2012 increased to 3.5% in 2016. As seen in Figure 3, in the retail e-commerce sector in which China has 17.1%, England 14.9% and USA 10.5%, Turkey has still room for improvement.

Despite its higher growth rate when compared to most of the other countries, it appears that Turkey's e-commerce total retail and total share of trade volume remain low, which is based on the past and the future expectations for e-commerce in Turkey. The other important issue is that Turkey is a country which aims at the exportation of 500 billion dollars. If this target is achieved by 2023, it means that Turkey's share of the world exports will be doubled and it will be one of the top 20 exporting countries. However, the current realizations indicate that it will be difficult to achieve this target. But, with the help of the opportunities that e-commerce presents, Turkey can increase its exportation more than before. Reducing the disadvantages caused by distance and even in some cases doing away with them are important advantages of e-commerce (TEPAV, 2014).[1]

The studies indicate that trade carried out with traditional means between two countries has a negative impact on their trade as the distance between the two countries increases. When the export made by e-commerce is taken into consideration, it is stated that the negative effect of distance on trade volume decreases. For example, the negative effect of the distance on the trade with e-buy is 65% lower than that of traditional exports (Figure 4).

E-Payment Systems

In modern societies, economic activities are only possible via payments and settlements. Therefore, payment systems could be stated as one of the most crucial and important factors of e-payments (Premchand & Choudhry, 2015). The developments of payment systems and technologies directly affect e-commerce. Globalization and advanced technology implications lead to very significant changes and developments

Figure 4. One Percent Increase in Distance Effect on Exports (%)
Source. TEPAV (2014)

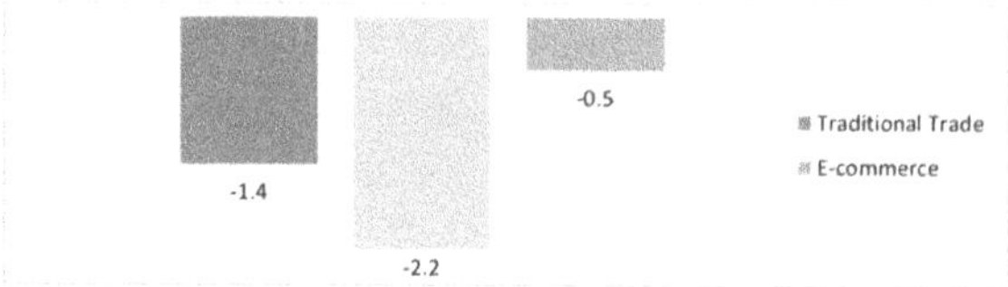

in e-payments as well. In this context, payment methods continue on evolving and varying to meet the changing necessities of users (Qin, 2009).The salient tendencies regarding the e-payments are; faster payments, more mobile payments, new payments, new payment options, improved security implications, Apps and some other integrated payment options (The Future of Payments, 2016).

E-payment is a system that provides tools for payment of services or goods carried on the internet. It provides the ease of transaction processing in e-commerce between consumers and sellers. Using the e-payment systems have many benefits for payers, payees, e-commerce, banks, organizations and governments. These benefits can lead to widespread e-payment systems in the world . An efficient and reliable e-payment system enables faster payouts, better tracking, transparent transactions, reduced time use, cost savings and increased trust between sellers and buyers (Fatonah et.al, 2018). E-commerce is built upon e-payment system and with the increasing volume of e-commerce, e-payment system is becoming more crucial for both businesses and consumers. E-payment systems are used for the completion of e-commerce transactions and can be defined as any payment system facilitating more secure e-commerce transactions between organizations and individuals.

Linck, Pousttchi, and Wiedemann (2006) stated that for businesses that operate electronically, e-payment systems are one of the most essential determinants of success. Sales of goods and services have increased significantly with the use of e-payment systems so that electronic payments have become an increasingly important part of the payment system. E-payment systems have come to replace cash payment systems. However, the emergence of e-commerce has created new financial needs that are not seen within traditional payment systems.

Characteristics of E-Payment Systems There are numbers of concepts characterize the electronic payment systems. These are as follows:

Anonymity

Anonymity means hiding the users' personal identity and the merchant only knows pseudonym of the user. Privacy means protecting the users' information from unauthorized parties (Tsiakis & Sthephanides, 2005). The user's information can be protected by technical activities or by not sharing with third parties. With the characteristics of anonymity and privacy, confidential payment information is not open for any party (Asokan et al., 1997; Neuman & Medvinsky, 1995; Tsiakis & Sthephanides, 2005). The payment system cannot trace the transections if these characteristics are provided. For instance; a customer makes his payment with a credit card; the purchase information is saved to the vendor's and bank's database. This allows other people/parties to find out the amount of the purchase and what the user has bought. Low et al. (1994) proposed a system like this and suggested an anonymous credit card to handle problematic scenarios. Wen (2010) proposed such a protocol to guarantee anonymity with complete security.

The users' identity and the purchase information can be anonymized by applying the technical actions mentioned in the related standards. Such as holding the last four digits of the card but not the sensitive data. Securing the users' information can be provided by encrypting the data and registering it to the database that way.

Traceability

Traceability means tracking the flow of money, the sources of the money or the link between the money spent and the customer. (Harris et al., 2011). In e-payment systems, money can be traced using records acquired during payment activities. These records should be kept in a safe and secure system. As we have mentioned before, securing data or information can be ensured by a strong encryption. The information of the credit card used in the payment is kept by the bank or the payment gateway. Traceability is associated with anonymity and privacy of the payment system (Abrazhevich, 2004). Traceability is important for law enforcements for preventing, detecting and prosecuting financial crimes.

Securit

Internet is a wide area network with no centralised control, which means there is no authorization responsible for security. By nature, the infrastructure of the e-commerce and e-payment systems should be secure as a fort, means resistant to attacks over the internet (Neuman & Medvinsky, 1995). Kim et al. (2010) and Hanzaee and Alinejad (2012) shared an opinion that users information can be secured by technical protection, transaction procedure and security. Gupta and Johari (2011) have proposed another approach that using mutual authentication procedure between cardholder and merchant increases the credit card security.

Authorisation Type

Authorization type controls validity of the transaction made (Asokan et al., 1997). Authorization type is a part of security characteristic that can be offline or online. Offline authorization helps users to perform transactions even when the system is not connected to the network, without an authorization server. When we are talking about e-commerce systems, we expect that the payment should be online. But in some occations paper check and payment by conventional cash can also be an option as an example of offline authorization. Within authorisation type there is a model that consists of three parties: customer, merchant and payment authority. Each uses payment order integrity concept. This model includes a merchant agreement to verify payment order (Raghuwanshi et al., 2009).

Trust

Trust, which also can be defined as customer trust, refers to the level of confidence of a customer. This level can vary depending on the security system. The system should guarantee the users' information to be protected, not to be stolen. A high level of trust also ensures that personal information will not be misused, and all parties will act according to the agreement. Reputation and previous experience with the merchant are also another argument of the trust. A good reputation or positive experience will definitely increase trust and vice versa (Egger, 2003). Customer trust can be increased by the two dimensions;

trust in the payment system provider and trust in the technology used that the merchant is providing via a web or mobile application.

Reliability

A reliable payment system depends on the infrastructure of e-commerce and the payment system. Uptime of the website is essential for reliability. It is also important for the merchant to provide an easy to use and well secured payment system to the customer. A user would not be happy to have a bad experience such as losing money due to a system crash (Asokan et al., 1997). Also, payment system would be expected to handle some threats, such as attacks from hackers. The payment service should quickly be restored if any failure occurs in the system. That can be done by a high-quality devops and security operations.

Convertibility

Modern banks and payment gateways provide users to make multi-currency payments. This is very important for the e-commerce websites which provide goods and service internationally. Also, customers can choose different payment systems according to their personal needs. It is also possible for each user to use different payment systems at the same time. To Neuman and Medvinsky, (1995), the electronic money in a payment system should be easily converted regarding the needs of the customer or the system that the merchant has. Conversion should be made without any limits. As Abrazhevich (2004) suggests, the multi-currency characteristic is considered as part of the convertibility.

Usability

Modern e-commerce systems provide users to save their payment information for their later purchases. This allows customers to make their payments with a free of effort as Davis (1989) suggested. According to Neuman and Medvinsky (1995), users should not be disturbed to provide payment information in each purchase. Payment process should be carried out automatically. That means the payment system should be user-friendly and easy to use. If not, the customers will probably not prefer to use it once more.

Interoperability

Interoperability relies on inter-development of the payment system. It is also important to work together with an efficient integration between the different solutions. An interoperable system could get a customer base more quickly, which is required for the development in the future with a higher adoption rate. Because the users are already familiar with that kind of payment systems they make payments without any hesitation.

Scalability

For an e-commerce website, the primary aim is to increase their customer number. That means the payment infrastructure must also be able to answer the increasing number of new customers. Researches show that slow payment systems make the customers cancel the purchase and leave the website. Fort hat reason, payment systems should work successfully without having any problems. It is also important to serve with high uptime and a good quality of service, even when there are huge numbers of users (Medvinsky & Neuman, 1993; Neuman & Medvinsky, 1995).

Efficiency

Efficiency is important for SMBs due to the characteristic of their payment model. Generally, SMBs need for micropayments and small payments. According to Hauser et al. (1996), a payment system must be able to process small payments and micropayments without any performance problems and high costs.

Applicability

The payment system should be applicable to the e-commerce system. The e-commerce system can be a free or commercial solution. Regardless of the technology used for the e-commerce solution, the payment system should be integrated easily and work properly. Applicability is also important for the customers. They most probably will prefer making payments via debit and credit cards. That means, the payment system should have a very high level of applicability for that payment systems.

Assessment of E-Payment Systems

There are four aspects to consider in assessing e-payment systems that are; technological, economic, social, and regulatory.[2] In assessing the technological aspect of a payment system, it would be accurate to consider efficiency and security of transactions, the system's expandability, and compatibility with other payment methods as well as user-friendliness. There are requirements to fulfill for companies to ensure security. These requirements include privacy, authenticity, integrity, and non-repudiation. Privacy requirement is related to anonymity protection of customers during transactions and the prevention of unauthorized parties from accessing customer information. Authenticity refers to verification of identities involved in transactions in order to prevent unauthorized access to information. Integrity requirement deals with prevention of data tampering during transactions while non-repudiation requirement is to prevent denial of commitments made during transactions. Thus, it is important to record and verify details of transactions. Economical feasibility is an important factor in terms of designing, building, maintaining e-payment systems. Economical feasibility depends on widespread use by customers. The Economic needs of e-payment systems include transaction costs, atomic exchange, accessibility, value mobility, and financial risk. Direct and indirect costs involved in a transaction as well as fixed costs should be considered in e-payment systems. Additionally, whether a system is widely accessible or not is another consideration.

In addition to economical and technical aspects, electronic payment systems should also consider the requirements of social aspects which include anonymity, user-friendliness, mobility, and regulations. An e-payment system should ensure its customers of protection of anonymity which is a critical factor. Also, user friendly and mobile systems would be more likely to be preferred by customers. Customers prefer systems that are easy to use and that can be used from anywhere. Regarding regulations, e-payment systems should ensure to follow government regulations of the country where e-commerce activities take place. These regulations include but are not limited to digital signatures, customs and taxation, international agreements, etc.

Table 2. Payment Methods[4]

Online Payment	The payment method is initiated by a user who has an access to the Internet.
Offline payment	The offline payment method is a method which mail/phone order or sales points or any other offline methods are used.
Mobile Payment	The mobile payment method is method which can be done via using the customer's cell phone or any other device's data function.

Source. İGEME (2009)

Categories of E-Payment System E-payment is and sub-category of an e-commerce transaction which encompasses e-payment for buying and selling goods or services through the Internet. Although there are many other types of e-payment options are available[3], we generally assume that e-payments are online transactions on the Internet (Premchand & Choudry, 2015). Payments methods according to the systems mentioned are given in Table 2.

Some of these systems are discussed in the following section.[5] Although the related literature which is used in e-commerce payment methods is quite similar, there are different classificiations. Please see the other classifications in Premchand and Choudhry (2015), TÜSİAD (2014), Hidayanto et al. (2015), Yang (2017), Turban et al. (2018). The other global e-payment options are Cash-On-Delivery, Electronic Cheque, Credit Cards, Debit Card, Virtual Card, Mobile Payment, Electronic wallets and cryptocurrency.[6] The mentioned payment methods will be explained here:

Cash-On-Delivery

Cash-on-delivery system, which gives clients the opportunity to make payment at the door to the courier company, both supports e-trade and promotes online-sales by adopting conventional payment habits to technology. Cash-on-delivery is a payment system that does not need any integration. Cash-on-delivery can be used in payment by in cash or by credit card. Its advantage is that you do not have to reveal your financial information like debit card, credit card or account information to the seller and payment is occurred upon delivery. Another advantage is that it rules out the dependency on credit or other payment cards.

Cash-on-delivery, which is one of the alternative payment systems that e-trade clients use, comes forward as an application for the undertakings to differentiate themselves from the others in competition. Accordingly, e-trade undertakings create an important opportunity by providing payment options in cash or by credit card for the clients who still continue their old consumption habits.

Electronic Cheque

Electronic cheque (e-cheque) is a payment system for e-commerce websites to accept payments by cheques. E-cheques have been designed for clients who do not want to make payment in cash as a virtual equivalent of cheques used in real life. There is no difference between e-cheques and paper cheques (Oney et al., p. 397). As different from the paper cheques, a digital signature is used on the e-cheques. A

Digital signature is an encryption system on a network, which has been created for security purposes in transactions that are not done face to face. In the e-cheque system, payments are made by entering only necessary bank account data to the e-commerce website. In other words, the user makes the payment by making out a cheque to the e-trade web site. Although it is an easy system, its use is not as widespread as the other mechanisms. For its more extensive use, it should be accepted by the financial sector.

In e-cheque system, there is a promise to buy a good with declaring a reason. Since the amount is fixed, there will be no transfer of any extra payment other than the fixed amount and if it is understood that the service will not be provided or badly done there is right to withdraw without making any payment. Therefore, it is a secure way for payment in e-commerce.

Credit Cards

Credit card systems are preferred more often than other e-commerce payment tools because they provide users several financial advantages such as insurance, bonuses, installment and security. While credit cards provide added value to customers, they incentivize businesses to meet the standards and reduce transaction costs through automated accounting.[7]

In addition to having a legal infrastructure that is standardized in the world and high security, credit cards are easy to use (Khan et al., 2017). The customer would only need to enter the credit card number and the expiration data on the website of the merchant. In order to improve security systems, several practices such as using card verification number (CVN) are implemented in online credit card payments. The CVN system helps identify fraud by comparing the CVN number with the information of the cardholder.[8]

When a customer makes a purchase with a credit card, the card issuer bank makes the payment on behalf of the customer which would allow the customer to have a time frame in which he can make the payment for the credit card. The actors involved in a credit card system are as follows:

Card holder – Customer **Merchant** – product seller who accepts credit card payments **Card issuer bank** – card holder's bank **Acquirer bank** – merchant's bank **Card brand** – such as Visa or Mastercard

Some of the companies that export and issue license of use credit card and card systems worldwide include Mastercard, Visa, American Express, Discover and JCB.

Debit Card

Debit card is also known as a bank card (Oney, 2017, p. 397) and it's a payment tool used in e-commerce and several transactions. It is one of the most popular payment methods without using cash (Kim et al., 2010). As this card does not provide a credit option for cardholders, it's not considered as a credit card. Debit card, in this context, is a card without credit card characteristics that allows the owner to withdraw and deposit money to checkings account. Debit card holders can withdraw money from ATMs of the bank they have an account with for 24/7 and make purchases through POS machines. During shopping, the amount of purchase is withdrawn from the cardholder's checking account and transferred to the merchant's bank account. Bank cards can be used as credit cards in payments made online. However, as they are not credit cards, the payment takes place as a money transfer from the user's checking account to the merchant's bank account. In comparison to credit cards, debit card costs incurred are lower which allows them to be used for micropayments. Additionally, the level of security of debit cards is higher than credit cards as the required identification processes demanded by banks are more rigorous (Khan et al., 2017). There are two kinds of debit cards that are; online and offline debit cards.

Virtual Card

Virtual card, as the name suggests, is a virtual product to reduce the risks of online shopping. This card that does not have a physical form but has digital information of the card user's bank account. Virtual card has a different card number and pin number from the physical card (Çakırer, 2013, p. 153).

Virtual card practices are provided by banks in Turkey. Banks issue virtual card or virtual credit cards with multiple functions to provide a safe environment for commercial activities, and to incentivize e-commerce customers. The most important aspect of virtual credit cards is that it is a card type that can onlu be used for online shopping within the limits the card owner determines via internet banking and that it can't be used in pos devices in stores. These cards are not printed as other cards and transactions are made only through the number determined by the bank (Zerenler, 2013, p. 103).

Mobile Payment

Online payments made through cell phones in e-commerce are called mobile payments. This method of payment is easy to use and in this method a payment request is sent to service provider via text instead of credit card use or cash payments. Prior to each online purchase, the mobile user authorizes the payment and the purchase amount is reflected on the user's phone bill. Consumers who have pre-paid phones make their payments through their balance on their phone.

There are several methods for using mobile payment services. While most of these methods use advanced technologies, some methods are considered as processes used through current technologies. The "new field communication" (NFC) method, one of the newer mobile payment methods, is designed with a focus on mobile payment solely. Several other mobile payment methods are performed through mobile networks and use traditional communication models such as SMS.

This method which is being used for the past few years in online purchases provides a possibility for payments to be made from anywhere which is a reason for being considered as advantageous and preferred. Also, mobile payment can not only be used in online shopping but also in stores. Mobile payment systems are safe payment systems as they make payments possible by using customers' cell phone numbers without sharing any card information or making cash payments. The concept of m-money emerged with mobile payment and it aims to replace cash for small transactions and removes disadvantages for cash use such as getting stolen or lost, or storing, etc.

Although there have been developments in current mobile payments during the past few years, payments are supported with SMS or e-mail with the 3D-secure system in terms of security. Along with payment models that center around banks in which mobile network service servers have the responsibility for secure communication, there are payment models that mobile network servers take on a bigger role. With the number increase in smartphone owners, the number of applications related to mobile payment services continue to increase. The number of mobile payment system users continue to increase worldwide. A study conducted by Gartner company showed that the number of mobile payment system users worldwide would be 200 million by 2012. This number increased to 245 million in the year 2013 and is expected to increase to 450 million by 2017 (McDermott, 2015, p. 6-7).

Mobile payments today are mostly used in the continents of Asia and Africa. Mobile applications that started with money transfer and mobile trade are being improved with applications that include invoices and pre-paid bank cards. Cell phones are not only communication devices anymore but also a small computer that's carried all the time. Today, all banking and payment transactions can be performed via cell phones. (Please see the other explanations of mobile payments; Bezhovski (2016); Kim, Mirsobit, and Lee (2010); Cabanillas and Rubio (2017).

Electronic Wallets

Electronic wallets are also referred to as digital wallets and provide the opportunity to store more than one credit cards, bank cards, and bank account numbers in a secure environment. Electronic wallets contain bank card numbers, electronic money, the owner's identity and communication information similar to an actual wallet. This removes the need to enter account information in every payment. Thus, entering card information to digital wallets one time and choosing the option of paying with e-wallet is sufficient rather than entering card information in every online purchase. Once the electronic wallet profile is created and saved, payments are made faster.

Electronic wallets are convenient for those who prefer to pay with a credit card Electronic wallets that make e-commerce faster and more practical are preferred mostly by consumers at the young age group. The number of e-wallet users increase in direct proportion with the number of e-commerce users which indicates that the digital wallet use will become even more frequent in the future. Amazon Pay, Google Pay, Apple Pay, Ali Pay, ByoWallet are among e-wallet providers that are mostly seen in international e-commerce activities.

Cryptocurrency

Cryptocurrency is a type of currency that draws on the cryptography science (Gandal & Halaburda, 2014). Cryptography is used in controling the processes of securing purchasing, selling, and payment activities as well as creating new currencies. Cryptocurrency (digital money) can be used both as an investment tool and as an alternative payment method which creates new opportunities for e-commerce companies. With its decentralized structure, it has characteristics such as being independent, low-cost, and fast transfer which attract more and more attention from users. Therefore, cryptocurrency is becoming a popular currency and a payment method. However, it is frequently mentioned that cryptocurrencies are still in the early adaptation phase which is why waiting for the industry to mature and technology to improve are recommended often. Despite different views, the number of companies accepting cryptocurrency in online payments is increasing every day.[9] Thus, the likelihood of cryptocurrency being a common payment method in e-commerce is very high.

Cryptocurrency was first introduced in 2009 through bitcoin which is positioned on a non-central architecture and it became a popular payment method in commerce with over 2000 types. Cryptocurrency is a kind of virtual money. The database algorythms that underlie the concept of cyrptocurrency and that are very different from traditional methods have been accepted. Banking sector has already started working on transitioning to this data base system. Commerce of a product occurs through transferring money from a digital wallet to another through electronic codes by eliminating mediators such as visa/mastercard and related commissions or costs. Within the frame of all these developments, the very first example of cryptocurrency application in the world is Bitcoin[4] and it's the most known cryptocurrency in the world.

The blockchain technology that provides high security due to cryptography method paved the way for cryptobased payment and money transfer as[10] well. Additionally, as cryptocurrency are not dependent on a central authority or an intermediary, it allows shopping to occur between the seller and the buyer only and thus, a faster payment. Within this context, unlike the slow speed of current payment methods and high costs, crypto payment methods provide a faster and less expensive way[11] for global payment activities. Despite the high potential and advantages it has, there are some negative aspects of cryptocurrency such as high price volatility, requirement of additional installment in order to accept crypto payments, and transactions in cryptocurrency being irreversible. Thus, it is important to be careful when making transactions and not saving personal information. Also, it should be known that legal infrastructure is not completed yet. Bitcoin constitutes 54% of the 220 billion dollar-cryptocurrency market.

In 110 countries out of 251, Bitcoin purchase/sales is free.[12] In the case of Bitcoin, the total currency units that can be in the market are limited to 21 million units (Ron & Shamir, 2013). From this aspect, it can be used in more than hundred countries as a payment method. Also, there are crypto payment gateways that allow the use, collection, and saving of several cryptocurrencies such as CoinPayments, PayCoiner. BitPAy, PumaPay, and Coingate.

Van Alstyne (2014) stated that the technical aspects of Bitcoin include that it can be used by its owner and one-time, the transaction fees are almost zero, that it is accepted as a payment method due to its success in identifying fraud with its open-access activity history. Additionally, the first day it was open by an online shopping portal, 125.000 USD-worth of transactions made. Churilov (2015) discusses the advantages and disadvantages of Bitcoin as a payment method, and its validity and taxation in international legal corporates. According to Churilov, Bitcoin is a currency unit that is immature and has high volatility. Thus, he warned companies using Bitcoin to be careful due to security problems and uncertainty in its legal status. Angel ve McCabe (2015) approached this from an ethical perspective and discussed the imbalance of power between the payer and the receiver. Within this context, they examined if reinforcement of Bitcoin as a payment method would be considered as misuse ethically and concluded that a potential misuse would not stem from the nature of Bitcoin.

Online Payment Gateway Model

Today's e-commerce world is less challenging then before. In the previous times of e-commerce, merchants have had to provide virtual POS services from each local banks of the base country. Now, there is a new and –relatively- better solution: Online Payment Gateways.This model is a service that sends credit card information from a website to credit card payment network to be processed and then sending transaction details and responses back to the website. If credit card payments are accepted online device, businesses need a payment network channel. This can be considered as the safe technology bridging for the customer and the business. In today's world where online shopping is popular, the use of online payments provides several advantages to both merchants and clients (customers). Online transactions are performed through a payment gateway during the process. Practically, payment gateways serve as a link between financial organizations and merchants' website. There are several factors involved in online payment processes during selling or purchasing products. Electronic Payment Gateway is fundamental for online transactions and they ensure reliable and safe exchange. An E-Commerce Payment Gateway is a part of infrastructure guaranteeing exchanges happen without any problems and electronic system security is maintained. A Payment Gateway is a point of access to national banking systems. Every online exchange takes place through a Payment Gateway which routes and confirms payment details securely between related banks and parties. Payment Gateway serves as an "encoded/encrypted" channel that sends transaction details from customers' online devices to banks for the purposes of authentication and countersignature. Once the approval is obtained, the Payment Gateway sends the data back to the merchant, completes the "order", and provides information of the payment process (Khan et al., 2017; Masihuddin et al., 2017). Stripe, Amazon Payments, Braintree, Authorize.Net, WePay, BlueSnap, Skrill, PayU, Dwolla, PaySimple, Paddle, PayPal, Payoneer, Yandex Checkout are among popular International Payment Gateways.[13]

FACTS AND TRENDS

Non-Cash Transaction

While the purchase of goods and services with cash payment is a traditional payment system reaching from past to present, e-payment systems have become a commonly used and preferred method instead of cash payment today. As a result of the evolvement of economies and commerce into a non-cash structure, e-payment systems instead of physical money come to the forefront in the commerce forms of the future. With the use of the internet, the system of payments has varied starting from the end of 1990s and although there was only one option as credit card before 1990, many payment systems are used today, and many payment systems are in the development process.

Within the context of our subject, the facts and trends regarding the usage density of domestic and foreign e-payment tools and systems are among the important issues to take into consideration for estimating the use of non-cash e-payment tools that are alternative to both cash and each other, healthy investment in terms of central banks, which are the determinants of monetary policies, as well as consumers and companies constituting the production and consumption side of goods and services in addition to making appropriate preferences.

According to World Payment Report (2018), during 2015-2016 global non-cash transaction volumes grew at 10.1% to reach 482.6 billion. Two regions fueled this growth: Emerging Asia (with 25.2% growth) and CEMEA(17.1%). Overall, the developing markets of Emercing Asia, CEMEA and Latin America recorded accelerated growth rate of 16.5% in 2016, driven by financial inclusion efforts and the adoption of mobile payments. It needs to be noted that overall volume of non-cash transactions grew significantly as shown below. All industry stakeholders will have to adopt e-payments and mobile payments channels as these channels are continuously driving growth of non-cash transactions. Following figure shows the Global number of non-cash transactions between 2012 and 2016 (Figure 5). As per World Payments

Figure 5. Non-Cash Transaction By Region (Billions Dollars)
Source. World Payments Report (2018), CEMEA (Cenral Europe, Middle East, Africa)

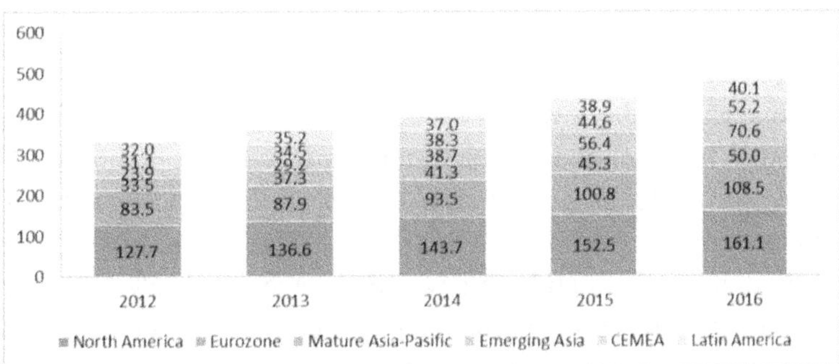

Report 2018, by 2021, there will be a major shift in payments industry - banks may not be at the centre of payment governance. Non-bank organizations and retailers will be encouraged more to participate in the payment chain. Total number of non-cash transactions are predicted to touch 876 billion by 2021.

In the North America and Europe, payments market is dominating, however, in the following years it is possible for this situation to change since developing markets share can be half of total non-cash transactions by 2021. Key areas where changes are estimated to go on will undergo some fragmentations and consolidations. Consumer protection will be provided with more anti-fraud measures. Some data policies could be applied, and it could affect this process. Such new currencies as reward points, mobile air time and digital currencies (bitcoin) can make a change in the way in which the payments are being made. There can be used some identification methods in other industries to protect the consumers. These methods can affect banks, payment processors and retailers.

The realization of noncash payments in Turkey show parallelism to developments in the world. The most preferred payment method in 2015 and 2017 was credit card with 61% and 68%, respectively. The decrease in cash payments and the increase in using credit card as payment method show parallelism. While the use of cash payment method was 35% in 2015, it decreased to 27% in 2017. Additionally, considering the fact that there are over 20 million consumers without a bank account or credit cards, and that the percentage of individuals considering getting a credit card increased from 11% in 2015 to 37% in 2017, it can be predicted that noncash payments will increase in economic activities and e-commerce. For details on the advantages and disadvantages of transitioning to non-cash economy in Turkey, you can refer to Elgin, Erzan & Kuzubas (2013) and BKM (2017). Within this context, compatibility should be established related to systems with credit card and other methods of payment in Europe and Asia as the first step in transitioning to a noncash society.[14]

E-Payments

As economies grow and globalize, the need for non-cash payment tools has increased. For example, while paper-based payment tools such as checks were initially used, the difficulties brought by the incredible increase in the number and amount of transactions in the international payments and the opportunities offered by the technology in these areas have expanded the use of e-payment tools. In parallel with the aforementioned developments, national and international payment systems and tools alternative to each other have been developed in many countries and are still being developed. In this context, the use of alternative e-payment methods, which both replace cash and increase its efficiency by relieving the use of e-commerce, has become widespread in almost every country.

In the context of national and international e-commerce practices, how to use the e-payment technologies and systems as well as which payment tools will be used is the key of performing online purchase and payment. E-payment systems are increasingly used throughout the world in parallel with the developments emerging in the fields of commerce and technology.

The expectations with regard to the development in international e-payment methods for e-commerce could be seen in Figure 6. There are two elements coming forward in Figure 6. First, the expectation for the rise of the share of e-wallet usage, which is one of the outstanding elements of digitalism, in the international e-payment methods from 18% to 46% by 2021; secondly, the expectation for the fall of the share of credit card, bonus card and pre-pay cards usage from 53% to 30% in the international e-payment methods. Consequently, although the payment method has been changed, the goods which are being paid have not changed. Accordingly, the share of international e-payment methods by cards

Figure 6. E-Payment Methods (%)
Source. Global Payments Report (2017).

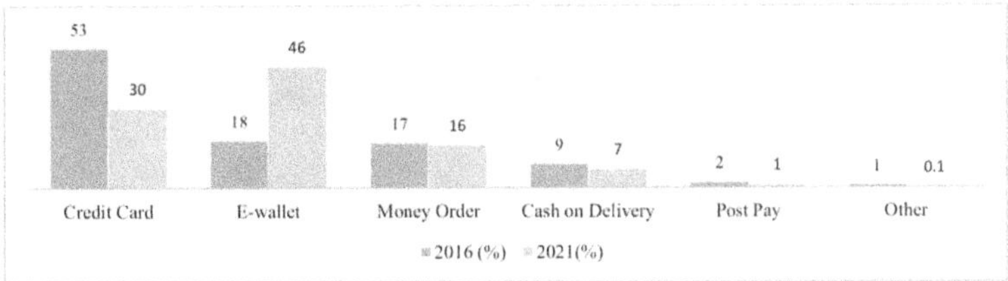

and e-wallet is expected to rise from 71% to 76% by 2021. It is because that the infrastructure of these payments is very appropriate for e-commerce. In this sense, the share of payment by cards is expected to be higher in the future.

In Turkey, 85% of payments are made by cards. It is very remarkable, as the share of payments made by card in the world is 71% today. Therefore, the card ownership rate is quite high in Turkey and the rise in the use of e-wallet could be expected as a result of change in composition or other payment tools special to Turkey might come forward. The facts regarding e-payment in Turkey are shown in Figure 7. Since credit card is mainly preferred for purchasing in e-commerce in Turkey, the development of the e-payment systems that will provide secure shopping and easy payment is very important for the growth of the sector.

In the near future, the retail sector and thus e-commerce will have to undergo a significant transformation in the countries where alternative e-payment systems cannot be commonly used today but seen as an important opportunity. In this sense, it will be inevitable for socities to direct to alternative e-payment methods rather than the use of cash.

If the companies, which want to carry out e-commerce activities in different places of the world, have infrastructure supporting as many payment methods as possible, they will gain many advantages and in this way, they will optimize their online incomes thanks to the ability of making the transaction process as easy as possible for their customers. Figure 8 given below details the e-payment systems used in e-commerce according to the geographical regions in the world. Although many alternative e-payment methods frequently mentioned in the recent period show a great increase in every period compared to the previous period, their shares in the total composition are extremely low.

Figure 7. E-Payment Methods in Turkey (%)
Source. Global Payments Report (2017).

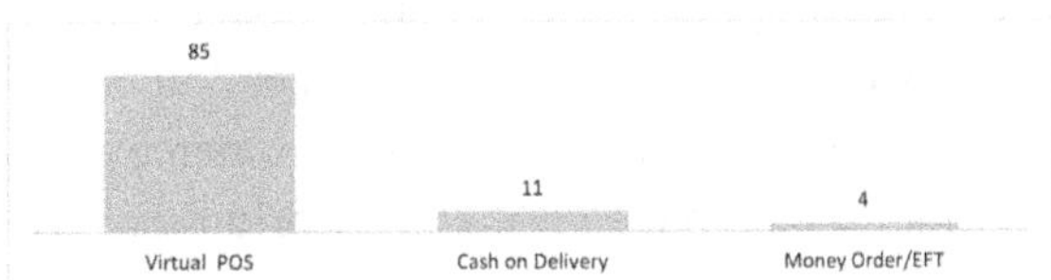

Figure 8. Preferred E-Payment Methods for E-Commerce (2018,%)
Source. Statista, https://www.statista.com/statistics/348004/payment-method-usage-worldwide/

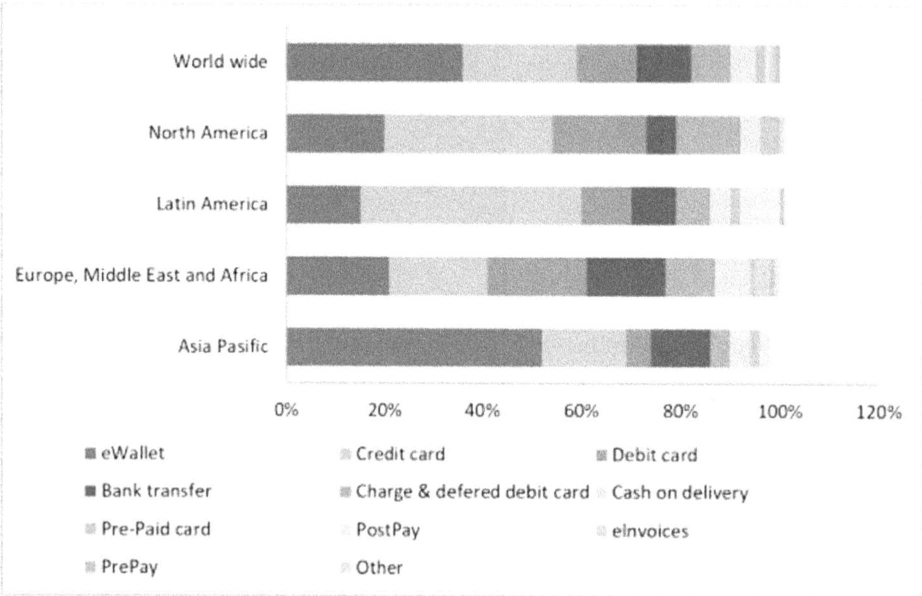

SOLUTIONS AND RECOMMENDATIONS

It is not possible to state that e-payment systems are the same in all continents or countries. Some of the important reasons for this include the demographic characteristics, the degree of financial literacy, the infrastructure provided by the financial system, the advantages and disadvantages of e-payments, the level of income of consumers and the extensity of e-commerce use. Therefore, it is a very natural situation that the e-payment methods preferred by consumers are different. In this context, having various e-payment options suitable for customers is crucial for companies in terms of not being devoid of important operations. Since the growth in global e-commerce significantly results from cross-border e-commerce, every company in e-commerce should aim at certain alternative payment systems and tools, which are popular in different countries or regions, for alternative e-payments. As e-commerce becomes widespread and develops, even the solutions that are seen as optimal today may not be permanent since e-payments will vary. Not integrating appropriate e-payment systems will cause companies to encounter problems in every field. The way of turning the problem into an advantage is to provide e-payment methods appropriate for customers.

FUTURE RESEARCH DIRECTIONS

With the rise of Industry 4.0, the concepts such as robots, artificial intelligence and artificial neural networks have started to be increasingly used in the production and sales process of goods and services. These developments will inevitably affect all sectors. The e-commerce sector will have the opportunity of using the big data constantly increasing in the digitalized world more effectively by benefitting from the artificial intelligence. Thanks to the artificial intelligence, e-commerce websites will be able to offer products special to the users who do shopping, make a voice call, their payment systems will be simpler and more user-friendly and there will be a more refined functioning logistically. The semantic web technologies of the past will give place to the web applications having artificial intelligence and with the use of developments such as artificial intelligence in e-commerce, significant returns will be achieved in terms of efficiency. This means that in the e-commerce of the future, more intelligent and self-learning shopping systems will be active thanks to machine learning. As a result, the involvement of Industry 4.0 and artificial intelligence, one of the basic elements of it, in e-commerce activities can affect many technological, economic and legal factors, it is important to conduct more studies on the field.

CONCLUSION

With the increasing interest in e-commerce, companies have started to look for alternative e-payment systems for themselves. In addition to this need, the widespread use of smart devices and Internet has diversified e-payment systems and extended them to a wide range and the use of alternative e-payment systems has become widespread in every country. The widespread of e-payment systems has increasingly caused economies to evolve into a non-cash structure. Considering the expectation that global e-commerce volume will reach 4 trillion dollars in 2020, the changes that will occur in e-payment systems, which are the most important elements for the healthy functioning of millions of online payment transactions to be made today and in the future, will affect the development of e-commerce directly. While having national and international different payment alternatives enables companies to reach more consumers from different sectors/geographies, it will also increase the chance of being preferred by the potential customers due to payment diversity. In this context, the relation between e-commerce companies and consumers enhances thanks to offering different payment alternatives. Today, many different e-payment methods such as payment with card, e-wallet, mobile payment, cryptocurrency etc. are offered by companies when purchase-sale is performed with e-commerce. Consumers' preference regarding alternative payment systems inland and abroad varies depending on many factors such as income level, demographic characteristics and financial literacy. While credit cards and debit cards are commonly used among the alternative e-payment tools, the use of e-wallet has outdistanced the use of credit card or they compete head to head in many countries. Mobile payments, which have a very high potential, have shown a significant progress, however, it is not possible for mobile devices to offer an experience similar to the one that consumers experience on WEB. The use of cryptocurrencies as a payment method is not possible today compared to mobile payments. Consequently, considering that the developing technology can change many things in the course of time, the determination of payment preferences is very important for the competitiveness of companies.

REFERENCES

Abrazhevich, D. (2004). *Electronic Payment Systems: A User-Centered Perspective and Interaction Design. Phd D.* Eindhoven: Eindhoven University of Technology.

Alstyne, M. V. (2014). Why Bitcoin Has Value, Association for Computing Machinery, 57(5), 30-32.

Angel, J., & McCabe, D. M. (2014). The Ethics of Payments: Paper, Plastic, or Bitcoin*? SSRN Electronic Journal, 132*(3). Retrieved From https://econpapers.repec.org/article/kapjbuset/v_3a132_ 3ay_3a2015 _3ai_3a3_3ap_3a603-611.htm

Asokan, N., Janson, P., Steiner, M., & Waidner, M. (1997). The State of The Art in Electronic Payment Systems. *Computer, 30*(9), 28–35. doi:10.1109/2.612244

Bansal, S., Bruno, P., Denecker, O., Goparaju, M., & Niederkorn, M. (2018). *Global Payments 2018: A Dynamic Industry Continues to Break New Ground.* McKinsey&Company. Retrieved From https://www.mckinsey.com/~/media/McKinsey/Industries/Financial%20Services/Our%20Insights/Global%20payments%20Expansive%20growth%20targeted%20opportunities/Global-payments-map-2018. ashx.

Bezhovski, Z. (2016). The Future of The Mobile Payment as Electronic Payment System. *European Journal of Business and Management, 8*(8), 127–133.

BKM. (2017). *Cashless Turkey by 2023.* Retrieved From https://www.burnmark.com/ uploads/reports/Burnmark_Report_BKM_Turkey1.pdf

Cabanillas, F. L., & Rubio, J. L. (2017). Predictive and Explanatory Modelling Regarding Adoption of Mobile Patment Systems. *Technological Forecasting and Social Change, 120*, 32–40. doi:10.1016/j.techfore.2017.04.002

Çakırer, M. A. (2013). *Elektronik Ticaret*. Bursa: Ekin Yayınları.

Churilov, A. (2015). *Practical Aspects of Bitcoin Usage in Business,* Retrieved From https://ssrn.com/abstract=2685646 or doi:10.2139srn.2685646

Coingape. (2018). *Jap based Yamada Denki Now Accepts Bitcoin Payments.* Retrieved From fhttps://coingape.com/japan-based-yamada-denki-now-accepts-bitcoin-payments/

Consuegra, R. A. A., & Garcia, M. A. Z. (2013). *A Study of Electronic Payments in B2C Ecommerce, Master of Science in Management Engineering*. Milano: Politecnico.

Criteo. (2015). *Criteo E-Commerce Industry Outlook 2015*, Retrieved From http://mobint.com.br/Downloads/criteo-ecommerce-industry-outlook-2015.pdf

Dapplife. (2019). *Switzerland's E-Commerce Giant Digitec Galaxus Accepts Bitcoin Payments.* Retrieved From https://dapplife.com/switzerlands-ecommerce-giant-digitec-galaxus-accepts-bitcoin-payments/

Davis, F. (1989). Perceived Usefulness, Perceived Ease of Use, and User Acceptance of Information Technology. *Management Information Systems Quarterly, 13*(3), 319–340. doi:10.2307/249008

Egger, F. (2003). From Interactions to Transactions: Designing the Trust Experience for BusinessTo-Consumer Electronic Commerce, PhD thesis, *Eindhoven University of Technology*, The Netherlands.

Elgin, C., Erzan, R., & Kuzubaş, U. (2013). *Türkiye' de Nakit ve Kart Ödemelerinin Karşılaştırmalı Maliyeti*. Boğaziçi Üniversitesi Ekonomi ve Ekonometri Merkezi.

Ersoy, N. F. (2002). Finansal Hizmetlerde Müşteri İlişkileri Yönetimi (CRM) Kavramı. Pazarlama Dünyası Dergisi, Sayı:2002-03, İstanbul.

Fatonah, S., Yulandari, A., & Wibowo, F. W. (2018). A Review of E-Payment System in E-Commerce, IOP Conf. Series. *Journal of Physics: Conference Series*, *1140*, 012033. doi:10.1088/1742-6596/1140/1/012033

Finnegan, P., Kilmartin, J.(2002). Electronic Payment Systems: An Empirical Investigation of Customer and Merchant Requirements, *Managing Business with Electronic Commerce: Issues and Trends*, 151-166.

Gandal, N., & Hałaburda, H. (2014). Competition in the Cryptocurrency Market, *Bank of Canada Working Paper* 2014-33 August 2014, Retrieved From https://www.bankofcanada.ca/wp-content/uploads/2014/08/wp2014-33.pdf

Gupta, S., & Johari, R. (2011). A New Framework For Credit Card Transactions Involving Mutual Authentication Between Cardholder and Merchant, Proceedings of The CSNT. *11: International Conference On Communication Systems and Network Technologies*, 22–26.

Hanzaee, K. H., & Alinejad, S. (2012). An Investigation About Customers Perceptions of Security and Trust In E-Payment Systems Among Iranian Online Consumers. *Journal of Basic and Applied Scientific Research*, *2*(2), 1575–1581.

Harris, H., Guru, B. K., & Avvari, M. V. (2011). Evidence of Firms Perceptions Toward Electronic Payment Systems (EPS) in Malaysia. *International Journal of Business and Information*, *6*(2), 226–245.

Harrop, P. (1989). New Electronics For Payments, *IEE Review, IX*, 35-45. Retrieved From https://ieeexplore.ieee.org/xpl/tocresult.jsp?isnumber=5642&punumber=2188

Hauser, R., Steiner, M., & Waidner, M. (1996), *Micro-Payments Based on IKP, Technical Report 2791* (#89269) [online] http://www.researchgate.net/publication/2669783_Micro-Payments_ based_on_iKP/file/79e41507d2ec8a3a97.pdf (accessed 3 April 2013).

Hidayanto, A. N., Hidayat, L. S., Sandhyaduhita, P. I., & Handayani, P. W. (2015). Examinin the Relations of Payment System Characteristics and Behavioual Intention in E-payment Adoption: A Case of Indonesia. *International Journal of Business Information Systems*, *19*(1), 58. doi:10.1504/IJBIS.2015.069065

İGEME. (2009). *Yurtdışına E-Ticaret*. Ankara.

Information Technology Faculty. (2016). *The Future of Payment*, Retrieved From https://www.icaew.com/-/media/corporate/files/technical/information-technology/technology/185-the-future-of-payments.ashx

Kaur, K., Pathak, A. (2015). E-Payment System on E-Commerce in India, *Karamjeet Kau Int. Journal of Engineering Research and Alications*, 5(2-part1) 79-87.

Khan, B. I., Olanrewaju, R. F., Baba, A. M., Langoo, A. A., Assad, S. (2017). A Compendious Study of Online Payment Systems: Past Developments, Present Impact, and Future Considerations, *(IJACSA) International Journal of Advanced Computer Science and Applications*, Vol. 8, No. 5.

Kim, C., Mirsobit, M., & Lee, I. (2010). An Empirical Examination of Facctors Influencing the Intention to Use Mobile Payment. *Computers in Human Behavior*, *26*(3), 310–322. doi:10.1016/j.chb.2009.10.013

Kim, C., Tao, W., Shin, N., & Kim, K. S. (2010). An Empirical Study of Customers Perceptions of Security and Trust in E-Payment Systems. *Electronic Commerce Research and Applications*, *9*(1), 84–95. doi:10.1016/j.elerap.2009.04.014

Lee, Z. Y., Yu, H. C., & Kuo, P. J. (2001). An Analysis and Comparison of Differen Types of Electronic Payment Systems, *Portland Int. Conference on*, IEEE., 38-45.

Linck, K., Pousttchi, K., & Wiedemann, D. G. (2010). Security Issues in Mobile Payment From The Customer Viewpoint In: Ljungberg, J. (Hrsg.). *Proceedings of the 14th European Conference on Information Systems (ECIS 2006)*. Göteborg, Schweden 2006, S.1-11.

Low, S., Paul, S., & Maxemchuk, N. (1994). Anonymous Credit Cards, *Proceedings of The 2nd ACM Conference on Computer and Communications Security*. 108–117.

Manzoor, A. (2010). *E-Commerce an Introduction*. Lawbert Academic Publishing USA.

Masihuddin, M., Khan, B.U.I., Mattoo, M. M. I., & Olanrewaju, R. (2017). A Survey on E-Payment Systems: Elements, Adoption, Architecture, Challenges and Security Concepts. *Indian Journal of Science and Technology*, *10*(20), 1-19.

McDermott, K. (2015). The Mobile Payments Revolution, *Payvision BV*, Retrieved From http://boletines.prisadigital.com/The-mobile-payments-revolution-2015.pdf

Medvinsky, G., & Neuman, B. C. (1993). Netcash: a Design for Practical Electronic Currency on the Internet, *Proceedings of the 1st ACM Conference on Computer and Communications Security, pp.* 102–106. 10.1145/168588.168601

Meral, Y. (2018). Documentary Risk in International Trade. In Strategic Design and Innovative Thinking in Business Operations. 413-431, Springer, Cham.

Miva. (2011) *The History of Ecommerce: How Did it All Begin.* Retrieved From https://www.miva.com/blog/the-history-of-ecommerce-how-did-it-all-begin/

Neuman, B. C., & Medvinsky, G. (1995). Requirements for Network Payment: Tthe Netcheque Perspective, *Proceedings of IEEE COMPCON'*95. 10.1109/CMPCON.1995.512360

OECD. (2006). *Online Payment Systems for E-commerce*, OECD Digital Economy Papers, No:117.

Öney, E., Öksüzoğlu, G. G., & Rizvi, W. H. (2017). The Determinants of Electronic Payment Systems Usage From Consumers' perspective. *Economic Research Journal*, *30*(1), 394–415.

Premchand, A., & Choudhry, A. (2015). Future of Payments – *E-Payments,* International Journal of Emerging Technology and Advanced Engineering, Website: www.ijetae.com (ISSN 2250-2459, ISO 9001:2008 Certified Journal, Volume 5, Issue 1, January 2015)

Qin, Z. (2009). *Introduction to E-Commerce*. Springer.

Raghuwanshi, S., Pateria, R. K., & Singh, R. P. (2009). *A New Protocol Model for Verification of Payment Order Information Integrity in Online E-Payment System. World Congress on Nature & Biologically Inspired Computing, NABIC 2009*, 1665–1668. 10.1109/NABIC.2009.5393641

Ray, A. (2017). *What are the different types of e-commerce payment systems?* https://services.amazon.in/resources/seller-blog/different-types-of-e-commerce-payment-systems.html

Read, R. J. (1989). *EFTPOS: Electronic Funds Transfer At Point Of Sale, Electronics & Communications Engineering Journal, I, 6* (pp. 17–25). Retrieved From; https://ieeexplore. ieee.org/ document/105349

ReportW. P. (2018). Retrieved From https://worldpaymentsreport.com/wp-content/uploads/sites/5/2018/10/World-Payments-Report-2018.pdf

Ron, D., & Shamir, A. (2013). *Quantitative Analysis of the Full Bitcoin Transaction Graph, in Financial Cryptography and Data Security*, 17th International, FC 2013,(Ahmad-Reza Sageghi ed., 2013), Retrieved From https://eprint.iacr.org/2012/584.pdf

Şahbaz, U., Sökmen, A., & Aytaç, A. Türkiye' de E-İhracat: Fırsatlar ve Sorunlar, *Tepav,* 2014, Retrieved From https://www.tepav.org.tr/upload/files/haber/1415973180-5.Turkiyede _E_Ihracat _ Firsatlar_ve_Sorunlar.pdf

Steemit. (2018). *Bitcoin: E-Ticaret İçin 2 Saniyede Kripto Ödeme Çözümü.* Retrieved From https://steemit.com/ethereum/@ioseta/bitcoinus-e-ticaret-icin-2-saniyede-kripto-oedeme-coezuemue

Suberg, W. (2018). South Korea E-Commerce Giant to Add 12 Cryptocurrencies With Bithumb, Cointelligence Research & Analysis For The Crypto Economy. Retrieved from https://www.cointelligence.com/content/south-korea-e-commerce-giant-add-12-cryptocurrencies-bithumb/

Sumanjeet, S. (2009). Emergence of Payment Systems in The Age of Electronic Commerce: The State of Art. *Global Journal of International Business Research, 2*(2), 17–36.

Tsiakis, T., & Sthephanides, G. (2005). The Concept of Security and Trust in Electronic Payments. *Computers & Security, 24*(1), 10–15. doi:10.1016/j.cose.2004.11.001

TÜBİSAD. Deloitte, Etid, *Türkiye'de E-Ticaret 2017 Pazar Büyüklüğü,* Mayıs 2018, Retrieved From http://www.tubisad.org.tr/tr/images/pdf/tubisad_2018_e-ticaret_sunum_tr.pdf https://www2. deloitte.com/content/dam/Deloitte/tr/Documents/technology-media-telecommunications/turkiyede-2017-e-ticaret-pazar-buyuklugu.pdf

Turban, E., Whiteside, J., King, D., & Outland, J. (2018). *Electronic Commerce 2018, A Managerial and Social Networks Perspective.* Springer. doi:10.1007/978-3-319-58715-8

TÜSİAD. (2014). *Dijital Pazarın Odak Noktası E-Ticaret: Dünyada ve Türkiye' nin Yeri, Mevcut Durum ve Geleceğe Yönelik Adımlar,* Yayın No: TÜSİAD-T/2014-06/553, İstanbul, Retrieved From https://tusiad.org/tr/yayinlar/raporlar/item/7891-dijital-pazarin-odak-noktasi-e-ticaret-dunyada-turkiyenin-yeri-mevcut-durum-ve-gelecege-yonelik-adimlar-raporu

TÜSİAD. (2017). *Dijitalleşen Dünyada Ekonominin İtici Gücü: E-Ticaret,* Yayın No: TÜSİAD-T/2017, 04-587, İstanbul, Retrieved From https://tusiad.org/tr/yayinlar/raporlar/item/9675-dijitallesen-dunyanin-itici-gucu-e-ticaret

Twentyfy. (2018). Kripto Para Birimleri Algı & Güven Araştırması Türkiye'nin Sanal Cüzdanı, 2018, Retrieved From https://www.twentify.com/hubfs/Turkish_Reports/Twentify_Kripto-Para-Arastirmasi.pdf?hsCtaTracking=9c0%20cee2f-c64d-4d79-80cf-ce5a46cf46c3%7Ca4dbb8fe-29ab-4c7a-b1be-1536d9de794e

Twentyfy. (2018). *Türkiye'de E-ticaret: Çevrimiçi Alışverişte Tüketici Davranışları Araştırması ve Marka Karşılaştırması,* Retrieved From https://www.twentify.com/tr/raporlar/turkiyede-e-ticaret-cevrimici-alisveriste-tuketici-davranislari-arastirmasi-ve-marka-karsilastirmasi

WEF. (2018). *Addressing E-Payment Challenges in Global E-Commerce, White Paper*, Retrieved From http://www3.weforum.org/docs/WEF_Addressing_E-Payment_Challenges_in_Global_E- Commerce _clean.pdf

Wen, X. (2010). An E-Payment System Based on Quantum Group Signature. *Physica Scripta, 82*(6), 065403. doi:10.1088/0031-8949/82/06/065403

Yang, W. (2017). Analysis On Online Payment Systems of E-Commerce. *Bachelor's Thesis, Business Information Technology Oulu University of Applied Sciences*, Retrieved From https://www.theseus.fi/bitstream/handle/10024/139600/Yang_Wenjing.pdf?sequence=1&isAllowed=y

Zerenler, M. (2013). *Dijital İş Yaşamı: Tüm Boyutlarıyla Elektronik Ticaret.* Ankara: Gazi Kitapevi.

KEY TERMS AND DEFINITIONS

Electronic Commerce: E-commerce is a concept covering the purchase and sales of any good or service by using information technologies, electronic communication channels and other relevant technologies through cyber space. According to a different definition, e-commerce refers to the traditional trade which is performed on a web environment or mobile. There is also another definition stating that e-commerce includes purchases-sales whose payment transaction is made through the internet. Contrary to the general view, e-commerce is not only performed through the internet, but also other wide networks as specified above with the term "cyber space".

Electronic Payment System: E-payment system is the means of making payment and/or transaction for goods and services on an e-commerce website or electronic environment without any need to use cash or check. E-payment system is also known as online payment system. It has many forms such as credit card, virtual card, mail order, e-wallet, mobile payment, cryptocurrency, etc.

Payment Gateway: Payment gateway is a system that facilitates payments in a strict sense. In a broad sense, it is a service that securely encypts confidential information regarding credit card, debit card and other electronic payment methods of users giving online order on e-commerce systems, conveys them to the e-commerce manager and to the bank or intermediary institutions from the e-commerce manager in compliance with the related standards (PCI DSS) and enables the processing of online transactions real-timely.

ENDNOTES

1 For risks in international trade see Meral (2018).

2 For more detailed information please see Lee, Yu, Kuo (2001).

3 Please see the comparative analysis regarding the chosen different characteristics of payment system OECD (2006), Consuegra and Garcia (2013), Turban et.al (2018), Sumanjeet (2009).

4 Please see the other features of payments Kaur and Pathak (2015), Masihuddin et.al (2017), Turban et.al (2019-8), Consuegra and Garcia (2013).

5 For more detailed information please see Manzoor (2010), Turban et.al (2018).

6 Please see the studies which are done to identify the preferences in e-payment systems of customers Oney, Oksuzoglu, Rizvi (2017), Kim, Tao, Shin, Kim (2010).

7 For advantages and disadvantages of credit card systems see Finnegan and Kilmartin (2002).

8 https://services.amazon.in/resources/seller-blog/different-types-of-e-commerce-payment-systems.html

9 The largest e-commerce website of South Korea, WeMake Price decided to integrate several cryptocurrency units into their payment system. https://www.cointelligence.com/content/south-korea-e-commerce-giant-add-12-cryptocurrencies-bithumb/.
Bic Camera and Yamada Denki, Japanese electronic retails, started to accept payments with Bitcoin https://coingape.com/japan-based-yamada-denki-now-accepts-bitcoin-payments/
E-commerce retail Digitec Galaxus in Sweden started to accept Bitcoin payments. https://dapplife.com/switzerlands-ecommerce-giant-digitec-galaxus-accepts-bitcoin-payments/.
Today, **Microsoft, CheapAir, Shopify, Bloomberg, Expedia ve Intuit**, accept payments with cryptocurrency.

10 Crypto-based payment methods function with a different logic from credit cards or other online payment systems. Instead of withdrawing money by the receiver upon authorization by card or account holder, money is transferred directly to the receiver. Documentation of each transaction and storage of this documentation across a network increases the safety of records which makes block chain technology a candidate for future payment and money transfer infrastructure.

11 For a detailed comparison of alternative payment methods, see https://steemit.com/ethereum/@ioseta/bitcoinus -e-ticaret-icin-2-saniyede-kripto-oedeme-coezuemue

12 https://www.twentify.com/hubfs/Turkish_Reports/Twentify_Kripto-Para-Arastirmasi.pdf?hsCtaTracking =9c0 cee2f-c64d-4d79-80cf-ce5a46cf46c3%7Ca4dbb8fe-29ab-4c7a-b1be-1536d9de794e

13 Please find the e-payment companies in developing and emerging economies, WEF (2018), Turban (2018).

14 For various statistics on Global Payments see Bansal, Bruno, Denecker, Goparaju, Niederkom (2018).

Chapter 7
Electronic Trade and Electronic Presentation of Export Documents in Documentary Credits

Yurdagül Meral
İstanbul Medipol University, Turkey

ABSTRACT

Documentation plays a very important role in international trade. Information technology has changed practises in international trade as well. In this chapter, international rules of electronic presentation of documents under documentary credit are defined to guide importers and exporters. This will enable them to speed up transactions to conduct their business as per these rules. Paperback presentation and electronic presentation international rules differences are explained. Electronic presentation will help import export management to facilitate transactions which will increase international trade volume. It is recommended that electronic presentation will help them to speed up their transactions. In the long run, electronic presentation will be cheaper compared to paper presentation and much safer.

INTRODUCTION

Electronic trade has increased with internet. Electonic transactions to be affected smoothly requires legal framework as well. As it is comparatevily new that is created and increased with internet, international electronic trade, which is a cross-border transaction, requires a legal system for a healthy progress (Weber, 2007). International trade is total of import and export of goods, across borders. In other words, buyers and sellers are in different countries. If buyers and sellers are in same country, then it is local trade. Whether local trade or international trade, main concern of seller is to receive money as soon as possible and main concern of buyer is to receive goods in time, in good condition as per sales contract. The same thing applies for international trade, receiving goods for importer and receiving money for exporter, main concerns are the same as local trade.

DOI: 10.4018/978-1-7998-0035-4.ch007

The main difference between local trade and international trade is that import- export is affected between two different countries, via customs clearance, across borders. Customs do not deal only with goods, passengers travelling abroad have to pass through borders, at the same time they pass through the customs as well. Just like passengers travelling abroad require documentation like passport, if necessary visa for the country they are travelling to, same thing applies for goods as well. Exported goods have to be cleared via exporter's country's border/customs and imported goods have to be cleared via importer's country's border/customs with these required documentations.

Documents are so important in international trade that payments are mainly based on shipping documents, namely payment against documents and documentary credit payments. Specification and presentation of the shipping documents are subject to worldwide accepted international rules set by ICC (International Chamber of Commerce). Importers and exporters must be aware of these rules and be careful to comply with these rules to receive payment and to receive goods in time.

Although majority of shipping documents are still presented physically paper-based by the exporter, with information technology impact in international trade which can be named as e-trade or e-export in international trade, e-presentation, electronic submission of documents has started to replace physical/manuel submission of paper documents.

With the increasing tendency for e-trade and expected increase in electronic presentation, International Chamber of Commerce (ICC) has published International Trade Rules for Electronic Submission of Documents (e-UCP) as a supplement to with the revision of UCP 600. This chapter covers the difference between the rules of physical submission and e-submission of shipping documents.

BACKGROUND

This chapter aims to provide information about international rules of electronic and paper based documentation presentation in documentary credits (known as letter of credit). The differences between electronic presentation and paper presentation of documentary credit documents. Providing information about main process of the transactions, reasons why either presentation method must be used. International rules of documentary credit issued by ICC (International Chamber of Commerce), interpretations with reference to literature review and with discussion and conclusion.

DOCUMENTS ROLE IN INTERNATIONEL TRADE

Documents play a very important role in international trade. International trade is trade between different countries, cross borders, which means importer and exporter most probably have never met, do not know each other, do not trust each other, do not know other country and their rules, traditions etc. Documentation is vital in customs clearance as well, clearance of goods require specific documentation, as all countries want to protect their borders, want to control not only people leaving and entering country, governments follow goods import and export as well. All is done via documentation in customs clearance. Not only for customs for international trade payments, the most important document is the unique, original bill of lading/transport document because original bill of lading/transport document is a negotiable document, representing ownership/title of the goods.

International organisations try to increase international trade by applying standard applications, standard rules to facilitate international trade transactions. Standardization of international rules help importers and exporters to avoid misunderstanding due to different languages, different cultures. As they are in different countries, in local trade it is easier to solve disputes because both parties are subject to same local law, but this is not the case in international trade, standard rules are important as well. Although paper documentations will not be used it is not that easy to apply to this in international trade because of complex processes of international trade (Civelek et al., 2017).

Open Account

If importer and exporter agree on open account, this means importer will clear goods first and then transfer the value of the goods to the exporter at a time agreed upon among themselves, must be able to clear goods through customs. In this case, exporter will ship the goods and bill of lading/transport document will be issued directly in the name of the importer and exporter will send the necessary documents to clear goods directly to importer, of which importer will clear goods with these documents.

Advance Payment

Same process only importer pays in advance to exporter, then the process is the same, exporter ships goods, prepares shipping documents and having received the value of the goods in advance, transportation document issued in the name of the importer will be sent directly to importer via special courrier to enable him clear goods through customs.

D/P Documents Against Payment (Payment Against Documents or Cash Against Documents)

Advance payment and open account payment terms are used where importer and exporter trust each other. They might know each other or in the contrary one of the parties might be so powerful that other weak party has to accept the terms and act accordingly. Payment against documents is a term where both parties do not trust each other, and banks are involved in the process as follows. They agree upon payment against documents basis, exporter ships goods, prepares original bill of lading/transport documents in the name of (usually importer's) BANK, sends shipping documents to importer's bank with instruction to deliver documents to importer documents against payment. Importer's bank advises exporter about import documents, importer applies to bank, pays documents value, in return, bank delivers documents by endorsing bill of lading/transport document in favour of the importer to enable importer to clear goods through customs.

Acceptance Payments

In addition to above mentioned payments acceptance payments are also used in international trade. Main difference between other payments and acceptance payments is there is an instrument called draft, which can be sight draft or time draft, called acceptance because a draft is issued by the beneficiary (drawer) and accepted by the debtor (drawee). If buyer and seller agree upon a payment derm to be paid in a future date and a time draft is required among other documents this payment order is called acceptance payments. If it is acceptable only by importer it is called trade acceptance. However, it is usually either a bank acceptance (bank accepting the draft) or bank guaranteed acceptance where (usually importer's) bank avalizes the draft which is accepted by the importer, of which bank guarantees payment in case importer does not pay at the maturity date of the draft.

In all these payment terms either one of the party is in a disadvantageous position. Even in documents against payment term, exporter is not sure whether importer will pay for the documents value and receive the documents in return. There is no enforcement on importer to the so, plus importer might go bankruptcy etc after sales contract and may not be able to pay, ICC 522 says that collecting bank will return documents if not heard within 60 days. There comes documentary credit payment a conditional payment order which protects both parties as follows.

DOCUMENTARY CREDIT

Documentary Credit (commonly known as letter of credit) is a payment method used in international trade. Documents play a very important role in international trade not only for payment terms, it is important for both importer and exporter because international trade is based on documentation for customs clearance as well. As the name 'documentary credit' itself is self-explanatory, documentary credit payment is a payment method where documents stipulated in letter of credit are presented in compliance payment is affected by the issuing bank. For these reasons, 'Documentary Credit' will be used hereinafter in this chapter.

There are two main groups of documentary credits (letters of credit) namely, Commercial documentary credit (letter of credit) and Standby documentary credit (letter of credit). The main difference between

Commercial Documentary Credit and Standby Documentary Credit can be defined as, 'Commercial' term inserted to distinguish from standby documentary credit, however sometimes the word 'documentary' is inserted and used as 'documentary letters of credit' is used which is not correct as 'document' is required in all letters of credit, in other words they are all documentary (Byrne, 2012).

In other words, the difference between commercial documentary credits and standby documentary credits are that commercial documentary credits are payable if conditions of documentary credit are met and stipulated documents are presented in compliance with documentary credit. However, in standby documentary credit, it is the opposite, in other words, if the conditions of standby documentary credit are not met by the beneficiary, bank will pay. Why does commercial documentary credit guarantee payment upon meeting conditions of documentary credit and why does standby documentary credit pay when the conditions of standby documentary credit are not met?

That is because especially in United States banking system, standby documentary credits are used in lieu of letter of guarantees. Letter of guarantees guarantee payment if applicant is in breach of a contract, like the following cases if importer does not affect payment of goods imported, if exporter does not refund advance payment, nor ship the goods, issuing bank of standby documentary credit has to pay upon presentation of e.g. a declaration signed by beneficiary stating that applicant is in breach of contract.

Whereelse in commercial documentary credits it is the contrary, if the beneficiary meets the conditions of documentary credit and presents stipulated documents in compliance with letter of credit, issuing bank of documentary credit has to pay.

Standby documentary credit can be issued as subject to ICC publication (ISP 98 - International Standby Practices) however if requested they can be issued as subject to UCP 600 as well, because both types of documentary credits require documentation presentation for payment. Documentary credit users must be aware of difference between commercial documentary credit and standby documentary credit and must be able to differentiate the difference especially if standby documentary credit is issued subject to ICC Uniform Customs and Practice for Documentary Credits-UCP 600 as well.

Documentary Credits are subject to Uniform Customs and Practice for Documentary Credits rules which are are not compulsory rules. In other words, these rules are not laws applied by governments. These rules are voluntarily accepted by importers and exporters and other related parties like banks, applicants (importers), beneficiaries (exporters), carriers, insurers etc. These rules are self-regulated industry rules issued by ICC (International Chamber of Commerce) located in Paris. ICC is an organisation consisting of local chamber of commerces of countries all over the World.

The first letter of credit rules was used since 1933. ICC has revised UCP several times since 1933. The latest version has been published in 2008. Documentary credit were used in ancient Egypt and Babylon and were common in 19th century, especially in Europe. It has been started to be used in United States as trade increased with Europe and 'letter of credit' has been started to be used worldwide. Documentary credit format has been started to be used for standby letter of credit, that is a bank guarantee which is subject to UCP 600 as well.

Documentary credit does not have to be issued by banks only and they can be issued by an individual or a by a company as well. As a nice example for this case is the hand-written letter and signed by Thomas Jefferson, the president of United States on 4th of July, 1803 in favour of explorers Captains Lewis and Clark for their expolaration of West Part of US (ICC, 2008). President Jefferson, authorised 'the explorers, Captain Lewis and Captain Clark' to draw on the United States Secretaries of State, Treasury, Consuls etc declared that the drawn amounts would be paid at the payment date.

In 19th century, merchants used to travel all around the world to find new markets and to sell their goods or buy raw materials etc. for trading. However, it was not safe to travel with large amount of cash therefore the merchants were offered a traveller's letter of credit by their banks, which enabled them to get cash from their bank's correspondent banks during their overseas visits to find new markets. The merchants with the traveller's 'letter of credit' applied to their bank's correspondent banks in overseas and applied for cash, if necesary. The origin traveller's 'letter of credit' document was delivered to the merchant. In addition to the 'letter of credit' the bank issued an introduction letter addressed and sent in advance to their overseas correspondent banks introducing the merchant and request them to pay upto the amount mentioned in letter of credit document. The original 'letter of credit' stated that the amount paid by the correspondent bank to the merchant, not exceeding the maximum amount of the 'letter of credit' and within the expiry date under the said 'letter of credit' would be paid by themselves i.e. the issuing bank. Each payment details (amount, date, etc.) under the traveller's 'letter of credit' would be written on the original letter of credit document and the merchant would keep the original letter of credit document.

Letter of credit issued by banks made merchants' lives easier so that they could make necessary arrangements for goods to be shipped from overseas without carrying large amounts of cash. Origin of 'letter' come from travellers 'letter of credit' issued by banks for their correspondents to enable their customers/merchants to receive money in their overseas trips for new markets and are widely used today in international trade as a payment method.

When importer and exporter agree on payment term as 'documentary credit' (letter of credit) they also agree upon documents required as well. Documentary credit issued by importer's bank covers the required documents to be presented for payment. In other words, documentary credit is a conditional payment order issued by issuing bank which is usually the importer's bank and advised to exporter, via advising bank, usually which is exporter's bank. Upon receipt of documentary credit from issuing bank, exporter has got a conditional payment order that is once he presents documents in compliance with documentary credit and complies with the conditions of letter of credit, issuing bank has to pay to exporter. This is a safe method which protects both importer and exporter because importer is sure that issuing bank will pay only upon receipt of documents in compliance with documentary credit and exporter is sure that he will paid once he presents documentary credit compliance documents whether importer may not be able to pay or not due to financial risks. Documentary credit rules are subject to UCP 600, the Uniform Customs and Practise issued by International Chamber of Commerce (ICC) latest revision published in 2007.

As documentary credit is a conditional payment order issued by a bank (usually buyer's or applicant's bank), in favour of beneficiary (seller). It is an irrevocable undertaking (in other words can not be cancelled). Issuing bank guarantees payment to beneficiary upon presentation of documents in complaince with required documents stated in documentary credit and if other conditions of documentary credit (like presented within latest presentation date and within expiry date etc) are met by beneficiary.

Documentary credit are not used only for import and export purposes. They can be used for services as well. It is a payment method used in international trade, although there is no restriction that it can not be used locally, if both parties agree, letter of credit payment method can be used in local payments, within the same country as well.

It can be issued by an individual or any company as well. If beneficiary accepts of course. As documents and conditions will be controlled by buyer/applicant himself, a beneficiary may not accept this. The main reason for choosing documentary credit payment method is that beneficiary/seller/exporter does not trust buyer and wants to make sure that payment will be affected upon presentation of documentary credit compliance documents and other documentary credit conditions are met.

Therefore, it is not a common practise that buyer company issues its own documentary credit in favour of beneficiary/seller. Issuing bank (applicant's bank) issuing documentary credit via (usually) authenticated swift is worldwide common practise. Sometimes due to political risks, country risks etc beneficiary might insist on another bank (usually in beneficiary's bank) to confirm said letter of credit, which means, the second bank will also pay upon credit complaince documents presentation and other documentary credit conditions are met.

Process of a simple letter of credit process can be summarized as four steps, four parties as follows;

(1) Sales Contract between importer and exporter, covering payment term as documentary credit, required documents, other terms like latest shipment date, latest presentation date, expiry date etc. Sales contract is beginning of process and actually documentary credit is a mirror of sales contract. Therefore, parties must be careful with conditions of sales contract to avoid documentary risks (Meral, 2018).

(2) Issuance of Documentary Credit by applicant's bank, as per applicant's instruction and and sends conditional payment order, i.e. documentary credit to usually beneficiary's (exporter) bank via authenticated swift to be advised to exporter.

(3) Shipment of goods by exporter (if documentary credit is accepted with conditions and stipulated documents) and presentation of documents in compliance with documentary credit to advising bank to be presented to issuing bank or for payment if advising bank has confirmed documentary credit.

(4) Payment if presented documents are found in compliance with documentary credit, and other conditions of documentary credit are met by exporter and delivers original documents to importer against payment for customs clearance. Bank is obliged to make payment to beneficiary even if applicant fails payment.
(5) Advising bank effects payment to beneficiary's account.

Documentary credit payment is preferred by both parties, importer and exporter because exporter knows that he will be paid if he presents documentary credit compliance documents and meets documentary credit terms. Importer knows that payment will be affected if exporter meets documentary credit terms and presents stipulated documents in complaince with documentary credit. Both parties trust their banks and banks proceed transaction as per Uniform Customs and Practice for Documentary Credits (UCP 600) rules.

UCP 600-UNIFORM CUSTOMS AND PRACTICE FOR DOCUMENTARY CREDITS

Documentary credit payment terms are subject to articles of UCP 600 (Uniform Customs and Practice for Documentary Credits). The first UCP (Uniform Customs and Practice for Documentary Credits) rules were published in 1933. With globalization increase international trade has also increased. ICC to update (International Chamber of Commerce) revised the Uniform Customs and Practice for Documentary Credits rules accordingly. The latest revision, which was the sixth revision of Uniform Customs and Practice for Documentary Credits, namely UCP 600 has been started to be used by as of July 2007.

The said rules are prepared by the Banking Commission of ICC which tries to standardize rules for world wide common practise. There are 39 articles in UCP 600, however any clause might be excluded with mutual agreement of importer and exporter.

However, it is strongly recommended that both parties must try to avoid to exclude these clauses as all clauses are prepared and accepted after long discussions and accepted only after all the related, interested parties' opinions. Exclusion request and acceptance of the exclusion request might end up with a loss of one of the parties.

Documentary credit is issued by applicant's (importer) bank. It is a reflection of sales contract conditions. Exporter must peruse the conditions of documentary credit and the documents stipulated in the documentary credit whether he can comply with the conditions and whether he can present the required documents in compliance. If exporter has any hesitations with the conditions and stipulated documents, exporter must request importer to amend the said conditions.

Documentary credits are payable against documents required in documentary credit are presented in compliance with the documentary credit and if other conditions of documentary credit are met. Therefore, if exporter can not meet the conditions of documentary credit exporter must request an amendment from importer, to instruct the issuing bank to amend the said clause.

Documents Presentation in Documentary Credit

Documentary credit issuance and payment processes are handled by banks electronically via swift system. Presentation of documents are presented electronically for examination within banks because international trade departments are located in head offices, therefore branches scan documents and send them to centralize international trade department in their head office. However, original of documents are sent via special courrier to head office for final checking and sent to issuing bank by international trade department. Presentation of documents plays a vital role in documentary credit payment process since merchants started using documentary credit payment term. Payment is affected against / upon presentation of complaince documents stipulated in documentary credit.

UCP 600-Uniform Customs and Practice for Documentary Credits requires that if there is no specified presentation period in documentary credit, beneficiary must present documents within maximum 21 calender-days after shipment within documentary credit expiry date (Article 14). Banks must check presented documents within five business days following presentation date and decide whether the documents are in compliance with documentary credit or not.

Original Bill of Lading/Transport Document Presentation Rule in Documentary Credits

Documentary credit presentation rule (Article 14) latest presentation date 21 days after shipment date requires original bill of lading/transport document to be presented. In other words, presentation period starts with presentation of original/unique negotiable bill of lading/transport document for presentation period to start.

As per UCP rules, presentation date is verified with presentation of original transport document. Original transport document is the most important document in documentary credits. Original bill of lading is a negotiable document. Bill of lading shows title of goods, in other words ownership of goods. Negotiable documents are endorsable documents and with delivery and endorsement new bona fide holder is the owner.

This rule protects both importer and exporter because importer knows that payment will be affected only after shipment as presentation requires original shipping/transportation document showing that goods are shipped.

Transport document, original bill of lading usually issued other than exporter and importer, are issued to order of bank which enables controlling ownership and title of goods. Exporter is protected as well because payment is affected before goods are delivered upon presentation of original shipping / transportation document showing that goods are shipped.

Although other transport documents are not negotiable documents however in practise, transportation companies take into consideration of whom original transportation document is issued in the name of to deliver goods. So, does customs authorities for example Turkish Customs officials do not permit clearance of goods through customs unless the endorsed transport document is presented whether it is original bill of lading which is negotiable and endorsable or any other transport document.

One of the reasons for banks to prefer negotiable documents, i.e. original bill of lading is that original bill of lading issued in the name of or to the order of themselves are used as a secondary collateral. They control possession of the goods, as original bill of lading represents ownership, title of the goods during the process. Therefore, documentary credits usually request original, unique, negotiable paper documents such as bill of lading issued or endorsed to order of themselves, thereby controlling goods ownership as carrier has to deliver goods to holder of original bill of lading of whose name bill of lading is issued.

To avoid non-payment or delays due to discrepancy of late presentation or non-presentation of original shipping document, parties must agree at the beginning about presentation of original bill of lading/

transport document. Paper-based, original bill of lading/transport document presentation is required to be in compliance with UCP600 article 14 in documentary credit payment term.

Banks have started long ago electronic issuance and payment process of documentary credit with telegraphic transmission. At the beginning, during transition period banks used both methods, that is, they sent the authenticated documentary credit followed with the paper backed original via post. However, as time passed, with the common practise accepted by all parties, banks started to send authenticated documentary texts, with a note that no original document would follow and that the authenticated documentary credit message would be the original. Documentary credits are issued with no signature, no paper original etc. are used worldwide with authenticated swift message transmissions today. Payments are affected electronically (telegraphic transfer) via swift sytem since 1977. Before swift payments were affected via telex was used between banks with manuel authentication tables. Today swift system automatically authenticated messages between banks. Today there are eleven thousand banks and financial institutions are members of the SWIFT system all over the world with an average of 28 million message per day (swift.com).

Although related legal frame is already published by ICC e-UCP-Supplement to the Uniform Customs and Practise for Documentary Credits for Electronic Presentation, paper-back presentation is still preferable by all parties.

Original of negotiable documents presentation is main issue of documentary credits payments. In addition to legal requirements of an 'original' negotiable documents, it is a legal requirement of documentary credits that original bill of lading/transport documentation is required to comply with presentation period condition of documentary credit as well.

Documentary credit process compared to other payment methods are more complex and requires specialisation for presented documentary examination. Although it is safe and protecting both parties, subject to common rules of UCP accepted worldwide, due to discrepant documents presented, payments may not be paid immediately upon presentation of documents. To avoid documentary risks both parties must be cautious.

Banks, by issuing documentary credit are aware of the potential risks and that once having sent documentary credit swift message know that independent from importer whether importer's financial status might be worse and may not be able to pay goods value upon credit complaince documents presentation, issuing bank itself has to pay documents value.

However, documentary credit is one of the most important basic finance technique of sellers/manufacturers especially in developing countries, where small manufacturers can not afford other alternative finance methods. Upon receipt of a documentary credit from importer's bank, whether deferred or sight payment, manufacturer or seller knows that upon credit compliance documents presentation and meeting conditions of documentary credit, issuing bank will affect payment independent from applicant/buyer. That is actually a bank guarantee for exporter. Even if it is a deferred documentary credit, exporter always can ask for discount of documentary credit, where he can receive payment before maturity date. Which will enable importer to pay at maturity whereelse exporter to receive upon presentation of stipulated documents in complaince with documentary credit. Actually, in this case documentary credit is financing both parties.

With globalisation, innovation, international trade increase helped developing countries to integrate with other countries via international trade. However, parties not knowing each other, not trusting each other, prefer payment methods which enabled them to bypass this barrier. Documentary credit is one of the best methods for parties who do not know and who do not trust each other and especially for manufacturers too who can not afford other payment methods.

ELECTRONIC PRESENTATION OF DOCUMENTS IN DOCUMENTARY CREDITS

Innovation with information technology changed everything in our lives as all sectors in economy, including international trade. With globalisation, digital certificates/documents have started replacing paper-based documents. Having foreseen trend increase ICC (International Chamber of Commerce) has started working on electronic presentation of digital documents and ICC published e-UCP as a supplement to UCP 600 (Uniform Customs and Practice for Documentary Credits) and named it as eUCP-Supplement to the Uniform Customs and Practice for Documentary Credits for Electronic Presentation of electronic documents submission of documentary credit documents in April 2002.

However electronic documentation presentation is not up to the expectation and majority of presentations are still manuelly paper-based documents. International trade documentation is complicated, involves too many parties along with importer and exporter, importer's bank, exporter's bank, insurance company, transportation company, chamber of commerces, expertise companies, customs consultant, customs authorities etc. and process of electronic presentation and paper-based presentation of documents are completely different. The standards for electronic documentation are not clear yet. Furthermore, paper documentation presentation has been used for years and trustable, and it is not easy for the parties to trust and use electronic documentation.

e-UCP-Supplement to the Uniform Customs and Practise for Documentary Credits for Electronic Presentation

As a supplement to UCP, eUCP allows both electronic and paper-based document presentation. It enables digital certificates equivalent of paper-based documents electronic presentation. In other words, electronic presentation is not in conflict with paper-based presentation, there is no need to make an amendment for electronic presentation. When taken into consideration together UCP and e UCP provide necessary rules for electronic presentation.

eUCP does not need for specific private technologies or specific systems to process electronic presentation easier. In other words, the technology and systems to be used in electronic presentation as per eUCP are subject to mutual agreement of documentary credit parties. eUcp, as a supplement to UCP600, is in compliance with UCP 600 except electronic presentation clauses. To avoid confusion between eUCP and UCP clauses, the letter 'e' is inserted in front of the numbers for eUCP clauses. The eUCP rules accompany UCP 600 rules of documentary credit issued by ICC.

Documentary credit issuance and payment is already handled electronically via swift system by the banks. Although eUCP has been published for electronic presentation, majority of documents are still paper based presented. Main reason for this is the unique, original, negotiable documents presentation requirement in letter of credits. Therefore, eUCP is a supplement of UCP600 and allows both paper and electronic presentation of documents under documentary credits.

UCP vs. EUCP

- eUCP is only a supplement to UCP 600 and must be used with UCP600, that is if a documentary credit is issued subject to eUCP, it is automatically subject to UCP 600, and there is no need to clarify or mention it in documentary credit text.
- A documentary credit issued subject to eUCP, articles of eUCP is valid or suppress UCP 600 rules if application of rules have different outcomes/results.
- If a documentary credit subject to eUCP credit allows beneficiary to choose either electronic presentation or paper-based presentation and if beneficiary chooses to present paper documents, then documentary credit is subject to UCP only.
- If a letter of credit issued subject to eUCP however only paper-based presentation is allowed, then UCP rules will apply to presented documents.
- Presentation place in eUCP is the mail address or the web site given in documentary credit.
    - Presentation place in UCP is the bank given in 41A available with bank in documentary credit text.
- Documents are received digitally via e-mail or web site in eUCP.
    - Documents are received physically, manually by the 41A available with bank in UCP.
- Documents can be presented partially or all of them electronically in eUCP,
    - Partially paper based presented documents are automatically subject to UCP.
- If all documents are paper based presented, they are subject to UCP.
- Electronic/digital document must be in any format (like word, exml, pdf) which can be opened and examined with the bank's system.
- Electronic presentation does not have to presented only with one presentation, at the same time, electronic documents can be presented seperately within presentation period given in documentary credit.
- Upon completion of seperate presentation of documents, beneficiary must give a notice to the bank that presentation has been completed (hereinafter called as 'letter of completeness' document) with documentary credit reference
- If 'Completeness notice' is not received by the bank, it is accepted as 'presentation is not completed' and bank has no responsibility, beneficiary is responsible from 'not presenting' documents, although all documents might have been presented separately.
- Electronic presentation must be authenticated, in other words with pin numbers etc like internet banking otherwise in other words if there is no authentication, presentation must not be done.
- If banking system is off/down and presentation can not be made, it is considered as 'force majeur' reason and the bank is accepted as closed (like weekend, official holiday, etc.). When bank system starts working and presentation is completed, it is considered as documents are presented the following business day.
- 'Completeness notice' document might be paper-based presented.
- If there is a link in an electronically presented document and if the link does not work, it is discussion and solution, future study recommendation, key term explanatitionas 'discrepant document'.
- If nominated bank, examines electronically presented documents and sends them to issuing bank, it is considered that electronically presented documents are presented with authentication.
- If banks define a format for presentation and upon presentation if bank can not open the defined format, bank can not reject the said documents.

- Examination period is the same with UCP, within five business days following 'letter of completeness' date.
- If presentation period is extended due to bank's system failure, examination period starts following next banking day, after the bank's system starts working and presentation is completed (following business day after 'Completeness notice').
- Electronic presentation can be rejected by the bank, if does not receive any instruction within 30 days, bank can return document or can delete electronically presented documents in eUCP.
    - Bank sends notice of refusal (MT734) in UCP
- If multiple originals are required, original digital document in the system is sufficient.
- In transport documents, date of sending is considered as issuance date of transport if there is no other dates like issuance date/notation date etc.
- If electronic/digital document is corrupted and can not be examined, bank requests re-presentation (re-submission) of the said document, the examination period is frozen / pending till the next resubmission date and upon re-submission, the following business day starts for the remaining dates of examination period (if re-presentation was requested on the 2.day, with re-presentation the remaining examination days are 3 business days, not five business days after presentation).
- If re-presentation is not done within 30 days, it is considered as not presented.
- eUCP version 1.1 can be used with UCP 600 and is a supplement document.
- eUCP can be used for both paper-based presentation and electronic presentation, or fully electronic presentation which enables a flexible approach, during transition period where parties will be used to the application.

eUCP articles can be summarized as follows:

1. UCP 600 articles which do not have an equivalent article in eUCP and which can be applied to an eUCP article can be applied.
2. UCP Articles 4-9 and article 12 remain unchanged.
3. eUCP clauses which do not contradict with UCP 600, give additional information about e.g. related with electronic / digital documents but do not affect or contradict with paper-based documents subject to UCP 600 like in eUCP, article e3(a) which defines terms of eUCP.
4. eUCP articles related with only electronic/digital documents (e.g. e11 and e12) so there is no change with UCP 600 articles under a documentary credit subject to eUCP.

SOLUTIONS AND RECOMMENDATIONS

Although ICC, International Chamber of Commerce, has done in advance forecasting the e-business boom, electronic/digital documentation, has released original version of electronic presentation in 2002 as a supplement to UCP 500 which was latest version of the year. eUCP was designed for both paper and electronic presentation for authenticity. At the same time for refusal of original, unique document (i.e. bill of lading/transport document, negotiable document, showing the title/ownership of the goods) by banks etc. which might lead to non-payment or delay in payment.

However, paper presentation of documentary credit documents are still widely used. Literature review resulted with no statistics found for electronic presentation. Only Bryne referred a case (KEB,

2010) where Korean Exchange Bank, has issued a letter of credit, subject to eUCP, in 2010. However electronic presentation of bill of lading, insurance and analysis and weight certificate presentation via Bolero's trade firm was not permitted by the bank.

Bolero, Electronic Bills of Lading (eB/Ls)

Electronic bill of lading has been used since 1980s (BCF, 2016), but due to the reasons already mentioned above in this chapter, banks and importers insist on receiving original, unique, paper bill of lading. Bill of lading, which is a paper negotiable document, showing title of goods prevent/avoid electronic bills of lading to be used worldwide. Although it was expected that with Bolero-SWIFT integration, there would be an increase in electronic presentation of bill of ladings, the majority of presentations are still paper-backed.

Another reason other than simply requesting original, signed, paper negotiable document, is the investment costs because system integration with Bolero is a cost which must be born by banks, importers, exporters, transportation companies etc.

Another reason might be bank's cost and charges which are reflected to customers. On paper-based documentation, of which they are accustomed, they do not pay swift charges. Although swift is non-profit center and do not charge their members extra, banks put additional mark up charges of which customers refrain using swift in their transactions if they have an alternative option during their transactions.

Banks must consider that electronic/digital documents are cheaper, to archieve, easy to process, secure and actually cheaper and that their investments will pay back in the long run for the customers as well avoiding courrier charges and speeding up transactions. Time is money, shorter process, cheaper cost.

Another important aspect of electronic/digital document presentation is to avoid fraud transactions. It is very difficult to differentiate an original document from a fake/fraud document because fraud documents are nearly exactly the same as the original document.

However, in electronic / digital documentation presentation, especially the most important document, bill of lading/transport document electronic version namely Electronic Bills of Lading (eB/Ls) which will be presented via swift bolero integration system will be much safer for banks, importers and all other related parties.

First of all, swift, of which 16 trillion dollars import, 16 trillion dollars export, total of 32 trillion dollars of total international trade volume communications are all effected via swift system. Their first priority is the security of these messages sent and received daily all over the world. They are trying hard to standardize message types. They are a non-profit organisation, working for international trade faciliation, with their technical infra structure and safe and standardized rules.

As a summary, eUCP standard rules application was a beginning to fill a gap in international trade to prevent paper documentation and motivate for electronic documentation however only ICC's effort is not enough. All parties involved must work hard, force to change legislation, systems infrastructure for application of said rules. E-trade has already increased and will increase more and more. It will be much cheaper with electronic presentation.

FUTURE RESEARCH DIRECTIONS

Reasons of paper-presentation or electronic presentatioin of documents under documentary credits might change according to countries. Future researches investigating in different countries might find out different reasons.

CONCLUSION

With the bloom of e-trade, electronic / digital documentation, e-international trade has increased and helped countries to connect with global integration. Therefore, ICC has published standard rules for electronic presentation. With parallel to this, ICC, namely International Chamber of Commerce, has updated international trade rules which are widely voluntarily accepted rules all over the world. Within this context, eUCP rules as a supplement to UCP, Uniform Customs and Practise rules of documentary credit were revised in 2007 as well. Market has a higher expectation for equivalence digital/electronic documents of paper docments. The aim was to meet the demand of the market for electronic/digital documents presentation of international trade documents under documentary credits.

This chapter aims to clarify the differences of paper-based documentation presentation and electronic presentation of documentary credit documents.

eUCP is restricted only with documentary credit documents presentation and does not cover other electronic documentation and majority of documents are still paper-based presented.

The main reason for this is that original, unique, paper negotiable documents like bill of lading / transport document, draft/bill of exchange etc are required in international trade and it is very difficult to change these in a short time. Therefore, ICC has issued eUCP rules which enables partial electronic and partial paper-based presentations, to be used with UCP which will help parties to get used to with e-presentation during transition period.

To increase electronic presentation which will faciliate international trade and increase international trade the following handicaps must be handled;

- Furthermore digital/electronic documents are not valid all over the world.
- Legislation does not allow electronic equivalant documents of original, unique, negotiable documents, which represent the title, ownership of the goods, which are used as secondary collateral in documentary credit.
- These negotiable original, unique paper documents of commercial documentary credits can not be presented electronically.
- All related parties, legal entities, institutions, banks, local chamber of commerces, transportation companies must motivate local authorities to update local legislation accordingly and motivate importers and exporters to use digital equivalant of these documents and electronic presentation to speed up transactions.

As they start electronic presentation even partially and it will help red tape reduction and speed up transactions and increase international trade volumes. Like payments and issuance of letter of credits, electronic presentation will also inrease immediately after these obstacles are handled. This will help the management of import and export to be much more easier and it will increase international trade volume all over the world, via international trade faciliation will help integration to globalization of trader countries.

REFERENCES

Byrne, J. E. (2012). The Four Stages in the Electrification of Letters of Credit. Geo. *Masan J. Int'l Com. L., 3,* 253-275.

Civelek, M. E., Çemberci, M., Uca, N., Çelebi, Ü., & Özalp, A. (2017). Challenges of Paperless Trade Redesign of the Foreign Trade Processes and Bundling Functions of Traditional Documents. *International Business Research*, *10*(2), 74. doi:10.5539/ibr.v10n2p74

Collyer, G., (2007), The guide to documentary credits, published by IFS School of Finance.

ICC. (1995) Uniform Rules for Collections, ICC Publication No. 522E.

ICC. (2002). eUCP-The Supplement to the Uniform Customs and Practice for Documentary Credits for Electronic Presentation.

ICC. (2007). *Practice for Documentary Credits, 2007 Revision, ICC Publication No. 600*. International Chamber of Commerce.

KEB, Korean Exchange Bank. (2010). Issues First Paperless LC Under eUCP, TRADE FIN., Dec. 14, 2010.

Meral, Y. (2018). Documentary Risk in International Trade. In *Strategic Design and Innovative Thinking in Business Operations* (pp. 413–431). Cham, Switzerland: Springer. doi:10.1007/978-3-319-77622-4_21

Swift.com. (n.d.). Retrieved from https://www.swift.com/about-us/highlights-2017

Weber, R.H. (2007). IT Markets, Asia's Chance for Revitalizing the WTO, 37 Hong Kong L. J. 185.

KEY TERMS AND DEFINITIONS

Bill of lading: An original, unique, signed, paper negotiable document, showing title/ownership of goods

Commercial Documentary Credit: Documentary credit used usually for goods import and export.

Documentary Credit: (Letter of Credit) Payment Method: International Trade payment method, where importer's bank sends exporter a conditional payment order, when exporter complies with documentary credit and presents documentary credit complaince documents, bank pays exporter independent from importer.

Documents: Documents used in international trade for customs clearance, required by importer. There are approximately more than 3000 documents in international trade.

Electronic Bills of Lading (eB/Ls, Bolero): With Bolero-SWIFT integration, expected to be used more in international trade, but due to lack of system investments, not used as expected.

Electronic Presentation: Electronic presentation of electronic / digital documents via system or e-mail given in documentary credit.

ICC: (International Chamber of Commerce): A non-governmental organisation, located in Paris, sets international trade rules, worldwide voluntarily accepted.

Paper-Based Presentation: Presentation of documents, which are original, paper, signed, usually negotiable issued to the order to the bank nominated by issuing bank.

Standby Documentary Credit: Documentary credit used for letter of guarantee purposes, like standby documentary credit for performance, for advance payment, for bid etc.

Chapter 8
E-Retailing Practices in Mobile Marketing:
The Case of Getir Application

Ihsan Eken
https://orcid.org/0000-0002-0401-8545
İstanbul Medipol University, Turkey

Basak Gezmen
İstanbul Medipol University, Turkey

ABSTRACT

Today, the Internet has become a frequently-used tool in trading information, products, and services. Together with the transformations in the Internet, new media, and mobile technologies, the retail sector is also developing its service area. With the development of mobile technologies, retail giants determine the expectations and needs of their consumers in a good and fast way with artificial intelligence applications. This situation transforms it into purchasing behavior with the reflection of customer preferences on products and increasing personalization. One of the key issues in the mobile retail sector is to make the purchasing behavior permanent by ensuring the satisfaction of consumers. In the study, Getir application, a mobile marketing application was analyzed with focus group research technique performed on university students selected in accordance with certain criteria. As a result of the research, the availability, awareness, and satisfaction status of the participants on Getir application were revealed.

INTRODUCTION

Communication technologies, which are seen as the most rapid development area of our age, together with the changes and transformations on societies, also provide the basis for the formation of a different culture. Nowadays, the possibility of distributing information very easily and quickly on the axis of new communication technologies encourages institutions to be positioned in different areas in many areas.

DOI: 10.4018/978-1-7998-0035-4.ch008

With different environments, individuals are offered the opportunity to be active in technology and various sharing areas are produced in this direction. A rapidly evolving technology has allowed the devices such as radio, television, computers, smartphones to be used with the Internet. At this point, many studies are being carried out in order to provide instant and effective communication to wider audiences especially in marketing. Organizations use mobile applications to inform their customers about their products and services and campaigns in accordance to their target audience. In the face of the rapidly evolving and continuously developing competitive environment, the institutions that constantly renew themselves develop their marketing and communication strategies in this context.

New communication technologies, especially the use of the Internet and the use of mobile telephones, have greatly improved in the area of traditional marketing. A brand new business area where digital tools are used extensively with the digital marketing shaped under the name of interactive platforms. In this new system, where the Internet is treated as a global market, advertising and sales activities and mobile marketing brands have been included in the marketing strategies.

As digital individuals who spend a large part of their daily lives on mobile phones, now they have a phobia such as inability of being without mobile telephones. In this context, in the sense of digital dependence, individuals no longer spend a moment without their mobile phones with them. This enabled many organizations to start running sales and marketing strategies through mobile phones. On-demand application is also functioning in metropolitan life at the point of solution to the individual's fast pace of life. The application aims to provide the individuals' needs in an instant and high-quality manner.

In the research section of the study, Getir application, which is a mobile marketing application, is analyzed with the focus group research technique performed on university students selected in accordance with certain criteria. As a result of the research, it was aimed to reveal the availability, awareness and satisfaction status of the participants on Getir application.

NEW TREND MOBILE MARKETING IN THE GLOBALIZING WORLD

New communication technologies and many new concepts, which meet societies and trying to make sense of them, emerge in the axis of social changes and transformations at a dizzying pace. Gambling underlines the rhetoric that societies can no longer be treated with old concepts and theories and it states that after the industry western societies have become post-modern and even post-history (Kumar, 1995). These concepts, which are used to express the new world order and are constantly renewed, constitute the center of the debate on globalization. Each society develops a technological infrastructure whose form belongs to them. The characteristic of information age related to computer and computer-oriented developments, microchip, which is the main element of information technologies, consists of almost all information. While the industrial society is shaped by the presence of steel and the products connected to it; it is the concept of information production that determines the development criterion of the information society. In this context, Bozkurt focuses on the determinism of the processing and distribution of the production of information and its distinctiveness from the industrial society. (Bozkurt, 1997) In the process of transition to an information society, the transformation is not only in the product services produced but also in the quality of human resources. The unqualified worker based on the arm power of the industrial society is now replaced by the information worker. Human resources are among the most important competitive instruments in terms of enterprises. The necessity of having knowledge about marketing philosophy, aims, and applications of enterprises has emerged. While industrial products are emerging as tangible assets at the center of industrial society, in information societies, the information itself, the concepts under the leadership of the creativity and the thought become important (Köseoğlu, 2006).

The dazzling developments in technology and globalization deeply affect all societies, predict new lifestyles by changing many things. Local habits are broken with striking developments in information and communication technology and the globalization phenomenon that is expanding our common living spaces. At this point, individuals are directed to a common lifestyle by going beyond the national borders. The concept of globalization, which primarily takes place in minds as an economic concept, is a concept that goes far beyond economy and finance. (Ulugay, 2001). The power underlying the phenomenon of globalization, which has a long history of development, is triggered by economic power. Globalization comes to existence on the paths of information and communication technologies. Today's globalization is spreading interactively over hundreds of thousands of channels satellite technologies, Internet technologies, mobile communications, stock market transactions, radio, tv, telephone, fax, www, e-mail systems, real-time chat rooms, interactive programs that allow all kinds of electronic data transfer. The phenomenon of globalization, which has continued to show its impact rapidly since the 1980s, also causes changes in marketing.

Globalization, which creates new opportunities for businesses, also brings with it many threats. Today, businesses are obliged to compete continuously in a hazy business environment of the concepts that are in intricate structure with each other such as globalization, the information society, new economy in a constantly changing. The new competitive conditions have made it necessary to create and implement new approaches in marketing. Globalization has brought new types of consumer models to life. In the face of new consumer types and competitive conditions, today's enterprises have to be very fast in order not to stay behind their competitors in adapting to the environment. Businesses that cannot provide fast and effective marketing solutions will be destined to disappear. While globalization offers new market opportunities, it makes it compulsory for enterprises to enter into a new market where other businesses will take place. This fast and competitive area eliminates the distinction of the national and international market. In the face of the new conditions of the globalizing world, another point that businesses face is the emergence of an increase in the number of brands centered on the same target group. The consumer population, which faces many types, is now looking for brands that offer the best prices or campaigns but may prefer another product at the end of the campaign. The digital environment can provide individuals with appropriate facilities for price researches. Research and development opportunities increase thanks to new communication technologies however, they eliminate opportunities to compete based on product differentiation. In this context, it requires an integrated way of sending messages at all points which will ensure the continuation of interaction between the consumers and the business with more promotional efforts (Köseoğlu, 2006). Philip Kotler, considered to be the marketing guru, also refers that companies which invent new ways of delivering value to their target markets will gain premiums today These companies can be defined as companies with marketing vision (Kotler, 2011). In the 2000s, Kotler refers to the cyberspace phenomenon, which will lead to an era in which trade is very much automated and easier. During this period, companies will be able to connect to each other and their customers continuously through virtual networks. It will be possible to transfer information from one end of the world to another without cost. Time and distances, causing huge obstacles to the cost and trade in the old times, will soon become shorter and the merchant mentality will be eliminated. Companies will be able to easily identify potential buyers, and consumers will be able to identify the best sellers and products more easily and meet their expectations in a short way. Along with the digital revolution, it has been possible to reach the companies that started with small capital and niche companies from all over the world (Kotler, 2011, p. 286).

The first stage in the marketing process is the emergence of the customer needs the next stage is the development of products or services for these needs. After this stage, two parallel processes are involved. These are: Presenting the product or service and communication and transmission of the product or service to the customer. Considering each of the marketing stages, it is not wrong to say that all these marketing sub-components are in an irreversible change with digital life. In Emre Açıkel and Mehmet Çelikol's naming "dijitoloji", along with being an evolution in the digital marketing process, dijitoloji is also a revolution for brands that understand themselves well and succeed in changing their genes in this direction. (Açıkel & Çelikol, 2014).

The advantages of new communication technologies now allow communication to be produced both from the manufacturer to the consumer and provides the ability to produce multiple options. In this way, more participation of consumers can be achieved. New technologies support the realization of fragmentation and decentralization, which are at the center of postmodern features. Instead of short-lived campaign messages and fast-consumed messages, the messages and information that can be stored are on the agenda. Being able to advertise and purchase at the same time puts sales and distribution, from marketing applications, into interaction with advertising (Odabaşı, 2014).

The history, which has lost its tangible base together with local time, is not something that has accelerated today. It is actually the plain truth. The moment of a new earthly time that has recently gained importance eliminates the reality of distances (Virilio, 2003). The speed captured with new communication technologies also changes the concepts of time and space. As Ulugay states in his discourse, it is increasingly difficult to find persistent and reliable reference points in a world in which everything has become liquid in a sense. Consumers are dragged from one place to another without knowing which values to hold on to. The keywords that make a premium in the new environments that shine as a result of change and transformation in today's environment are motility, flowability, and mobility. In particular, mental mobility and adaptability to changing conditions are decisive. It does not enable those who cannot adapt to this situation to continue their lives under market conditions. (Ulugay, 2001).

Kimberly Clark's CMO Clive Sirkin says that he believes in marketing in a digital world, not digital marketing. Now marketing in the digital world is becoming a digital specialty, and digital marketing is tagged as Internet sites, e-mail, online advertising, search engine marketing and social media (Brinker, 2017). With the new communication technologies of smartphones and tablets take their place on the Internet in a very fast way with their constantly renewed shapes and search engines such as Google have become the sources where individuals search for all kinds of information and apply to each question. The instant and fast circulation of knowledge and the fact that individuals immediately reach and share all the information they want makes the world a global village. Social media appears to be among the triggering elements of information sharing, even as the main actor. Customers influence the purchasing decisions of digital channels and contact points for each product and service at all stages of the purchasing process.

The digital world and the real world are intertwined and the consumers who become dependent on the virtual world in any purchase decisions cannot be isolated from the digital world. The dynamics of the virtual world confines the real world to itself. At every stage of purchasing decisions, consumers started to take risks in brands that position their marketing activities in a digital environment different from traditional marketing missions when they began to introduce behavioral models on the basis of voluntary service and approval (Brinker, 2017).

Mobility refers to the technology that is carried out without creating mobile solutions that enable individuals to access information and act on this information. The advantages of mobility include secure, real-time information access or data entry from multiple locations. (Özgüven, 2013). Mobile technologies allow not only mobile phones but also tablet computers and many devices in our daily life to be connected to each other and the Internet. Mobile systems that offer mobile phones to our lives are called the letter G of the word generation neo.

Re-regulating music and entertainment industry according to e-commerce sites, corporate web pages, mobile phones are investing heavily in the mobile world. The search engine continues to change the rules in the marketplace with mobile searches (Karahasan, 2014). The main features of mobility are being portable, having a moving structure, being interactive and minimizing. Mobility brings a new dimension to traditional marketing and advertising environments, reaching the target audience in terms of location and time. In addition, it helps with measuring the consumer's interest in the product and the effects of advertising. It is also possible to send personalized offers via mobility to individuals and to send new offers based on previous shopping habits. It accelerates continuous sending of the programs and the organization of contests. Mobile communication technologies provide a connection from point to point or as a network community. They can be independent of time and space and they have freedom of movement (Özgüven, 2013).

Nowadays, individuals feel detached from the world when they forget their mobile phones. All GSM companies now have an in-depth knowledge of the individuals from the things they talk about, the messages they send, the calls they make to the content they share. In this context, mobile marketing offers a great database in terms of communicating directly with customers. It allows mobile applications to be based on the real data about the phone owner who carry their phones for 24 hours (Karahasan, 2014).

Hopkins and Turner emphasize that mobile marketing is not just an evolutionary technology, but a revolutionary technology. There is a change in the way that customers establish a connection with brands. This change is very rare. It has a greater impact than mass media tools, radio, television, and personal computers. Mobile applications often intimidate organizations. But with a mobile app, preparing, launching and executing any campaign is much easier than it is thought. Large masses, which have not used yet, can be transformed into customers as buyer candidates through mobility. Individuals always respond to mobile devices with a built-in payment system and it provides advantages with a low-cost structure. It is possible to have an idea about how effective campaigns are through mobile devices that have a physical presence from a specific location. Every message can be delivered to the individuals who spend most of their day with smartphones and whose every movement can be followed (Hokins & Turner, 2013, pp. 19-22). Some of the disadvantages are navigation difficulties, different operating systems and some adverse situations regarding privacy. (Hokins & Turner, 2013)

For a successful mobile marketing app, it is necessary to have knowledge about everything that the age requires from social media to e-mail technology, from online community management to cybersecurity and law besides creating of a digital communication strategy. It is necessary to establish a partner ecosystem and appropriate teams and perform in an organized manner (Açıkel & Çelikol, 2014).

POSITIONING OF DISTRIBUTION CHANNELS IN MOBILE MARKETING: E-RETAILING

The rise of mobile has changed the form of trade in the last 5 years and has started to affect the sales of computers. As of 2011, smartphone sales in the world have surpassed computer sales and smartphones have begun to replace computers. In 2016, worldwide computer sales reached the lowest level in the last few years with 258 million units. According to the research company IDC, sales of computers will continue to fall by 1.9% on average and the sales volume of 315 million units in 2013 will decrease to 250 million level in 2020. Contrary to the decrease in computer sales, smartphone sales continue to increase. Smartphone sales between 2012 and 2015 increased 26% annually, reaching a level of 1.5 billion a year. After 2015, there is a slowdown in growth and an increase of approximately 4% per annum by 2020 is foreseen. Saturation of the market, especially in developed countries, is the most important factor for slowing down. Areas, where there are a large number of individuals who have not yet received their first smartphone, will be the sector's new focus areas for growth. For example, India, where smartphone penetration is still at 17%, and mobile phone sales are still largely made with non-smartphones, is currently the most critical market for manufacturers. Increasing smartphone sales and fast-growing mobile Internet penetration have begun to change e-commerce despite falling computer sales, making mobile one of the most important channels of e-commerce. As such, the share of mobile in e-commerce, which was 10% in 2012, reached 44% in just 4 years. Mobile commerce, which will continue to grow after 2016, will be one of the main factors in the formation and development of new generation trade (Kantarcı, Özalp, Sezginsoy, Özaşkınlı, & Cavlak, 2017).

According to Deloitte's "The Role of Mobile Technologies 2017 in Our Digitalized Lives", in Turkey smartphone penetration continues to increase with each passing year. 92% of the users who participated in the 2017 Global Mobile User Market research stated that they had access to a smartphone, 81% to laptop computers and 63% to the tablet (Deloitte, 2018).

The Internet penetration which was 45% in 2012 in our country increased rapidly and by the year 2016, Turkey has reached 58% Internet penetration with 46.2 million Internet user3. Compared to the previous year's report published in 2014, the number of Internet users in Turkey increased by 6.6 million in just two years. The estimate of 2020 is that with 62 million Internet users Turkey's Internet penetration will reach 76%. Turkey which was quite below the world average 9.6% in 2010 with the smartphone penetration of around 6%, has reached 65% penetration and has increased by five points above the world average, with smartphone growth in the last six years. Only since 2014, 16 million new smartphones have been bought in the country and as of 2021, 84% of the population of Turkey is expected to use smartphones. According to a study made in conjunction with ethidium TUBISAD and ETİD, with increasing Internet penetration and smartphone use, as of 2016, Turkey's e-commerce market volume reached 30.8 billion TL. While this size covers all sectors, the retail segment of the market, which we will focus on in this report, has reached to 17.5 billion TL from 7.3 billion in 2016 with an average annual growth of 34% since 2013. It is estimated that approximately 70% of the retail e-commerce volume amounting to TL 17.5 billion is made up of marketplaces that sell only through online channels, multi-category shopping sites, vertical sites specialized in certain sectors and private shopping sites. The remaining companies below 30% are those which took a step from classic retail to e-commerce and realized sales on the electronic platform took a step from classic retail to e-commerce. Online betting, entertainment, and travel ticket sales, as well as holiday expenses, are excluded from this amount (Kantarcı, Özalp, Sezginsoy, Özaşkınlı, & Cavlak, 2017).

Today, due to the development of technology, the increase in Internet usage and the use of the Internet by approximately 3.4 billion people worldwide, the Internet has become one of the main sources of the global economy (OECD, 2019). Due to the fact that the Internet is one of the cornerstones of the global economy, time and space constraints have disappeared. Consumers have access to the information they need at the time and place they want. Today's intense competition environment, changing customer behavior, caused organizations to change the ways of business. The radical changes brought about by the Internet have reorganized the economic balances. The Internet, which offers the opportunity to realize economic activities on a global scale, has begun to virtualize its retailing activities. The e-retailing (electronic retailing) that has emerged with the Internet is the purchase of goods and services by the consumers through the Internet or other channels in accordance with the personal or household needs and requests (Harris & Dennis, 2008). In other words, e-retailing is commercial transactions performed on the Internet, realized in the commercial transactions made from the company to consumers. All transactions that enable companies to make sales from their Internet sites / mobile applications are included in this scope. The main objective here is to market products and services to target audiences.

There are different types of models in the classification made looking at products and services taking the type of players/users into consideration. The term covering the purchase and sale of products and services via the Internet; is also called with names such as Internet retailing in B2C market (business to consumers), online retailing, e-retailing (Wang, Head, & Archer, 2002). In other words, B2C can be examined in two dimensions by considering the type of product sold and the way the product is sold. While the type of product sold may be physical (such as clothing, electronics, etc.) or digital (software, music, books, etc.), the media in which the product is sold may be the vendor's own website, or a third person shopping platform. Shopping platforms collect products from more than one vendor on the same website and offer customers diversity and price advantages (Ministry of Development, 2013). Shopping platforms such as Amazon, eBay, Ali express, Hepsiburada, and Getir in the world and in our country undertake the position of intermediary between the seller and the consumer in the e-retailing process.

In today's challenging competitive environment, businesses are committed to retail activities in order to survive. Being able to respond to ever-changing customer demands and needs is one of the most important factors, which enables an enterprise to hold on to a competitive environment, is to use the Internet effectively. Knowing the behaviors of consumers during shopping, providing products and services suitable for them will lead to significant increases in market share as well as competitive advantage. Developments in information technologies have made consumers more independent of time and space constraints created by traditional retailing. Thanks to the Internet and the technology provided by the Internet, consumers experience a different shopping experience, thus, they can compare the desired products without having to go to the traditional retailer stores and can contact the different people and solve the problems before the purchase (Bozkurt, 2015).

Internet retailing, expressed as e-retailing, has some characteristics in terms of physical properties, customer relations, technology, competition, and customer structure. In case of an increase in the number of visitors, it extends the e-retail platform to increase network capacity and deployment capabilities. In case of an increase in the number of visitors, it extends the e-retail platform to increase network capacity and deployment capabilities. As technology, the latest technology is used in all areas that the customer sees, the latest technology is used in all the backgrounds that the customer does not see and information technologies are used. Customer relationship is less stable to older customers, more intolerant to controversial situations and establishes logical relations. In competition, it has global and more rivals.

Customer-based, global customers are involved and more resources are needed to increase customer loyalty (Lee & Brandyberry, 2003).

E-retailing has advantages and disadvantages for companies. Advantages of e-retailing; no place to select, no limitation of square measure, cost advantages, access to masses, open 24 hours, CRM (Customer Relationship Management), easiness in implementing such applications. Besides, e-retailing has disadvantages. The disadvantages of e-retailing include the need for know-how and technology, basic installation, operational costs and maintenance costs, complex logistics requirements, face-to-face (with technology this problem is being overcome), lack of smell and taste, legal difficulties (work on this issue is ongoing worldwide), after-sales service problems (Harris & Dennis, 2008).

Nowadays, e-retailing has gained a different dimension thanks to smartphones and the Internet. Smartphones, in other words, the mobile ecosystem is rapidly changing and evolving both in terms of consumer use and infrastructure. Mobile is a very flexible channel. It enables companies to reach their customers in many different ways. Mobile Marketing aims to reach consumers via mobile channels; It is an additional channel integrated into traditional marketing channels, enabling to reach the target audience in the desired way in terms of location and time. It is a brand-new communication method for brands that are trying to reach their target audience that has become different through mobile marketing. While it is a new and close communication channel between the brand and the customer, it is a channel that adds value to marketing communication solutions by using the power of mobility for institutions (Mobil Dev, 2014). Mobile Marketing also aims to reach consumers through mobile channels; It is an additional channel integrated into traditional marketing channels, enabling to reach the target audience in the desired way in terms of location and time. In other words; mobile marketing refers to marketing activities through mobile phones. One of the most important ways of achieving a new, different and fast way to reach the spirit of the client is to convey messages with different means. The fastest way to transmit messages is to use a direct marketing device, such as a telephone or a mobile phone.

The mobile phones' use is rapidly spreading and penetration rate is above 100% in most countries. It was also introduced as a means of continuous communication between people while on the move when it was first introduced to the market. However, recent developments in mobile technologies have led to the differentiation of mobile phones and the emergence of mobile devices of different qualities. On the one hand, these tools have started to have advanced multimedia features and on the other hand, they have started to use the Internet (Akyan, Zalluhoğlu, & Tatlıdil, 2012). By gaining these features, mobile phones have become smartphones becoming extensions of people, in McLuhan's words. It is estimated that world retail e-commerce has reached a transaction volume of $1.6 trillion in 2016 and its high growth rate will continue also in the coming years. Investment bank Goldman Sachs predicts that in 2020 the global transaction volume will reach the $3 trillion limit (Deloitte, 2018).

Considering the share of e-commerce in total retail; the share of e-commerce in 2016 increased to 8.5% in 2011, which was 3.6% in total retail in the world. This is an indication that the e-commerce sector receives about a 1% share of the classic retail sector every year. Due to decreasing profit margins in classic retail, change in consumer behavior, technological innovations, and new business models, the share of e-commerce in total retail is expected to reach 13% in 2021 (Deloitte, 2018).

There are various marketing techniques used in mobile retailing. Among these, mobile applications are of particular importance. Mobile applications used for multipurpose in the retail sector are used for mobile shopping, payment and marketing purposes. In the context of stimulating and encouraging the use of consumers, it should have a user-friendly interface of applications, reach the desired product and service with at least button and perhaps most importantly, with increased security (Becker & Arnold, 2010).

Nowadays, almost every retailer has a mobile application. However, the features of these applications vary considerably from retailer to retailer. Some offer relatively limited options such as finding stores, downloading coupons, or electronically viewing a weekly catalog of actual products whereas some applications offer an integrated channel (omnichannel) experience.

In mobile retailing activities, there are some facilities that provide easiness to businesses. These features are (Yüce, Deniz, & Gödekmerdan, 2012):

- **They have a one-to-one marketing approach:** One-to-one marketing approach is valid for mobile marketing activities. The communication is established directly with the consumer, not through mass media. In this communication, a direct marketing channel is used.
- **The authorized marketing method is used:** Mobile marketing application is made with permission from the target audience. It is a personalized understanding based on giving the communication messages that they expect and want to receive.
- **Measurable:** Mobile marketing provides businesses with clear information on how effective their campaigns are and how they use their products. Many information such as the hours and days of participation in the campaign, the average number of attendances, how many times a user consumes the product during the campaign, and the rate of preference among the products if there are different products included in the campaign are reported at the end of the campaign and conveyed to the brand authorities.
- **It has a low cost:** Due to the fact that mobile marketing is also one of the direct marketing applications, the costs are low.
- **It creates a high level of awareness for the brand:** The level of perception of mobile marketing applications is high. The customer can be reached by using personal channels.
- **It may be single or double sided:** Mobile marketing applications are marketing applications that have an interactive structure. In this regard, in some cases, the customer may be in the position of an active member of these applications.
- **Fast:** Thanks to mobile infrastructure technologies, the message can be delivered to the consumer in seconds. In this way, it is possible to get feedback within a few minutes.

RESEARCH: GETIR AS A MOBILE MARKETING APPLICATION

As Nazım Salur, one of the founders of Getir which is a mobile commerce application, states "*It is a model that has no similar model in the world yet* " (CallCenterLife, 2018). Getir, was modeled by taking bitaksi application of Nazım Salur. Bitaksi is a mobile application that provides advantages to its users such as providing the possibility of paying by credit card for the first time in Turkey,registration of journeys,rating of drivers, not matching with non-preferred drivers,voice guidance system for visually impaired people and many interactions The difference between the world's fastest-delivering application Getir and Bitaksi is the absence of a system like Getir in the past (StartupMarketBlog, 2018).

Getir application, which has grown by 5 times in 2017, was established by Nazım Salur, Serkan Borançılı (founder of Gittigidiyor) and Tuncay Tütek (Entrepreneur). Salur, calling themselves as*business chaser*, emphasized the importance of creativity in new ideas by drawing attention to the innovative structure in entrepreneurship. Salur particularly emphasizes the contribution of new communication technologies and digitalization to marketing. (Karahan, 2018) Thanks to the steady expansion of smartphone usage and instant access to millions of people, a new marketing field has been born with applications instead of traditional methods.

Getir is an organization that can bring a 7/24 thousand products based on an on-demand business model to your desired point. On-demand business model provides advantages when compared to traditional shopping practices. Consumers, visiting major retail stores to shop on weekends in the past, used to create long queues in the cash desk by placing their products in the store trolleys. Consumers, who paid after a long waiting period, spent time to carry these bags to their vehicles and then go their homes with their vehicles. Moving and placing these products at home were also a waste of time. Getir, based on on-demand business model, eliminates time and effort loss. Getir, which is as close as a phone for the consumers who spend most of their daily life on mobile phones thanks to the Internet, displays the power of the present (Saygılı, 2019).

For the separation of mobile marketing applications in today's competitive conditions, they should Getir different advantages to their retailers and consumers. According to the similar features of other applications such as payment by credit card, credit card security transactions, there are important features that distinguish Getir application from other mobile applications. In these days when time has become so precious, the biggest advantage of a mobile shopping app is the delivery of products in 10 minutes to consumers despite traffic density and distances (Sakarya Pehlivan, 2017). Another important feature of the product is that it gives information about the product to both retailers and consumers. Getir provides a variety of data to retailers. If we take a market as an example, it is difficult for the consumer to find information about the extent to which a product is searched and loved or how much has been purchased. Collecting information for retailers and consumers together, Getir increases and decreases the variety of products. Moreover, Getir brings this data to brands for free. One of the most important features that distinguishes Getir from other applications it is the sensitivity of the distribution channels (motor couriers). In practice, a great deal of attention is paid to the training of couriers. Couriers do not act on the basis of fast delivery; compliance with life safety and traffic rules is prioritized. Life insurance is provided to each courier in order to provide courier satisfaction, their salaries are kept high compared to the market rate, their insurances are paid. The courier endangering life safety, especially for company policy, in violation of more than one traffic rule is terminated.(for example, a courier passing through a red light is fired if he repeats it after being warned once). This application is carried out by courier tracking 24/7 system (Saygılı, 2019).

As a mobile application, Getir is downloaded from iOS and Android smartphone application centers. After the application is downloaded, the GSM number and necessary information are entered in the system to register for Getir. The consumer who opens the application can add his/her preferred products to the basket by selecting a delivery address. Then a payment option is added and the order is confirmed. With Getir application, without the need of cash or POS devices, the information you have approved is deducted from your credit card by protecting your information with MasterCard security system. With the MasterCard security system, your card information is stored and saved to the system only once. With the Getir app, you can instantly follow a product you order with mobile technology. With the map feature on smart phones, individuals can determine their position directly, however, in some cases the maps may not find your location. In similar cases, Getir is useful in positioning the map on the smartphones to the consumer with the ability to pin the map. Consumers can use it 24/7 at any time and the customer service of the application is also consulted 24/7. Besides this, it responds to consumers' wishes via social media application such as twitter, Facebook and Instagram (Getir). Customer-oriented employee, Getir uses a friendly communication language through social media. For example, Say Getir and we bring, bring happiness etc. thanks to "you and me" communication language, preferred for feedback, a friendly atmosphere is provided.

The same intimate communication language is also seen in the slogans included in the application.

"Getir happiness, Getir happiness to your happiness with safe mobile payment", Getir happiness to you wherever you are ", slogans The importance of customer satisfaction is emphasized by the concepts of happiness and happiness. (Getir).

In the Getir application, inventory tracking is performed instantaneously. When you purchase a product, the product you purchased is automatically deducted from the stock and the product deducted from the stock cannot be seen another consumer. Also, Getir uploads all of his products to the system as arrival date and expiration date and if a product is out of date, that product is automatically removed from the system. There is no product refund in the Getir app, If the customer wants to return a product for a variety of reasons, a gift voucher is given same as the price value of that product instead of the change of product. However, even if a product has not been out of date, if the customer is not satisfied with the product for a variety of reasons, a gift voucher / discount is provided instead of that product. Getir provides satisfaction with this application (Saygılı, 2019).

Perhaps the most important reason for the success of the Getir application is that they invite those who use the application most to their office and receive evaluation about the application. This method is, in a way, a test of usability of the application with real users. In the Getir application, which does not intend to switch to physical retailing, prices are kept constant according to the number of products, varieties etc., but the price is not changed according to the supplier's position. In app product prices are parallel to the prices in neighborhood, street etc. it is approximately 10% more expensive than supermarkets in some products (Saygılı, 2019).

In the Getir application, all products are packaged individually according to the type of products in terms of consumer satisfaction and health. For example, a bread and a detergent are separately packaged. The consumer pays separately for each of packages[1].

Nazim Salur emphasized that there is no Getir application in anywhere the world and has also stated that İstanbul is the only city where an average of thousand products are brought to their feet within 10 minutes. Salur said that similar practices would be made in other cities of the world soon and they would like to put this successful model into practice abroad without others doing it. He states that there are various studies on this subject and they want to realize this as a Turkish initiative (Salur, 2018).

The Aim and the Significance of the Research

As the use of smart phones all over the world and Turkey is increasing the rate of using mobile apps accordingly. Mobile applications that come into our lives with technology have become one of the distinguishing features of reaching consumers in a highly competitive environment besides daily entertainment, transportation, knowledge and information etc. Therefore, many businesses reach consumers by using mobile applications. The aim of the study is to examine the Getir application in the context of mobile marketing (e-retailing) and to evaluate the satisfaction of the consumers using the application.

In Salur's words on Getir app *"The only city in the world, which has a unique model with the average of thousand products brought to their doors within 10 minutes, is İstanbul.* Getir, based on such a model, plans to expand abroad by increasing each year compared to the figures of the previous year.

Getir, aiming to grow in a global dimension and in particular with a Turkish name, continues its works on this matter. With this feature, Getir aims to be the first Turkish brand in mobile marketing.

The Limitations of the Research

In the scope of the research, considering the width of the population, a study was conducted with the students residing in İstanbul Medipol University dormitory which is the foundation university accepting the highest number of students according to the 2018 YKS placement results. In this study, at least one student from each faculty representing the Faculty of Medicine and International Medicine students in eight faculties (Dentistry, Education, Pharmacy, Fine Arts Design and Architecture, Law, Humanities and Social Sciences, Communication, Business and Management Sciences, Engineering and Natural Sciences, Health Sciences, Medipol University) participated in the research.

Methodology of the Study

The focus group is defined as a carefully planned discussion in an environment where individuals can express their thoughts freely. Focus group interviews can be defined as a qualitative data collection technique carried out within the pre-defined guidelines in accordance with the logic of this method, which prioritize the subjectivity of the interviewees and in which attention should be paid to the discourse of the participants and to the social context of this discourse. According to Kreuger (1994), the aim of focus group interviews was not to make sense of meaning, generalization or explanation about the participants, but the way participants perceive the situation (Çokluk, Yılmaz, & Oğuz, 2011).

When the focus group technique is examined, this study is characterized by defining diversity and determining the existing situation, and it is not possible to test any generalization or hypothesis. The results of the study are to reveal the satisfaction, awareness, usability and perception of the participants about the application.

In 2007, marketing academician David Stewart estimated that the use of focus groups has grown steadily since the 1970s, and that business spending in the focus group accounts for at least 80% of the $ 1.1bn qualitative research expenditure per year. ESOMAR, a market research trade group, found that the ratio of focus group within the market research expenditures of companies remained constant at 11% in both 2007 and 2013. (Even increased by a few points in 2011 and 2012). Other organizations in the sector agree that the use of focus groups protects the liveliness. Greenbook noted that despite the above-mentioned blog post, there was no significant change in focus group spending from 2013 to 2014. Almost half of the companies participating in the Greenbook survey in 2013 reported that they used the traditional focus group method more than any other market research method in the same year. Market Research Association estimates that Fortune 500 companies will spend nearly seventy percent of their spending on market research in focus groups (Featherstone, 2019).

Fokus group method, whether Internet or neuroscience, is said to have died because of technology. Nevertheless, the unpredictability and possible insights presented by face-to-face and group dynamics still maintain their value. Not only do focus groups maintain their importance, but also the culture of consultancy, which is based on this method, is more vivid and more diverse than ever, and as consumers and citizens, it has much more space in our daily lives (Featherstone, 2019).

İstanbul Medipol University (4051), the foundation university that has the highest number of students according to the 2018 Higher Education Institutions Exam (YKS) placement number of the Higher

Education Council (YÖK), constitutes the population of the research (Torlak, 2018). 2420 students (Medipol University) from 26412 students studying at Medipol University live in dormitories provided by the university on campus. Firstly, questions were asked about the demographic information and online shopping habits of the students. The participants were informed about the focus group work with the questions in the questionnaire, and a button (option) was added to the participants' voluntary participation in the focus group work. Among the 243 students who wanted to participate in the study voluntarily and who were using the Getir application, 24 participants were selected from each section of the Medipol University in order to represent all the students in the universe. For the focus group study, three groups (first group, second group and third group control group) were established and in each group, the number of boys and girls were determined to be equal in order to ensure homogeneity of the group.

Findings of the Research

Demographic data of the participants in the study are given in Table 1 and Table 2.

Each question in the questionnaire formed in focus group study is explained respectively according to the distributions. Table 1 shows the age, gender, and the faculties of the first group participants who formed the focus group. When the age characteristics of the participants in the first group focus study were examined, three of them were 19 years old, three were 20 years old and two were 21 years old. When the gender status of the participants who participated in the first group focus study were examined, four of them were female and four of them were male. When the participants of the first group focus study were examined, they are Faculty of Dentistry, Fine Arts Design and Architecture, Law, Humanities and Social Sciences, Communication, Medicine, International Medicine and Business and Management Sciences.

Each question in the questionnaire formed in focus group study is explained respectively according to the distributions. Table 2 shows the age, gender, and the faculties of the first group participants who formed the focus group. When the age characteristics of the participants in the second group focus study were examined, two of them were 19 years old, four were 20 years old and two were 21 years old. When the gender status of the participants who participated in the second group focus study were examined, four of them were female and four of them were male. When the participants of the second group focus study were examined, they are Law, Communication, Engineering and Natural Sciences, Education, Pharmacy, Humanities and Social Sciences, Business and Management Sciences and Health Sciences Faculties.

Table 1. Demographic Information of Participants in the First Group Study

USER	AGE	GENDER	FACULTY
Participant 1	21	Male	Dentistry
Participant 2	19	Female	Fine Art Design and Architecture
Participant 3	19	Male	Law
Participant 4	20	Male	Department of Humanities and Social Sciences
Participant 5	19	Female	Communication
Participant 6	21	Female	Medicine
Participant 7	20	Male	International Medicine
Participant 8	20	Female	Business Administration and Management

Table 2. Demographic Information of the Participants in the Second Group Study

USER	AGE	GENDER	FACULTY
Participant 1	19	Female	Law
Participant 2	21	Male	Communication
Participant 3	20	Male	Engineering and Natural Sciences
Participant 4	20	Female	Education
Participant 5	19	Male	Pharmacy
Participant 6	20	Female	Department of Humanities and Social Sciences
Participant 7	20	Male	Business Administration and Management
Participant 8	21	Female	Health Sciences

In Table 3, when respondents who participated in the first focus group study were asked to do their shopping for virtual shopping or traditional shopping methods to meet their needs; the participants were found to buy virtual shopping in general for food, drink, ready to eat food etc. to be bought without trying; however, in the type of clothes and shoes, it has been found out that consumers are shopping with traditional shopping method in stores. In addition, it was determined that the two participants did virtual shopping for the items including clothes and shoes. In Table 4, it has been found that the participants in the second focus group study, like in the first group, use the virtual shopping method for food, drink, ready to eat food etc. which are to be bought without trying. In the products such as clothes and shoes, it has been found that all five participants shop in stores, however, it has been determined that they prefer shopping online, as it is cheaper, after trying items such as clothes and shoes in stores.

In Table 3, when the thoughts of the participants in the first focus group study are examined about shopping on Internet or mobile, in general, it has been seen that the participants do not emphasize that Internet and mobile made life easier, save time, is not comfortable, practical, fast and easy. In addition, one of the participants have emphasized that the Internet and mobile have more security than before and therefore, they are used by the larger masses. In Table 4, when the thoughts of the participants about shopping from Internet or mobile in the second focus group study were examined, it was observed that they gave similar answers to the participants who participated in the first focus group study. In addition, the participants have emphasized that they are alternative and cheaper than the store and they do shopping according to comparisons made by seeing all campaigns without going out especially when feeling lazy. In addition to this, one of the participants stated that they did not trust shopping on Internet or mobile except some products (food and beverage supplies, cleaning products, etc.).

In Table 3, all of the participants in the first focus group study stated that they made purchases via Internet or mobile. The most recent purchases made by the participants on the Internet or mobile are food and beverage supplies and ready to eat food orders. In Table 4, all of the participants in the second focus group study also make purchases via Internet or mobile. Participants in the second focus group also stated that they bought items such as sand and food for cats and dogs besides food and drink ingredients.

In Table 3, when the answers of the participants in the first focus group study, which frequently used the tool, were examined; it has been found that participants generally shop once or twice a week on the Internet and some participants shop online several times a month. It has been seen that the participants generally shop over the smartphone and also laptops were used in terms of comparing and seeing products more easily. In Table 4, it was found that the participants in the second focus group study did

Table 3. General Questions About the First Focus Group

	F1	F2	F3	F4	F5	F6	F7	F8
Shopping in a virtual/store	Virtual	Virtual	Virtual	Virtual	Virtual and store	Virtual	Virtual and store	Virtual
Opinion about shopping on the Internet or mobile	Simplifying our lives, easy and practical	Saving time, easy	Comfortable, practical and fast	Easy and practical	Comfortable, practical, fast and time saving	Safer than before	Practical, easy and fast	Time saving and comfort
Latest product purchases via Internet or mobile shopping	Yes, food and beverage and ready to serve food	Yes, food and beverage	Yes, food and beverage and ready to serve food	Yes, food and beverage	Yes, food and beverage	Yes, food and beverage and ready to serve food	Yes, food and beverage	Yes, food and beverage and ready to serve food
How often do they shop using which tool	1-2 times per week, smartphone	1-2 times per month, smartphone	1-2 times per week, smartphone	1-2 times per week, smartphone	1-2 times per week, smartphone, laptop	1-2 times per month, smartphone	1-2 times per week, smartphone	1-2 times per week, smartphone, laptop
Which product or products is/ are bought on mobile app	Water	Water	Book	Water	Water	Book	Water	Water
a problem or complaint regarding the products you buy from mobile	No problem	Courts	No problem	Social Media	No problem	No problem	Social Media	No problem
shopping with credit card while shopping on mobile	Credit card	Credit card	Credit card	Credit card	Credit card	Credit card	Credit card	Credit card
What they pay attention to when choosing a mobile app	fast delivery and recommendation	available	fast delivery and recommendation	available	available	to its design and logo	available	fast delivery and recommendation
Purchasing a product after the store is closed	Getir	by another product or sleeping	by another product or sleeping	Getir	by another product or sleeping	by another product or sleeping	by another product or sleeping	by another product or sleeping
advantages and disadvantages of mobile marketing	fast and practical, saves time, product range, instant notifications, none	saves time, everything is available at any moment, sending wrong	fast and practical, product range, problem in returning product	fast and practical, saves time, instant notifications, none	saves time, type of product, everything can be reached at any moment, shipping fee	fast and practical, everything is available at any time, wrong information about the stock	fast and practical, saves time, product range, none	fast and practical, product range, problem in returning product

online shopping a few times per week, while the two users did online shopping twice a month. Besides online shopping on smartphone in general, some users have been seen to shop on laptops and desktops.

In Table 3, when the answers of the participants in the first focus group study about which product or products was/were purchased on the mobile, it was observed that six participants mostly preferred the water products and two participants mostly bought the most books. In Table 4, it was seen that four of the participants who participated in the second focus group ordered water, one of them ordered books and three of them ordered food.

In Table 3, when the participants in the first focus group study were asked if they encountered a problem or complaint in the products they bought on the mobile, five of the participants stated that they did not experience any problems, two participants said that they complained on social media and companies called them back and the problem was solved; one participant stated that he/she had a defect in the product he/she bought and that he/she had a court case with the company because of this problem and

Table 4. General Questions About Second Focus Group

	F 1	F 2	F 3	F 4	F 5	F 6	F 7	F 8
Shopping in a virtual/store	Virtual	Virtual and store	Virtual	Virtual and store	Virtual and store	Virtual	Virtual and store	Virtual and store
Opinion about shopping on the Internet or mobile applications	Practical, easy and fast	Easy and practical	Comfortable, practical and fast	Comfortable, practical and fast	Simplifying our lives, easy and practical	Safer and cheap compared to before	Practical but I do not trust	Saving time, easy
Latest product purchases via Internet or mobile shopping	Yes, food and drink, ready to serve food with sand and feed	Yes, food and beverage	Yes, food and drink with sand and feed	Yes, food and drink with sand and feed	Yes, food and beverage	Yes, food and drink, ready to serve food with sand and feed	Yes, food and beverage	Yes, food and beverage, ready to serve food and sand and feed
How often do they shop using which tool	1-2 times per week, smartphone	1-2 times per week, smartphone	1-2 times per week, smartphone	1-2 times per month, smartphone	1-2 times a week, smartphone, laptop and desktop	1-2 times a week, smartphone, laptop and desktop	1-2 times per month, smartphone	1-2 times per week, smartphone
Which product or products is/are bought on mobile app	Water	Book	Ready to serve food	Water	Ready to serve food	Water	Water	Ready to serve food
a problem or complaint regarding the products you buy from mobile	No problem	No problem	No problem	No problem	Social Media	No problem	No problem	Social Media
shopping with credit card while shopping on mobile	Credit card	Credit card	Credit card	Credit card	Credit card	Credit card	Credit card	Credit card
What they pay attention to when choosing a mobile app	available	design, logo, ease of payment options and friend recommendation	free	available	design, logo, ease of payment options and friend recommendation	free	design, logo, ease of payment options and friend recommendation	available
Purchasing a product after the store is closed	Getir	Getir	by another product or sleeping	Getir	by another product or sleeping	by another product or sleeping	by another product or sleeping	by another product or sleeping
advantages and disadvantages of mobile marketing	fast and practical, saves time, instant notifications, none	fast and practical, saves time, product range, instant notifications, none	fast and practical, saves time, instant notifications	fast and practical, saves time, product range, none	saves time, everything is available at any moment, lack of addressee	saves time, product range, everything is available at any moment, problem with size	fast and practical, everything is available at any moment, ineligible people	it saves time, everything is available at any moment, wrong images related to the product

as a result of the court, the company changed the product and gave a gift voucher. In Table 4, six of the participants from the second focus group stated that they did not experience any problems or complaints and two participants reported that the problem was solved through twitter and sikayetvar.com website.

Table 3 and 4, it was seen that all participants who participated in the first and the second focus group used a credit card while shopping via mobile. Participants emphasized that Internet shopping has become very secure, especially thanks to technological innovations. All of the participants have emphasized that they use the 3D Secure security system for a secure way and that there is no question mark on their mind regarding credit card security.

In Table 3, while participants in the first focus group study prefer a mobile application, when they were asked what they mostly paid attention to, four of the participants said availability, in other words finding the things they wanted to reach in a short time, three of them said fast delivery together with the recommendation of friends and people in the immediate vicinity, and one of them stated that he/she prefers according to the application design and logo. In Table 4, three of the participants who participated in the second focus group study, like the participants who participated in the first focus group study, chose the application according to reaching the end from the beginning easily and quickly. three participants stated that they prefer applications that do not advertise constantly while using the application; two participants said that they preferred the applications free of charge, three participants chose according to the design of the application, the logo, the ease of payment options and the recommendation of friends.

In Table 3, it was asked to the participants who participated in the first focus group study, how they would obtain a product that they wanted after closing time of the places such as grocery stores and supermarkets, which are close to where they lived. When the answers were examined6 of the participants said if they wanted chocolate for example, they would provide another product or they would sleep and buy it next morning. two participants said that they could provide the product 24/7 with the Getir application. In Table 4, the participants who participated in the second focus group gave similar answers to the participants in the first focus group. Five of the participants said that they would request the item/items from their friends and if they didn't also have it they would sleep and buy it the next morning. Three participants who participated in the study stated that they would use the Getir application.

When the answers of the participants who participated in the first focus group study about the advantages and disadvantages of mobile marketing in Table 3 were examined, the following were found to be the advantages for the participants: being fast and practical, saving time, product diversity availability of everything at any time. In addition, thanks to instant notifications on mobile, it is also seen as an important advantage to follow the products instantly without having to go to shopping. The disadvantages stated by the participants are; sending the product incorrectly, knowingly and unknowingly entering the wrong information about the stock of the product thus keeping the consumer waiting, problems with the return of the product, extra shipping charges, deceptive information about the product. In Table 4, the participants' answers in the second focus group study about the advantages and disadvantages of mobile marketing were examined, it was seen that similar answers were given to the participants in the first focus group. However, when the answers of the participants of the second focus group were examined, the problems especially stated are; there is no addressee when there is a problem with the product, insufficient information about the product, even if there is an addressee, differences between the visual of the product and the actual product, the problems related to the size especially in clothing. In addition, one participant emphasized that the finishing of his/her money as a disadvantage due to shopping every moment when he/she got bored since 7/24 shopping is available.

In Table 5, the participants who participated in the first focus group were asked about the reasons for using the getir application; it is seen that the application is preferred for reasons such as being fast, practical, time saving and always accessible, having a warm language. In addition to these answers, the participants reveal the fact that delivering the products without being deformed and offering personalized discounts are the reasons for preferring Getir application. In Table 6, when the participants who participated in the second focus group study preferred reasons to choose the Getir application, in particular, the kind language used by couriers and social media are considered to be one of the most important reasons for participants to choose Getir application. In addition to this, making life easier, being always available for delivery, taking care of product delivery, product variety are the other features that make the application preferred.

In Table 5, when the respondents who participated in the first focus group were asked about how much they purchased and how much they paid for these products by using the Getir application; It is seen that five of them buy two or more than two products a week and in contrast they spend 35 pounds on average, three of them have ordered once a week and on the other hand they pay 50 TL. Table 6 shows the answers of the participants participating in the second focus group study; five of them buy two or more than two products a week and in spite of this they spend an average of 30 pounds. It is seen that three of them order once a week and on the other hand they pay an average of 26 lira.

In Table 5, when the participants in the first focus group were asked about the products they bought most from Getir application; six participants ordered water most and two participants bought sand and feed for their domestic animals. In Table 6, when the answers of the participants of the second focus group were examined; seven participants mostly ordered water and one participant bought sand and feed for the domestic animals.

When the answers of the participants from the first focus group were asked about where they heard Getir app from, in Table 5 are examined, five of them said they became aware due to the sponsored ads on social media, two people have learned from a moto-courier due to their curiosity and one of them expressed that he/she saw Getir storage which brought awareness to him/her. Besides, one of the important factors that provide the spread of the application appears to be a friend's recommendation. When the Table 6, showing the answers of the second focus group, is examined, it is seen that six participants learned through social media sponsored advertising, two participants learned through the circle of friends and that the moto courier was one of the important factors to raise awareness about the application.

When the answers related to the packaging and service times of the products of the Getir application of the participants of the first focus group study is examined in Table 5, all of the participants stated that they did not have any problems with the packaging of the products and that the service period was within reasonable time (average 10 minutes) and that the products were delivered on time. The participants who stated that the application is very sensitive in the packaging of the products have suggestions for the plastic bags used during the packaging of the products. When the answers of the second focus group study in Table 6 are examined, it is seen that they stated that there were no packaging problems as in the first focus group participants and that the products were properly packaged and thus there was no deterioration in the forms of the products. It is seen that the participants, who have stated that the couriers delivered the products in about 10 minutes, have various suggestions about plastic bagging.

Table 5. Questions Related to the First Focus Group Application

	F 1	F 2	F 3	F 4	F 5	F 6	F 7	F 8
Reasons to choose the application	Facilitating work, no timeout, saving time	Fast, practical and delivery of products without being deformed	Night delivery and warm language	Fast, practical, product range and personalized discounts	Delivery to wherever you want whenever you want	Being available every hour	Warm language, night delivery and warm language used.	Fast delivery and time saving
How long and at what amount do you use per week?	2-3/30 TL	4-5/40 TL	1/20 TL	2/35 TL	1/40 TL	4-5 / 30 TL	1/100 TL	2/50 TL
Mostly which product?	Water	Water	Water	Feed and sand	Water	Feed and sand	Water	Water
Where did you hear it from?	Social Media	Social media and friends	Moto-couriers	Social media and friends	Social Media	Moto-courier and friend	Social Media	Storage and friend
Packaging and service time	No problem, normal	No problem, normal	No problem, normal	No problem, normal	No problem, normal	No problem, normal	No problem, normal	No problem, normal
Opinions about Courier	Educated, friendly	Educated, friendly, smiling	Educated, friendly	Educated, friendly, kind	Educated, friendly and solution-oriented	Educated, friendly, smiling	Educated, friendly	Educated, friendly
Minimum order amount	Reasonable, student	Reasonable, student	Reasonable	Reasonable, student	Reasonable	Reasonable	Reasonable, student	Reasonable
return	no	no	no	no	no	no	no	no
Social media content	No	No	Yes	No	Yes	No	No	No
Opinions on campaigns	Good	Good	Good	Good	Good	Good	Good	Good
Plastic bag practice	cloth	transformation	cloth	Cloth, pouch	transformation	net	pouch	cloth
Recommendations for application development	bag	product diversification	Category, plastic bag, student	Bag, campaign	Tobacco products	Plastic bag, student	Plastic bag, category	Category, plastic bag

When the answers of the participants, who were in the first focus group, about their thoughts on the courier are examined in Table 5, all participants describe couriers as educated, respectful, sincere, polite, solution-oriented, friendly. However, one of the participants stated that although one of the moto couriers did not comply with the traffic rules but he or she did not complain about it and stated that they were very satisfied with the behavior of the couriers in general. The participants in the second focus group study in Table 6 gave similar answers to the answers of the participants in the first focus group study. One of the participants shared an event he/she experienced in order to indicate his/her satisfaction with the courier. Although the order was delivered at 04.00 at night, the courier delivered the product with a friendly and warm speech and the participant stated that he/she could not act in this way if he/she had been the courier.

When the answers on the opinions of the participants in the first focus group about the minimum wage amount used in the Getir application are examined in Table 5, it is stated that the wage amount is reasonable. However, in some mobile applications (spotify) an extra discount is made when registered with a student certificate. Participants specifically want this feature to be included in the Getir application. On the other hand, one of the participants considers giving priority to the consumers with more urgent need by increasing the minimum wage amount during the day as a positive decision. In Table 6, all of the participants of the second focus group study found that the minimum wage amount of the application is reasonable. When the participants are examined in terms of benefit-cost, they think that the fee is a suitable price for everyone. Another participant prefers having products come to his/her door whenever he wants rather than going out from home, office, etc. to shop.

In Table 5, when the participants in the first focus group were asked whether they returned a product they bought from Getir application, it was seen that no participant returned the product they bought. In Table 6, the participants in the second focus group study did not return the products in a similar way to the participants in the first focus group study.

Table 6. Questions Related to the Second Focus Group Application

	F 1	F 2	F 3	F 4	F 5	F 6	F 7	F 8
Reasons to choose the application	Makes life easier, delivery can be made any time	Care in product delivery, warm language used	Warm language used and campaigns made	Product type and language	Delivery can be made any time	Warm language used	Fast and practical	Fast delivery, product diversity and language used
How long and at what amount do you use per week?	1/20 TL	4/30 TL	2 /25 TL	2-3/35 TL	1-2 /30 TL	4-5 / 30 TL	1-2/30 TL	3-4/30 TL
Mostly which product?	Water	Water	Feed and sand	Water	Water	Water	Water	Water
Where did you hear it from?	Social Media	Social media and friends	Social Media and Moto Courier	Friend	Social Media and Friends and Moto Courier	Social Media	Moto courier and friend	Social media and friends
Packaging and service time	No problem, normal	No problem, normal	No problem, normal	No problem, normal	No problem, normal	No problem, normal	No problem, normal	No problem, normal
Opinions about Courier	Educated, friendly, smiling	Educated, friendly	Educated, friendly, respectful	Trained, friendly, kind	Educated, friendly, caring	Educated, friendly	Educated, friendly	Educated, friendly
Minimum order amount	Reasonable, student	Reasonable	Reasonable	Reasonable, student	Reasonable, student	Reasonable	Reasonable, student	Reasonable
return	no	no	no	no	no	no	no	no
Social media content	No	Yes	No	No	no	No	No	No
Opinions on campaigns	Good	Good	Good	Good	Good	Good	Good	Good
Plastic bag practice	Cloth, transformation	cloth	Cloth, net	Single bag	cloth	Cloth, pouch	cloth	deposit
Recommendations for application development	Gift vouchers, bag selection, product diversity, sachet	Product diversity, more frequent discounts, plastic bag	Category, plastic bag, student	Tobacco products	Plastic bag, student	Plastic bag, student	Tobacco products	Plastic bag, student

In Table 5, when the participants' answers about whether they shared a content with a hashtag of Getir on social media were examined, it was seen that six of the participants stated that they had not shared any content from social media and two participants had shared some content on social media. One of the participants stated that he/she shared a content on twitter and Getir application added the shared content to its favorites and reached him/her; another participant said that he/she shared a content regarding health products on twitter and Getir application reached him/her directly via e-mail stating that they were working on the issue and he/she was surprised by this situation. In Table 6, seven of the participants who participated in the second focus group study stated that they did not share any content on social media and one of them stated that he/she a content via twitter and he/she was contacted via dm.

In Table 5, when the answers of the participants, who participated in the first focus group, about the campaigns carried out by Getir application were examined, it was seen that they found the campaigns of Getir application positive. According to the participants, campaigns are encouraging to shop. The welcome campaign / discount check made especially for new members is encouraging for the participants. One of the participants says that the ability to select the desired campaign, especially among the opportunities offered by the campaigns, as well as the gifts given within the application make shopping attractive. In Table 6, participants participating in the second focus group have supportive attitudes towards the campaigns conducted by Getir application. Although the behaviors of the participants seem to be positive, some of the participants have criticism about the campaigns. It is among the expectations of the consumers that the campaigns are made more frequently and the institution plays a more active role in gift certificates.

In Table 5, when the answers of the participants of the first focus group about the plastic bag charge applied by the Getir application as a result of companies' charging for plastic bags due to the new law entered into force in Turkey against plastic bags, it is obvious that the participants offered a variety of pouches that would be more suitable for the Getir application. Especially, solution methods such as cloth bags, mesh, paper bags are recommended instead of charging for the use of plastic bags, an application emerged to protect nature. In Table 6, while the participants participating in the second focus group study gave similar answers to the answers of the participants in the first focus group study, in addition to these answers, it can establish a more sensitive system to the environment by using paper bag as an example to other institutions due to brand positioning. These were the expressions they used. Another participant recommends a returnable plastic bag system. He/she suggests that a system can be established by giving a bag in the orders and returning the other with the two cloth bags to be bought by the consumer. A participant opposed to these ideas recommends that all products should be placed and delivered in a bag regardless of the type of product instead of using packages according to the variety of the product.

When the recommendations of the participants in the first focus group on the development of the application are examined in Table 5, the following expressions attract attention; it can be ensured that greater variety can be created by increasing the product categories, gift vouchers can be created, extra discounts can be made for the students and disabled people by making separate memberships for them. In order to increase the market share, it is possible to sell tobacco products, replace plastic bags with cloth bags which are more susceptible to nature or completely transformed bags, include some medications, in other words simple medication, such as painkillers, can be added in terms of product diversity. In Table 6, when the participants of the second focus group were asked about their recommendations regarding Getir application, they shared the following recommendations; selection of plastic bags, increase in the gift vouchers, increased product variety, especially the sale of tobacco products, making extra discounts on the records created through the student, giving the plastic bags, which are completely soluble in nature.

SOLUTIONS AND RECOMMENDATIONS

Based on the literature researches and the results obtained, it is seen that institutions have started to use digital marketing methods and applications in an increasing competitive environment with constantly changing and developing new communication technologies in the world and Turkey. Especially due to the power of mobile, it is seen that some institutions operate only through mobile marketing applications. With the on-demand business model, Getir application, which delivers products one thousand types of product, 24 hours a day in an average of 10 minutes, it aims to be an example to other applications and differs from other applications with this feature.

With this feature, it aims to be an example to the entrepreneurs in Turkey and abroad. Getir is the model of the application comes to the fore due to the reasons such as increase in mobile use, time saving (gain) and traffic intensity etc in Turkey and world. With entrepreneurial activities abroad and government support for mobile marketing applications, it will be easier for enterprises to gain a place in the global market. If the State and private enterprises support such practices, it may be the first application to enter the global market with its Turkish name (existing in its own name) and with this business model. This can be a source of motivation for the country and for new entrepreneurs.

FUTURE RESEARCH DIRECTIONS

As one of the founders, Salur, mentioned, this study aims one of the founders of Salur aims to analyze Getir application, which brings thousands of products in 10 minutes on average wherever and whenever consumers wants, with a focus group method which is a qualitative research method in terms of knowledge, awareness and satisfaction mobile on the marketing axis. In this context, the students who stay in İstanbul Medipol University dormitories, which accept the highest number of students according to YKS results in 2018, and who use the application have been taken into consideration. The needs of the university students will be determined by the counseling culture and the inferences will be made on these needs. The students who participated in the research were selected from people who use smart phones and make purchases through mobile marketing applications. With these individuals, the reasons behind the success of the Getir application can be examined and inferences can be made on the satisfaction of the actual users about the Getir application. Through these inferences, the study will be a resource for entrepreneurs serving on-demand method in Turkey, following the example of on-demand app that want to develop new applications and aiming to expand abroad in the future. In this way, it is thought that the study will support the literature.

CONCLUSION

In today's competitive globalized world, changes in consumer choice and behavior models have started to be seen. The effects of this situation are also reflected in the world of marketing. When creativity is taken to the center, new marketing approaches, completely customer-oriented and shaped within the framework new communication technologies, are trying to be produced.

The instant changes and development of the digital world enable this field to be considered as an area of opportunity in the world of marketing. With the interaction and communication of Internet and mobile phones, mobile phone usage is increasing. Mobile phones, which have become a part of individuals, continue to cover a large part of their living practices. This requires new applications focused on mobile phones in the new world. The concepts such as speed, instantaneous and customer satisfaction have been placed at the top, and the applications that accelerate the race discourse have sped up.

Now, consumers can save time by choosing 24/7 applications, and have the products they want and desire in a short time only by touching a few keys on the phones or tablets. Mobile marketing applications, which are considered as a magic wand with which the digital world touches on individuals, are being renewed continuously. On-demand application is among the most preferred products by consumers with its features of speed, timeliness, interaction and satisfaction.

In this study, the availability on college students, awareness and satisfaction status of the application Getir, as mobile marketing applications operating in Turkey, are discussed. Getir has been a role model for entrepreneurs, as the founders say, in an area of store retailing, such as big market chains, supermarkets and grocery stores, where it entered by using on-demand business model in mobile marketing. Getir is a mobile marketing application that brings every product (about a thousand items) anytime and anywhere by saving the consumers, who have to go to the big retail stores or the stores like grocery store in alleys during week/weekends for shopping, from time and effort loss. Today, smart phones function as an extension of individuals and consumers spend a large part of the day on the Internet with their smart phones. In this context, Getir is as close to the consumers as a smartphone. In addition to the on-demand business model, the Getir application is an example for the courier companies in all sectors other than the retail system with its courier (moto-courier or car courier) system, as revealed in the findings of the study, due to the special and systematic trainings given. Getir, especially responding to the needs of consumers by interaction via social media, minimize the consumers' problems and increase their satisfaction levels by using a friendly language with consumers. With this application, Getir carries the virtual dialogue between the small tradesmen and the consumers in the neighborhood culture to the virtual environment through the Internet. In addition to this, with the business model Getir application has established, it brings the product to the consumers by always keeping each product fresh according to product usage dates and product sales situation.

When the data collected from the participants in the study of the Getir application were analyzed, it was seen that the participants purchased the food, drink and ready meals on the mobile without any problem, but some of the participants preferred buying items which are bought by trying on such as shoes and clothing from the stores instead of the Internet. In addition, some of the participants have been observed to be shopping on mobile even for products such as clothes and shoes which are bought by trying on. These participants emphasized that after trying out the products they want, looking at the sizes, numbers when they go out to meet their needs such as walking around, having fun, they did shopping on the mobile because it is cheaper and more convenient.

Participants have stressed that Internet/mobile shopping makes life easier, saves time, is comfortable, practical, fast, easy alternative and cheaper than stores, they are able to make comparisons with seeing all the campaigns without going out, especially when feeling lazy and it has become safer to shop online through security systems such as 3D Secure, especially for purchases made by credit card thanks to technological innovations that are developing today.

Participants stated that they had been shopping at least once a week on Internet/mobile. While all of the participants shop via smart phones, some of the participants are shopping on their laptop or desktop computers. Participants usually buy water, ready to eat food and books on the Internet. With the development of technology, there have been changes in all business lines. These changes have brought many innovations to both consumers and organizations. Consumers can sometimes experience problems with organizations and this problem can continue without being resolved. Through social media, consumers can find solutions more easily by writing about problems. Participants expressed that they could easily solve the problem they experienced with platforms such as Twitter and şikayet.var.

Participants consider these elements when selecting mobile applications; being able to do the jobs they want the most easily and quickly, fast delivery for shopping applications, the color, logo and application design used in the design of the application, friend recommendation, applications's being free. However, due to the fact that the application is free, the advertisements given in every step disturb consumers. Therefore, if the advertisements within the applications are reduced within the framework of certain criteria, consumer satisfaction will increase in this way. In this context, one of the most important reasons why the participants prefer this application is that they can provide everything 24/7 whenever and wherever they want. Participants emphasize that the types of shopping places such as market, grocery store etc. are closed on certain hours or on certain days. Therefore, consumers cannot obtain the materials they need during these hours and days. In the study, while the participants stated that they would sleep in such a situation and meet their needs the next day, some users stated that they would use the Getir application in such a case.

The reasons why the participants prefer Getir application are similar to the reasons of their choosing mobile applications in general. Although the common reasons for choosing mobile application can be listed as being fast, practical, making life easier, care shown in product delivery, warm language used through social media, product variety, delivery of products without deformation, personalized discounts, warm way of communication used by couriers and time saving, the fact that the product can be reached at any time and that the products can be delivered in an average of 10 minutes seems to be one of the most important reasons for using the Getir application.

Participants use the Getir application at least once a week on average. In addition, according to a research conducted on Getir prior to the study, it is seen that the most sold product is water. Within the study, it is observed that the most common bought product among the participants is water. Participants have started to use the Getir application by hearing it from different places. Moto-courier and car couriers, which have become a part of advertising, are among the most important reasons that increase the awareness of the Getir application. Besides that friend advertisements and sponsored advertising via social media are among the other reasons that increase the recognition of the Getir application.

The participants stated that they did not experience any problems with the packing time of the Getir application. Especially, the sincere, warm and respectful language the couriers working in the Getir application use on problem solving as a result of the training, is among the important reasons why consumers use the application. The articles shared by the participants on the social media with Getir hashtag, Getir application, which provides feedback and solution by means of DM (direct message) in a warm and friendly language ensure consumer satisfaction.

Getir, delivering orders without any deformation in the product within an average of 10 minutes, has not experienced any issue on products received by users using the application. Participants offer different solutions for different packaging instead of plastic bags. It is said that the practice, which is exemplified by the participants in many subjects, should be an example to other organizations about being sensitive to the environment. Rather than plastic bag, they may be more sensitive to the environment environmentally sensitive solutions such as mesh, cloth and paper bag. Some of the participants suggest that a similar deposit system applied in glass bottle should be used for cloth bag in the Getir application. With this proposition, instead of plastic bags, consumers will give the cloth bag they have while buying the product they ordered so with such a transformation the use of plastic bags will be eliminated.

While the campaigns involved in the Getir application are frequently used by the participants, most of the participants have expressed that the 20-TL gift voucher given to the members, especially to those new members, is very important for the consumers and they want special campaigns for the students. It is requested that Spotify's special campaign for students is done by the Get application and it is recommended to apply for both students and disabled consumers.

Salur states that Getir with an uninterrupted service during the day,*"Istanbul is the only city in the world with a unique model and the average thousand products are brought to their feet within 10 minutes*". Getir plans to expand abroad by growing each year compared to the figures of the previous year. In an increasingly competitive marketing world, Getir, aiming to grow in a global dimension and in particular with a Turkish name, continues its works in this direction. With this feature, Getir aims to be the first Turkish brand in mobile marketing.

REFERENCES

Açıkel, E., & Çelikol, M. (2014). *Dijitoloji Dijital Çağ:Satış ve Pazarlamada Uçmanın Yolları*. İstanbul, Turkey: Mediacat Kitapları.

Akyan, C., Zalluhoğlu, A. E., & Tatlıdil, R. (2012). *Mobil Perakendecilik ve Tüketici Eğilimlerinin Analizine Yönelik Bir Pilot Çalışma. 11.Ulusal İşletmecilik Kongresi* (pp. 10–11). Konya: Selçuk Üniversitesi İ.İ.B.F.

Becker, M., & Arnold, J. (2010). *Mobile Marketing For Dummies*. Hoboken, NJ: Wiley.

Bozkurt, D. (2015). *Elektronik Perakendecilikte Pazarlama Uygulamalari Üzerine Bir Araştirma*. İzmir, Turkey: Dokuz Eylül Üüniversitesi Sosyal Bilimler Enstitüsü İşletme Anabilim Dalı Pazarlama Programı Yayınlanmamış Yüksek Lisans Tezi.

Bozkurt, V. (1997). *Enformasyon Toplumu ve Türkiye*. İstanbul, Turkey: Sistem Yayıncılık.

Brinker, S. (2017). *Pazarlamayı Hacklemek*. İstanbul, Turkey: Mediacat Kitapları.

CallCenterLife. (2018, March). *BiTaksi & Getir Kurucusu Nazım Salur*. Retrieved from http://www.callcenterlife.com.tr/bitaksi-getir-kurucusu-nazim-salur/

Çokluk, Ö., Yılmaz, K., & Oğuz, E. (2011). Nitel Bir Görüşme Yöntemi: Odak Grup Görüşmesi. *Kuramsal Eğitimbilim*, 95-107.

Deloitte. (2018). *Dijitalleşen Hayatımızda Mobil Teknolojilerin Yeri Deloitte Global Mobil Kullanıcı Anketi 2017: Türkiye Yönetici Özeti.* İstanbul, Turkey: Deloitte.

Featherstone, L. (2019). *Arzuyu Sezmek.* İstanbul, Turkey: The Kitap.

Getir. (n.d.). *Getir nedir?* Retrieved from http://static.getir.com/faq_tr.html

Getir. (n.d.). *Neden Getir?* Retrieved from https://www.getir.com/

Harris, L., & Dennis, C. (2008). *Marketing the E-Business.* New York, NY: Routledge Press.

Hokins, J., & Turner, J. (2013). *Mobil Pazarlama Hakkında Herşey.* İstanbul, Turkey: Optimist Yayınları.

Kantarcı, Ö., Özalp, M., Sezginsoy, C., Özaşkınlı, O., & Cavlak, C. (2017). *Dijitalleşen Dünya'da Ekonominin İtici Gücü: E-Ticaret.* İstanbul, Turkey: TÜSİAD.

Karahan, P. (2018, July 22). *Hissedip Getir'di vurdu gol oldu.* Retrieved from http://www.gazetevatan.com/hissedip-getir-di-vurdu-gol-oldu-1184450-ekonomi/

Karahasan, F. (2014). *Taşlar Yerinden Oynarken- Dijital Pazarlamanın Kuralları.* İstanbul, Turkey: CEO Plus.

Köseoğlu, Ö. (2006). Bilgi İletişim Teknolojilerinin Pazarlamaya Etkisi. In *B. Akıncı Vural, Bilgi İletişim Teknolojileri ve Yansımaları* (pp. 145–185). Ankara, Turkey: Nobel Yayınları.

Kotler, P. (2011). *Kotler ve Pzarlama Pzar Yaratmak, Para Kazanmak ve Pazara Egemen Olmak.* İstanbul, Turkey: Sistem Yayıncılık.

Kumar, K. (1995). *Sanayi Sonrası Toplumdan Post-modern Topluma Çağdaş Dünyanın Yeni Kuramları.* Ankara, Turkey: Dost Kitabevi Yayınları.

Lee, S. C., & Brandyberry, B. A. (2003). The E-tailer's Dilemma. *Advanced Information Systems*, *34*(2), 10–22. doi:10.1145/784580.784584

Medipol University. (n.d.). *Sık Sorulan Sorular.* Retrieved from http://www.medipol.edu.tr/Sayfa/413/SSS.aspx

Mobil Dev. (2014, Feb. 6). *Mobil Pazarlama.* Retrieved from http://www.mobildev.com/393/Mobil-Pazarlama.htm

Odabaşı, Y. (2014). *Post Modern Pazarlama Tüketim ve Tüketici.* İstanbul, Turkey: Mediacat Kitapları.

OECD. (2019, Feb. 28). High-speed fibre makes up one quarter of fixed Internet in OECD countries. *OECD Broadband Statistics.* Retrieved from http://www.oecd.org/Internet/broadband-statistics-update.htm

Özgüven, N. (2013). *Mobil Pazarlama ve Mobil Reklam Tüketicilerin Mobil Reklamcılığa Karşı Tutumlarının Analizi.* İstanbul, Turkey: Babil Yayınları.

Sakarya Pehlivan, A. (2017, Feb. 28). *Getir tüm dünyada başarı hikayesi olacak.* Retrieved from https://www.ekonomist.com.tr/girisim-kobi/getir-tum-dunyada-basari-hikayesi-olacak.html

Salur, N. (2018, March 1). Talks2018: Nazım Salur. (A. E. Tamer, Interviewer)

Saygılı, Z. (2019, Jan. 22). Mobil Perakendecilik: Getir Uygulaması. (İ. Eken, & B. Gezmen, Interviewers)

StartupMarketBlog. (2018, Oct. 2). *Nazım Salur ile Girişimciliği ve Girişimlerinin Hikayesini Konuştuk.* Retrieved from https://blog.startupmarket.co/2018/10/02/nazim-salur-ile-girisimciligi-ve-girisimlerinin-hikayesini-konustuk/

Torlak, O. (2018, Sept. 6). *2018 Türkiye Geneli Vakıf Üniversiteleri Lisans - Önlisans Doluluk Yerleşme ve Bursluluk Oranları.* Retrieved from https://univerlist.com/blog/2018-turkiye-geneli-vakif-universiteleri-lisans-onlisans-doluluk-yerlesme-ve-bursluluk-oranlari/

Ulugay, O. (2001). *Küreselleşme Korkusu.* İstanbul, Turkey: Timaş Yayınları.

Virilio, P. (2003). *Enformasyon Bombası.* İstanbul, Turkey: Metis Yayınları.

Wang, F., Head, M., & Archer, N. (2002). E-Tailing: An Analysis Of Web İmpacts On The Retail Market. *The Journal of Business Strategy, 19*(1), 73.

Yüce, A., Deniz, A., & Gödekmerdan, L. (2012). Tüketicilerin Mobil Pazarlama Faaliyetlerini Benimsemesi: Üniversite Öğrencileri Üzerine Bir Araştırma. *Süleyman Demirel Üniversitesi İktisadi ve İdari Bilimler Fakültesi Dergisi*, 183-184.

KEY TERMS AND DEFINITIONS

Customer Satisfaction: It is revealing the level of satisfaction and dissatisfaction with the sales and services of consumers, institutions through interaction and feedback. With the positive increase in the satisfaction of the consumers, loyalty situation arises. The loyalty status of the consumer is also one of the criteria of success and continuity in your business.

E-retailing: Nowadays, with the concept of retailing what comes to our minds is the grocery stores, supermarkets, chain stores, shopping centers and so on. Together with the rapid development of the digital world, retailing carried on via Internet is also evolving and transforming. With the penetration of Internet usage, mobile applications spread among consumers have brought retailing to a different point. Today, thanks to electronic retailing, consumers can order and receive the products whenever and wherever they want.

Focus Group: The focus group is defined as a carefully planned discussion in an environment where individuals can express their thoughts freely.

Getir: It is a mobile marketing application that delivers approximately one thousand products every hour of the week to consumers in an average of 10 minutes in Turkey. The basis of the Getir application is based on on-demand business model. Bringing the products that consumers want, especially through moto-courier, Getir becomes an example distinguished from the similar distributors in terms of their sensitivity in the training of moto-couriers.

Mobile Application: Mobile application is the name given to spellings with special codes and designs for mobile devices (smartphone and tablet).

Mobile Marketing: It is all applications that enable the consumer to reach their consumers in an interactive way by means of the Internet via mobile devices such as smart phones and tablets. Thanks to mobile applications, consumers can meet their needs by introducing different experiences at the place and time they want. Organizations can interact with their consumers every minute with the modern marketing strategies provided by the new communication technologies.

Mobile Technology: Electronic equipment such as smartphone, mobile phones, tablets.

ENDNOTE

1 Considering the issues encountered in the first periods of the application starting across the country in line with the Procedures and Principles for the Charging of Plastic Bags, the need to reorganize the Procedures and Principles emerged and Procedures and Principles for the Charging of Plastic Bags have been revised and put into effect with the approval dated 9/1/2019 and No. 66745475-145.07-6267.

Chapter 9
E-Trading Decision Making:
An Integrated Digital Marketing Approach With Theory and Cases

Fatih Pınarbaşı
https://orcid.org/0000-0001-9005-0324
Istanbul Medipol Universitesi, Turkey

Habib Mehmet Akpınar
Istanbul Esenyurt University, Turkey

ABSTRACT

Electronic trade has a key role for today's companies with help of technology affecting marketing environment. The emergence of the Internet has led to huge changes in both the production and strategy channels and the consumer's purchasing process. Previous studies from different contexts examine electronic trade focusing on different aspects on concept. An integrative approach combining theory with cases can help to a better understanding of electronic trade and competitive markets. This study aims to examine electronic trading decision making with digital marketing approach. The study identifies a three-step marketing plan for competitive advantage about electronic trading. First step includes identifying standards, seasonalities, and anomalies related to market. Second step continues with further evaluation of market environment by including sentiment analysis and network analysis cases. Third step goes further with predicting cases by focusing on future. The study also contains solutions and recommendations, future research directions, and conclusion sections.

INTRODUCTION

Electronic Trade and the business world are affected by many factors such as developing technology, changing competition conditions and differentiating consumers. One of the results of this intense change in recent years is the need to understand the factors in the market correctly for the competitive advantage. When compared with the business world in the 20th century, there are a quite different market and competition conditions. When the business history is examined as a timeline in the 20th century, it

DOI: 10.4018/978-1-7998-0035-4.ch009

is observed that many different factors such as mass production, world wars, developments in quality and technology are effective. When the 21st century is examined, it is concluded that technology and globalization factors are effective in competition conditions. As a result of these factors, there have been changes in the market actors and consumer expectations. The main aim of this study is to understand the changes and to develop strategies for them.

The concept of electronic trade has become one of the issues of global markets and the business world, especially with the spread of technology and the Internet. The existence of a more global commercial world has created a market environment in which electronic commerce can be reached by the whole world and commercial actors can participate. Commercial markets, which approach the concept of full competition in economics at this stage, have both advantages and disadvantages for the business world. Factors related to advantages generally include access to the market and access to customers, while the factors associated with disadvantage include increasing competition in the market and changing consumer expectations.

One of the changes for electronic trade refers to the consumer side of the market. "Consumer" in this change can refer to companies for business to business markets and refers to individual customers for a business to customer markets. The processes of consumer decision making are changing day by day due to technological advancements. Consumers of 80s, consumers of 90s and today's consumers have different characteristics. Main consumer decision making processes have three different stages including; information seeking, comparing alternatives, forwarding information. Information seeking step has lots of changes due to the speed of internet and social media. Today, companies can reach to different suppliers from different countries/regions of the world. This information availability causes second steps to be complex. Comparing alternatives is easier than past times, as there are lots of alternative suppliers and buying options. Third step forwarding information refers to information exchange between both sides. Consumers affect each other fast with help of social media and electronic communication mediums.

Complexity of electronic trade, changing of competitive environment and consumer beliefs are main factors affecting electronic trade today. These factors make strategic decision making necessary for competitive advantage. This study focuses on this gap and suggests a three-step action plan for competitive advantage in an electronic trade context. Contents of the study start with electronic trade concept and continue with digital marketing and competitive advantage concepts. Case section of study starts with detecting standards and norms since they signal about marketing environment. This section also has an anomaly detection part as it would include insights for further steps. Second case section includes network analysis and sentiment analysis methodologies for evaluating market conditions better. Last case section focuses on the future as it includes prediction of future values of variables. All three case sections have marketing focus and competitive positions either. Therefore, it is aimed to have integrated and comprehensive view for electronic trade. The study also includes solutions and recommendations, suggestions for further research, and discussion parts.

LITERATURE REVIEW

Electronic Trade

One of the most important factors that ensure the survival and prosperity of human beings is to establish organizations that provide the means and methods for the trade of goods and services. These organizations have led to the establishment and management of the human race in trade. The first demand for the beginning of the trade emerged in the Stone Age. The exchange system that emerged in the Stone Age was the basis of trade (Gibreel, AlOtaibi, & Altmann, 2018). In the 21st century, business performs their activities over the Internet. The way in which the Internet has entered business life has become a major transformation. Businesses carry their business to online environments due to the development of the Internet. Thanks to the Internet, the new initiatives are evaluating the opportunities offered by the Internet (Amit & Zott, 2001).

The development of technology supports worldwide trade. Consumers do research on the Internet before buying products or services. The Internet has deeply influenced all businesses and has led to a major transformation. Especially with the spread of technological developments, consumers have become a part of internet consumers' lives. As a result of this situation, it was inevitable for companies to adopt the Internet. The Internet has made all its activities available to the Internet (Anvari & Norouzi, 2016). The increase in e-commerce depends on the transformation of the Internet. The advancement of the Internet has emerged from a device of communication to one of economic benefits. The emergence of the Internet has facilitated national and international trade. Besides, it allows easy access large consumer groups at lower costs (Malkawi, 2007). With the use of electronic tools and the Internet in trade, the process of trading transactions become much easier, faster and cheaper (Terzi, 2011). The spread of electronic commerce has led to a reduction in overall prices. By means of electronic commerce, consumers have reached goods and services more easily and their welfare levels have increased.

Earl (2000) explained the transformation of electronic commerce in six stages: external communications, internal communications, e-commerce, e-business, e-enterprise, and transformation. The stage of external communication is the stage where the company has established its first internet site. At this stage, businesses use their websites as a brochure in which they can describe their business promotions and activities. The vision behind creating such websites is to communicate with those outside the organization. In this period, there was a period of unilateral communication by electronic mail. The internal communication phase is followed by the external communication phase. One of the most important developments of the internal communication period is the emergence of the IT departments responsible for the internet. With the emergence of IT teams, work on the internet has increased. The most important issue in the development of these studies was the emergence and development of intranets. Interanet increased the information and communication cover of organizations. With the help of technology, knowledge management has spread much faster within the organization and increased efficiency and efficiency. In the third stage of electronic commerce, enterprises were successful in selling their products and services via internet. Very important initiatives that have changed the fate of trade emerged in this period. One of the most successful companies in the history of e-commerce at the beginning of Amazon emerged. The term e-commerce was used to quickly buy and sell products online. For the first time, businesses have begun to develop strategies for online channels, except for general communication channels. They went to support both physical and digital product sales. In the fourth stage of electronic commerce, enterprises developed new business systems in accordance with electronic activities. The most important motto of the period was to quickly respond to customer requests and needs. They digitized their traditional processes to respond to the wishes and needs of the customer. The transfer of management processes and operational activities to the internet has led to the digital footprint of the customers. This enabled the online collection of information. Methods for analyzing this data have been developed. All these developments mean that consumer behavior can be continuously monitored, analyzed and understood. By conducting market tests in real time, businesses have led to the emergence of market opportunities and new business ideas. This situation led to the transformation of enterprises by revealing electronic initiatives. This period is called electronic entrepreneurship. At the last stage of the transformation phase, how the company has spent its e-commerce journey and whether it has successfully reached its goal is examined. The previous steps were completed respectively. It has adapted to the new economy by digitizing business management and operational activities. The most important situation that will bring success to the business is closely related to the harmony with the electronic world and environment (Earl, 2000).

Globalization, which has gained speed with the introduction of internet in the world, has created a digital world where people can communicate with each other 24/7, through the emergence of smartphones and social media platforms. The physical boundaries of the world have disappeared owing to the rapid dissemination of information, trends, and trends through smartphones. In other words, the world has turned into a digital village. According to We Are Social (2019) report, which publishes the world's most up-to-date Internet usage statistics and social media statistics, there are 4.38 billion internet users worldwide, accounting for 56% of the world's population. There are a total of 3.48 billion social media users in the world, accounting for 45% of the world's population. When the total number of mobile users is examined, there are 5.11 billion mobile users in the world and this ratio constitutes 67% of the world's population. When the last published data are compared with the previous year, it is seen that the most important growth is in Internet usage. More than 360 million people have met the Internet for the first time. This rate corresponds to more than 1 million users online each day. 57 percent of the world's population is connected to the internet. According to the results of the study, it is expected that this ratio will increase significantly in the next year. When the 2019 financial data are analyzed in the published report, 69% of the world's population finds a bank account and only 16% has a credit card. As a result of the increased use of mobile payment systems, 4.4% of the world's population has a mobile money account. When the electronic commerce data crossing over the world are analyzed, 29% of transactions in the world were realized through online purchases. Consumers have spent most of their fashion and beauty materials according to current data. These categories are followed by food & personal care and furniture items respectively. 2018 According to E-Commerce statistics, expenditures on consumer goods increased by 37% and realized as 1.78 trillion dollars.

There are many business e-commerce models proposed and explained in the literature. In this study, e-commerce sector is examined with two main business models: B2C and B2B. Business-to-consumer (B2C) business model, in which online companies look for to reach consumers, is the most popular and common type of e-commerce. The B2C business model has many sub-business models in itself. These are e-tailer (Amazon, Walmart, Dell, & LLBean), community provider (Facebook, Instagram, Twitter, & Pinterest), content provider (WSJ, CNN, & BBC), portal (Google, Bing, Yandex, & Firefox), transaction broker (Monster, Hotels.com, & Orbitz), market creator (eBay, Aliexpress, & Gearbest), service provider (Airbnb, Uber, & Udemy) provider business models. B2B is the e-commerce of businesses with other businesses. While the public is generally giving attention to B2C, the e-commerce that businesses make to other businesses is 10 times more than B2C e-commerce. The sub-business models that make up the B2B model are as follows: e-distributor, e-procurement, ocean connect, industry consortium (Laudon & Traver, 2016).

Understanding of electronic business models is extremely important in the competitive advantage of the companies. When we look at the companies that have recently emerged and are on their way to becoming the most valuable companies in the world, it has been seen that they have developed highly innovative business models. The digital world will be the world of enterprises that are open to innovations and that provide innovative solutions to the demands and needs of consumers.

Digital Marketing

A thorough understanding of digital marketing requires a clear definition of traditional marketing. The American Marketing Association (2013) defines marketing as:

Marketing is the activity, set of institutions, and processes for creating, communicating, delivering, and exchanging offerings that have value for customers, clients, partners, and society at large.

There are three concepts to be considered in this definition. The first is related to offering a unique value for customers. Nowadays, brands should offer their customers more than products and services in order to stand out in a competitive environment. This is possible by creating value for customers. The second refers to creating value for stakeholders. Marketing making decision should create values for its stakeholders with a sharing structure rather than a centralized one. When a business is considered a ship, marketing can be described as a captain. Third and perhaps most importantly, marketing is customer-oriented thinking. Marketers put the customer in the center of the enterprise and every step they think like a customer. In addition, it will play a key role in the success of the enterprise in providing customer-oriented thinking with all its departments.

One of the most important rules and principles of success in marketing is understanding the customer and it can be implemented in many contexts (Pınarbasi & Türkyılmaz, 2017; Pınarbaşı & Canbolat, 2018; Canbolat & Pınarbaşı, 2018). Marketing professionals should be familiar with the target markets and should be able to better understand their customers. Compared to traditional marketing, the geographical and cultural distribution in digital marketing is larger. From this point of view, it is vital to understand customers in digital marketing in terms of being successful. Digital customers have very different attitudes in information acquisition and purchasing decision making. The behaviors and thoughts of the customers differ from each other. Accordingly, customers may behave differently in digital and non-digital environments. Therefore, businesses that want to succeed in marketing activities should carefully follow the footprints of electronic consumers and conduct market research to understand their wishes and needs (Chaffey, Smith, & Smith, 2013).

Digital marketing has great benefits to buyers and sellers. When considered in terms of buyers, digital marketing is convenient, accessible, easy and private. Buyers can make the purchase they want from anywhere and almost unlimited product variety. For example, Amazon.com's website and mobile app have detailed information on products, expert reviews, reviews and comments from customers who have previously purchased that product. This offers much more information than we can reach in any traditional way. In terms of sellers; Digital marketing provides vendors a low cost, efficiency, quick alternative. Through digital marketing, sellers can target small groups and individual customers in their target markets. With the direct marketing activities of digital marketing, businesses can interact with consumers on mobile or online. In this way, they can learn more about the needs and needs of their target audience and can further personalize products and services to specific target audiences. In addition, customers can ask questions and receive feedback on the products and services they offer (Kotler, Armstrong, & Harris, 2017).

The understanding of the environment in which the business is located in one of the most important requirements of being successful in digital marketing. Environmental factors play a key role in the development of marketing strategies and in the decision-making process of the consumer. They should understand the environment in which they operate and develop their strategies according to these environmental factors. In the study conducted by Chaffey and Ellis-Chadwick (2019), the macro and microenvironments of digital marketing are determined. The customers, suppliers and intermediaries, competitors constitute the microenvironment of digital marketing. The macro environment is composed of forces, economic forces, political forces, social forces, and cultural forces.

Digital marketing which defined as an adaptive technology-enabled process in which marketers collaborate with customers and partners in order to create, transit, present and sustain value for all stakeholders (Kannan & Li, 2017). Due to Internet, access to information, organizing and communication are remarkably easy. From this point of view, the Internet including communication types and technologies ranging from written and verbal words to visual images. Digital marketing is one of the newest distribution channels used by marketers to reach customers. Digital marketing is different from conventional channels and marketing because it benefits from the Internet network and its channels. Compared to traditional networks, people on the Internet can communicate with each other more easily. (Yelkur & Nêveda DaCosta, 2001).

Considering today's digital consumer, customers care more about others' views. It not only cares about it, but it also shares its own views, creating a large pool of information about the goods and services they have experienced. Customers respond to the brand perception businesses want to create their own perceptions and their own company definitions. This will continue to drive this way. Almost everyone in the world will soon be able to connect to the internet. The Internet was mainly introduced to the launch of cheap smartphones. According to researches, mobile data traffic is predicted to increase by 33 times in 2020 compared to 2010. With this situation, the behaviors of the customers will be different. Mobile connections enable customers to reach information more easily and make better purchasing decisions (Kotler, Kartajaya, & Setiawan, 2016). Marketing academics and practitioners have notice extensive revolution of marketing last decade. Social marketing and mobile marketing play an important role in the development of digital marketing. Moreover, the progress of marketing in parallel with technological developments accelerated the developments. Especially the widespread use of the Internet in the households, the emergence of social media platforms and the adaptation of users to smart mobile devices have resulted in a great transformation (Lamberton & Stephen, 2016). Thanks to the Internet, consumers' relationships with brands have increased. The Internet has transformed the economy in which businesses are located and has made the fashion of traditional strategies and structures out of date. Businesses cannot continue their activities with traditional and old methods (Edelman, 2010).

When digital marketing is considered in terms of consumers, it makes their lives considerably easier. A new concept of word of mouth communication has gained a new dimension, especially with the production of content that has emerged with the widespread use of the internet. This digital concept of word of mouth communication is the comments that consumers have made on the internet about the goods and services they have purchased. When this situation is evaluated in terms of marketing, it has created a new distribution channel via internet (Sparks & Browning, 2011). With increased word-of-mouth communication, consumers pay attention to user reviews before purchasing a product or service. Todays' consumers make purchasing decisions based on these interpretations rather than advertising or sales representatives. Electronic word of mouth has a deep impact on consumer purchase decision and lots of goods and services. For instance, hotels (Ye, Law, & Gu, 2009), restaurants (Zhang, Ye, Law,

& Li, 2010), online shopping malls (Han, Lee, & Park, 2011), books (Chevalier & Mayzlin, 2006), e-commerce (Duan, Gu, & Whinston, 2008).

If customers are interested in and use of social media, businesses should also attend to social media and develop social media strategies. In the past, businesses have used conventional marketing instruments, such as direct mail, telephone marketing, print, broadcast (TV, radio, etc.) communicate with a customer. With the introduction of the Internet this process entirely different and possible to reach a number of people in a short span of time. Web sites and social media networks use for marketing messages (Tiago & Veríssimo, 2014).

Today, people expose themselves to more digital and social media. These consumers are constantly searching for information about products, buying, consuming, and sharing their experiences with other people on these digital platforms. In recent years, there has been an increase in studies on issues related to digital consumer behavior. However, digital marketing literature is still new needs further research. In a world where consumers are constantly interacting with brands, digital marketing will find more research areas (Stephen, 2016). Kannan and Li (2017) gathered studies on digital technology and marketing under five headings. These are consumer behavior, social media, platforms, search engines, and content interaction. In order to understand the impact of digital marketing, it is necessary to carefully examine the pre-purchase, purchase and post-purchase phases of the consumers. Social media is the positive and negative conversations of digital media customers on products and services in social media platforms. Their comments and reviews reach far more potential customers. Platforms are companies that emerged in digital environments. In addition to platforms such as individual sellers (eBay), there are businesses that face customers with a large number of sellers (Alibaba, Amazon). Search engines are searched by the internet through search engines to get information about customers' products and services. Internet sites search engines include organic and paid word lists. Finally, studies on content interaction have focused on three points. These are the geography and location where the contents are developed, regulations related to private life and legal regulations against content piracy.

Digital marketing shows several differences in terms of activity. Digital marketing is measurable and therefore digital marketing applications are increasing day by day. Thanks to digital marketing instruments, the recycling rates of the investments made by the enterprises are easily calculated. This is a clear calculation of the contribution of the expenditures made to the business compared to traditional marketing activities. Content marketing, influencers, affiliate marketing, search engine optimization (SEO), email marketing, social media marketing are among the most widely used digital marketing applications (Charlesworth, 2014).

The main purpose of the enterprises is to gain a profit by providing a competitive advantage against their competitors. The ability of businesses to create competitive advantage today depends on how effectively they use digital marketing activities. Businesses that have adapted to the digital world make their competitors competitive with their processes by adapting their processes to the technology. Considering today's conditions, it can be said that the biggest dimension of competition is experienced in digital marketing environments when consumers are living in a digital world.

Competition and Competitive Advantage

In literature, the competition is generally defined by the researchers at the level of countries (Chung 2016). The OECD's (2013) definition:

Competition refers to a situation in a market in which firms or sellers independently strive for the patronage of buyers in order to achieve a particular business objective, e.g., profits, sales and/or market share.

Although there are many definitions in the literature, Porter's competitive strategies are prominent in the literature. According to Porter (1985), the competition strategy can be defined as the activities that a firm has carried out to achieve a sustainable competitive advantage in a given sketch.

As a result of the developments of globalization and technology, a major revolution started for the world. There have been major changes in the transportation of consumers to goods and services owing to technological transformation. Historically, consumers reached a limited number of goods and services in a particular region, and today, with the help of technological developments, the purchase of goods and services can be purchased with one touch.

Although there are different classifications and different studies in the literature, Porter's competitive strategies have been adopted more than other competitive strategies (Linton & Kask, 2017). Prior to the work of Michael Porter, other researchers attempted to explore the relationships between industrial structure and performance with experimental studies focusing on structural variables in a limited number of studies (Nikolopoulos, Georgopoulos, & Karagiannopoulos, 2005). According to Porter's competitive strategies, two main strategies are distinguished in order to meet customer requirements. These are cost leadership and differentiation strategies (Porter & Porter, 1985). According to Porter, businesses have to decide on one of two competitive strategies to have a competitive advantage. Otherwise, companies will have a higher cost than their competitors (Dombrowski, Krenkel, & Wullbrandt, 2018). In contrast, According to Porter (1980), the cost leadership and differentiation strategy used simultaneously are extremely low in achieving competitive advantage and the company will be stuck in the middle.

In the study conducted by Karagiannopoulos et al. (2005) in the literature, Porter's five competitive strategies are briefly described as follows:

Force 1: The Degree of Rivalry

The most pronounced competition intensity from the five powers in a sector helps to determine how the distances generated by an industry will be distributed through head-to-head competition. Porter's most valuable contribution to this issue within the framework of his five power strategies may be that he argues that competition is only one of the most fundamental forces determining the attractiveness of the sector.

Force 2: The Threat of Entry

Potential and existing competitors affect the profitability of the enterprise in the market. Market entry barriers are the most important part of the analysis of new enterprises. Entry barriers vary according to the markets to be entered. When profits, rise above zero, firms resort to various strategies to prevent entry into the industry. Basically, the most commonly used entry barriers are investments to enter a sector, with the exception of physical or legal barriers.

Force 3: The Threat of Substitutes

The threat of substitution for industries depends on the price-performance ratios of different types of products or services that customers can purchase to meet the same basic need. The threat of substitution is also affected by the change in costs; In other words, when a customer chooses a different product or service, replacement costs arise such as retraining, retooling, and redesigning.,

Force 4: Buyer Power

The power of the buyers is one of the most important forces in the allocation of the value created by an industry. The most important determinants of the buyer's power are the size of the enterprise and customer density. Other factors determining the buyer power are the extent to which the recipients are informed, the concentration and differentiation of the competitors.

Force 5: Supplier Power

Supplier power is the reflection of the receiver power in the mirror. As a result, its analysis first focuses on the relative size of the suppliers and secondly on the degree of differentiation used in the inputs. The ability to demand different prices for the value created from customers indicates that the market is associated with high supplier power and low buyer power at the same time.

The Internet allows firms to exceed physical boundaries and distances. This allows businesses to offer more goods and services to a wider audience. At the same time, with the development of the Internet, it is possible to know more about the consumers who are at the focal point of the enterprises and make more effective targeting to consumer group Secondly, the internet provides more detailed, comprehensive and high-quality information about customers. Information obtained from sales points generally uses information technologies, inventory management, and customer analysis, while the information gathered over the internet provides significant advantages in terms of targeting the customers to which they have identified their products and services (Kim, Nam, & Stimpert, 2004). In other words, the Internet allows more data on consumers to be collected. In this way, marketing decision makers have more information about consumer behaviors and they form their marketing strategies more effectively and successfully.

COMPETITIVE ADVANTAGE FOR E-TRADE: SAMPLE CASES AND INTEGRATED APPROACH

Competitive advantage for e-trade operations includes several methodologies and strategies regarding variety of e-trade contexts. As e-trade concept has practitioner side, sample cases and scenarios can be helpful for understanding competitive advantage methodologies. This study suggests a three-stage action plan for competitive advantage regarding e-trade. It has a deductive approach which examines market strategically then implements specific methods for evaluating details.

The application section of this study has three stages. As the study has a deductive approach, the first stage includes a general view for evaluating key performance metrics or variables in the market. This stage can be a starting point for different types of contexts and scopes. Norms and seasonalities are determined in this stage and anomalies can be detected after determination of these. The second stage starts with conclusions of the first stage. Factors behind norms, seasonalities or anomalies must be examined in detail for better understanding of e-trading environment. Sentiment analysis and network analysis are included in this study, but the methodologies are not limited to these. First two stages require determination of current characteristics which focus on "now". The last stage focuses on "future"

Figure 1. Three Stage Action Plan For Competitive Advantage

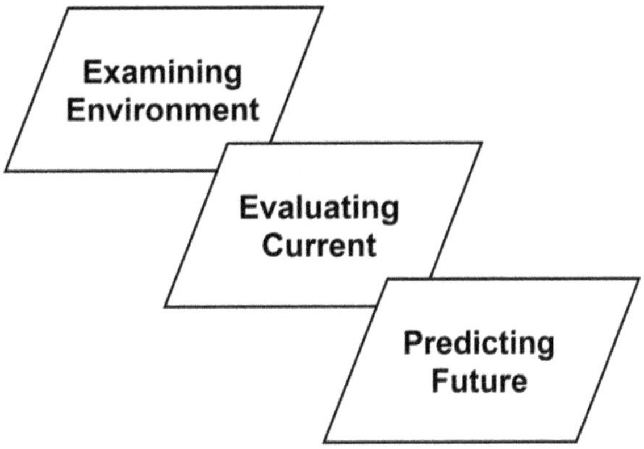

while it employs the data from the first two stages and makes predictions for future events. The plan can be summarized as; 1) understanding norms of "now", 2) understanding details of "now", 3) predicting "future" with "now".

For the content part of three-stage plan consists of nine scenarios which have different metrics regarding competitiveness. Company sizes, industries, e-trade types, and competitive positions are varied for scenarios and three scenarios for each case are included. It is aimed to examine cases with different scenarios to a better understanding of e-trade competitiveness.

Case 1: Examining Competition Environment: Norms, Seasonality, Anomalies

Strategic decision-making process starts with strategic planning. The scope of case mainly refers to a macro view of the competitive environment since it includes actors and their behaviors. The goal of competitive advantage for electronic trade requires strategic thinking and targeted marketing campaigns since the environment includes a wide range of actors and conditions.

The first case includes characteristics of the environment which refers to market conditions in our case. When we examine market conditions, we recognize some pattern due to the dynamic structure of markets. For example, each country can have a certain amount of demand, which is referring to norms for our case. Norms are average values for certain actions, these actions include total sales, total website visits, total social media interactions, etc. Another variable is seasonality which refers to certain loop/patterns in periods. For example, spring and autumn are potentials for stock movement for e-trade due to seasonality. The last variable, in this case, refers to the anomaly which can be explained as standard changes of norms and seasonalities.

Table 1 includes three different e-trade organizations which have different characteristics regarding market conditions. Three different scenarios will follow according to these characteristics. Norms, seasonality, and anomalies will be included in three scenarios as it is aimed to understand each concept in real life examples.

Scenario 1 includes a company named "A Technology" as an example. The company is a market leader in its market and have e-trade services for B2B industry, while it is a large organization. Norms can be defined as average annual demand, the volume of export, cost of goods periodically. Therefore, these sample metrics guide company to evaluate factors influencing them. The questions for these metrics

Table 1. Scenarios for Case 1

	A Technology	B Fashion	C Sports
Industry	Tech goods	Textile	Sport Goods
Company Size	Large	Medium Size	Small
E-Trade Type	B2B	B2B	B2C
Competition Position	Market Leader	Market Challenger	Follower

include; factors affecting demand for worldwide, factors affecting demand by region and by country, current trade laws affecting the volume of export and import and lastly technological stock costs. Next question regarding company is related to seasonalities for long periods. Detection of long-range increasing or decreasing which repeats periodically can guide decision making for evaluating predictions better. Seasonalities related to first company refers to technological launches since there are specific launch periods in a year. The three months before a special product launch can guide the company to prepare stocks for the event since demand would increase. Detecting anomalies in trends and seasonalities are the last part of this case. As the company tracks trends of metrics and seasonalities, it has the opportunity to detect any anomaly in the market. For example, demand for a specific product can increase regarding successful launch, customer e-wom, etc. Case 2 examines factors affecting metrics in detail.

Scenario 2 includes a textile trade company named "B Fashion". Similar to the first company it is in the B2B market, but it is at market challenger position in a competitive environment. Due to this position, there are some differences related to metrics. For example, standards for B Fashion company is affected by the market leader, therefore a plan in more detail must be evaluated. Seasonality can be helpful for this company, while anomalies have important potential. Market challenger position of competitiveness can use anomalies for competition in the market. Market challenger company can use anomalies for competitive advantage if it uses marketing intelligence for decision making. For B Fashion, there would be a surprising demand for a specific product. Following discovering demand anomaly for a specific product, the company can implement an emergency marketing/production plan for this product. Therefore, the timing of production/marketing implementation related to anomaly detection can guide "B Fashion" company.

Scenario 3 includes a company named "C Sports" in a follower position in a competitive market. This company is in a B2C market, therefore understanding individual consumers is important. C Sports company can examine seasonalities regarding consumers' lifestyles and holidays. For example, valentine's day can be a demand opportunity for sports products, since people want to buy gifts. Some specific events like basketball or football matches can be also helpful for C Sports. According to the follower position in the competitive market, C Sports does not have to use specific marketing plans. Examining trends and seasonalities are enough for the majority of marketing decision making.

Case 1 includes three different companies from three different industries and competitive positions. It is aimed to examine three different concepts (trends, seasonality, anomaly) together with three different situations. Each e-trade type and situation have its own characteristics, therefore marketing decision making must examine specific situations. The nature of information processing in case 1 refers to quantitative data which includes volume of demand, average website visits, etc. Evaluation of dynamic data helps the decision-making process, as it explains the marketing structure. In this step, creating dashboards consist of different key performance metrics, defining trends and seasonalities are suggested for e-trade decision making.

Case 2 will include details of understanding market conditions, unlike number-based Case 1. Numbers regarding consumers and companies in macro scale express market conditions. It is a good starting point for e-trade marketing decision making, but it must be supported by marketing intelligence. Next section includes different methodologies for evaluating the market in terms of consumers and companies.

Case 2: Evaluating Current Customers / Companies: From Sentiment Analysis to Network Analysis

Case 2 starts with the results of case 1 for further e-trade decision making. Detecting anomalies, trends or seasonalities signal important starting points for e-trade decision making, but it would be incomplete unless further action is taken. Examining the factors behind anomalies or seasonalities would be helpful for better marketing decision making. For example, total interaction on Twitter can be important KPI to evaluate e-trade performance, any increasing interaction could be a signal for potential market gaps for company. On the contrary, any decreasing interaction regarding competitor's can be helpful too. Case 1 deals with a numerical section of KPI management. Case 2 starts with examining factors, while it employs specific methodologies including; network analysis, sentiment analysis.

Understanding customers regarding purchase and continue process is a key element of managing the customer relationship. Bhattacherjee (2001) examines antecedents of electronic commerce service continuance and concludes that continuance intention is shaped by;

i) Consumers' satisfaction with initial service use,
ii) Consumers' perceived usefulness of service use,
iii) Interaction between perceived usefulness and loyalty incentives for service use.

The first methodology, in this case, refers to sentiment analysis which is simply sensemaking of content of users share. For example, "I love Brand X shoes!" can be signal for positive sentiment regarding user interaction. From this point, the macro view of user interactions which consist of thousands of user interactions makes sense for understanding consumers. This macro view employs several methodologies including lexicon-based sentiment analysis, machine learning, etc. The process underlying sentiment analysis mostly refers to examining the content, relating to positive/negative polarities and calculating sentiment scores.

The second methodology, in this case, refers to network analysis. Network analysis simplifies the relationship of actors and calculates some distance/centrality scores to evaluate actors regarding all network. For example, sportswear consumers to interact with each other in a network structure. There would be some users who have a "larger" effect of influence to others, marketing literature defines them as "influencers". There would be sub-groups consist of different characteristics in this network, there would be conservatives, open to innovation, introvert and extroverts. Therefore, it is important to understand how information flow in networks, especially for consumer-focused markets.

Table 2 includes three different scenarios consist of three companies in terms of industry, e-trade type, and competitiveness situation. It is aimed to examine methodologies in this case with different market and competitiveness types.

Table 2. Scenarios for Case 2

	computer	jewelry	F Games
Industry	Computer Parts	Jewelry	Games and Related Materials
Company Size	Large	Medium Size	Small
E-Trade Type	B2B	B2C	B2C
Competition Position	Market Leader	Market Challenger	Market Nicher

Scenario 4 includes a company named "D Computer" which is a large company and market leader. This company can use network analysis for evaluating supplier networks for specific regions or cities of markets. For example, a new entry strategy for a market can employ network analysis methods to detect most influential actors for the supply chain management. This could reduce costs of distribution and help e-trade decision making regarding logistics management. Market Leader position of D Computer requires strategic thinking, therefore network analysis could help this process.

Scenario 5 includes a jewelry company named "E Jewellery" which has market challenger position in a competitive environment. Sentiment analysis and network analysis can be employed integrated for consumers regarding jewelry industry, as emotions and social networks have an important role for consumer minds. Evaluating marketing environment through social media websites can employ network analysis to detect influential actors in networks. These actors can be traditional celebrities, social media celebrities or bloggers. After this detection, sentiment analysis can be employed to evaluate which specific sentiments take place in a marketing environment. For this methodology, time dimension also can help for better decision making.

Scenario 6 includes "F Games" company, different from previous scenarios this company has marketing niche position in the game industry. This niche position requires specific thinking regarding consumers, as they have "niche" specific characteristics. Understanding reactions of game players to specific events, for example, game console launches, game expeditions, etc can help for F Games, as they signal market potentials for company. Sentiment analysis in this scenario requires detail process beyond main polarities (positive, negative, and neutral) and include several sentiments like anger, fear, anticipate, love, joy, and hate.

As scenario 4-5 and 6 includes three different competitive positions and industries, sentiment analysis and network analysis can be employed separately or together for several e-trading cases including; supply chain management, consumer relationship management, social media advertising. Companies must evaluate e-trading goals first, then implement these methodologies.

Case 2 starts with findings of the first case and results with a general understanding of the marketing environment. This understanding helps marketing decision making about current marketing environment characteristics. It would be enough for competitiveness, but competitive advantage requires more strategical thinking. Case 3 includes further details for predicting the future in the marketing environment, not limited to current characteristics. Therefore, the third case will be related to competitive advantage.

Case 3: Predicting Future of Competition: Opportunities or Threats

The third case starts with understanding the current marketing environment and continues with predicting future events. Prediction action simply means that understanding current characteristics and converting them into formulas or plans to evaluate future events. This can be portrayed as linear regression methodology. As independent variables change (increase or decrease) the dependent variable is affected. Therefore, detecting a formula for current e-trading event can be employed for predicting future events. For example, total interactions of social media users regarding e-trading launch activity can be monitored for long periods (six months to several years), this can lead to a pattern of user reactions. Therefore, next event can be evaluated with past events' information and a total number of reactions can be estimated.

Chong et al. (2016) examine online reviews, sentiments and promotion strategies variables together to predict online product sales. They conclude that interplay effects of variables are more important than variables themselves. For consumer side of electronic commerce and trade, prediction and forecasting of customer churn is an important topic and studied by many researchers (Yu et al., 2011; Tsai & Lu, 2009; Huang et al., 2012).

As prediction methodologies require several methods including regression analysis, decision trees, and other machine learning algorithms, many different examples can be included for case 3. In this study two strategic elements; opportunities and threats are selected for explaining prediction phrase of e-trading activities. This approach is also consistent with the SWOT analysis approach.

Opportunities and threats which are two opposite sides of the marketing environment have the same starting points for decision making. Regularities or standards for metrics must be determined to understand the market correctly. Therefore, evaluating gaps/threats could be easy if standards/trends are measured periodically.

Table 3. includes three different scenarios for case 3 as they are in different competitive positions.

Scenario 7 includes a furniture company named "G Furniture" which is a medium-size company and market leader. The metrics company examine for current marketing environment are related to the volume of sales, average demand for specific countries and macro politic and economic variables including average income and customer index. G Furniture can evaluate a regression formula including average income, customer index and company related KPI's as independent variables; average demand for X country as a dependent variable. From this point when the company employs ten years of data, it can predict next year average demand. The prediction results can be implemented as opportunities or threats regarding country-specific situations. For example, instability of a specific country forwards the result of regression to negative prediction, therefore it can be classified as threats.

Scenario 8 includes a finance company named "H Finance" which has marketing challenger position in a competitive environment. This company can examine credit returns globally or continent-based, therefore a logistic regression formula which consists of return possibilities can be helpful. The unemployability ratios regarding continents and other economic variables like interest ratios and company related ratios can be helpful for logistic regression. Different from scenario 7, this company can use other

Table 3. Scenarios for Case 2

	G Furniture	H Finance	I Machine
Industry	Furniture	Finance and Banking	Machine Materials
Company Size	Medium	Medium Size	Large
E-Trade Type	B2B	B2B	B2B
Competition Position	Market Leader	Market Challenger	Market Follower

cities or regions as reference data, instead of previous timezones. For example, cities which are in an economically unstable situation can be reference data for predicting the next critic city for this company.

Lastly, scenario 9 includes a B2B machine company named "I Machine" as an example. This company can use machine learning methodologies for evaluating opportunities in markets. The company can use market competitiveness data from market and segment customers into different groups regarding possibility/cost indexes. Including thousands of companies to this analysis can help to create a classification machine learning algorithm to predict next companies' segment. Therefore, any potential customer can be used for this marketing follower company.

Case 3 includes three different scenarios regarding the competitive environment for the e-trading decision-making process, while it aims to reach opportunities or threats for companies. As prediction methodologies have different kind of targets like classification, segmentation, etc., companies must examine which KPI's to examine for their dependent variable for e-trading decision making.

SOLUTIONS AND RECOMMENDATIONS

The solutions part of the study has a three-step plan for e-trade decision making. The plan has a strategic approach while starts with a general view of markets by employing standards, trend, and anomalies. This approach can be helpful for marketing entry strategies or starting of e-trade campaigns. Understanding of market in details follows this step while it employs sentiment analysis and network analysis. The methodologies for this step are not limited to these methodologies, but they show that each e-trading case can be improved with this step. Third and the last step is not mandatory but helpful for competitive advantage since it deals with the future. Predicting future event for e-trading can be helpful for competitive advantage. Summarily the study suggests three step-plan for e-trading companies regarding understand market and consumers.

As this study covers lots of issues about electronic trade, there are some uncovered search areas for the future of electronic trade. For example, blockchain technology and virtual coin products can influence electronic trade in the next years. On the other handi new types of economic structures like sharing economy, have the potential for next years. Electronic trade decision making must examine all market conditions for better management.

FUTURE RESEARCH DIRECTIONS

Future research directions about this study have three parts consistent to the case section of the study. The first part refers to norms/seasonalities of different market types as they can have unique characteristics. The electronic/traditional difference can be also examined for this purpose. Examining different parts of markets would create new research questions for e-trading companies. The second part refers to examining market in detail. This study includes two methodologies (sentiment analysis and network analysis) for scenarios, but several methodologies could be considered for a better understanding of e-trade. Third part refers to prediction of future elements for e-trade. This study examines prediction in a simple situation which prediction of future with current information takes place. But different types of data can be helpful for better decision making. For example, time-series data can be useful for long-time prediction.

Second research direction is related to scope of e-trade research since global e-trade researches have different scopes regarding target areas. City-based, region-based, continent-based and global researches have a unique, therefore, size of the market also has an important role in addition to market characteristics.

CONCLUSION

Electronic trade market has a complex structure due to globalization and technological advancements. Companies that want to achieve a competitive advantage in the competitive electronic trade market should make long-term, strategic plans. The complex and global structure of electronic commerce affects firms in various categories, including environmental factors, competitive factors, and consumer factors. One of the important implications of this study is that it is necessary to make a strategic plan and think long term. An initial stage of this will be useful for companies, in which the environmental factors are first examined and the current situation is addressed. A good examination of market movements and decision-making on key market indicators will be useful in measures related to strategic planning. In the following stages, detailed statistical and technical data should be analyzed. In this study, network analysis and sentiment analysis were chosen as examples. Different methods can be used depending on the sector of the firm and the market. In the last stage of this study, different from the existing stages, it is included to make predictions about the future. Long-term thinking requires not only to focus on the past and the present situation but also to make inferences about the future. In this respect, the applications of enterprises to predict the future will be useful in electronic trade.

REFERENCES

Amit, R., & Zott, C. 2001. Value Creation in E-Business. *Strategic Management Journal 22*(6-7), 493-520.

Anvari, R. D., & Norouzi, D. (2016). The Impact of E-commerce and R&D on Economic Development in Some Selected Countries. *Procedia: Social and Behavioral Sciences, 229*, 354–362. doi:10.1016/j.sbspro.2016.07.146

Bhattacherjee, A. (2001). An empirical analysis of the antecedents of electronic commerce service continuance. *Decision Support Systems, 32*(2), 201–214. doi:10.1016/S0167-9236(01)00111-7

Canbolat, Z. N., & Pınarbaşı, F. (2018). Mobil Uygulamalara Yönelik Olumsuz Kullanıcı Değerlendirmelerinin İncelenmesi: İçerik Analizi ve Metin Madenciliği Yöntemleriyle Bir Uygulama. V. Yıldız Sosyal Bilimler Kongresi, 102.

Chaffey, D., & Smith, P. R. (2013). Emarketing Excellence: Planning and Optimizing Your Digital Marketing. New York, NY: Routledge.

Chaffey, D., & Ellis-Chadwick, F. (2019). Digital marketing. London, UK: Pearson.

Charlesworth, A. (2014). Digital marketing: A practical approach. New York, NY: Routledge. doi:10.4324/9780203493717

Chevalier, J. A., & Mayzlin, D. (2006). The Effect of Word of Mouth on Sales: Online Book Reviews. *JMR, Journal of Marketing Research*, *43*(3), 345–354. doi:10.1509/jmkr.43.3.345

Chong, A. Y. L., Li, B., Ngai, E. W., Ch'ng, E., & Lee, F. (2016). Predicting online product sales via online reviews, sentiments, and promotion strategies: A big data architecture and neural network approach. *International Journal of Operations & Production Management*, *36*(4), 358–383. doi:10.1108/IJOPM-03-2015-0151

Chung, T. W. (2016). A Study on Logistics Cluster Competitiveness among Asia Main Countries using the Porter's Diamond Model. *The Asian Journal of Shipping and Logistics*, *32*(4), 257–264. doi:10.1016/j.ajsl.2016.12.010

Dombrowski, U., Krenkel, P., & Wullbrandt, J. (2018). Strategic Positioning of Production within the Generic Competitive Strategies. *Procedia CIRP*, *72*, 1196–1201. doi:10.1016/j.procir.2018.03.007

Duan, W., Gu, B., & Whinston, A. B. (2008). The dynamics of online word-of-mouth and product sales—An empirical investigation of the movie industry. *Journal of Retailing*, *84*(2), 233–242. doi:10.1016/j.jretai.2008.04.005

Earl, M. J. (2000). Evolving the E-Business. *Business Strategy Review*, *11*(2), 33–38. doi:10.1111/1467-8616.00135

Edelman, D. C. (2010). Branding in the Digital Age: You're Spending Your Money in All the Wrong Places. *Harvard Business Review, Aralık 1.*

Gibreel, O., AlOtaibi, D. A., & Altmann, J. (2018). Social commerce development in emerging markets. *Electronic Commerce Research and Applications*, *27*, 152–162. doi:10.1016/j.elerap.2017.12.008

Han, I., Lee, J., & Park, D. (2011). The different effects of online consumer reviews on consumers' purchase intentions depending on trust in online shopping malls: An advertising perspective. *Internet Research*, *21*(2), 187–206. doi:10.1108/10662241111123766

Huang, B., Kechadi, M. T., & Buckley, B. (2012). Customer churn prediction in telecommunications. *Expert Systems with Applications*, *39*(1), 1414–1425. doi:10.1016/j.eswa.2011.08.024

Kannan, P. K., & Li, H. A. (2017). Digital marketing: A framework, review and research agenda. *International Journal of Research in Marketing*, *34*(1), 22–45. doi:10.1016/j.ijresmar.2016.11.006

Kim, E., Nam, D.-I., & Stimpert, J. L. (2004). The Applicability of Porter's Generic Strategies in the Digital Age: Assumptions, Conjectures, and Suggestions. *Journal of Management*, *30*(5), 569–589. doi:10.1016/j.jm.2003.12.001

Kim, E., Nam, D.-I., & Stimpert, J. L. (2004). The Applicability of Porter's Generic Strategies in the Digital Age: Assumptions, Conjectures, and Suggestions. *Journal of Management*, *30*(5), 569–589. doi:10.1016/j.jm.2003.12.001

Kotler, P., Armstrong, G., & Harris, L. C. (2017). *Principles of Marketing.*

Kotler, P., & Kartajaya, H., & Setiawan, I. (2016). Marketing 4.0: Moving from Traditional to Digital. Hoboken, NJ: John Wiley & Sons.

Lamberton, C., & Stephen, A. T. (2016). A Thematic Exploration of Digital, Social Media, and Mobile Marketing: Research Evolution from 2000 to 2015 and an Agenda for Future Inquiry. *Journal of Marketing*, *80*(6), 146–172. doi:10.1509/jm.15.0415

Laudon, K. C., & Guercio Traver, C. (2016). *E-commerce: business, technology, society.* Upper Saddle River, NJ: Pearson Prentice Hall/Pearson Education.

Linton, G., & Kask, J. (2017). Configurations of entrepreneurial orientation and competitive strategy for high performance. *Journal of Business Research*, *70*, 168–176. doi:10.1016/j.jbusres.2016.08.022

Malkawi, B. H. (2007). E-Commerce in Light of International Trade Agreements: The WTO and the United States-Jordan Free Trade Agreement. *International Journal of Law and Information Technology*, *15*(2), 153–169. doi:10.1093/ijlit/eal017

Nikolopoulos, K., Georgopoulos, N., & Karagiannopoulos, G. D. (2005). Fathoming Porter's five forces model in the Internet era. *Info*, *7*(6), 66-76. doi:10.1108/14636690510628328

Pınarbaşı, F., & Canbolat, Z. N. (2018). Evaluation of augmented reality mobile applications in turkey market: a data mining approach to consumer reviews. *Changing organizations,* 187.

Pinarbasi, F., & Türkyılmaz, C. A. (2017). Retro Marka Deneyiminin Yeniden Satın Alma Niyeti & Marka Bağlılığı Yaratmadaki Rolü. *International Journal of Research in Business and Social Science* (2147-4478), 6(2), 13-25.

Porter, M. E., & Porter, M. (1985). Competitive Advantage: Creating and Sustaining Superior Performance. New York, NY: Free Press.

Sparks, B. A., & Browning, V. (2011). The impact of online reviews on hotel booking intentions and perception of trust. *Tourism Management*, *32*(6), 1310–1323. doi:10.1016/j.tourman.2010.12.011

Stephen, A. T. (2016). The role of digital and social media marketing in consumer behavior. *Current Opinion in Psychology*, *10*, 17–21. doi:10.1016/j.copsyc.2015.10.016

Terzi, N. (2011). The impact of e-commerce on international trade and employment. *Procedia: Social and Behavioral Sciences*, *24*, 745–753. doi:10.1016/j.sbspro.2011.09.010

Tiago, M. T. P. M. B., & Veríssimo, J. M. C. (2014). Digital marketing and social media: Why bother? *Business Horizons*, *57*(6), 703–708. doi:10.1016/j.bushor.2014.07.002

Tsai, C. F., & Lu, Y. H. (2009). Customer churn prediction by hybrid neural networks. *Expert Systems with Applications*, *36*(10), 12547–12553. doi:10.1016/j.eswa.2009.05.032

Ye, Q., Law, R., & Gu, B. (2009). The impact of online user reviews on hotel room sales. *International Journal of Hospitality Management*, *28*(1), 180–182. doi:10.1016/j.ijhm.2008.06.011

Yelkur, R., & Nêveda DaCosta, M. M. (2001). Differential pricing and segmentation on the Internet: The case of hotels. *Management Decision*, *39*(4), 252–262. doi:10.1108/00251740110391411

Yu, X., Guo, S., Guo, J., & Huang, X. (2011). An extended support vector machine forecasting framework for customer churn in e-commerce. *Expert Systems with Applications*, *38*(3), 1425–1430. doi:10.1016/j.eswa.2010.07.049

Zhang, Z., Ye, Q., Law, R., & Li, Y. (2010). The impact of e-word-of-mouth on the online popularity of restaurants: A comparison of consumer reviews and editor reviews. *International Journal of Hospitality Management*, *29*(4), 694–700. doi:10.1016/j.ijhm.2010.02.002

KEY TERMS AND DEFINITIONS

Decision Making: The overall process of deciding regarding to specific targets.

Digital Marketing: Using digital technologies for marketing strategies and actions.

Electronic Trade: The type of trade action takes place in electronic mediums where people/companies use digital tools for communication and trade.

Network Analysis: The activity of evaluating structure, segments or relationships between actors of networks.

Sentiment Analysis: The activity of detecting polarities (positive, negative or neutral) or specific emotions from content.

Chapter 10
New Economy, E-Commerce Businesses, and E-Businesses:
Types, Similarities, and Differences

Duygu Toplu Yaşlıoğlu
https://orcid.org/0000-0002-5637-8999
Istanbul University, Turkey

ABSTRACT

Electronic commerce and electronic business concepts are highly researched in recent management literature. Network economy has revealed e-commerce, a new trade route that is carried out over the interlinked computers and mobile devices. E-commerce is a method used by almost all businesses that are physically processing. Therefore, there should be a significant distinction between e-business and e-commerce. With the development of e-commerce, new ways of doing business have emerged. Thus, many e-commerce companies have emerged, traditional businesses have started trading in electronic networks, and new business models have begun to be created in digital environments. In order to understand how e-businesses make money, many business models have been studied. For this reason, the concept of business model in the new economy and the transformation of business models into e-business models are examined. In line with this, it is aimed in this chapter to examine e-businesses, to clarify e-business models, and to explain e-commerce types and e-business model types in detail, with examples.

INTRODUCTION

E-business models, which have many similarities with classical business models, continue to develop and diversify along with e-commerce. In the new economy, many studies are being conducted to examine new business models in order to understand how e-commerce enterprises survived or why they could not survive (Persson & Stirna, 2001). Many researches indicate there has been an organizational transformation in some sectors and enterprises with the development of information and communication technologies.

E-commerce is defined as "doing things electronically", in general. European Union Commission defines e-commerce as "selling goods and services over the Internet" and OECD defines it as "trading

DOI: 10.4018/978-1-7998-0035-4.ch010

of products or services through computer networks". E-commerce includes the electronic trading of physical goods and nonphysical products such as information and data, and this trading includes steps such as online marketing, orders, payment, and post-delivery services (Timmers, 1998). This concept is also referred as "Internet-based business", "e-trading" and "e-market". Even though the product and services are ordered electronically, payment and delivery processes are not necessarily online. In other words, while e-commerce businesses perform their operations in the traditional sense, they can fulfill the transactions through the Internet (Zott et al., 2011).

Identifying e-commerce as a world-wide trading on the network will be a depreciatory assumption. Although e-commerce is perceived as a buying-selling process only because of its trading concept, it is understood that it has a much wider meaning with the use of e-business term (Özmen, 2013). E-business term was first used by IBM in 1997. According to IBM's definition, e-business is defined as "transforming the main business processes using Internet technologies" (https://www-03.ibm.com/ibm/history/ibm100/us/en/icons/ebusiness/transform/ accessed at 11.01.2019).

It is understood that e-business is a term that includes not only buying-selling but also other processes, from accounting to human resources, production to marketing, from the acceptance of the order to automation and the use of information technologies. In short, e-business includes new ways of doing business, new business methods. It is the restructuring of all processes from e-business supply chain to customer relations (Dubosson-Torbay et al., 2002).

New business models have started to surface with the emergence of e-commerce and have become powerful components in e-commerce environment (Kalakota & Robinson, 2001). However, e-commerce is a method used by almost all businesses that are now physically processing. Therefore, there should be a significant distinction between e-business and e-commerce. Every e-commerce business cannot be referred as e-business, but every e-business has to include electronic commerce.

In order to understand how e-businesses make money, many business models that emerged in the new economy have been studied in various ways. In fact, although e-businesses are in a different perspective from each other, they actually have the same purpose and working on the same subject. The most critical issue in the e-business models is whether these companies can be compared and whether they can be examined under the categories. Common point in the planning of e-business models is to clarify the revenue models and to develop the business processes and strategies to the finest detail. (Dubosson-Torbay et al., 2002). Some researchers have made classifications of e-business according to the degree of functionality and innovation (Timmers, 1998), some according to the ability of economic control (Tapscott et al., 1999), the type and degree of relationships and the power of buyers and sellers (Pigneur, 1996).

E-commerce and e-business concepts are highly debated and researched in the recent management literature. With the development of information technologies, businesses in the digital age have had to adapt themselves and their business models to this era. Thus, many e-commerce companies have emerged, traditional businesses have started to trading in electronic networks and new business models have begun to be created in digital environments. In line with these developments, it is aimed in this chapter to examine e-businesses, to clarify e-business models, to explain e-commerce types and e-business model types in detail with examples.

BACKGROUND

New Economy and New Businesses

Changes triggered by computers, Internet and communication technologies have led to the formation of an economy called network economy. The network economy has also revealed the electronic commerce, a new trade route that is carried out over the interlinked computers and mobile devices. In the digitalization process, formed by the network economy, problems related to customers and business life have also been differentiated. Old ways of doing business have been insufficient from time to time to solve these problems. Thus, parameters of business management have changed, especially in terms of risks and gains. Organizational structures of businesses have changed and organizational structures based on information and information technologies have emerged instead of the old hierarchical organization structures.

The very first rule of business in the new economy is being agile and creative. Frame of time is expanded and can be offered every hour of the day, every day of the year through the Internet. Importance of distance has reduced. Value is created with abstract services and information creation rather than tangible products (Meyer & Davis, 2000). Businesses in the new economy, must be agile. They have to offer their products and services faster than before. Hence, process of production should be finalized rapidly in order to proceed offerings. That is, business now needs to supply, produce and market faster. In order to carry out these transactions fast, they have to utilize their management skills better at every stage and have to perform business functions faster.

In global competition, being agile is an important advantage. Thanks to the Internet, users have the opportunity to reach the information they want from any location and at any time. Internet, along with wired and wireless connections, led to an abundance of data and information. Increasing number of subscriptions to social networks through Internet, interactions and sharing add value to the business as long as it is managed correctly. As the number of Internet users, the number of transaction and shoppers on networks, number of buyers and sellers (who are members of virtual market places) increase, the potential value created through these networks also starts to raise (Amit & Zott, 2001; Wirtz et al., 2010). As an e-retail company begin operating on the Internet, the more visitors to its website are attracted, and therefore more value is created in the virtual environment. Because of the traces left by those visitors, it is possible to gather feedback on product preferences, product or service advices, and negative opinions. These can be clearly identified in all types of business models operating on the Internet (Dubelaar et al., 2005).

Another important factor that changes the business rules of the new economy is the increase in the number of production factors. Creativity and innovation are added to the factors of production, which formerly were only enlisted as capital, labor, land and entrepreneur (Kim & Mauborgne, 1999). Accordingly, Internet-based new business models have emerged. Companies that were born in the Internet and which did not exist in the tradition trade life, were called "virtual" formerly. During this period, not only dot-com companies but also the companies which are trading in the traditional sense have increased their productivity and earnings by being included in network-based practices. Using information and network technologies, companies bring innovation not only in the products and services, but also in their business models, processes and management approaches. So, businesses that can develop their skills and abilities in new ways of doing business have come forward (Morris et al., 2005; Onetti et al., 2012).

Digitalization of information and communication infrastructures is economy based. Developments in the digital economy have significant impact on the creation of economic systems and economic value.

Basic features of digital economy are structures, processes, products and infrastructure (Zimmermann, 2000). Not to be the best in the market or to produce products in the most efficient way important in the digital economy; it is important to win the customer, to satisfy their needs, to have the best strategy and business model (van Eijsden, 2000). Powerful new digital technologies have created a serious change in customer behaviors. When a product, interaction, or device starts to digitize, there is no power to stand in the face of this, and in this case the old business models cannot be flexible, adaptable or unable to adapt so the old business model has to be deleted (Rogers, 2016).

BUSINESS MODEL CONCEPT

The concept of the business model, which includes all the processes of a business, covering its activities and describing the business plan, is closely related with the economy. Nowadays, when the digital transformation is experienced, the business structures that are transformed with the development and expansion of the Internet are also affected by this. The geographical distance is no longer a problem with the new economy, also markets expanded globally. Sales, production and marketing activities have become independent of the place. The globalization of the markets has led to the globalization of competitors. Thus, the definition of competition and the expectations of customers have changed as well.

Drucker's 1994 work in Harvard Business Review did not explicitly mention the business model, but there are a number of assumptions about what a business should and should not do. Moreover, some of the assumptions suggested by Porter, in an article published in Harvard Business Review in 1996, were also accepted as a starting point of the business model concept by some researchers (Ovans, 2015). While defining the business model, it is necessary to take Drucker's assumptions into account and to answer the questions by Porter such as "who is the customer?", "what creates the customer value?", "how can we earn money in this business?", "how can we provide value to customers?". The reason to answering those questions is the definition is that the business model is a set of elements of explaining how businesses operate (Magretta, 2002).

According to some researchers, the business model is defined as the concept that explains the business logic (Timmers, 1998; Teksten, 2001; Petrovic et al., 2001), while others refer to it as the link between business strategy, business processes and information systems (Nilsson, 1999; Osterwalder & Pigneur, 2002). Difference between these two interpretations of the business model roots from the relation of the business model with the concepts of strategy, business processes and technology. In the first interpretation, these three concepts are included in the definition of business model, while the second interpretation accepts them as interconnected components, which are set at different levels of pyramid structure. In this case, a business model is considered as the conceptual and architectural implementation of the business strategy and represents the basis of the implementation of business processes and information systems (Pateli, 2003). Many businesses are designing and evaluating their business models independently from the environment. However, especially without an examination of the business models of competitors, this can lead to failure (Casadesus-Masanell & Ricart, 2011).

Timmers, who mentioned the concept of business model for the first time, describes it in three different ways in his article published in 1998;

- Design of product, service and information flow where many different elements and their roles are combined.

- Identification of potential profits created or will be created by different business elements.
- Definition of income sources.

There are many different studies that define the concept of business model in various ways. Some of them define it as the technical capacity as an experiment-based logic that brings together the realization of economic value (Chesbrough & Rosenbloom, 2002), some as the basic logic of creating and retaining value within the network of values (Shafer et al., 2005).

According to Dubosson-Tobay et al. (2002) business model frame is divided into four basic elements. First of all, the product or service offered by the business should create value for the target customer, secondly, the relationship capital created by the business is used to satisfy the customer and generate sustainable income. Thirdly, designing of a structure to create value and creation of a network of stakeholder relations; and finally, the expected financial effects such as cost and revenue as a result of the previous three.

More specifically, Osterwalder et al. (2005) described the business model as a concept consisting of series of elements. These elements are value propositions (product, service offerings, customer segment identification and customer relations), activities, resources, shareholders, distribution channels, cost structure and revenue model. In 2010, Zott and Amit's approach to the business model was activity-based perspective and refers to the selection of some activities, system's activity structure and answering for questions concerning the realization of those activities. Referring to these perspectives, it is argued that the supply chain should be taken into consideration while developing a business model. In this respect, the business model consists of two main elements. First, everything related to production/service activity (design, raw material procurement, manufacturing, planning etc.), secondly everything related to the sales and marketing (finding and accessing customers, realizing the sale, distributing the product, or performing the service, etc.) (Ovans, 2015).

Three features of a good business model are listed below (Casadesus-Masanell & Ricart, 2011).

- It should be consistent with goals of the business. Choices made while designing business models should be aimed at achieving the goals.
- It should be self-strengthening. The choices made when designing business models must complement each other and must have internal consistency.
- It should be stable and durable. A good business model should be able to maintain its effectiveness and integrity against various threats.

For the success of the business model, implementation is as important as formulation. It should be checked whether there is a difference between the activities carried out during the implementation and the results and the plans. In case in a change of circumstances and conditions, corrections should be made in the business plan if necessary. Initially planning of a business model may be more successful or less successful than expected. In both cases, the plan is unlikely to have been made properly. If the result is unsuccessful, it may be considered that the planned business model is not working properly. Therefore, if it is more successful than expected, it can also be assumed that the positive developments could not have been predicted well enough (Özmen, 2013).

It has always been important for businesses to achieve competitive advantage and make it sustainable. However, since digital copying and replication is quite easy nowadays, businesses need to be innovative not only in products and services but also in processes and business models to be successful. In the past, competition has taken place between competing companies that are similar to each other, with fixed boundaries and clearly defined sectors, and now competition can still be experienced among unrelated businesses. Previously, businesses used to create value through their suppliers, sales channels. But now, because of digital revolution, boundaries between sectors have become transparent, distinction between stakeholders and competitors is changing, and the value creation can be made through different channels (Rogers, 2016).

E-COMMERCE AND E-BUSINESS MODELS

E-commerce, in the most general sense, is defined as "doing business electronically". European Union Commission has defined e-commerce as "the goods and services being sold on the Internet", OECD has defined it as "trading of products or services through computer networks" and World Trade Organization definition is "the production, advertisement, sales and distribution of goods and services over the Internet". E-commerce involves the electronic trading of physical goods and intangible products such as information and data. And this includes the steps of online marketing, ordering, payment and post-delivery services. It also facilitates the provision of e-commerce services and electronic transactions such as after-sales support and online assistance (Timmers, 1998). Even though the product or services are ordered electronically, payment and delivery processes do not have to be online. In other words, e-commerce companies perform their operations in the traditional sense, while they can do their job through the Internet (Zott et al., 2011).

New ways of doing business with the Internet are constantly improving. Most of these business practices attract the attention of consumers/customers and customer focus is prioritized. For those who are not directly in relation with the consumers, e-commerce can also be used to carry out business to business (B2B) transactions. New models in e-commerce are run in all types of business forms, sucha as business to business, business to consumer and business to government (Timmers, 1998). In a study which examined the strategies of e-commerce companies conducted by Mohapatra (2013), e-commerce companies are classified as business to consumer (B2C), business to business (B2B), consumer to consumer (C2C), consumer to business (C2B), business to employee (B2E), government to government (G2G), government to business (G2B), business to government (B2G), government to consumer (G2C) and consumer to government (C2G). From this point on, it is important to determine the direction of e-commerce.

E-commerce, which has been growing very rapidly especially in the last 10 years, has reshaped the shopping habits of consumers and therefore the business models of enterprises. Benefits of e-commerce, which continues to grow rapidly for both society and economy, are listed below (TÜSİAD, 2017);

- Restrains the hidden economy, increases productivity and supports the growth of enterprises.
- Contributes to the development of industries such as logistics and information technologies.
- Eliminates the costs of physical transactions and enables SMEs to compete with large enterprises.
- Increases the export potential by ensuring that products and services are promoted globally more easily, faster and at lower costs.

Defining e-commerce as a world-wide trade ground on the network is the main assumption. Although e-commerce is perceived as a trading process only because of its trading concept, it is understood that it has a much broader meaning with the use of e-business term (Özmen, 2013). E-commerce, which is perceived as the use of Internet in business functions such as communication, marketing and sales channels, continues evolve even though it moderately changed the business models. However, besides the evolution of e-commerce, it should be said that it is in fact a revolutionary development (Zimmermann, 2000; Kalakota & Robinson, 2001). This development will radically change the processes and structures within and between industries, and will help the digital economy pave the way for businesses. This situation is clearly predicted to have a major impact on basic business models. Most importantly, digital technologies are increasing the power of business models that enable an enterprise to create value by improving its interaction with other businesses or customers (Rogers, 2016).

E-business term was first used by IBM in 1997. According to IBM's definition, e-business is defined as "transforming the main business processes using technologies". Thus, it is understood that e-business is a term that includes not only trading but also other processes, from accounting to human resources, production to marketing, acceptance of order to automation to delivery and using information technologies. In short, e-business includes new ways of doing business, business model and business methods. E-business is an enterprise that covers the restructuring of all processes from supply chain to customer relations.

A business model is to build the business and its partners in order to create value and create a profitable and sustainable revenue stream. E-business models have the purpose of creating value by providing information to related parties, providing communication, buying and selling of activities, providing an exchange of ideas. It has been suggested that e-business model should consist of the following elements (Dubosson-Torbay et al., 2002):

- Product innovation (value creation, definition of target market, capabilities)
- Customer relations (customer feedback, customer service, brand building)
- Design management (resources/assets, activities/processes, shareholder relations)
- Financial aspects (revenue, cost, profit)

As mentioned above, new business models have started to emerge with the emergence of e-commerce and have become powerful components in e-commerce environment (Kalakota & Robinson, 2001). There should be a significant difference between e-business and e-commerce. Every e-commerce company cannot be defined as an e-business, but every e-business has to make e-commerce.

E-business models have the same objectives as the traditional models. Business models help businesses to identify their vision and strategies, redesign and regulate their business operations, facilitate the sharing of information about their processes and visions, and to ensuring that the decisions made are shared with shareholders (Persson & Stirna, 2001). In e-business models, there are targets such as increasing efficiency, the number of customers and the number of transactions. Traditional enterprises involved in the digital transformation, experience significant challenges in terms of ensuring integration of their business processes using information technologies. In order to accomplish digitalization of all processes, various databases, different software and hardware must be integrated. A business within the digital transformation process should not only build and manage a website, but should also be able to transform all its processes into e-business (Özmen, 2013).

E-business models create value by combining two or more sides within the framework of the work done instead of creating the value alone. For example, while e-marketplaces such as eBay and AliExpress bring together all kinds of buyers and sellers, Uber serves through a system that brings together people who need a vehicle and drivers who use their own vehicles (Rogers, 2016). In addition to the previously mentioned Timmers' business model definition, Klose and Lechner defines business model as design of products and services that meet customer needs, determination of the many different actors, their roles, relationship between them and benefits of different actors and sources of income. It is important to analyze and understand current developments to answer the questions within this definition and to design effective business models for the future. Analyzing them reveals four key elements that characterize the evolving digital economy. This analysis process, which includes observations, researches and experiences related to the real world, makes it necessary to concentrate on issues including the structure, business processes, products or services and infrastructure of enterprises (Klose & Lechner, 1999; Zimmermann, 2000).

E-Transformation Process and Being E-Business

E-businesses add value to all parties (customers, manufacturers, suppliers, employees, and managers) provide convenience, comfort, benefit and cost savings. It is essential that enterprises adapt to new technologies and new management approaches in order to sustain in the competitive environment. In recent years, it has become more important to start e-transformation process with the correct goals and strategies and to take a quick lead.

The most important success factors for the transformation of business processes into e-business, are the re-definition of enterprises into being a successful e-business, being visionary and making strategic decisions. It is not the old paradigms that are important in the process of transforming traditional businesses and their ways of doing business, but the realities of new economy and the realities of e-commerce. One of the main reasons for the negativity of e-transformation efforts, is the lack of business and management skills (Lee, 2001; Osterwalder et al., 2005).

Process of transforming businesses into e-businesses, managers to e-managers, requires strategic direction. This process starts with the enterprise deciding how to position itself in the market. In other words, it must first decide how it wants to see itself in the future. A business can carry through the stages of e-transformation process by spreading them to a certain time period, or it may initially emerge as an e-business, designing all business processes as e-processes (Hanna, 2009; Özmen, 2013).

Efforts of companies to differentiate themselves from their competitors have gained a different momentum in recent years due to the opportunities offered by Internet technologies. One of them is to set up the website. Companies want to reach more customers by establishing a website and communicate better and continuously with their existing customers. The first thing an e-business has to do is to build a website that users will like and enjoy during their visit. If the website visitors cannot access the information they want in the first few seconds, they may get lost on the site. Or if the pages are visually choking, visitors may prefer another website (Reichheld & Schefter, 2000). Taking care of such issues is the first rule of being an e-business.

Purpose of e-business models is to inform the relevant parties, to create value, to communicate, to buy/sell, to exchange ideas and to share (Zott et al., 2010). Also, a revenue model is extremely important.

In recent years, people have been exchanging ideas with each other, sharing their comments and complaints in social networking sites and blogs. Those shares reach very large audiences on aforementioned channels (Harris & Rae, 2009). For this reason, companies should visit at least certain portals frequently and should examine the negative comments about the products and services.

Basic elements that must be integrated for strategic activities in e-business ecosystem are; customers, markets, products, processes, organizations (structure and relations), shareholders, financing, social values and government policies. E-business ecosystem, that emerged from this point of view, is a network of customers, suppliers, distributors and trading service providers. E-businesses use the Internet for business-related basic communications and operations, including creation of value for new customers, transforming competition rules, moving people and resources to unprecedented performance levels (Pateli, 2003).

Zimmermann (2000) defines four elements that are changing for e-business models, and in the light of these elements given below, points to be taken into consideration while creating new business models are listed as;

- In today's e-commerce models, there is a value chain in which the customers and suppliers interact directly. E-commerce has changed the industry structures and differentiated the value creation process. Businesses can be divided into units or transformed into a modular structure. Technological ventures, especially called "start-ups", are often a single product enterprise that focus on one or more services or products (Sarkar et al., 1995). Rather than focusing on the entire value chain, businesses have started to pay attention on customer relations by focusing on their core competences.
- Process of creating value reversed, focusing on the customers' wishes and needs has come to the fore. In a structure focused on delivering personalized products or services, business processes have made the customer an element of market value that should be deemed as an individual. Industrial mechanisms have constituted the necessity for the processes coordination not only within the business, but also between enterprises.
- Especially in information intensive products, content is usually prepared with multiple contexts and infrastructures. Thanks to the infrastructure of information and communication technologies, each unit of a product is prepared in a flexible and diverse context. For example, latest breaking news are available through a large number of websites. Thus, information needs to be updated continuously. There are also many ads and other content on these websites.
- Many innovations in value creation processes and many technical platform infrastructures are needed to produce new products. These technical platforms are required for the actualization of the business models. Especially from business to business (B2B) perspective, businesses from different industries should meet the needs of different actors.

In addition to the above-mentioned elements, it is necessary to perform some basic functions for the success of the e-businesses. One of these is the planning of business processes. It is determined by whom these processes will be managed and which tasks will be maintained. It is necessary to revise the business functions within the framework of the business model. It should be noted that the purpose it to generate revenue while preparing a business plan. It is important to calculate the costs well and identify the return of the investment for this revenue to turn into profits (Özmen, 2013). It should be kept in mind that it is difficult to create a sustainable business model and provide a competitive advantage in the digital age where product life cycles are very short.

E-businesses often come to the forefront with the value created by the customer and achieve success. These business models often have a lot in common with the value they offer. E-businesses generally make it possible to offer the same product or service at a cheaper price. In addition, many new e-business models offer a system where some service is provided free of charge. The most common value source for e-business models is that the content or services can be accessed remotely from anywhere. Most e-businesses make purchasing easy and simple by eliminating any problem in the sales process. E-businesses give importance to personalization, allowing people to choose and use the service or product that suits their needs (Rogers, 2016).

E-Business Types and Examples

In order to understand how e-businesses earn money or not, various business models have been studied. Common point in the planning of e-business models is to clarify the income model and to develop business processes and strategies to the finest detail. The most critical issue in e-business models is whether it can be used to compare the companies that implement these models and whether they can be examined in categories (Dubosson-Torbay, 2002).

When e-business models are examined in general terms, can be listed as: virtual market places that bring buyers and sellers together and offering auction opportunities, private shopping opportunity sites that offer products or services at discounted prices, search engines, portals, supply chain enterprises that bring together suppliers and manufacturers, social networks that provide social interaction and information sharing, blogs, service providers that provide e-commerce solutions, distribution networks performing electronic and physical distribution (Özmen, 2013). According to the e-business model classifications in the literature, some of them have been classified according to the degree of functionality and innovation (Timmers, 1998), some according to the ability of economic control (Tapscott et al., 1999), some according to the type and degree of relations and some according to the power of buyers and sellers (Pigneur, 1996).

According to Tapscott et al. (2000)'s study, e-business models should be evaluated by the main theme, the value offered to the customer, the customer's role and knowledge and finally by main business processes. Main theme and main business process criteria refer to the mission, purpose and tasks of the enterprise to achieve its goal. Main business processes will be shaped around the main objectives of an enterprise. Value proposition criteria should answer the question of how the business model offers benefits to its users. For example, Amazon offers buyers the opportunity to get the product they want, while seller provide income for Amazon. Thus, it creates value for both sides. Another factor in the evaluation of e-business models is the role of the customer. Customers often play an important role in business processes. Customers who evaluate the product they buy in shopping sites, make comments on the books they buy in book sales sites, evaluate their vacation and the hotel they stayed on tour and travel sites. These factors affect business processes and sales directly. Usability of knowledge acquired by the business while implementing e-business models is related to how the business analyzes the information obtained and how it benefits from the findings of the analysis (TÜSİAD, 2017; Özmen, 2013). For example, in online book sales sites such as Barnes & Noble, all of the products that the user looks at, buys or discontinues to look for are recorded with a profile of his or her personal characteristics, such as his or her age, gender. These are all the information they need to focus on and analyze. When this information is analyzed correctly, customer satisfaction and loyalty can be improved.

Researchers working to examine the business model have developed many different schematic presentations about the applicability of models. In a study conducted by Weill and Vitale in 2001, tools necessary for the design and analysis of the e-business models included in these presentations were examined and analyzed in a simple manner. The "business model schematic" as a result is divided into three. The first is roles and relationships (electronic and primary, its customers, suppliers and collaborators), the second is major flows of product, information and money, and the third is revenue and other benefits each participant receives (Fielt, 2014). In that study, various e-business models were examined in accordance with these components.

Many different researchers have classified e-business models in various ways (Tapscott, 2000; Timmers, 1998; Applegate, 2001; Rappa, 2003). All types of e-business models are described by examining three of the most accepted classifications. First of these classifications was made by Timmers (1998) and the other was by Tapscott et al. (1999), and third, by Zott et al. (2011). E-business models discussed according to these classifications are briefly explained below.

One type of e-business model is so-called *e-shops,* which refers to Internet marketing and promotion of a business or a store. The priority of e-shop is the promotion of the company's products and services through the Internet. It is often used in conjunction with traditional marketing channels. Customers have the opportunity to compare product offerings, evaluate more options, get better information and make transactions such as selection, purchasing and acquisition easier (Timmers, 1998; Zott et al., 2011). An example of this business model is the online ticket sales of airlines, online stores of brands such as Zara, Gap or Walgreens.

Another e-business model is the where e-shops of well-known brands are often found. This business model, *e-mall*, provides a common technological platform for different e-shops. Thus, e-shops, which are members of e-malls, have some benefits such as lowering some of their costs and not having to deal with services like electronic payment and promotion. Besides, for customers, it is possible to examine and compare many brands at once (Timmers, 1998). It brings customers who want to shop over the Internet together with sellers who do not have the opportunity to host or cannot sell through a web site. Zimmermann (1997) acknowledges that an e-mall is a regional marketplace with multi-national products within the same region. An e-mall may also contain products from multiple contiguous regions (Laudon & Traver, 2016). Globally, e-malls are the most important purchase sites and their revenue model involves advertising, subscription, sales, affiliates, and transaction fees (Bahaddad et al., 2012). There are many examples of this business model. An e-mall hosts many online merchants. Examples of this model are Yahoo!Shopping, zShops and so on (Wen et al., 2001).

Another e-business model, *e-procurement*, depends on the products and services by offering them electronically. Large enterprises or government authorities can operate the e-procurement process over the Internet. Products or services offered to the large supplier network offer advantages such as lower cost, better quality products/services, better delivery and lowering of procurement costs (Timmers, 1998; Zott et al., 2011).

Similar to auction or traditional bidding, electronic version is called *e-auction*, which is an auction and bidding environment over the Internet (Zott et al., 2011). Such models are usually implemented with multi-media presentations of products and are carried through the integration of stages such as bidding, making deals, payment and delivery. Revenues of the e-auctioneers' businesses consist of the use of technology environment, payments made through the transaction and advertising revenues. For buyers and suppliers, there are benefits such as being more efficient, time-saving and global trading (Timmers, 1998). This business model is used by many different industries. There are e-auction websites established for different areas ranging from antiques and artworks to housing sales.

Virtual communities are based on the acquisition of the final value from members (customers or suppliers). Members enter the basic knowledge of the virtual community and obtain the necessary environmental elements from them. The virtual community offers the necessary marketing operations to create customer loyalty and receive customer feedback. In such models, revenue is generated from membership fees and advertisements (Zott et al., 2011).

Companies that want to meet their products with more customers and to test their operational processes and competencies use *e-marketplaces*. These businesses, in agreement with the e-marketplace, benefit from their systematic infrastructure, network, knowledge and traffic (Brunn et al., 2002). The e-marketplace concept provides the opportunity for companies to coordinate complex and multifunctional activities of supply chain processes through web-based applications (Eng, 2004). Ebay is one of the most important enterprises of the group of e-marketplaces in the world. Ebay, Amazon and Alibaba, the pioneers of e-marketplaces in different formats, have been very successful and have achieved a significant market share in the retail sector with thousands of suppliers and millions of customers.

Another e-business model is the third-party marketplace where an enterprise leaves the web marketing of the business to a third party (usually in addition to other channels). Generally, it serves as an interface where product catalogs are provided to suppliers, it ensures the secure execution of the processes such as branding, payment, logistics and ordering (Timmers, 1998; Zott et al., 2011). For example; "Google My Business" application operates as a digital media that manages business information that the business does not have.

Enterprises that specialize in one step of the value chain such as electronic payment or logistics, called *value chain service providers* (Timmers, 1998; Van de Vorst et al., 2002). Freight operators such as FedEx or UPS, payment businesses such as PayPal are examples of this model. Especially, e-businesses that specialize in terms of delivery, have created many different models.

Another business model focuses on many steps of the value chain, which creates value through the flow of information between these steps. Revenues of *value chain integrators* are usually obtained from consulting and processing fees (Timmers, 1998; Cagliano et al., 2003). Business called "Global Value Web" can be used as an example. The business defines itself as a company that serves to connect global businesses and creates a global value chain (https://global-value-web.com/index.html). It is a company that integrates the value chain steps among many companies in various industries, provides quality solutions and engineering services.

Business model of the enterprises that provide the necessary tools and information environment to ensure cooperation between enterprises also called *collaboration platforms*. Businesses in this model are focused on specific functions such as design and engineering, or do project-based work through virtual teams (Timmers, 1998). There are many companies that have a business model in the form of a collaboration platform. Looking at the examples of this model, it is seen that there are many different companies that provide environment and human resource for project based works.

Yet another e-business model is a large number of new information provisioning services, which are created by large amounts of data on open networks. These type of enterprises are called *information brokers*. In brief, they have emerged to provide services such as information search, customer profiling, investment advice and commercial business information services (Timmers, 1998; Hayes & Finnegan, 2005). Acxiom, for example, collects customer information to provide some businesses with information for marketing activities.

Another e-business model is *trust or other third party services*. They usually provide trust services, that are provided by certification authorities and electronic notaries. These services may charge subscription fees or service fees, combined with software sales and consultancy revenues (Timmers, 1998; Rappa, 2003).

Types of e-business models discussed in this part, have been obtained by considering many different sources. Such a viewpoint, which makes it easy to classify e-business types, of course, can be transformed and changed by the development of digital technologies. Increase in digitalization leads to different factors in the transformation from e-business models to digital business models. For this reason, new business models will lead to different classifications or different types of e-business models.

Internet entrepreneurs who set up an e-business model, or businesses planning to survive in the digital economy, were generally inspired by business models that first emerged in the United States. For example, entrepreneurs inspired by eBay's business model have implemented similar business models in many countries and have been successful.

Amazon, founded in 1994, has become a stand-alone brand thanks to its e-business model. As an enterprise that started to work primarily by selling books, it has achieved great success by selling twenty thousand books in the first two weeks of its establishment. Today, Amazon is an e-business with more than 350 centers across the globe (Eczacıbaşı, 2018), selling almost all of the products. Along with this, cloud technology systems called Amazon Cloud, have become an important opportunity for technology entrepreneurs today. Amazon's business model is based on an innovation that provides interface connectivity to more than two million stores that it doesn't own or manage (Keen & Wiliams, 2013).

Another important example of e-business model was the establishment of Uber company, which led to the birth of a new sector as a result of dream of an entrepreneur named Garrett Camp. E-business models similar to Uber company redefine the concept of transportation, through sharing economy, as competing with taxis all over the world. In US, Lyft, BlaBlaCar in France and Addison Lee in London are companies using the similar e-business models (Rogers, 2016).

Another example is the business model of Airbnb, which was founded in 2008. Airbnb is growing rapidly and has more rooms than the most important hotel chains in the world (such as Hilton, Inter Continental). According to 2015 statistics, Airbnb provided accommodation for over 25 million tourists in more than 190 countries. Airbnb's business model is a platform that brings together the homeowners who want to rent part or all of their houses and customers looking for accommodation. The most important feature of Airbnb in terms of business model is that the value offered to customers is different from other enterprises (Kavadias et al., 2016).

It would not have been possible for Amazon to change the concept of shopping 20 years ago. Also, the idea that the world's largest hospitality company would not have a single hotel could not be understood five years ago. A similar example is that Apple has become the world's largest digital music company in almost 10 years, thanks to its business model, not products such as iPod and iPhone. Apple has created 92% of the market by supporting the iTunes app with smartphones. What is important here is that the new and different business model is transformed into one of the world's largest shops, selling not only music but all kinds of products and services (Eczacıbaşı, 2013).

Another e-business model application, known as TaskRabbit, was established in 2008 as an individual outsourcing site. Operation of the business model starts by logging into the system by describing what kind of service is needed and by continuing to communicate with them by selecting the most appropriate person to perform the requested service. Person who receives the service is responsible for payment via the application or website when the job is completed (Ay et al., 2018).

E-business models, sometimes creating a new sector from scratch, sometimes appearing as a different formation of the existing sector, can disable other players in the sector. For example, business model of Craigslist, a classified ads service, has had a very negative effect on the newspapers that obtained most of its revenue from classified ads. The most profitable section of the newspapers with high production costs, is the classified ads sections that readers want to sell or rent for their various needs. However, a new e-business model created by Craig Newmark, a software programmer in the USA, with the idea that everyone is free to submit their ads online. With this idea, in a short period of time, it has become a global company which has been broadcasting in 70 countries and 13 languages and its contents have been read 50 billion times as day (https://www.feedough.com/how-does-craigslist-make-money/ accessed at 06.11.2018; Rogers, D. (2016). The Digital Transformation Playbook. Columbia University Press.)

Companies in several countries, such as GrubHub in US, Seamless in UK and Delivery Hero in Germany are another example of an e-business model. People can order online by ordering the most suitable meal by scanning the restaurants around their house or workplace. Value created by this model is that, it offers a more convenient experience than examining different restaurants websites, brochures and trying to order by phone (https://mediacat.com/caginin-otesinde/ accessed at 6.11.2018).

Examples given above are those that have created a unique business model and even give insight to those who come after. Different e-business model types and examples examined in this section. These e-business models continue to be added every day with the development and utilization of technology.

DISCUSSION AND CONCLUSION

Since the mid-1990s, commercial websites have become widespread. Success of e-commerce businesses, established since the 2000s, have attracted attention and the business models they implement are different from traditional business models. First enterprises operating in the early stages of e-commerce, are businesses that appear directly on the Internet. Many of them failed because of the proliferation of these enterprises and their activity only on the Internet. Later on, enterprises that are successful in traditional commerce and also integrate the Internet into their business model have been successful.

Effects of technology and Internet on our lives have increased with the beginning of the transformation of enterprises digitally. However, it is clear that digitalization is much more than just Internet usage. Business practices, workplace structures, relationships between employees, information sharing, customer relations and even competition are affected by digital transformation. In an e-business model, it is necessary to integrate the value network with technology, and most importantly, to use technology in every process of the business.

As it can be seen from detailed examples in the chapter, it is very common for businesses with traditional business models to convert their business model into e-business models. Companies invest in digital channels in order to create different experience from their competitors, and businesses in the service industry are trying to bring their business processes to a digital environment.

One of the most important effects of digital transformation is, its impact on business structures and therefore on business models. Nowadays, it is an inevitable necessity for businesses that sell to end customers to transform themselves in digital transformation. For this reason, it is thought that the differentiation of the business processes of all enterprises which are born in digital environment and trying to exist in digital environment, will bring a transformation to the business model literature and there are many opportunities to make research in this direction.

REFERENCES

Amit, R., & Zott, C. (2001). Value creation in e-business. *Strategic Management Journal, 22*(6-7), 493–520. doi:10.1002mj.187

Applegate, L. M. (2001). E-business Models: Making sense of the Internet business landscape. *Information technology and the future enterprise: New models for managers*, 49-94.

Ay, C., Yakın, V., & Kacar, A. İ. (2018). *Paylaşım Ekonomisi, A'dan Z'ye Tüm Boyutlarıyla* (pp. 41–42). Ankara, Turkey: Akademisyen Kitabevi.

Bolumole, Y. A. (2003). Evaluating the supply chain role of logistics service providers. *International Journal of Logistics Management, 14*(2), 93–107. doi:10.1108/09574090310806620

Brunn, P., Jensen, M., & Skovgaard, J. (2002). e-Marketplaces: Crafting A Winning Strategy. *European Management Journal, 20*(3), 286–298. doi:10.1016/S0263-2373(02)00045-2

Cagliano, R., Caniato, F., & Spina, G. (2003). E-business strategy: How companies are shaping their supply chain through the Internet. *International Journal of Operations & Production Management, 23*(10), 1142–1162. doi:10.1108/01443570310496607

Casadesus-Masanell, R., & Ricart, J. E. (2011). How to design a winning business model. *Harvard Business Review, 89*(1/2), 100-107. Retrieved from https://hbr.org/2011/01/how-to-design-a-winning-business-model

Chesbrough, H., & Rosenbloom, R. S. (2002). The role of the business model in capturing value from innovation: Evidence from Xerox Corporation's technology spin-off companies. *Industrial and Corporate Change, 11*(3), 529–555. doi:10.1093/icc/11.3.529

Dubosson-Torbay, M., Osterwalder, A., & Pigneur, Y. (2002). E-business model design, classification, and measurements. *Thunderbird International Business Review, 44*(1), 5–23. doi:10.1002/tie.1036

E-business. (n.d.). Retrieved from https://www.ibm.com/ibm/history/ibm100/us/en/icons/ebusiness/transform/

Eczacıbaşı, F. (2018). *Daha Yeni Başlıyor: Geleceğin Dünyasında Esneklik, Yakınsama, Ağ Yapısı ve Karanlık Taraf* (pp. 60–62). İstanbul, Turkey: Koç Üniversitesi Yayınları.

Eng, T. Y. (2004). The role of e-marketplaces in supply chain management. *Industrial Marketing Management, 33*(2), 97–105. doi:10.1016/S0019-8501(03)00032-4

Fielt, E. (2014). Conceptualising business models: Definitions, frameworks and classifications. *Journal of Business Models, 1*(1), 85–105.

Global Value Web. (n.d.). Retrieved from https://global-value-web.com/index.html

Glossary: E-commerce. (n.d.). Retrieved from https://ec.europa.eu/eurostat/statistics-explained/index.php/Glossary:E-commerce

Hanna, N. K. (2009). e-Transformation: Enabling new development strategies. Berlin, Germany: Springer Science & Business Media.

Harris, L., & Rae, A. (2009). Social networks: The future of marketing for small business. *The Journal of Business Strategy*, *30*(5), 24–31. doi:10.1108/02756660910987581

Hayes, J., & Finnegan, P. (2005). Assessing the of potential of e-business models: Towards a framework for assisting decision-makers. *European Journal of Operational Research*, *160*(2), 365–379. doi:10.1016/j.ejor.2003.07.013

Kalakota, R., & Robinson, M. (2001). E-business 2.0: Roadmap for Success. Boston, MA: Addison-Wesley Longman Publishing

Kavadias, S., Ladas, K., & Loch, C. (2016). Dönüştürücü İş Modeli, *Harvard Business Review Türkiye*. Retrieved from https://hbrturkiye.com/dergi/donusturucu-is-modeli

Keen, P., & Williams, R. (2013). Value architectures for digital business: Beyond the business model. *Management Information Systems Quarterly*, *37*(2), 643–648.

Kim, W. C., & Mauborgne, R. (1999). Strategy, value innovation, and the knowledge economy. *Sloan Management Review*, *40*(3), 41–42.

Klose, M., & Lechner, U. (1999). Design of business media-an integrated model of electronic commerce. *AMCIS 1999 Proceedings*, 193.

Lee, C. S. (2001). An analytical framework for evaluating e-commerce business models and strategies. *Internet Research*, *11*(4), 349–359. doi:10.1108/10662240110402803

Magretta, J. (2002). Why business models matter? *Harvard Business Review*, *80*(5), 86–92. PMID:12024761

Meyer, C., & Davis, S. (2000). Blur: The speed of change in the connected economy. *Work Study*, *49*(4). doi:10.1108/ws.2000.07949dae.003

Mohapatra, S. (2013). E-commerce Strategy. In *E-Commerce Strategy* (pp. 155–171). Boston, MA: Springer. doi:10.1007/978-1-4614-4142-7_7

Morris, M., Schindehutte, M., & Allen, J. (2005). The entrepreneur's business model: Toward a unified perspective. *Journal of Business Research*, *58*(6), 726–735. doi:10.1016/j.jbusres.2003.11.001

Nilsson, J. (1999). Co-operative organisational models as reflections of the business environments. *The Finnish Journal of Business Economics*, *4*(99), 449–470.

Onetti, A., Zucchella, A., Jones, M. V., & McDougall-Covin, P. P. (2012). Internationalization, innovation and entrepreneurship: Business models for new technology-based firms. *The Journal of Management and Governance*, *16*(3), 337–368. doi:10.100710997-010-9154-1

Osterwalder, A., & Pigneur, Y. (2002). An eBusiness model ontology for modeling eBusiness. BLED 2002 Proceedings, 2.

Osterwalder, A., Pigneur, Y., & Tucci, C. L. (2005). Clarifying business models: Origins, present, and future of the concept. *Communications of the Association for Information Systems*, *16*(1), 1.

Ovans, A. (2015). What is a business model? *Harvard Business Review*, 1–7.

Özmen, Ş. (2013). *Ağ Ekonomisinde Yeni Ticaret Yolu – E-Ticaret*. İstanbul Bilgi Üniversitesi Yayınları.

Pateli, A. (2003). A framework for understanding and analysing ebusiness models. *BLED 2003 Proceedings*, 4.

Persson, A., & Stirna, J. (2001, June). Why enterprise modelling? an explorative study into current practice. In *International Conference on Advanced Information Systems Engineering* (pp. 465-468). Berlin, Germany: Springer. 10.1007/3-540-45341-5_31

Petrovic, O., Kittl, C., & Rappa, M. (2001). Managing the digital enterprise - Business models on the Web. North Carolina State University.

Pigneur, Y. (1996). A Framework for designing new information systems. In F. Bodart (Ed.), *Future of Information Systems – Challenge and Pitfalls* (pp. 61–102).

Porter, M. E. (2017, Oct. 3). *What Is Strategy?* Retrieved from https://hbr.org/1996/11/what-is-strategy

Rappa, M. (2003). Business models on the web. *Managing the Digital Enterprise website.* Available at http://digitalenterprise. org

Reichheld, F. F., & Schefter, P. (2000). E-loyalty: Your secret weapon on the web. *Harvard Business Review*, *78*(4), 105–113.

Rogers, D. (2016). The Digital Transformation Playbook. New York, NY: Columbia University Press. doi:10.7312/roge17544

Sarkar, M. B., Butler, B., & Steinfield, C. (1995). Intermediaries and cybermediaries: A continuing role for mediating players in the electronic marketplace. *Journal of Computer-Mediated Communication*, *1*(3), 1–14.

Shafer, S. M., Smith, H. J., & Linder, J. C. (2005). The power of business models. *Business Horizons*, *48*(3), 199–207. doi:10.1016/j.bushor.2004.10.014

Statistics Directorate, O. E. C. D. (n.d.). Electronic Commerce. Retrieved from https://stats.oecd.org/glossary/detail.asp?ID=4721

Tapscott, D. (2000). Digital capital: Harnessing the power of business webs. Brighton, MA: Harvard Business School Press.

Tapscott, D., Ticoll D., & Lowy, A. (1999). The rise of the business web. *Business 2.0,* November, 198-208.

Teksten, R. (2001). Developing Business Models for eBusiness. *Proceedings of the International Conference on Electronic Commerce.*

Timmers, P. (1998). Business models for electronic markets. *Electronic Markets*, *8*(2), 3–8. doi:10.1080/10196789800000016

TÜSİAD. (2017). *Dijitalleşen Dünyada Ekonominin İtici Gücü: E-Ticaret.* 04-587.

Van der Vorst, J. G., Van Dongen, S., Nouguier, S., & Hilhorst, R. (2002). E-business initiatives in food supply chains; definition and typology of electronic business models. *International Journal of Logistics*, *5*(2), 119–138. doi:10.1080/13675560210148641 van Eijsden, G. A. I. (2000). *Banking in the Digital Economy* (Doctoral dissertation, Technical University Eindhoven, The Netherlands).

Wirtz, B. W., Schilke, O., & Ullrich, S. (2010). Strategic development of business models: Implications of the Web 2.0 for creating value on the Internet. *Long Range Planning*, *43*(2-3), 272–290. doi:10.1016/j.lrp.2010.01.005

WTO. (n.d.) Retrieved from https://www.wto.org/english/rese/bookspe/ecombrochuree.pdf

Zimmermann, H. D. (2000) Understanding the Digital Economy: Challenges for new Business Models. In: *Proceedings of the 2000 Americas Conference on Information Systems*. 10.2139srn.2566095

Zott, C., Amit, R., & Massa, L. (2010). The business model: Theoretical roots, recent developments, and future research. *IESE business school-University of Navarra*, 1-43.

Zott, C., Amit, R., & Massa, L. (2011). The business model: Recent developments and future research. *Journal of Management*, *37*(4), 1019–1042. doi:10.1177/0149206311406265

Chapter 11
The Effect of Consumer Emotions on Online Purchasing Behavior

Dilaysu Cinar
Beykent University, Turkey

ABSTRACT

This chapter was written to demonstrate the effect of consumer emotion on online purchasing behavior. According to the results obtained from 418 data, it was observed that both positive and negative emotions impacted online buying behavior. In this context, as the positive emotions of the online consumer increases, the frequency of purchases increases, but as the negative emotions of the online consumer increases, the frequency of purchases decreases. In addition, user interface quality, product information quality, service information quality, site awareness, security perception, information satisfaction, and relational benefit factors are factors that negatively affect consumers emotionally in purchasing online. On the other hand, only product information quality, user interface quality, and security perception factors positively affect emotions of online consumers.

INTRODUCTION

Businesses target certain feelings, values, and emotions in consumers in order to achieve competitive advantage, to make their ads memorable and to ensure that consumers select the product offered by them. In this case, the fundamental aim is to create the attitudes and actions on buying behavior of consumers. It has been proved that almost all of the purchases made by consumers are done with their emotional motivation. For this reason, it is clear that companies need to give a place emotional content in order to provide a competitive advantage. To achieve this, a company follows the steps such as; to determine the consumer's needs and desires, to develop a marketing communication strategy that can position the product emotionally and establish a relationship between consumer emotions and the concrete product features. Almost every product offers similar advantages. For this reason, firms take steps to create strategies parallel to consumer sentiments and, above all, emphasizes the values related to the inner desires, wants and

DOI: 10.4018/978-1-7998-0035-4.ch011

ambitions of potential customers. Therefore, the secret of business is to create an emotional relationship between the consumer and the product. Studies argued that the attention of consumers would be drawn not by logical arguments but by creating images that created emotions. Therefore, the more intense the emotion, the deeper the neurological connection in the brain of the consumer. In this sense, companies have the goal of eliminating expectations with products that can address consumer feelings. Therefore, it is necessary to know how the consumers think, what the consumers feel and what emotions can be produced to reveal their dreams. In other words, firms should leave a mark on the consumer in order to be catchy, to create consumer loyalty and to turn potential customers into existing customers. The way to achieve this is to stimulate the networks that create a sense of pleasure and goodness in the consumer.

In this study, first of all, it has been examined whether there is a statistically significant difference between online purchasing behavior and demographic variables. Then, the factors affecting the consumer's emotions in the online shopping channel has been revealed. For this, it has benefited from the scale developed by Park and Kim (2003). The factors discussed in this scale are; user interface quality, product information quality, service information quality, site awareness, security perception, information satisfaction, and relational benefit. The scale developed by Laros and Steenkamp (2003) was used to determine how the aforementioned factors affect consumer emotions. The factors have been discussed in this scale are; anger, fear, sadness, shame, contentment, and happiness. Finally, the impact of these emotional factors on online purchasing behavior have been measured in this study.

BACKGROUND

Customer Emotions

Emotion is the body reactions that is acquired in parallel with the evolutionary development of human beings, affected to human behavior, occurs depending on events, factors, objects. Emotion is also mostly uncontrollable. (Taylor, 2000). Although there are different typologies related to emotions, when evaluated as a whole, they can be classified in two ways: basic emotions and complex (secondary) emotions. The basic emotions are instinctive reactions that do not require any cognitive evaluation, which arise suddenly, and that apply to all people and are constantly changing (Bellman, 2007). On the other hand, complex emotions are a mixture and a combination of basic emotions (Plutchik, 1980). The complex emotion set consists of differentiated emotions that require cognitive evaluation such as love, anger, empathy, nostalgia and desire (Blossom, 2001).

Emotions are examined in the marketing literature on issues such as advertising (Stayman & Aaker, 1988), retailing (Babin et. al., 2005), pleasure (Alcan˜iz et. al, 2005), behavioral trends (Hicks et. al, 2005) and decision-making process (Stayman & Batra, 1991). Emotions affect consumer and executive decisions closely (Bagozzi et. al, 1999). According to this, positive feelings of consumption lead to positive behaviors and re-purchase (Karakaya, 2017)

Emotional experiences during the shopping by consumers are very important. Because consumers will evaluate their next purchase in line with their emotional experiences. Therefore, consumer emotions are used to define consumption experiences and to create an impact on the consumer. In order to be successful in marketing strategies, it is necessary to identify the emotions that are effective throughout the consumption (Cacioppo & Gardner, 1999). The subjective emotions that are experienced in evaluating, buying or using a product are consumption emotions (Cohen & Areni, 1991). Richins (1997) also describes the various feelings, moods or emotions gained during the consumption of a product or service as consumption emotions (Deveci, 2014).

Consumption emotions are a conceptualized classification of different primary emotions such as entertainment, interest, sadness and happiness. According to his research, which is called as the marketing literature, Consumption Emotion Set, Richins (1997) states that there are 16 consumption emotions and that this consumption emotion set is only used to measure direct emotions about product consumption and not to measure indirect feelings about advertisements. Richins (1997) dealt with these emotions as a combination of emotions such as anger, dissatisfaction, anxiety, unhappiness, fear, shame, jealousy, loneliness, romantic love, affection, tranquility, freshness, optimism, fun, enthusiasm, astonishment. On the other hand, according to Hansen et al. (2006), consumers choose the ones closest to their emotions from adjectives (happiness, anger, etc.) that are presented to them, even though they do not fully represent the main emotions when talking about their emotions. In other words; presenting adjectives that consumers can use to express their feelings are not enough to catch true emotions of consumers about that advertising or brand. For this reason, the Net Emotional Response Strength (NERS) approach was developed by Hansen et al. (2006) in order to capture the emotions felt by the consumers towards advertising or brand. According to this approach, by calculating the absolute value of the positive and negative emotions that the consumers feel for the brand, the NERS value that the consumer has to the brand or the advertising is calculated. The NERS value that the consumer possesses against that the brand or the advertising is calculated. If this value is greater than 0, the consumer feeds positive emotions towards that brand / advertisement, if it is less than 0, consumer feeds negative emotions against that brand / advertisement. Consumption emotions are the main reason for motivation of the individual. Holbrook and Gardner (1993) discussed the relationship between emotion dimensions and consumption experiences in terms of satisfaction and mobilization dimensions. As a result of the study, they determined that positive emotions motivated the consumer. Emotions are important at this point. Because the emotional importance of the situation in terms of the individual determines the level of motivation (Allen et al., 2003).

Emotional reactions that may occur pre-purchase, during purchase and post- purchase, the use of the product and other consumption processes can be in the form of contentment, joy, enthusiasm, pride, relaxation, nerve, fear, sadness and guilt (Holbrook & Hirschman, 1982). In order to evaluate the product, the effects of the product feelings and product satisfaction on the post-consumer experience were examined in a study by Mano and Oliver (1993). To evaluate emotions about the product; they have applied to adjectives such as good mood, fear, bad mood, action, boredom, calmness, confusion, guilt and content (Mano & Oliver, 1993) In general terms, emotions related to consumption are examined at two levels as positive and negative emotions (King & Meiselman, 2010). Customers seek positive emotional experiences in their purchasing or consumption processes and avoid negative emotional experiences (Karakaya, 2017). According to Westbrook (1987), consumption emotion is the main determinant of consumer behavior and the direction of oral communication. Not fulfilling expectations plays a role in determining consumption feelings. Westbrook (1987) stated that both positive and positive emotions are related to surprise and interest, while negative emotions are associated with hostility. There is a significant relationship between positive word of mouth communication with consumption emotions and being willing to share more and also changing preference (White & Yu, 2005). Positive consumer emotions create positive word of mouth communication, more and more positive shares with other consumers and brand loyalty, while negative consumer emotions result in negative word of mouth communication, sharing of negative emotions for business or products with the environment and changing the brand preference

(White & Yu, 2005). According to Tronvoll (2010) negative emotions occur when a consumer experiences a situation or experience that he does not want. This situation ends with the complaint behavior of the consumer. Inman et al. (1997) found that negative emotions had a much stronger impact on subsequent purchasing evaluations than positive feelings. Because consumers remember the negative feelings they experience more clearly than positive emotions. Such feelings are frequently encountered in services. As a result, it is useful to know what emotions lead to negative consumer behavior in order to provide positive word of mouth communication behavior and to create customer loyalty (Karakaya, 2017).

Consumer emotions may also be caused by advertising. Batra and Ray (1986), who examined the state of advertising positively in consumers, show that advertising can cause emotions such as excitement, happiness, relaxation, sincerity, compassion and sympathy. On the other hand, promotional efforts such as a cigarette advertisement involving the use of health harmful substances for young children, a cosmetic advertisement containing a thin woman, and a public spot that resulted in death could lead to feelings such as anger, disgust, shame, sadness and fear. In another study by Batra and Halbrook (1990) measures to basic reactions that are created by the ads on consumers. According to their study, mood, emotions, and motives are effective reactions towards advertising. Another study related to advertising is the study by Derbaix (1995). Derbaix (1995) examined the effect of television commercials on emotions and mentioned two important variables about advertising to evaluate this. These are; consumer attitude towards advertisements and brand attitude after exposure to advertising. Then, Ekman (1999) examined the effect of these two important variables, which are evaluated using the oral and nonverbal emotion scales, on the emotional responses of those exposed to the ad. At the end of the research, verbal expressions have a significant effect on these variables while non-verbal expressions (mimic, gesture, etc.) have no significant effect on these variables (Kabadayı & Alan, 2013).

Customer emotion is also examined in the context of customer complaint behavior. To explain the behavior after purchasing is simply insufficient to understand the phenomenon of dissatisfaction, as in question that unsatisfactory behavior of the customers that harm to company (abandonment, negative communication, etc.) instead of forwarding the complaint to the business. Consumer emotion may also affect consumer behavior before buying. If the consumer focuses on emotions in the decision-making process, as in the case of fast-moving consumer goods where preferences based on emotions occur, attention should be given to product characteristics that will create positive emotional responses such as the picture on the package. On the other hand, if customers are seeking concrete reasons, the advantages of the product are primarily suitable (Scarabis et al., 2006). For example, for a product such as ice cream or chocolate, consumers are more likely to make decisions depending on emotions and internal reactions. Consumer emotion can also be examined in terms of the effectiveness of the specific promotion activity. For example, the emotional response to advertising may affect the relationship between the consumer's advertising message processing and the attitudes towards advertising and brand (Edell & Marjon, 1987). Hence, it is understood that in marketing communication, emotions are an issue that should be examined from different perspectives. Consequently, it is expected that people will develop positive attitudes and have behavioral tendencies against businesses, products, stores, salespeople, brands or advertisers who create positive emotions in the customer (Karakaya, 2017).

Online Purchasing Behavior

The continuous changes in consumer demands and the behaviors in the purchasing process are of great importance for marketing today. The elasticity of this demand in consumers is due to new and different information acquired continuously. Because consumers now have a lot of choice. Therefore, businesses should remind consumers of their assets frequently. For this, the best way to follow in terms of enterprises is to be on the internet environment where consumers spend most of their time. Thus, it will be possible to meet the consumers' demands and needs by reaching them in a shorter time (Leinbach & Reyhle, 2015). Previously, shopping was done to spend time and socialize, over time it becomes a tedious activity by some consumers. This is is the most important indicator of changes in consumer behavior. The rapid development of the Internet and the spread of marketing from the internet has been a good alternative for consumers who think that shopping is boring or time consuming. As the number of online shoppers increased, it became important to investigate consumers' online buying behavior (Gültaş & Yıldırım, 2016). In addition, the internet is not limited to an environment where consumers can use it only at the time of shopping. the Internet is also able to master many functions in the traditional shopping area both pre- purchase and post-purchase (Cengiz & Şekerkaya,2010)

Experience is the first factor that influences consumers' online purchase. It has been demonstrated in various studies that the experiences related to internet channel are effective to evaluation of the benefits offered by the internet channel to the consumers (Montoya et al., 2003). While consumers with adequate internet experience may feel more comfortable when using online channels; others may be more hesitant about using the online channel due to perceived uncertainty and risk (Murray & Schlacter, 1990). Dahle'N (1999), who researched on the shoppers in the online environment, revealed that individuals with a lot of internet experience are more engaged in online shopping than individuals with less internet experience. Hofmann et al. (1995) found in their research that people who connect to the internet more often do more online shopping than those who are not frequently connected. Rangaswamy and Gupta, (1999) also found that individuals who spend more time on the internet prefer more than online shopping the consumer's beliefs regarding the perceived benefit and perceived ease of use also affect to buy on the online channels (Karahanna & Straub, 1999).

Another factor effective in online purchasing is privacy. Privacy is defined as the protection of information provided in a communication system or network and hiding against access by others. Privacy is also consumers concerning about making online purchases that is most frequently mentioned by them (56). Another factor that is effective in online purchasing is security. The security risks are perceived by consumers against online shopping more than they perceive against a physical store. This is due to the fact that consumers are most often afraid of stealing credit card information or using them for different purposes. In order to increase online shopping, it is necessary to minimize this risk perceived by the consumer. The online shopping site should close the gaps in financial security and build trust in consumer perception (Akbar & James, 2014)). Time factor is another factor in online purchasing. According to Becker, time is very limited for the modern time consumer and efficient use of time is a critical issue. The Internet is seen as a time saver for the consumer in this sense. Not having to visit the store, looking for products in the crowd and preventing queues in the trial cabins has a positive effect on increasing online purchasing (Kim, 2004). In fact, ease of use also allows consumers to buy online. The ease of use is associated with the ability of the consumer to use the relevant shopping site effortlessly. The easier the consumer can use the online store, the more positive the buying behavior will be (Alcan˜iz et al., 2008)). Touching is another factor that has an impact on consumer purchasing decision-making processes in online purchasing. The consumer wants to touch, see and try that product before buying a product. In a way, this is to test whether the product meets the performance desired by the consumer. Since there is no physical contact in online shopping, the consumer can perceive this as a risk (Perry et al., 2013)

On the other hand, marketing related factors affecting the online purchasing behavior are; product quality, diversity and characteristics, product promotion, delivery methods, returning policy and customer service (Özdemir and Taşkın, 2017). While shopping, consumers pay attention to product variety and quality. It is a fact that online stores have more products than a physical store. Selling quality products will increase online store's sales performance. Both factors have the potential to increase online sales (Sebastianelli et al., 2008). The characteristics and types of products listed for customers' selection in the online store can affect the purchasing decisions of customers. Product promotion is another factor in influencing consumers' buying behavior. Through online channels (e-mail messages, advertisements, etc.), the online store's poster and logo are tried to be conveyed to the consumer to gain awareness. These promotional activities have positive effects on informing the consumer and referring them to the website. (Gallagher et. al., 2001). The use of delivery service, which is another factor, is required because there is a physical separation between the buyer and the seller in an online purchase. The time difference between the product order and delivery reduces the consumer's concern. These concerns have a negative impact on the consumers' online shopping (Yrjola, 2001). Another factor is that the consumer will not have any trouble in returning the product, the consumer will not hesitate to make purchases in the online environment. A problem that may arise during the returning phase will also negatively affect future online purchases. Unlike a shopping in a physical store, it is not possible to examine the product in a shop online. This situation makes application of product returning more important (Kim, 2004). As the last factor that keeps its importance in online stores, customer service includes order fulfillment and order tracking. Providing personalized service gives competitive advantage and customer satisfaction in online retailers (Luo et al., 2012).

In studies on online consumer behavior, researchers generally adopted two accepted views; these are consumer-oriented and technology-oriented views. Consumer-oriented view focuses on consumers' beliefs about online shopping and the impact of these beliefs on the shopping channel. To give an example, online consumer behavior has been studied in terms of shopping orientation, motivation, personal characteristics and internet experience (Monsuwe, Dellart, & Ruyter, 2004). On the other hand, technology-oriented view is used to estimate consumers' online shopping adoption by examining web site designs, content and system usability. Researchers have developed socio-psychological-based theories to explain and predict consumers' online buying behavior and decision-making process by adhering to technology-oriented and consumer-oriented perspectives. Theory of Reasoned Action, Theory of Planned Behavior, Technology Adoption Model, Expectation-Confirmation Theory and and Process Cost Theory are some of them. These theories, based on attitude and intention, are the most common and dominant cognitive models and have been used as an important tool to explain individual behavior. These models provide an infrastructure for evaluating the cognitive basis of behavioral decisions. Among the mentioned models, the studies conducted to understand the consumer behavior in the online environment are basically based on two models. These two models have been widely studied are; Theory of Reasoned Action (TRA) and Theory of Planned Behaivor (TPB) (Cheung, Chan, & Limayem, 2005).

Fishbein and Ajzen (1975) was developed the Theory of Reasoned Action in order to describe the behavior of a particular purchase. The TRA recognizes that the individual's behavior is determined by the behavioral intention of that individual. There are two main determinants of behavioral intention according to TRA. These are subjective norms that can be defined as attitude towards behavior and normative social pressure. The attitude towards behavior can be considered as a combination of the beliefs about the behavior and the evaluation of the behavior results. In addition, subjective norms are considered as a combination of a particular reference group's views on behavior and the motivation of adherence to the individual's reference group (Fishbein & Ajzen, 1975). Although this model is widely used in experimental research on online behavior, Kim (2005) concluded in their studies that this model showed a poor performance for explaining the behavioral intention compared to other models. Therefore, Theory of Planned Behaivor has been developed as a result of the addition of perceived behavioral control variable to the basic model Ajzen's Theory of Planned Behaivor is an extended version of TRA. TPB has been developed taking into account the conditions in which individuals do not have full control over their behavior. In order to better predict the consumer behavior in the online environment, the Theory of Reasoned Action, which includes the individual's attitude towards behavior and subjective norm factors, was expanded by adding a Perceived Behavioral Control (PBC) variable. PBC expresses the perception of how easy or difficult it can be for an individual to perform a behavior (Ajzen, 1991). According to TPB, actual behavior is determined by both behavioral intent and perceived behavioral control. Behavioral intent can be estimated respectively by looking at subjective norms, attitudes and ADC factors. Using this model, which focuses on understanding and predicting the behaviors of individuals, many studies have been conducted for a specific behavior in different areas. Empirical research has shown that TPB is well suited for predicting consumer behavior in online shopping (George, 2004). Hansen, Jensen and Solgaard (2004) tested both TRA and TPB in his studies and found that TPB was a better model than TRA in explaining online consumer behavior.

While there are different models related to the consumer buying process in the online environment, this study will be based on the consumer purchasing decision model, which was developed in 1968 by Engel Kollat Blackwell. The reason why EKB model is preferred is that it is widely accepted in the literature and it is used in other scientific studies investigating consumers' buying behavior from the internet. The model consists of five stages: determination of needs (identification of the problem), information collection, evaluation of alternatives, purchase decision and post-purchase evaluation (Cengiz & Sekerkaya, 2010).

The pre-purchase period consists of the first three stages of the online consumer purchase decision process. The stages of determining the needs, collecting information and evaluating the alternatives constitute the stages that the consumers spend before making the decision to buy. Recognition of the need arises from the perception of the difference between the current situation of the consumer and the ideal situation and this phase is characterized by the identification of needs. At this stage, it is possible to be aware of the needs by informing to online consumers (Blackwell et al., 2001). Moreover, websites and some referral agencies can also enable consumers to recognize their undiscovered needs (Maes et al., 1999). The Internet increases consumer efficiency by facilitating more convenient access to consumption-related information, and helps to save time, energy and money expenditure to collect information. The Internet also enhances consumer effectiveness by offering a mix of visual tools (sound, image, text) to facilitate consumer information and help consumers to select products that best meet their needs (McGaughey & Mason, 1998) The Internet provides consumers with fast and convenient information as well as the ability to compare products and services (Keeney, 1999). Thus, it makes easier to compare various alternatives. The Internet has created some differences in terms of the consumer. Consumers have started to need new things together with the Internet. When considering there is a much wider market on the internet than traditional markets and obtaining information is extremely easy, it can be thought that the needs of consumers increased compared to the traditional ones (Özcan, 2010).

The consumer searches for information by utilizing internal and external sources. Internal resources are the consumer's past experiences and knowledge about the product. The main external sources for which information can be obtained are advertisements, internet and business web pages, mass media, experienced reference groups, magazines and consumer reports (Aksoy, 2006, p. 63). Consumers do not only meet their needs in the online environment, but also perform recreational activities in the search stage of pre- purchase. Sometimes they do a continuous scan to avoid lagging behind developments in the market (Solomon et al., 2006). Consumers can search the internet for active information in three ways. The first one is that the consumer can reach the information that he is looking for on the website. When the consumer clicks on any of the internal or external links while browsing any web site, he gets the information that he is looking for. The second one is that consumers reach the information they want through the browsers. If the consumer knows the exact address of the source of the information he wants, it will be quite useful. The latter is the result of the consumers questioning the information they need by entering their keywords into the search engineering. There are many search engines serving this purpose. Google.com, yahoo.com etc. portals are the best-known search engines.

In the process of evaluating alternatives, the consumer is in a selection process. Characteristics of products and services, the relative importance given to the different properties of the product, the brand image, individual utility functions and attitudes for each product feature of the consumer are considered in this selection process (Tek & Ozgul, 2005). Businesses in the virtual environment help the consumer to make decisions in a shorter time and effortless way by contributing to the evaluation process of alternatives. Through the Internet, the set of alternatives can be created in a much shorter time and on a global scale. Even a lack of knowledge of foreign languages is not considered as a problem. Because many businesses can prepare their pages on the Internet in accordance with their target audiences' mother tongue (Aksoy, 2009). E-commerce sites can create a price and property comparison of their products on their site. At the same time, there are also Internet businesses that offer different product groups and products' prices and features comparatively to consumers. It is also possible to access consumer reviews via the Internet. Consumer reviews are used as an application of the interaction with the internet. Comments are an important feature, especially for consumers who care about others' evaluations. In addition, it is possible to prevent the possibility of misinformation that can be perceived as risk by taking measures such as receiving feedback from a large number of users and asking a user to comment whether other users find the correct one (Özcan, 2010).

The purchase decision is taken after the analysis and comparison of the products. Two decisions must be made at the time of purchase. The first one is where to buy and the second one is how to make the purchase. The Internet can be used as a means of exchange at the stage of purchase. Therefore, more consumers can be reached, income can be increased and individualized messages can be delivered to consumers (Kiang et al., 2000) When the point of payment is reached, support is provided to consumers and firms during the purchase process via online payment facilities (credit card, electronic cash, and official approval procedures from the bank) (Zwass, 1996).

In terms of consumers, buying behavior in the virtual environment is more risky than traditional markets, and these risks affect the sense of trust depending on the attitude and functioning of the enterprises. These risks can be financial, time, personal and product functions. When the consumer decides to purchase goods or services, he or she thinks about these risks and probabilities until the time of obtaining the product, the enterprises are trying to minimize these risks in order to increase their trust and keep their customers in the competitive environment (Fah, Choo, 2010, p. 135).

The final stage of the buying decision process is the post-purchase behavior. The experience of the consumers, who make their evaluations about the product or service they buy, will have a great deal of influence on the product and service choices they will make in the future. In this stage, where satisfaction or dissatisfaction is experienced, it is seen that consumers make appraisal by evaluating their decisions.

In addition, timely delivery of products received via internet quality and use of products, quality of service, warranty, refund conditions, resolution of complaints and suggestions are important components of this phase. Consumers who are satisfied with this experience are researching new products, collecting information and buying again by turning again to the website they purchase these products (Cengiz & Sekerkaya, 2010).

Final stage of purchasing decision process should not be separated from the purchase process and should be seen as a component of the process. In this way, a clearer view can be obtained about the overall online consumer buying behavior. In the development of the relationship with the customer, the purchase phase should be seen as a starting point, not an end. Thus, critical factors in understanding customer behavior are how the customer receives the product, how the customer uses the product, how satisfied the customer is, the service quality of the product, the complaints and suggestions about the product (Butler & Peppard, 1998). The online consumers buy any product in order to meet their needs. The online consumer makes an assessment on the suitability of the product purchased on the post-purchase stage. As a result of the evaluation he thinks that he satisfies his needs or not. The online consumer who satisfies his needs will probably buy the same product again and even recommend it to others (Aksoy, 2009). Inactivity of consumers in case of dissatisfaction is a detrimental condition for the enterprise. In such a case, the business loses both the customer and the dissatisfaction. This is even more important for businesses operating on the Internet. The structure of the Internet, which provides high interaction, provides significant benefits to the consumer at many stages as well as providing support in post-purchase stage. An unsatisfied consumer can request the solution of the problem by contacting the enterprise on the Internet without any cost. Furthermore, if the consumer believes that the business is insufficient to solve the problem, he/she can express his/her dissatisfaction on different social media platforms. This may mean a negative word of mouth marketing about the business and the business may therefore lose reputation. Enterprises dealing with electronic commerce need to know how the consumer is going through the process of making a purchase decision in order to determine the consumer's decision to make an impact on consumer behavior (Özcan, 2010).

METHODOLOGY

In order to measure the effect of consumer emotions on online purchasing behavior, a questionnaire method was used in this study. Since the original language of the questions was in English, the questions were translated into Turkish and re-adapted and then back translation was done. The total number of questions in the survey is 69 and consists of four parts. Demographic questions were asked to the participants in the first part. In the second part, questions were asked to determine the factors affecting the emotions of consumers through online shopping channel. For this, it was benefited from the scale developed by Park and Kim (2003). The factors discussed in this scale are; user interface quality, product information quality, service information quality, site awareness, security perception, information satisfaction, and relational benefit. In the third part, questions were asked to measure the emotions of consumers towards the online shopping site which is the subject of the study. For this, it was benefited from the scale developed by Laros and Steenkamp (2003). The factors have been discussed in this scale are; anger, fear, sadness, shame, contentment, and happiness. In the last section, how often the consumers were buying through the online shopping site which is the subject of the research was asked in order to measure the consumers' purchasing behavior. The answers in the questionnaire were classified with 5-point Likert

Figure 1. Research Model

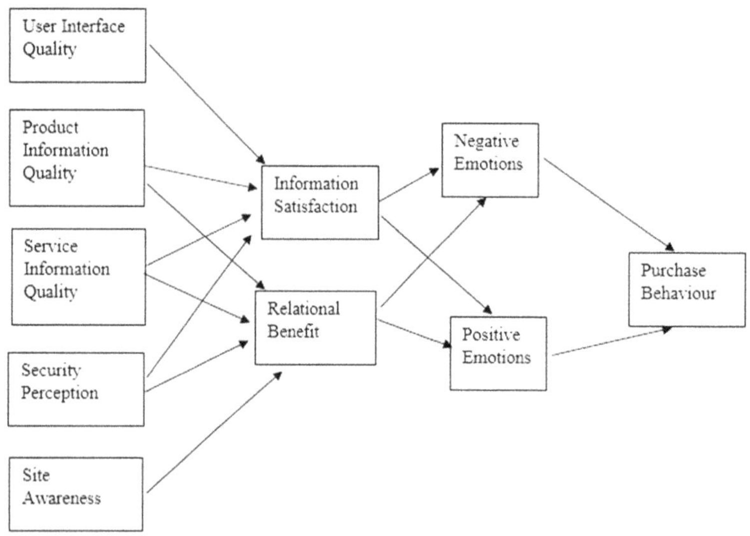

scale (1: Strongly agree, 2: Agree, 3: Undecided, 4: Disagree and 5: Strongly disagree). Four hundred eighteen participants over the age of 18 who were residing in Istanbul were chosen as the universe of research. In addition, random sampling method was chosen in the study.

The Research Model and Hypotheses

The main purpose of this study is to reveal what emotions in the consumer should be satisfied on the basis of purchasing behavior in the online environment. For this purpose, one of the most preferred online shopping sites in Turkey discussed. Sub-objectives created in line with the main purpose mentioned in the study are; examining whether there is a statistically significant difference between online purchasing behavior and demographic variables and revealing the factors affecting the consumer's emotions in the online shopping. The model created for these purposes is given below. This model is derived from the model created by the model created by Park and Kim (2003).

The following hypotheses were taken into consideration as a result of the model created for the purposes of the research:

H_1: There is a statistically significant relationship between information satisfaction and production information quality

H_2: There is a statistically significant relationship between information satisfaction and service information quality

H_3: There is a statistically significant relationship between information satisfaction and user interface quality

H_4: There is a statistically significant relationship between information satisfaction and security perception

H_5: There is a statistically significant relationship between relational belief and production information quality

H_6: There is a statistically significant relationship between relational belief and service information quality

H_7: There is a statistically significant relationship between relational belief and security perception
H_8: There is a statistically significant relationship between relational belief and site awareness
H_9: There is a statistically significant relationship between information satisfaction and negative emotions
H_{10}: There is a statistically significant relationship between relational belief and negative emotions
H_{11}: There is a statistically significant relationship between information satisfaction and positive emotions
H_{12}: There is a statistically significant relationship between relational belief and positive emotions
H_{13}: There is a statistically significant relationship between negative emotions and purchase behavior
H_{14}: There is a statistically significant relationship between positive emotions and purchase behavior

In addition, whether there is a statistically significant difference between online purchasing behavior and demographic variables has been examined.

Analysis of the Research Data

The "SPSS 16.0" package program was used for the analysis of the data obtained as a result of the research. Validity and reliability analysis, descriptive statistics, One Way Anova Test and multiple linear regression analysis were performed through this program.

Frequency Distributions of Demographic Variables

According to the results obtained by frequency analysis, the majority of the participants are 18-25 years old, female, single, a monthly income of between TL 2001 and TL 3000, and undergrate education. In addition, sometimes and often were found as the frequency value of the majority of the participants to buy products from the online site which is the subject of research. The results of frequency analysis are given in the table below.

After the frequency analysis, One Way Anova test was used to test whether there is a significant difference between the participants' demographic variables regarding the purchasing behavior from the online site subject to the study. The results of the test are given in the table below.

An analysis of variance has showed that the effect of age and monthly income on the online purchasing behavior were significant. When the results in multiple comparisons are analyzed, there is a significant difference in online purchasing behavior among participants with monthly income of less than TL 1000 and those with monthly income of TL 2001-3000 and more than TL 5000 monthly income. In addition, when the age situation is examined, a significant difference in online purchasing behavior among participants with aged 18-25, 26 -30 and over the age of 40. Similarly, there is a significant difference in online purchasing behavior between participants aged 31-40 and over 40.

Reliability and Validity Analysis of the Scales

Firstly, internal consistency test was performed in order to find out whether the scales were reliable or not. Factors affecting online behavior are user interface quality, product information quality, service information quality, site awareness, security perception, information satisfaction, and relational benefit factors considered as factors affecting consumer behavior in online purchasing in the study conducted by Park and Kim (2003). The reliability ratio of this scale was found as 0,940. In addition, the factors such as anger, fear, sadness, shame, contentment, and happiness are considered as factors that reveal

Table 1. Descriptive Statistics on Demographic Characteristics of The Participants

Measure	Items	Frequency	%
Age	18-25	189	45,2
	26-30	112	26,8
	31-40	90	21,5
	>40	27	6,5
Gender	Female	187	44,7
	Male	231	55,3
Marital Status	Married	112	26,8
	Single	306	73,2
Monthly Income	<TL 1000	66	15,8
	TL 1000- TL 2000	82	19,6
	TL 2001- TL 3000	115	27,5
	TL 3001- TL 4000	88	21,1
	TL 4001- TL 5000	28	6,7
	>TL 5001	39	9,3
Education Level	Middle School	5	1,2
	High School	53	12,7
	College	74	17,7
	Undergraduate	226	54,1
	Postgraduate	44	10,5
	Doctorate	16	3,8
Purchasing behavior within a year from the site which is subject of the study	Never	44	10,5
	Rarely	35	8,4
	Sometimes	122	29,2
	Often	125	29,9
	Always	92	22,0

online consumer emotions in the study conducted by Laros and Steenkamp (2003). The reliability rate of

Table 2. One-Way-Anova Test Results

Measure	F	Sig.
Age	10,571	,000
Gender	,149	,700
Marital Status	1,420	,234
Monthly Income	3,346	,006
Education Level	1,030	,400

the scale used was found to be 0,867. As a result of internal consistency analysis, it can be said that the scale is reliable since the alpha coefficients of the factors constituting both scales are greater than 0.70.

Then, explanatory factor analysis was performed in order to determine the variables that are high in the study as factors with high explanatory variables, to identify those who are unrelated or weak in the variables and finally to determine the prominent ones in the variable. In the study conducted by Park and Kim (2003), the Kaiser-Meyer-Olkin Measure of Sampling Adequacy value was 0,838 and the value of Bartlett's Test of Sphericity was 0,000. In the study conducted by Park and Kim (2003), the Kaiser-Meyer-Olkin Measure of Sampling Adequacy value was 0,838 and the value of Bartlett's Test of Sphericity was 0,000. For the 30 items constituting a total of seven factors on the said scale, it was determined that there were seven components with eigenvalues over one, and the total contribution of these factors to the variance was 72.81%. In addition, the value of the Kaiser-Meyer-Olkin Measure of Sampling Adequacy was 0.840 and the value of Bartlett's Test of Sphericity was 0.000 in the study performed by Laros and Steenkamp (2003). It was found that there were five components with eigenvalues over one in total for 33 items which constitute five factors in the scale and the total contribution of these factors to variance was found to be 82.41%. In both scales, the KMO value is higher than 0.60, indicating that the sample size is appropriate. In addition, a p value in the Bartlett Sphericity Test for both scales less than 0.05 indicates that the expressions on the scale are related to each other. The reliability and validity results of the factors included in the aforementioned studies are summarized in the table below.

After the reliability and validity analysis of the scales, multiple linear regression analysis was performed to test the hypotheses. The findings obtained from the analysis are given in the table below.

SOLUTIONS AND RECOMMENDATIONS

Adjusted R^2 value of each model discussed in the table above was investigated by multiple linear regression analysis. The Adjusted R^2 value was taken into account because the research model was built in the form of multiple linear regressions. This value is calculated as 0,583 for the first model. In other words, four independent variables (Product Information Quality, Service Information Quality, Security Perception) can explain 58.3% of the change in the dependent variable (Information Satisfaction). Adjusted R2 value was found to be 0.503 in the second model, 0.278 in the third model, 0.342 in the fourth model and 0.481 in the fifth model. In this case, it can be stated that variables of information satisfaction and relational belief are insufficient to explain negative emotions change.

In the next step, the results of the Anova test for each model were examined. As a result of the Anova test, the p value of each model was 0.000. Therefore, it can be said that the multiple linear regression model can be considered as a whole. Then, the coefficients and the significance values of each multiple linear egression model were analyzed. According to this, p value of constant term coefficient for each model was found as 0.000. In this case, it can be said that the constant term is meaningful. As can be seen from the table above, it can be stated that the significance level of each factor, other than the relational factor, is significant as it is less than 0.05. Therefore, all hypotheses, aside from the H_{12} were accepted in the study. Then, regression coefficients of each model were examined in the study. Accordingly, it can be stated that there is a direct proportion between dependent and independent variables in the most models. On the other hand, it can be said that there is an inverse relationship between information satisfaction and relational belief variables and negative emotions. In addition, can be expressed that there is an inverse relationship between negative emotions and the purchasing behavior. According to this; as the level of

Table 3. The Reliability and The Validity Analysis of Factors Used

Factors	Cronbach's Alpha	Eigenvalue	Total Variance Explanation Rate
User Interface Quality	0,854	11,581	38,604
Product Information Quality	0,860	3,156	10,520
Service Information Quality	0,819	1,786	5,952
Site Awareness	0,717	1,500	4,999
Security Perception	0,749	1,373	4,576
Information Satisfaction	0,843	1,243	4,143
Relational Benefit	0,854	1,016	3,386
Kaiser-Meyer-Olkin Measure of Sampling Adequacy Bartlett's Test of Sphericity Approx. Chi-Square: df: sig.:		,838 9,809E3 435 ,000	
Anger	0,941	18,307	55,475
Fear	0,936	5,351	16,216
Sadness	0,952	1,967	4,745
Shame	0,933	1,883	2,929
Contentment	0,925	1,566	2,676
Kaiser-Meyer-Olkin Measure of Sampling Adequacy Bartlett's Test of Sphericity Approx. Chi-Square: df: sig.:		,840 2,295E4 528 ,000	

information satisfaction and relational belief increases, negative emotions can be reduced. Finally, the rates of Collinearity statistics were analyzed for each model in the analysis. Accordingly, it can be stated that there is no correlation between the independent variables because VIF ratio is not 5 or higher in any model. In this case, it can be stated that it would be appropriate to keep the variables in the models.

According to the above results, companies should create strategies to increase the consumers' positive emotions in order to achieve competitive advantage in online environment, to ensure consumer loyalty, to improve brand image in a positive way and to increase brand value. In order to provide this, e-commerce sites should give weight the product information quality, user interface quality and security perception factors. In addition, firms should also identify strategies to avoid from situations that create negative emotions. In order to provide this, e-commerce sites should give weight the user interface quality, product information quality, service information quality, site awareness, security perception, information satisfaction, and relational benefit factors.

FUTURE RESEARCH DIRECTIONS

In future studies, it is thought that the examination of the enterprise which exists both in the traditional environment and online environment and then comparing the emotions of the consumer towards the business in these two environments will contribute to the study. In addition, it can be examined whether

Table 4. Hypothesis Testing According to the Results of Multiple Linear Regression Analysis

Model	Unstandardized Coefficients		T	Sig	Tolerance	VIF	Ad. R^2	Hypothesis Results
	B	Std. Error						
Information satisfaction= Product Information Quality+ Service Information Quality+ User Interface Quality + Security Perception+ ε	,226	,056	4,042	,000	,426	2,345	,583	H1 was supported
	,539	,057	9,457	,000	,429	2,330		H2 was supported
	,168	,041	4,059	,000	,588	1,699		H3 was supported
	,101	,042	2,403	,017	,764	1,309		H4 was supported
Relational Belief= Product Information Quality+ Service Information Quality+ Security Perception+ Site Awareness + ε	,369	,056	6,571	,000	,453	2,210	,503	H5 was supported
	,295	,058	5,101	,000	,446	2,243		H6 was supported
	,245	,047	5,247	,000	,667	1,499		H7 was supported
	,069	,036	1,920	,046	,729	1,371		H8 was supported
Negative Emotions= Information satisfaction + Relational Belief + ε	-,349	,062	-5,585	,000	,467	2,141	,278	H9 was supported
	-,247	,066	-3,752	,000	,467	2,141		H10 was supported
Positive Emotions= Information satisfaction + Relational Belief + ε	,583	,062	9,332	,000	,467	2,141	,342	H11 was supported
	,068	,066	1,031	,303	,467	2,141		H12 was rejected
Online Purchasing Behavior= Negative Emotions+ Positive Emotions + ε	-,239	,059	4,047	,000	,695	1,439	,481	H13 was supported
	,781	,056	13,835	,000	,695	1,439		H14 was supported

there is a significant difference between the consumer's feelings towards the different product groups that offer various products in the online environment. Finally, it is possible to compare consumer emotions between companies that provide services in online environment and companies offering products in the online environment.

CONCLUSION

It is becoming more and more difficult for businesses to maintain their existing customers in the competitive environment and to add potential customers to their portfolio. While the production understanding in enterprises is dominant in old times, today's enterprises need to carry out their activities at the level of global competition in order to sustain their assets and to be one step ahead in the competition due to developments in globalization and communication technologies. In addition, the developments in communication technologies enable many businesses to reach customers by creating virtual stores and offer their products and services to the customer faster and more affordable price compared to a traditional retail store. Developments in recent years cause businesses to build more and more e-commerce sites and to place their brands in virtual stores. The main reason for this orientation is to reach out to consumers who have limited time or have no opportunity to go to a store for shopping. and to ensure the use of its products by consumers. Whether the business is a traditional store or a virtual store, its purpose is to make more sales to customers, to allow customers to visit its own store again and to increase its profits by gaining new customers through existing customers. The realization of this aim by the enterprises depends mainly on the creation of positive emotions on the online consumers. The identification and understanding of the online customer's emotions by e-businesses will provide ease to customer satisfaction and loyalty.

By the reason of the importance of online consumer emotion discussed in background section, the main purpose of this study is to reveal what emotions in the consumer should be satisfied on the basis of purchasing behavior in the online environment. Due to the absence of any studies on the subject previously in Turkey, this research is important in terms of contributing to the literature and helping practitioners to understand the importance of consumer emotions. As a result of the multiple regression analysis conducted for the main purpose of the study, it was observed that both positive and negative emotions had an impact on the online buying behavior. In this context, when the coefficients related to the factors are examined, it can be stated that as the positive emotions of the online consumer increases, the frequency of purchases increases but as the negative emotions of the online consumer increases, the frequency of purchases decreases.

The first of the sub-objectives in the study is to examine whether there is a statistically significant difference between online purchasing behavior and demographic variables. As a result of the One Way Anova Test performed for this purpose, the effect of age and monthly income on the online purchasing behavior were significant. When the results in multiple comparisons are analyzed, there is a significant difference in online purchasing behavior among participants with monthly income of less than TL 1000 and those with monthly income of TL 2001-3000 and more than TL 5000 monthly income. In addition, when the age situation is examined, a significant difference in online purchasing behavior among participants with aged 18-25, 26 -30 and over the age of 40. Similarly, there is a significant difference in online purchasing behavior between participants aged 31-40 and over 40. Another sub-objective of the study is to reveal the factors affecting the consumer's emotions in the online shopping. As a result of multiple linear regression analysis, user interface quality, product information quality, service information quality, site awareness, security perception, information satisfaction, and relational benefit factors that can be expressed as factors that negatively affect consumers emotionally in purchasing online. On the other hand, it can be stated that only product information quality, user interface quality and security perception factors are effective on the positive emotions of online consumers.

REFERENCES

Ajzen, I. (1991). The theory of planned behavior. *Organizational Behavior and Human Decision Processes*, *50*, 179–211.

Akbar, S., & Paul, T. J. (2014). Consumers' attitude towards online shopping: Factors influencing employees of crazy domains to shop online. *Journal of Management and Marketing Research, 14*(1), 1–11.

Aksoy, R. (2009). *İnternet ortamında pazarlama*. Ankara, Turkey: Seçkin Yayıncılık.

Alcan˜iz, E. B., Andreu, L., & Gnoth, J. (2005). The theme park experience: An analysis of pleasure, arousal and satisfaction. *Tourism Management, 26*, 833–844.

Alcan˜iz, E. B., Mafe, C. R., Manzano, J. A., & Blas, S. S. (2008). Influence of online shopping information dependency and innovativeness on internet shopping adoption. *Online Information Review, 32*(5), 648–667.

Allen, C. T., Machleit, K. A., Kleine, S. S., & Notani, A. S. (2005). A place for emotion in attitude models. *Journal of Business Research, 58*, 494–499.

Babin, B. J., Lee, Y. K., Kim, E. J., & Griffin, M. (2005). Modeling consumer satisfaction and word-of-mouth: Restaurant patronage in Korea. *Journal of Services Marketing, 19*, 133–139.

Bagozzi, R. P., Mahesh, G., & Prashanth, U. N. (1999). The Role of Emotions in Marketing. *Journal of the Academy of Marketing Science, 27*(2), 184–206.

Batra, R., & Ray, M. L. (1986). Affective responses mediating acceptance of advertising. *The Journal of Consumer Research, 13*, 234–249.

Bellman, S. (2007). Theory and measurement of type 1 & type 2 emotions. *Australasian Marketing Journal, 15*(1), 14–22.

Blackwell, R. D., Miniard, P. W., & Engel, J. F. (2001). Consumer Behavior. Fourth Worth. San Diego, CA: Harcourt College Publishers.

Blossom, D. (2001). *Theoretical, methodological and analytical methods for exploring emotional episodes: Applications to consumption emotions and emotional satisfaction* (Unpublished doctoral dissertation). The Arizona University.

Butler, P., & Peppard, J. (1998). Consumer purchasing on the internet: Processes and prospects. *European Management Journal, 16*(5), 600–610.

Cacioppo, J. T., & Gardner, W. L. (1999). Emotion. *Annual Review of Psychology, 50*, 191–214. PMID:10074678

Cengiz, E., & Şekerkaya, A. (2010). Internet kullanicilarinin internetten alişverişe yönelik satin alma karar süreçlerinin incelenmesi ve kullanim yoğunluklari açisindan siniflandirilmasi üzerine bir araştirma. *Öneri Dergisi, 9* (33), 33-49.

Christy, C., Chan, M. K., Gloria, W. W., & Limayem, M. (2005). A critical review of online consumer behavior: Empirical research. *Journal of Electronic Commerce in Organizations, 3*(4), 1–19.

Cohen, J. B., & Charles, S. A. (1991). Affect and Consumer Behavior, In Thomas S. Robertson, & Harold H. Kassarjian (Eds.), Handbook of Consumer Behavior. Englewood Cliffs, NJ: Prentice Hall.

Crosby, L. A., Evans, K. R., & Cowles, D. (1990). Relationship quality in services selling: An interpersonal influence perspective. *Journal of Marketing*, *54*, 68–81.

Dahle, N. M. (1999). *Closing in on the web consumer*. Amsterdam, The Netherlands: Elsevier.

Derbaix, C. M. (1995). The impact of affective reactions on attitudes toward the advertisement and the brand: A step toward ecological validity. *JMR, Journal of Marketing Research*, *32*(4), 470–479.

Deveci, F. G. (2014). *Mücevher satin aliminda yaşanan duygusal çelişkilerde etkili olan değişkenlerin belirlenmesi* (Unpublished master's dissertation). The Ataturk University.

Ekman, P. (1999). *Basic emotions. Handbook of cognition and emotion. Sussex*. UK: John Wiley & Sons.

Fah, B., & Choo, B. (2010). Undergraduates online purchasing behavior. *Asian Social Science*, (October), 133–138.

Fishbein, M., & Ajzen, I. (1975). Belief, attitude, intention, and behavior: An introduction to theory and research. Boston, MA: Digital Press, Addison-Wesley.

Gallagher, K., Foster, K. D., & Parsons, J. (2001). The medium is not the message: Advertising effectiveness and content evaluation in print and on the web. *Journal of Advertising Research*, *41*(4), 57–70.

George, J. F. (2004). The theory of planned behavior and Internet purchasing. *Internet Research*, *14*(3), 198–212.

Gültaş, P., & Yıldırım, Y. (2016). Internetten alişverişte tüketici davranişini etkileyen demografik faktörler. *Dicle Üniversitesi İktisadi ve İdari Bilimler Fakültesi Dergisi*, *6*(10), 32–50.

Hannu, Y. (2001). Physical distribution considerations for electronic grocery shopping. *International Journal of Physical Distribution ve Logistics Management*, *31*(10), 750.

Hansen, F., Percy, L., & Lundsteen, S. (2006). Outstanding brands "emotionally speaking. *European Advances in Consumer Research*, *6*, 511–515.

Hansen, T., Jensen, J. M., & Solgaard, H. S. (2004). Predicting online grocery buying intention: A comparison of the theory of reasoned action and the theory of planned behavior. *International Journal of Information Management*, *24*(6), 539–550.

Hicks, J. M., Page, T. J., Behe, B. K., Dennis, J. H., & Fernandez, R. T. (2005). Delighted consumers buy again. *Journal of Consumer Satisfaction, Dissatisfaction & Complaining Behavior*, *18*, 94–104.

Hoffman, D. L., & Novak, T. P. (1995). Marketing in hypermedia computer-mediated environments: Conceptual foundations. *Journal of Marketing*, *60*(3), 50–68.

Holbrook, M. B., & Batra, R. (1987). Assessing the role of emotions as mediators of consumer responses to advertising. *The Journal of Consumer Research*, *14*(3), 404–420.

Inman, J. J., Dyer, J. S., & Jia, J. (1997). A generalized utility model of disappointment and regret effects on post-choice valuation. *Marketing Science*, *16*, 97–111.

Kabadayı, E. T., & Alan, A. K. (2013). Duygu tipolojilerinin tüketici davranışları üzerindeki etkisi ve pazarlamadaki önemi, *İşletme Araştırmaları Dergisi*, *5*(1), 93-115

Karahanna, E., & Straub, D. W. (1999). The psychological origins of perceived usefulness ad ease-of-use. *Information ve Management, 35*(4), 237–250.

Karakaya, E. (2017). Müşteri duygulari ile müşteri memnuniyeti, sadakati ve satin alma sonrasi kolaylik arasindaki ilişkilerin incelenmesi: Yüksekokul öğrencileri ile gerçekleştirilen bir saha çalişmasi. *Uluslararası Sosyal Araştırmalar Dergisi, 10*(50), 747–757.

Keeney, R. L. (1999). The value of internet commerce to the customer. *Management Science, 45*(4), 533–542.

Kiang, M. Y., Raghu, T. S., & Shang, K. (2000). Marketing on the Internet: Who can benefit from an online marketing approach? *Decision Support Systems, 27*(2), 383–393.

Kim, E. Y. (2004). Online purchase intentions for products categories: The functions of internet motivations and online buying tendencies. *Journal of the Korean Society of Clothing and Textiles, 32*(6), 890–901.

Kim, H. S. (2005). Consumer profiles of apparel product involvement and values. *Journal of Fashion Marketing and Management: An International Journal, 9*(2), 207–220.

King, S. C., & Meiselman, H. L. (2010). Development of a method to measure consumer emotions associated with foods. *Food Quality and Preference, 21*, 168–177.

Laros, F. J. M., & Steenkamp, J. B. (2005). Emotions in consumer behavior: A hierarchical approach. *Journal of Business Research, 10*, 1437–1445.

Leinbach-Reyhle, N. (2015). *The single most important reason why online marketing is more important than ever.* Retrieved from https://www.forbes.com/sites/nicoleleinbachreyhle/2015/06/16/the-single-most-important-reason-why-online-marketing-is-more-important-than-ever/#43583aa53bff

Luo, J., BA S., & Zhang, H. (2012). The effectiveness of online shopping characteristics and well-designed websites on satisfaction. *Management Information Systems Quarterly, 36*(4), 1131–1144.

Maes, P., Gutman, R. S., & Maukas, A. G. (1999). Agents that buy and sell. *Communications of the ACM, 42*(3), 81–91.

Mano, H., & Oliver, R. L. (1993). Assessing the dimensionality and structure of the consumption experience: Evaluation, feeling, and satisfaction. *The Journal of Consumer Research, 20*(3), 451–466.

McGaughey, R. E., & Mason, K. H. (1998). The Internet as a marketing tool. *Journal of Marketing Theory and Practice, 6*(3), 1–11.

Monsuwe, T. P., Dellaert, G. C., & Ruyter, K. D. (2004). What drives consumers to shop online? A literature review. *International Journal of Service Industry Management, 15*(1), 102–121.

Montoya-Weiss, M. M., Voss, G. B., & Grewal, D. (2003). Determinants of online channel use and overall satisfaction with a relational, multichannel service provider. *Journal of the Academy of Marketing Science, 31*(4), 448–458.

Murray, K. B., & Schlacter, J. L. (1990). The impact of services versus goods on consumers' assessment of perceived risk and variability. *Journal of the Academy of Marketing Science, 18*(1), 51–65.

Özcan, S. O. (2010). Internet pazarlama faaliyetlerinde tüketici satin alma karar süreci. *IUYD, 1*(2), 30–39.

Özdemir, Ö., & Taşkın, Ç. (2017). *Online itkisel satin alma davranişi: PLS-SEM ile bir model önerisi.* Bursa, Malaysia: Dora Basım Yayın.

Park, C. H., & Kim, Y. G. (2003). Consumer purchase behavior in an online shopping context. *International Journal of Retail & Distribution Management, 31*(1), 16–29.

Perry, P., Martai, B., & Stefano, P. (2013). Translating the need for touch to online fashion shopping via digital technology. *Proceedings of The First International Conference on Digital Technologies for the Textile Industries the University of Manchester*, 8.

Plutchik, R. (1980). *Emotion: A Psycho-evolutionary synthesis.* New York, NY: Harper and Row Publishing.

Rangaswamy, A., & Gupta, S. (1999). Innovation adoption and diffusion in the digital environment: Some research opportunities. *E-business Research Center Working Paper*, 02(1999), Penn State.

Richins, M. L. (1997). Measuring emotions in the consumption experience. *The Journal of Consumer Research, 24*, 127–146.

Sebastianelli, R., Tamimi, N., & Rajan, M. (2008). Perceived quality of online shopping: Does gender make a difference? *Journal of Internet Commerce, 7*(4), 445–469.

Solomon, M., Bamossy, G., Askegaard, S., & Hogg, M. K. (2006). *Consumer behavior a European perspective.* UK: Prentice Hall.

Stayman, D. M., & Aaker, D. A. (1988). Are all the effects of ad-induced feelings mediated by ad*? The Journal of Consumer Research, 15*, 368–373.

Stayman, D. M., & Batra, R. (1991). Encoding and retrieval of ad affect in memory. *Journal of Marketing Research, 28*, 232–239.

Taylor, R. K. (2000). Marketing strategies: Gaining a competitive advantage through the use of emotion. *Competitiveness Review, 10*(2), 146–152.

Tek, Ö. B., & Özgül, E. (2005). *Modern pazarlama ilkeleri.* İzmir, Turkey: Birleşik Matbaacılık.

Tronvoll, B. (2010). Negative emotions and their effect on customer complaint behavior. *Journal of Service Management, 22*, 111–134.

Westbrook, R. A. (1987). Product-consumption-based affective responses and post purchase process. *Journal of Marketing Research, 24*, 258–270.

White, C., & Yu, Y. T. (2005). Satisfaction emotions and consumer behavioral intentions. *Journal of Services Marketing, 19*(6), 411–420.

Yrjola, H. (2001). Physical distribution considerations for electronic grocery shopping. *International Journal of Physical Distribution & Logistics Management, 31*(10), 746–761.

Zwass, V. (1996). Electronic commerce: Structure and issues. *International Journal of Electronic Commerce, 1*(1), 3–23.

KEY TERMS AND DEFINITIONS

Consumer Emotions: It is used to define consumption experiences and to create an impact on the consumer.

Online Purchasing Behavior: It is used to purchase of products or services through the online environment for consumers' personal use or the use of their households.

Chapter 12
Understanding Shopping Behaviors With Category- and Brand-Level Market Basket Analysis

İnanç Kabasakal
https://orcid.org/0000-0003-0098-0144
Ege University, Turkey

ABSTRACT

In a digital transformation environment, most businesses shift towards e-business and encounter businesses and customer interaction on digital channels. Information Technology renders data access and processing more efficient, and use of customer data in decision making has become a focal interest area that attracts researchers. Customer data is a relevant subject for numerous studies in Data Mining. In this chapter, Association Rule Mining has been utilized to extract purchase behavior patterns with a multilevel approach. Basket data obtained from an online retailer was analyzed to discover purchase behaviors with a focus on category and brand attributes of products. Brands and categories purchased together frequently were discovered. Brand and category-wise association rules were also presented in the results. The analysis differs from the majority of prior analyses, by referring to the category and brand attributes in basket data. It could be noted that generalized rules obtained with this approach might prove useful in recommending new items of existing brands or categories.

INTRODUCTION

Information Technology is a crucial driver of radical transformation in various industries. Over the last decades, the businesses have put substantial effort to adapt to an inevitable wave of digitalization. Moreover, the emergence of electronic trade stresses the game-changing nature of digitalization for businesses. Such transformation has introduced customer data as an enormous resource. Especially in a

DOI: 10.4018/978-1-7998-0035-4.ch012

global market that turns out as a compelling environment for businesses, the utilization of digital assets is a vital requirement for business management.

The Internet had a game-changing role over the competition as well. The introduction of e-commerce had quickly pushed businesses to extend to the global market. The decline in transportation costs has been one of the most critical factors that increased global trade over the last five decades (Hummels, 2007). It might be noted that the progress in global trade, the prevalence of e-commerce and Internet technologies have also created various opportunities for businesses. For instance, businesses have the opportunity to reach out to more distant markets and connect to a higher number of customers around the globe. In this context, it could also be argued that the significant role of Information Technology in the rise of an integrated global market is worth emphasis. Such developments offer global opportunities for both individuals and small businesses with electronic commerce. A customer has the opportunity to search a particular product from numerous rivals in the global market, explore various alternatives, evaluate corresponding transportation costs and arrival options, and pick a product for purchase among various options by many competitors.

For businesses, the global market powered by electronic commerce has a specific challenge of anonymity. A local dealer might easily get acquainted with hundreds of citizens over time. Such acquaintance then enables a more detailed and individually developing conversation with customers. Moreover, customer response can be captured unconsciously. In contrast, electronic commerce is far from offering such personal contact. For instance, an online visitor who has not performed a login becomes anonymous. Technically, such a visitor is hiding his or her personal identity from the owner of the website. Moreover, the interaction established with the customer involves actions limited to mouse clicks, gestures, and some text entered over search forms. Far from a regular encounter with a personal conversation, it might be reasonable to mention the challenge of understanding an online customer. For salespeople or practitioners, scarceness of behavioral patterns might constitute a troublesome endeavor in an online setting.

Fuciu and Dumitrescu (2015) underlined the ever-changing nature of the marketing discipline and argued that there is a shift of focus on customer behavior and social media in marketing. In particular, customer data can be highlighted as an important asset that has been a focus of interest with the prevalence of digitalization in marketing. Besides, it can be argued that a customer-focused approach had become prevalent in marketing researchers and practitioners, especially since the introduction of Customer Relations Management (CRM). Within this context, Payne and Frow (2005) identified the role of customer data in CRM; and emphasized the importance of collection and utilization of customer data to enhance customer experience and endure the existing relationships with customers.

In their book published recently, namely 'Marketing 4.0', Kotler et al. (2017) have mentioned the importance of capturing customer data for marketers regarding various decisions in tactical level; including layout selection, promotion launching, customer purchase prediction, and fixing real-time offerings online. Likewise, Saarijärvi et al. (2013) explored the role of customer data in customer-business interaction; and has come up with a notion of shared customer data that emphasizes the social connections among customers.

In order to create value from data, quantitative models are employed to reach out to useful conclusions. Concerning the high volume of customer data in a typical e-business, analyses without the utilization of proper techniques might lead to information overload. Eppler and Mengis (2004) provided an overview of prior research on information overload problem and addressed its consequences in decision-making. The authors noted that the problem decreases decision quality and effectiveness, and argued that Management Information Systems (MIS) studies have the advantage to provide solutions concerning its focus on the solutions based on Information Technologies (IT), and their effect of on individual-level, group-level or organizational level. Moreover, Ellis et al. (2010) argued that models developed to handle large volumes of data should also fundamentally define the relevance of information as well in order to prevent potential information overload.

Techniques, such as data mining are put into use to discover unknown patterns; thereby, to extract useful information for the use of decision makers. Proposed chapter broadly aims to provide a review of prior research on data mining techniques in market basket analysis. The use of discovered information will be mentioned for various marketing-related decisions with regard to the metrics defined in the data mining domain. Moreover, a real case will be demonstrated for cross-category and brand-level market basket analysis, over the data obtained from an e-retailer in Turkey. The results will be presented with a discussion over the purchase behavior patterns discovered through the chapter.

ANALYTICAL CRM

As the primary source of income for businesses, customers have been regarded with high importance. In this regard, Gupta and Lehmann (2003) advocate defining customers as 'intangible assets for businesses'. Furthermore, the relationship between the businesses and their customers has been a topic of interest in the marketing domain. The terms 'customer loyalty', 'customer retention', 'customer value' demonstrate various approaches that intent to identify distinct aspects of the relationship between businesses and customers.

The marketing literature hosts quantitative models (Jain & Singh, 2002; Berger & Nasr, 1998; Dwyer, 1997; Blattberg & Deighton, 1996; Pfeifer & Carraway, 2000) which propose measurements to estimate the lifetime value of those relationships. Such models propose estimations for the future profits obtained from the customers and also provide a tool to designate customer segments. Compared to mass marketing, engaging with customer segments indicate a more detailed effort to consider the customer characteristics, at least within a group level.

In businesses, practitioners in marketing departments often employ customer-focused practices in order to hold their existing customers for longer. Customer retention is a problem often studied in prior studies, that hosts quantitative models over the customer data. In fact, Customer Relationship Marketing (CRM) receives intensive attention from both practitioners and researchers as an essential tactical tool, as well as a strategy for businesses.

In prior research, CRM has been often covered with an emphasis on its strategic, operational and analytical aspects. Moreover, CRM provides a basis for a transformation in marketing management. In this context, Rygielski et al. (2002) noted that the introduction of CRM techniques provides opportunities to act with a customer-oriented approach, instead of a product-oriented view.

With the introduction of CRM strategy in organizations, it can be argued that marketing managers seek to establish profitable and long-lasting relationships with their customers and potential buyers. On the other hand, the adaptation of CRM strategy into tactical or routine decisions require further efforts beyond a mere embracement of a customer-centric philosophy. In particular, the analysis of customer data is often required to support decision makers. In this context, the use of Information Technology (IT) has an outstanding role in exploiting customer data in various decisions. Tanner et al. (2005) described CRM as a strategy to create beneficial relations with customers and noted the supportive function of technology for CRM. In particular, Analytical CRM incorporates analysis of customer data with quantitative techniques.

In practice, CRM is mostly associated with software-based solutions in order to improve relationships with customers (Farooqi & Raza, 2011). Businesses essentially use database software to keep track of their products, customers, orders, deliveries, etc. Accordingly, various models have been proposed to extract useful information over customer data. The next section presents a brief introduction of data mining and its applications in marketing research.

DATA MINING IN MARKETING DOMAIN

Customer data is an essential input in marketing decisions. Utilization of customer data with efficient methods could provide the opportunity to employ more customer-focused strategies. The integration of information technologies in businesses has paved the way to store large quantities of data, and access to required information more swiftly with lower costs. In the 2010s, Business Intelligence (BI) techniques utilized in businesses still make use of data stored on relational databases, and heavily utilize statistical methods and data mining techniques (Chen et al., 2012).

Ling and Li (1998) noted that decisions such as identifying the potential buyers of products and designating mail lists for promotions require more specific practices than mass marketing; and advocated for the role of data mining as a crucial enabler for direct marketing.

In this section, the concept of data mining will be introduced at first. Secondly, data mining tasks and several types of data mining models will be described. Subsequently, the role of data mining in marketing-related studies will be addressed. with references to prior studies. Finally, the problem of market basket analysis will be introduced as a well-known application of data mining within the marketing research.

Data Mining

Data Mining is a field of research in Computer Science, that hosts various problems and applications on other domains. With a broad meaning, the term *Data Mining* corresponds to various tools that are used to discover interesting patterns and to extract meaningful knowledge from large datasets (Liu et al., 2004). Moreover, the term 'Data Mining' is an expression with a metaphorical meaning. An activity such as mining stands for a practice that defines a search activity to find precious items within large masses. Accordingly, data mining involves techniques to explore a large volume of data and discover valuable information through data processing.

In a managerial perspective, an analysis that involves data mining is often utilized to support various decisions, and the information extracted with such analysis should support the decision-making process. In data mining studies, a flow is frequently mentioned to delineate a transition from data to information, as demonstrated in Figure 1.

The definitions for data mining mostly involve discovering valuable information, and such statements imply a metric about a value metric for information to be discovered. Mostly, lots of information might be discovered, and it becomes crucial to find out how to use that information in business objectives. The adoption of a data mining technique into a problem might require expertise, as well as attention while evaluating the results.

Figure 1. An intuitive flow to demonstrate the use of data with data mining in decision making

Data Mining stands as a part of Knowledge Discovery in Databases (KDD), which denotes the process of extracting interesting patterns from large masses of data (Sahar, 2009). In this manner, data mining studies are concerned with the discovery of information from data. Subsequently, the information being discovered is also evaluated regarding the decision makers' problem. Typically, such evaluation involves the selection of information that connects to the problem with better relevance. The evaluation process also includes the use of measures for the patterns being discovered. In the following sections, our chapter will reference several measures for association rules obtained through a specific data mining technique.

It could be noted that using data and obtaining information have been mentioned as two crucial terms to reinforce decision making in Figure 1. Furthermore, those terms have been addressed as subsequent steps in the DIKW Pyramid that demonstrates a hierarchy about the nature of data (Rowley, 2007). The hierarchy in Figure 2 adds two additional steps that describe the extraction of knowledge from information and reaching up to a final level of wisdom.

As Figure 2 suggests, the volume of items decreases through the higher steps of the hierarchy. Logically, such decrease points to a requirement of data to be summarized or eliminated with some methods or criteria. Bernstein (2009) noted that the DIKW hierarchy depends on filtration, reduction, and transformation across levels. Due to the function of data mining in information discovery from data, data mining can be described as a part of the DIKW hierarchy to extract knowledge and obtain organizational wisdom. More precisely, the DIKW hierarchy is related to data mining in the discovery of information within data.

Data Mining Models and Tasks

Data mining methods have distinct functionality, and those methods are usually classified into several categories based on their function and objective. Data mining models are labeled as descriptive or

Figure 2. Data Information Knowledge Wisdom (DIKW) Hierarchy

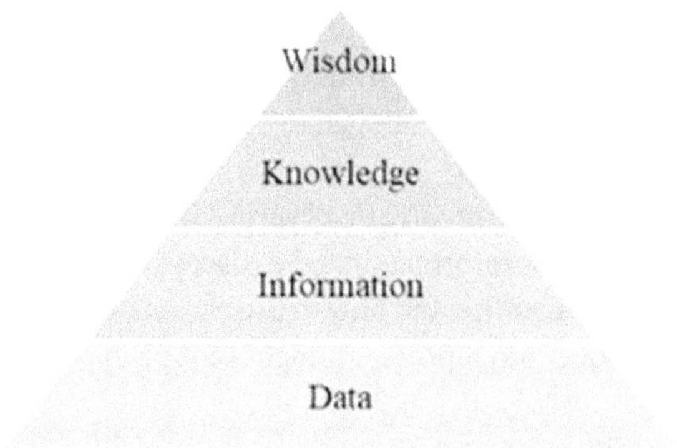

Table 1. Data Mining tasks

Data Mining Task	Description	Patterns Discovered
Summarization	Abstraction or generalization of data that provide a smaller overview of the entire data set	*Aggregate Totals*, that demonstrate total results to be obtained from financial data
Classification	Discovering a function or model to map objects into existing classes, according to objects' attributes	*Classification Models* that classify websites into either 'Safe' or 'Unsafe'
Association	Discovering how objects connect with other objects, how they come together	*Associations and Association Rules* derived from basket data in supermarkets, that demonstrate which products are often sold together
Clustering	Identifying groups among data, namely 'clusters'; with minimum similarity across groups, and maximum similarity across the objects in the same group	*Customer Segments* that are identified to demonstrate distinct groups of customers whose purchase habits are similar to each other
Trend Analysis	Identifying the patterns in the data over time, that might also lead to predictions	*Identification of an Increase or Decrease Trend* over sales data that provides a prediction for the next months

Source: Adapted from Sumathi & Sivanandam (2006, p. 204)

predictive, based on their functionality; descriptive models provide characteristics about the data being analyzed, the predictive models suggest predictions through inference over data (Han & Kamber, 2006, p. 21). A distinctive capability of predictive models that deserve mentioning is their ability to guess unknown fields in datasets based on the patterns discovered (Sumathi & Sivanandam, 2006, p. 601), possibly with descriptive models.

Data mining models are characterized as supervised, or unsupervised learning models based on the obscurity of the output before the analysis. In supervised models, the desired output objectives are formerly known; on the other hand, unsupervised models learn without any predefined output objective (Sumathi & Sivanandam, 2006, p. 42). As an example, clustering models are described as unsupervised techniques since they require no specific target at the beginning; on the contrary, classification models require supervised techniques since they aim to target a predefined value among alternatives (Tsiptsis & Chorianopoulos, 2009).

Data mining methods also differ according to the characteristics of information to be discovered. Initially, it could be noted that data mining models result in the discovery of patterns. Subsequently, such patterns are evaluated, and useful ones are chosen to find out interesting information. However, the patterns discovered within the data are not uniform; they depend on the data mining task, and the model in use. Such variation in patterns brings out another classification over data mining methods. Data mining models produce several types of patterns that also correspond to data mining tasks as listed below:

Among the data mining models being covered, association rule mining is an unsupervised model that is used to discover patterns that represent the co-occurrence (Ishibuchi et al., 2001) of items. The main objective in association rule mining is to discover frequent items in large data sets efficiently and to provide representations that demonstrate how those items come together. In particular, association rules provide a specific formulation for the co-occurrence of items. In the next section, the technique will be revisited with applications over several problems across various domains.

Data Mining in the Marketing Context

In the marketing context, data mining can be described as a set of methods that look for patterns of customer behaviors (Laudon & Traver, 2014). With the introduction of the Internet, e-trade, social media, and mobile applications; businesses have the opportunity to accumulate customer data in various forms. For an alert business, such technologies provide a basis to maintain high volumes of customer data through multiple channels, such as websites and mobile applications.

The use of data mining over customer data has been subject to numerous marketing studies. Customer data is analyzed with data mining methods to extract patterns that provide useful outputs about customer behaviors, especially over the data captured online.

Clustering of data is a frequent task in data mining studies that relate to marketing. Data clustering techniques identify groups of samples in a dataset that have similarities with each other and attach members to the clusters being identified. For instance, a clustering technique that depends on a few attributes to measure item similarity, might calculate distances between records based on those attributes, and result in a given number of clusters that minimize the total distances from the gravity center of connected clusters. As a related task in data mining is the outlier analysis, that mostly looks for the discovery of distant samples from the clusters previously created. Moreover, classification is a data mining task in which new samples are matched to one of the existing clusters based on some similarity criteria.

In marketing, data clustering mostly corresponds to methods developed to perform customer segmentation. Besides, prior research hosts customer segmentation models that propose clustering algorithms of data mining. McCarty and Hastak (2007) noticed that segmentation methods in direct marketing employ quantitative methods including Recency - Frequency and Monetary Model (RFM), Chi-square Automatic Interaction Detection (CHAID), and logistic regression; and commented out for both simplicity and effectiveness of RFM model despite its maturity among others being mentioned. In a study that depends on RFM model; Chen et al. (2012) formulated customers' purchase behaviors by three RFM variables; namely: recency, frequency, monetary; and proposed a model to identify customer segments with a clustering technique over RFM variables.

Association Rule Mining is another key data mining technique that has been applied to accomplish various tasks in business management. In particular, Market Basket Analysis (MBA) is one of the most popular problems that have rejoiced intensive attention from data mining research community. In this analysis, the objective is to figure out the frequent products purchased within the same shopping basket. With MBA, practitioners have the ability to identify which products are bought together based on their customers' purchase history, and use such findings in several decisions.

In the next section, MBA will be described along with its implications in marketing. Moreover, the application of the analysis with ARM will be briefly introduced.

MARKET BASKET ANALYSIS WITH DATA MINING

Market Basket Analysis (MBA) is a technique in marketing research that aims to figure out which products are frequently purchased together. In this way, the customers' purchase behaviors are analyzed, and results are evaluated and taken into account in order to increase sales and profits. The objective is to sell products in larger quantities (up-selling) or selling different products from other categories (cross-selling) to increase the total number of sales (Videla-Cavieres & Ríos, 2014).

In some studies, the MBA is used in conjunction with the data mining technique of Association Rule Mining. However, it could be noted that MBA has been revisited in numerous studies before the introduction of techniques for ARM in data mining studies. However, both concepts are often mentioned together for a reason. Hegland (2003) demonstrates the necessity of data mining in MBA as follows: with 10.000 products, there are $\sim 10^{3000}$ possible combinations for unique market baskets. Obviously, the increase in the input size forces solutions that rely on data mining techniques.

Association Rule Mining

In data mining techniques, Association Rule Mining (ARM) is a novel technique by Agrawal et al. (1993) that aims to discover frequent item sets hidden in transactional data. The study has received a huge interest over the years and had been utilized in various applications, especially within the marketing domain. The objective of finding association rules involve discovery of co-occurring data that possibly corresponds to concurrent events. For instance, the purchase of different products in the same basket by customers is a typical example of co-occurrence for such problems.

Despite the use of ARM in conjunction with MBA in various studies, the applicability of ARM is much broader, due to the fact that concurrency is not limited to a single incident or basket. In contrast, Agrawal et al. (1993) underlined that basket data might refer to a group of products that have been purchased over a specific time interval by a customer.

To discover association rules from data; several techniques have been proposed including Apriori, Frequent Pattern Growth (FP Growth), and ECLAT. Apriori and FP-Growth have been proposed to handle transactional data, and ECLAT operates over vertically organized data, after a transformation phase from the transactional form (Han & Kamber, 2006). In the next subsection, the rule mining process with Apriori algorithm will be explored with detail and along with the MBA.

Apriori Algorithm

Apriori algorithm is a data mining technique that aims to discover frequent itemsets from transactional data and generate representations that demonstrate how items come together in a specialized form: association rules. The algorithm was initially proposed by Agrawal et al. (1993). The technique relies on the necessity that, frequent item groups can only consist of items or sub-items that are also frequent (Agrawal & Srikant, 1994). Accordingly, Hegland (2003) briefly provided the idea as the following rule of thumb:

If pattern A is frequent and B A, then B is frequent.

The term *frequent* remarks a qualification for a pattern in this context. In particular, a pattern qualifies as frequent if the ratio of samples matching that pattern exceeds a predefined threshold. Such threshold is referred as Support in ARM. With such consideration; item groups that have support below a threshold are assumed redundant, thus can be safely eliminated. This step is often referred as pruning in data mining textbooks.

The algorithm discovers frequent items in consecutive iterations, where frequent items and itemsets are combined to find out larger frequent itemsets, over and over again. Each itemset is checked against the support threshold and removed immediately unless the support criteria are not met. The itemsets being generated are either picked or pruned; thus, the itemsets are named as *candidates*. A detailed pseudo-code for the algorithm has been presented in Han and Kamber (2006, p. 239), and the candidate generation phase has been detailed in Agrawal et al. (1993, p. 209).

After the discovery of frequent itemsets, the algorithm follows a rule generation phase. In rule generation, each frequent itemset is repeatedly partitioned into two subsets to form association rules. A formal definition of a rule is as follows.

For a non-empty itemset *I*, rules are derived for its non-empty subsets A and B where A∩B=∅, and such rules are formulated as A → B; in such rules, the sets A and B are respectively named as the antecedent and consequent of the rule (McNicholas et al., 2008). In such formulation, the sets A and B in the rule A→B are also named as left-hand side and right-hand side of the rule.

For a frequent itemset such as {A, B, C}, the Apriori algorithm generates the following rules:

A → B & C
B → A & C
C → A & B
A and B → C
A and C → B
B & C → A

As it can be noticed, the association rules generated involve all combinations of the set {A, B, C}. The meaning of such rules depends on the problem and the data being analyzed. For basket data, a rule such as Milk → Biscuits indicates a purchase pattern, that verbalizes a result such as 'the customers who purchase milk also purchase biscuits'. However, the evaluation of such findings in decision making requires further details, including some metrics.

Interpretation of the association rules requires measures such as confidence and support. Confidence is a percentage calculated for a rule, which assesses the degree of certainty of the pattern (Han & Kamber, 2006, p. 28). A rule Milk → Biscuits with a confidence of 0.7 might indicate the following statement: 'Within the baskets where milk was purchased, the ratio of baskets that also involve biscuits is 70%'.

Intuitively, lower rule confidence indicates less certainty and vice versa. In fact, Apriori algorithm has a confidence threshold as a parameter. Each rule is checked against that ratio, and strong rules that satisfy the threshold are chosen.

Rules that satisfy confidence criteria are misleading in some cases. For instance, a rule such as "80% of customers who purchase milk also purchase water" points to a high ratio, thus indicates a possibly interesting finding. In addition, let's extend the example with a fact that 90% of customers already purchase water. With this ratio, the interpretation of the rule would be subject to change. A marketer would possibly interpret such finding as an example of substitute goods, and consider both products as alternatives. In this example, it can be argued that an analyst should have evaluated the findings with the use of multiple measures. The interestingness of such rules must be evaluated with criteria augmented with a correlation measure such as lift (Han & Kamber, 2006, p. 274).

Applications of Association Rule Mining

Association Rule Mining (ARM) technique is used to discover items that frequently come together in data sets. The technique has been utilized in various domains for numerous problems, including prediction tasks (Toivonen et al., 1995). Moreover, association rules are also useful in classification. In associative classification technique introduced by Yin and Han (2003), an instance is matched with a class based on the evaluation of relevant association rules. Due to the applicability of ARM for different data mining

Table 2. Sample applications in prior research that utilize Association Rule Mining

Domain	Authors	Objective
Security	Chen et al. (2004)	ARM was utilized to analyze the historical crime data prepared by law enforcement, and extract criminal relations based on co-occurrence
Direct Marketing	Wang et al. (2005)	Association rules were used in a data mining model that ranks customers based on customer value and estimate those that are more likely to respond for direct marketing.
Manufacturing	Chen et al. (2005)	A defect detection method was proposed in manufacturing, that utilizes association rules to discover patterns with defects
Medicine	Karabatak and İnce (2009)	In an analysis for detection of breast cancer, a model that depends on association rules and utilizes neural networks was introduced
Finance	Sánchez et al. (2009)	ARM was used to find out fuzzy association rules that might identify potential fraud in credit card usage data
Web	Forsati et al. (2009)	Personalizing web pages using weighted association rules that represent the web page navigation patterns of online users
Security	Tajbakhsh et al. (2009)	Association rules were used for classification of actions as a threat or regular activity, and to detect possible intrusions
Store Layout	Çil (2012)	Association rules based on purchase data were utilized to suggest a new layout for a supermarket chain
Finance	Paranjape-Voditel and Deshpande (2013)	Recommendation of stocks for portfolio, with a novel methodology that involves the discovery of association rules
Hazard Prediction	Harun et al. (2017)	A model was proposed to predict flood areas, based on ARM over hydrological data.

tasks, rule mining has been often utilized by researchers from various disciplines. The table below lists several applications that make use of ARM in prior research.

Models based on ARM has been developed for various problems in prior research. However, analyses over the market basket data constitute a prominent area of interest that takes attention. Even in the original study (Agrawal et al., 1993) where the Apriori Algorithm was introduced, the authors analyzed purchase records in a transactional database. It could be remarked that basket data is mostly valued as a substantial resource to explore customer purchase patterns.

In the following subsection, the problem of MBA will be introduced along with a popular application of ARM for basket data.

Market Basket Analysis with Data Mining

The prior research in CRM hosts various studies where market basket data has been regarded as a resource to explore the behavioral patterns. As identified by Russell (2000), such studies rely on the assumption that market basket choice is a decision-making process with limitations such as ignorance of availability and price variability of products. Kaur and Kang (2016) noted the informative outputs of basket analysis for retailers in several marketing decisions such as store and shelf layout, preparing coupons, bundling product, online recommendations and etc. Specifically, MBA helps to identify the relations among items chosen by customers and analyze the customers' purchase habits (Han & Kamber, 2006).

Analyses of customer data, including MBA, are performed with the assistance of software over the last few decades. The volume of data in large databases requires specialized algorithms that handle such data efficiently. In this regard, the application of data mining for market basket data is very popular in prior research. Specifically, the problem has been addressed in frequent item-set mining or associative rule mining. Several algorithms including Apriori, ECLAT, and FP-Growth were proposed in prior research to discover frequent item-sets in datasets (Heaton, 2016).

In Apriori, frequent itemsets are incrementally built from frequent items and smaller itemsets. The algorithm runs efficiently thanks to the pruning of non-frequent items, regarding a support threshold. For MBA, the algorithms mentioned brings out the products frequently purchased together. Moreover, the association rules exhibit relations among frequently purchased products.

A typical market analysis might involve preparation of transactional purchase data, performing ARM by Apriori with arguments that set the support & confidence thresholds, and selection & evaluation of useful rules with respect to interestingness measures. The case study presented in the chapter demonstrates a typical application of ARM, with a slightly different approach of handling purchase data in category-wise and brand-wise level.

Product Recommendations with Association Rules

In prior studies, various cases have been presented that benefit from the use of ARM technique as well as the resulting association rules in marketing management. Mostly, such applications take place within the context of Analytical CRM, and the cases involve scenarios in which the primary objective involves exploiting customer data to guide for decisions. Association rules are useful to generate recommendations (Tsiptsis & Chorianopoulos, 2009, p. 51) since they represent how the purchase decisions over products are linked to each other.

Generating product recommendations is an important task that host data mining studies. Online or mobile users often provide their personal information to use online services. With such information, businesses have the opportunity to create profiles for their existing, or potential customers. Cookies stored in browsers are often used to identify an online user that had been identified before. Based on the identification of a user; profile information, browsing history might become available to provide personalized content in web sites.

Matching users with appropriate web contents became an important task for web servers. Accordingly, opportunities that might be achieved with personalized websites, have led to the introduction of Recommender Systems (RS). Schafer et al. (1999) noted that RS help businesses to choose which products are to be recommended to customers, and highlighted the potential benefits of RS in e-commerce in cross-selling, and increasing loyalty.

RS are mostly described either as collaborative, content-based based on their approach in providing recommendations. Burke (2000) noted that collaborative filtering is the prominent approach in RS context that utilizes customers' purchase habits & preferences, and argued that such RS could provide more personalized recommendations that even improve in quality over time through data collection.

Different types of RS have been proposed in various studies that provide a personalized experience to users. Several applications of RS have been presented in Table 3.

As mentioned in some of the studies listed in Table 3, websites provide personalized content and item offerings to enhance user experience. In the context of marketing, RS is often employed in order to increase the chances of cross-sales. For instance, RS integrated into e-retail websites provide relevant suggestions while the customer is ordering products. In such occurrences, both of product attributes and customer ratings are processed to suggest relevant items. In particular, the selection of appropriate

Table 3. Recommendation models based on Association Rule Mining

Domain	Authors	Objective
Education	Lu (2004)	In e-learning, personalization for a recommender system was introduced that makes use of association rules
Education	Bendakir and Aïmeur (2006)	In the educational data mining context, past transcript data were analyzed with a model that intends to generate course recommendations based on association rules
E-Business	Lee at al. (2001)	Personalization on a movie website with recommendations generated with a method that utilizes association rule mining
Online Product Recommendations	Kim et al. (2011)	Association rules derived from navigational and behavioral patterns were used to generate product recommendations
Movie Recommendations	O'Sullivan et al. (2002)	Recommendations for an online movie recommender system were generated with association rules that demonstrate patterns across movies and profile data.

items for users is one of the most challenging problems in RS. Furthermore, choosing appropriate users for new items is even harder, described as the cold-start problem (Schein et al., 2002). The challenge in new items or new users is the lack of previous data to utilize when choosing among alternatives.

In prior research, several researchers have considered an item as a group of attributes within the context of rule mining; and proposed specialized mining techniques accordingly. For instance, Leung et al. (2007) introduced a novel rule mining approach in which item attributes are taken into account to discover association rules, and enable recommendations that overcome with the cold-start problem.

Websites can list products with filtering on attributes such as categories and brands. Accordingly, new products without prior basket data are listed under a specific category. In this manner, a category-wise basket analysis might be useful to obtain sufficient input in the recommendation process. Mostly, the cross-category purchase patterns attract practitioners (Bandyopadhyay, 2009), rendering MBA useful at the categorical level. Furthermore, analysis of shopping baskets at the brand level might be useful to predict customer purchase behaviors based on the purchase history of brand products.

In the next section, a case study of an online supermarket is presented that involves consecutive rule mining analyses that explore basket data, considering brand & category attributes of products. At first, the focus is on the discovery of frequently purchased product categories. In such an analysis, the transaction data is transformed and analyzed with a category-level approach. Next, purchase history data was mined for discovering rules that represent interconnection of products at a brand-wise perspective. Findings for both analyses are presented along with groups of frequent items and association rules that demonstrate how categories or brands come together in baskets.

CASE STUDY

The case covered in this chapter involves a data mining analysis to discover the relationships of basket products with a brand-level and category-level approach. Specifically, the data analyzed was obtained from an online supermarket in Turkey. The transaction records consist of monthly purchase data recorded in November 2013. By that time, the business was located and operative in İzmir, one of the populous cities in Turkey, and responded to online orders from both individual and corporate customers within the same neighborhood. In particular, purchase data involved records that were ordered from 13 districts of the city.

In prior research, several attributes of products that indicate a taxonomy was used for categorization in order to obtain generalized association rules. For a setting where product data involves attributes of category and brand, De Graaf et al. (2001) exemplified this categorization as the elimination of brand attribute from products, and obtain generalized association rules with categories. On the other hand, prior studies that focus on developing product recommendations with a category-wise and brand-wise rule mining approach have been found meager, despite the excessive count of rule mining studies. Correspondingly, the cast study presented in our chapter aims to obtain and present generalized rules to be used in recommendations for online visitors. The recommendations are intended to be defined based on brand-level and category-level association rules so that the cold-start problem could be dealt with.

The analysis involves data preprocessing, MBA with Apriori algorithm, and generation of association rules. Each step is presented in the corresponding subsections below.

Data Preprocessing

The data obtained for the analysis was contained as a large spreadsheet and consists of 3163 baskets purchased by 1717 customers. The data was preprocessed and converted into a relational database. In particular, the following tables were created in a local database on the Microsoft SQL Server. Subsequently, the brands, categories, customer demographics, delivery locations, products, orders, and baskets were located within the spreadsheet for migration into corresponding tables. The products, baskets, customers have been stored in individual tables demonstrated in Figure 3. Moreover, a table was created that matches products with corresponding baskets, namely *BasketProducts*. The table *Entity* was designed as a generic table to store brands and categories.

As an exception, the products in the vegetable and fruit categories are not related to any of the brands. Thus, those products were marked with a dummy brand and excluded from the brand-level MBA. Even so, the two categories mentioned are still counted in the category-level analysis.

Descriptive Summary of Basket Data after Preprocessing Phase

The basket data involves of 4390 distinct products. In the raw data obtained from the e-retailer, there were 395 products with a standard label that manifests inactive products. Because of the ambiguity of the product information, those products without a proper description were regarded as redundant data. Accordingly, those products and corresponding sale records were eliminated. As a result, the data involved 3995 distinct products.

Because of the characteristics of the MBA conducted in the introduction of the Apriori Algorithm (Agrawal et al., 1993), it is essential to note how the algorithm handles baskets data. The algorithm requires transactional data in the Boolean type. Specifically, the count of identical products in a basket is not required for analysis. For instance, purchasing an additional product that already exists in a basket does not change the results. In summary, the total list of distinct products involved in baskets makes a difference. With such consideration, it should be cleared that, from the 51667 combinations of product – basket relations in the original data, 2643 were eliminated due to inactive products. After the elimination of redundant products, the count of distinct products in baskets decreased to a total of 49024.

Figure 3. Entity-Relationship diagram for the relational database

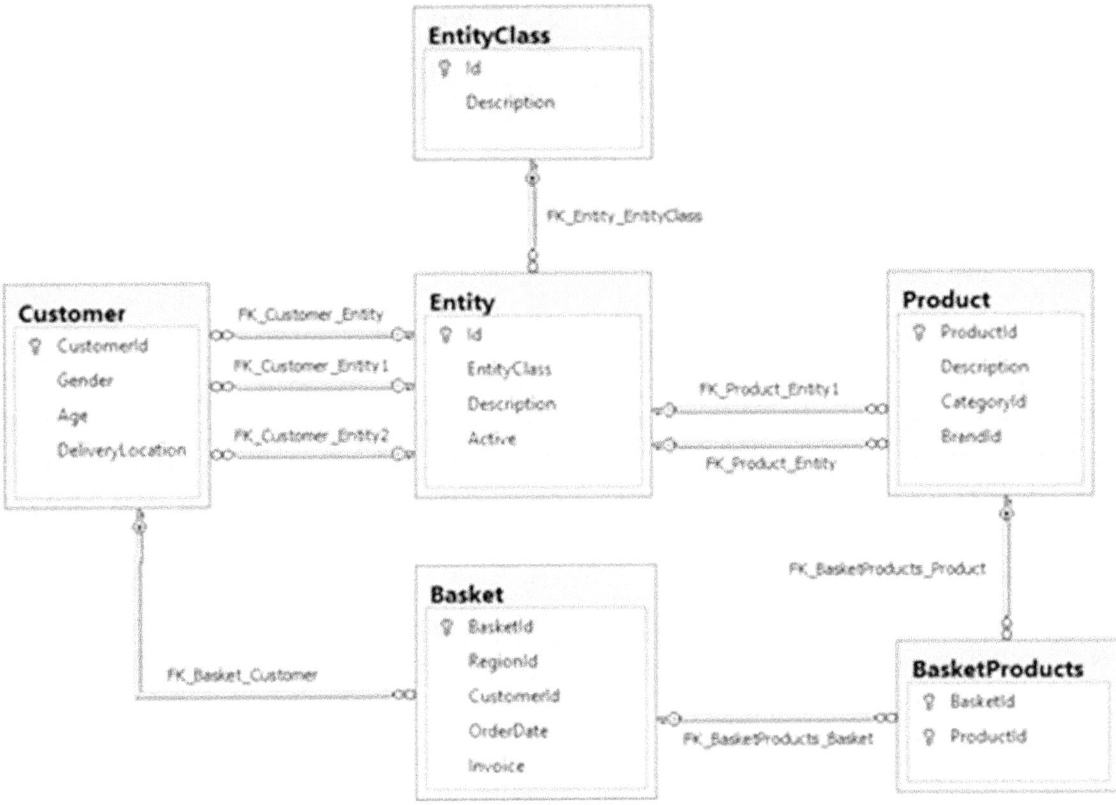

The product descriptions obtained for the study had been named in a standard fashion. All product descriptions precisely start with the brand name before the product title. Accordingly, a total of 442 brands were matched from the product spreadsheet. Because of the relevance of brands to our study, the product-brand relationship was established in the relational database. As an essential step in data preprocessing phase, each brand was assigned with a unique integer. Then, the products of that brand were marked with corresponding brand identifiers.

The spreadsheet involved 335 category definitions, declared with unique identifiers. Each product corresponds to a category. The popularity of product categories is measured and demonstrated with the support criterion.

In a market basket analysis, support for a product is calculated by counting baskets in which the product has been put into. For the support of categories in our case, it should be noticed that the supports do not correspond to the total count of products within that category. As mentioned above, finding the support of an item is a Boolean task that returns either one, or zero. In our case, the support column listed in categories indicates the count of baskets in which at least one product of that category had been purchased.

Table 4 below demonstrates the most popular categories that exist in baskets, ranked with their support. Accordingly, the most popular categories were vegetables, milk, fruits, yogurt, paper towels. The top row indicates that 1315 baskets out of a total of 3163 (41.57%) involve at least one product in the vegetable category.

Table 4. Top categories in purchase data

Rank	Category	Support	%	Rank	Category	Support	%
1	Vegetables	1315	0.4157	21	Black Tea	389	0.1230
2	Milk (UHT)	1170	0.3699	22	Chicken	382	0.1208
3	Fruits	836	0.2643	23	Turkish Coffee	362	0.1144
4	Normal **Yogurt**	683	0.2159	24	Wet Towels Napkins	361	0.1141
5	Paper Towels	681	0.2153	25	Instant Coffee	355	0.1122
6	Coke	647	0.2046	26	Sunflower Oil	351	0.1110
7	Pasta	604	0.1910	27	Liquid Detergent	348	0.1100
8	Eggs	604	0.1910	28	Rice	347	0.1097
9	Soda Water	527	0.1666	29	Washing Powder	325	0.1028
10	Biscuits	481	0.1521	30	Liquid Soap	306	0.0967
11	Granulated Sugar	458	0.1448	31	Flour	305	0.0964
12	Double-Layered Toilet Paper	452	0.1429	32	White Cheese	300	0.0948
13	Household Cleaners	448	0.1416	33	Black Tea Bags	294	0.0929
14	Cube Sugar	448	0.1416	34	Spices	280	0.0885
15	Trash Bag	444	0.1404	35	Ice Tea	279	0.0882
16	Concentrated Bleach	440	0.1391	36	Cheddar	276	0.0873
17	Fabric Softener	433	0.1369	37	Fruit Nectar	273	0.0863
18	Paper Napkins	415	0.1312	38	Bread	269	0.0850
19	Purpose Cleaner	403	0.1274	39	Beans	267	0.0844
20	Washing Up Liquid	390	0.1233	40	Butter	259	0.0819

Table 5 lists the top-40 most popular brands, according to the support criterion. The top row in this table demonstrates a product for Pınar exists in 864 baskets out of a total of 3163 (27.32%). As noticed for the previous table, the ranking was performed considering the total count of baskets that involve at least one product of each brand.

SOLUTIONS AND RECOMMENDATIONS

Association Rule Mining was employed to discover interesting purchase patterns regarding the category and brand attributes. As a prominent data mining task, the discovery of association rules takes place in various applications. The use of rule mining was explored in previous subchapters. Two analyses have been conducted consecutively, in order to extract association rules that figure out category-wise and brand-wise purchase behaviors. For such reason, basket data was transformed into transactional datasets that summarize the existence of categories and brands in baskets.

The transformation of basket data involves selection of brand or category attributes instead of product identifiers; and elimination of repeating transaction rows. As an example, suppose that basket data involves a single order for a customer who purchased Pepsi and Coca-Cola together. Such basket data

Table 5. Top brands in purchase data

Rank	Brand	Support	%	Rank	Brand	Support	%
1	Pınar	864	0.2732	**21**	Karmez	318	0.1005
2	Sütaş	689	0.2178	**22**	Cif	315	0.0996
3	Doğuş	644	0.2036	**23**	Mehmet Efendi	312	0.0986
4	Coca Cola	629	0.1989	**24**	Doğadan	302	0.0955
5	Ülker	606	0.1916	**25**	Pril	300	0.0948
6	Eti	512	0.1619	**26**	Sarıkız	296	0.0936
7	Lipton	505	0.1597	**27**	Nescafe	292	0.0923
8	Keskinoğlu	477	0.1508	**28**	ÇAYKUR	290	0.0917
9	Nestle	446	0.1410	**29**	Selpak	285	0.0901
10	Domestos	408	0.1290	**30**	Tire	275	0.0869
11	Filiz	402	0.1271	**31**	Perwoll	264	0.0835
12	Yayla	386	0.1220	**32**	Cook	257	0.0813
13	Solo	381	0.1205	**33**	SuperFresh	242	0.0765
14	Viking	379	0.1198	**34**	Barilla	237	0.0749
15	Dr. Oetker	361	0.1141	**35**	Tahsildaroğlu	236	0.0746
16	Moova	360	0.1138	**36**	Günbak	236	0.0746
17	Sek	354	0.1119	**37**	Senso	229	0.0724
18	Nar	336	0.1062	**38**	Söke	226	0.0715
19	Tat	333	0.1053	**39**	Bağdat	224	0.0708
20	Koroplast	326	0.1031	**40**	Bingo	213	0.0673

would transform into {Basket#1, Cokes} with the category-level approach. Likewise, data is transformed into {Basket#1, Pepsi} and {Basket#1, Coca-Cola} with the brand-level approach.

The Apriori algorithm was chosen as the technique to discover the association rules. Thresholds were specified as 1% for itemset support, and 10% for confidence.

The analyses were conducted with the RuleGenerator software (http://rulegenerator.inanc.biz), which had been developed for research by the author of this chapter. Specifically, the software had been developed in C# as a Windows application on the Microsoft ASP.NET platform. The software is an implementation for the Apriori algorithm, with the user interface as presented in Figure 4.

For a rule mining task, RuleGenerator lets to create a *warehouse* and requires the definition of a data source along with queries for items and transactions. Such queries should be prepared to return a standard data table. Each warehouse can be assigned individual support and confidence criteria. When an analysis runs, RuleGenerator can be used to list itemsets (associations) and rules in result windows and to export the findings in a spreadsheet. Furthermore, for curious readers, various options exist to mine association rules, such as Weka (Hall et al., 2009).

Figure 4. The user interface of the RuleGenerator software for a sample analysis

Category-Level Association Rules and Purchase Patterns

To discover useful patterns of categories that were purchased together, basket data was initially queried for data transformation. As mentioned in the methodology, transactional data for this analysis involves a list of basket-category pairs. Initially, 3808 frequent itemsets were discovered. The transactional data was transformed into categories; accordingly, the results in Table 6 demonstrate the frequent categories purchased together.

The next phase of the Apriori algorithm discovers the association rules in Table 7 that were generated from frequent itemsets. As mentioned before, rule combinations are generated; subsequently, the rules below the confidence threshold are eliminated in Apriori.

Itemset supports for antecedent, consequent, and both are listed respectively in the columns {X}, {Y} and {XY}. Top 20 among a total of 271 strong rules were listed, referring to the lift measure that signifies the correlation. A lift for a rule measured over 1 indicates a positive correlation. Accordingly, the high lift scores calculated in the results indicate relatively high correlations in association rules.

The first association rule indicates that the customers that purchase vanilla are likely to purchase baking powder. Such implication comes from the high confidence of 66.67%. Such statistics suggest

Table 6. Top categories frequently purchased together

Rank	Categories	Support	Rank	Categories	Support
1	Vegetables & Fruits	697	11	Vegetables & Pasta	304
2	Vegetables & Milk (UHT)	593	12	Normal Yogurt & Fruits	294
3	Normal Yogurt & Vegetables	429	13	Pasta & Milk (UHT)	288
4	Normal Yogurt & Milk (UHT)	409	14	Normal Yogurt & Eggs	261
5	Vegetables & Eggs	393	15	Normal Yogurt & Vegetables & Fruits	260
6	Fruits & Milk (UHT)	391	16	Fruits & Eggs	258
7	Vegetables & Fruits & Milk (UHT)	334	17	Biscuits & Milk (UHT)	254
8	Coke & Vegetables	316	18	Normal Yogurt & Vegetables & Milk (UHT)	251
9	Milk (UHT) & Eggs	309	19	Paper Towels & Milk (UHT)	250
10	Coke & Milk (UHT)	308	20	Soda & Milk (UHT)	243

Table 7. Top category-level association rules

Rank	Association Rules X → Y		Support for Item-sets			Rule Measures (X→Y)	
			{X}	{Y}	{XY}	Confidence	Lift
1	Vanilla	Baking Powder	75	87	50	0.6667	24.2375
2	Baking Powder	Vanilla	87	75	50	0.5747	24.2375
3	Coffee Cream & Cube Sugar	Instant Coffee & Black Tea	102	95	39	0.3824	12.7303
4	Instant Coffee & Black Tea	Coffee Cream & Cube Sugar	95	102	39	0.4105	12.7303
5	Coffee Cream & Cube Sugar	Trash Bag & Instant Coffee	102	88	35	0.3431	12.3334
6	Trash Bag & Instant Coffee	Coffee Cream & Cube Sugar	88	102	35	0.3977	12.3334
7	Trash Bag & Coffee Cream	Paper Towels & Instant Coffee	68	122	32	0.4706	12.2006
8	Paper Towels & Instant Coffee	Trash Bag & Coffee Cream	122	68	32	0.2623	12.2006
9	Cube Sugar & Instant Coffee	Trash Bag & Coffee Cream	139	68	35	0.2518	11.7123
10	Trash Bag & Coffee Cream	Cube Sugar & Instant Coffee	68	139	35	0.5147	11.7123
11	Trash Bag & Instant Coffee	Paper Towels & Coffee Cream	88	101	32	0.3636	11.3879
12	Paper Towels & Coffee Cream	Trash Bag & Instant Coffee	101	88	32	0.3168	11.3879
13	Coffee Cream & Cube Sugar	Paper Towels & Instant Coffee	102	122	41	0.4020	10.4213
14	Paper Towels & Instant Coffee	Coffee Cream & Cube Sugar	122	102	41	0.3361	10.4213
15	Trash Bag & Cube Sugar & Instant Coffee	Coffee Cream	52	206	35	0.6731	10.3347
16	Cube Sugar & Instant Coffee	Coffee Cream & Black Tea	139	87	39	0.2806	10.2007
17	Coffee Cream & Black Tea	Cube Sugar & Instant Coffee	87	139	39	0.4483	10.2007
18	Trash Bag & Paper Towels & Instant Coffee	Coffee Cream	50	206	32	0.6400	9.8268
19	Sunflower Oil & Lentil	Cracked Wheat	59	192	35	0.5932	9.7727
20	Coffee Cream	Instant Coffee & Black Tea	206	95	60	0.2913	9.6975

that, among three customers who ordered vanilla, two also ordered baking powder. Furthermore, the correlation is better explained with the lift score. Accordingly, baking powder is present 24x more frequently in baskets, where vanilla was also ordered.

When suggesting recommendations over a product in a basket, category-level association rules listed helps to focus on the relevant categories. Since the results indicate the most frequent patterns, 271 strong rules in the results will most likely cover most purchased products. In this manner, it could be argued that the category-wise results in Table 7 might lead to suggestions that help to increase cross-sales.

Brand-Level Association Rules and Purchase Patterns

The analysis with the Apriori algorithm was repeated for discovering brands frequently purchased together. For such purpose, basket data was transformed into a transactional list of basket and brand pairs. Then, the RuleGenerator software was executed with predefined thresholds of support and confidence. As noted before, the initial phase of the algorithm discovers pairs of frequent brands in basket data. A total of 1215 patterns were discovered, each of which indicates a list of frequently purchased brands. Top 20 among those patterns are listed in Table 8.

In Table 9, the top 20 among a total of 2555 strong rules were listed in descending order regarding the lift measure. According to the first rule, 38% of the baskets that involve products of *Nescafe* and *Lipton*, also involve products of *Nestle* and *Doğuş*. Moreover, the customers who purchased *Nescafe* & *Lipton* together have additionally bought *Nestle* and *Doğuş* in the same basket more often (~8x) than others in the entire population.

The category-level and brand-level relations discovered through the study lets a variety of product recommendations that might increase the chance of cross-sales. Moreover, a rule mining approach that utilizes brand attributes might also provide feedback for marketers and brand managers. Besides, the technique might help to find relevant products in case the findings include relevant rules either in category-level or in brand-level.

Table 8. Top brands frequently purchased together

Rank	Brands	Support	Rank	Brands	Support
1	Sütaş & Pınar	272	**11**	Keskinoğlu & Sütaş	174
2	Ülker & Eti	270	**12**	Eti & Sütaş	164
3	Coca Cola & Pınar	261	**13**	Lipton & Pınar	161
4	Ülker & Pınar	206	**14**	Ülker & Coca Cola	161
5	Keskinoğlu & Pınar	202	**15**	Nestle & Doğuş	155
6	Eti & Pınar	193	**16**	Nestle & Pınar	151
7	Ülker & Sütaş	187	**17**	Pınar & Filiz	147
8	Doğuş & Lipton	185	**18**	Doğuş & Sütaş	145
9	Doğuş & Pınar	185	**19**	Eti & Coca Cola	144
10	Coca Cola & Sütaş	177	**20**	Karmez & Pınar	143

Table 9. Top brand-level association rules

Rank	Association Rules X → Y		Support for Item-sets			Rule Measures (X→Y)	
			{X}	{Y}	{XY}	Confidence	Lift
1	Nescafe & Lipton	Nestle & Doğuş	94	155	36	0.3830	7.7782
2	Doğuş & Nescafe	Nestle & Lipton	115	131	36	0.3130	7.5226
3	Nestle & Lipton	Doğuş & Nescafe	131	115	36	0.2748	7.5226
4	Şölen	Ülker & Eti	59	270	34	0.5763	6.7189
5	Nestle & ÇAYKUR	Nescafe	58	292	33	0.5690	6.1339
6	Nestle & Mehmet Efendi	Nescafe	92	292	52	0.5652	6.0935
7	Nestle & Doğuş & Lipton	Nescafe	64	292	36	0.5625	6.0642
8	Artı	Bağdat	105	224	39	0.3714	5.2199
9	Nestle & Doğadan	Nescafe	98	292	45	0.4592	4.9504
10	Nestle & Doğuş	Nescafe	155	292	71	0.4581	4.9383
11	Doğadan & Nescafe	Mehmet Efendi	72	312	35	0.4861	4.9047
12	Ülker & Şölen	Eti	43	512	34	0.7907	4.8616
13	ÇAYKUR & Nescafe	Nestle	48	446	33	0.6875	4.8526
14	Doğuş & Nescafe & Lipton	Nestle	53	446	36	0.6792	4.7943
15	Şölen	Eti	59	512	45	0.7627	4.6895
16	Nestle & Ülker	Eti & Pınar	129	193	37	0.2868	4.6783
17	Nestle & Nescafe	Doğuş & Lipton	131	185	36	0.2748	4.6762
18	Nestle & Mehmet Efendi	Doğadan	92	302	41	0.4457	4.6454
19	Nestle & Lipton	Nescafe	131	292	56	0.4275	4.6086
20	Doğadan & Mehmet Efendi	Nescafe	82	292	35	0.4268	4.6016

FUTURE RESEARCH DIRECTIONS

In our case, a variant of market basket analysis was conducted with a brand-wise and category-wise approach. As in the original analysis of basket data, association rules were discovered that represent customer behaviors. However, the discovered rules indicate relations across brands and categories, rather than products in contrast with the conventional approach. In this manner, it should be noted that rules over brands or categories might lead to recommendations of multiple products. Picking the appropriate product over a generalized rule set requires further effort in future studies.

In the study, brand and category data were taken as product attributes, and both data were individually mined to discover interesting patterns. Furthermore, a more thorough analysis might be conducted with rule mining to figure out more complex patterns that involve combinations of both attributes.

CONCLUSION

The digital transformation, triggered with Information Technologies and the Internet, has various effects on businesses. Notably, the rise of e-business has been a game-changer for global competition. In such progress, the customer-business interaction has extended towards the Internet, and the volume of customer data has increased along with the reduced cost of data storage and processing. With the prevalence of digitalization in global competition, businesses have been in a transformation to adopt a more customer-focused strategy to establish better relationships with their customers. For marketing researchers, various forms of customer data have become a valuable asset.

The importance of customer data and the role of IT has been more critical with this transformation. Various data analysis models on such data were proposed to analyze consumer behaviors and provide managerial support in the operational and tactical levels. In this regard, data mining techniques perform an essential role in the extraction of useful information from data and provide a supportive function in various decisions.

In this chapter, data mining techniques were mentioned with a focus on problem areas in marketing. In particular, data mining tasks such as clustering, classification, and association discovery has proven useful in many problems including customer segmentation, shelf layout planning, product bundling, online recommendations, and launching campaigns. In our case study, two attribute-level association rule analyses have been presented over the data obtained from an e-retailer in İzmir. The objective of the analysis is to discover association rules that demonstrate how purchased categories and brands are chosen together in basket data.

Unlike a typical basket rule mining scenario, the data were analyzed with a focus on product categories and brands rather than products. In particular, each product in the analysis had been assigned with a brand and category attributes. For such purpose, basket data was transformed into transactional datasets that correspond to basket-brand basket-category relationship. Subsequently, rules were mined using Apriori algorithm on both datasets. After the discovery of frequent itemsets, category-level and brand-level association rules were obtained.

The results were presented with corresponding interestingness measures of confidence and lift criteria. The category-wise and brand-wise rules in findings are generalized, and each rule might correspond to a set of products. With such consideration, the rules with a high lift score might indicate strong positive correlations among product sets. The primary utility in category-wise and brand-wise rules is the adaptability in various situations. Even one rule that relates two brands might trigger hundreds of alternative recommendations. On the other hand, such generalized rules might bring out complexity in recommendation selection.

In summary, our rule mining approach with the data transformation step mentioned reveals useful generalized rules to derive alternative recommendations. In this manner, the approach might take part to overcome the cold-start problem in various cases. However, such an approach also brings up an additional challenge in recommendation selection, that requires further studies.

REFERENCES

Agrawal, R., Imieliński, T., & Swami, A. (1993). Mining association rules between sets of items in large databases. In *Proceedings of the International Conference on Management of Data*, *22*(2), 207-216. 10.1145/170035.170072

Agrawal, R., & Srikant, R. (1994). Fast algorithms for mining association rules. In *Proceedings of 20th International Conference on Very Large Data Bases*, 1215, 487-499.

Bandyopadhyay, S. (2009). A dynamic model of cross-category competition: Theory, tests and applications. *Journal of Retailing*, *85*(4), 468–479. doi:10.1016/j.jretai.2009.05.001

Bendakir, N., & Aïmeur, E. (2006). Using association rules for course recommendation. In *Proceedings of the AAAI Workshop on Educational Data Mining*, 3, 1-10.

Berger, P. D., & Nasr, N. I. (1998). Customer lifetime value: Marketing models and applications. *Journal of Interactive Marketing*, *12*(1), 17–30. doi:10.1002/(SICI)1520-6653(199824)12:1<17::AID-DIR3>3.0.CO;2-K

Bernstein, J. H. (2009). The Data-Information-Knowledge-Wisdom Hierarchy and its Antithesis. In *Proceedings of the North American Symposium on Knowledge and Organization*, 2, 68-75.

Blattberg, R. C., & Deighton, J. (1996). Manage marketing by the customer equity test. *Harvard Business Review*, *74*(4), 136–144. PMID:10158473

Burke, R. (2000). Knowledge-based recommender systems. Encyclopedia of library and information systems, 69(32), 175-186.

Chen, D., Sain, S. L., & Guo, K. (2012). Data mining for the online retail industry: A case study of RFM model-based customer segmentation using data mining. *Journal of Database Marketing & Customer Strategy Management*, *19*(3), 197–208. doi:10.1057/dbm.2012.17

Chen, H., Chiang, R. H., & Storey, V. C. (2012). Business intelligence and analytics: From big data to big impact. *Management Information Systems Quarterly*, *36*(4), 1165–1188. doi:10.2307/41703503

Chen, H., Chung, W., Xu, J. J., Wang, G., Qin, Y., & Chau, M. (2004). Crime data mining: A general framework and some examples. *Computer*, *37*(4), 50–56. doi:10.1109/MC.2004.1297301

Çil, İ. (2012). Consumption universes based supermarket layout through association rule mining and multidimensional scaling. *Expert Systems with Applications*, *39*(10), 8611–8625. doi:10.1016/j.eswa.2012.01.192

De Graaf, J. M., Kosters, W. A., & Witteman, J. J. (2001). Interesting fuzzy association rules in quantitative databases. In *Proceedings of European Conference on Principles of Data Mining and Knowledge Discovery*, 140-151. 10.1007/3-540-44794-6_12

Dwyer, F. R. (1997). Customer Lifetime Valuation to Support Marketing Decision Making. *Journal of Direct Marketing*, *11*(4), 6–13. doi:10.1002/(SICI)1522-7138(199723)11:4<6::AID-DIR3>3.0.CO;2-T

Ellis, G., & Mansmann, F. (2010). Mastering the information age solving problems with visual analytics. In *Proceedings of the Eurographics 2010*, 2, 1-6.

Eppler, M. J., & Mengis, J. (2004). The concept of information overload: A review of literature from organization science, accounting, marketing, MIS, and related disciplines. *The Information Society*, *20*(5), 325–344. doi:10.1080/01972240490507974

Farooqi, M., & Raza, K. (2012). A Comprehensive Study of CRM through data mining Techniques. In *Proceedings of the National Conference: NCCIST-2011*.

Forsati, R., Meybodi, M. R., & Neiat, A. G. (2009). Web page personalization based on weighted association rules. In *IEEE 2009 International Conference on Electronic Computer Technology*, 130-135.

Fuciu, M., & Dumitrescu, L. (2018). From Marketing 1.0 To Marketing 4.0–The Evolution of the Marketing Concept in the Context of the 21st Century. In *Proceedings of International Conference Knowledge-Based Organization*, *24*(2), 43-48. 10.1515/kbo-2018-0064

Gupta, S., & Lehmann, D. R. (2003). Customers as assets. *Journal of Interactive Marketing*, *17*(1), 9–24. doi:10.1002/dir.10045

Hall, M., Frank, E., Holmes, G., Pfahringer, B., Reutemann, P., & Witten, I. H. (2009). The WEKA data mining software: An update. *ACM Special Interest Group on Knowledge Discovery and Data Mining. Explorations Newsletter*, *11*(1), 10–18. doi:10.1145/1656274.1656278

Han, J., & Kamber, M. (2006). *Data Mining Concepts and Techniques* (2nd ed.). Burlington, MA: Morgan Kaufmann.

Harun, N. A., Makhtar, M., Aziz, A. A., Zakaria, Z. A., Abdullah, F. S., & Jusoh, J. A. (2017). The application of apriori algorithm in predicting flood areas. *International Journal on Advanced Science, Engineering and Information Technology*, *7*(3), 763–769.

Heaton, J. (2016). Comparing dataset characteristics that favor the Apriori, Eclat or FP-Growth frequent itemset mining algorithms. In *Proceedings of the 2016 SoutheastCon Conference*, 1-7. 10.1109/SECON.2016.7506659

Hegland, M. (2003). Algorithms for association rules. In *Proceedings of the Advanced Lectures on Machine Learning*, 226-234.

Hummels, D. (2007). Transportation costs and international trade in the second era of globalization. *The Journal of Economic Perspectives*, *21*(3), 131–154. doi:10.1257/jep.21.3.131

Ishibuchi, H., Nakashima, T., & Yamamoto, T. (2001). Fuzzy association rules for handling continuous attributes. In *Proceedings of 2001 IEEE International Symposium on Industrial Electronics*, 1, 118-121. 10.1109/ISIE.2001.931767

Jain, D., & Singh, S. S. (2002). Customer lifetime value research in marketing: A review and future directions. *Journal of Interactive Marketing*, *16*(2), 34–46. doi:10.1002/dir.10032

Karabatak, M., & Ince, M. C. (2009). An expert system for detection of breast cancer based on association rules and neural network. *Expert Systems with Applications*, *36*(2), 3465–3469. doi:10.1016/j.eswa.2008.02.064

Kaur, M., & Kang, S. (2016). Market Basket Analysis: Identify the changing trends of market data using association rule mining. *Procedia Computer Science*, *85*, 78–85. doi:10.1016/j.procs.2016.05.180

Kim, Y. S., & Yum, B. J. (2011). Recommender system based on click stream data using association rule mining. *Expert Systems with Applications*, *38*(10), 13320–13327. doi:10.1016/j.eswa.2011.04.154

Kotler, P., Kartajaya, H., & Setiawan, I. (2016). *Marketing 4.0: Moving from traditional to digital.* Hoboken, NJ: John Wiley & Sons.

Laudon, K. C., & Traver, G. C. (2014). *E-Commerce.* New Jersey: Pearson Education.

Leung, C. W. K., Chan, S. C. F., & Chung, F. L. (2007). Applying cross-level association rule mining to cold-start recommendations. In *Proceedings of the 2007 IEEE/WIC/ACM International Conferences on Web Intelligence and Intelligent Agent Technology-Workshops*, 133-136.

Ling, C. X., & Li, C. (1998). Data mining for direct marketing: Problems and solutions. In *Proceedings of the Fourth International Conference on Knowledge Discovery and Data Mining*, 98, 73-79.

Liu, J., Li, J., Xu, W., & Shi, Y. (2004). Data mining approach in scientific research organizations evaluation via clustering. In *Proceedings of Chinese Academy of Sciences Symposium on Data Mining and Knowledge Management*, 128-134.

Lu, J. (2004). A personalized e-learning material recommender system. In *Proceedings of International Conference on Information Technology and Applications.* Australia: Macquarie Scientific Publishing.

McCarty, J. A., & Hastak, M. (2007). Segmentation approaches in data-mining: A comparison of RFM, CHAID, and logistic regression. *Journal of Business Research*, *60*(6), 656–662. doi:10.1016/j.jbusres.2006.06.015

McNicholas, P. D., Murphy, T. B., & O'Regan, M. (2008). Standardising the lift of an association rule. *Computational Statistics & Data Analysis*, *52*(10), 4712–4721. doi:10.1016/j.csda.2008.03.013

O'Sullivan, D., Wilson, D., & Smyth, B. (2002, September). Improving case-based recommendation. In *Proceedings of European Conference on Case-Based Reasoning*, 278-291. 10.1007/3-540-46119-1_21

Paranjape-Voditel, P., & Deshpande, U. (2013). A stock market portfolio recommender system based on association rule mining. *Applied Soft Computing*, *13*(2), 1055–1063. doi:10.1016/j.asoc.2012.09.012

Payne, A., & Frow, P. (2005). A strategic framework for customer relationship management. *Journal of Marketing*, *69*(4), 167–176. doi:10.1509/jmkg.2005.69.4.167

Pfeifer, P. E., & Carraway, R. L. (2000). Modeling Customer Relationships as Markov Chains. *Journal of Interactive Marketing*, *14*(2), 43–55. doi:10.1002/(SICI)1520-6653(200021)14:2<43::AID-DIR4>3.0.CO;2-H

Rowley, J. (2007). The wisdom hierarchy: Representations of the DIKW hierarchy. *Journal of Information Science*, *33*(2), 163–180. doi:10.1177/0165551506070706

Russell, G. J., & Petersen, A. (2000). Analysis of cross category dependence in market basket selection. *Journal of Retailing*, *76*(3), 367–392. doi:10.1016/S0022-4359(00)00030-0

Rygielski, C., Wang, J. C., & Yen, D. C. (2002). Data mining techniques for customer relationship management. *Technology in society*, *24*(4), 483–502. doi:10.1016/S0160-791X(02)00038-6

Saarijärvi, H., Karjaluoto, H., & Kuusela, H. (2013). Customer relationship management: The evolving role of customer data. *Marketing Intelligence & Planning*, *31*(6), 584–600. doi:10.1108/MIP-05-2012-0055

Sahar, S. (2009). Interestingness measures on determining what is interesting. In *Data mining and knowledge discovery handbook* (pp. 603–612). Boston, MA: Springer. doi:10.1007/978-0-387-09823-4_30

Sánchez, D., Vila, M. A., Cerda, L., & Serrano, J. M. (2009). Association rules applied to credit card fraud detection. *Expert Systems with Applications*, *36*(2), 3630–3640. doi:10.1016/j.eswa.2008.02.001

Schafer, J. B., Konstan, J., & Riedl, J. (1999). Recommender systems in e-commerce. In *Proceedings of the 1st ACM conference on Electronic Commerce*, 158-166.

Schein, A. I., Popescul, A., Ungar, L. H., & Pennock, D. M. (2002). Methods and metrics for cold-start recommendations. In *Proceedings of the 25th annual international ACM SIGIR conference on Research and development in information retrieval*, 253-260.

Sumathi, S., & Sivanandam, S. D. (2006). *Introduction to Data Mining and its Applications*. Berlin, Germany: Springer-Verlag. doi:10.1007/978-3-540-34351-6

Tajbakhsh, A., Rahmati, M., & Mirzaei, A. (2009). Intrusion detection using fuzzy association rules. *Applied Soft Computing*, *9*(2), 462–469. doi:10.1016/j.asoc.2008.06.001

Tanner, J. F. Jr, Ahearne, M., Leigh, T. W., Mason, C. H., & Moncrief, W. C. (2005). CRM in sales-intensive organizations: A review and future directions. *Journal of Personal Selling & Sales Management*, *25*(2), 169–180.

Toivonen, H., Klemettinen, M., Ronkainen, P., Hätönen, K., & Mannila, H. (1995). Pruning and grouping discovered association rules. In *Workshop Notes of ECML Workshop on Statistics, Machine Learning, and Knowledge Discovery in Databases*, 47-52.

Tsiptsis, K. K., & Chorianopoulos, A. (2009). *Data mining techniques in CRM: Inside Customer Segmentation*. Hoboken, NJ: John Wiley & Sons.

Videla-Cavieres, I. F., & Rios, S. A. (2014). Extending market basket analysis with graph mining techniques: A real case. *Expert Systems with Applications*, *41*(4), 1928–1936. doi:10.1016/j.eswa.2013.08.088

Wang, K. W., Zhou, S., Yang, Q., & Yeung, J. M. S. (2005). Mining customer value: From association rules to direct marketing. *Data Mining and Knowledge Discovery*, *11*(1), 57–79. doi:10.100710618-005-1355-x

Yin, X., & Han, J. (2003). CPAR: Classification based on predictive association rules. In *Proceedings of the International SIAM Conference on Data Mining*, 331-335 10.1137/1.9781611972733.40

KEY TERMS AND DEFINITIONS

Association Rule Mining: A technique in data mining to discover patterns that represent the relationship among items that frequently exist together in a data set.

Customer Relationship Management: CRM is an approach and strategy to establish strong and long-lasting relations with customers and emphasize the interaction between business and its customers.

Data Mining: Data Mining is a research field, and a set of methods that are developed with intention to extract interesting and useful patterns from existing data.

DIKW Pyramid: A pyramid proposed to demonstrate the relationship among the concepts of data, information, knowledge and wisdom.

KDD: Knowledge Discovery in Databases, the overall process of extracting knowledge from large masses of data.

Market Basket Analysis: An analysis over previous purchase records that helps to discover products frequently purchased together.

Recommender Systems: a term to describe the software developed to suggest appropriate products/content to online shoppers/visitors.

RFM: Recency, Frequency and Monetary Model, a technique that is used to perform segmentation for customers considering three different quantitative aspects of their purchase history.

Chapter 13
Digitalization of Human Resources:
e-HR

Elif Baykal
İstanbul Medipol University, Turkey

ABSTRACT

Recent decades brought about astonishing technologies that affected organizations in several ways. With the latest developments, organizations earned the capabilities to carry out their functions more efficiently and rapidly. Having several tasks affecting both interior and exterior customers, human resources departments also benefited from these technological developments. Owing to the digital revolution, e-HR emerged as a new way of practicing HRM activities with the latest web-based and computer-based tools and applications. These applications eased the work of HR professionals and served them the opportunity to focus on their core work, namely strategic human resources activities rather than procedural paperwork of the department. With a holistic and integrative approach, this digital transformation in HRM has been dispersed among all services in human resources including recruitment, career management, training and development, performance management, and compensation.

INTRODUCTION

Latest technological and competitive developments in the markets enabled the creation of real-time, knowledge-based, self-managed and interactive business atmosphere. This knowledge based interactive work atmosphere was impossible to believe throughout most of the twentieth century. After 1990s digitalization in all spheres of life have become prominent. Latest developments in web based technologies have given birth to production of large bulks of online data varying from social media posts to digitalized libraries. This new body of knowledge and data provided a significant source of data complimenting classical quantitative and qualitative data and allowing individuals to unravel sound patterns regarding managerial and social phenomena (Platanou, Mäkelä, Beletskiy, & Colicev, 2018). The creation of huge online data sets, namely Big Data has also grown significantly recently owing to the astonishing

DOI: 10.4018/978-1-7998-0035-4.ch013

developments in data storage Technologies and digital monitoring mechanisms. This "Big Data" can help individuals understand collective patterns of events, behaviors, perceptions, and attitudes better and easier than other methods (Hannigan, 2015). And its use disseminated in a considerable wide scope of managerial functions including even human resources management.

In fact, use of technology is a new realm of study in management literature. When the related literature is examined as Orlikowski and Scott (2008) suggest there are two streams regarding use of technology in organizations. The first stream explains technological determinism reflecting an underlying positivist approach wherein technology can be conceived as a independent qualitative variable predicting organizational consequences. The second stream considers technology as a new construct evolving over time reflecting a more post-positivist perspective. In the first stream, technology is an entity interacting with different organizational aspects (Orlikowski & Scott, p. 439). It is considered as an independent variable that have a quiet noteworthy number of impacts in organizational life at various analysis levels including individual level, group level, enterprise level, and inter-organizational level. Moreover, it is effective on various organizational outputs when considered as an independent variable including effectiveness, agility, resilience, profitability, etc. (Orlikowski & Scott, 2008). This approach has a rather deterministic perspective, since it views technology as a causal factor which can create assessable, theoretically-determined results. For example, the number of IT projects accomplished in a certain organizations, the number and quality of technical tools used, the qualifications of IT personnel etc. can all be conceived as independent variables in the kind of researched that exist in this first stream of research. The second main stream of studies regarding technology which is prominent in management literature is the stream known with its focus on dynamic interactions between people factor and technology factor over time. This approach can be considered as less deterministic compared to the first one. It views technology as a component of complex process wherein organization of the structure can be accomplished. However, today technology should not be understood with a limited perspective. It is no longer a discrete entity. That is why it cannot be conceived as a quantifiable independent or dependent dimension. In fact, technology is emergent and cannot be determined fully. There are many factors, complicated relationships and grey areas in understanding effects of technology in organizational setting. That is why, Strohmeier (2009) explains the second stream of studies as studies of moderated organizational imperatives wherein there multiple actors interact with the aim of creating an outcome which is in fact cannot be predicted entirely.

In practice, although latest digital technologies have been utilized in HR information systems since 1980s, it was a different application when compared to e-HR. HRISs was focusing on automating HR systems that were used by HR department's itself, namely its sole 'customer' was HR professionals themselves. Moreover, HRISs were not successful in creating the ideal internal virtual value chain. On the other hand, e-HR is more about the application of the internet, including use of social media, and mobile communications technologies are important in changing the nature of interactions among HR professionals, managers and employees. Its aim was changing these relationships from a pure face-to-face relationship to a technology-based one (Martin and Redington, 2010). Nonetheless, HRISs can be accepted as the first step before transition to e-HR.

In technology research the term "e-HR" first emerged after 1990s. Emergence of the term "e-commerce" namely electronic commerce was the antecedent of the term. E- HR is a way of implementing HR activities, strategies and policies through a conscious and directed support of latest technology (Ruël, Bondarouk, & Looise, 2004). E-HR can be explained as a way of conducting HR strategies in companies through a willing, conscious and directed support of full use of internet-based technologies (Ruel et al.; 2004). As in the case in the term e-commerce, e-HR refers to conducting human resources transactions with the help of internet. The use of Internet ensured human resources function with the ease to reach and use information in any time when needed and wanted. (Lengnick-Hall & Moritz, 2003).With the help of e-HR, organizations and employees can administer their own information. E-HR gives them the opportunity to update records and make decisions easily using this records (Lengnick-Hall & Moritz, 2003). E-HR is positively related with both efficiency and effectiveness. Efficiency is possible through reducing the required time for processing paperwork. It also increases accuracy of the data obtained and stored. Moreover, it reduces the time human resource employees spend for their daily activities. On the other hand, effectiveness is also another product of e-HR. With latest technologies and newly adopted know- how to these Technologies companies using E-HR can administer their activities more effectively. Since e -HR improved the capabilities of organizations and organizational members in making more satisfying, more timely and more meaningful decisions (Lengnick-Hall & Moritz, 2003).

In order to understand e-HR, it is necessary to first understand the nature of HR activities.Thite and Kavanagh (2009) grouped human resources management functions into three basic groups: transactional activities, involving daily transactions and record keeping; traditional human resources management activities, encompassing activities like recruitment, selection, HR planning, training and development, compensation and performance appraisal; and transformational activities, activities adding value to the company, like organizational development, talent management and organizational learning. Recently, a shift occurred in the delivery of transactional human resources activities which are often labour intensive to the more technology-intensive activities such as e-recruitment, e-coaching, e-mentoring etc. (Florkowski & Olivas-Lujan, 2006). E-HR has become more pervasive after companies adopted this new more technology-based form of doing business. The introduction of e-HRM had significantly reduced the traditional transactional workload of the HR professionals (Parry & Tyson, 2011). And it increased transformational outcomes like more transparent and detailed information or more time available to human resources practitioners (Parry & Tyson, 2011). Moreover, the use of a common technological system led to more consistent HR processes, contributing to higher levels of standardization (Parry & Tyson, 2011). E-HR seems to be more involved in this standardization and homogenization process within larger, more bureaucratic and mostly international companies (Ruel et al., 2004).

In fact, e-HR development has been seen in three main forms. The easiest and most common way to implement e-HR is to publish information. This first form is known as the simplest form of e-HR involving one-way communication in the organization that has a top-down flow, namely top managers or owners tend to disclose information for the use of employees. In this form of e-HR companies mostly prefer to use intranets as the main source information delivery. Earliest examples of this e-HR method encompass some generic content information publishing such as company policies, service directories, informing employees about daily events etc. The second mainstream use of e-HR involves the automation of HR processes and transactions. In this e-HR form it is preferred to use intranets with extranets simultaneously. This form combines different digital applications. In this HR mode, paperwork is mostly replaced by digital input. In the third, and most developed form of e-HR we can talk about transformation of HR functions almost to a fully electronic mode. In this journey, from information to automation and from automation to transformation, e-HR has gone beyond its traditional focus to a more modern and digitalized mode. And through this transformation, e-HR liberated HR from being operational-focused and has been redirected towards being a more strategic function. On the other hand, while some companies embrace a more evolutionary approach to implementing e-HR, others can prefer embracing more radical ways in directly to transforming the HR activities (Lengnick-Hall & Moritz, 2003).

BENEFITS OF E-HR

First of all, e-HR is a cost saving way of conducting HR processes. In organizations that wherein e-HR is used, fewer human resource professionals and lower working hours are required due to the fact that e-HR eliminates the need for HR middleman. Besides reducing costs and increasing efficiency, use of e-HR also can create new revenue sources. Human resources professional earn the ability to direct their energy to new realms in doing their business more effectively and professionally after they have met with e-HR. But, establishing direct and objective methods to measure benefits of these new ways of conducting HR functions are difficult to achieve. For instance, e-HR can increase employee productivity, motivation and can speed up decision-making processes but these issues are difficult to measure (Lengnick-Hall & Moritz, 2003). Moreover, in companies using e-HR, transactions are held with a higher speed, lower levels of information errors are seen, and tracking and control of human resource functions are handled more professionally. Thus, with the help of e-HR companies can improve their HRM service delivery (Lengnick-Hall & Moritz, 2003).

On the one hand, costs can also occur linked with using an e-HR system. For instance, using high technology in HR process may make it necessary to buy expensive technological devices for each personnel that carry on these processes (Lengnick-Hall & Moritz, 2003). For example, making online meetings with HR account managers from other geographies makes it necessary to buy high-tech cameras and computers in each geographical location of the company. On the other hand, variation in e-HR activities, creates variations in organizational capabilities supporting increasingly coordinated and automated HR processes encompassing those kinds of activities such as data processing and stocking, internal and external communication and conducting HR operations using internet-based technologies (Marler & Parry, 2015). In fact, use of e-HR is a planned strategic activity regarding provision of HRM services through modern technologies (Marler & Parry, 2015)

Today, most prominent e-HR systems often include enterprise resource planning software systems, automated HR operations, interactive voice responses (IVR) of HR call centers, web applications of career portals that are used in applications, and most pervasively interior employee portals (Lengnick-Hall, & Moritz, 2003). Using these systems e-HR systems increase efficiency and ensure a change in HR that shifts to a more strategic level (Parry & Tyson, 2011). By the help of these systems, organizations can be successful in attaining five probable goals including e-HRM-efficiency, high-quality service delivery, long-term strategic orientation, more-empowered employees and standardisation in HR processes (Parry & Tyson, 2011).

When considered with a different perspective, e-HR is found to be more pervasive in those kinds of companies wherein a more sophisticated and complex HR functioning is prominent. In this point, Voermans and van Veldhoven (2007) claims that in those kinds of organizations wherein in there is a system of HR strategic partnership, it is more likely to see an inclination towards e- HRM. In HR partnership system, HR professionals are considered as strategic partners of business units or geographical subunits of the main organization. In this system HR professionals are considered as HR account managers in their own strategic business unit. They have intimate contact with the business unit they are responsible for. And they are often working in the location their business unit is located rather than in HR Office that is why the HR department needs using electronic communication and information sharing tools in getting in touch with these professionals.

As mentioned before, researchers like Thite and Kavanagh (2009) divide HR function into two main activities: transactional activities, involving day-to-day activities, daily transactions and record keeping; such as recruitment of new employees, selection, training and development, wage management and performance management; and rather more transformational activities, including organisational development, career management, performance appraisal, mentoring and talent management. In the practice we see that organizations preferring a more strategic HR management tend to engage in e-HR systems (Voermans & Veldhoven, 2007). It is more advantageous to carry on human resources functions through online portals and technological communication tools. It makes HR function more effective on multiple stakeholders such as potential candidates, existing employees, middle and top managers and line managers. In such organizations, a negative possible result of E-HR is losing personal contact with HR professionals. In fact, personal contact with human resources agents is one of the strongest needs when in strategic human resources management, where the human resources professional has employee champion role for HR (Voermans & Veldhoven, 2007). Thus, e-HR is expected to confer many advantages on organizations, such as a more efficient and strategically-oriented HR function and an increased competitive advantage (Lazaaara & Galanaki, 2018).

ANTECEDENTS OF E-HR ADOPTION

Extant literature shows that companies operating in technology-intensive sectors tend to embrace IT tools in order to enhance their external image (Teo, Lim, & Fedric, 2007). But this is a contagious perception for most contemporary companies. Today even those companies that has little to do with technology prefer to use technological tools and mechanisms to create a more modern image. In the digital age human resources professionals started to prefer online domains more frequently, wherein they can learn about the latest trends in the field, they can share their experiences and best practices, and they can embrace in carrying out their daily activities. Of course, there are many reasons underlying the preference of companies and human resources professional regarding the usage of e-HR technologies.

In fact, the task characteristics in an organization or in an industry, that is to say the inclination or necessity to have more or less clerical or stationary tasks is useful in predicting technological adoption, and without doubt e-HR adoption. Sometimes too much clerical work, sometimes disjointed geographical organization structure and sometimes excessive levels of recruitment and selection may result in more frequent use of e-HR. Companies having too many bureaucratic tasks prefer to follow-up their daily routine through web-based applications. Again companies having complicated recruitment, career management or performance management processes prefer to use technological tools to carry on their task more effectively and efficiently.

Moreover, organizational size also effective on the use of technological tools in HRM functions. Namely, number of people working in the organization, span of control, number of departments and organizational structure are all important in designating the use of e-HRM adoption. More crowded companies having too much employees and several hierarchical levels and myriad managers are compelled to embrace web-based e-HR processes in order to ease the complicated and exhausting task of HR professionals dealing with several people and procedures simultaneously. Workload of human resources professionals are heavier the bigger the size of the company. And this necessitates mechanisms and tools for making the job easier for human resources professionals.

Furthermore, the kind of companies that are actors in global competition, namely, international companies tend to engage in e-HRM more frequently. The need to collaborate with their partners and subunits in different geographies and the higher educational levels of their employees are effective on e-HRM adoption. In those kind of companies we can come across lower levels of failure in e-HR adoption since employees are well educated and the characteristics of the tasks that are carried out are proper for web-based procedures (Lazazzara & Galanaki 2018). On the one hand, isomorphic pressures at the industry level namely, the pressured applied by the other competitors in an industry to resemble each other effects the use of e-HR. If in an industry most companies prefer to engage in use of web-based HR tools, rest of the companies also start to engage in a e- HR with the aim of achieving organizational legitimacy. Without doubt employees working in these companies and all the other stakeholders will compare their company with the other companies using e-HR and this will create a pressure on the company to engage in e-HR.

After a company decides on engaging in e-HR, the company decides on the kind of activities that the company should benefit from e-HR. In some companies all e-HR functions are carried out with the help of e-HR, and in some cases, companies prefer to adopt and use e-HR in a limited manner, that is to say only in some functions of e-HR. This id sometimes a preference and sometimes a requirement. In some cases as a strategic decision, companies prefer a limited or a generalized use of e-HR, or in some cases financial limitations end up with a more limited use of e-HR. Nevertheless, technology proponents claim that, the IT possibilities for human resource management are endless: in principal all human resources functions can be supported by technology (Ruël, Bondarouk, & Looise, 2004). In the next part of this chapter, most prominent human resources functions that are benefiting from web-based technologies will be discussed.

E-RECRUITMENT

E-recruitment systems have become quiet popular in the last few years due to its advantages in allowing HR professionals to target a great number of candidates at a small cost (Faliagka, Tsakalidis, & Tzimas, 2012). E-recruitment is carrying out recruitment functions through web-based Technologies. E-recruitment implies publishing job posts, namely open positions in a compony online, having an online fill-in form available for applicants and a web-based database existing to store the resumes of applicants (Brandão, Silva, & dos Santos, 2019). Using e-HR systems companies can be seen in myriad career portals and can attract the attention of astronomic number of candidates with various qualifications. In most e-recruitment processes, companies use an automated system wherein candidates are ranked by using a set of objective and credible criteria, that are easy to apply for companies (Faliagka, Tsakalidis, & Tzimas, 2012). And they use an online career portal in reaching their applicants. By the help of digital Technologies these criteria are applied to all candidates that make a job application through company's internet portal or a common recruitment portal. E-recruitment starts with candidates intend to apply for a job in a certain organization. During this process, in case a new position opens, the human resources professional creates a job post in the internet portal of the company or in a web-based career portal. Predetermined selection criteria and weights of that criteria is used in determining the suitability of each candidate. Selection criteria and position requirements are posted by the recruiter through the job post. The recruitment process starts when the candidates apply for an open position at the e-recruitment portal (Faliagka, Tsakalidis, & Tzimas, 2012). In fact, e-recruitment allows candidates to have contact with more job opportunities and reach a greater flow of information (Sylva & Mol, 2009). In e-recruitment candidates upload their resumes to the system that should be examined by an HR expert in the organization (Faliagka, Tsakalidis, & Tzimas, 2012). And the applicant can get information from the company about his process through the web-based recruitment portal or through the internet site of the company. There are some additional applications in e-recruitment system. For instance, specialized selection tests such as knowledge tests and personality tests can be applied through internet which provide online feedback to the recruiters and the applicants about the qualifications of the candidates. And in e-recruitment, various preliminary online procedures can be applied through internet enabling the elimination of applicants that do not fit the position (Brandão, Silva, & dos Santos, 2019). If their process is negative, namely if after the resume is examined, the evaluation about the resume is negative, the candidate is directly informed about the negative evaluation via the web-based portal. Companies can also use their organizational website in informing their potential applicants regarding new job opportunities, but they mostly prefer to have a permanent recruitment portal for receiving applications of new candidates even when there is not an urgent need for new candidates (Brandão, Silva, & dos Santos, 2019). In fact, organizational websites are communication channels between companies and job seekers (Araújo & Ramos, 2002). Sometimes companies merely use their corporate websites to attract new applications. Whether the tool for receiving applications is their corporate website or a recruitment portal is not important. In both cases their aim That is why companies prefer to have a pool of candidates attracted and collected via their web-based portal that are stocked for a certain period of time that are ready to be evaluated in case there occurs an urgent need. However, it is an inevitable fact that only a small number of overall applicants are selected and receives a call for a job interview (Faliagka, Tsakalidis, & Tzimas, 2012). And this can make the company notorious among applicants if their applicant hiring/applicant stocking rate is too low.

On the one hand, there are also some disadvantages of e-recruitment especially for candidates. Specifically, privacy can be perceived as a problem by the candidates. In their empirical study Petre et al. (2016) found that while applying to online job posts, applicants sometimes perceive a certain privacy risk. They can become anxious about sharing their personal information. They may be suspicious about the possibility that the information they shared in their resumes may be shared by third parties without their permission. Moreover, some people are not accustomed to using technological tools and they may avoid making applications via internet due to their technology bias. That is to say, in e-recruitment candidates' reactions to the online system and job advertisements in this system are influenced by the perceived efficiency and user-friendliness, namely, if or not the applicant views the job advertisement easy to conceive and apply for (Sylva & Mol, 2009).

E-TRAINING

E-training can be considered as a way of distance training through the use of web-based Technologies encompassing either Internet or Intranet that provide individuals with the required knowledge on specific selected themes or a specific specialty, with the help of the computer-based technologies, sound tracks, videos, multimedia messages, e-books, emails, and discussion groups (Amara, & Atia, 2016). In e-training, the use of technology to educate is prominent (Mohsin & Sulaiman, 2013). This kind of training can be either in the form of face to face education or in the form of distance mediated or pure online education. Origins of this term e-training goes back to the 1980s, as in the case with emergence of the term online training. There are various terms indicating e-training such as distance training; virtual training; online training or web-based training (Amara & Atia, 2016). And E-training systems encompass myriad tools including writing technologies, communication technologies, visualization, and storage (Aparicio, Bacao, & Oliveira, 2016). Furthermore, e-training activities are not bounded merely using a computer or we-based technology as an artifact in the training process. Students can be individual students or company employees that prefer using these modules in congruent with the development policies of their employees (Aparicio, Bacao, & Oliveira, 2016). Some organizations embrace knowledge management and virtual collaboration in their e-training strategies, broadly including any system generating and disseminating information and improving organizational and individual performance (Welsch et al., 2003).

E-learning is also a pervasive term used in e-training processes. E-learning is the implementation of Internet-based technologies with the aim of delivering a satisfactory number of alternative solutions enhancing knowledge acquisition (Esterhuyse & Scholtz, 2016). And it seems sound to companies due to its ability to ensure cost-effective training. Moreover, e-learning is also useful for ensuring consistency in learning materials and learning techniques. Each people benefiting from a certain learning material reach the same kind of content. It also ensures flexibility in the time period that the learner prefers to benefit from the learning material, it provides ease of access, it is capable of just- in-time delivery, have low costs, and high customer value (Esterhuyse & Scholtz, 2016). In fact, we can talk about six main elements of e-learning encompassing; computer that have an access to internet, utilization of the system by both the learner and the HR, curriculum development by the HR professionals, content creation by the educator (often a specialist in the topic), content management that is mostly carried out by the related HR professional, learning management, delivery of the education program and development of the program (Riahi, 2015). These processes are mostly carried by HR department of the company with the help of a special institute or education company that is specialist on the related subject.

Companies prefer e-training to decrease their costs of education they spend for training their personnel. Considering the cost of training employees working in different geographies, it is an important solution to get rid of both waste of time and travel costs. In fact, different from the traditional face-to- face training techniques, e-training techniques help companies reach a considerably large number of education contents with low costs (Jackson et al., 2018). It is a more egalitarian way of educating employees when compared to classical methods of education, owing to the greater number and quality it serves to employees from various hierarchical levels and geographies. In the table below a good summary of the differences between classical face to face training and web-based digital e-training can be found.

E-MENTORING

E-mentoring is a specific kind of mentoring that get use of technology-based programmes in providing flexibility in time management and scheduling. E-mentoring is helpful in decreasing problems caused by geographical barriers. People that cannot otherwise get mentoring benefit from mentoring opportunities thanks to e-mentoring. In this mentoring style mentor and mentee do not experience adversities related to scheduling. Pairs are not bounded by constraints like a proper place or a proper time to meet, if they can access to a proper computer and the Internet. Mentoring is easier and more comfortable through e-mentoring for the kind of people who are unable to access this service previously (Kasprisin, Single, Single, & Muller, 2003).

In classical mentoring, organizations appoint higher rank employees or managers having more experience or higher performance as mentors to the ones with lower ranks, less experience or lower performance levels. Unfortunately, this can give way to some discomforting feelings on the side of mentee. E-mentoring can lower this discrepancies and unequal power relationship, since in e-mentoring status symbols are often unidentified. That is why, although a bit discomforting for individuals that are not

Table 1. Training vs. E-Training

Traditional training	E-training
-The trainer is the main source of knowledge	-The trainer is a kind of facilitator and mentor of in the training process
- One-way, from trainer to trainee, flow of knowledge	-Interactive training process
-The trainee receives or takes knowledge from the trainer	-Flexible and more self-involving learning process
-Inflexible and routine processes	-Developing and flexible content
-Static content	-Relatively low cost
-High cost	-Emphasis on individual differences
-Ignorance of individual differences	

Source: Omar Ahmad El-Kabir, Distance training in the context of evolving techniques of training, National symposium on education and vocational e-training, General People's Committee for Workforces, Training and Employment, Tripoli, 2006, P. 7.

comfortable with digital communication, it is more equalitarian way of mentoring (Kasprisin, Single, Single, & Muller, 2003).

Moreover, unlike classical mentoring programmes encompassing face-to face mentoring relationships, e-mentoring makes it possible for huge organizations design large-scale programmes encompassing many mentor-mentee pairs from different locations (Kasprisin, Single, Single, & Muller, 2003). Individuals can be matched with various alternatives which creates prosperity regarding alternatives. Companies can match mentors and mentees more freely without considering geographical obstacles, financial matters and fear of spending too much time in making peers come together.

E-CAREER MANAGEMENT

Computer-based and web-based career management mechanisms are important tools in identifying and putting across the necessities required for the employee's development. And, these mechanisms ensures the facilities in comparing the knowledge and capabilities hold by employees with the skills and competences necessary for the existing or future tasks and positions (Rothwell et al., 2005, pp. 122-124). E-career management is one of these mechanisms making HR function work profoundly more effective. In classical career management programs HR professionals try to understand properties and potentials of employees and mostly group them according to their performance, potential and career plans. And there occurs a huge data related to all that information that should be stocked and analyzed year by year for a long period of time, which is really a burdensome and exhausting task. With the help of e-career management this difficult and tiring task can be accomplished more easily through computer-based and we-based technologies.

Moreover, with the help of e-career management, employees can follow their own career processes. They can store their own personal data, they can make updates about change in their tasks, roles or positions. Moreover, they can even make decisions on their own, getting help from HR professionals only if they need help. For instance, an individual making a retirement plan can plan it by using the Internet (Lengnick-Hall & Moritz, 2003). Or they can develop their technical capabilities or soft skills that are needed for a promotion through web-based learning modules. And by using intranet they can search open positions in their organizations that can pave the way for a promotion if they are found suitable. Moreover, with the help of e-career management tools human resources professional can also draw career maps of individuals in their organizations comfortably. They can store the necessary data for each employee and can reach the necessary data when creating a pool for candidates for certain position.

E-COMPENSATION

E-compensation can be described as the use computer-based and web-based technologies for planning employees' compensation (Swaroop, 2012). Dulebohn and Marler (2005) explains e-compensation as the use of web-based software applications in allowing managers' effective administration and disclosure of information regarding compensation and benefits procedures and information in an organization. In fact, payroll administration can be considered as one of the earliest forms of e-HR processes. (Lengnick-Hall & Moritz, 2003). After 1990s, growth in integrated human resources information systems ensured administration of several human resources functions simultaneously and resulted in more sophisticated human resources management and reporting opportunities. These technological developments enabled companies to provide their employees and managers access to real-time and trustworthy information. Thus, these technological self-service systems gave organizational members the opportunity to manage HR processes. Organizational members can use these systems in updating their records, and HR Professional can use them for accommodating wages and fringe benefits and managers can use generate reports to develop plans (Stone & Dulebohn, 2013). Most importantly, bureaucratic tasks are conducted by e-compensation mechanisms with the help of real-time data. Web-based technologies ensures more updated, quick and reliable workflows.

The use of e-compensation mechanisms helps HR professionals and line managers access to higher levels of data that can contribute to more effective and accurate compensation initiatives. Having the necessary information whenever needed HR professional can also serve the paperwork needs of employees easily without making them wait for tedious time periods. On the other hand, e-compensation decreases the levels of error regarding compensation function of HR. For example, companies embracing e-compensation experience lower level of errors about wages or other kinds of payments made to the employees.

Moreover, e-compensation can also be beneficial for maintaining wage equality (Dulebohn & Marler, 2005, pp. 166-167). Giving the opportunity to control and report all the wages in an organization simultaneously and giving the change to make analysis on this huge data, a fair HR team can take steps to provide wage equality comfortably with the help of e-compensation. Inequalities made before can be seen and corrected easily. During daily processes if a subordinate makes a mistake regarding compensation function for example if they send wrong payroll to the wrong employee, it can be easily detected by the HR manager and corrective action can be taken quickly.

E-PERFORMANCE APPRAISAL

E-performance systems can be explained as the mechanisms using company's web-based portals and applications in order to conduct an evaluation of the employees' potential, knowledge and performance through internet (Swaroop, 2012). In e-performance appraisal systems all the processes are online. HR

Professional do not waste time with paperwork. They can trace the performance evaluation process via web-based performance management tools. All the stakeholders of performance appraisal system, namely the employee whose performance is evaluated, the line manager who is one of the evaluators and the HR professional who is responsible of the success of the process can all benefit from the comfort and easiness of the system.

In e-performance appraisal, all the stakeholders of performance management have access to the online performance module. Namely, the employee whose Performance is evaluated, the line manager evaluating the Performance and the HR Professional coaching the process can reach to the related workflow, but each one can only see and control the part related to his own task in the process. For example, the employee whose Performance is evaluated can see his latest records and his updated situation regarding his performance goals bur cannot change approved performance grades he had earned before. Similarly, a line manager cannot change previous years' performance grades of his staff after they have been approved by the related HR professional.

E-HR GOALS

By embracing e-HR, companies direct their HR function to a more systematized, mode digitalized and more convenient state. It often results in an improvement in HR'S strategic orientation, namely by the help of e-HR, HR function can better accommodate itself with the higher strategies of their organization more comfortably. For example, with the help of using e-performance appraisal systems even huge organizations can cascade their organization's strategic goals and can appoint goals to the people working even in the lowest hierarchical levels. And this goal can be traced by multiple stakeholders in the performance appraisal system including the employee's himself, line manager and the HR account manager. By this way all activities in the organization can be directed towards the highest goal, towards the strategic goal. Moreover e-HR results in cost reductions in the organization. Having their most functions computerized and automatized after e-HR adoption, most HR departments start to need less people working in their services. A quieted significant part of the activities are held by computers. The bulk of paperwork's diminishes. On the other hand, most routine tasks no longer take as much time as they took before. So, e-HR can be accepted as a time saving way of doing business in HRM department. Furthermore, it is a comfortable way of doing business when HR account managers are in different geographies or external stakeholders such as new applicants are from various different geographies. In huge companies having different HR services in different strategic business units or in different geographies, most spontaneous communication is ensured via web-based applications such as corporate intranet, corporate messaging applications and e-mails. And most communication from external stakeholders are again ensured via emails, voicemails, video conferences and online meetings. For example, an international bank attracting applicant from all over the world can prefer to make their job interviews in the form of online interview. It will be both time and cost saving method of doing an interview.

On the one hand, according to Ruel et al. (2004) e-HR also creates more committed employees and HR professionals. Experiencing newest technologies in their daily organizational life, both subjects and objects of HR processes benefit from more rapid, more effective and more satisfying HR processes which leads to more committed organizational members. For instance, in a company using e-career management portals, being aware of the fact that his career data is being stocked and administered objectively and securely in e-HR portals, an employee can feel trust for the career management mechanisms in his organizations and can feel secure regarding his future in the organization which will lead to organizational commitment. In the digital age most employees are millennium children that are below their 30s which means that they like technology and they like doing business with the help of latest technological tools and mechanisms. Having HR applications designed with highest technology, employees feel that their organization is technology-friendly, and it creates the perception that they are working in an open-minded organization. On the other hand, the next generations and Z generations, are also even more prone to use technological devices in their daily life and coming across digitalized processes and tools make job more enjoyable for them.

CONCLUSION

As mentioned before, e-HRM or e-HR can be conceived as a concept involving the use of internet and Web-based technologies in the provision of human resources services in organizations. E-HR is the conceptualization of the application of web-based and internet-based strategies, procedures, policies and implications in human resources management function (Ruel, Bondarouk, & Looise, 2004). In 1990s Internet entered the lives of people as an important phenomenon in the digitalization business life. Emergence of internet facilitated previously non-existing spontaneous and cheap two-way communication among people. It was a revolutionary step in creating instant worldwide information that can be easily disseminated with considerably low costs. After 1990s, Web-based started to be used for the benefit of human resources management function. Similar technologies used in managerial functions and e trade has been replicated and acidulated to the human resources. From then on human resources software programs became more congruent with Internet architecture. In the early 2000s, this novel trend ensured centralization of all human resources and administrative data for the use of Web browsers, namely organizational members whenever and wherever they want (Stone & Dulebohn, 2013). After digitalization of HR functions, HR data has become more available and disseminated in organizations.

With the help of electronic human resources management practices, various stakeholders in organizations such as employees, HR agents and managers can access to organizational data and human resources data timelier and easily (Berber, Dordevic, & Milanovic, 2018). E-HR speeds up HRM activities and contributes to more accurate and transparent transactions. In e-HR we can talk about full support and full reliance on web-based technologies in organizational setting. It is not merely the use of internet or computer in carrying out HR activities but also designing tasks and procedures incompatible with latest technologies. After e-HR adoption most companies reevaluate their task designs and processes and embrace more updated versions of their procedures that makes e-HR adoption easier and convenient. E-HR usage ensures more simplistic and more encompassing processes on all over organizations. After e-HR adoption many tools and portals are shared with various stakeholders that somehow has something to do with HR activities. For example, in order to share resumes collected from online e recruitment portal and online job posts with the related line managers. Online accounts are opened for each line manager in the organization. Having their own accounts and these line managers can filter applicants, can evaluate their short lists and can share their comments on these resumes with the related HR account manager. Or they can learn about new applicants quickly without getting any help from the related HR account manager. Thus, this fastens daily activities of both HR department and the other functional departments.

Moreover, e-HR can result in more dedicated and more satisfying HR professionals with considerable heightened customer focus (Ruel et al., 2004). This heightened focus is mostly seemed to be valid for internal customers, namely organizational members. After embracing e-HR, human resources professionals earn the opportunity to act as internal coaches or consultants to the departments that they are responsible for. Being available each time an organizational member wants to reach, being more transparent and informing, an HR agent would create the perception of a friendly strategic partner that can act as an interior consultant. As it is known by almost all HR professionals having a close contact with employee and being in touch with them constantly will make the HR agent more reliable in the eyes of organizational members. Good relationships with the rest of the company will empower HR agents and will make it easy for them to get information from different segments of the organization. The information obtained through good relationship with organizational members will create a mutual understanding between the parts and will lead parties to act in accordance with each other's interests. Both the HR professional and the employees will cooperate in doing business in order to benefit from their mutually nourishing relationship.

Automating human resources management function is about transforming the classical paper-and-pencil, labor-intensive human resources function, into more efficient, more fast-response and more effective functions enabling organizations to expect and benefit from environmental changes creating competitive advantage (Olivas-Lujan, Ramirez, & Zapata-Cantu, 2007). That is to say, human resources function is converted to a strategic tool making organizations more adaptable, flexible and competitive structure benefiting from highest human resources technologies, web based human resources applications and computer programs. These applications are helpful in accommodating daily routines to strategic goals of the organization in a user-friendly manner. By adapting newest Technologies to human resources management function, companies learn and embrace more about latest improvement in human resources realm and they can successfully integrate these improvements to the other functions in the organization. For example, a modern recruitment system will market the company better candidates more quickly compared to their rivals and sophisticated orientation and training modules will make these new employees better adopt to the organizational realities and processes which will make the organization more successful in the long run.

Moreover, e-HR is also effective on the development of capabilities of human resources professional in the organizations that embraced it. In this point, Bell, Lee, & Young (2006) applied a study on senior HR professionals from 19 Fortune 500 companies with the aim of examining the relationships between eHR and the reshaping of HR professionals' competences. Results of the study showed that, e-HR adoption necessitates higher skills in adapting HR practices and strategic competence to the organization. These requirements create a synthesis of HR professionals' expertise in Human resources functions and their business knowledge regarding their organizations' business. Moreover, latest e-HR tools necessitate technical knowledge and some technological knowhow in order to be able to benefit from them. An HR professional that does not know how to get use of this technological applications and tools cannot be successful in carrying out his daily tasks.

Moreover, e-HR is effective on individual productivity in organizations. Generally, companies utilize HRM technologies with the aim of boosting employee productivity (CedarCrestone, 2013). Since, e-HRM creates possibilities of enhancing individual's capabilities in organizations, giving way to improved employee productivity (Bissola & Imperatori, 2013). For example, in a company using e-career management module, everyone should learn the technical details of the system in order to get benefit from it. Or in an organization wherein e-coaching system is prevalent, more organizational members can benefit from the coaching service compared to the case that is seen where classical coaching methodologies are embraced. e-HRM has the potential to boost productivity by increasing automation and by changing low-value processes with high value-added tasks (Marler & Parry, 2016). This increase in productivity also comes about through quick, updated, and reliable data that managers can get from the system in order to make appropriate decisions. Specifically, operational e-HRM tools increase productivity of companies by streamlining classical HR practices, speeding up processes and reducing headcounts (Parry, 2011). In fact, e-HRM has the potential to reduce costs and save organizational members' time by letting them carry out more transactions with fewer fixed costs" and, thus, improving employee productivity (Hendrickson, 2003). Supporting this view Ruel, Bondarouk, and Van der Velde (2007) applied a study. In their study in the Ministry of Internal Affairs in The Netherlands, wherein e-HR was used Ruel, Bondarouk, and Van der Velde (2007) examined whether e-HRM is useful for organizations. Results of their study showed that HRM perceived as technically and strategically effective. Especially perceived quality of the e-HR Services and the structure of e-HR applications have found to be perceived effective by individuals.

SOLUTIONS AND RECOMMENDATIONS

As discussed above, e-HR has the potential to lower Human resources transaction costs thus, the number of people working in human resources department. For instance, by supplying human resources information to several people on a basis e-HR is conceived as an economic way of doing business in HR department. It is a good alternative for re-using information on an infinite number of occasions at little costs. For instance, by e-training large numbers of people can benefit from a specific learning module or training program. Once the company pays for that program in the beginning afterwards many people can use it with little costs. Or once a career portal is established all the personnel can benefit from the portal without creating an expense for the HR department. Furthermore, with the help of e-HR companies may build effective customer relationships both with the internal and external customers (Martin & Reddington, 2010). It increases the frequency and richness of both internal and external communication with the related parts. These improved flows of information are mostly witnessed during e-recruitment process, e-career development and e-performance appraisal. Moreover, e-HR can change the strategic focus of the HR department. With e-HR transformation of classical HR approach to a business model that is more value-focused is possible. E-HR creates more strategic HR departments supporting flexible organizational structures, remote working opportunities, holistic performance management systems and strategic goal tracing.

Organizations with considerably challenging strategic goals, often require unique HR functions privileging transformational goals that spare time for human resources personnel to address strategic issues. Through e-HR transformation, human resources department can provide the necessary means for changing its business model. These attempts range from extending human resource functions to reach all over the organization with the aim of creating a sense of corporateness. This can be achieved by internal integration through human resources portals. On the one hand, the use of more sophisticated recruitment tools, utilizing deep learning through online interactions with potential candidates; increasing the organizational IQ through organizational learning; using technology-based communication tools and creating higher levels of work–life balance through remote and virtual working can ease e-HR integration and make e-HR usage easier (Florkowski & Olivas-Lujan 2006).

According to Schalk et al. (2013), for e-HR to be successful regarding strategic goals, strategic considerations should be considered in HRM decision-making processes. All the goals regarding e-HR should be compatible with the strategic goals of the organization. For example; in a company wherein a cost-reduction strategy has been embraced, adopting new career portals with huge costs would be unmeaningful. It would be more strategy-friendly if the human resources department can solve this requirement with the inner sources like their own IT department. In fact, strategy alignment should be on all over the company especially encompassing critic departments such as human resources management that has very important strategic goal on the lives of employees and managers. Many decisions taken in HR department can create considerable changes in the lives of organizational members. For instance, a company that embraced a strategic orientation towards internalization may prefer to adopt new recruitment that necessitates hiring new candidates that knows more than two foreign languages and giving importance to the knowledge of foreign language in promotions.

On the one hand, e-HR implications can also contribute to the creation of a learning organization. Feeling compelled to keep pace with latest technologies in e-HR companies can become more outwitted, more open-minded and more learning focused structures. Moreover, once the organization adopt a certain e-HR module, routine trainings and routine updates are needed in order to use the tool efficiently. So, companies, send their HR agents to trainings in order to make them benefit from the tools better. Or sometimes companies learn how to update and revise the tools on their own, which necessitates a serous learning process. Once organizations learn how to use and update these e-HR applications, users in the organizations start to teach the usage of this applications to the newcomers and make the learning process continuous. After a certain time, organizational members do not need any more external support regarding the usage of these computer-based tools.

To sum up, E-HR enables HR employees to focus on more strategic, value-added activities. With e-HR adoption, less administrative and paperwork lets the human resources staff to develop other, more strategic functions regarding their jobs. And through self-service, e-HR increase the involvement of employees and line managers in human resources practices (Moran & Anan, 2018). E-HR usage transform some routine tasks from human resources professionals to functional departments and their managers, making it unnecessary to hold too much staff in human resources department. Specifically, sharing operational tasks with related departments would lower the workload of human resources department. Thus, the human resources professionals can earn the opportunity to focus on more differentiated strategic tasks and becomes more and more professional in time.

FURTHER RESEARCH

Although we can talk about a growing body of literature regarding e-HR, it is still an under-theorized and under-explored realm of study (Strohmeier, 2007). And there is a scarcity of empirical study in this topic. This study attempted to have a contribution in filling this gap. In this study, the term e-HR has been explained in details and the use of e-HR in each HRM function has been handled separately with the aim of understanding its positive functional outputs. Moreover, the advantages of e-HR on the effectiveness and efficiency of HRM have been analyzed with a technology-based perspective. However, it will be meaningful to add an empirical research to this study in further studies will be more explanatory in making our assumption clearer regarding the use of e-HR in increasing positive HRM outputs and organizational outputs.

REFERENCES

Agrawal, A. (2017, March). *HRM Effectiveness through E-HRM*. In National Conference on "Contemporary Issues in Management & Entrepreneurship", jointly organized by The Confederation of Indian Industry.

Amara, N. B., & Atia, L. (2016). E-training and its role in human resources development. *Global Journal of Human Resource Management*, *4*(1), 1–12.

Aparicio, M., Bacao, F., & Oliveira, T. (2016). An e-learning theoretical framework. *Journal of Educational Technology & Society*, *19*(1), 292–307.

Araújo, S., & Ramos, A. (2002). *Recrutamento On-line: Estudo da Percepção de Utilização da Internet em Empresa de Consultoria de Recursos Humanos* [Online recruitment: Study of the perception of Internet use in a human resources consulting firm]. Curitibia, Brasil: ENEGEP.

Bell, B. S., Lee, S. W., & Yeung, S. K. (2006). The impact of e-HR on professional competence in HRM: Implications for the development of HR professionals. Human Resource Management: Published in Cooperation with the School of Business Administration, *The University of Michigan and in alliance with the Society of Human Resources Management*, *45*(3), 295-308.

Berber, N., Đorđević, B., & Milanović, S. (2018). Electronic human resource management (e-HRM): A new concept for digital age. *Strategic Management*, *23*(2), 22–32.

Bhatnagar, J., & Sharma, A. (2005). The Indian perspective of strategic HR roles and organizational learning capability. *International Journal of Human Resource Management*, *16*(9), 1711–1739.

Bissola, R., & Imperatori, B. (2013). Facing e-HRM: E consequences on employee attitude towards the organisation and the HR department in Italian SMEs. *European Journal of International Management*, *7*(4), 450–468.

Brandão, C., Silva, R., & dos Santos, J. V. (2019). Online recruitment in Portugal: Theories and candidate profiles. *Journal of Business Research*, *94*, 273–279.

Chen, H., & Tseng, H. (2012). Factors That Influence Acceptance of Web-Based E-Learning System for the in-Service Education of Junior High School Teachers in Taiwan. *Evaluation and Program Planning*, *35*(3), 398–406. PMID:22321703

Dulebohn, J. H., & Marler, J. H. (2005). E-Compensation: The Potential to Transform Practice. In Greutal, & Stone (Eds.), The Brave New World of e-HR (166-189). San Francisco, CA: Jossey-Bass.

Esterhuyse, M., & Scholtz, B. (2016). The Intention to Use e-Learning in Corporations. In CONF-IRM (p. 12).

Faliagka, E., Tsakalidis, A., & Tzimas, G. (2012). An integrated e-recruitment system for automated personality mining and applicant ranking. *Internet Research*, *22*(5), 551–568.

Florkowski, G. W., & Olivas-Luján, M. R. (2006). The diffusion of human-resource information-technology innovations in US and non-US firms. *Personnel Review*, *35*(6), 684–710.

Hannigan, T. (2015). Close encounters of the conceptual kind: Disambiguating social structure from text. *Big Data & Society*, *2*(2), 1–6.

Hendrickson, A. R. (2003). Human resource information systems: Backbone technology of contemporary human resources. *Journal of Labor Research*, *24*(3), 381–394.

Iqbal, N., Ahmad, M., Raziq, M. M., & Borini, F. M. (2019). Linking e-hrm practices and organizational outcomes: Empirical analysis of line manager's perception. *Revista Brasileira de Gestão de Negócios*, *21*(1), 48–69.

Jackson, C. B., Quetsch, L. B., Brabson, L. A., & Herschell, A. D. (2018). Web-based training methods for behavioral health providers: A systematic review. *Administration and Policy in Mental Health*, 1–24. PMID:29352459

Kasprisin, C. A., Single, P. B., Single, R. M., & Muller, C. B. (2003). Building a better bridge: Testing e-training to improve e-mentoring programmes in higher education. *Mentoring & Tutoring*, *11*(1), 67–78.

Lazazzara, A., & Galanaki, E. (2018). E-HRM Adoption and Usage: A Cross-National Analysis of Enabling Factors. In *Digital Technology and Organizational Change* (pp. 125–140). Cham, Switzerland: Springer.

Lengnick-Hall, M. L., & Moritz, S. (2003). The impact of e-HR on the human resource management function. *Journal of Labor Research*, *24*(3), 365–379.

Marler, J. H., & Parry, E. (2016). Human resource management, strategic involvement and e-HRM technology. *International Journal of Human Resource Management*, *27*(19), 2233–2253.

Martin, G., & Reddington, M. (2010). Theorizing the links between e-HR and strategic HRM: A model, case illustration and reflections. *International Journal of Human Resource Management*, *21*(10), 1553–1574.

Mohsin, M., & Sulaiman, R. (2013). A Study on e-Training Adoption for Higher Learning Institutions. *International Journal of Asian Social Science*, *3*(9), 2006–2018.

Olivas-Lujan, M. R., Ramirez, J., & Zapata-Cantu, L. (2007). e-HRM in Mexico: Adapting innovations for global competitiveness. *International Journal of Manpower*, *28*(5), 418–434.

Omran, K., & Anan, N. (2018). Studying the impact of using E-HRM on the effectiveness of HRM practices: An exploratory study for the internet service providers (ISP) in Egypt. *International Journal of Academic Research in Business and Social Sciences*, *8*(4), 458–492.

Parry, E. (2011). An examination of e-HRM as a means to increase the value of the HR function. *International Journal of Human Resource Management*, *22*(5), 1146–1162.

Parry, E., & Tyson, S. (2011). Desired goals and actual outcomes of e-HRM. *Human Resource Management Journal*, *21*(3), 335–354.

Petre, A., Osoian, C., & Zaharie, M. (2016). Applicants' perceptions on online recruitment. *Managerial Challenges of the Contemporary Society*, *9*(1), 63–67.

Platanou, K., Mäkelä, K., Beletskiy, A., & Colicev, A. (2018). Using online data and network-based text analysis in HRM research. *Journal of Organizational Effectiveness: People and Performance*, *5*(1), 81–97.

Riahi, G. (2015). E-learning systems based on cloud computing: A review. *Procedia Computer Science, 62*, 352–359.

Rothwell, W. J., Jackson, R. D., Knight, S., & Lindholm, J. (2005). *Career Planning and Succession Management: Developing Your Organization's Talent-for Today and Tomorrow*. Westport, CT: Greenwood Publishing Group.

Ruël, H., Bondarouk, T., & Looise, J. K. (2004). E-HRM: Innovation or irritation. An explorative empirical study in five large companies on web-based HRM. *Management Review*, 364–380.

Ruel, H. J., Bondarouk, T. V., & Van der Velde, M. (2007). The contribution of e-HRM to HRM effectiveness: Results from a quantitative study in a Dutch Ministry. *Employee Relations, 29*(3), 280–291.

Schalk, R., Timmerman, V., & Van den Heuvel, S. (2013). How strategic considerations influence decision making on e-HRM applications. *Human Resource Management Review, 23*(1), 84–92.

Stone, D. L., & Dulebohn, J. H. (2013). Emerging issues in theory and research on electronic human resource management (eHRM).

Strohmeier, S. (2007). Research in e-HRM: Review and Implications. *Human Resource Management Review, 17*, 19–37.

Strohmeier, S., & Kabst, R. (2009). Organizational adoption of e-HRM in Europe: An empirical explanation of major adoption factors. *Journal of Managerial Psychology, 24*(6), 482.

Swaroop, K. R. (2012). E-HRM and how it will reduce the Cost in Organization. *Asia Pacific Journal of Marketing & Management Review, 1*(4), 133–139.

Sylva, H., & Mol, S. T. (2009). E-recruitment: A study into applicant perceptions of an online application system. *International Journal of Selection and Assessment, 17*(3), 311–323. doi:10.1111/j.1468-2389.2009.00473.x

Teo, T. S. H., Lim, G. S., & Fedric, S. A. (2007). The adoption and diffusion of human resources information systems in Singapore. *Asia Pacific Journal of Human Resources, 45*, 44–62.

Thite, M., & Kavanagh, M., & Johnson, R. D. (2009). Evolution of human resource management and human resource information systems: the role of information technology. In *M.* Thite, M. Kavanagh, & R. D. Johnson (Eds.), *Evolution of human resource management and human resource information systems*.

Voermans, M., & van Veldhoven, M. J. P. M. (2007). Attitude towards E-HRM: An empirical study at Philips. *Personnel Review, 36*(6), 887–902.

Welsh, E. T., Wanberg, C. R., Brown, K. G., & Simmering, M. J. (2003). E-learning: Emerging uses, empirical results and future directions. *International Journal of Training and Development, 7*(4), 245–258.

Zainab, B., Awais Bhatti, M., & Alshagawi, M. (2017). Factors affecting e-training adoption: An examination of perceived cost, computer self-efficacy and the technology acceptance model. *Behaviour & Information Technology, 36*(12), 1261–1273.

KEY TERMS AND DEFINITIONS

E-Compensation: The use computer-based and web-based technologies for planning employees' compensation.

E-HR: Electronic Human Resources, Use of web-based computer technologies in carrying on HRM tasks.

E-Mentoring: The kind of menoring method wherein mentor and mentee meet through internet.

E-Performance Appraisal: Pursuing the necessary steps of performance appraisal process on online performance portals.

E-Recruitment: Using online portals for selection and recruitment, attracting applicants through online career portals or corporate websites.

E-Training: Using online learning modules for training staff.

Chapter 14
Examination of Effects of Competitive Strategies on the E-Commerce Companies in Terms of Achieving Sustainable Competitive Advantage

Zafer Adiguzel
Istanbul Medipol University, Turkey

ABSTRACT

E-commerce brings companies and customers together in an exchange market environment, beyond any physical, cultural, and legal boundaries, and on an unimaginable scale, which was considered to be technically impossible before. The companies' online facilities have been improved and become accessible to everyone through smart phones, tablets, etc. as the web pages and social networks started to direct individuals towards e-commerce. E-commerce not only raises economic concerns related to competition and pricing, but also reveals new social and environmental threats that can be quite widespread and viral. Several studies have been conducted to examine the transformation of traditional business models into e-businesses, the impact of e-commerce businesses on traditional business activities, or opportunities brought by technological innovations. For this reason, the effects of the competitive strategies will be explained in terms of ensuring sustainable competitive advantage within e-commerce companies.

INTRODUCTION

E-commerce is becoming increasingly important for companies due to increasing technological opportunities. The companies that want to reach more customers and present their product range can use their web pages to conduct marketing and sales activities and share corporate information. As a result, technological and managerial strategies are becoming increasingly widespread in the political, social, and regulatory environments of e-commerce. The growing development of e-commerce has caused an

DOI: 10.4018/978-1-7998-0035-4.ch014

intensely competitive environment where only strong companies can survive and the weaker ones are eliminated. The power wars in a competitive environment can create new markets, increase or decrease existing legal regulations, create market entry barriers, affect prices, decrease or increase competition costs, and re-structure interactions between companies and customers (Chen, 2001). E-commerce brings companies and customers together in an exchange market environment, beyond any physical, cultural, and legal boundaries, and on an unimaginable scale, which was considered to be technically impossible before. Because of competition, consumers can make a selection by comparing products and/or services as they wish. E-commerce is defined as the transactions of financial, marketing, and human resources management or similar functional activities by means of information technologies and through web-based networks (Zhang & Gai, 2005).

E-commerce companies use IT and communication technologies to interact with their customers for commercial purposes in order to gain a competitive advantage. According to the definition of e-commerce, it includes sales activities by telephone or e-mail or through online shopping systems over the Internet. The most important factor behind the thrive of e-commerce is the accessibility of the thousands of networks by individuals around the world. E-commerce began to boom, especially after the development of the World-Wide-Web and establishments of sector networks. The companies' online facilities have been improved and become accessible to everyone through smart phones, tablets, etc. as the web pages and social networks started to direct individuals towards e-commerce. Furthermore, e-commerce companies have changed the market rules and the role of information technology (IT) in the sectors. Before, information technology was just another option within market strategy; however, in today's world, information technology has a power all its own since the Internet is accessible by everyone (Venkatraman & Henderson, 1998). Indeed, some companies established their market strategies based on information technology. When we look at today's successful e-commerce models, we see that marketing and technological activities interlock with each other in a competitive environment (Ghosh, 1998).

E-commerce not only raises economic concerns related to competition and pricing, but also reveals new social and environmental threats that can be quite widespread and viral. One of the advantages is that e-commerce reduces the cost of organising activities in every sector and this is an issue companies should give necessary importance to. In the last decade, significant studies have been carried out on e-commerce technologies and multi-dimensional applications. It is clear that ever-expanding and developing e-commerce opportunities affect the organizational management field; therefore, studies on new e-business technologies and e-business modelling have been carried out (Brynjolfsson & Hitt, 2003; Rust & Kannan, 2003; Yunus, Moingeon, & Lehmann-Ortega, 2010). Several studies have been conducted to examine the transformation of traditional business models into e-businesses, the impact of e-commerce businesses on traditional business activities, or opportunities brought by technological innovations. There are entangled applications such as Internet business models, web business models, e-commerce business models, and e-market business models (Koellinger, 2008).

The e-commerce concept can transform organisations and industries into virtual networks where customers and suppliers come together to create value-added processes, a concept that challenges long-accepted business models. Thus, it is important to analyse the transformational effects of e-commerce on the critical and fundamental processes of organizations (Fahey et al., 2001). E-business strategies, funding, and governance are considered critical issues that require efficient planning, and effective control of information technologies in private and public organizations (Gottschalk, 2006). For this reason, the effects of the competitive strategies will be explained in terms of ensuring sustainable competitive advantage within e-commerce companies.

WHAT IS E-COMMERCE?

According to the world trade organization, the definition of e-commerce is the advertising, sales, and distribution of products and services through the Internet network (Ussahawanitchakit & Intakhan, 2011). E-commerce is the realization of all commercial activities through computer networks, as from the design of the products to the production and promotion. Furthermore, E-commerce is the implementation of all business activities in an electronic environment (Ramanathan, 2010) and refers to all business transactions of processing, transmission, and storage of digital information in the form of text, sound, and image either over the Internet (reached by all the individuals and institutions) or over the intranet (accessed by limited number of users) (Chaffey, 2007). E-commerce can be defined as the process of delivering products and services to the customer after payment transactions, performing after-sales support, and also providing information and search opportunities to consumers, organisations, and public institutions by means of presenting data in Internet or intranet environments (Canpolat, 2001).

Different Definitions of E-Commerce

In terms of communication; e-commerce is the promotion of products and services by telephone, fax, computer networks, Internet or similar electronic tools for the purpose of sales.

In terms of business; e-commerce uses information technologies for the work- related activities of companies (Dal & Özbek, 2006).

E-commerce is the advertising, sales, and distribution of products and services through communication networks (Canpolat, 2001).

E-commerce is the new commercial understanding of the new century where the exchange of products and services is carried out on electronic environments, a result of the rapid changes and developments of information technologies (Mucuk, 2012).

E-commerce is all kinds of transactions related to commercial activities through computer networks (Erbaşlar & Dokur, 2012).

These definitions include wide and multi-dimensional relationships between provider and the consumer and also all the possible commercial transactions. Therefore, it can be said that e-commerce covers large scopes of transactions conducted in an electronic environment for providing information, carrying out promotions, and advertising and public information activities for commercial purposes (Canpolat, 2001). E-commerce activities started with telephone, fax, telex, television sales and electronic payments and money transfer systems (EFT) but reached a point where all commercial activities can be carried out over the Internet as a result of the developments in information technologies (Coşkun, 2004).

Today, the 'Information Society' or 'Knowledge Society' is seen as post- industrial societies, with the advancement of knowledge causing significant developments in commercial activities as technological developments are used to process and manage information or resources (Marangoz, 2014). E-commerce is a concept that includes the sale and purchase of all kinds of products and services with the use of computer technology, electronic communication channels, and related technologies (smart card, electronic fund transfer EFT, POS terminals, fax, etc.) (Ersoy, 1999). E-commerce refers to the purchase and sales of products and services and payment transactions over the Internet. The economy generated by e-commerce is called 'digital economy' or 'e-economy' (Erbaşlar & Dokur, 2012). Globalization makes it necessary for companies to closely follow the developments in information and communication technologies in order to obtain a permanent and firm position in competitive markets.

In a highly competitive environment, e-commerce is the most efficient and fastest way for companies to reach and communicate with their customers if they use the right tools. In particular, e-commerce enables companies to operate in global markets, easily make differentiations, reduce operational costs, expand their customer portfolio and control the risk structure, as well as having a key role in the efficient use of distribution channels. E-commerce is about the management of consumption activities between manufacturers, consumers, and the public and private organizations in an electronic environment (Erbaşlar & Dokur, 2012). E-commerce is the realisation of promotions, sales, insurance, and the distribution and payment of products and services through Internet networks.

E-commerce is the implementation of commercial transactions in an electronic environment and has three stages;

- Advertising and market research
- Order and payment
- Delivery

With the rapid expansion and development of Internet technology, e-commerce has become a new and very effective tool of commercial transactions and has emerged as a result of technological developments and the liberalization of trade.

The Actions of E-Commerce (Akgöz, 2009)

- Providing/getting information and conducting search activities in an electronic environment.
- Meeting of both parties in an electronic environment and during the transaction of payments
- Fulfilment of the commitment to the delivery of goods or services to the customer
- After-sales maintenance, support, etc.

E-commerce is about the activities carried out by the companies in an electronic environment in order to provide faster services, decrease service costs, and improve the quality of products. E-commerce enables products and services to be bought, sold, and shared over the Internet and by means of other electronic services (Görkey, 2001). E-commerce companies responds faster to customers' expectations and needs in line with the rapid changes and developments in a global world. E-commerce also offers the possibility of choosing the best supplier from widespread sales networks (Akgöz, 2009).

Common grounds of e-commerce (Erbaşlar & Dokur, 2012);

1. E-commerce can be carried out via Internet or intranet.
2. Interest holders of e-commerce including producers, consumers, public and private sector companies, and other organisations.
3. Tools of e-commerce: TV, Radio, Fax, EFT, EDI, ATM, Telephone, Internet.

These definitions not only cover the relationships between the seller and the buyer but also cover a wide and multi-dimensional relationship, together with all possible commercial transactions. Therefore, the context of e-commerce include activities such as promotions, advertising, training, and public information (Canpolat, 2001).

E-commerce Activities are Carried out in 4 Stages (Akgöz, 2009)

- **1st Stage:** Sharing information and documents of foreign trade in the Internet. For example, standards such as BM / EDI-FACT, SWIFT must be introduced.
- **2nd Stage:** Transactions for ordering, proforma invoice, e-contract, insurance, transportation and payments should be carried out in an electronic environment.
- **3rd Stage:** Legal structures should be established such as e-signature, e-tax, customs, and exchange legislation.
- **4th Stage:** Necessary importance should be given to e-security. Internet security should be provided and foreign trade operations should be conducted over a secure electronic environment.

According to this view, the presentation of the product, supplying to customers, company searches, transportation, payments, transactions and customs operations are an inseparable part of the process (Akgöz, 2009).

The acquisition, internalization, production and efficient use of information have a key role in the success of organisations and the national economy. In the information age, digital data regarding the world economy has significant value for organizations. A new and rather large sector has been structured for knowledge ownership, information sharing, and the reshaping of information. The information has become an essential capital of organizational life and is considered raw material like any product or service or other production tool that can be obtained from suppliers if necessary (Marangoz, 2014).

The characteristics of the new world economy (also called 'digital economy' by some researchers) are briefly stated below (Fırlar, 2010):

- Knowledge is the main source of production.
- The most important resource of a knowledge-based economy is brain power, which is the tool encompassing the production of information.
- A virtual world is formed by the digitalization of knowledge, so the relationship, interaction, etc. between all beings in the real world changes accordingly.
- New management processes of organizations are shaped according to micro-partitioning and are structured on an individual basis.
- In the new economy, communication provides the transfer of the knowledge and the role and function communication changes according to the digital network.
- The communication sector is leading the way in the economies of almost all world countries.
- One of the main rules of the new economy is planned obsolescence of products and the innovation and servicing of new products.
- In the new economy, the individuals/customers can participate in the production process through the elimination of boundaries by means of new information technologies and personal-oriented products that will therefore gain importance.
- Speed is another key factor in the effectiveness of organizational success and economic activity. In this respect, the importance of web-based interactive environments is increasing daily.
- In the new economy, organizations must operate in an environment that is constantly changing and developing without borders due to globalization.

The common feature of these factors is the importance of generating information, specifically because of the intense use of communication and computer technologies. Therefore, the concepts of an old or new economy do not refer to an economy as getting older or younger. These concepts are about the changes in the same economy in terms of value creation, relationships with customers and employees, methods of conduct, behaviour, and management methods, etc. (Marangoz, 2014). Increasing global competition and the formation of advanced technologies manifests itself in every aspect of the economy and the production, distribution, and consumption of goods and services are deeply affected by this processes.

Today, there are three concepts that direct the new economy (Dal & Özbek, 2006);

a) Informatics
b) Communication
c) Information.

Changes in macro factors affects the organisations and create pressure for the following reasons (Dal & Özbek, 2006);

a) Globalization
b) Rapid changes in technology
c) Increased production
d) Increased use of computers by individuals and organisations
e) Constantly up-to-date concepts of new products and services
f) Fast and short delivery of new products and services to the consumers
g) The opening of new business areas such as e-commerce, the opportunity of the seller and the buyer to meet without any intermediary and beyond the national boundaries
h) Emergence of new business opportunities
i) Expansion of value-added concepts such as communication and information exchange for the products and services
j) Intense competition
k) Focus on consumer-oriented marketing approaches
l) Investing in research and development activities

DEVELOPMENT OF E-COMMERCE

There are two important elements in the development of e-commerce.

The first is development in the IT sector. The development of new communication environments, the increasing interest in information communication technologies from all sections of society, and the increasing power of social media adds a new dimension to the concept of socialization (Vural & Bat, 2010). Investments in information technologies increase each year and positively affects e-commerce because, information technologies form the basis of development tools of e-commerce (Coşkun, 2004).

Second is the globalization of the markets, which accelerates the development of e-commerce or vice versa. The globalization of markets accelerates the development of e-commerce, at which point e-commerce eliminates the borders of the country leading to an ease in customs rules, and an increase in globalization (Coşkun, 2004).

History of the Development of E-commerce

According to Smith (2011), the timeline of e-commerce development:

1946: ENIAC (first computer) was structured at the University of Pennsylvania.
1957: The Soviet Union launched the first artificial satellite (Sputnik).
1958: USA established ARPA to gain the science and technological leadership and to withstand the technological superiority of the Soviet Union.
1969: ARPANET (pioneer of the Internet) was founded at UCLA, Stanford, UC-Santa Barbara and the University of Utah.
1970: Application of EDI-Electronic Information Exchange
1973: The first international communication to the ARPANET was implemented at the University College of London.
1974: BBN company announced the establishment of Telnet, the first commercial version of ARPANET.
1982: ARPA established TCP and IP.
1984: The number of Internet users exceeded 1000.
1987: The number of Internet users exceeded 10000.
1989: The number of Internet users exceeded 100000.

- In the 1990s, the development and dissemination of the World Wide Web (www) began.

1990: The ARPANET was shut down.
1992: www (world wide web) was founded in Cern.
1994: Pizza Hut started to sell its products over the Internet.
1994: The first cyber bank First Virtual was founded.
1997: B2B (Business to Business) trading activity started.
2000: The number of Internet users exceeded 360 million.
2011: The number of Internet users exceeded 2 billion.
2011: More than 200 countries connected.
2017: The number of Internet users is about 3.7 billion (Kemp 2017).

It is a fact that the number of Internet users increased almost six-times in a period of 10 years between 2000-2010. It is expected that the volume of e-commerce will continue to increase as Internet technology is more widely used (Porter, 2001). The reason for this expectation is that Internet technology will positively affect the general development of e-commerce.

The advantages of e-commerce, such as the wide range of products offered to customers, price comparison and time savings, are important factors in e-commerce development (Hamad, Elbeltagi, & El-Gohary, 2018). In the coming years, it is thought that e-commerce will continue to grow due to factors such as the tendency of the young population to use the Internet, the increase in the mobile device usage rate, and the growth of emerging markets.

The most significant difference of e-commerce from traditional trade is in communication and approval processes. Transactions carried out in the traditional method are not expected to be faster than any e-commerce methods, such as e-mail or other types of electronic data transmissions ((Elibol & Kesici, 2004; Erbaşlar & Dokur, 2012).

E-commerce has caused radical changes in the marketing methods, shopping life, and payment of purchased products as a result of the widespread use of computers, the Internet, and the high volume of

Table 1.

Traditional Trade	E-commerce
Information about the products can be obtained by talking to the companies or examining magazines, brochures, and catalogues.	The customers can easily obtain information about the products or services of companies through their web pages on the Internet.
The customers should file a request and fill in a form regarding the product or service in order to purchase.	E-mail makes it possible to perform processes easily and quickly.
The Purchasing Department starts the price survey with the approval of the form from the customer. Catalogues and price lists are reviewed and interviews are made.	The web sites of companies already provide requested information that is easily reachable.
Forms are filled, faxed, or mailed to the supplier at the time of ordering.	E-mail or electronic data exchange (EDI) methods makes the ordering process more convenient.

commercial networks. In the Internet environment, consumers can browse the web pages of companies, order products and services from shopping sites, and then have the products and services delivered to their location (Damanpour & Damanpour 2001).

It is very easy for stakeholders (internal and external) to reach business registry and partnership data by visiting the website of the company (Marangoz, 2014).

The main objective of e-commerce is to make commercial transactions in the electronic environment easy, reliable, fast and efficient (Kiennan, 2002).

E-commerce is not a one-sided activity and provides advantages to customers and sellers.

E-Commerce Types

E-commerce is about the sales and marketing of products and services over the Internet and transmissions between two or more parties. A classification of e-commerce is made in terms of the parties of the trade who are the businesses, consumers, and the government (Doğaner, 2007). Considering this trilateral mechanism, e-commerce types are:

Companies can gain a competitive advantage by maintaining their loyal customers who are constantly shopping through their websites (Guthrie & Austin, 1996). In periods of intense competition or economic/financial problems, companies tend to establish e-commerce activities by setting up websites in order to reduce costs and survive in the market, thus they also increase the possibility of achieving sustainable competitive advantages (Morrison & King, 2002; Tse, 2003). The reason for the private property arrangement of B&B is the lack of systematic performance data caused by competition and differing financial situations (Poorani & Smith, 1995). Therefore, it is necessary to pay attention to the financial performance of B&B. In short, it is important to achieve a sustainable competitive advantage in terms of organizational learning skills, as they have an impact on organizational performance in the field of e-commerce (Ruiz-Mercader, Merono-Cerdan, & Sabater-Sanchez 2006).

Selecting Definitive Partners for Strategic Alliances

Another way to succeed in competition in the field of e-commerce is building strategic alliances. The aim of strategic alliances is to eliminate or wipe out the other competitors in the market. B2B companies are rival companies that combine their power to distribute their products in bulk, and also, they have

Figure 1. Characteristics of e-commerce
Source: Dolanbay, C. (2000). Elektronik ticaret stratejiler ve yöntemler, Ankara: Meteksan.

access to new geographical markets through strategic alliances (Hamad, Elbeltagi, Jones, & El-Gohary, 2015). B2B allows information to be disseminated easily and swiftly. In a competitive environment, a partner company should only leave the strategic alliance after gaining basic competencies, knowledge, and developing a stronger strategic position (Stiles, 2001).

E-commerce is an important element for organisations to gain cost effectiveness against their competitors (Oum & Zhang, 2001). With B2B, partners have the opportunity to share strategic resources and capabilities that are scarce or absent in one or both companies (Gultai, 1999). Therefore, strategic alliance relations secure a wider distribution area, increase the efficiency of distribution, and facilitate the management of strategic resources, capabilities, and qualifications from a single source (Rowley, 2002). According to the findings of Stafford (1994), three strategic factors are necessary in order to be successful in competition: strategic goals, resources, and a corporate culture. Geringer (1991) explained that the collaboration, experience, and similarities in organizational culture can affect alliance performances. A strategic alliance is perhaps the most important step in forming a successful partnership in a highly competitive environment (Elmuti, & Kathawala 2001).

Figure 2. E-Commerce Types. Source: Doğaner, M., (2007). A study on the development of electronic commerce in Turkey and electronic trade from business to consumer. Master Thesis. Konya: Selcuk University Faculty of Economics and Administrative Sciences.

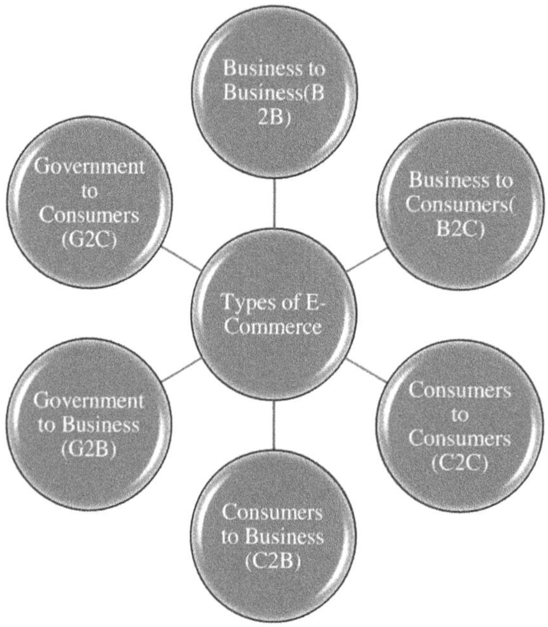

Achieving Expected Performance for Strategic Alliances

The growing reputation of a strategic alliance can reduce the damage caused by opportunist companies in a competitive environment. Trust is the essential factor for a strategic alliance to be successful in a competitive environment (Dale, 2003). However, inter-company diversity can lead to the opportunistic behaviour of a partner and this may adversely affect alliance performance in terms of the cost of transactions (Park & Ungson, 1997). Profit, growth, adaptability, and participation are often mentioned during the evaluation of alliance performance (Boersma & Ghauri, 1997). In strategic alliances, profit and growth are also often used as measurement elements (Hyder & Abraha, 2004). It is necessary to analyze the success of a strategic alliance by comparing alliances to competitors in a competitive environment (Tinnila, 2002). A strategic alliance provides both low transaction costs and a simultaneous tracking of products or services with high added value. In a highly competitive environment, e-commerce companies are expected to increase their competitive advantages by adopting to B2B strategic alliances (Wise & Morrison, 2000). In short, the performance of strategic alliances is influenced by the industry environment, the experience of cooperation of alliance members, and by the motivation of selected partners (Harrigan, 1988; Kalakota, 2000; Chen & Tseng, 2005). At the same time, environmental characteristics affect alliance formation and motivation (Xie & Johnston, 2004). In a strategic alliance, high-quality partnerships increase performance (Lee & Lim, 2005).

Figure 3. Different Types Of E-Commerce
Source: Nemat, R. (2011). Taking a look at different types of e-commerce. World Applied Programming, 1(2), 100-104.

Business to Consumer (B2C)	•The most known e-commerce application; in the business-to-consumer system, the customers order the products from company's web site or from web portals or e-commerce sites where the products are marketed.
Business to Business (B2B)	•Business sell goods and services to each other over the internet, in addition, it also allows companies to exchange information and perform financial transactions between each other. It offers significant advantages such as expanding dealer network and providing more efficient service to dealers. In the trading process, all transactions are carried out electronically, which reduce the costs radically.
Consumer to Consumer (C2C)	•In this e-commerce model, consumers come together on a website to display their products or services, and other consumers buy that products / services online. The website is the mediator of the trade. For example, the most known consumer-to-consumer e-commerce models are the pioneers such as eBay, Amazon, Alibaba.
Consumer to Business (C2B)	•It is an e-commerce form in which individuals present their products or services to companies and companies make the payment. For example, we can say that the editors of websites or blogs sell their work to companies like Amazon.com and earn membership revenue for successful sales.
Government to Business (G2B)	•Government-to-business e-commerce is the online interaction between government and non-commercial local businesses or commercial business sectors. It is an environment where businesses learn and get advice about the applications of e-commerce.
Government to Consumers (G2B)	•Government-to-consumer e-commerce is a link for establishing communication between the state and individuals. Government-to-consumer e-commerce can occur in federal, state or local dimensions (Nemat, 2011).

Strategic Planning in E-Commerce

In the 21st century, e-commerce businesses can achieve success by integrating new job- processes into their organizations, giving importance to human resources, determining necessary skills/talents and bringing appropriate management roles and knowledge management systems (Okrent & Vokurka, 2004). Furthermore, in order to be successful in the field of e-commerce, organizations need to learn about new planning perspectives and manage innovation cycles suitable for e-commerce (Zahra & Gerard, 2002).

There is a strategically accepted fact that the Internet is now widespread throughout all countries. As a result, the e-commerce sector can be managed from even a home office environment, and this situation may have a devastating effect on companies in the normal trading environment, possibly bringing alarming change and threatening businesses. 'Alarming change' means that if companies do not conduct e-commerce activities through their web pages and continue their traditional trading activities, they may disappear from the competitive market. We know that there are 3 important strategies for achieving competitive advantage: cost leadership, differentiation, and focus strategies. It is only a matter of time before the new strategic approaches arise in the face of the change brought by e-commerce companies and their destructive impact (Lumpkin, Droege, & Dess, 2002). For example, if you look at potential customer populations and annual revenues of companies such as Amazon, Alibaba, or E-bay, which only trade over the Internet, you can better understand the impact of these potentially destructive changes of these companies.

From a strategic point of view, organizations must be able to adeptly measure, evaluate, and manage their skills. These skills are necessary for organizations to create value and to respond to the needs of customers (McAdam, & Galloway, 2005). In order to be successful in a competitive environment, the organizations need to control strategic processes (planning processes, management changes, accountability, and returns on investment) (Ho et al., 2004). In order to evaluate the assets, resources, and qualifications of the organization, e-business strategies must be aligned with organizational strategies, and the results of the implemented strategies should be related to organizational efficiency (Chang et al., 2003).

STRENGTH AND WEAKNESSES OF E-COMMERCE

Although e-commerce provides a number of advantages to businesses and individuals, there are also some questions about the reliability of e-commerce transactions as individuals have to share their personal information and credit card details on the Internet.

Strengths of E-Commerce

Advantages of E-Commerce (Budak 2010):

E-Commerce allows businesses to operate in the global market, allowing businesses to reach out to almost all countries and different cultures, and sell their products/services.

E-Commerce provides businesses not only new customers but also an opportunity to work with better suppliers and select partners, access to low-cost financing resources, and a qualified workforce.

E-Commerce businesses process, transmit, and record information in the electronic environment, instead of written paper format, reducing costs and eliminating time losses.

E-Commerce systems use visual images and personal support services in order to enable companies to promote their products and services at the most appropriate cost.

E-commerce provides an opportunity to offer quality after-sales support services to increase customer satisfaction and loyalty.

E-Commerce allows companies to identify and respond to customer demands and needs quickly and effectively.

The Advantages of E-Commerce for Customers (Yeşil, 2008):

E-Commerce allows customers to shop at almost any place where the Internet is available.

E-Commerce provides consumers/customers with an opportunity to compare products and services, and select the reasonable priced ones.

E-Commerce companies use the complaints and suggestions of the customers for the purpose of improving customer service.

Weaknesses of E-Commerce

The web pages created by the e-commerce companies may have a number of security-related problems, which may lead to theft crime in the Internet environment.

Another security problem may arise if e-commerce companies share personal information of their customers.

In an e-commerce environment, communities should be made aware of fraudsters who use credit card copying technology on the Internet.

Customers can not try or test the products online, therefore returns and refund transactions are carried out, subsequently resulting in a loss of time and money. This is one of the issues that receives the most complaints from customers.

Tax problems that may arise due to the gains of enterprises in e-commerce,

The need for human resources in the field of e-commerce technology can be seen as a weakness as it brings extra costs to companies.

Advantages and Disadvantages Of E-Commerce

Advantages of E-Commerce

The advantages of e-commerce for businesses are as follows:

- **Customer Relationship Management:** Through e-commerce, companies are able to manage customer experiences easily, and provide solutions to any problems. Companies can create a more effective brand perception by online advertising through their e-commerce sites (Porter, 2005).
- **Reduction in Offline Store Cost:** Online stores reduce the costs of rent, office, and staff expenses. In the supply chain, it is very important to ensure accurate and fast information flow from the customer to suppliers and the delivery of correct materials from the supplier to the customer (Pavic,

Koh, Simpson, & Padmore, 2007). The lack of stock requirements and the need of fewer numbers of staff can even make it possible to organise e-commerce sales from home.

- **Effective Use of Time:** Online, time effectiveness is an element of commercial transactions between the seller and the buyer (Porter, 2001).
- **Documentation Process***:* E-commerce activities are conducted with e-documents, which reduce stationery costs and make it possible for transactions to be carried out with minimum errors.
- **International Sales and Marketing:** Through online stores, companies have an opportunity to virtually conduct their sales and marketing activities in an international market without making any physical investments (Porter, 2001).
- **Competitive Advantage:** Online trading companies, unlike offline trading companies, provide competitive advantages by promoting their products and services more easily in the national and international arena without time and space restrictions (Lumpkin, Droege, & Dess, 2002).
- **365 Days 24 Hours Open Store:** E-commerce companies can provide uninterrupted service 365 days, 24/7 hours. If the website's software and technical infrastructure is strong, the companies can ensure uninterrupted regular services to their customers at all times (Hidayanto, Ovirza, Anggia, Budi, & Phusavat, 2017). E-commerce decreases informality in the economy and increases competition. In addition, within related sectors, it creates new employment areas through dynamic new business lines and specializations. Furthermore, it contributes to regional development, education, and social solidarity (Afra, 2014).
- **The benefits of e-commerce for the customer are as follows:** Consumers can carry out online transactions around the clock, save time, and get the product they want through the Internet. Thanks to e-commerce, consumers can easily compare different types of brand products. Furthermore, consumers can read the comments of previous buyers of products or services, gleaning different perspectives.

Disadvantages of E-Commerce

E-commerce has several disadvantages for customers and sellers.

Disadvantages of E-Commerce for Sellers are as Follows:

- **Security Problem:** The biggest disadvantage of e-commerce is the security vulnerability, as there is a possibility that the web sites can be hacked and user information can be captured by the hackers (Baldwin & Currie, 2000).
- **E-Commerce Costs:** The databases and applications of e-commerce companies should be very well maintained. The need for serious infrastructure and the cost for effective e-commerce activity is a disadvantage for the seller.
- **Security-Reliability:** The biggest disadvantage of e-commerce for customers is that of security vulnerability, there is risk that all personal information such as identity details, home address, phone number, etc., can be served to third parties (Baldwin & Currie, 2000).
- **Quality Uncertainties:** It may not always be enough to obtain information about the product in a virtual environment. The return process of the unwanted products often creates a great time loss for customers (Corbitt, Thanasankit, & Yi, 2003).

- **Delivery Delays:** Delivery delays may occur due to weather conditions, public holidays, and a lack of product in a seller's stock. Delivery delays can cause customer dissatisfaction.

Competition Concepts and Competition Strategies

Competition has five points.

First, the goal. There must be an objective, and the existence of others might cause difficulties in the realization of this objective.

The second is rule and restrictions. In a competitive environment, the prevention of opponents into the game or their elimination by either force, abuse of the dominant position, agreement between the competitors, or cheating etc. is prohibited. If a race does not have any rules and restrictions, we cannot call it a competition. In such cases, it can be said that there is a violation in competition or unfair competition.

The third is the guarantee of fundamental freedoms and human rights. It is not enough to recognise freedom on paper. The full guarantee of freedom is possible by the existence of a well-functioning, independent, and effective justice system.

Fourth, there should be no discrimination. The position of the state in the competitive environment is very important. The state should not give privilege or priority to some players for various reasons and should not discriminate or tolerate incompliances with rules and obligations.

Fifth, the number of players should be more than one. In a competitive environment, in some cases, certain number of players are required to play, so the players can not dominate the game and can not affect the result of the game. In fact, all the players should have free access to the game, and none of the players should dominate the play on their own. In some exceptional cases, even if there is only a single player, it still may be considered a competitive environment if the entry into the race is free. However, in such special cases, the existing player should feel the competitive pressure from the potential players who want to enter the market (http://www.rekabetdernegi.org/rekabethakkinda.htm, Access: 01.02.2019).

Benefits of Competition

Competitive power is the key to the success for companies in national and international fields. Companies should give necessary importance to research and development, information, and training of employees in order to improve their technological infrastructure. In today's intense competitive environment, only robust companies can survive, whereas weaker ones are forced out of the market, both in production and service sectors. Therefore, these factors become more significant as they provide flexibility for the companies. Flexibility is an essential factor in a competitive environment because it allows companies to survive in the market by differentiating their products or services. Furthermore, the companies need to work efficiently to be successful in a competitive environment, and in this way, they can transform their savings into investments and ensure capital accumulation in a country (Su, Guo, & Sun, 2017). The companies in the e-commerce sector have flexibility, which is a significant step towards efficiency. In comparison with traditional companies, the e-commerce companies have many advantages such as reduction of costs, allowing flexibility and providing product/service diversity. Companies operating in the field of e-commerce can gain more advantages and achieve sustainability if they can open up to international economic areas and integrate with the world (Mess, 1997).

Competitive Advantage

There are other factors that may be important for the competitive advantage. One of them is the content of the web page. The Internet makes it possible for companies to display large amounts of content at a very low cost. For example, REI.com is a supplier of recreation equipment and ready-to-wear clothes and has more than 78,000 items on its 45,000-page web site. However, the company could not manage its website content effectively in order to gain added value. Similarly, Garden.com had a strong start in 1999, raising tremendous venture capital but failing to create detailed and compelling content (but its name is still used by Burpee, a 125-year-old garden products supplier).

Three types of content can improve the value of a web site: customer feedback, expertise, and entertainment programming:

Customer Feedback

Buyers often rely on other buyers' comments more than a company's promise. The customer comments and customer feedback can help to improve the content of a website.

For example, if you want to buy a piece of furniture online, you can't touch, feel or try it. In this case, you can make the purchase decision by reading or evaluating the objective references of other buyers who have previously purchased the product you want to buy. Such references can create trust or play a significant role in the purchasing decision by highlighting the 'unwanted or unappreciated' sides of the product or services as experienced by the previous buyers. This can also be a competitive advantage source for the competitors because they follow each other. It is necessary for the companies to examine the responses of customers and read their experiences to understand their opinions about the products and services in order to create new product or improve services in a competitive environment (Kakalejčík, Bucko, & Vejačka, 2019).

Expertise

The Internet is a very important learning tool and it is constantly developing. Fifty percent of users regard the Internet as a kind of library, because search-oriented web pages such as Google, Yandex, etc. allow access to a vast amount of information quite quickly. As a result, users have the opportunity to improve their knowledge. Furthermore, some websites provide valuable new or objective information. At the same time, its problem-solving function often educates consumers on various options and outcomes. For example, several online web pages such as Sikayetvar.com, Sikayetim.com, or Sikayet.com can provide information about products and services, and customers can read about the problems they face before buying them. The expertise function is not limited to regions. In the case of B2B businesses, web sites share their expertise by creating communities or professional groups in the industry (Kaplan, & Sawhney, 2000).

Entertainment Programming

The Internet is used for entertainment purposes by more and more people. Technologies such as streaming media allow the Internet to send TV-like images and sound allowing computers to broadcast breaking news, offer video games and movies, and provide fun time online. In fact, we can say that TV viewing has been reduced and online activity has been increased among people with high-speed broadband service because the technology has an interactive approach, which means the viewers not only passively watch but are involved in creating art and playing a game etc. Of course, e-commerce companies noticed this trend and have started to create web content that is not only informative but also fun.

These three types of contents-customer feedback, expertise, and entertainment programming- are sources of potential competitive advantage and can strengthen the value creation process. However, if they are used negatively, they can also reduce performance. Strategically displayed quality content enables companies to effectively differentiate their offer of product or services. This can be particularly important in an environment where differentiation strategies provide more gains compared to a low-cost strategy.

STRATEGIES TO GAIN A COMPETITIVE ADVANTAGE

There are many methods and strategies to achieve a competitive advantage. The analysis of the competitive situation of a company within the market is called competition analysis. The determination of the competitive situation of a company reveals whether the investment was successful and if it has the ability to gain above average profits (Lu & Wang, 2016). This skill increases the chance of being successful in the free market. Competitive strategies also allow companies to find the most suitable position within a competitive environment and achieve their main objectives (Porter, 2008).

There are many methods and strategies for companies to achieve a competitive advantage. Competitive strategies that can be implemented according to their sector;

1. Competitive Strategy: Porter's Model
2. Competitive Strategy: Resource-Based Model
3. Competition Strategy: Game Theory Approach

According to the Porter's competition strategy, it is necessary for companies to determine conditions affecting competition in order to ensure a competitive advantage (Porter, 2008). After that, the generic competition strategies can be implemented in every sector.

Main Conditions Affecting Competition

If the company(s) are entering the sector for the first time, they need to obtain a market share in order to stay in the market. From the moment they enter the competition, the companies should bring their resources. However, every company may not enter the market as they wish. This situation is called market entry barriers which is explained below (Porter, 2008):

Economies of Scale

The increase of absolute production volume per period can cause a decrease in unit costs per product. Companies may reverse their decisions for two reasons:

Figure 4. Competitive strategies

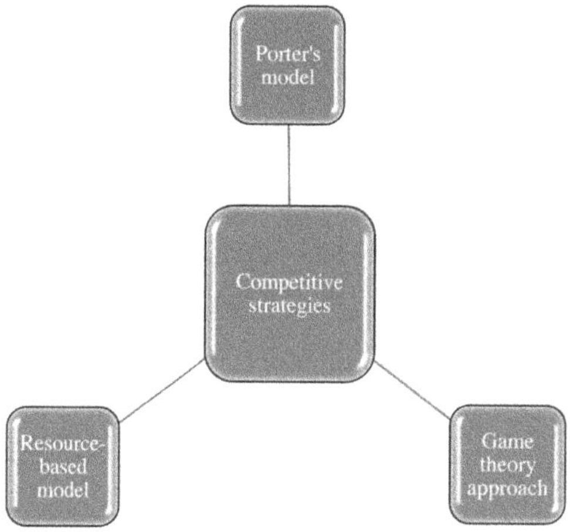

- They cannot take the risk of the reactions from companies already in the market.
- Or, they can't afford the cost resulting from the disadvantageous situation.

Product Differentiation

Newly entered companies may have to spend more money to create satisfaction and gain loyalty of the customers as this is a barrier for companies.

Figure 5. There are five powers that influence competition (Porter 2008)

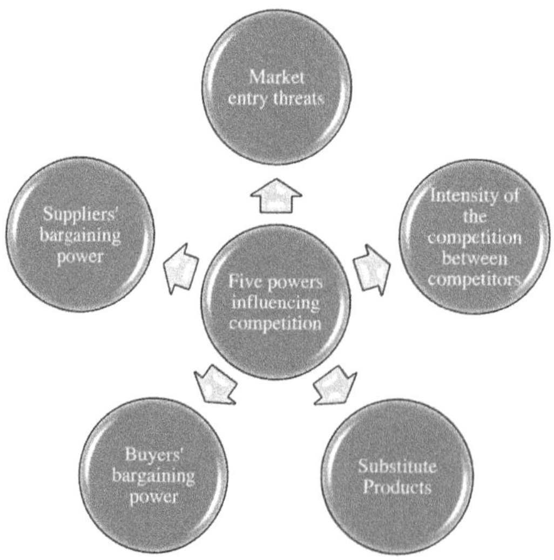

Capital Requirements

New companies in the market should spend on advertising and/or R&D activities in order to compete. This means that they should have more financial resources. For companies that are unable to handle this burden, insufficient capital is an barrier to entry.

Transition Costs

If a company does not like its supplier or does not agree with its supplier, the transition process to a new supplier may create a barrier to entry as it may be reflected in costs.

Access to Distribution Channels

When the company enters the market, it must have a good distribution channel to respond to the demand from the buyers. The need to guarantee the delivery of the product to the buyer may create a barrier to entry.

Cost Disadvantages

One of the biggest entry barriers for new entrants to the market is the position of the companies that have already taken place in the market. Their superiority gained from experience, image, reputation, or location can be a barrier to the market for possible entrants.

Government Policies

A number of state policies, restrictions, prohibitions, penalties, etc. or similar elements can be entry barriers for new entrants to the market.

Intense Competitiveness Between Competitors

From the moment of market entry, there will be competitive manoeuvres of competitors within the market. In many sectors, the competition of companies can have a significant impact on competitors in the market. In the face of these moves, opponents will tend to retaliate against their counterparts. In fact, as a result of these mutual moves, the firms become dependent on each other because they re-develop and renew themselves through retaliation.

Substitute Products

If the products of a company are also available from the competitors, and if buyers have the right to choose, this may cause a reduction in profits. The most important move of the company (s) against substitution products is to explain to consumers the difference of their products from other products in a positive way. Because, what is important for consumers is the relationship between price/performance/quality (Porter, 2008).

The Bargaining Power of Buyers

One of the most important situations for companies is that there are buyers who will benefit from competition in the market because buyers have the right to buy a product according to their budgets. The buyers gain this power as a result of competition among companies (Porter, 2008).

The Bargaining Power of Suppliers

When companies enter the market, they may see that suppliers can play with the price or decrease the quality of products and services. In this case, the suppliers can have power in the market. This power can reduce the profitability of the companies due to the cost increase caused by suppliers (Porter, 2008).

Generic Competitive Strategies

Businesses who want to be active in e-commerce should be able to satisfy their customers or consumers much better than their competitors in order to be successful in a competitive environment (Coltman, Devinney, & Midgley, 2007). The degree of satisfaction is directly proportional to loyalty. In a competitive environment, competitive analysis has a strategic importance enabling survival in the market. The two most important elements of competitive analysis is the determination of strengths and weaknesses. If senior management has ego problems, if they cannot have a result-oriented mindset, and if they are not visionaries, they might ignore weaknesses within the firm. This means that the company's life in the market will be short-lived. Status/position title can change people. Real leadership is seen in those who do not show any change in character/personality after receiving a office/title/status. Naturally, during competitive analysis, companies should identify their weaknesses and turn their strengths into opportunities within the market (Tek, 1999).

The differentiation and cost-leadership strategy are parts of the Generic Competitive Strategy and also for companies operating under industry conditions. The focus strategy is for businesses with a narrow field of activity (Porter, 1985).

Industry 5.0: This means the existence of unmanned technologies in life. It is a fact that robots can do every job that people can, while also allowing artificial intelligence to communicate among themselves. The unlimited advancement of technology highlights the continuing problem of 'unemployment'. Furthermore, industries are now able to be managed by only one group of people while all other jobs can be carried out by artificial robots. The development of the capabilities of humanoid robots will push companies to generate new strategic moves. It is worthy paying attention to the question of how e-commerce companies will be affected by the attempts to bring the virtual world and the real world together. In this case, we need to ask if generic competitive strategies need a 4th strategy? Companies operating in the field of e-commerce should focus on technology-based activities in order to be ready for industry 5.0. It will be possible that new strategies will be generated as a result of this atmosphere in the competition environment.

However, Strategic Transformation should focus on;

- Reducing costs and ensuring operational efficiency; the supply chain must be functioning smoothly and technological integration, which is the pioneer of change, must be sustained successfully (Coltman et al., 2001).

Figure 6. Generic Competitive Strategy (Porter 1985)

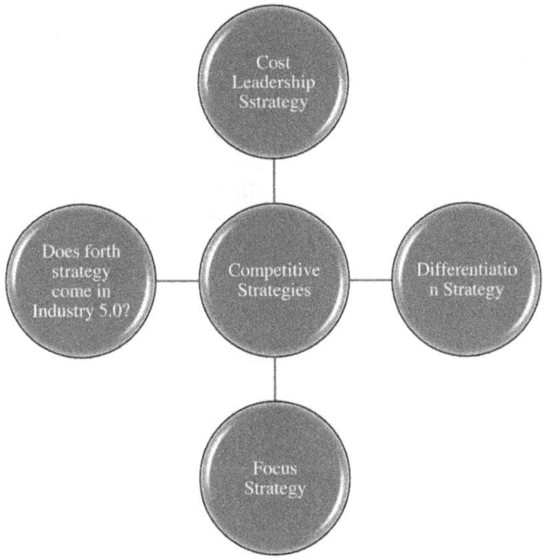

- In order to have a good position in the e-commerce market, it is necessary to differentiate products and/or services and use the resources in the supply chain effectively (Chang et al., 2003).
- It is necessary to create a superior economic value that will provide a competitive advantage (Riggins, 1999).

Cost Leadership Strategy

Cost leadership strategy is about businesses gaining advantages over its competitors and obtaining above average income above in line with the reduction of costs in all activities and ensuring positive differences between costs and prices (Porter, 1985).

The cost leadership strategy has several risks (Porter, 1985);

- With the continuous development and change of technology, past investments or experiences may become invalid.
- The low cost of new entrants in the sector by imitating or investing in very good facilities,
- The fact that product or market changes may not be seen due to the company's concentration on cost.

Differentiation Strategy

By differentiating product or services, businesses can create something that is considered unique by consumers and customers. Carrying out business activities the same as other companies does not allow a company to progress beyond imitation. However, the basis of the differentiation strategy is to generate different applications, become distinct among competitors, and direct customer preferences to a company's products and services. Then, differentiation can be made based on the design, brand name, brand

Table 2.

Advantages of Differentiation Strategy	Risks of Differentiation Strategy
- Generates customer loyalty, as well, customers become insensitive to prices and this provides protection against competition. - Customer loyalty and the uniqueness of the company, due to differentiation, creates barriers for new competitors, - Creates high margins against the power of suppliers; this also destroys the need for a low-cost market situation. - The company that differentiates itself and achieves customer loyalty is better protected than its competitors in the case of substitution products (Porter 2008).	- If the cost difference between low-cost competitors and the differentiated enterprise increase too much, differentiation cannot maintain brand loyalty, and buyers stop buying the products for certain features, services, or the image of the enterprise. -Buyers' need for the differentiating factor may decrease. This occurs when buyers become more complex. -Imitation can reduce the perceived differentiation. This situation becomes more common in widespread sectors (Porter 1985).

image, stores, technology, support services, customer services etc. In order for the differentiation strategy to provide a competitive advantage, the value created must exceed the cost. In addition, differentiation must be valuable for the consumer.

From the Technological Aspect

There are a range of outsourcing options from total outsourcing to partial outsourcing. It is possible for an organization to try to differentiate itself in the market by focusing only on one main factor. This can shift the strategic focus to an external supplier and generates additional strategic issues but does not generally lead to a comprehensive organizational culture change. However, if a comprehensive relationship in management is needed, there may be a significant gap between strategic expectations and fulfilment (Levina & Ross, 2003).

From the Products and Services Aspect

When e-branding becomes a critical issue, and when a difference occurs between brand identity and brand totality, a significant cultural change is seen (Venkatraman & Henderson, 1998). This requires all members of the organization to think 'out of the box' and distinguish between corporate customers and end consumers.

Business Models, E-Positioning

At this stage, the organization regains its position in the market through e-services to a wider community. Fujitsu and Dell have been exemplary for successful differentiation through e-business. These pioneers developed their public relations and established a special relationship between suppliers and buyers. This created an organizational culture that embraces 'community culture' throughout the organization.

Focus Strategy

Businesses choose a specific part of the market. For example; it may be certain consumer populations, a specific production and distribution line, or a geographic location. With the focus strategy, a company attempts to reach a specific target, market and provide better service.

Table 3.

Advantages of Focus Strategy	Risks of Focus Strategy
- It can be considered a type of competitive strategy which reduces the threats that new entrants may create. - The threat of substitution products for businesses is very low. - The number of competitors in private and differing markets decreases and competition occurs at a different severity (lower level) (Porter, 2008).	-In the case of a wide range of products, the company with a focus strategy may lose the cost advantage of serving a narrow target. - Differences in products or services begin to decrease as a whole. -Competitors find sub-markets within the strategic target and exclude the orientation focus (Porter, 1985).

Resource-Based Competition Strategy

Resources of Business

The competitive strategy based on resources emerged after 1980, and started to develop in order to achieve a sustainable competitive advantage in the sector. The aim of this strategy is to determine the strengths and weaknesses of the organisation and focus on strong resources (Van Hooft & Stegwee 2001). It is a perspective based on gaining competitive advantage by focusing on a company's strong resources (Karacaoğlu, 2006). Resources (tangible assets, intangible assets, and organizational skills) are the tools for organisations to develop and implement a strategy to achieve a competitive advantage (Seviçin, 2006).

There are two basic assumptions of the Resource Based Competition Strategy:

Figure 7. The Tools for Organisations
Source: Seviçin, A. (2006). Kaynaklara Dayalı Rekabet Stratejisi Geliştirme. Dumlupınar Üniversitesi Sosyal Bilimler Dergisi, (15).

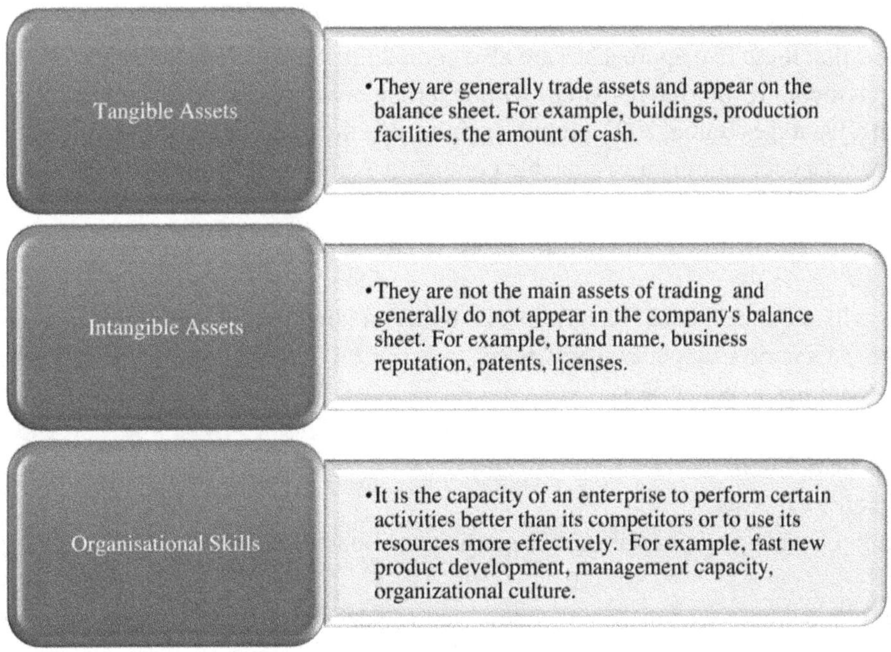

- Businesses may have different strategic resources in the sector. In other words, the resources of similar production processes may have different characteristics compared to other enterprises. This situation may cause different productivity and efficiency levels and can lead to distinctive performance gaps. At the same time, it can generate competitive advantages.
- Resource differences between businesses may be long-term. This situation indicates that the resources are specific to the enterprises and are very valuable. At the same time, it ensures a sustainable competitive advantage.

Characteristics of Resources

The characteristics of the strategic resources are:

Stages of Resource-Based Competition Approach

Prahalad and Hamel, Grant and Rumelt stated that the Resource-Based Competition Strategy, carried out from internal to external dimension, and companies should use resources and skills effectively.

Hamel and Prahalad explain certain stages of competition (Köseoğlu, 2007):

- Establishing basic skills by predicting customer demands and future opportunities.
- Creating an alternative product variety to reshape the customer approach
- Creating and managing necessary coalitions for the sector
- Forcing competitors to progress styles that will be expensive and time consuming
- Ensuring suppliers have worldwide networks
- Entering key markets before competitors by identifying a suitable market positioning strategy
- Differentiating product and production processes to increase efficiency and effectiveness.

The Porter's approach and Resource-based approach are alternatives to each other, however Barca (2002) explains that these two approaches are also complementary. Barca states that 'strategy development is about associating internal resources with external environments in order to achieve a competitive long-term advantage (Barca, 2002). Barca explains that the good 'market position' and 'basic skills position' is necessary for gaining a sustainable competitive advantage (Barca, 2002).

The Effect of E-Commerce on Competitive Strategies

E-Commerce will require radical changes in our understanding of competing enterprises. When we consider Porter's Generic Competition Strategies,

Through e-commerce, businesses;

- can focus on different markets
- reduce their total costs
- can develop a wide range of services or products compared to their competitors (Porter, 2008).

If we analyse e-commerce from the recourse-based perspective, we can say that e-commerce companies should have effective and efficient approaches in using their resources. If we analyse e-commerce's

Figure 8. The Characteristics of The Strategic

competitive strategy, in terms of game theory, e-companies will affect all companies in the sector, in terms of added-value rules.

The reciprocal moves of companies operating in the field of e-commerce will also affect their strategies and naturally have an impact on the conditions of competition (Ma, Jin and Huo 2019). If companies want to turn these effects of a competitive environment into an opportunity and gain an advantage, they should ensure that their strategic moves are complementary to each other.

Adding Value

Companies need to collect information and data to analyse their customers and competitors in the sector. At the same time, customers need information to compare the products and/or services of companies to make a purchase. The Internet provides a great convenience both in terms of accessing and gathering information. The Internet reduces search costs and brings multiple benefits. For example, we can use the Google search engine to gather information and compare products and services of several companies and then buy from the appropriate company according to our budget. Google scans 3 billion web pages in an average of 500 milliseconds and provides instant information. Imagine if you had to do the same search without the Internet; If you spend 1-minute per page, you will need to spend 5707 years to navigate 3 billion web pages. This example helps us to better understand what kind of technological invention the Internet is. Therefore, Google has become of interest for people of all ages and at all educational levels. Companies allocate significant portions of their budget to appear on the first page of Google. Because, if you want to gain a competitive advantage, you should use the technology very effectively (both in the manufacturing and in the service sector).

In order to achieve a sustainable competitive advantage, strong support is needed to create value in productivity and customer service because the quality of the products and/or services or customer satisfaction determines the value of the product/service offered. Customers value the product together with the service received. The value created by the service will be an advantage in a competitive environment, and a competitive advantage depends on increasing the efficiency and positive return on investments. Therefore, trainings should be provided for employees and organisational plans should be done with the utmost care. Continuous development and change will make it possible for companies to achieve their targets and reach their goals. Especially in today's business world, where there is intense competition, it is not possible for companies to be successful if they do not learn and not keep up with the changes or are slow to adopt to developments. Success in a competitive environment also depends on planning and implementing non-disruptive supply chain practices and providing innovative product and/or services compared to competitors.

SOLUTIONS AND RECOMMENDATIONS

It is accepted that 'policy' is an important factor for the new e-commerce concept. Indeed, technology and management strategy options are very much linked to the political, social, and regulatory environments of e-business. Policies can be quite complex or change regularly; therefore, their impact on e-commerce is not fully understood yet. Policies can change market conditions, increase or decrease regulations, create market entry barriers, influence prices, increase or decrease competition costs, and configure interactions between companies and customers. E-commerce companies have different options, and they can either act passively and obey the rules or become an actor in managing policy limits as a part of a company's overall strategy (Hackney, & Burn, 2001). E-commerce brings customers and traders together in a commercial, translational, cultural market beyond imagined technical boundaries.

E-businesses use computers and communication technologies for commercial purposes; therefore, they should pay attention to the automation of communication and interaction activities. E-business includes telephone, e-mail sales, or systems that support commercial activities over the Internet and exploded with the growth of the Internet (global gathering of thousands of individual networks in the world), particularly the World Wide Web. E-commerce has changed the market rules and the role of information technology (IT). Before, market strategies determined the use of IT systems; however, now, IT has power of its own (Venkatraman, & Henderson, 1998). Indeed, companies that want to be successful in e-commerce are planning their market strategies based on IT. Today's successful e-commerce models are market and technology-oriented, but at the same time, it requires the seamless integration of both marketing and technological skills (Ghosh, 1998). Tomorrow's e-business model will be technology oriented, and information technologies will be an integral part of the company strategy, in dealings with governments, interest groups, and the public. In other words, policies will be closely managed with strategy and technology options. Tomorrow's e-businesses will need to design, structure, and create relationships that allow technology and policy-driven dynamic and cost-effective options to be present.

FUTURE RESEARCH DIRECTIONS

There is a deep concern in many circles that e-commerce may be increasing the power of traders, reducing the power of consumers, challenging the government's ability to protect local industries, and threatening the income sources of both the state and governments. E-commerce not only raises economic concerns related to competition and pricing but also reveals new social and environmental threats that can be quite widespread and viral (Kakalejčík, Bucko, & Vejačka, 2019). Moreover, the regulation of a country may need global cover rather than being limited to a sovereign state. Finally, as the Internet reduces the cost of the organization, there is an increasing number of interest groups, and their opinions about policies should be taken into consideration. These interest groups can be formed and solved in a short time and e-businesses should develop interactions with them regarding forming policy. Up until now, there has been little awareness or interest in public policies in the field of management within e-commerce. Therefore, companies that want to be successful in competition conditions should thoroughly analyze their external stakeholders before starting their activities in the field of e-commerce. Then, they need to create their own organizational culture with a better dynamic structure than their competitors. However, in doing so, the most important point is to make sure that their investment has a visionary perspective and is integrated with technology.

CONCLUSION

The most important feature of e-commerce is that it provides an opportunity for customers to evaluate and compare products and services. The customer/consumer can conduct cost and benefit analysis and purchase the most appropriate product and/or service according to his/her budget. However, it is also necessary to point out the disadvantages of e-commerce. There are some products that even if comparisons are made on the Internet, it will not be enough, and a customer will need to go and look or try. For example, textile products may not always be same as the one on the web page, and a customer may have to go to the store and try it on and purchase the goods there. Similarly, furniture may not be same as it appears on web pages. One of the indicators of success for e-business is whether the company is ready to meet the demands of customers/consumers. From a strategic point of view, the important factor is the organisation's adaptation process to technology (Spathis & Constantinides, 2003). The success of the e-business initiative also depends on having a compelling vision that radically changes the organization's performance. Another way of being successful is to have open communication between the leader and employees, and also have strong organisational participation and determination. In order to achieve this, it is necessary to establish an appropriate organizational culture (Yu, 2005). Another key point for the success of e-business is that its vision of change should be adopted by all stakeholders within the organization. In order to gain this, intra-organizational communication should be successfully implemented at all levels. A further factor of success of e-business initiative lies in the adoption of a transparent management approach, which is very important in providing trust for all internal stakeholders and external stakeholders. Managers need to use resources in line with organisational objectives and they should prepare the structure of the organization for competition in order to achieve organizational change (Huang et al., 2004; Zhao, 2004; McAdam & Galloway, 2005). A digital economy has changed the cost structures of certain sectors, as well, the applications of Internet-based technologies have already had a tremendous impact. It is clearly understood that the Internet reduces costs and speeds up processes. For example, transactions between a seller and customer can be mutually agreed and implemented on E-bay.com very easily and quickly. Similarly, payments can be made between the parties through services such as Paypal, without any need of seeing each other. Amazon offers One-Click technology that enables high-speed purchases and is very successful in fulfilling orders and conducting fast and reliable transactions. These examples show that companies should focus on every detail in e-commerce, such as the variety of payment methods they offer in their web pages, in order to be successful in a competitive environment.

REFERENCES

Afra, S. (2014). *Dijital Pazarın Odak Noktası eTicaret: Dünya'da Türkiye'nin Yeri, Mevcut Durum ve Geleceğe Yönelik Adımlar*. İstanbul, Turkey: TÜSİAD.

Akgöz, S. S. (2009). E-dış ticaret işlemleri. *BETA Bulletin of Experimental Treatments for AIDS*.

Baldwin, L. P., & Currie, W. L. (2000). Key issues in electronic commerce in today's global information infrastructure. *Cognition Technology and Work*, *2*(1), 27–34.

Barca, M. (2002). *Stratejik Yönetim Yaklaşımları: Rekabet Avantajı Yaratmada Sinerjik Etki, Stratejik Boyutlarıyla Modern Yönetim Yaklaşımları*. İstanbul, Turkey: Beta Yayınevi.

Boersma, M. F., & Ghauri, P. N. (1997). A qualitative meta analysis of performance measures and factors affecting international joint venture performance. *Proceedings of the 24th Annual Conference at the UK Academy of International Business* (pp. 119–142). Leeds, UK: CIBUL, April.

Brynjolfsson, E., & Hitt, L. M. (2003). Computing productivity: Firm-level evidence. *The Review of Economics and Statistics*, *85*(4), 793–808.

Budak, B. (2010). *E-Ticaret İnternet Ortamında Ticaret*. İstanbul, Turkey: Etap Yayınevi.

Canpolat, Ö. (2001). *E-Ticaret ve Türkiye'deki gelişmeler*. Ankara, Turkey: Sanayi ve Ticaret Bakanlığı Hukuk Müşavirliği.

Chaffey, D. (2007). E-business and e-commerce management: Strategy, implementation and practice. London, UK: Financial Times.

Chang, K. C., Jackson, J., & Grover, V. (2003). E-commerce and corporate strategy: An executive perspective. *Information & Management, 40*(7), 663–675.

Chen, H. M., & Tseng, C. H. (2005). The performance of marketing alliances between the tourism industry and credit card issuing banks in Taiwan. *Tourism Management, 26*(1), 15–24.

Chen, S. (2001). *Strategic management of e-business*. New York, NY: John Wiley and Sons.

Coltman, T., Devinney, T. M., Latukefu, A., & Midgley, D. F. (2001). E-business: Revolution, evolution, or hype? *California Management Review, 44*(1), 57–86.

Coltman, T. R., Devinney, T. M., & Midgley, D. F. (2007). e-Business strategy and firm performance: A latent class assessment of the drivers and impediments to success. *Journal of Information Technology, 22*(2), 87–101.

Corbitt, B. J., Thanasankit, T., & Yi, H. (2003). Trust and e-commerce: A study of consumer perceptions. *Electronic Commerce Research and Applications, 2*(3), 203–215.

Coşkun, A. G. D. N. (2004). Elektronik ticaretin gelişiminde temel dinamikler ve gelişimi önünde engeller, Çukurova Üniversitesi Sosyal Bilimler Enstitüsü Dergisi, *13*(2), 243-258

Dal, V. & Özbek, A. (2006). Avrupa Birliği ve Türk hazır giyim sanayiindeki e-ticaret uygulamalarının karşılaştırılmalı olarak incelenmesi. Elektronik Sosyal Bilimler Dergisi, *5*(18).

Dale, C. (2003). The competitive networks of tourism e-mediaries: New strategies, new advantages. *Journal of Vacation Marketing, 9*(2), 109–118.

Damanpour, F., & Damanpour, J. A. (2001). E-business e-commerce evolution: Perspective and strategy. *Managerial Finance, 27*(7), 16–33.

Doğaner, M. (2007). *Elektronik ticaret Türkiye'de elektronik ticaretin gelişimi ve işletmeden tüketiciye elektronik ticaret üzerine bir araştırma. Yüksek Lisans Tezi.* Konya, Turkey: Selçuk Üniversitesi İİBF.

Dolanbay, C. (2000). *Elektronik ticaret stratejiler ve yöntemler*. Ankara, Turkey: Meteksan.

Elibol, H., & Kesici, B. (2004). Çağdaş İşletmecilik Açisindan Elektronik Ticaret. Selçuk Üniversitesi Sosyal Bilimler Enstitüsü Dergisi, (11), 303-329.

Elmuti, D., & Kathawala, Y. (2001). An overview of strategic alliances. *Management Decision, 39*(3), 205–217.

Erbaşlar, G., & Dokur, Ş. (2012). *Elektronik ticaret: e-ticaret*. Nobel Yayın Dağıtım.

Ersoy, Z. (1999). *Elektronik ticaret ve ticaret noktaları*. Ankara, Turkey: İgeme.

Fahey, L., Srivastava, R., Sharon, J. S., & Smith, D. E. (2001). Linking e-business and operating processes: The role of knowledge management. *IBM Systems Journal, 40*(4), 889–907.

Fırlar, B. G. (2010). Dijital geleceğe hazırlanmak: bilgi ve yenilik yaratma. Sinem Yeygel Çakır (Ed.). Teknolojinin pazarlama iletişimine etkileri içinde, Ankara, Turkey: Nobel.

Geringer, J. M. (1991). Strategic determinants of partner selection criteria in international joint ventures. *Journal of International Business Studies*, *22*(1), 41–62.

Ghosh, S. (1998). Making business sense of the Internet. *Harvard Business Review*, *76*(2), 126–135. PMID:10177862

Görkey, A., & Küçük, S. (2001). *Elektronik ticaret*. İstanbul, Turkey: Yüksek Lisans Tezi, Marmara Üniversitesi, Sosyal Bilimler Enstitüsü.

Gottschalk, P. (2006). *IS/IT Outsourcing E-Business Strategy*. Sourcing and Governance.

Gultai, R. (1999). Network location and learning: The influence of network resources and firm capabilities on alliance formation. *Strategic Management Journal*, *20*, 397–420.

Guthrie, R. A., & Austin, L. D. (1996). Competitive implications of the Internet. *Information Systems Management*, *13*(3), 90–92.

Hackney, R. A., & Burn, J. (2001). SPECS-Strategic planning for e-commerce systems: Towards an e-customer focus. *International Journal of E-Business Strategic Management*, *2*(4), 281–291.

Hamad, H., Elbeltagi, I., & El-Gohary, H. (2018). An empirical investigation of business-to-business e-commerce adoption and its impact on SMEs competitive advantage: The case of Egyptian manufacturing SMEs. *Strategic Change*, *27*(3), 209–229.

Hamad, H., Elbeltagi, I., Jones, P., & El-Gohary, H. (2015). Antecedents of B2B e-commerce adoption and its effect on competitive advantage in manufacturing SMEs. *Strategic Change*, *24*(5), 405–428.

Harrigan, K. R. (1988). Joint ventures and competitive strategy. *Strategic Management Journal*, *9*, 141–158.

Hidayanto, A. N., Ovirza, M., Anggia, P., Budi, N. F. A., & Phusavat, K. (2017). The Roles of Electronic Word of Mouth and Information Searching in the Promotion of a New E-Commerce Strategy: A Case of Online Group Buying in Indonesia. *Journal of Theoretical and Applied Electronic Commerce Research*, *12*(3), 69–85.

Ho, C. F., Wu, W. H., & Tai, Y. M. (2004). Strategies for the adaptation of ERP systems. *Industrial Management & Data Systems*, *104*(3), 234–251.

Huang, S. M., Chang, I. C., Li, S. H., & Lin, M. T. (2004). Assessing risk in ERP projects: Identify and prioritize the factors. *Industrial Management & Data Systems*, *104*(8), 681–688.

Hyder, A. S., & Abraha, D. (2004). Product and skills development in small- and medium-sized high-tech firms through international strategic alliances. *Singapore Management Review*, *26*(2), 1–24.

Kakalejčík, L., Bucko, J., & Vejačka, M. (2019). Differences in buyer journey between high-and low-value customers of e-commerce business. *Journal of Theoretical and Applied Electronic Commerce Research*, *14*(2), 47–58.

Kalakota, R. (2000). Next generation B2B solutions: The revolution's winners. Supply chain. *Management Review*, 14–79.

Kaplan, S., & Sawhney, M. (2000). E-hubs: The new B2B marketplaces. *Harvard Business Review, 78*(3), 97–106. PMID:11183982

Karacaoğlu, K. (2006). *Rekabet Üstünlüğü Sağlamada Endüstri Temelli ve Kaynak Temelli Bakış Açısı: Kayseri'de Faaliyet Gösteren İmalat Sanayi İşletmeleri İçin Bir Model Önerisi. Yayınlanmamış Doktora Tezi*. Ankara, Turkey: Ankara Üniversitesi Sosyal Bilimler Enstitüsü.

Kemp, S. (2017). Digital in 2017: Global overview. *We are social, 24.*

Kiennan, B. (2002). *İşletmeler için çözümler elektronik ticaret, (Çev. Kaan Öztürk, Okan Cem Çırakoğlu, Serdar Özkaya)*. Ankara, Turkey: Arkadaş.

Koellinger, P. (2008). The relationship between technology, innovation, and firm performance—Empirical evidence from e-business in Europe. *Research Policy, 37*(8), 1317–1328.

Köseoğlu, M. A. (2007). *Etik Kodların Rekabet Stratejilerine Etkileri ve Bir Alan Araştırması.* Yayınlanmamış Doktora Tezi. Afyonkarahisar Kocatepe Üniversitesi Sosyal Bilimler Enstitüsü.

Lee, S., & Lim, G. G. (2005). The impact of partnership attributes on EDI implementation success. *Information & Management Amsterdam, 42*(4), 503–516.

Levina, N., & Ross, J. W. (2003). From the vendor's perspective: Exploring the value proposition in information technology outsourcing. *Management Information Systems Quarterly*, 331–364.

Lu, B., & Wang, H. (2016). Research on the Competitive Strategy of Cross-Border E-Commerce Comprehensive Pilot Area Based on the Spatial Competition. *Scientific Programming*, 12.

Lumpkin, G., Droege, S., & Dess, G. (2002). E-commerce strategies: Achieving sustainable competitive advantage and avoiding pitfalls. *Organizational Dynamics, 30*(4), 325–340.

Ma, L., Jin, C., & Huo, Y. (2019). Strategy Of E-Commerce Market Entry Based On Vertical Complementarity Of Service Supply Chain. *International Journal of Innovative Computing, Information, & Control, 15*(2), 757–772.

Marangoz, M. (2014). *İnternette pazarlama*. İstanbul, Turkey: Beta.

McAdam, R., & Galloway, A. (2005). Enterprise resource planning and organisational innovation: A management perspective. *Industrial Management & Data Systems, 105*(3), 280–290.

Mess. (1997). Dünya'da ve Türkiye'de Rekabet. İstanbul, Turkey: Mess Yayınları.

Morrison, A. J., & King, B. E. (2002). Small tourism businesses and e-commerce: Victorian tourism online. *Tourism and Hospitality Research, 4*(2), 104–115.

Mucuk, İ. (2012). *Pazarlama ilkeleri. 19. Basım*. İstanbul, Turkey: Türkmen.

Nemat, R. (2011). Taking a look at different types of e-commerce. *World Applied Programming, 1*(2), 100–104.

Okrent, M. D., & Vokurka, R. J. (2004). Process mapping in successful ERP implementations. *Industrial Management & Data Systems, 104*(8), 637–643.

Oum, T. H., & Zhang, A. (2001). Key aspects of global strategic alliances and the impacts on the future of Canadian airline industry. *Journal of Air Transport Management, 7*, 287–301.

Park, H. P., & Ungson, G. R. (1997). The effect of national culture, organizational complementarities, and economic motivation on joint venture dissolution. *Academy of Management Journal, 40*(2), 279–307.

Pavic, S., Koh, S., Simpson, M., & Padmore, J. (2007). Could e-business create a competitive advantage in UK SMEs? Benchmarking. *International Journal (Toronto, Ont.), 14*(3), 320–351.

Poorani, A. A., & Smith, D. R. (1995). Financial characteristics of bed and breakfast inns. *The Cornell Hotel and Restaurant Administration Quarterly, 36*(5), 57–63.

Porter, M. (2001). Strategy and the Internet. *Harvard Business Review, 79*(3), 62–79. PMID:11246925

Porter, M. E. (1985). *Competitive Advantage: Creating and Sustaining Superior Performance.* New York, NY: The Free Press.

Porter, M. E. (2008). *Competative Strategy. Çev. Gülen Ulubilgen.* İstanbul, Turkey: Sistem Yayıncılık.

Porter, Q. (2005). Internet and Competitive advantage: an empirical study of UK retail banking sector (Doctoral dissertation, University of Warwick).

Ramanathan, R. (2010). E-commerce success criteria: Determining which criteria count most. *Electronic Commerce Research, 10*(2), 191–208.

Rekabetdernegi (n.d.). Retrieved from http://www.rekabetdernegi.org/rekabethakkinda.htm

Riggins, F. J. (1999). A framework for identifying web-based electronic commerce opportunities. *Journal of Organizational Computing and Electronic Commerce, 9*(4), 297–310.

Rowley, J. (2002). *E-business: Principles and practice.* Basingstoke, UK: Palgrave.

Ruiz-Mercader, J., Merono-Cerdan, A., & Sabater-Sanchez, R. (2006). Information technology and learning: Their relationship and impact on organizational performance in small businesses. *International Journal of Information Management, 26*(1), 16–29.

Rust, R. T., & Kannan, P. K. (2003). E-service: A new paradigm for business in the electronic environment. *Communications of the ACM, 46*(6), 36–42.

Seviçin, A. (2006). Kaynaklara Dayalı Rekabet Stratejisi Geliştirme. Dumlupınar Üniversitesi Sosyal Bilimler Dergisi, (15).

Smith, K. T. (2011). Consumer perceptions regarding e-commerce and related risks, B>Quest, 1-20.

Spathis, C., & Constantinides, S. (2003). The usefulness of ERP systems for effective management. *Industrial Management & Data Systems, 103*(9), 677–685.

Stafford, E. R. (1994). Using co-cooperative strategies to make alliances work. *Long Range Planning, 27*(3), 69–70.

Stiles, J. (2001). Strategic alliances. In H. Volberda, & T. Elfi-ing (Eds.), *Rethinking strategy.* London, UK: Sage.

Su, Z., Guo, H., & Sun, W. (2017). Exploration and firm performance: The moderating impact of competitive strategy. *British Journal of Management*, *28*(3), 357–371.

Tek, Ö. B. (1999). *Pazarlama İlkeleri Global Yönetimsel Yaklaşım Türkiye Uygulamaları*. İzmir, Turkey: Beta.

Tinnila, M. (2002). Service processes in electronic travel services: A summary. *Information Technology & Tourism*, *4*, 203–214.

Tse, A. C. B. (2003). Disintermediation of travel agents in the hotel industry. *Journal of Hospitality Management*, *22*(4), 453–460.

Ussahawanitchakit, P., & Intakhan, P. (2011). Internet strategy of e-commerce business in Thailand. *International Journal of Business Strategy*, *11*(1), 1–15.

Van Hooft, F. P., & Stegwee, R. A. (2001). E-business strategy: How to benefit from a hype. *Logistics Information Management*, *14*(1/2), 44–54.

Venkatraman, N., & Henderson, J. C. (1998). Real strategies for virtual organizing. *Sloan Management Review*, *40*(1), 33–49.

Vural, Z., & Bat, M. (2010). Yeni bir iletişim ortamı olarak sosyal medya: Ege üniversitesi iletişim fakültesine yönelik bir araştırma. *Journal of Yaşar University*, *20*(5), 3348–3382.

Wise, R., & Morrison, D. (2000). Beyond the exchange--the future of B2B. *Harvard Business Review*, *78*(6), 86–96. PMID:11184979

Xie, F. T., & Johnston, W. J. (2004). Strategic alliances: Incorporating the impact of e-business technological innovations. *Journal of Business and Industrial Marketing*, *19*(3), 208–222.

Yeşil, A. (2008). E-Ticaret İnternet Ortamında Ticaret. İstanbul, Turkey: Kum Saati Yayın Dağıtım LTD. ŞTİ.

Yu, C. S. (2005). Causes influencing the effectiveness of the post-implementation ERP system. *Industrial Management & Data Systems*, *105*(1), 115–132.

Yunus, M., Moingeon, B., & Lehmann-Ortega, L. (2010). Building social business models: Lessons from the Grameen experience. *Long Range Planning*, *43*(2-3), 308–325.

Zahra, S. A., & George, G. (2002). The net-enabled business innovation cycle and the evolution of dynamic capabilities. *Information Systems Research*, *13*(2), 147–150.

Zhang, G., & Gai, J. (2005, August). Strategic choice for being e-business. In *Proceedings of the 7th international conference on Electronic commerce* (pp. 184-187). ACM.

Zhao, F. (2004). Management of information technology and business process re-engineering: A case study. *Industrial Management & Data Systems*, *104*(8), 674–680.

Chapter 15
Data Mining-Based Evaluating the Customer Satisfaction for the Mobile Applications:
An Analysis on Turkish Banking Sector by Using IT2 Fuzzy DEMATEL

Hasan Dinçer
Istanbul Medipol University, Turkey

Serhat Yüksel
İstanbul Medipol University, Turkey

Zehra Nur Canbolat
İstanbul Medipol University, Turkey

Fatih Pınarbaşı
https://orcid.org/0000-0001-9005-0324
Istanbul Medipol University, Turkey

ABSTRACT

The aim of this study is to evaluate the customer satisfaction for mobile applications in the Turkish banking industry. For this purpose, the last 500 customer comments of 24 different Turkish deposit banks' mobile applications are analyzed with data mining approach. In this process, the most frequent one keyword, two keywords and three keywords are identified, and the most important dimensions are classified into four different categories. Secondly, IT2 fuzzy DEMATEL methodology is considered to weight these dimensions. The findings show that operational and usability are the most important dimensions regarding the customer satisfaction in mobile applications. This situation explains that customers give importance to the quality and variability of the services given by the mobile applications. Hence, it is recommended that different services, such as credit card payment and money transferring should be provided in these applications by the banks. Another important point is that these applications should be designed effectively so that the customer can easily make their operations.

DOI: 10.4018/978-1-7998-0035-4.ch015

INTRODUCTION

Customer satisfaction is a significant concept for all industries. The main reason is that if companies can satisfy their customers, they can be preferred more. This situation has a positive influence on the competitive power of these companies. The concept of customer satisfaction also plays a very crucial role for banking industry because of the high competition. Therefore, banks try to generate new products to attract the attention of the customers to survive in such a difficult environment (Gera et al., 2017; Iglesias et al., 2019).

Generating mobile applications is one example for these strategies. With these applications, banks provide chances to their customers to make some banking operations very easily (Brunette, 2017). For instance, customers can transfer their money to the others by using mobile applications. In addition to this issue, it is also possible to pay the bills through the mobile applications. In summary, these mobile applications can increase customer satisfaction since they can make their operations without going to the branches (Tunay et al., 2019).

On the other side, customers can have some problems while using mobile applications. For example, there may be problems related to the connection to these applications. Additionally, it takes too much time to make operations in the applications. Moreover, the design of these applications may not be user friendly. In other words, customers may not find the necessary menus in the applications easily. Hence, if these problems cannot be solved, they negative affect customer satisfaction (Francis et al., 2018).

Therefore, customer satisfaction regarding mobile application usage should be measured periodically by the banks. This condition provides an opportunity to stop the problem at an early stage. There are some different methods to evaluate the customer satisfaction. As an example, a survey can be conducted with some users of these applications. However, it has some difficulties, such as reaching high number of customers or obtaining the evaluations accurately. It is obvious that applied method for this condition should be selected appropriately (Dinçer et al., 2018; Koçak et al., 2018).

The important point in mobile application is that customers can share their comments about these applications. That is to say, the customers can write their positive or negative opinions to the system. It means that there is high number of information about customer satisfaction for mobile applications (Shilton & Greene, 2017). However, it is very difficult to evaluate this big data. If all comments are examined in a detailed manner, it will not be an efficient way because it takes too much time. For this purpose, data mining approach provides many opportunities to evaluate this big data because it analyzes most frequent keywords in this data (Storey & Song, 2017).

The aim of this study is to evaluate the customer satisfaction for the mobile applications. For this purpose, an analysis is performed for Turkish banking sector by using data mining and interval type-2 DEMATEL approaches. In the first process of the analysis, data mining method is used to evaluate the customer comments about mobile applications so that different dimension can be identified. After that, interval type-2 fuzzy DEMATEL approach is considered to rank these dimensions.

This study has some important novelties. The main novelty is to introduce an integrated model by using DEMATEL and data mining approaches firstly in this study to evaluate customer satisfaction for mobile applications. The DEMATEL method was preferred in comparison with AHP or ANP methodologies. The main reason is that it is possible to make impact and relationship analysis in DEMATEL. In addition to this issue, some strategies can be presented for the banks to increase customer satisfaction in this process. The satisfied customers become willing to work with these banks. Therefore, by attracting the customers, banks can get a chance to increase financial profitability. In other words, it can be possible to gain a competitive power in the market. Furthermore, these strategies can also be taken into the consideration for the companies which aim to develop mobile applications.

This study has four different sections. In this introduction section, general information regarding the chosen subject is given. Next, in the second section, literature is reviewed for the scope of customer satisfaction, mobile applications, data mining and interval type-2 fuzzy DEMATEL. Moreover, the third section is related to the application on Turkish banking industry. In the first part, methods used in this study are defined. After that, analysis results are given. In the last stage, some strategies for the banking industry are developed.

LITERATURE REVIEW

The subject of customer satisfaction for banking industry was evaluated by many different researchers in the literature. For instance, Ozatac et al. (2016) focused on the customer satisfaction for banking sector in Cyprus. In this study, SERVQUAL is used in this study for examining determinants of customer satisfaction. It is concluded that good and firm relations and building trust between customers and bank employees are related to customer satisfaction. Similarly, Kasiri et al. (2017) and Ong et al. (2017) determined that customer loyalty is significantly affected by customer satisfaction for the banking industry. Mihelis et al. (2001) and Arbore and Busacca (2009) also analyzed the ways of increasing customer satisfaction in retail banks. They defined different indicators for this purpose and weighted them according to the importance.

Additionally, customer satisfaction in online banking also attracted the attention of some researchers. Yoon (2010) investigated customer satisfaction for online banking in China. For this purpose, multi group model which includes a high-experience group and a low-experience group is employed. It is concluded that design, security, information content, speed and customer support service variables are influencing customer satisfaction for both groups. Parallel to this study, Casaló et al. (2008), Ariff et al. (2013), and Ling et al. (2016) also evaluated customer satisfaction in online banking for different countries. They identified that web design and content is the most important factor that affects customer satisfaction for online banking. In addition to them, there are also some other studies in the literature which examined the importance of online banking in customer satisfaction (Jha & Dubey, 2019; Al-Otaibi et al., 2018; Dharmavaram & Nittala, 2018; de Oliveira Santini et al., 2018; Azemi et al., 2019)

Moreover, some studies examined mobile application subject for many different purposes. As an example, Alnawas and Aburub (2016), Mahatanankoon et al. (2005), Verkasalo et al. (2010), and Hsiao et al. (2016) tried to define customer perceptions on mobile applications. They conducted a survey analysis with a high number of mobile application users. They concluded that effective mobile application service provides a close connection with the banks. Nilsson (2009) and Munoz-Leiva et al. (2017) aimed to identify the determinants of customer satisfaction in mobile applications. They underlined that design of the mobile application plays the most important role in this context. Some researchers also defined the way of increasing customer satisfaction, such as advertisement (Kim et al., 2015) and ease of use (McLean et al., 2018). On the other side, some studies defined the factors which have a decreasing effect on this aspect like high purchase price of mobile application (Hsu & Chin, 2015; Noulas et al., 2018; Bochem et al., 2018) and technological risk (Shen, 2015; Choong et al., 2018; Abia et al., 2018; Bento et al., 2019).

Data mining approach is used in this study to identify the significant dimensions by analyzing customer comments. It is seen that this approach is very popular in the literature. Some researchers preferred this approach to evaluate online customer reviews in different purposes, such as travel blogs (Ye et al., 2009) and machine learning (Singh et al., 2017). Similarly, Hargreaves et al. (2018), Moro et al. (2018), Kasemsap (2018), Cao et al. (2011) and Salehan and Kim (2016) focused on the ways to improve the online consumer reviews by using data mining approach. Hsieh (2004) integrated data mining and behavioral scoring methods to evaluate customers of banks. Also, Grover et al. (2018), Marconi et al. (2019), Wang et al. (2018) and Liu and Shih (2005) considered data mining methodology for product recommendation based on customer lifetime value. Furthermore, Mostafa (2013), He et al. (2013), Lahuerta-Otero and Cordero-Gutiérrez (2016) and Singh et al. (2018) used data mining approach to evaluate customer brand sentiments on social media.

Interval type-2 DEMATEL methodology is used in this study to weight the dimensions according to their importance. DEMATEL model was preferred by many researchers for various subjects, such as supplier selection (Liu et al., 2018; Abdel-Basset et al., 2018; Kumar et al., 2018; Ashtarinezhad et al., 2018), evaluating job satisfaction (Tsai, 2018), procurement (Bakir et al., 2018), performance measurement (Dinçer & Yüksel, 2018; Yüksel et al., 2017) and knowledge management (Gopal et al., 2018). On the other side, Dinçer et al. (2019), Asan et al. (2018), Dinçer et al. (2018) and Han et al. (2018) considered fuzzy DEMATEL approach under the hesitancy in their studies. In addition to them, interval type-2 DEMATEL is a new method in the literature in comparison with the others. It was also used for human resource management (Abdullah & Zulkifli, 2015) and strategy selection (Baykasoğlu & Gölcük, 2017).

As a result of literature review, it is understood that there are lots of studies in the literature for the subject of customer satisfaction in various industries, such as manufacturing, health and banking. Also, mobile application subject was also considered by many different researchers to understand customer perception or the ways of increasing satisfaction. The missing part of the literature in this framework is that there is need a new study which focuses on customer satisfaction in mobile application with a new and original methodology. Another important point is that both data mining and interval type-2 fuzzy DEMATEL approaches are used in the literature for many different purposes. However, there is not a study in which these methods are used for customer satisfaction in mobile application.

METHODOLOGY

Data Mining

Data mining; it is a data analysis method used to explore information, that has not been previously explored and explicitly, used by using many disciplines such as statistics, database management and machine learning (Kavakiotis et al., 2017). The concept of text mining, a sub-branch of data mining, is a science that reveals the undiscovered information in textual documents with the help of computer systems (Gholizadeh et al., 2017). The main objective of this discipline is to make an inference and discovery through from non-structural structures with natural language processing methods. Text mining is thought to have a higher commercial potential than data mining because the most natural storage information form is text. In this respect, there is a recent study in the literature showing that 80% of a company's knowledge is included in text documents. Text mining, however, performs a much more complex function than data mining, since it deals with text data that is naturally unstructured and fuzzy (Leech et al., 2017).

The N-gram is an adjacent n sequence from a specific text or speech instance (Majumder et al., 2017). The context can also be provided by a well-defined procedure, as is valid for documenting similarity. N-gram size; 1 n-gram "unigram", 2 n-gram "bigram", and 3 n-gram is called "trigram". N-gram creator was used to find the most frequently used 2- and 3-word groups side by side in the text mining operations performed with KNIME software. N-gram creator creates N-grams from the documents of the input table and counts their frequencies. Word or character is used to specify N-grams (Wang et al., 2018).

Interval Type-2 Fuzzy Sets

Interval type-1 fuzzy sets are very popular methods and many different researchers considered them in their analysis. However, because some of these researchers think that they are not sufficient in decision making for uncertain issues (Qin et al., 2017; Sola et al., 2015). Owing to this aspect, interval type-2 fuzzy sets were developed. In this circumstance, $\tilde{A}$ represents type-2 fuzzy set and $¼_{\tilde{A}(x,u)}$ identifies type-2 membership function which can get the value between 0 and 1 (Li et al., 2016; Jhang et al., 2018; Castillo et al., 2016). The following equation gives information about type-2 fuzzy sets.

$$\tilde{A} = \left\{\left(\left(x,u\right), \mu_{\tilde{A}(x,u)}\right) | \forall_x \in X, \forall_u \in J_x \subseteq \left[0,1\right]\right\} \text{ or } \tilde{A} = \int_{x\in X} \int_{u \in J_x} \mu_{\tilde{A}}\left(x,u\right) / \left(x,u\right) J_x \subseteq \left[0,1\right]. \quad (1)$$

This set can also be represented as in the following equation when the membership function equals to "1".

$$\tilde{A} = \int_{x\in X} \int_{u \in J_x} 1 / \left(x,u\right) J_x \subseteq \left[0,1\right]$$

On the other side, $\tilde{A}_i^L$ and $\tilde{A}_i^U$ explain "lower trapezoidal membership function" and "the upper trapezoidal membership function" that are identified in the following equation.

$$\tilde{A}_i = \left(\tilde{A}_i^U, \tilde{A}_i^L\right) = \left(\left(a_{i1}^U, a_{i2}^U, a_{i3}^U, a_{i4}^U; H_1\left(\tilde{A}_i^U\right), H_2\left(\tilde{A}_i^U\right)\right), \left(a_{i1}^L, a_{i2}^L, a_{i3}^L, a_{i4}^L; H_1\left(\tilde{A}_i^L\right), H_2\left(\tilde{A}_i^L\right)\right)\right)$$

In addition to them, the calculation of interval type-2 fuzzy sets is defined in the following equations.

$$\begin{aligned}
&\tilde{A}_1 \oplus \tilde{A}_2 = \left(\tilde{A}_1^U, \tilde{A}_1^L\right) \oplus \left(\tilde{A}_2^U, \tilde{A}_2^L\right) = \\
&\left(\left(a_{11}^U + a_{21}^U, a_{12}^U + a_{22}^U, a_{13}^U + a_{23}^U, a_{14}^U + a_{24}^U; \min\left(H_1\left(\tilde{A}_1^U\right), H_1\left(\tilde{A}_2^U\right)\right), \min\left(H_1\left(\tilde{A}_1^U\right), H_2\left(\tilde{A}_2^U\right)\right)\right),\right. \\
&\left.\left(a_{11}^L + a_{21}^L, a_{12}^L + a_{22}^L, a_{13}^L + a_{23}^L, a_{14}^L + a_{24}^L; \min\left(H_1\left(\tilde{A}_1^L\right), H_1\left(\tilde{A}_2^L\right)\right), \min\left(H_1\left(\tilde{A}_1^L\right), H_2\left(\tilde{A}_2^L\right)\right)\right)\right)
\end{aligned}$$

$$\tilde{A}_1 \ominus \tilde{A}_2 = \left(\tilde{A}_1^U, \tilde{A}_1^L\right) \ominus \left(\tilde{A}_2^U, \tilde{A}_2^L\right) =$$
$$\left(\left(a_{11}^U - a_{21}^U, a_{12}^U - a_{22}^U, a_{13}^U - a_{23}^U, a_{14}^U - a_{24}^U; \min\left(H_1\left(\tilde{A}_1^U\right), H_1\left(\tilde{A}_2^U\right)\right), \min\left(H_1\left(\tilde{A}_1^U\right), H_2\left(\tilde{A}_2^U\right)\right)\right),\right.$$
$$\left.\left(a_{11}^L - a_{21}^L, a_{12}^L - a_{22}^L, a_{13}^L - a_{23}^L, a_{14}^L - a_{24}^L; \min\left(H_1\left(\tilde{A}_1^L\right), H_1\left(\tilde{A}_2^L\right)\right), \min\left(H_1\left(\tilde{A}_1^L\right), H_2\left(\tilde{A}_2^L\right)\right)\right)\right)$$

$$\tilde{A}_1 \otimes \tilde{A}_2 = \left(\tilde{A}_1^U, \tilde{A}_1^L\right) \otimes \left(\tilde{A}_2^U, \tilde{A}_2^L\right) =$$
$$\left(\left(a_{11}^U \times a_{21}^U, a_{12}^U \times a_{22}^U, a_{13}^U \times a_{23}^U, a_{14}^U \times a_{24}^U; \min\left(H_1\left(\tilde{A}_1^U\right), H_1\left(\tilde{A}_2^U\right)\right), \min\left(H_1\left(\tilde{A}_1^U\right), H_2\left(\tilde{A}_2^U\right)\right)\right),\right.$$
$$\left.\left(a_{11}^L \times a_{21}^L, a_{12}^L \times a_{22}^L, a_{13}^L \times a_{23}^L, a_{14}^L \times a_{24}^L; \min\left(H_1\left(\tilde{A}_1^L\right), H_1\left(\tilde{A}_2^L\right)\right), \min\left(H_1\left(\tilde{A}_1^L\right), H_2\left(\tilde{A}_2^L\right)\right)\right)\right)$$

$$k\tilde{A}_1 =$$
$$\left(k \times a_{11}^U, k \times a_{12}^U, k \times a_{13}^U, k \times a_{14}^U; H_1\left(\tilde{A}_1^U\right), H_2\left(\tilde{A}_1^U\right)\right), \left(k \times a_{11}^L, k \times a_{12}^L, k \times a_{13}^L, k \times a_{14}^L; H_1\left(\tilde{A}_1^L\right), H_2\left(\tilde{A}_1^L\right)\right)$$

$$\frac{\tilde{A}_1}{k} =$$
$$\left(\frac{1}{k} \times a_{11}^U, \frac{1}{k} \times a_{12}^U, \frac{1}{k} \times a_{13}^U, \frac{1}{k} \times a_{14}^U; H_1\left(\tilde{A}_1^U\right), H_2\left(\tilde{A}_1^U\right)\right), \left(\frac{1}{k} \times a_{11}^L, \frac{1}{k} \times a_{12}^L, \frac{1}{k} \times a_{13}^L, \frac{1}{k} \times a_{14}^L; H_1\left(\tilde{A}_1^L\right), H_2\left(\tilde{A}_1^L\right)\right)$$

Fuzzy DEMATEL

The word DEMATEL comes from the expression of "Decision making trial and evaluation laboratory". Mainly, the interdependence between the factors is evaluated. Moreover, it is also possible to identify the significance of these factors by using this method. This approach can also be used with internal type-2 fuzzy sets. This situation can be examined in 5 different steps (Dinçer et al., 2017). The evaluations of the decision makers are provided and converted in the fuzzy sets in the first step. Also, the second step is related to the calculation of "the initial direct-relation fuzzy matrix" ($\tilde{Z}$). This process is identified in the following equations.

$$\tilde{Z} = \begin{bmatrix} 0 & \tilde{z}_{12} & \cdots & \cdots & \tilde{z}_{1n} \\ \tilde{z}_{21} & 0 & \cdots & \cdots & \tilde{z}_{2n} \\ \vdots & \vdots & \ddots & \cdots & \cdots \\ \vdots & \vdots & \vdots & \ddots & \vdots \\ \tilde{z}_{n1} & \tilde{z}_{n2} & \cdots & \cdots & 0 \end{bmatrix}$$

$$\tilde{Z} = \frac{\tilde{Z}^1 + \tilde{Z}^2 + \tilde{Z}^3 + \ldots \tilde{Z}^n}{n}$$

Additionally, this matrix is normalized with the help of the following equations.

$$\tilde{X} = \begin{bmatrix} \tilde{x}_{11} & \tilde{x}_{12} & \cdots & \cdots & \tilde{x}_{1n} \\ \tilde{x}_{21} & \tilde{x}_{22} & \cdots & \cdots & \tilde{x}_{2n} \\ \vdots & \vdots & \ddots & \cdots & \cdots \\ \vdots & \vdots & \vdots & \ddots & \vdots \\ \tilde{x}_{n1} & \tilde{x}_{n2} & \cdots & \cdots & \tilde{x}_{nn} \end{bmatrix}$$

$$\tilde{x}_{ij} = \frac{\tilde{z}_{ij}}{r} = \left(\left(\frac{Z_{a_{ij}}}{r}, \frac{Z_{b_{ij}}}{r}, \frac{Z_{c_{ij}}}{r}, \frac{Z_{d_{ij}}}{r}; H_1\left(z_{ij}^{U}\right), H_2\left(z_{ij}^{U}\right) \right), \left(\frac{Z_{e_{ij}}}{r}, \frac{Z_{f_{ij}}}{r}, \frac{Z_{g_{ij}}}{r}, \frac{Z_{h_{ij}}}{r}; H_1\left(z_{ij}^{L}\right), H_2\left(z_{ij}^{L}\right) \right) \right)$$

$$r = max\left(max_{1\le i\le n} \sum_{j=1}^{n} Z_{d_{ij}}, max_{1\le i\le n} \sum_{j=1}^{n} Z_{d_{ij}} \right)$$

Moreover, the fourth step includes the calculation of "the total influence fuzzy matrix". In this process, the following equations are considered.

$$X_a = \begin{bmatrix} 0 & a'_{12} & \cdots & \cdots & a'_{1n} \\ a'_{21} & 0 & \cdots & \cdots & a'_{2n} \\ \vdots & \vdots & \ddots & \cdots & \cdots \\ \vdots & \vdots & \vdots & \ddots & \vdots \\ a'_{n1} & a'_{n2} & \cdots & \cdots & 0 \end{bmatrix}, \ldots, X_h = \begin{bmatrix} 0 & h'_{12} & \cdots & \cdots & h'_{1n} \\ h'_{21} & 0 & \cdots & \cdots & h'_{2n} \\ \vdots & \vdots & \ddots & \cdots & \cdots \\ \vdots & \vdots & \vdots & \ddots & \vdots \\ h'_{n1} & h'_{n2} & \cdots & \cdots & 0 \end{bmatrix}$$

$$\tilde{T} = \lim_{k\to\infty} \tilde{X} + \tilde{X}^2 + \ldots + \tilde{X}^k$$

$$\tilde{T} = \begin{bmatrix} \tilde{t}_{11} & \tilde{t}_{12} & \cdots & \cdots & \tilde{t}_{1n} \\ \tilde{t}_{21} & \tilde{t}_{22} & \cdots & \cdots & \tilde{t}_{2n} \\ \vdots & \vdots & \ddots & \cdots & \cdots \\ \vdots & \vdots & \vdots & \ddots & \vdots \\ \tilde{t}_{n1} & \tilde{t}_{n2} & \cdots & \cdots & \tilde{t}_{nn} \end{bmatrix}$$

$$\tilde{t}_{ij} = \left(a''_{ij}, b''_{ij}, c''_{ij}, d''_{ij}; H_1\left(\tilde{t}_{ij}^{\,U}\right), H_2\left(\tilde{t}_{ij}^{\,U}\right) \right), \left(e''_{ij}, f''_{ij}, g''_{ij}, h''_{ij}; H_1\left(\tilde{t}_{ij}^{\,L}\right), H_2\left(\tilde{t}_{ij}^{\,L}\right) \right)$$

$$\left[a''_{ij}\right] = X_a \times \left(I - X_a\right)^{-1}, \ \ldots, \ \left[h''_{ij}\right] = X_h \times \left(I - X_h\right)^{-1}$$

In the final step, "the defuzzified total influence matrix" is calculated. The following equations give information about this process.

$$Def_T = \frac{\frac{\left(u_U - l_U\right) + \left({}^{2}{}_{U} \times m_{1U} - l_U\right) + \left(\pm_U \times m_{2U} - l_U\right)}{4} + l_U + \left[\frac{\left(u_L - l_L\right) + \left({}^{2}{}_{L} \times m_{1L} - l_L\right) + \left(\pm_L \times m_{2L} - l_L\right)}{4} + l_L\right]}{2}$$

$$Def_T = T = \left[t_{ij}\right]_{n\times n},\ i,j = 1,2,\ldots,n$$

$$\tilde{D}_i^{def} = r = \left[\sum_{j=1}^{n} t_{ij}\right]_{n\times 1} = \left(r_i\right)_{n\times 1} = \left(r_1,\ldots,r_i,\ldots,r_n\right)$$

$$\tilde{R}_i^{def} = y = \left[\sum_{i=1}^{n} t_{ij}\right]'_{1\times n} = \left(y_j\right)'_{1\times n} = \left(y_1,\ldots,y_i,\ldots,y_n\right)$$

With respect to the defuzzification, $\left(\tilde{D}_i + \tilde{R}_i\right)^{def}$ and $\left(\tilde{D}_i - \tilde{R}_i\right)^{def}$ are considered. For this purpose, the sum of all vector rows is indicated with $\tilde{R}_i^{def}$. Therefore, the value of $\left(\tilde{D}_i + \tilde{R}_i\right)^{def}$ gives information about the closeness to the central point. On the other hand, the degree of causality is shown with $\left(\tilde{D}_i - \tilde{R}_i\right)^{def}$. DEMATEL approach was considered by many researchers in the literature for different purposes, such as supplier selection (Abdel-Basset et al., 2018; Kumar et al., 2018; Ashtarinezhad et al., 2018; Luthra et al., 2018), supply chain management (Kazancoglu et al., 2018; Sharma et al., 2018; Bhagawati et al., 2019) and financial performance (Dinçer et al., 2019; Dinçer, Uzunkaya, & Yüksel, 2019; Dinçer & Yüksel, 2019; Yüksel et al., 2019).

AN APPLICATION ON TURKISH BANKING SECTOR

Step 1: Identifying the Dimensions of Customer Satisfaction in Mobile Banking Applications by Using Text Mining

First of all, the last 500 comments of 24 different Turkish deposit banks are obtained from the Apple Store. This data is analyzed according to the most frequent keywords. Within this framework, three different analyses are performed which are most frequent one keyword, two keywords and three keywords. The most frequent keywords are demonstrated on Table 1.

By considering these keywords, the most important dimensions are classified into four different categories that are functionality, timing, usability and operational. The details of these dimensions are illustrated on Table 2.

Table 1. List of the Most Frequent Keywords related to the Customer Satisfaction

Keywords	Frequency
Credit	1,811
Nice	1,751
Entrance	1,710
Login	1,701
Transaction	1,679
Error	1,525
Money	1,458
Time	1,286
Update	1,186
Notification	1,179
Easy	1,164
Password	1,148
Fast	1,116
Practical	1,103
Payment	1,007
Useful	993
Account	981
Slow	866
Simple	739
Card	404
Connection	306
Closing	301

Table 2 shows that with respect to the dimension of the functionality (D1), the problems in the process of connection to the mobile applications are considered. In other words, the errors while connection to the applications are stated in this dimension. Therefore, the keywords of "error", "login", "connection", "closing" and "notification" are taken into the consideration because they show the problems regarding to the functionality of the applications.

In addition, it is also understood that the timing (D2) is also significant for customer satisfaction. The main reason is that customers prefer to make their operations quickly. On the other hand, the ap-

Table 2. List of the Dimensions

Dimensions	Related Keywords
Functionality (D1)	Error; Login; Connection; Closing; Notification
Timing (D2)	Time; Fast; Practical; Slow; Update
Usability (D3)	Easy; Simple; Useful; Nice; Password; Entrance
Operational (D4)	Credit; Money; Payment; Account; Card; Transaction

plication, which takes too much time, has a decreasing effect on the customer satisfaction. Within this framework, "time", "fast", "practical", "slow" and "update" are the significant keywords which give information about this purpose.

Moreover, regarding the dimension of usability (D3), the customers prefer to use the applications very easily. For this purpose, these applications should be designed that users can understand each step very easily. In this context, the difficulties in entering the applications and using the sections in these applications lead to customer dissatisfaction. Hence, the keywords of "easy", "simple", "useful", "nice", "password" and "entrance" represent this dimension.

The last dimension, operational (D4), gives information about the quality of the services. That is to say, the different services provided by the application are taken into the consideration in this dimension. The main reason is that if the customers can perform many different operations, they can prefer to use this mobile banking application. In this circumstance, "credit", "money", "payment", "account", "card" and "transaction" are the keywords which explain the different services provided by this application.

Step 2: Calculation of the Weights of These Dimensions by Considering Interval Type-2 Fuzzy DEMATEL

Three different decision makers have provided their linguistic evaluations for the dimensions by considering seven-point scales. Table 3 presents the linguistic evaluations and their values converted into the interval type 2 numbers.

Table 4 represents the linguistic scales of each decision maker for measuring dependency degrees among the dimensions.

Linguistic evaluations are converted into the fuzzy numbers based on IT2 fuzzy numbers and averaged values are used for the initial direct relation matrix for the dimensions. The results are seen in Table 5

The initial direct relation matrix has been normalized for the total relation matrix. Table 6 illustrates the normalized values.

Table 7 examines the total relation matrix for the defuzzified values of the dimensions.

Impact-relation degrees and importance of the dimensions have been computed by using the defuzzified values. The details of the results are given on Table 8.

Table 8 shows that functionality (D1) is the most influenced factor among the dimensions while operational (D4) is the most influencing dimension. However, operational (D4) and usability (D3) have

Table 3. Linguistic Evaluations and Interval Type 2 Fuzzy Numbers for the Dimensions

Linguistic Scales	Interval Type 2 Fuzzy Numbers
Very very low (VVL)	((0,0.1,0.1,0.2;1,1), (0.05,0.1,0.1,0.15;0.9,0.9))
Very low (VL)	((0.1,0.2,0.2,0.35;1,1), (0.15,0.2,0.2,0.3;0.9,0.9))
Low (L)	((0.2,0.35,0.35,0.5;1,1), (0.25,0.35,0.35,0.45;0.9,0.9))
Medium (M)	((0.35,0.5,0.5,0.65;1,1), (0.4,0.5,0.5,0.6;0.9,0.9))
High (H)	((0.5,0.65,0.65,0.8;1,1), (0.55,0.65,0.65,0.75;0.9,0.9))
Very high (VH)	((0.65,0.8,0.8,0.9;1,1), (0.7,0.8,0.8,0.85;0.9,0.9))
Very very high (VVH)	((0.8,0.9,0.9,1;1,1), (0.85,0.9,0.9,0.95;0.9,0.9))

Source: Baykasoglu and Golcuk (2017)

Table 4. Linguistic evaluations of the decision makers for the dimensions

	D1			D2			D3			D4		
	DM1	**DM2**	**DM3**	**DM1**	**DM2**	**DM3**	**DM1**	**DM2**	**DM3**	**DM1**	**DM2**	**DM3**
D1	-	-	-	L	VL	M	L	M	M	M	M	L
D2	L	M	M	-	-	-	L	M	VL	L	M	L
D3	VH	H	H	H	M	H	-	-	-	M	H	M
D4	VH	VH	H	VVH	VH	VH	VH	M	H	-	-	-

Table 5. Initial direct relation matrix for the dimensions

	D1	D2	D3	D4
D1	((0,0,0,0;1,1), (0,0,0,0;0.90,0.90))	((0.22,0.35,0.35,0.50;1,1), (0.27,0.35,0.35,0.45;0.90 ,0.90))	((0.30,0.45,0.45,0.60;1,1), (0. 35,0.45,0.45,0.55;0.90,0.90))	((0.30,0.45,0.45,0.60;1,1), (0.35 ,0.45,0.45,0.55;0.90,0.90))
D2	((0.30,0.45,0.45,0.60;1,1), (0. 35,0.45,0.45,0.55;0.90,0.90))	((0,0,0,0;1,1), (0,0,0,0;0.90,0.90))	((0.22,0.35,0.35,0.50;1,1), (0. 27,0.35,0.35,0.45;0.90,0.90))	((0.25,0.40,0.40,0.55;1,1), (0.30 ,0.40,0.40,0.50;0.90,0.90))
D3	((0.55,0.70,0.70,0.83;1,1), (0. 60,0.70,0.70,0.78;0.90,0.90))	((0.45,0.60,0.60,0.75;1,1), (0.50,0.60,0.60,0.70;0.90 ,0.90))	((0,0,0,0;1,1), (0,0,0,0;0.90,0.90))	((0.40,0.55,0.55,0.70;1,1), (0.45 ,0.55,0.55,0.65;0.90,0.90))
D4	((0.60,0.75,0.75,0.87;1,1), (0. 65,0.75,0.75,0.82;0.90,0.90))	((0.70,0.83,0.83,0.93;1,1), (0.75,0.83,0.83,0.88;0.90 ,0.90))	((0.50,0.65,0.65,0.78;1,1), (0. 55,0.65,0.65,0.73;0.90,0.90))	((0,0,0,0;1,1), (0,0,0,0;0.90,0.90))

also highest importance in a set of dimensions whereas timing (D2) is the weakest important dimension. It gives information that customers mainly focus on the quality of the services given by the mobile applications. By considering this issue, it can be said that the banks' mobile applications should provide different services effectively such as giving credit, money transferring, credit card debt payment. Thus, if the banks can design their mobile applications in this framework, it can be much easier to attract the attentions of the customers.

In addition to this situation, it is also identified that the customers prefer to use the applications very easily. Thus, the applications should be designed for the customers to understand different steps easily. Hence, customer satisfaction can be provided by the banks. The threshold value has been defined by

Table 6. The normalized direct-relation matrix for the dimensions

	D1	D2	D3	D4
D1	((0,0,0,0;1,1), (0,0,0,0;0.90,0.90))	((0.08,0.14,0.14,0.19;1,1), (0. 10,0.14,0.14,0.17;0.90,0.90))	((0.12,0.17,0.17,0.23;1,1), (0. 14,0.17,0.17,0.21;0.90,0.90))	((0.12,0.17,0.17,0.23;1,1), (0.14 ,0.17,0.17,0.21;0.90,0.90))
D2	((0.12,0.17,0.17,0.23;1,1), (0. 14,0.17,0.17,0.21;0.90,0.90))	((0,0,0,0;1,1), (0,0,0,0;0.90,0.90))	((0.08,0.14,0.14,0.19;1,1), (0. 10,0.14,0.14,0.17;0.90,0.90))	((0.10,0.15,0.15,0.21;1,1), (0.12 ,0.15,0.15,0.19;0.90,0.90))
D3	((0.21,0.27,0.27,0.32;1,1), (0. 23,0.27,0.27,0.30;0.90,0.90))	((0.17,0.23,0.23,0.29;1,1), (0. 19,0.23,0.23,0.27;0.90,0.90))	((0,0,0,0;1,1), (0,0,0,0;0.90,0.90))	((0.15,0.21,0.21,0.27;1,1), (0.17 ,0.21,0.21,0.25;0.90,0.90))
D4	((0.23,0.29,0.29,0.34;1,1), (0. 25,0.29,0.29,0.32;0.90,0.90))	((0.27,0.32,0.32,0.36;1,1), (0. 29,0.32,0.32,0.34;0.90,0.90))	((0.19,0.25,0.25,0.30;1,1), (0. 21,0.25,0.25,0.28;0.90,0.90))	((0,0,0,0;1,1), (0,0,0,0;0.90,0.90))

Table 7. The total relation matrix for the dimensions

	D1	D2	D3	D4
D1	((0.10,0.26,0.26,0.73;1,1), (0.14,0.26,0.26,0.50;0.90 ,0.90))	((0.17,0.37,0.37,0.86;1,1), (0. 22,0.37,0.37,0.62;0.90,0.90))	((0.17,0.36,0.36,0.82;1,1), (0.22,0.36,0.36,0.60;0.90,0.90	((0.17,0.35,0.35,0.81;1,1), (0.22 ,0.35,0.35,0.59;0.90,0.90))
D2	((0.19,0.40,0.40,0.90;1,1), (0.25,0.40,0.40,0.65;0.90 ,0.90))	((0.08,0.23,0.23,0.67;1,1), (0. 12,0.23,0.23,0.45;0.90,0.90))	((0.14,0.32,0.32,0.77;1,1), (0. 19,0.32,0.32,0.55;0.90,0.90))	((0.15,0.33,0.33,0.77;1,1), (0.20 ,0.33,0.33,0.56;0.90,0.90))
D3	((0.32,0.57,0.57,1.16;1,1), (0.39,0.57,0.57,0.87;0.90 ,0.90))	((0.28,0.52,0.52,1.10;1,1), (0. 35,0.52,0.52,0.82;0.90,0.90))	((0.11,0.28,0.28,0.78;1,1), (0. 15,0.28,0.28,0.53;0.90,0.90))	((0.24,0.45,0.45,0.99;1,1), (0.29 ,0.45,0.45,0.73;0.90,0.90))
D4	((0.37,0.64,0.64,1.26;1,1), (0.44,0.64,0.64,0.94;0.90 ,0.90))	((0.39,0.64,0.64,1.23;1,1), (0. 46,0.64,0.64,0.93;0.90,0.90))	((0.29,0.53,0.53,1.09;1,1), (0. 36,0.53,0.53,0.81;0.90,0.90))	((0.13,0.32,0.32,0.85;1,1), (0.17 ,0.32,0.32,0.58;0.90,0.90))

using the averaged value of the defuzzified total relation matrix and higher values than the threshold have been defined as the influencing factors in the relation matrix.

SOLUTIONS AND RECOMMENDATIONS

According to these findings, it is recommended that customers give importance to the quality of the services given by the mobile applications. Therefore, different services should be provided in the mobile applications of the banks effectively, such as money transferring, paying bills. In this context, mobile applications of the banks should be user-friendly and satisfy the needs of the customers properly. This situation mainly attracts the attentions of the customers to prefer these applications. Moreover, customers want to make their operations easily in these applications. Thus, banks should design these applications significantly so that it should be understandable by the customers. With the help of these actions, it can be possible to provide customer satisfaction. The satisfied customers prefer to work with these banks so that they can increase profitability. In other words, these banks gain a competitive power in the market in comparison with the rivals.

Table 8. Defuzzified total relation matrix and the weights for the dimensions

	D1	D2	D3	D4	r	y	r+y	r-y	Weights
D1	0.31	0.41	0.40	0.39	1.51	2.04	3.55	-0.53	0.245
D2	0.44	0.28	0.36	0.37	1.44	1.93	3.37	-0.49	0.232
D3	0.61	0.57	0.33	0.50	2.01	1.66	3.66	0.35	0.253
D4	0.68	0.68	0.57	0.37	2.30	1.62	3.92	0.67	0.270

FUTURE RESEARCH DIRECTIONS

In this study, an essential topic is evaluated with the original methodology. Nevertheless, for the future studies, another industry can be assessed with different approaches like interval type-2 fuzzy TOPSIS.

CONCLUSION

The concept of customer satisfaction also plays a very significant role for banking industry due to the high competition. Thus, banks try to implement new strategies in order to gain a competitive advantage over their rivals. Generating mobile applications is one way to reach this objective. By providing many different services in these applications like money transferring and debt payment, banks aim to increase customer satisfaction. Thus, they can be preferred by the customers more and this situation has a positive influence on their financial performance.

In this study, it is aimed to evaluate the customer satisfaction for the mobile applications. In this context, Turkish banking sector is taken into the consideration. First of all, by using data mining approach, customer comments related to the mobile applications are analyzed. In this framework, the last 500 comments of 24 different Turkish deposit banks' mobile applications are obtained from the Apple Store. Next, the most frequent one keyword, two keywords and three keywords are defined with this methodology. As a result, the most important dimensions are classified into four different categories that are functionality, timing, usability and operational.

After that, interval type-2 fuzzy DEMATEL methodology is considered to weight these dimensions according to their importance. This method was preferred by comparing with AHP and ANP approaches because it gives opportunity to make impact and relationship analysis. It is concluded that operational and usability are the most important dimensions regarding the customer satisfaction in mobile applications. On the other side, timing dimension is on the last rank. In addition to them, usability and operational have the impact on each dimension. However, functionality and timing have no impact on the other dimensions.

REFERENCES

Abdel-Basset, M., Manogaran, G., Gamal, A., & Smarandache, F. (2018). A hybrid approach of neutrosophic sets and DEMATEL method for developing supplier selection criteria. *Design Automation for Embedded Systems*, 1–22.

Abdullah, L., & Zulkifli, N. (2015). Integration of fuzzy AHP and interval type-2 fuzzy DEMATEL: An application to human resource management. *Expert Systems with Applications*, *42*(9), 4397–4409. doi:10.1016/j.eswa.2015.01.021

Abia, D., Ajayi, S., & Iwegbu, M. (2018, August). Technological Risk Assessment: A Panacea to Preventing Major Process Incidents-A Case Study of Amenam Kpono. In *SPE Nigeria Annual International Conference and Exhibition*. Society of Petroleum Engineers. 10.2118/193429-MS

Al-Otaibi, S., Aljohani, N. R., Hoque, M. R., & Alotaibi, F. S. (2018). The satisfaction of Saudi customers toward mobile banking in Saudi Arabia and the United Kingdom. [JGIM]. *Journal of Global Information Management*, *26*(1), 85–103. doi:10.4018/JGIM.2018010105

Alnawas, I., & Aburub, F. (2016). The effect of benefits generated from interacting with branded mobile apps on consumer satisfaction and purchase intentions. *Journal of Retailing and Consumer Services*, *31*, 313–322. doi:10.1016/j.jretconser.2016.04.004

Arbore, A., & Busacca, B. (2009). Customer satisfaction and dissatisfaction in retail banking: Exploring the asymmetric impact of attribute performances. *Journal of Retailing and Consumer Services*, *16*(4), 271–280. doi:10.1016/j.jretconser.2009.02.002

Ariff, M. S. M., Yun, L. O., Zakuan, N., & Ismail, K. (2013). The impacts of service quality and customer satisfaction on customer loyalty in internet banking. *Procedia: Social and Behavioral Sciences*, *81*, 469–473. doi:10.1016/j.sbspro.2013.06.462

Asan, U., Kadaifci, C., Bozdag, E., Soyer, A., & Serdarasan, S. (2018). A new approach to DEMATEL based on interval-valued hesitant fuzzy sets. *Applied Soft Computing*, *66*, 34–49. doi:10.1016/j.asoc.2018.01.018

Ashtarinezhad, E., Sarfaraz, A. H., & Navabakhsh, M. (2018). Supplier evaluation and categorize with combine Fuzzy Dematel and Fuzzy Inference System. *Data in Brief*, *18*, 1149–1156. doi:10.1016/j.dib.2018.03.077 PMID:29900289

Ashtarinezhad, E., Sarfaraz, A. H., & Navabakhsh, M. (2018). Supplier evaluation and categorize with combine Fuzzy Dematel and Fuzzy Inference System. *Data in Brief*, *18*, 1149–1156. doi:10.1016/j.dib.2018.03.077 PMID:29900289

Azemi, Y., Ozuem, W., Howell, K. E., & Lancaster, G. (2019). An exploration into the practice of online service failure and recovery strategies in the Balkans. *Journal of Business Research*, *94*, 420–431. doi:10.1016/j.jbusres.2018.08.035

Bakir, S., Khan, S., Ahsan, K., & Rahman, S. (2018). Exploring the critical determinants of environmentally oriented public procurement using the DEMATEL method. *Journal of Environmental Management*, *225*, 325–335. doi:10.1016/j.jenvman.2018.07.081 PMID:30099147

Baykasoğlu, A., & Gölcük, İ. (2017). Development of an interval type-2 fuzzy sets based hierarchical MADM model by combining DEMATEL and TOPSIS. *Expert Systems with Applications*, *70*, 37–51. doi:10.1016/j.eswa.2016.11.001

Bento, N., Gianfrate, G., & Groppo, S. V. (2019). Do crowdfunding returns reward risk? Evidences from clean-tech projects. *Technological Forecasting and Social Change*, *141*, 107–116. doi:10.1016/j.techfore.2018.07.007

Bhagawati, M. T., Manavalan, E., Jayakrishna, K., & Venkumar, P. (2019). Identifying Key Success Factors of Sustainability in Supply Chain Management for Industry 4.0 Using DEMATEL Method. In *Proceedings of International Conference on Intelligent Manufacturing and Automation* (pp. 583-591). Springer, Singapore. 10.1007/978-981-13-2490-1_54

Bochem, A., Leiding, B., & Hogrefe, D. (2018, August). Unchained Identities: Putting a Price on Sybil Nodes in Mobile Ad hoc Networks. In *International Conference on Security and Privacy in Communication Systems* (pp. 358-374). Springer, Cham, Switzerland. 10.1007/978-3-030-01701-9_20

Brunette, W. (2017, June). Building Mobile Application Frameworks for Disconnected Data Management. In *Proçeedings of the 2017 Workshop on MobiSys 2017 Ph. D. Forum* (pp. 15-16). ACM. 10.1145/3086467.3086475

Cao, Q., Duan, W., & Gan, Q. (2011). Exploring determinants of voting for the "helpfulness" of online user reviews: A text mining approach. *Decision Support Systems*, *50*(2), 511–521. doi:10.1016/j.dss.2010.11.009

Casaló, L. V., Flavián, C., & Guinalíu, M. (2008). The role of satisfaction and website usability in developing customer loyalty and positive word-of-mouth in the e-banking services. *International Journal of Bank Marketing*, *26*(6), 399–417. doi:10.1108/02652320810902433

Castillo, O., Amador-Angulo, L., Castro, J. R., & Garcia-Valdez, M. (2016). A comparative study of type-1 fuzzy logic systems, interval type-2 fuzzy logic systems and generalized type-2 fuzzy logic systems in control problems. *Information Sciences*, *354*, 257–274. doi:10.1016/j.ins.2016.03.026

Choong, C. K., Hamid, M. S. R. B. A., & Chew, B. C. (2018). Technological Disaster Prevention: Technological Risks Assessment Process on High Technological Risk Supply Chain Activities. [JAMT]. *Journal of Advanced Manufacturing Technology*, *12*(1 (1)), 285–300.

de Oliveira Santini, F., Ladeira, W. J., Sampaio, C. H., & Perin, M. G. (2018). Online banking services: A meta-analytic review and assessment of the impact of antecedents and consequents on satisfaction. *Journal of Financial Services Marketing*, *23*(3-4), 168–178. doi:10.105741264-018-0059-4

Dharmavaram, V., & Nittala, R. (2018). Service quality and customer satisfaction in online banking. [IJOM]. *International Journal of Online Marketing*, *8*(2), 45–56. doi:10.4018/IJOM.2018040103

Dinçer, H., Hacıoğlu, Ü., & Yüksel, S. (2017). Balanced scorecard based performance measurement of European airlines using a hybrid multicriteria decision making approach under the fuzzy environment. *Journal of Air Transport Management*, *63*, 17–33. doi:10.1016/j.jairtraman.2017.05.005

Dincer, H., Uzunkaya, S. S., & Yüksel, S. (2019). An IT2-Based Hybrid Decision-Making Model Using Hesitant Fuzzy Linguistic Term Sets for Selecting the Development Plan of Financial Economics. *International Journal of Computational Intelligence Systems*, *12*(2), 460–473. doi:10.2991/ijcis.d.190312.001

Dinçer, H., & Yüksel, S. (2018). Financial Sector-Based Analysis of the G20 Economies Using the Integrated Decision-Making Approach with DEMATEL and TOPSIS. In *Emerging Trends in Banking and Finance* (pp. 210–223). Cham, Switzerland: Springer. doi:10.1007/978-3-030-01784-2_13

Dinçer, H., & Yüksel, S. (2019). Multidimensional evaluation of global investments on the renewable energy with the integrated fuzzy decision-making model under the hesitancy. *International Journal of Energy Research*.

Dinçer, H., Yuksel, S., & Bozaykut-Buk, T. (2018). Evaluation of Financial and Economic Effects on Green Supply Chain Management With Multi-Criteria Decision-Making Approach: Evidence From Companies Listed in BIST. In Handbook of Research on Supply Chain Management for Sustainable Development (pp. 144–175). Hershey, PA: IGI Global. doi:10.4018/978-1-5225-5757-9.ch009

Dinçer, H., Yüksel, S., & Martínez, L. (2019). Balanced scorecard-based Analysis about European Energy Investment Policies: A hybrid hesitant fuzzy decision-making approach with Quality Function Deployment. *Expert Systems with Applications*, *115*, 152–171. doi:10.1016/j.eswa.2018.07.072

Dinçer, H., Yüksel, S., & Martínez, L. (2019). Interval type 2-based hybrid fuzzy evaluation of financial services in E7 economies with DEMATEL-ANP and MOORA methods. *Applied Soft Computing*.

Dinçer, H., Yüksel, S., & Şenel, S. (2018). Analyzing the Global Risks for the Financial Crisis after the Great Depression Using Comparative Hybrid Hesitant Fuzzy Decision-Making Models: Policy Recommendations for Sustainable Economic Growth. *Sustainability*, *10*(9), 3126. doi:10.3390u10093126

Francis, B., Hasan, I., Liu, L., & Wang, H. (2018). Employee Treatment and Contracting with Bank Lenders: An Instrumental Approach for Stakeholder Management. *Journal of Business Ethics*, 1–18.

Gera, R., Mittal, S., Batra, D. K., & Prasad, B. (2017). Evaluating the effects of service quality, customer satisfaction, and service value on behavioral intentions with life insurance customers in India. [IJSSMET]. *International Journal of Service Science, Management, Engineering, and Technology*, *8*(3), 1–20. doi:10.4018/IJSSMET.2017070101

Gholizadeh, A., Carmon, N., Klement, A., Ben-Dor, E., & Borůvka, L. (2017). Agricultural Soil Spectral Response and Properties Assessment: Effects of Measurement Protocol and Data Mining Technique. *Remote Sensing*, *9*(10), 1078. doi:10.3390/rs9101078

Gopal, J., Sangaiah, A. K., Basu, A., & Gao, X. Z. (2018). Integration of fuzzy DEMATEL and FMCDM approach for evaluating knowledge transfer effectiveness with reference to GSD project outcome. *International Journal of Machine Learning and Cybernetics*, *9*(2), 225–241. doi:10.100713042-015-0370-5

Grover, V., Chiang, R. H., Liang, T. P., & Zhang, D. (2018). Creating strategic business value from big data analytics: A research framework. *Journal of Management Information Systems*, *35*(2), 388–423. doi:10.1080/07421222.2018.1451951

Han, W., Sun, Y., Xie, H., & Che, Z. (2018). Hesitant fuzzy linguistic group DEMATEL method with multi-granular evaluation scales. *International Journal of Fuzzy Systems*, *20*(7), 2187–2201. doi:10.100740815-017-0397-8

Hargreaves, I., Roth, D., Karim, M. R., Nayebi, M., & Ruhe, G. (2018). Effective customer relationship management at atb financial: A case study on industry-academia collaboration in data analytics. In *Highlighting the Importance of Big Data Management and Analysis for Various Applications* (pp. 45–59). Cham, Switzerland: Springer. doi:10.1007/978-3-319-60255-4_4

He, W., Zha, S., & Li, L. (2013). Social media competitive analysis and text mining: A case study in the pizza industry. *International Journal of Information Management*, *33*(3), 464–472. doi:10.1016/j.ijinfomgt.2013.01.001

Hsiao, C. H., Chang, J. J., & Tang, K. Y. (2016). Exploring the influential factors in continuance usage of mobile social Apps: Satisfaction, habit, and customer value perspectives. *Telematics and Informatics*, *33*(2), 342–355. doi:10.1016/j.tele.2015.08.014

Hsieh, N. C. (2004). An integrated data mining and behavioral scoring model for analyzing bank customers. *Expert Systems with Applications*, *27*(4), 623–633. doi:10.1016/j.eswa.2004.06.007

Hsu, C. L., & Lin, J. C. C. (2015). What drives purchase intention for paid mobile apps?–An expectation confirmation model with perceived value. *Electronic Commerce Research and Applications*, *14*(1), 46–57. doi:10.1016/j.elerap.2014.11.003

Iglesias, O., Markovic, S., & Rialp, J. (2019). How does sensory brand experience influence brand equity? Considering the roles of customer satisfaction, customer affective commitment, and employee empathy. *Journal of Business Research*, *96*, 343–354. doi:10.1016/j.jbusres.2018.05.043

Jha, M. B. K., & Dubey, A. K. (2019). Analysis of Customer Satisfaction on Online Banking: A Case Study of Nalanda District of Bihar. *European Journal of Business and Social Sciences*, *7*(4), 55–63.

Jhang, J. Y., Lin, C. J., Lin, C. T., & Young, K. Y. (2018). Navigation Control of Mobile Robots Using an Interval Type-2 Fuzzy Controller Based on Dynamic-group Particle Swarm Optimization. *International Journal of Control, Automation, and Systems*, *16*(5), 2446–2457. doi:10.100712555-017-0156-5

Kasemsap, K. (2018). Multifaceted Applications of Data Mining, Business Intelligence, and Knowledge Management. In Intelligent Systems: Concepts, Methodologies, Tools, and Applications (pp. 810-825). Hershey, PA: IGI Global.

Kasiri, L. A., Cheng, K. T. G., Sambasivan, M., & Sidin, S. M. (2017). Integration of standardization and customization: Impact on service quality, customer satisfaction, and loyalty. *Journal of Retailing and Consumer Services*, *35*, 91–97. doi:10.1016/j.jretconser.2016.11.007

Kavakiotis, I., Tsave, O., Salifoglou, A., Maglaveras, N., Vlahavas, I., & Chouvarda, I. (2017). Machine learning and data mining methods in diabetes research. *Computational and Structural Biotechnology Journal*, *15*, 104–116. doi:10.1016/j.csbj.2016.12.005 PMID:28138367

Kazancoglu, Y., Kazancoglu, I., & Sagnak, M. (2018). Fuzzy DEMATEL-based green supply chain management performance: Application in cement industry. *Industrial Management & Data Systems*, *118*(2), 412–431. doi:10.1108/IMDS-03-2017-0121

Kim, S. J., Wang, R. J. H., & Malthouse, E. C. (2015). The effects of adopting and using a brand's mobile application on customers' subsequent purchase behavior. *Journal of Interactive Marketing*, *31*, 28–41. doi:10.1016/j.intmar.2015.05.004

Koçak, O., Beki, A., & Eti, S. (2018). Farklı Aktivitelerin Yaşlıların Depresyon Seviyeleri Üzerine Etkileri. *OPUS Uluslararası Toplum Araştırmaları Dergisi*, *8*(15), 25–25.

Kumar, A., Pal, A., Vohra, A., Gupta, S., Manchanda, S., & Dash, M. K. (2018). Construction of capital procurement decision making model to optimize supplier selection using Fuzzy Delphi and AHP-DEMATEL. *Benchmarking: An International Journal*, *25*(5), 1528–1547. doi:10.1108/BIJ-01-2017-0005

Lahuerta-Otero, E., & Cordero-Gutiérrez, R. (2016). Looking for the perfect tweet. The use of data mining techniques to find influencers on Twitter. *Computers in Human Behavior*, *64*, 575–583. doi:10.1016/j.chb.2016.07.035

Leech, N. L., Collins, K. M., & Onwuegbuzie, A. J. (2017). Collecting Qualitative Data to Enhance Social Network Analysis and Data Mining. Encyclopedia of Social Network Analysis and Mining, 1-11.

Li, H., Wang, J., Lam, H. K., Zhou, Q., & Du, H. (2016). Adaptive sliding mode control for interval type-2 fuzzy systems. *IEEE Transactions on Systems, Man, and Cybernetics. Systems*, *46*(12), 1654–1663. doi:10.1109/TSMC.2016.2531676

Ling, G. M., Fern, Y. S., Boon, L. K., & Huat, T. S. (2016). Understanding customer satisfaction of internet banking: A case study in Malacca. *Procedia Economics and Finance*, *37*, 80–85. doi:10.1016/S2212-5671(16)30096-X

Liu, D. R., & Shih, Y. Y. (2005). Integrating AHP and data mining for product recommendation based on customer lifetime value. *Information & Management*, *42*(3), 387–400. doi:10.1016/j.im.2004.01.008

Liu, T., Deng, Y., & Chan, F. (2018). Evidential supplier selection based on DEMATEL and game theory. *International Journal of Fuzzy Systems*, *20*(4), 1321–1333. doi:10.100740815-017-0400-4

Luthra, S., Mangla, S. K., Shankar, R., Prakash Garg, C., & Jakhar, S. (2018). Modelling critical success factors for sustainability initiatives in supply chains in Indian context using Grey-DEMATEL. *Production Planning and Control*, *29*(9), 705–728. doi:10.1080/09537287.2018.1448126

Mahatanankoon, P., Wen, H. J., & Lim, B. (2005). Consumer-based m-commerce: Exploring consumer perception of mobile applications. *Computer Standards & Interfaces*, *27*(4), 347–357. doi:10.1016/j.csi.2004.10.003

Majumder, N., Poria, S., Gelbukh, A., & Cambria, E. (2017). Deep learning-based document modeling for personality detection from text. *IEEE Intelligent Systems*, *32*(2), 74–79. doi:10.1109/MIS.2017.23

Marconi, M., Germani, M., Mandolini, M., & Favi, C. (2019). Applying data mining technique to disassembly sequence planning: A method to assess effective disassembly time of industrial products. *International Journal of Production Research*, *57*(2), 599–623. doi:10.1080/00207543.2018.1472404

McLean, G., Al-Nabhani, K., & Wilson, A. (2018). Developing a Mobile Applications Customer Experience Model (MACE)-Implications for Retailers. *Journal of Business Research*, *85*, 325–336. doi:10.1016/j.jbusres.2018.01.018

Mihelis, G., Grigoroudis, E., Siskos, Y., Politis, Y., & Malandrakis, Y. (2001). Customer satisfaction measurement in the private bank sector. *European Journal of Operational Research*, *130*(2), 347–360. doi:10.1016/S0377-2217(00)00036-9

Moro, S., Cortez, P., & Rita, P. (2018). A divide-and-conquer strategy using feature relevance and expert knowledge for enhancing a data mining approach to bank telemarketing. *Expert Systems: International Journal of Knowledge Engineering and Neural Networks*, *35*(3), e12253. doi:10.1111/exsy.12253

Mostafa, M. M. (2013). More than words: Social networks' text mining for consumer brand sentiments. *Expert Systems with Applications*, *40*(10), 4241–4251. doi:10.1016/j.eswa.2013.01.019

Munoz-Leiva, F., Climent-Climent, S., & Liébana-Cabanillas, F. (2017). Determinants of intention to use the mobile banking apps: An extension of the classic TAM model. *Spanish Journal of Marketing-ESIC, 21*(1), 25-38.

Nilsson, E. G. (2009). Design patterns for user interface for mobile applications. *Advances in Engineering Software*, *40*(12), 1318–1328. doi:10.1016/j.advengsoft.2009.01.017

Noulas, A., Salnikov, V., Hristova, D., Mascolo, C., & Lambiotte, R. (2018, October). Developing and deploying a taxi price comparison mobile app in the wild: Insights and challenges. In *2018 IEEE 5th International Conference on Data Science and Advanced Analytics (DSAA)* (pp. 424-433). IEEE.

Ong, K. S., Nguyen, B., & Syed Alwi, S. F. (2017). Consumer-based virtual brand personality (CBVBP), customer satisfaction and brand loyalty in the online banking industry. *International Journal of Bank Marketing*, *35*(3), 370–390. doi:10.1108/IJBM-04-2016-0054

Ozatac, N., Saner, T., & Sen, Z. S. (2016). Customer satisfaction in the banking sector: The case of North Cyprus. *Procedia Economics and Finance*, *39*, 870–878. doi:10.1016/S2212-5671(16)30247-7

Qin, J., Liu, X., & Pedrycz, W. (2017). An extended TODIM multi-criteria group decision making method for green supplier selection in interval type-2 fuzzy environment. *European Journal of Operational Research*, *258*(2), 626–638. doi:10.1016/j.ejor.2016.09.059

Salehan, M., & Kim, D. J. (2016). Predicting the performance of online consumer reviews: A sentiment mining approach to big data analytics. *Decision Support Systems*, *81*, 30–40. doi:10.1016/j.dss.2015.10.006

Sharma, Y. K., Mangla, S. K., Patil, P. P., & Uniyal, S. (2018). Sustainable Food Supply Chain Management Implementation Using DEMATEL Approach. In *Advances in Health and Environment Safety* (pp. 115–125). Singapore: Springer. doi:10.1007/978-981-10-7122-5_13

Shen, G. C. C. (2015). Users' adoption of mobile applications: Product type and message framing's moderating effect. *Journal of Business Research*, *68*(11), 2317–2321. doi:10.1016/j.jbusres.2015.06.018

Shilton, K., & Greene, D. (2017). Linking platforms, practices, and developer ethics: Levers for privacy discourse in mobile application development. *Journal of Business Ethics*, 1–16.

Singh, A., Shukla, N., & Mishra, N. (2018). Social media data analytics to improve supply chain management in food industries. *Transportation Research Part E, Logistics and Transportation Review*, *114*, 398–415. doi:10.1016/j.tre.2017.05.008

Singh, J. P., Irani, S., Rana, N. P., Dwivedi, Y. K., Saumya, S., & Roy, P. K. (2017). Predicting the "helpfulness" of online consumer reviews. *Journal of Business Research*, *70*, 346–355. doi:10.1016/j.jbusres.2016.08.008

Sola, H. B., Fernandez, J., Hagras, H., Herrera, F., Pagola, M., & Barrenechea, E. (2015). Interval type-2 fuzzy sets are generalization of interval-valued fuzzy sets: Toward a wider view on their relationship. *IEEE Transactions on Fuzzy Systems*, *23*(5), 1876–1882. doi:10.1109/TFUZZ.2014.2362149

Storey, V. C., & Song, I. Y. (2017). Big data technologies and management: What conceptual modeling can do. *Data & Knowledge Engineering*, *108*, 50–67. doi:10.1016/j.datak.2017.01.001

Tsai, S. B. (2018). Using the DEMATEL model to explore the job satisfaction of research and development professionals in China's photovoltaic cell industry. *Renewable & Sustainable Energy Reviews*, *81*, 62–68. doi:10.1016/j.rser.2017.07.014

Tunay, N., Yüksel, S., & Tunay, K. B. (2019). The Effects of Technology on Bank Performance in Advanced and Emerging Economies: An Empirical Analysis. In Handbook of Research on Managerial Thinking in Global Business Economics (pp. 263–280). Hershey, PA: IGI Global. doi:10.4018/978-1-5225-7180-3.ch015

Verkasalo, H., López-Nicolás, C., Molina-Castillo, F. J., & Bouwman, H. (2010). Analysis of users and non-users of smartphone applications. *Telematics and Informatics*, *27*(3), 242–255. doi:10.1016/j.tele.2009.11.001

Wang, F., Quach, T. T., Wheeler, J., Aimone, J. B., & James, C. D. (2018). Sparse Coding for N-Gram Feature Extraction and Training for File Fragment Classification. *IEEE Transactions on Information Forensics and Security*, *13*(10), 2553–2562. doi:10.1109/TIFS.2018.2823697

Wang, W. M., Li, Z., Tian, Z. G., Wang, J. W., & Cheng, M. N. (2018). Extracting and summarizing affective features and responses from online product descriptions and reviews: A Kansei text mining approach. *Engineering Applications of Artificial Intelligence*, *73*, 149–162. doi:10.1016/j.engappai.2018.05.005

Ye, Q., Zhang, Z., & Law, R. (2009). Sentiment classification of online reviews to travel destinations by supervised machine learning approaches. *Expert Systems with Applications*, *36*(3), 6527–6535. doi:10.1016/j.eswa.2008.07.035

Yoon, C. (2010). Antecedents of customer satisfaction with online banking in China: The effects of experience. *Computers in Human Behavior*, *26*(6), 1296–1304. doi:10.1016/j.chb.2010.04.001

Yüksel, S., Dinçer, H., & Emir, Ş. (2017). Comparing the performance of Turkish deposit banks by using DEMATEL, Grey Relational Analysis (GRA) and MOORA approaches. *World Journal of Applied Economics*, *3*(2), 26–47. doi:10.22440/wjae.3.2.2

Yüksel, S., Dinçer, H., & Meral, Y. (2019). Financial Analysis of International Energy Trade: A Strategic Outlook for EU-15. *Energies*, *12*(3), 431. doi:10.3390/en12030431

KEY TERMS AND DEFINITIONS

DEMATEL: The decision-making trial and evaluation laboratory. This methodology is mainly used to weight different issues.

SERVQUAL: A methodology which is used to evaluate the service quality of the companies.

Compilation of References

Abate, G. T., Rashid, S., Borzaga, C., & Getnet, K. (2016). Rural finance and agricultural technology adoption in Ethiopia: Does the institutional design of lending organizations matter? *World Development, 84*, 235–253. doi:10.1016/j.worlddev.2016.03.003

Abdel-Basset, M., Manogaran, G., Gamal, A., & Smarandache, F. (2018). A hybrid approach of neutrosophic sets and DEMATEL method for developing supplier selection criteria. *Design Automation for Embedded Systems*, 1–22.

Abdullah, L., & Zulkifli, N. (2015). Integration of fuzzy AHP and interval type-2 fuzzy DEMATEL: An application to human resource management. *Expert Systems with Applications, 42*(9), 4397–4409. doi:10.1016/j.eswa.2015.01.021

Abia, D., Ajayi, S., & Iwegbu, M. (2018, August). Technological Risk Assessment: A Panacea to Preventing Major Process Incidents-A Case Study of Amenam Kpono. In *SPE Nigeria Annual International Conference and Exhibition*. Society of Petroleum Engineers. 10.2118/193429-MS

Abrazhevich, D. (2004). *Electronic Payment Systems: A User-Centered Perspective and Interaction Design. Phd D.* Eindhoven: Eindhoven University of Technology.

Acha, I. A., Michael, E. I., & Essien, J. M. (2017). Nigeria's Investment Environment: Issues of Economic Growth and Development. *Expert Journal of Finance, 5*, 1–11.

Açıkel, E., & Çelikol, M. (2014). *Dijitoloji Dijital Çağ:Satış ve Pazarlamada Uçmanın Yolları*. İstanbul, Turkey: Mediacat Kitapları.

Ada, E., Ventura, K., Aracioglu, B., Savasci, I., & Kazancoglu, Y. (2008). KOBI'lerin Rekabet Gucu ve E-Ticarete Gecis Sureci: Bir Model Onerisi. *Ege Academic Review, 8*(1), 53–68.

Adam, B. E., & Ahmed, S. B. (2005). On the experience of Islamic agricultural finance in Sudan: Challenges and sustainability. *Islamic Econ, 18*, 63–65.

Adnan, K. M., Ying, L., Sarker, S. A., Hafeez, M., Razzaq, A., & Raza, M. H. (2018). Adoption of Contract Farming and Precautionary Savings to Manage the Catastrophic Risk of Maize Farming: Evidence from Bangladesh. *Sustainability, 11*(1), 1–19. doi:10.3390u11010029

Afra, S. (2014). *Dijital Pazarın Odak Noktası eTicaret: Dünya'da Türkiye'nin Yeri, Mevcut Durum ve Geleceğe Yönelik Adımlar*. İstanbul, Turkey: TÜSİAD.

Agrawal, A. (2017, March). *HRM Effectiveness through E-HRM*. In National Conference on "Contemporary Issues in Management & Entrepreneurship", jointly organized by The Confederation of Indian Industry.

Agrawal, R., Imieliński, T., & Swami, A. (1993). Mining association rules between sets of items in large databases. In *Proceedings of the International Conference on Management of Data, 22*(2), 207-216. 10.1145/170035.170072

Agrawal, R., & Srikant, R. (1994). Fast algorithms for mining association rules. In *Proceedings of 20th International Conference on Very Large Data Bases*, 1215, 487-499.

Ahmed, R. R., Vveinhardt, J., Štreimikienė, D., Ashraf, M., & Channar, Z. A. (2017). Modified SERVQUAL model and effects of customer attitude and technology on customer satisfaction in banking industry: Mediation, moderation and conditional process analysis. *Journal of Business Economics and Management*, *18*(5), 974–1004. doi:10.3846/16111699.2017.1368034

Ajzen, I. (1991). The theory of planned behavior. *Organizational Behavior and Human Decision Processes*, *50*, 179–211.

Akbar, S., & Paul, T. J. (2014). Consumers' attitude towards online shopping: Factors influencing employees of crazy domains to shop online. *Journal of Management and Marketing Research*, *14*(1), 1–11.

Akgöz, S. S. (2009). E-dış ticaret işlemleri. *BETA Bulletin of Experimental Treatments for AIDS.*

Aksoy, R. (2009). *İnternet ortamında pazarlama.* Ankara, Turkey: Seçkin Yayıncılık.

Akyan, C., Zalluhoğlu, A. E., & Tatlıdil, R. (2012). *Mobil Perakendecilik ve Tüketici Eğilimlerinin Analizine Yönelik Bir Pilot Çalışma. 11.Ulusal İşletmecilik Kongresi* (pp. 10–11). Konya: Selçuk Üniversitesi İ.İ.B.F.

Alcan˜iz, E. B., Andreu, L., & Gnoth, J. (2005). The theme park experience: An analysis of pleasure, arousal and satisfaction. *Tourism Management*, *26*, 833–844.

Alcan˜iz, E. B., Mafe, C. R., Manzano, J. A., & Blas, S. S. (2008). Influence of online shopping information dependency and innovativeness on internet shopping adoption. *Online Information Review*, *32*(5), 648–667.

Ali, M., & Raza, S. A. (2017). Service quality perception and customer satisfaction in Islamic banks of Pakistan: The modified SERVQUAL model. *Total Quality Management & Business Excellence*, *28*(5-6), 559–577. doi:10.1080/14783363.2015.1100517

Allahverdi, M. (2006). *Elektronik İnsan Kaynakları Yönetimi ve Türkiye'deki Uygulamalarına Yönelik Bir Araştırma.* Konya: Selçuk Üniversitesi Sosyal Bilimler Enstitüsü Yüksek Lisans Tezi.

Allen, C. T., Machleit, K. A., Kleine, S. S., & Notani, A. S. (2005). A place for emotion in attitude models. *Journal of Business Research*, *58*, 494–499.

Alnawas, I., & Aburub, F. (2016). The effect of benefits generated from interacting with branded mobile apps on consumer satisfaction and purchase intentions. *Journal of Retailing and Consumer Services*, *31*, 313–322. doi:10.1016/j.jretconser.2016.04.004

Al-Otaibi, S., Aljohani, N. R., Hoque, M. R., & Alotaibi, F. S. (2018). The satisfaction of Saudi customers toward mobile banking in Saudi Arabia and the United Kingdom. [JGIM]. *Journal of Global Information Management*, *26*(1), 85–103. doi:10.4018/JGIM.2018010105

Alstyne, M. V. (2014). Why Bitcoin Has Value, Association for Computing Machinery, 57(5), 30-32.

Altaf, M., Iqbal, N., Mohd. Mokhtar, S. S., & Sial, M. H. (2017). Managing consumer-based brand equity through brand experience in Islamic banking. *Journal of Islamic Marketing*, *8*(2), 218–242. doi:10.1108/JIMA-07-2015-0048

Amara, N. B., & Atia, L. (2016). E-training and its role in human resources development. *Global Journal of Human Resource Management*, *4*(1), 1–12.

Amin, M. (2016). Internet banking service quality and its implication on e-customer satisfaction and e-customer loyalty. *International Journal of Bank Marketing*, *34*(3), 280–306. doi:10.1108/IJBM-10-2014-0139

Amit, R., & Zott, C. 2001. Value Creation in E-Business. *Strategic Management Journal* *22*(6-7), 493-520.

Amit, R., & Zott, C. (2001). Value creation in e-business. *Strategic Management Journal*, *22*(6-7), 493–520. doi:10.1002mj.187

Ammirato, S., Sofo, F., Felicetti, A. M., & Raso, C. (2019). A methodology to support the adoption of IoT innovation and its application to the Italian bank branch security context. *European Journal of Innovation Management*, *22*(1), 146–174. doi:10.1108/EJIM-03-2018-0058

Angel, J., & McCabe, D. M. (2014). The Ethics of Payments: Paper, Plastic, or Bitcoin*? SSRN Electronic Journal*, *132*(3). Retrieved From https://econpapers.repec.org/article/kapjbuset/v_3a132_ 3ay_3a2015_3ai_3a3_3ap_3a603-611.htm

Antón, J., & Cattaneo, A. (2019). Agricultural Risk Management and Climate Change: What Role for Policy? *Global Challenges For Future Food And Agricultural Policies*, *1*, 281–306. doi:10.1142/9789813235403_0015

Anvari, R. D., & Norouzi, D. (2016). The Impact of E-commerce and R&D on Economic Development in Some Selected Countries. *Procedia: Social and Behavioral Sciences*, *229*, 354–362. doi:10.1016/j.sbspro.2016.07.146

Aparicio, M., Bacao, F., & Oliveira, T. (2016). An e-learning theoretical framework. *Journal of Educational Technology & Society*, *19*(1), 292–307.

Applegate, L. M. (2001). E-business Models: Making sense of the Internet business landscape. *Information technology and the future enterprise: New models for managers*, 49-94.

Araújo, S., & Ramos, A. (2002). *Recrutamento On-line: Estudo da Percepção de Utilização da Internet em Empresa de Consultoria de Recursos Humanos* [Online recruitment: Study of the perception of Internet use in a human resources consulting firm]. Curitibia, Brasil: ENEGEP.

Arbore, A., & Busacca, B. (2009). Customer satisfaction and dissatisfaction in retail banking: Exploring the asymmetric impact of attribute performances. *Journal of Retailing and Consumer Services*, *16*(4), 271–280. doi:10.1016/j.jretconser.2009.02.002

Ariff, M. S. M., Yun, L. O., Zakuan, N., & Ismail, K. (2013). The impacts of service quality and customer satisfaction on customer loyalty in internet banking. *Procedia: Social and Behavioral Sciences*, *81*, 469–473. doi:10.1016/j.sbspro.2013.06.462

Arıkan, A. S. (1999). *Dünyada ve Türkiye'de Elektronik Ticaret Çalışmalarına Hukuki Bir Yaklaşım*. Ankara, Turkey: Yetkin Yayınları.

Armstrong, M. (2011). Armstrong's handbook of strategic human resource management. London, UK: Kogan Page Publishers.

Arpacı, T., & Uluçay, U. (2012). Dünyada ve Türkiye'de E-Ticaret: Tüketicilerin İnternet Üzerinden Alışveriş Alışkanlıkları Üzerine Bir Uygulama.

Asan, U., Kadaifci, C., Bozdag, E., Soyer, A., & Serdarasan, S. (2018). A new approach to DEMATEL based on interval-valued hesitant fuzzy sets. *Applied Soft Computing*, *66*, 34–49. doi:10.1016/j.asoc.2018.01.018

Ashtarinezhad, E., Sarfaraz, A. H., & Navabakhsh, M. (2018). Supplier evaluation and categorize with combine Fuzzy Dematel and Fuzzy Inference System. *Data in Brief*, *18*, 1149–1156. doi:10.1016/j.dib.2018.03.077 PMID:29900289

Asokan, N., Janson, P., Steiner, M., & Waidner, M. (1997). The State of The Art in Electronic Payment Systems. *Computer*, *30*(9), 28–35. doi:10.1109/2.612244

Atay, Ş. (2006). *Kariyer Yönetiminin Örgütsel Bağlılığa Etkisi.* Afyon Kocatepe Üniversitesi, Sosyal Bilimler Enstitüsü, Yüksek Lisans Tezi, Afyon.

Ayanso, A., & Yoogalingam, R. (2009). Profiling retail web site functionalities and conversion rates: A cluster analysis. *International Journal of Electronic Commerce*, *14*(1), 79–114. doi:10.2753/JEC1086-4415140103

Ay, C., Yakın, V., & Kacar, A. İ. (2018). *Paylaşım Ekonomisi, A'dan Z'ye Tüm Boyutlarıyla* (pp. 41–42). Ankara, Turkey: Akademisyen Kitabevi.

Aydın, K. (2016). *Elektronik İnsan Kaynakları Yönetimi Uygulamaları ve İnovasyon Performansı.* İstanbul, Turkey: Bahçeşehir Üniversitesi, Sosyal Bilimler Enstitüsü, Yüksek Lisans Tezi.

Azemi, Y., Ozuem, W., Howell, K. E., & Lancaster, G. (2019). An exploration into the practice of online service failure and recovery strategies in the Balkans. *Journal of Business Research*, *94*, 420–431. doi:10.1016/j.jbusres.2018.08.035

Babin, B. J., Lee, Y. K., Kim, E. J., & Griffin, M. (2005). Modeling consumer satisfaction and word-of-mouth: Restaurant patronage in Korea. *Journal of Services Marketing*, *19*, 133–139.

Bagozzi, R. P., Mahesh, G., & Prashanth, U. N. (1999). The Role of Emotions in Marketing. *Journal of the Academy of Marketing Science*, *27*(2), 184–206.

Bakir, S., Khan, S., Ahsan, K., & Rahman, S. (2018). Exploring the critical determinants of environmentally oriented public procurement using the DEMATEL method. *Journal of Environmental Management*, *225*, 325–335. doi:10.1016/j.jenvman.2018.07.081 PMID:30099147

Baldwin, L. P., & Currie, W. L. (2000). Key issues in electronic commerce in today's global information infrastructure. *Cognition Technology and Work*, *2*(1), 27–34.

Bamakhramah, A. S. (2005). Book Review: On the Experience of Islamic Agricultural Finance in Sudan: Challenges and Sustainability. *Journal of King Abdulaziz University: Islamic Economics*, *18*(2).

Bandyopadhyay, S. (2009). A dynamic model of cross-category competition: Theory, tests and applications. *Journal of Retailing*, *85*(4), 468–479. doi:10.1016/j.jretai.2009.05.001

Bansal, S., Bruno, P., Denecker, O., Goparaju, M., & Niederkorn, M. (2018). *Global Payments 2018: A Dynamic Industry Continues to Break New Ground.* McKinsey&Company. Retrieved From https://www.mckinsey.com/~/media/McKinsey/Industries/Financial%20Services/Our%20Insights/Global%20payments%20Expansive%20growth%20targeted%20opportunities/Global-payments-map-2018. ashx.

Barani, N., Menhaj, M. H., Ramezanpoor, E., & Borazjani, M. A. (2015). Investigating the Impacts of Credits Granted by Agricultural Bank of Iran on Economic Conditions of Farmers in Hirmand Region. *International Journal of Agricultural Management and Development (IJAMAD)*, *5*(1047-2017-1604).

Barber, L. (2006). *E-recruitment Developments.* Brighton, MA: Institute for Employment Studies.

Barca, M. (2002). *Stratejik Yönetim Yaklaşımları: Rekabet Avantajı Yaratmada Sinerjik Etki, Stratejik Boyutlarıyla Modern Yönetim Yaklaşımları.* İstanbul, Turkey: Beta Yayınevi.

Barlow, A., & Birkhahn, T. (2005). Traditional Marketing Not Ready for the Junk Heap Just Yet. *PR News*, *61*(43), 1.

Barney, J. B., & Wright, P. M. (1998). On Becoming A Strategic Partner: The Role Of Human Resources İn Gaining Competitive Advantage. Human Resource Management: Published in Cooperation with the School of Business Administration, *The University of Michigan and in alliance with the Society of Human Resources Management,* 37(*1*), pp. 31-46.

Barua, A., Konana, P., Whinston, A. B., & Yin, F. (2004). An empirical investigation of net-enabled business value. *Management Information Systems Quarterly*, *28*(4), 585–620. doi:10.2307/25148656

Basfirinci, C., & Mitra, A. (2015). A cross cultural investigation of airlines service quality through integration of Servqual and the Kano model. *Journal of Air Transport Management*, *42*, 239–248. doi:10.1016/j.jairtraman.2014.11.005

Basu, A., & Muylle, S. (2003). Online support for commerce processes by web retailers. *Decision Support Systems*, *34*(4), 379–395. doi:10.1016/S0167-9236(02)00065-9

Batra, R., & Ray, M. L. (1986). Affective responses mediating acceptance of advertising. *The Journal of Consumer Research*, *13*, 234–249.

Baykasoğlu, A., & Gölcük, İ. (2017). Development of an interval type-2 fuzzy sets based hierarchical MADM model by combining DEMATEL and TOPSIS. *Expert Systems with Applications*, *70*, 37–51. doi:10.1016/j.eswa.2016.11.001

Becker, A. (Ed.). (2007). Electronic Commerce: Concepts, Methodologies, Tools, and Applications: Concepts, Methodologies, Tools, and Applications. Hershey, PA: IGI Global.

Becker, M., & Arnold, J. (2010). *Mobile Marketing For Dummies*. Hoboken, NJ: Wiley.

Beheshtinia, M. A., & Farzaneh Azad, M. (2017). A fuzzy QFD approach using SERVQUAL and Kano models under budget constraint for hotel services. *Total Quality Management & Business Excellence*, 1–23.

Bell, B. S., Lee, S. W., & Yeung, S. K. (2006). The impact of e-HR on professional competence in HRM: Implications for the development of HR professionals. Human Resource Management: Published in Cooperation with the School of Business Administration, *The University of Michigan and in alliance with the Society of Human Resources Management*, *45*(3), 295-308.

Bellman, S. (2007). Theory and measurement of type 1 & type 2 emotions. *Australasian Marketing Journal*, *15*(1), 14–22.

Bendakir, N., & Aïmeur, E. (2006). Using association rules for course recommendation. In *Proceedings of the AAAI Workshop on Educational Data Mining*, 3, 1-10.

Benjamin, R. I., & Levinson, E. (1993). A framework for managing IT-enabled change. *Sloan Management Review*, *34*(4), 23–33.

Bento, N., Gianfrate, G., & Groppo, S. V. (2019). Do crowdfunding returns reward risk? Evidences from clean-tech projects. *Technological Forecasting and Social Change*, *141*, 107–116. doi:10.1016/j.techfore.2018.07.007

Berber, L. K. (2002). *İnternet üzerinden yapılan işlemlerde elektronik para ve dijital imza*. Yetkin Yayınları.

Berber, N., Đorđević, B., & Milanović, S. (2018). Electronic human resource management (e-HRM): A new concept for digital age. *Strategic Management*, *23*(2), 22–32.

Berger, P. D., & Nasr, N. I. (1998). Customer lifetime value: Marketing models and applications. *Journal of Interactive Marketing*, *12*(1), 17–30. doi:10.1002/(SICI)1520-6653(199824)12:1<17::AID-DIR3>3.0.CO;2-K

Bernstein, J. H. (2009). The Data-Information-Knowledge-Wisdom Hierarchy and its Antithesis. In *Proceedings of the North American Symposium on Knowledge and Organization*, 2, 68-75.

Bezhovski, Z. (2016). The Future of The Mobile Payment as Electronic Payment System. *European Journal of Business and Management*, *8*(8), 127–133.

Bhagawati, M. T., Manavalan, E., Jayakrishna, K., & Venkumar, P. (2019). Identifying Key Success Factors of Sustainability in Supply Chain Management for Industry 4.0 Using DEMATEL Method. In *Proceedings of International Conference on Intelligent Manufacturing and Automation* (pp. 583-591). Springer, Singapore. 10.1007/978-981-13-2490-1_54

Bhasin, H. (2019). *Marketing91.* Marketing Management. Promotional mix – What are the different types of promotions? Retrieved from https://www.marketing91.com/promotional-mix/adresinden alındı

Bhatnagar, J., & Sharma, A. (2005). The Indian perspective of strategic HR roles and organizational learning capability. *International Journal of Human Resource Management, 16*(9), 1711–1739.

Bhattacherjee, A. (2001). An empirical analysis of the antecedents of electronic commerce service continuance. *Decision Support Systems, 32*(2), 201–214. doi:10.1016/S0167-9236(01)00111-7

Bissola, R., & Imperatori, B. (2013). Facing e-HRM: E consequences on employee attitude towards the organisation and the HR department in Italian SMEs. *European Journal of International Management, 7*(4), 450–468.

BKM. (2017). *Cashless Turkey by 2023.* Retrieved From https://www.burnmark.com/ uploads/reports/Burnmark_Report_BKM_Turkey1.pdf

Blackwell, R. D., Miniard, P. W., & Engel, J. F. (2001). Consumer Behavior. Fourth Worth. San Diego, CA: Harcourt College Publishers.

Blattberg, R. C., & Deighton, J. (1996). Manage marketing by the customer equity test. *Harvard Business Review, 74*(4), 136–144. PMID:10158473

Blossom, D. (2001). *Theoretical, methodological and analytical methods for exploring emotional episodes: Applications to consumption emotions and emotional satisfaction* (Unpublished doctoral dissertation). The Arizona University.

Bochem, A., Leiding, B., & Hogrefe, D. (2018, August). Unchained Identities: Putting a Price on Sybil Nodes in Mobile Ad hoc Networks. In *International Conference on Security and Privacy in Communication Systems* (pp. 358-374). Springer, Cham, Switzerland. 10.1007/978-3-030-01701-9_20

Boersma, M. F., & Ghauri, P. N. (1997). A qualitative meta analysis of performance measures and factors affecting international joint venture performance. *Proceedings of the 24th Annual Conference at the UK Academy of International Business* (pp. 119–142). Leeds, UK: CIBUL, April.

Bogdanovych, A., Berger, H., Simoff, S., & Sierra, C. (2006). Travel agents vs. online booking: Tackling the shortcomings of nowadays online tourism portals. *Information and communication technologies in tourism 2006*, 418-428.

Bolumole, Y. A. (2003). Evaluating the supply chain role of logistics service providers. *International Journal of Logistics Management, 14*(2), 93–107. doi:10.1108/09574090310806620

Bondarouk, T., Ruël, H., & Kees Looise, J. (Eds.). (2011). Electronic HRM in theory and practice. Bingley, UK: Emerald Group Publishing Limited. doi:10.1108/S1877-6361(2011)8

Bondarouk, T. V., & Ruel, H. J. M. (2009). Electronic Human Resource Management: Challenges in the digital era. *International Journal of Human Resource Management, 20*(3), 505–514. doi:10.1080/09585190802707235

Bonti, M., & Cori, E. (2004). The Communication of Company Values and Internetland empirical evidence. In Information, Knowledge and Management: Re-assessing the Role of ICTs in Public and Private Organization.

Bozkurt, V. (2000). Elektronik Ticaret, stanbul: Alfa Basım Yayım Dağıtım Ltd.

Bozkurt, D. (2015). *Elektronik Perakendecilikte Pazarlama Uygulamalari Üzerine Bir Araştirma*. İzmir, Turkey: Dokuz Eylül Üüniversitesi Sosyal Bilimler Enstitüsü İşletme Anabilim Dalı Pazarlama Programı Yayınlanmamış Yüksek Lisans Tezi.

Bozkurt, V. (1997). *Enformasyon Toplumu ve Türkiye*. İstanbul, Turkey: Sistem Yayıncılık.

Brandão, C., Silva, R., & dos Santos, J. V. (2019). Online recruitment in Portugal: Theories and candidate profiles. *Journal of Business Research*, *94*, 273–279.

Bratawisnu, M. K., Giri, R. R. W., & Rinaldi, R. (2017, May). Association perception customer feedback with text network analysis in social media (case study on internet banking BRI, BCA, Mandiri in Indonesia). In *2017 5th International Conference on Information and Communication Technology (ICoIC7)* (pp. 1-6). IEEE.

Brinker, S. (2017). *Pazarlamayı Hacklemek*. İstanbul, Turkey: Mediacat Kitapları.

Brunette, W. (2017, June). Building Mobile Application Frameworks for Disconnected Data Management. In *Proceedings of the 2017 Workshop on MobiSys 2017 Ph. D. Forum* (pp. 15-16). ACM. 10.1145/3086467.3086475

Brunn, P., Jensen, M., & Skovgaard, J. (2002). e-Marketplaces: Crafting A Winning Strategy. *European Management Journal*, *20*(3), 286–298. doi:10.1016/S0263-2373(02)00045-2

Brynjolfsson, E., & Hitt, L. M. (2003). Computing productivity: Firm-level evidence. *The Review of Economics and Statistics*, *85*(4), 793–808.

Budak, B. (2010). *E-Ticaret İnternet Ortamında Ticaret*. İstanbul, Turkey: Etap Yayınevi.

Buhalis, D., & Laws, E. (2008). Progress in information technology and tourism management: 20 years on and 10 years after the Internet - The state of eTourism research. *Tourism Management*, *29*(4), 609–623. doi:10.1016/j.tourman.2008.01.005

Burke, R. (2000). Knowledge-based recommender systems. Encyclopedia of library and information systems, 69(32), 175-186.

Burt, S., & Sparks, L. (2003). E-commerce and the retail process: A review. *Journal of Retailing and Consumer Services*, *10*(5), 275–286. doi:10.1016/S0969-6989(02)00062-0

Butler, P., & Peppard, J. (1998). Consumer purchasing on the internet: Processes and prospects. *European Management Journal*, *16*(5), 600–610.

Byrne, J. E. (2012). The Four Stages in the Electrification of Letters of Credit. Geo. *Masan J. Int'l Com. L.*, *3*, 253-275.

Cabanillas, F. L., & Rubio, J. L. (2017). Predictive and Explanatory Modelling Regarding Adoption of Mobile Patment Systems. *Technological Forecasting and Social Change*, *120*, 32–40. doi:10.1016/j.techfore.2017.04.002

Cacioppo, J. T., & Gardner, W. L. (1999). Emotion. *Annual Review of Psychology*, *50*, 191–214. PMID:10074678

Cagliano, R., Caniato, F., & Spina, G. (2003). E-business strategy: How companies are shaping their supply chain through the Internet. *International Journal of Operations & Production Management*, *23*(10), 1142–1162. doi:10.1108/01443570310496607

Çakırer, M. A. (2013). *Elektronik Ticaret*. Bursa: Ekin Yayınları.

Çakırer, M. A. (2013). *Elektronik ticaret*. Ekin Basım Yayın Dağıtım.

Caldwell, R. (2003). The changing roles of personnel managers: Old ambiguities, new uncertainties. *Journal of Management Studies*, *40*(4), 983–1004. doi:10.1111/1467-6486.00367

CallCenterLife. (2018, March). *BiTaksi & Getir Kurucusu Nazım Salur*. Retrieved from http://www.callcenterlife.com.tr/bitaksi-getir-kurucusu-nazim-salur/

Canbolat, Z. N., & Pınarbaşı, F. (2018). Mobil Uygulamalara Yönelik Olumsuz Kullanıcı Değerlendirmelerinin İncelenmesi: İçerik Analizi ve Metin Madenciliği Yöntemleriyle Bir Uygulama. V. Yıldız Sosyal Bilimler Kongresi, 102.

Canpolat, Ö. (2001). *E-Ticaret ve Türkiye'deki gelişmeler*. Ankara, Turkey: Sanayi ve Ticaret Bakanlığı Hukuk Müşavirliği.

Canpolat, Ö. (2001). *E-ticaret ve Türkiye'deki gelişmeler*. Sanayi ve Ticaret Bakanlığı.

Cao, Q., Duan, W., & Gan, Q. (2011). Exploring determinants of voting for the "helpfulness" of online user reviews: A text mining approach. *Decision Support Systems*, *50*(2), 511–521. doi:10.1016/j.dss.2010.11.009

Cao, Y., Gruca, T. S., & Klemz, B. R. (2003). Internet pricing, price satisfaction, and customer satisfaction. *International Journal of Electronic Commerce*, *8*(2), 31–50. doi:10.1080/10864415.2003.11044291

Cappelli, P. (2001). Making the most of on-line recruiting. *Harvard Business Review*, *79*(3), 139–148. PMID:11246921

Card, J. A., Chen, C. Y., & Cole, S. T. (2003). Online travel products shopping: Differences between shoppers and non-shoppers. *Journal of Travel Research*, *42*(2), 133–139. doi:10.1177/0047287503257490

Casadesus-Masanell, R., & Ricart, J. E. (2011). How to design a winning business model. *Harvard Business Review, 89(*1/2), 100-107. Retrieved from https://hbr.org/2011/01/how-to-design-a-winning-business-model

Casaló, L. V., Flavián, C., & Guinalíu, M. (2008). The role of satisfaction and website usability in developing customer loyalty and positive word-of-mouth in the e-banking services. *International Journal of Bank Marketing*, *26*(6), 399–417. doi:10.1108/02652320810902433

Castillo, O., Amador-Angulo, L., Castro, J. R., & Garcia-Valdez, M. (2016). A comparative study of type-1 fuzzy logic systems, interval type-2 fuzzy logic systems and generalized type-2 fuzzy logic systems in control problems. *Information Sciences*, *354*, 257–274. doi:10.1016/j.ins.2016.03.026

Celep, M. (2017). *Elektronik İnsan Kaynakları Uygulamalarının Örgütsel Çıktılar Üzerindeki Etkileri: Türkiye'de Yabancı İştirakli Sigorta Şirketlerinde Bir Araştırma*. İstanbul, Turkey: Bahçeşehir Üniversitesi Sosyal Bilimler Enstitüsü Yüksek Lisans Tezi.

Celep, M., & Fındıklı, M. A. (2018). Elektronik İnsan Kaynakları Uygulamalarının Örgütsel Çıktılar Üzerindeki Etkileri: Türkiye'de Yabancı İştirakli Sigorta Şirketlerinde Bir Araştırma. *Bilgi Ekonomisi ve Yönetimi Dergisi*, *13*(1), 63–77.

Cengiz, E., & Şekerkaya, A. (2010). Internet kullanicilarinin internetten alişverişe yönelik satin alma karar süreçlerinin incelenmesi ve kullanim yoğunluklari açisindan siniflandirilmasi üzerine bir araştirma. *Öneri Dergisi*, *9* (33), 33-49.

Çetinkaya, Ş. (2016). E-ticaret uygulamalarının makro ekonomik göstergelere etkisi SWOT Analizi ve Türkiye'de e-ticaret gelişimi için bir eylem planı önerisi. *Yalova Üniversitesi Sosyal Bilimler Dergisi*, *6*(11), 235–256.

Chaffey, D. (2007). E-business and e-commerce management: Strategy, implementation and practice. London, UK: Financial Times.

Chaffey, D., & Ellis-Chadwick, F. (2019). Digital marketing. London, UK: Pearson.

Chaffey, D., & Smith, P. R. (2013). Emarketing Excellence: Planning and Optimizing Your Digital Marketing. New York, NY: Routledge.

Chaffey, D., Chadwick, F. E., Johnston, K., & Mayer, R. (2000). Internet Marketing: Strategy, Implementation and Practice. London, UK: Pearson Education Limited.

Chan, E., & Swatman, P. M. (1999, November). Electronic commerce: a component model. In *Proceedings of the 3rd Annual CollECTeR Conference on Electronic Commerce* (p. 1999).

Chang, K. C., Jackson, J., & Grover, V. (2003). E-commerce and corporate strategy: An executive perspective. *Information & Management, 40*(7), 663–675. doi:10.1016/S0378-7206(02)00095-2

Charlesworth, A. (2014). Digital marketing: A practical approach. New York, NY: Routledge. doi:10.4324/9780203493717

Chatterjee, D., Grewal, R., & Sambamurthy, V. (2002). Shaping up for e-commerce: Institutional enablers of the organizational assimilation of web technologies. *Management Information Systems Quarterly, 26*(2), 65–89. doi:10.2307/4132321

Chen, D., Sain, S. L., & Guo, K. (2012). Data mining for the online retail industry: A case study of RFM model-based customer segmentation using data mining. *Journal of Database Marketing & Customer Strategy Management, 19*(3), 197–208. doi:10.1057/dbm.2012.17

Chen, H. M., & Tseng, C. H. (2005). The performance of marketing alliances between the tourism industry and credit card issuing banks in Taiwan. *Tourism Management, 26*(1), 15–24.

Chen, H., Chiang, R. H., & Storey, V. C. (2012). Business intelligence and analytics: From big data to big impact. *Management Information Systems Quarterly, 36*(4), 1165–1188. doi:10.2307/41703503

Chen, H., Chung, W., Xu, J. J., Wang, G., Qin, Y., & Chau, M. (2004). Crime data mining: A general framework and some examples. *Computer, 37*(4), 50–56. doi:10.1109/MC.2004.1297301

Chen, H., & Tseng, H. (2012). Factors That Influence Acceptance of Web-Based E-Learning System for the in-Service Education of Junior High School Teachers in Taiwan. *Evaluation and Program Planning, 35*(3), 398–406. PMID:22321703

Chen, S. (2001). *Strategic management of e-business*. New York, NY: John Wiley and Sons.

Chesbrough, H., & Rosenbloom, R. S. (2002). The role of the business model in capturing value from innovation: Evidence from Xerox Corporation's technology spin-off companies. *Industrial and Corporate Change, 11*(3), 529–555. doi:10.1093/icc/11.3.529

Chevalier, J. A., & Mayzlin, D. (2006). The Effect of Word of Mouth on Sales: Online Book Reviews. *JMR, Journal of Marketing Research, 43*(3), 345–354. doi:10.1509/jmkr.43.3.345

Chisasa, J., & Makina, D. (2013). Bank credit and agricultural output in South Africa: A Cobb-Douglas empirical analysis. *The International Business & Economics Research Journal (Online), 12*(4), 387–398.

Chong, A. Y. L., Li, B., Ngai, E. W., Ch'ng, E., & Lee, F. (2016). Predicting online product sales via online reviews, sentiments, and promotion strategies: A big data architecture and neural network approach. *International Journal of Operations & Production Management, 36*(4), 358–383. doi:10.1108/IJOPM-03-2015-0151

Choong, C. K., Hamid, M. S. R. B. A., & Chew, B. C. (2018). Technological Disaster Prevention: Technological Risks Assessment Process on High Technological Risk Supply Chain Activities. [JAMT]. *Journal of Advanced Manufacturing Technology, 12*(1 (1)), 285–300.

Christy, C., Chan, M. K., Gloria, W. W., & Limayem, M. (2005). A critical review of online consumer behavior: Empirical research. *Journal of Electronic Commerce in Organizations, 3*(4), 1–19.

Chung, T. W. (2016). A Study on Logistics Cluster Competitiveness among Asia Main Countries using the Porter's Diamond Model. *The Asian Journal of Shipping and Logistics, 32*(4), 257–264. doi:10.1016/j.ajsl.2016.12.010

Chung, T., & Law, R. (2003). Developing a performance indicator of hotel websites. *International Journal of Hospitality Management, 22*(1), 119–125. doi:10.1016/S0278-4319(02)00076-2

Chunling, W. (2015). Research on economic growth and information exchange based on b2b e-commerce. *The Open Cybernetics & Systemics Journal*, *9*(1), 2065–2069. doi:10.2174/1874110X01509012065

Churilov, A. (2015). *Practical Aspects of Bitcoin Usage in Business,* Retrieved From https://ssrn.com/ abstract=2685646 or doi:10.2139srn.2685646

Çil, İ. (2012). Consumption universes based supermarket layout through association rule mining and multidimensional scaling. *Expert Systems with Applications*, *39*(10), 8611–8625. doi:10.1016/j.eswa.2012.01.192

Civelek, M. E., Çemberci, M., Uca, N., Çelebi, Ü., & Özalp, A. (2017). Challenges of Paperless Trade Redesign of the Foreign Trade Processes and Bundling Functions of Traditional Documents. *International Business Research*, *10*(2), 74. doi:10.5539/ibr.v10n2p74

Clarke, R. (1999). Electronic commerce definitions. Retrieved from http://www.anu.edu.au/people/Roger.Clarke/EC/ECDefns.html

Clemons, E. K., Hitt, L. M., & Hann, I.-H. (2002). Price dispersion and differentiation in online travel: An empirical investigation. *Management Science*, *48*(4), 534–549. doi:10.1287/mnsc.48.4.534

Clemons, E., Hann, I.-H., & Hitt, L. (1998). *The Nature of Competition in Electronic Markets: An Empirical Investigation of Online Travel Agent Offerings.* The Wharton School of the University of Pennsylvania.

Cliquet, G., Hendrikse, G., Tuunanen, M., & Windsperger, J. (Eds.). (2007). Economics and management of networks: Franchising, strategic alliances, and cooperatives. Berlin, Germany: Springer Science & Business Media. doi:10.1007/978-3-7908-1758-4

Cohen, J. B., & Charles, S. A. (1991). Affect and Consumer Behavior, In Thomas S. Robertson, & Harold H. Kassarjian (Eds.), Handbook of Consumer Behavior. Englewood Cliffs, NJ: Prentice Hall.

Coingape. (2018). *Jap based Yamada Denki Now Accepts Bitcoin Payments.* Retrieved From fhttps://coingape.com/japan-based-yamada-denki-now-accepts-bitcoin-payments/

Çokluk, Ö., Yılmaz, K., & Oğuz, E. (2011). Nitel Bir Görüşme Yöntemi: Odak Grup Görüşmesi. *Kuramsal Eğitimbilim*, 95-107.

Collyer, G., (2007), The guide to documentary credits, published by IFS School of Finance.

Coltman, T. R., Devinney, T. M., & Midgley, D. F. (2007). e-Business strategy and firm performance: A latent class assessment of the drivers and impediments to success. *Journal of Information Technology*, *22*(2), 87–101.

Coltman, T., Devinney, T. M., Latukefu, A., & Midgley, D. F. (2001). E-business: Revolution, evolution, or hype? *California Management Review*, *44*(1), 57–86.

Commission of the European Communities. (1997). *A European initiative in electronic commerce.* Brussels, Belgium.

Consuegra, R. A. A., & Garcia, M. A. Z. (2013). *A Study of Electronic Payments in B2C Ecommerce, Master of Science in Management Engineering.* Milano: Politecnico.

Conway, E. (2009). *Gerçekten bilmeniz gereken 50 ekonomi fikri.* İstanbul, Turkey: Domingo Yayınevi.

Cook, J., Oviatt, K., Main, D. S., Kaur, H., & Brett, J. (2015). Re-conceptualizing urban agriculture: An exploration of farming along the banks of the Yamuna River in Delhi, India. *Agriculture and Human Values*, *32*(2), 265–279. doi:10.100710460-014-9545-z

Cook, M. F. (1999). *Outsourcing Human Resources Functions: Strategies For Providing Enhanced HR Services At Lower Cost*. New York, NY: American Management Association.

Corbitt, B. J., Thanasankit, T., & Yi, H. (2003). Trust and e-commerce: A study of consumer perceptions. *Electronic Commerce Research and Applications*, *2*(3), 203–215.

Coşkun, A. G. D. N. (2004). Elektronik ticaretin gelişiminde temel dinamikler ve gelişimi önünde engeller, Çukurova Üniversitesi Sosyal Bilimler Enstitüsü Dergisi, *13*(2), 243-258

Coşkun, A. G. D. N. (2004). Elektronik ticaretin gelişiminde temel dinamikler ve gelişimi önündeki engeller. Çukurova Üniversitesi Sosyal Bilimler Enstitüsü Dergisi, 13(2).

Coşkun, N. (2004). Elektronik ticaretin gelişiminde temel dinamikler ve gelişimi önündeki engeller. Çukurova Üniversitesi Sosyal Bilimler Enstitüsü Dergisi, 13(2).

Cowden, A. (2014). *Effect of Social Media Marketing on Traditional Marketing Campaigns in Young Icelandic Companies*. (Master thesis, Reykjavic University, Iceland).

Criteo. (2015). *Criteo E-Commerce Industry Outlook 2015*, Retrieved From http://mobint.com.br/Downloads/criteo-ecommerce-industry-outlook-2015.pdf

Crosby, L. A., Evans, K. R., & Cowles, D. (1990). Relationship quality in services selling: An interpersonal influence perspective. *Journal of Marketing*, *54*, 68–81.

Çubukcu, A., & Bayzan, Ş. (2013). Türkiye'de dijital vatandaşlık algısı ve bu algıyı internetin bilinçli, güvenli ve etkin kullanımı ile artırma yöntemleri. *Middle Eastern & African Journal of Educational Research*, *5*, 148–174.

Da Costa, E. (2003). *Global e-commerce strategies for small businesses*. Cambridge, MA: MIT Press.

Dahle, N. M. (1999). *Closing in on the web consumer*. Amsterdam, The Netherlands: Elsevier.

Dal, V. & Özbek, A. (2006). Avrupa Birliği ve Türk hazır giyim sanayiindeki e-ticaret uygulamalarının karşılaştırılmalı olarak incelenmesi. Elektronik Sosyal Bilimler Dergisi, *5*(18).

Dale, C. (2003). The competitive networks of tourism e-mediaries: New strategies, new advantages. *Journal of Vacation Marketing*, *9*(2), 109–118.

Daly, A., & Gebremedhin, T. A. (2015). Can An "Indigenous Employment Program" Work? A Case Study of National Australia Bank. *Economic Papers: A journal of applied economics and policy, 34*(3), 128-138.

Damanpour, F., & Damanpour, J. A. (2001). E-business e-commerce evolution: Perspective and strategy. *Managerial Finance*, *27*(7), 16–33.

Dapplife. (2019). *Switzerland's E-Commerce Giant Digitec Galaxus Accepts Bitcoin Payments*. Retrieved From https://dapplife.com/switzerlands-ecommerce-giant-digitec-galaxus-accepts-bitcoin-payments/

Daud, K. İ. (2010). *İnsan Kaynakları Yönetim Süreçlerinde Bilgi Teknolojilerinin Kullanımı ve E-İK Uygulamaları*. İstanbul, Turkey: İstanbul Teknik Üniversitesi, Fen Bilimleri Enstitüsü, Yüksek Lisans Tezi.

Davis, F. (1989). Perceived Usefulness, Perceived Ease of Use, and User Acceptance of Information Technology. *Management Information Systems Quarterly*, *13*(3), 319–340. doi:10.2307/249008

Dawson, S. K., Warton, D. I., Kingsford, R. T., Berney, P., Keith, D. A., & Catford, J. A. (2017). Plant traits of propagule banks and standing vegetation reveal flooding alleviates impacts of agriculture on wetland restoration. *Journal of Applied Ecology*, *54*(6), 1907–1918. doi:10.1111/1365-2664.12922

De Graaf, J. M., Kosters, W. A., & Witteman, J. J. (2001). Interesting fuzzy association rules in quantitative databases. In *Proceedings of European Conference on Principles of Data Mining and Knowledge Discovery*, 140-151. 10.1007/3-540-44794-6_12

de Oliveira Santini, F., Ladeira, W. J., Sampaio, C. H., & Perin, M. G. (2018). Online banking services: A meta-analytic review and assessment of the impact of antecedents and consequents on satisfaction. *Journal of Financial Services Marketing*, *23*(3-4), 168–178. doi:10.105741264-018-0059-4

Deloitte. (2018). *Dijitalleşen Hayatımızda Mobil Teknolojilerin Yeri Deloitte Global Mobil Kullanıcı Anketi 2017: Türkiye Yönetici Özeti.* İstanbul, Turkey: Deloitte.

Delone, W. H., & Mclean, E. R. (2004). Measuring e-commerce success: Applying the DeLone & McLean information systems success model. *International Journal of Electronic Commerce*, *9*(1), 31–47. doi:10.1080/10864415.2004.11044317

Derbaix, C. M. (1995). The impact of affective reactions on attitudes toward the advertisement and the brand: A step toward ecological validity. *JMR, Journal of Marketing Research*, *32*(4), 470–479.

Deveci, F. G. (2014). *Mücevher satin aliminda yaşanan duygusal çelişkilerde etkili olan değişkenlerin belirlenmesi* (Unpublished master's dissertation). The Ataturk University.

Dharmavaram, V., & Nittala, R. (2018). Service quality and customer satisfaction in online banking. [IJOM]. *International Journal of Online Marketing*, *8*(2), 45–56. doi:10.4018/IJOM.2018040103

Dholakia, R. R., & Kshetri, N. (2004). Factors impacting the adoption of the Internet among SMEs. *Small Business Economics*, *23*(4), 311–322. doi:10.1023/B:SBEJ.0000032036.90353.1f

Dictionary, B. D. (2019). *Heterogeneity*. BD Dictionary. Retrieved from http://www.businessdictionary.com/definition/heterogeneity.htmladresinden alındı

Dinçer, H., Yuksel, S., & Bozaykut-Buk, T. (2018b). Evaluation of Financial and Economic Effects on Green Supply Chain Management With Multi-Criteria Decision-Making Approach: Evidence From Companies Listed in BIST. In Handbook of Research on Supply Chain Management for Sustainable Development (pp. 144–175). Hershey, PA: IGI Global. doi:10.4018/978-1-5225-5757-9.ch009

Dinçer, H., Yüksel, S., & Pınarbaşı, F. (2019b). SERVQUAL-Based Evaluation of Service Quality of Energy Companies in Turkey: Strategic Policies for Sustainable Economic Development. In The Circular Economy and Its Implications on Sustainability and the Green Supply Chain (pp. 142-167). Hershey, PA: IGI Global.

Dinçer, H., Hacıoğlu, Ü., & Yüksel, S. (2017). A Strategic Approach to Global Financial Crisis in Banking Sector: A Critical Appraisal of Banking Strategies Using Fuzzy ANP and Fuzzy Topsis Methods. [IJSEM]. *International Journal of Sustainable Economies Management*, *6*(1), 1–21. doi:10.4018/ijsem.2017010101

Dinçer, H., Hacıoğlu, Ü., & Yüksel, S. (2017). Balanced scorecard based performance measurement of European airlines using a hybrid multicriteria decision making approach under the fuzzy environment. *Journal of Air Transport Management*, *63*, 17–33. doi:10.1016/j.jairtraman.2017.05.005

Dincer, H., Uzunkaya, S. S., & Yüksel, S. (2019d). An IT2-Based Hybrid Decision-Making Model Using Hesitant Fuzzy Linguistic Term Sets for Selecting the Development Plan of Financial Economics. *International Journal of Computational Intelligence Systems*, *12*(2), 460–473. doi:10.2991/ijcis.d.190312.001

Dinçer, H., & Yüksel, S. (2018). Financial Sector-Based Analysis of the G20 Economies Using the Integrated Decision-Making Approach with DEMATEL and TOPSIS. In *Emerging Trends in Banking and Finance* (pp. 210–223). Cham, Switzerland: Springer. doi:10.1007/978-3-030-01784-2_13

Dincer, H., & Yuksel, S. (2019). IT2-Based Fuzzy Hybrid Decision Making Approach to Soft Computing. *IEEE Access: Practical Innovations, Open Solutions*, *7*, 15932–15944. doi:10.1109/ACCESS.2019.2895359

Dinçer, H., & Yüksel, S. (2019). Multidimensional evaluation of global investments on the renewable energy with the integrated fuzzy decision-making model under the hesitancy. *International Journal of Energy Research*.

Dinçer, H., Yüksel, S., Korsakienė, R., Raišienė, A. G., & Bilan, Y. (2019c). IT2 Hybrid Decision-Making Approach to Performance Measurement of Internationalized Firms in the Baltic States. *Sustainability*, *11*(1), 296. doi:10.3390u11010296

Dinçer, H., Yüksel, S., & Martínez, L. (2019). Balanced scorecard-based Analysis about European Energy Investment Policies: A hybrid hesitant fuzzy decision-making approach with Quality Function Deployment. *Expert Systems with Applications*, *115*, 152–171. doi:10.1016/j.eswa.2018.07.072

Dinçer, H., Yüksel, S., & Martínez, L. (2019a). Analysis of Balanced Scorecard-based SERVQUAL Criteria based on Hesitant Decision-making Approaches. *Computers & Industrial Engineering*.

Dinçer, H., Yüksel, S., & Martínez, L. (2019e). Interval type 2-based hybrid fuzzy evaluation of financial services in E7 economies with DEMATEL-ANP and MOORA methods. *Applied Soft Computing*.

Dinçer, H., Yüksel, S., & Şenel, S. (2018a). Analyzing the global risks for the financial crisis after the great depression using comparative hybrid hesitant fuzzy decision-making models: Policy recommendations for sustainable economic growth. *Sustainability*, *10*(9), 3126. doi:10.3390u10093126

Dinçer, Ö. (2007). *Stratejik Yönetim ve İşletme Politikası*. İstanbul, Turkey: Alfa Yayınları.

Dixon, H., & Quinn, B. (2004). Franchising and the Internet: An exploratory study of franchisor Web sites. *Internet Research*, *14*(4), 311–322. doi:10.1108/10662240410555324

Doğan, A. (2011)... *Elektronik İnsan Kaynakları Yönetimi ve Fonksiyonları, İnternet Uygulamaları ve Yönetimi Dergisi*, *2*(2), 51–80.

Doğaner, M. (2007). *Elektronik ticaret Türkiye'de elektronik ticaretin gelişimi ve işletmeden tüketiciye elektronik ticaret üzerine bir araştırma. Yüksek Lisans Tezi*. Konya, Turkey: Selçuk Üniversitesi İİBF.

Doherty, N. F., & Ellis-Chadwick, F. E. (2006). New perspectives in internet retailing: A review and strategic critique of the field. *International Journal of Retail & Distribution Management*, *34*(4/5), 411–428. doi:10.1108/09590550610660305

Doherty, N., Ellis-Chadwick, F., & Hart, C. (2003). An analysis of the factors affecting the adoption of the Internet in the UK retail sector. *Journal of Business Research*, *56*(11), 887–897. doi:10.1016/S0148-2963(01)00275-2

Dolanbay, C. (2000). E-Ticaret: Strateji ve Yöntemler. Meteksan Sistem Yayınları, 229-230.

Dolanbay, C. (2000). *Elektronik ticaret stratejiler ve yöntemler*. Ankara, Turkey: Meteksan.

Dombrowski, U., Krenkel, P., & Wullbrandt, J. (2018). Strategic Positioning of Production within the Generic Competitive Strategies. *Procedia CIRP*, *72*, 1196–1201. doi:10.1016/j.procir.2018.03.007

Duan, W., Gu, B., & Whinston, A. B. (2008). The dynamics of online word-of-mouth and product sales—An empirical investigation of the movie industry. *Journal of Retailing*, *84*(2), 233–242. doi:10.1016/j.jretai.2008.04.005

Dubosson-Torbay, M., Osterwalder, A., & Pigneur, Y. (2002). E-business model design, classification, and measurements. *Thunderbird International Business Review*, *44*(1), 5–23. doi:10.1002/tie.1036

Dulebohn, J. H., & Marler, J. H. (2005). E-Compensation: The Potential to Transform Practice. In Greutal, & Stone (Eds.), The Brave New World of e-HR (166-189). San Francisco, CA: Jossey-Bass.

Dulebohn, H., & Marler, J. H. (2005). E-Compensation: The Potential to Transform Practice? In *H. G. Gueutal, & D. L. Stone (Eds.), The Brave New World of eHR: Human Resources Management in the Digital Age* (pp. 166–189). San Francisco, CA: Jossey Bass.

Dündar, İ. G. (1995). *Stratejik İKY'de İK Bilgi Sistemleri'nden Yararlanılması ve Kariyer Yönetimi Sistemine İlişkin Bir Model Önerisi*. İstanbul, Turkey: İstanbul Üniversitesi, Sosyal Bilimler Enstitüsü, Yayınlanmamı Doktora Tezi.

Dwyer, F. R. (1997). Customer Lifetime Valuation to Support Marketing Decision Making. *Journal of Direct Marketing*, *11*(4), 6–13. doi:10.1002/(SICI)1522-7138(199723)11:4<6::AID-DIR3>3.0.CO;2-T

Earl, M. J. (2000). Evolving the E-Business. *Business Strategy Review*, *11*(2), 33–38. doi:10.1111/1467-8616.00135

E-business. (n.d.). Retrieved from https://www.ibm.com/ibm/history/ibm100/us/en/icons/ebusiness/transform/

Eczacıbaşı, F. (2018). *Daha Yeni Başlıyor: Geleceğin Dünyasında Esneklik, Yakınsama, Ağ Yapısı ve Karanlık Taraf* (pp. 60–62). İstanbul, Turkey: Koç Üniversitesi Yayınları.

Edelman, D. C. (2010). Branding in the Digital Age: You're Spending Your Money in All the Wrong Places. *Harvard Business Review, Aralık 1.*

Egger, F. (2003). From Interactions to Transactions: Designing the Trust Experience for BusinessTo-Consumer Electronic Commerce, PhD thesis, *Eindhoven University of Technology*, The Netherlands.

Eimer, M. (2000). B&B internet marketing: The inside story. *Library Journal*, *125*(18), 150.

Ekman, P. (1999). *Basic emotions. Handbook of cognition and emotion. Sussex.* UK: John Wiley & Sons.

Ekwere, G. E., & Edem, I. D. (2014). Effects of agricultural credit facility on the agricultural production and rural development. *International Journal of Environment*, *3*(2), 192–204. doi:10.3126/ije.v3i2.10529

El Sawy, O. A., Malhotra, A., Gosain, S., & Young, K. M. (1999). IT-intensive value innovation in the electronic economy: Insights from Marshall Industries. *Management Information Systems Quarterly*, *23*(3), 305–335. doi:10.2307/249466

Elgin, C., Erzan, R., & Kuzubaş, U. (2013). *Türkiye' de Nakit ve Kart Ödemelerinin Karşılaştırmalı Maliyeti*. Boğaziçi Üniversitesi Ekonomi ve Ekonometri Merkezi.

Elhiraika, A. B. (2003). On the experience of Islamic agricultural finance in Sudan: challenges and sustainability. Jeddah, Saudi Arabia: Islamic Development Bank.

Elibol, H., & Kesici, B. (2004). Çağdaş İşletmecilik Açisindan Elektronik Ticaret. Selçuk Üniversitesi Sosyal Bilimler Enstitüsü Dergisi, (11), 303-329.

Ellis, G., & Mansmann, F. (2010). Mastering the information age solving problems with visual analytics. In *Proceedings of the Eurographics 2010*, 2, 1-6.

Elmuti, D., & Kathawala, Y. (2001). An overview of strategic alliances. *Management Decision*, *39*(3), 205–217.

Elseoud, M. S. A. (2014). Electronic commerce and economic growth in Saudi Arabia. *International Journal of Economics, Commerce and Management*, *2*(5), 1–16.

Emmerichs, R. M., Marcum, C. Y., & Robbert, A. A. (2004). An operational process for workforce planning. Santa Monica, CA: Rand Corporation.

Encyclopedia.com. (2002a). *Infomediary Model.* Encyclopedia.com. Retrieved from https://www.encyclopedia.com/economics/encyclopedias-almanacs-transcripts-and-maps/infomediary-modeladresindenalındı

Encyclopedia.com. (2002b). *Manufacturer Model*. Encyclopedia.com. Retrieved from https://www.encyclopedia.com/economics/encyclopedias-almanacs-transcripts-and-maps/manufacturer-modeladresindenalındı

Encyclopedia.com. (2002c). *Merchant Model*. Encyclopedia.com. Retrieved from https://www.encyclopedia.com/economics/encyclopedias-almanacs-transcripts-and-maps/merchant-modeladresindenalındı

Encyclopedia.com. (2002d). *Utility Model*. Encyclopedia.com. Retrieved from https://www.encyclopedia.com/economics/encyclopedias-almanacs-transcripts-and-maps/utility-modeladresindenalındı

Ene, S. (2002). *Elektronik ticarette tüketicinin korunması ve bir uygulama*. Pusula Yayıncılık ve İletişim.

Eng, T. Y. (2004). The role of e-marketplaces in supply chain management. *Industrial Marketing Management*, *33*(2), 97–105. doi:10.1016/S0019-8501(03)00032-4

Eppler, M. J., & Mengis, J. (2004). The concept of information overload: A review of literature from organization science, accounting, marketing, MIS, and related disciplines. *The Information Society*, *20*(5), 325–344. doi:10.1080/01972240490507974

Erbaşlar, G., & Dokur, Ş. (2012). *Elektronik ticaret: e-ticaret*. Nobel Yayın Dağıtım.

Eren, E. (2010). *Staretjik Yönetim ve İşletme Politikası*. İstanbul, Turkey: Beta Yayınevi.

Erkan, M. (2012). *E-ticaret çağı: profesyoneller için Türkiye'de ve dünyada e-ticaret*. Optimist Yayın Dağıtım.

Ersoy, N. F. (2002). Finansal Hizmetlerde Müşteri İlişkileri Yönetimi (CRM) Kavramı. Pazarlama Dünyası Dergisi, Sayı:2002-03, İstanbul.

Ersoy, Z. (1999). *Elektronik ticaret ve ticaret noktaları*. Ankara, Turkey: İgeme.

Esen, M. (2011). *Bireysel Ve Kurumsal Hazır oluşun Teknolojik Kabulüne Etkisi: Elektronik İnsan Kaynakları Yönetimi (E-İKY)*. Alanında Ampirik Bir Araştırma, Kocaeli Üniversitesi Sosyal Bilimler Enstitüsü, Doktora Tezi, Kocaeli.

Esterhuyse, M., & Scholtz, B. (2016). The Intention to Use e-Learning in Corporations. In CONF-IRM (p. 12).

Evanschitzky, H., Gopalkrishnan, R., Hesse, J., & Dieter, A. (2004). E-satisfaction: A re-examination. *Journal of Retailing*, *80*(3), 239–247. doi:10.1016/j.jretai.2004.08.002

Evans, N., Stonehouse, G., & Campbel, D. (2012). *Strategic management for travel and tourism*. Abingdon, UK: Taylor & Francis. doi:10.4324/9780080498294

Fah, B., & Choo, B. (2010). Undergraduates online purchasing behavior. *Asian Social Science*, (October), 133–138.

Fahey, L., Srivastava, R., Sharon, J. S., & Smith, D. E. (2001). Linking e-business and operating processes: The role of knowledge management. *IBM Systems Journal*, *40*(4), 889–907.

Faliagka, E., Tsakalidis, A., & Tzimas, G. (2012). An integrated e-recruitment system for automated personality mining and applicant ranking. *Internet Research*, *22*(5), 551–568.

Farah, M. F. (2017). Consumers' switching motivations and intention in the case of bank mergers: A cross-cultural study. *International Journal of Bank Marketing*, *35*(2), 254–274. doi:10.1108/IJBM-05-2016-0067

Farooqi, M., & Raza, K. (2012). A Comprehensive Study of CRM through data mining Techniques. In *Proceedings of the National Conference: NCCIST-2011*.

Fatonah, S., Yulandari, A., & Wibowo, F. W. (2018). A Review of E-Payment System in E-Commerce, IOP Conf. Series. *Journal of Physics: Conference Series*, *1140*, 012033. doi:10.1088/1742-6596/1140/1/012033

Featherstone, L. (2019). *Arzuyu Sezmek*. İstanbul, Turkey: The Kitap.

Fielt, E. (2014). Conceptualising business models: Definitions, frameworks and classifications. *Journal of Business Models*, *1*(1), 85–105.

Filieri, R., & McLeay, F. (2014). E-WOM and accommodation: An analysis of the factors that influence travelers' adoption of information from online reviews. *Journal of Travel Research*, *53*(1), 44–57. doi:10.1177/0047287513481274

Finnegan, P., Kilmartin, J.(2002). Electronic Payment Systems: An Empirical Investigation of Customer and Merchant Requirements, *Managing Business with Electronic Commerce: Issues and Trends*, 151-166.

Fiore, F., Shawn, C., & Foreword By-Marciano, J. (2001). *Successful affiliate marketing for merchants*. Hoboken, NJ: Que Corp.

Fırlar, B. G. (2010). Dijital geleceğe hazırlanmak: bilgi ve yenilik yaratma. Sinem Yeygel Çakır (Ed.). Teknolojinin pazarlama iletişimine etkileri içinde, Ankara, Turkey: Nobel.

Fishbein, M., & Ajzen, I. (1975). Belief, attitude, intention, and behavior: An introduction to theory and research. Boston, MA: Digital Press, Addison-Wesley.

Florkowski, G. W., & Olivas-Luján, M. R. (2006). The diffusion of human-resource information-technology innovations in US and non-US firms. *Personnel Review*, *35*(6), 684–710.

Forman, C. (2005). The corporate digital divide: Determinants of Internet adoption. *Management Science*, *51*(4), 641–654. doi:10.1287/mnsc.1040.0343

Forman, C., Goldfarb, A., & Greenstein, S. (2005). How did location affect adoption of the commercial Internet? Global village vs. urban leadership. *Journal of Urban Economics*, *58*(3), 389–420. doi:10.1016/j.jue.2005.05.004

Forsati, R., Meybodi, M. R., & Neiat, A. G. (2009). Web page personalization based on weighted association rules. In *IEEE 2009 International Conference on Electronic Computer Technology*, 130-135.

Forsythe, S. M., & Shi, B. (2003). Consumer patronage and risk perceptions in Internet shopping. *Journal of Business Research*, *56*(11), 867–875. doi:10.1016/S0148-2963(01)00273-9

Fotis, J., Buhalis, D., & Rossides, N. (2012). Social media use and impact during the holiday travel planning process. Berlin, Germany: Springer-Verlag, 13-24.

Francis, B., Hasan, I., Liu, L., & Wang, H. (2018). Employee Treatment and Contracting with Bank Lenders: An Instrumental Approach for Stakeholder Management. *Journal of Business Ethics*, 1–18.

Fuciu, M., & Dumitrescu, L. (2018). From Marketing 1.0 To Marketing 4.0–The Evolution of the Marketing Concept in the Context of the 21st Century. In *Proceedings of International Conference Knowledge-Based Organization*, *24*(2), 43-48. 10.1515/kbo-2018-0064

Galeeva, R. B. (2016). SERVQUAL application and adaptation for educational service quality assessments in Russian higher education. *Quality Assurance in Education*, *24*(3), 329–348. doi:10.1108/QAE-06-2015-0024

Gallagher, K., Foster, K. D., & Parsons, J. (2001). The medium is not the message: Advertising effectiveness and content evaluation in print and on the web. *Journal of Advertising Research*, *41*(4), 57–70.

Gandal, N., & Hałaburda, H. (2014). Competition in the Cryptocurrency Market, *Bank of Canada Working Paper* 2014-33 August 2014, Retrieved From https://www.bankofcanada.ca/wp-content/uploads/2014/08/wp2014-33.pdf

Gardner, S. D., Lepak, D. P., & Bartol, K. M. (2003). Virtual HR: The Impact of Information Technology on the Human Resource Professional. *Journal of Vocational Behavior*, *63*(2), 159–179. doi:10.1016/S0001-8791(03)00039-3

George, J. F. (2004). The theory of planned behavior and Internet purchasing. *Internet Research*, *14*(3), 198–212.

Gera, R., Mittal, S., Batra, D. K., & Prasad, B. (2017). Evaluating the effects of service quality, customer satisfaction, and service value on behavioral intentions with life insurance customers in India. [IJSSMET]. *International Journal of Service Science, Management, Engineering, and Technology*, *8*(3), 1–20. doi:10.4018/IJSSMET.2017070101

Geringer, J. M. (1991). Strategic determinants of partner selection criteria in international joint ventures. *Journal of International Business Studies*, *22*(1), 41–62.

Getir. (n.d.). *Getir nedir?* Retrieved from http://static.getir.com/faq_tr.html

Getir. (n.d.). *Neden Getir?* Retrieved from https://www.getir.com/

Ghazzawi, K., & Accoumeh, A. (2014). Critical success factors of the e-recruitment system. *Journal of Human Resources Management and Labor Studies*, *2*(2), 159–170.

Gholizadeh, A., Carmon, N., Klement, A., Ben-Dor, E., & Borůvka, L. (2017). Agricultural Soil Spectral Response and Properties Assessment: Effects of Measurement Protocol and Data Mining Technique. *Remote Sensing*, *9*(10), 1078. doi:10.3390/rs9101078

Ghosh, S. (1998). Making business sense of the Internet. *Harvard Business Review*, *76*(2), 126–135. PMID:10177862

Gibbs, J. L., & Kraemer, K. L. (2004). A cross-country ınvestigation of the determinants of scope of e-commerce use: An ınstitutional approach. *Electronic Markets*, *14*(2), 124–137. doi:10.1080/10196780410001675077

Gibreel, O., AlOtaibi, D. A., & Altmann, J. (2018). Social commerce development in emerging markets. *Electronic Commerce Research and Applications*, *27*, 152–162. doi:10.1016/j.elerap.2017.12.008

Gilbert, C. G. (2005). Unbundling the structure of inertia: Resource versus routine rigidity. *Academy of Management Journal*, *48*(5), 741–763. doi:10.5465/amj.2005.18803920

Global Value Web. (n.d.). Retrieved from https://global-value-web.com/index.html

Glossary: E-commerce. (n.d.). Retrieved from https://ec.europa.eu/eurostat/statistics-explained/index.php/Glossary:E-commerce

Goeldner, C., & Ritchie, B. J. (2009). *Tourism Principles, Practices, Philosophies* (11th ed.). Hoboken, NJ: John Wiley & Sons.

Goode, M. M., & Harris, L. C. (2007). Online behavioural intentions: An empirical investigation of antecedents and moderators. *European Journal of Marketing*, *41*(5/6), 512–536. doi:10.1108/03090560710737589

Gopal, J., Sangaiah, A. K., Basu, A., & Gao, X. Z. (2018). Integration of fuzzy DEMATEL and FMCDM approach for evaluating knowledge transfer effectiveness with reference to GSD project outcome. *International Journal of Machine Learning and Cybernetics*, *9*(2), 225–241. doi:10.100713042-015-0370-5

Gottschalk, P. (2006). *IS/IT Outsourcing E-Business Strategy*. Sourcing and Governance.

Grandon, E. E., & Pearson, J. M. (2004). Electronic commerce adoption: An empirical study of small and medium US businesses. *Information & Management*, *42*(1), 197–216. doi:10.1016/j.im.2003.12.010

Granger, C. W. J., & Newbold, P. (1974). Spurious regressions in econometrics. *Journal of Econometrics*, *2*(2), 111–120. doi:10.1016/0304-4076(74)90034-7

Gretzel, U., & Yoo, K. (2008). Use and impact of online travel reviews. *Information and communication technologies in tourism*, 35-46.

Grover, V., Chiang, R. H., Liang, T. P., & Zhang, D. (2018). Creating strategic business value from big data analytics: A research framework. *Journal of Management Information Systems*, *35*(2), 388–423. doi:10.1080/07421222.2018.1451951

Güçlü, N. (2003). Stratejik yönetim. Gazi Üniversitesi Gazi Eğitim Fakültesi Dergisi, 23(2).

Gueutal, H. G. (2003). *The Brave New World of E-HR: Advances in Human Performance and Cognitive Engineering Research*. USA: Emerald Group Publishing Limited.

Güler, E. Ç. (2006). İşletmelerin E-İnsan Kaynakları Yönetimi ve E-İşe Alım Süreçlerindeki Gelişmeler. *Ege Akademik Bakış Dergisi*, *6*(1), 17–23.

Gultai, R. (1999). Network location and learning: The influence of network resources and firm capabilities on alliance formation. *Strategic Management Journal*, *20*, 397–420.

Gültaş, P., & Yıldırım, Y. (2016). Internetten alişverişte tüketici davranişini etkileyen demografik faktörler. *Dicle Üniversitesi İktisadi ve İdari Bilimler Fakültesi Dergisi*, *6*(10), 32–50.

Gupta, S., & Johari, R. (2011). A New Framework For Credit Card Transactions Involving Mutual Authentication Between Cardholder and Merchant, Proceedings of The CSNT. *11: International Conference On Communication Systems and Network Technologies*, 22–26.

Gupta, S., & Lehmann, D. R. (2003). Customers as assets. *Journal of Interactive Marketing*, *17*(1), 9–24. doi:10.1002/dir.10045

Guthrie, R. A., & Austin, L. D. (1996). Competitive implications of the Internet. *Information Systems Management*, *13*(3), 90–92.

Hackbarth, G., & Kettinger, W. J. (2004). Strategic aspirations for net-enabled business. *European Journal of Information Systems*, *13*(4), 273–285. doi:10.1057/palgrave.ejis.3000511

Hackney, R. A., & Burn, J. (2001). SPECS-Strategic planning for e-commerce systems: Towards an e-customer focus. *International Journal of E-Business Strategic Management*, 2(4), 281–291.

Hagel, J., & Armstrong, A. (1997). *Net Gain - Expanding Markets through Virtual Communities*. Boston, MA: Harvard Business School Press.

Hall, M. L., & Moritz, S. (2003). The Impact of e-HR on the Human Resource Management Function. *Journal of Labor Research*, *14*(3), 365–379. doi:10.100712122-003-1001-6

Hall, M., Frank, E., Holmes, G., Pfahringer, B., Reutemann, P., & Witten, I. H. (2009). The WEKA data mining software: An update. *ACM Special Interest Group on Knowledge Discovery and Data Mining. Explorations Newsletter*, *11*(1), 10–18. doi:10.1145/1656274.1656278

Hamad, H., Elbeltagi, I., & El-Gohary, H. (2018). An empirical investigation of business-to-business e-commerce adoption and its impact on SMEs competitive advantage: The case of Egyptian manufacturing SMEs. *Strategic Change*, *27*(3), 209–229.

Hamad, H., Elbeltagi, I., Jones, P., & El-Gohary, H. (2015). Antecedents of B2B e-commerce adoption and its effect on competitive advantage in manufacturing SMEs. *Strategic Change*, *24*(5), 405–428.

Handfield, R., & Nichols, E. (2002). *Supply Chain Redesign: Transforming Supply Chains into Integrated Value Systems*. Upper Saddle River, NJ: Financial Times Prentice Hall.

Han, I., Lee, J., & Park, D. (2011). The different effects of online consumer reviews on consumers' purchase intentions depending on trust in online shopping malls: An advertising perspective. *Internet Research*, *21*(2), 187–206. doi:10.1108/10662241111123766

Han, J., & Kamber, M. (2006). *Data Mining Concepts and Techniques* (2nd ed.). Burlington, MA: Morgan Kaufmann.

Hanna, N. K. (2009). e-Transformation: Enabling new development strategies. Berlin, Germany: Springer Science & Business Media.

Hannigan, T. (2015). Close encounters of the conceptual kind: Disambiguating social structure from text. *Big Data & Society*, *2*(2), 1–6.

Hannu, Y. (2001). Physical distribution considerations for electronic grocery shopping. *International Journal of Physical Distribution ve Logistics Management*, *31*(10), 750.

Hansen, F., Percy, L., & Lundsteen, S. (2006). Outstanding brands "emotionally speaking. *European Advances in Consumer Research*, *6*, 511–515.

Hansen, T., Jensen, J. M., & Solgaard, H. S. (2004). Predicting online grocery buying intention: A comparison of the theory of reasoned action and the theory of planned behavior. *International Journal of Information Management*, *24*(6), 539–550.

Han, W., Sun, Y., Xie, H., & Che, Z. (2018). Hesitant fuzzy linguistic group DEMATEL method with multi-granular evaluation scales. *International Journal of Fuzzy Systems*, *20*(7), 2187–2201. doi:10.100740815-017-0397-8

Hanzaee, K. H., & Alinejad, S. (2012). An Investigation About Customers Perceptions of Security and Trust In E-Payment Systems Among Iranian Online Consumers. *Journal of Basic and Applied Scientific Research*, *2*(2), 1575–1581.

Hargreaves, I., Roth, D., Karim, M. R., Nayebi, M., & Ruhe, G. (2018). Effective customer relationship management at atb financial: A case study on industry-academia collaboration in data analytics. In *Highlighting the Importance of Big Data Management and Analysis for Various Applications* (pp. 45–59). Cham, Switzerland: Springer. doi:10.1007/978-3-319-60255-4_4

Harrigan, K. R. (1988). Joint ventures and competitive strategy. *Strategic Management Journal*, *9*, 141–158.

Harris, H., Guru, B. K., & Avvari, M. V. (2011). Evidence of Firms Perceptions Toward Electronic Payment Systems (EPS) in Malaysia. *International Journal of Business and Information*, *6*(2), 226–245.

Harris, L., & Dennis, C. (2008). *Marketing the E-Business*. New York, NY: Routledge Press.

Harris, L., & Rae, A. (2009). Social networks: The future of marketing for small business. *The Journal of Business Strategy*, *30*(5), 24–31. doi:10.1108/02756660910987581

Harrop, P. (1989). New Electronics For Payments, *IEE Review, IX*, 35-45. Retrieved From https://ieeexplore.ieee.org/xpl/tocresult.jsp?isnumber=5642&punumber=2188

Hart, C., Doherty, N., & Ellis-Chadwick, F. (2000). Retailer adoption of the Internet–Implications for retail marketing. *European Journal of Marketing*, *34*(8), 954–974. doi:10.1108/03090560010331441

Harun, N. A., Makhtar, M., Aziz, A. A., Zakaria, Z. A., Abdullah, F. S., & Jusoh, J. A. (2017). The application of apriori algorithm in predicting flood areas. *International Journal on Advanced Science, Engineering and Information Technology*, *7*(3), 763–769.

Hauser, R., Steiner, M., & Waidner, M. (1996), *Micro-Payments Based on IKP, Technical Report 2791* (#89269) [online] http://www.researchgate.net/publication/2669783_Micro-Payments_ based_on_iKP/file/79e41507d2ec8a3a97.pdf (accessed 3 April 2013).

Hayes, J., & Finnegan, P. (2005). Assessing the of potential of e-business models: Towards a framework for assisting decision-makers. *European Journal of Operational Research, 160*(2), 365–379. doi:10.1016/j.ejor.2003.07.013

Heaton, J. (2016). Comparing dataset characteristics that favor the Apriori, Eclat or FP-Growth frequent itemset mining algorithms. In *Proceedings of the 2016 SoutheastCon Conference*, 1-7. 10.1109/SECON.2016.7506659

Hegland, M. (2003). Algorithms for association rules. In *Proceedings of the Advanced Lectures on Machine Learning*, 226-234.

Hendrickson, A. R. (2003). Human resource information systems: Backbone technology of contemporary human resources. *Journal of Labor Research, 24*(3), 381–394.

Heung, V. C. (2003). Barriers to implementing E-commerce in the travel industry: A practical perspective. *International Journal of Hospitality Management, 22*(1), 111–118. doi:10.1016/S0278-4319(02)00075-0

He, W., Zha, S., & Li, L. (2013). Social media competitive analysis and text mining: A case study in the pizza industry. *International Journal of Information Management, 33*(3), 464–472. doi:10.1016/j.ijinfomgt.2013.01.001

Hibbard, J. (1998). Airlines, Online Agencies Battle for Customers–Enhancements to Web Sites Aimed at Getting More People to Book Travel Online. *Information Week*, 685 words.

Hicks, J. M., Page, T. J., Behe, B. K., Dennis, J. H., & Fernandez, R. T. (2005). Delighted consumers buy again. *Journal of Consumer Satisfaction, Dissatisfaction & Complaining Behavior, 18*, 94–104.

Hidayanto, A. N., Hidayat, L. S., Sandhyaduhita, P. I., & Handayani, P. W. (2015). Examinin the Relations of Payment System Characteristics and Behavioual Intention in E-payment Adoption: A Case of Indonesia. *International Journal of Business Information Systems, 19*(1), 58. doi:10.1504/IJBIS.2015.069065

Hidayanto, A. N., Ovirza, M., Anggia, P., Budi, N. F. A., & Phusavat, K. (2017). The Roles of Electronic Word of Mouth and Information Searching in the Promotion of a New E-Commerce Strategy: A Case of Online Group Buying in Indonesia. *Journal of Theoretical and Applied Electronic Commerce Research, 12*(3), 69–85.

Hitt, M. A., Ireland, R. D., & Hoskisson, R. E. (2012). Strategic management cases: competitiveness and globalization. Boston, MA: Cengage Learning.

Ho, C. F., Wu, W. H., & Tai, Y. M. (2004). Strategies for the adaptation of ERP systems. *Industrial Management & Data Systems, 104*(3), 234–251.

Hoffman, D., & Novak, T. (2000). Advertising Pricing Models for the World Wide Web. *Internet Publishing and Beyond: The Economics of Digital Information and Intellectual Property MIT Press.*

Hoffman, D. L., & Novak, T. P. (1995). Marketing in hypermedia computer-mediated environments: Conceptual foundations. *Journal of Marketing, 60*(3), 50–68.

Hoffman, D. L., & Novak, T. P. (2000). How to acquire customers on the web. *Harvard Business Review, 78*(3), 179–188. PMID:11183979

Hokins, J., & Turner, J. (2013). *Mobil Pazarlama Hakkında Herşey*. İstanbul, Turkey: Optimist Yayınları.

Holbrook, M. B., & Batra, R. (1987). Assessing the role of emotions as mediators of consumer responses to advertising. *The Journal of Consumer Research, 14*(3), 404–420.

Hsiao, C. H., Chang, J. J., & Tang, K. Y. (2016). Exploring the influential factors in continuance usage of mobile social Apps: Satisfaction, habit, and customer value perspectives. *Telematics and Informatics*, *33*(2), 342–355. doi:10.1016/j.tele.2015.08.014

Hsieh, N. C. (2004). An integrated data mining and behavioral scoring model for analyzing bank customers. *Expert Systems with Applications*, *27*(4), 623–633. doi:10.1016/j.eswa.2004.06.007

Hsu, C. L., & Lin, J. C. C. (2015). What drives purchase intention for paid mobile apps?–An expectation confirmation model with perceived value. *Electronic Commerce Research and Applications*, *14*(1), 46–57. doi:10.1016/j.elerap.2014.11.003

Huang, B., Kechadi, M. T., & Buckley, B. (2012). Customer churn prediction in telecommunications. *Expert Systems with Applications*, *39*(1), 1414–1425. doi:10.1016/j.eswa.2011.08.024

Huang, C. Y. (2011). Excess loyalty in online retailing. *International Journal of Electronic Commerce*, *16*(2), 115–134. doi:10.2753/JEC1086-4415160206

Huang, J. H., Jin, B. H., & Yang, C. (2004). Satisfaction with Business-to-Employee Benefit Systems and Organizational Citizenship Behavior: An Examination of Gender Differences. *International Journal of Manpower*, *25*(2), 195–210. doi:10.1108/01437720410535990

Huang, S. M., Chang, I. C., Li, S. H., & Lin, M. T. (2004). Assessing risk in ERP projects: Identify and prioritize the factors. *Industrial Management & Data Systems*, *104*(8), 681–688.

Hudson, S., Roth, M., Madden, T., & Hudson, R. (2015). The effects of social media on emotions, brand relationship quality, and word of mouth: An empirical study of music festival attendees. *Tourism Management, 47*, 68-76.

Hummels, D. (2007). Transportation costs and international trade in the second era of globalization. *The Journal of Economic Perspectives*, *21*(3), 131–154. doi:10.1257/jep.21.3.131

Hyder, A. S., & Abraha, D. (2004). Product and skills development in small- and medium-sized high-tech firms through international strategic alliances. *Singapore Management Review*, *26*(2), 1–24.

Hye, Q., & Wizarat, S. (2011). Impact of financial liberalization on agricultural growth: A case study of Pakistan. *China Agricultural Economic Review*, *3*(2), 191–209. doi:10.1108/17561371111131317

ICC. (1995) Uniform Rules for Collections, ICC Publication No. 522E.

ICC. (2002). eUCP-The Supplement to the Uniform Customs and Practice for Documentary Credits for Electronic Presentation.

ICC. (2007). *Practice for Documentary Credits, 2007 Revision, ICC Publication No. 600*. International Chamber of Commerce.

ICCA. (2017). *ICCA Statistics Report Country & City Rankings Public Abstract*. International Congress and Convention Association.

İGEME. (2009). *Yurtdışına E-Ticaret*. Ankara.

Iglesias, O., Markovic, S., & Rialp, J. (2019). How does sensory brand experience influence brand equity? Considering the roles of customer satisfaction, customer affective commitment, and employee empathy. *Journal of Business Research*, *96*, 343–354. doi:10.1016/j.jbusres.2018.05.043

Information Technology Faculty. (2016). *The Future of Payment*, Retrieved From https://www.icaew.com/-/media/corporate/files/technical/information-technology/technology/185-the-future-of-payments.ashx

Inman, J. J., Dyer, J. S., & Jia, J. (1997). A generalized utility model of disappointment and regret effects on post-choice valuation. *Marketing Science*, *16*, 97–111.

Internet World Stats. (2019). *Internet World Stats*. Internet Users in the World by Region - March 2019. Retrieved from https://www.internetworldstats.com/stats.htmadresindenalındı

Inversini, A., & Masiero, L. (2014). Selling rooms online: The use of social media and online travel agents. *International Journal of Contemporary Hospitality Management*, *26*(2), 272–292. doi:10.1108/IJCHM-03-2013-0140

Iqbal, N., Ahmad, M., Raziq, M. M., & Borini, F. M. (2019). Linking e-hrm practices and organizational outcomes: Empirical analysis of line manager's perception. *Revista Brasileira de Gestão de Negócios*, *21*(1), 48–69. doi:10.7819/rbgn.v21i1.3964

Ishibuchi, H., Nakashima, T., & Yamamoto, T. (2001). Fuzzy association rules for handling continuous attributes. In *Proceedings of 2001 IEEE International Symposium on Industrial Electronics*, 1, 118-121. 10.1109/ISIE.2001.931767

İşler, D. B. (2008). Rekabetçi Avantaj Yaratma Çerçevesinde Kobi'lerde E-Ticaret ve E-Ticaretin Stratejik Kullanımı. Süleyman Demirel Üniversitesi İktisadi ve İdari Bilimler Fakültesi Dergisi, 13(3).

Jackson, C. B., Quetsch, L. B., Brabson, L. A., & Herschell, A. D. (2018). Web-based training methods for behavioral health providers: A systematic review. *Administration and Policy in Mental Health*, 1–24. PMID:29352459

Jain, D., & Singh, S. S. (2002). Customer lifetime value research in marketing: A review and future directions. *Journal of Interactive Marketing*, *16*(2), 34–46. doi:10.1002/dir.10032

Jarvenpaa, S. L., & Todd, P. A. (1996). Consumer reactions to electronic shopping on the World Wide Web. *International Journal of Electronic Commerce*, *1*(2), 59–88. doi:10.1080/10864415.1996.11518283

Jentzsch, R., & Miniotas, A. (1999, December). The application of e-commerce to a sme. In *Proceedings 10th Australasian Conference on Information Systems* (pp. 435-448).

Jha, M. B. K., & Dubey, A. K. (2019). Analysis of Customer Satisfaction on Online Banking: A Case Study of Nalanda District of Bihar. *European Journal of Business and Social Sciences*, *7*(4), 55–63.

Jhang, J. Y., Lin, C. J., Lin, C. T., & Young, K. Y. (2018). Navigation Control of Mobile Robots Using an Interval Type-2 Fuzzy Controller Based on Dynamic-group Particle Swarm Optimization. *International Journal of Control, Automation, and Systems*, *16*(5), 2446–2457. doi:10.100712555-017-0156-5

Johnson, G., Scholes, K., & Whittington, R. (2008). Exploring corporate strategy: text & cases. London, UK: Pearson Education.

Johnson, G. (1988). Rethinking incrementalism. *Strategic Management Journal*, *9*(1), 75–91. doi:10.1002mj.4250090107

Johnson, R., Lukaszweski, K. M., & Stone, D. L. (2015). The Evolution of The Field of Human Resource Information Systems: Co-Evolution of Technology and HR Processes. *Communications of the Association for Information Systems*, *38*(28), 533–553.

Kaaya, E. A. (2014). *Assesment Of Marketıng Strategıes Tour Operators Use For Marketıng And Promotıon Of Tanzanıa Tourısm Products: A Case Of Arusha Cıty. Open University Of Tanzania.* Yüksek Lisans Tezi.

Kabadayı, E. T., & Alan, A. K. (2013). Duygu tipolojilerinin tüketici davranışları üzerindeki etkisi ve pazarlamadaki önemi, *İşletme Araştırmaları Dergisi*, *5*(1), 93-115

Kakalejčík, L., Bucko, J., & Vejačka, M. (2019). Differences in buyer journey between high-and low-value customers of e-commerce business. *Journal of Theoretical and Applied Electronic Commerce Research*, *14*(2), 47–58.

Kalakota, R., & Robinson, M. (2001). E-business 2.0: Roadmap for Success. Boston, MA: Addison-Wesley Longman Publishing

Kalakota, R., & Whinston, A. B. (1997). Electronic commerce: a manager's guide. Boston, MA: Addison-Wesley Publishing.

Kalakota, R. (2000). Next generation B2B solutions: The revolution's winners. Supply chain. *Management Review*, 14–79.

Kandampully, J., & Hu, H. (2007). Do hoteliers need to manage image to retain loyal customers? *International Journal of Contemporary Hospitality Management*, *19*(6), 435–443. doi:10.1108/09596110710775101

Kannan, P. K., & Li, H. A. (2017). Digital marketing: A framework, review and research agenda. *International Journal of Research in Marketing*, *34*(1), 22–45. doi:10.1016/j.ijresmar.2016.11.006

Kantarcı, Ö., Özalp, M., Sezginsoy, C., Özaşkınlı, O., & Cavlak, C. (2017). *Dijitalleşen Dünya'da Ekonominin İtici Gücü: E-Ticaret*. İstanbul, Turkey: TÜSİAD.

Kantarcı, Ö., Özalp, M., Sezginsoy, C., Özaşkınlı, O., & Cavlak, C. (2017). *Dijitalleşen dünyada ekonominin itici gücü: E-ticaret*. İstanbul, Turkey: TUSIAD Yayınları.

Kao, C. (1999). Spurious regression and residual-based tests for cointegration in panel data. *Journal of Econometrics*, *90*(1), 1–44. doi:10.1016/S0304-4076(98)00023-2

Kaplan, S., & Sawhney, M. (2000). E-hubs: The new B2B marketplaces. *Harvard Business Review*, *78*(3), 97–106. PMID:11183982

Karabatak, M., & Ince, M. C. (2009). An expert system for detection of breast cancer based on association rules and neural network. *Expert Systems with Applications*, *36*(2), 3465–3469. doi:10.1016/j.eswa.2008.02.064

Karacaoğlu, K. (2006). *Rekabet Üstünlüğü Sağlamada Endüstri Temelli ve Kaynak Temelli Bakış Açısı: Kayseri'de Faaliyet Gösteren İmalat Sanayi İşletmeleri İçin Bir Model Önerisi. Yayınlanmamış Doktora Tezi*. Ankara, Turkey: Ankara Üniversitesi Sosyal Bilimler Enstitüsü.

Karahan, P. (2018, July 22). *Hissedip Getir'di vurdu gol oldu*. Retrieved from http://www.gazetevatan.com/hissedip-getir-di-vurdu-gol-oldu-1184450-ekonomi/

Karahanna, E., & Straub, D. W. (1999). The psychological origins of perceived usefulness ad ease-of-use. *Information ve Management*, *35*(4), 237–250.

Karahasan, F. (2014). *Taşlar Yerinden Oynarken- Dijital Pazarlamanın Kuralları*. İstanbul, Turkey: CEO Plus.

Karakaya, E. (2017). Müşteri duygulari ile müşteri memnuniyeti, sadakati ve satin alma sonrasi kolaylik arasindaki ilişkilerin incelenmesi: Yüksekokul öğrencileri ile gerçekleştirilen bir saha çalişmasi. *Uluslararası Sosyal Araştırmalar Dergisi*, *10*(50), 747–757.

Karcıoğlu, F., & Öztürk, Ü. (2009). İşletmelerde Performans Değerleme ile İnsan Kaynakları Bilgi Sistemleri (İKBS) Arasındaki İlişkisi-İstanbul İlinde Bir Araştırma. *Atatürk Üniversitesi Sosyal Bilimler Enstitüsü Dergisi*, *13*(1), 343–366.

Kasemsap, K. (2018). Multifaceted Applications of Data Mining, Business Intelligence, and Knowledge Management. In Intelligent Systems: Concepts, Methodologies, Tools, and Applications (pp. 810-825). Hershey, PA: IGI Global.

Kasiri, L. A., Cheng, K. T. G., Sambasivan, M., & Sidin, S. M. (2017). Integration of standardization and customization: Impact on service quality, customer satisfaction, and loyalty. *Journal of Retailing and Consumer Services*, *35*, 91–97. doi:10.1016/j.jretconser.2016.11.007

Kasprisin, C. A., Single, P. B., Single, R. M., & Muller, C. B. (2003). Building a better bridge: Testing e-training to improve e-mentoring programmes in higher education. *Mentoring & Tutoring*, *11*(1), 67–78.

Kaufmann, P. J., Cliquet, G., & Achabal, D. D. (2010). Implementing multi-channel strategies: Issues and opportunities for franchise system websites. In *Proceedings of the 24th ISoF Conference*, Sydney, Australia.

Kaur, K., Pathak, A. (2015). E-Payment System on E-Commerce in India, *Karamjeet Kau Int. Journal of Engineering Research and Alications*, 5(2-part1) 79-87.

Kaura, V., Durga Prasad, C. S., & Sharma, S. (2015). Service quality, service convenience, price and fairness, customer loyalty, and the mediating role of customer satisfaction. *International Journal of Bank Marketing*, *33*(4), 404–422. doi:10.1108/IJBM-04-2014-0048

Kaur, M., & Kang, S. (2016). Market Basket Analysis: Identify the changing trends of market data using association rule mining. *Procedia Computer Science*, *85*, 78–85. doi:10.1016/j.procs.2016.05.180

Kavadias, S., Ladas, K., & Loch, C. (2016). Dönüştürücü İş Modeli, *Harvard Business Review Türkiye*. Retrieved from https://hbrturkiye.com/dergi/donusturucu-is-modeli

Kavakiotis, I., Tsave, O., Salifoglou, A., Maglaveras, N., Vlahavas, I., & Chouvarda, I. (2017). Machine learning and data mining methods in diabetes research. *Computational and Structural Biotechnology Journal*, *15*, 104–116. doi:10.1016/j.csbj.2016.12.005 PMID:28138367

Kaynama, S., & Black, C. (2008). A Proposal to Assess the Service Quality of Online Travel Agencies: An Exploratory Study. *Journal of Professional Services Marketing*, *21*(1), 63–88. doi:10.1300/J090v21n01_05

Kazancoglu, Y., Kazancoglu, I., & Sagnak, M. (2018). Fuzzy DEMATEL-based green supply chain management performance: Application in cement industry. *Industrial Management & Data Systems*, *118*(2), 412–431. doi:10.1108/IMDS-03-2017-0121

KEB, Korean Exchange Bank. (2010). Issues First Paperless LC Under eUCP, TRADE FIN., Dec. 14, 2010.

Keeney, R. L. (1999). The value of internet commerce to the customer. *Management Science*, *45*(4), 533–542.

Keen, P., & Williams, R. (2013). Value architectures for digital business: Beyond the business model. *Management Information Systems Quarterly*, *37*(2), 643–648.

Kemp, S. (2017). Digital in 2017: Global overview. *We are social, 24.*

Kepenek, Y. (1999). *Ekonomik Yönleriyle Elektronik Ticaret*. Ankara, Turkey: ODTÜ İktisat Bölümü ve Tekpol.

Khan, B. I., Olanrewaju, R. F., Baba, A. M., Langoo, A. A., Assad, S. (2017). A Compendious Study of Online Payment Systems: Past Developments, Present Impact, and Future Considerations, *(IJACSA) International Journal of Advanced Computer Science and Applications*, Vol. 8, No. 5.

Kiang, M. Y., Raghu, T. S., & Shang, K. (2000). Marketing on the Internet: Who can benefit from an online marketing approach? *Decision Support Systems*, *27*(2), 383–393.

Kiennan, B. (2002). *İşletmeler için çözümler elektronik ticaret, (Çev. Kaan Öztürk, Okan Cem Çırakoğlu, Serdar Özkaya)*. Ankara, Turkey: Arkadaş.

Kim, A. (2000). Community Building on the Web: Secret Strategies for Successful Online Communities. San Francisco, CA: Peachpit Press.

Kim, C., Mirsobit, M., & Lee, I. (2010). An Empirical Examination of Facctors Influencing the Intention to Use Mobile Payment. *Computers in Human Behavior*, *26*(3), 310–322. doi:10.1016/j.chb.2009.10.013

Kim, C., Tao, W., Shin, N., & Kim, K. S. (2010). An Empirical Study of Customers Perceptions of Security and Trust in E-Payment Systems. *Electronic Commerce Research and Applications*, *9*(1), 84–95. doi:10.1016/j.elerap.2009.04.014

Kim, E. Y. (2004). Online purchase intentions for products categories: The functions of internet motivations and online buying tendencies. *Journal of the Korean Society of Clothing and Textiles*, *32*(6), 890–901.

Kim, E., Nam, D.-I., & Stimpert, J. L. (2004). The Applicability of Porter's Generic Strategies in the Digital Age: Assumptions, Conjectures, and Suggestions. *Journal of Management*, *30*(5), 569–589. doi:10.1016/j.jm.2003.12.001

Kim, H. S. (2005). Consumer profiles of apparel product involvement and values. *Journal of Fashion Marketing and Management: An International Journal*, *9*(2), 207–220.

Kim, S. J., Wang, R. J. H., & Malthouse, E. C. (2015). The effects of adopting and using a brand's mobile application on customers' subsequent purchase behavior. *Journal of Interactive Marketing*, *31*, 28–41. doi:10.1016/j.intmar.2015.05.004

Kim, W. C., & Mauborgne, R. (1999). Strategy, value innovation, and the knowledge economy. *Sloan Management Review*, *40*(3), 41–42.

Kim, Y. S., & Yum, B. J. (2011). Recommender system based on click stream data using association rule mining. *Expert Systems with Applications*, *38*(10), 13320–13327. doi:10.1016/j.eswa.2011.04.154

King, R. C., Sen, R., & Xia, M. (2004). Impact of web-based e-commerce on channel strategy in retailing. *International Journal of Electronic Commerce*, *8*(3), 103–130. doi:10.1080/10864415.2004.11044297

King, S. C., & Meiselman, H. L. (2010). Development of a method to measure consumer emotions associated with foods. *Food Quality and Preference*, *21*, 168–177.

Klose, M., & Lechner, U. (1999). Design of business media-an integrated model of electronic commerce. *AMCIS 1999 Proceedings*, 193.

Koçak, O., Beki, A., & Eti, S. (2018). Farklı Aktivitelerin Yaşlıların Depresyon Seviyeleri Üzerine Etkileri. *OPUS Uluslararası Toplum Araştırmaları Dergisi*, *8*(15), 25–25.

Koellinger, P. (2008). The relationship between technology, innovation, and firm performance—Empirical evidence from e-business in Europe. *Research Policy*, *37*(8), 1317–1328.

Körfez, E. P. (2008). *Elektronik İse Alım ve Seçimin İnsan Kaynakları Yönetimi Açısından Yeri ve Önemi ve Bir Uygulama*. İstanbul, Turkey: Yıldız Teknik Üniversitesi, Sosyal Bilimler Enstitüsü, Yüksek Lisans Tezi.

Korkmaz, N. (2002). *Sorularla internet ve e-ticaret rehberi*. İTO.

Köseoğlu, M. A. (2007). *Etik Kodların Rekabet Stratejilerine Etkileri ve Bir Alan Araştırması*. Yayınlanmamış Doktora Tezi. Afyonkarahisar Kocatepe Üniversitesi Sosyal Bilimler Enstitüsü.

Köseoğlu, Ö. (2006). Bilgi İletişim Teknolojilerinin Pazarlamaya Etkisi. In *B. Akıncı Vural, Bilgi İletişim Teknolojileri ve Yansımaları* (pp. 145–185). Ankara, Turkey: Nobel Yayınları.

Kotler, P. (2003). *Marketing Management*. Upper Saddle River, NJ: Prentice Hall (11th edition).

Kotler, P., & Kartajaya, H., & Setiawan, I. (2016). Marketing 4.0: Moving from Traditional to Digital. Hoboken, NJ: John Wiley & Sons.

Kotler, P., Armstrong, G., & Harris, L. C. (2017). *Principles of Marketing*.

Kotler, P. (2011). *Kotler ve Pzarlama Pzar Yaratmak,Para Kazanmak ve Pazara Egemen Olmak*. İstanbul, Turkey: Sistem Yayıncılık.

Kotler, P., Kartajaya, H., & Setiawan, I. (2016). *Marketing 4.0: Moving from traditional to digital*. Hoboken, NJ: John Wiley & Sons.

Kozak, N., & Kozak, M. (2008). Information sources available to visitors: A segmentation analysis. *Tourism Review, 63*(4), 4–12. doi:10.1108/16605370810912173

Kumar, A., Pal, A., Vohra, A., Gupta, S., Manchanda, S., & Dash, M. K. (2018). Construction of capital procurement decision making model to optimize supplier selection using Fuzzy Delphi and AHP-DEMATEL. *Benchmarking: An International Journal, 25*(5), 1528–1547. doi:10.1108/BIJ-01-2017-0005

Kumar, K. (1995). *Sanayi Sonrası Toplumdan Post-modern Topluma Çağdaş Dünyanın Yeni Kuramları*. Ankara, Turkey: Dost Kitabevi Yayınları.

Kumar, M., Sujit, K. S., & Charles, V. (2018). Deriving managerial implications through SERVQUAL gap elasticity in UAE banking. *International Journal of Quality & Reliability Management, 35*(4), 940–964. doi:10.1108/IJQRM-10-2016-0176

Kusluvan, S. (2003). *Managing employee attitudes and behaviors in the tourism and hospitality industry*. Hauppage, NY: Nova.

Kusluvan, S. (2019). *Tourism Marketing Lecture Notes*. İstanbul, Turkey: İstanbul Medeniyet Üniversitesi.

Lahuerta-Otero, E., & Cordero-Gutiérrez, R. (2016). Looking for the perfect tweet. The use of data mining techniques to find influencers on Twitter. *Computers in Human Behavior, 64*, 575–583. doi:10.1016/j.chb.2016.07.035

Lamberton, C., & Stephen, A. T. (2016). A Thematic Exploration of Digital, Social Media, and Mobile Marketing: Research Evolution from 2000 to 2015 and an Agenda for Future Inquiry. *Journal of Marketing, 80*(6), 146–172. doi:10.1509/jm.15.0415

Laros, F. J. M., & Steenkamp, J. B. (2005). Emotions in consumer behavior: A hierarchical approach. *Journal of Business Research, 10*, 1437–1445.

Laudon, K. C., & Guercio Traver, C. (2016). *E-commerce: business, technology, society*. Upper Saddle River, NJ: Pearson Prentice Hall/Pearson Education.

Laudon, K. C., & Traver, G. C. (2014). *E-Commerce*. New Jersey: Pearson Education.

Law, R. (2000). Internet and travel and tourism marketing part I. *Journal of Travel & Tourism Marketing, 9*(3), 65–71. doi:10.1300/J073v09n03_05

Law, R., & Chen, F. (2000). Internet in Travel and tourism - Part I. *Journal of Travel & Tourism Marketing, 9*(4), 83–87. doi:10.1300/J073v09n04_05

Law, R., & Huang, T. (2008). Internet and Tourism-Part XII. *Journal of Travel & Tourism Marketing, 14*(2), 105–109. doi:10.1300/J073v14n02_06

Law, R., Leung, K., & Wong, J. (2004). The impact of the Internet on travel agencies. *International Journal of Contemporary Hospitality Management, 16*(2), 100–107. doi:10.1108/09596110410519982

Lazazzara, A., & Galanaki, E. (2018). E-HRM Adoption and Usage: A Cross-National Analysis of Enabling Factors. In *Digital Technology and Organizational Change* (pp. 125–140). Cham, Switzerland: Springer.

Lazazzara, A., & Galanaki, E. (2018). E-HRM Adoption and Usage: A Cross-National Analysis of Enabling Factors. In C. Rossignoli, F. Virili, & S. Za (Eds.), *Digital, Technology and Organizational Change: Reshaping Technology, People, and Organizations Towards a Global Society*. Lecture Notes in Information Systems and Organisation. doi:10.1007/978-3-319-62051-0_11

Le Nguyen, C. (2018). Preventing the use of financial institutions for money laundering and the implications for financial privacy. *Journal of money laundering control, 21*(1), 47-58.

Le Roux, I. (2015). The influence of online travel agent performance on customer satisfaction levels at a selected hotel. Nelson Mandela Metropolitan University. Yüksek Lisans Tezi.

Lee, C. S. (2001). An analytical framework for evaluating e-commerce business models and strategies. *Internet Research, 11*(4), 349–359. doi:10.1108/10662240110402803

Leech, N. L., Collins, K. M., & Onwuegbuzie, A. J. (2017). Collecting Qualitative Data to Enhance Social Network Analysis and Data Mining. Encyclopedia of Social Network Analysis and Mining, 1-11.

Lee, H. L., & Whang, S. (2001). Winning the last mile of e-commerce. *MIT Sloan Management Review*, *42*(4), 54–62.

Lee, I. (2005). The Evolution of E-Recruiting: A Concent Analysis of Fortune 100 Career Web Sites. *Journal of Electronic Commerce in Organizations*, *3*(3), 57–68. doi:10.4018/jeco.2005070104

Lee, S. C., & Brandyberry, B. A. (2003). The E-tailer's Dilemma. *Advanced Information Systems*, *34*(2), 10–22. doi:10.1145/784580.784584

Lee, S., & Lim, G. G. (2005). The impact of partnership attributes on EDI implementation success. *Information & Management Amsterdam*, *42*(4), 503–516.

Lee, Z. Y., Yu, H. C., & Kuo, P. J. (2001). An Analysis and Comparison of Differen Types of Electronic Payment Systems, *Portland Int. Conference on*, IEEE., 38-45.

Legge, K. (1989). Human resource management: a critical analysis. New perspectives on human resource management. In J. Storey (Ed.), New Perspectives on Human Resource Management. Abingdon, UK: Routledge, pp. 19-40.

Leinbach-Reyhle, N. (2015). *The single most important reason why online marketing is more important than ever.* Retrieved from https://www.forbes.com/sites/nicoleleinbachreyhle/2015/06/16/the-single-most-important-reason-why-online-marketing-is-more-important-than-ever/#43583aa53bff

Leiper, N. (2004). Tourism Management. London, UK: Pearson.

Lengnick-Hall, M. L., & Moritz, S. (2003). The impact of e-HR on the human resource management function. *Journal of Labor Research*, *24*(3), 365–379.

Lepak, D. P., & Snell, S. A. (1998). Virtual HR: Strategic human resource management in the 21st century. *Human Resource Management Review*, *8*(3), 215–234. doi:10.1016/S1053-4822(98)90003-1

LeTart, J. F. (1998). Virtual HR, HR Magazine, p. 62.

Leung, C. W. K., Chan, S. C. F., & Chung, F. L. (2007). Applying cross-level association rule mining to cold-start recommendations. In *Proceedings of the 2007 IEEE/WIC/ACM International Conferences on Web Intelligence and Intelligent Agent Technology-Workshops*, 133-136.

Levenburg, N. M. (2005). Delivering customer value online: An analysis of practices, applications, and performance. *Journal of Retailing and Consumer Services*, *12*(5), 319–331. doi:10.1016/j.jretconser.2004.11.001

Levina, N., & Ross, J. W. (2003). From the vendor's perspective: Exploring the value proposition in information technology outsourcing. *Management Information Systems Quarterly*, 331–364.

Levy, M., & Weitz, B. A. (2004). *Retailing Management.* New York, NY: McGraw Hill Irwin.

Le, X. (2010). Analysis of China's e-commerce and economic development by VAR model. *The Conference on Web Based Business Management.* pp. 621-624.

Liautaud, B., & Hammond, M. (2000). *E-Business Intelligence: Turning Information into Knowledge into Profit.* New York, NY: McGraw-Hill.

Lifsitz, R. (1998). Net As an Opportunity. *Travel Weekly*, *57*(45), F6.

Li, H., Wang, J., Lam, H. K., Zhou, Q., & Du, H. (2016). Adaptive sliding mode control for interval type-2 fuzzy systems. *IEEE Transactions on Systems, Man, and Cybernetics. Systems*, *46*(12), 1654–1663. doi:10.1109/TSMC.2016.2531676

Linck, K., Pousttchi, K., & Wiedemann, D. G. (2010). Security Issues in Mobile Payment From The Customer Viewpoint In: Ljungberg, J. (Hrsg.). *Proceedings of the 14th European Conference on Information Systems (ECIS 2006).* Göteborg, Schweden 2006, S.1-11.

Ling, C. X., & Li, C. (1998). Data mining for direct marketing: Problems and solutions. In *Proceedings of the Fourth International Conference on Knowledge Discovery and Data Mining*, 98, 73-79.

Ling, G. M., Fern, Y. S., Boon, L. K., & Huat, T. S. (2016). Understanding customer satisfaction of internet banking: A case study in Malacca. *Procedia Economics and Finance*, *37*, 80–85. doi:10.1016/S2212-5671(16)30096-X

Linton, G., & Kask, J. (2017). Configurations of entrepreneurial orientation and competitive strategy for high performance. *Journal of Business Research*, *70*, 168–176. doi:10.1016/j.jbusres.2016.08.022

Lituchy, T. R., & Rail, A. (2000). Bed and breakfast, small inns, and the internet: The impact of technology on the globalization of small businesses. *Journal of International Marketing*, *8*(2), 77–86. doi:10.1509/jimk.8.2.86.19625

Liu, D. R., & Shih, Y. Y. (2005). Integrating AHP and data mining for product recommendation based on customer lifetime value. *Information & Management*, *42*(3), 387–400. doi:10.1016/j.im.2004.01.008

Liu, J., Li, J., Xu, W., & Shi, Y. (2004). Data mining approach in scientific research organizations evaluation via clustering. In *Proceedings of Chinese Academy of Sciences Symposium on Data Mining and Knowledge Management*, 128-134.

Liu, S. (2013, June). An empirical study on e-commerce's effects on economic growth. In *2013 Conference on Education Technology and Management Science (ICETMS 2013).* Atlantis Press. 10.2991/icetms.2013.260

Liu, T., Deng, Y., & Chan, F. (2018). Evidential supplier selection based on DEMATEL and game theory. *International Journal of Fuzzy Systems*, *20*(4), 1321–1333. doi:10.100740815-017-0400-4

Londre, L. (2014). *Marketing, IMC, Advertising, Promotion, Media and More.* Los Angeles, CA: Londre Marketing Consultants.

Loureiro, S. M. C., & Sarmento, E. M. (2017, September). The Impact of Generation Y's Customer Experience on Emotions: Online Banking Sector. In *Conference on Creativity in Intelligent Technologies and Data Science* (pp. 616-639). Cham, Switzerland: Springer. 10.1007/978-3-319-65551-2_45

Low, S., Paul, S., & Maxemchuk, N. (1994). Anonymous Credit Cards, *Proceedings of The 2nd ACM Conference on Computer and Communications Security.* 108–117.

Lu, B., & Wang, H. (2016). Research on the Competitive Strategy of Cross-Border E-Commerce Comprehensive Pilot Area Based on the Spatial Competition. *Scientific Programming*, 12.

Lu, J. (2004). A personalized e-learning material recommender system. In *Proceedings of International Conference on Information Technology and Applications*. Australia: Macquarie Scientific Publishing.

Lumpkin, G., Droege, S., & Dess, G. (2002). E-commerce strategies: Achieving sustainable competitive advantage and avoiding pitfalls. *Organizational Dynamics*, *30*(4), 325–340.

Lunce, S. E., Lunce, L. M., Kawai, Y., & Maniam, B. (2006). Success and failure of pure-play organizations: Webvan versus Peapod, a comparative analysis. *Industrial Management & Data Systems*, *106*(9), 1344–1358. doi:10.1108/02635570610712618

Luo, J., BA S., & Zhang, H. (2012). The effectiveness of online shopping characteristics and well-designed websites on satisfaction. *Management Information Systems Quarterly*, *36*(4), 1131–1144.

Luo, Y., Hongxin Zhao, J., & Du, J. (2005). The internationalization speed of e-commerce companies: An empirical analysis. *International Marketing Review*, *22*(6), 693–709. doi:10.1108/02651330510630294

Luthra, S., Mangla, S. K., Shankar, R., Prakash Garg, C., & Jakhar, S. (2018). Modelling critical success factors for sustainability initiatives in supply chains in Indian context using Grey-DEMATEL. *Production Planning and Control*, *29*(9), 705–728. doi:10.1080/09537287.2018.1448126

Machlouzarıdes, H. (2009). *Improvıng The Deployment Model Of Modern Electronıc Marketıng Methods For The Cyprus Tourısm Organısatıon*. Doktora Tezi.

Mack, R., Blose, J., & Pan, B. (2008). Believe it or not: Credibility of blogs in tourism. *Journal of Vacation Marketing*, *14*(2), 133–144. doi:10.1177/1356766707087521

Maes, P., Gutman, R. S., & Maukas, A. G. (1999). Agents that buy and sell. *Communications of the ACM*, *42*(3), 81–91.

Magretta, J. (2002). Why business models matter? *Harvard Business Review*, *80*(5), 86–92. PMID:12024761

Mahatanankoon, P., Wen, H. J., & Lim, B. (2005). Consumer-based m-commerce: Exploring consumer perception of mobile applications. *Computer Standards & Interfaces*, *27*(4), 347–357. doi:10.1016/j.csi.2004.10.003

Majumder, N., Poria, S., Gelbukh, A., & Cambria, E. (2017). Deep learning-based document modeling for personality detection from text. *IEEE Intelligent Systems*, *32*(2), 74–79. doi:10.1109/MIS.2017.23

Ma, L., Jin, C., & Huo, Y. (2019). Strategy Of E-Commerce Market Entry Based On Vertical Complementarity Of Service Supply Chain. *International Journal of Innovative Computing, Information, & Control*, *15*(2), 757–772.

Malhotra, Y. (2000). Knowledge Management for E-Business Performance: Advancing Information Strategy to 'Internet Time'. *Information Strategy, The Executives Journal, [Online] 16(4),* 5-16 .

Malkawi, B. H. (2007). E-Commerce in Light of International Trade Agreements: The WTO and the United States-Jordan Free Trade Agreement. *International Journal of Law and Information Technology*, *15*(2), 153–169. doi:10.1093/ijlit/eal017

Mangold, W., & Faulds, D. (2009). Social Media: The New Hybrid Element of The Promotion Mix. *Business Horizons*, *52*(4), 357–365. doi:10.1016/j.bushor.2009.03.002

Mano, H., & Oliver, R. L. (1993). Assessing the dimensionality and structure of the consumption experience: Evaluation, feeling, and satisfaction. *The Journal of Consumer Research*, *20*(3), 451–466.

Manzoor, A. (2010). *E-Commerce an Introduction*. Lawbert Academic Publishing USA.

Marangoz, M. (2014). İnternette Pazarlama, Beta yayınları.

Marangoz, M. (2014). *İnternette pazarlama*. İstanbul, Turkey: Beta.

Marconi, M., Germani, M., Mandolini, M., & Favi, C. (2019). Applying data mining technique to disassembly sequence planning: A method to assess effective disassembly time of industrial products. *International Journal of Production Research*, *57*(2), 599–623. doi:10.1080/00207543.2018.1472404

Mariıssen, A. (2012). *A grounded theory of affiliate marketing performance measurement in the tourism and hospitality context.* (Doctoral thesis, Business School, Oxford Brookes University).

Mariz-Pérez, R., & García-Álvarez, T. (2009). The Internationalization strategy of Spanish indigenous franchised chains: A resource-based view. *Journal of Small Business Management*, *47*(4), 514–530. doi:10.1111/j.1540-627X.2009.00281.x

Marler, J. H. (2009). Making human resources strategic by going to the Net: Reality or myth? *International Journal of Human Resource Management*, *20*(3), 515–527. doi:10.1080/09585190802707276

Marler, J. H., & Parry, E. (2016). Human resource management, strategic involvement and e-HRM technology. *International Journal of Human Resource Management*, *27*(19), 2233–2253.

Martin, L., & Pénard, T. (2005). Investing in a website: a top dog or a resource-based strategy for firms?.

Martin, G., & Reddington, M. (2010). Theorizing the links between e-HR and strategic HRM: A model, case illustration and reflections. *International Journal of Human Resource Management*, *21*(10), 1553–1574.

Martin, L. (2004). E-innovation: Internet impacts on small UK hospitality firms. *International Journal of Contemporary Hospitality Management*, *16*(2), 82–90. doi:10.1108/09596110410519964

Martin, S. J., & Clapp, J. (2015). Finance for agriculture or agriculture for finance? *Journal of Agrarian Change*, *15*(4), 549–559. doi:10.1111/joac.12110

Masihuddin, M., Khan, B.U.I., Mattoo, M. M. I., & Olanrewaju, R. (2017). A Survey on E-Payment Systems: Elements, Adoption, Architecture, Challenges and Security Concepts. *Indian Journal of Science and Technology*, *10*(20), 1-19.

McAdam, R., & Galloway, A. (2005). Enterprise resource planning and organisational innovation: A management perspective. *Industrial Management & Data Systems*, *105*(3), 280–290.

McAfee, A., & Brynjolfsson, E. (2008). Investing in the IT that makes a competitive difference. *Harvard Business Review*, *86*(7/8), 98. PMID:18271321

McCarty, J. A., & Hastak, M. (2007). Segmentation approaches in data-mining: A comparison of RFM, CHAID, and logistic regression. *Journal of Business Research*, *60*(6), 656–662. doi:10.1016/j.jbusres.2006.06.015

McDermott, K. (2015). The Mobile Payments Revolution, *Payvision BV,* Retrieved From http://boletines.prisadigital.com/The-mobile-payments-revolution-2015.pdf

McGaughey, R. E., & Mason, K. H. (1998). The Internet as a marketing tool. *Journal of Marketing Theory and Practice*, *6*(3), 1–11.

McLean, G., Al-Nabhani, K., & Wilson, A. (2018). Developing a Mobile Applications Customer Experience Model (MACE)-Implications for Retailers. *Journal of Business Research*, *85*, 325–336. doi:10.1016/j.jbusres.2018.01.018

McNicholas, P. D., Murphy, T. B., & O'Regan, M. (2008). Standardising the lift of an association rule. *Computational Statistics & Data Analysis*, *52*(10), 4712–4721. doi:10.1016/j.csda.2008.03.013

Medipol University. (n.d.). *Sık Sorulan Sorular*. Retrieved from http://www.medipol.edu.tr/Sayfa/413/SSS.aspx

Medvinsky, G., & Neuman, B. C. (1993). Netcash: a Design for Practical Electronic Currency on the Internet, *Proceedings of the 1st ACM Conference on Computer and Communications Security, pp.* 102–106. 10.1145/168588.168601

Mendel, J. M. (2017). Type-2 fuzzy sets. In *Uncertain rule-based fuzzy systems* (pp. 259–306). Cham, Switzerland: Springer. doi:10.1007/978-3-319-51370-6_6

Meral, Y. (2018). Documentary Risk in International Trade. In Strategic Design and Innovative Thinking in Business Operations. 413-431, Springer, Cham.

Meral, Y. (2018). Documentary Risk in International Trade. In *Strategic Design and Innovative Thinking in Business Operations* (pp. 413–431). Cham, Switzerland: Springer. doi:10.1007/978-3-319-77622-4_21

Mess. (1997). Dünya'da ve Türkiye'de Rekabet. İstanbul, Turkey: Mess Yayınları.

Meyer, C., & Davis, S. (2000). Blur: The speed of change in the connected economy. *Work Study*, *49*(4). doi:10.1108/ws.2000.07949dae.003

Middleton, V., Fyall, A., & Morgan, M. (2009). *Marketing in Travel and Tourism* (4th ed.). Oxford, UK: Butterworth-Heinemann.

Mihelis, G., Grigoroudis, E., Siskos, Y., Politis, Y., & Malandrakis, Y. (2001). Customer satisfaction measurement in the private bank sector. *European Journal of Operational Research*, *130*(2), 347–360. doi:10.1016/S0377-2217(00)00036-9

Min, S., & Wolfinbarger, M. (2005). Market share, profit margin, and marketing efficiency of early movers, bricks and clicks, and specialists in e-commerce. *Journal of Business Research*, *58*(8), 1030–1039. doi:10.1016/j.jbusres.2004.02.005

Mintzberg, H., Ghoshal, S., Lampel, J., & Quinn, J. B. (2003). The strategy process: concepts, contexts, cases. London, UK: Pearson Education.

Miva. (2011) *The History of Ecommerce: How Did it All Begin.* Retrieved From https://www.miva.com/blog/the-history-of-ecommerce-how-did-it-all-begin/

Mobil Dev. (2014, Feb. 6). *Mobil Pazarlama.* Retrieved from http://www.mobildev.com/393/Mobil-Pazarlama.htm

Mohapatra, S. (2013). E-commerce Strategy. In *E-Commerce Strategy* (pp. 155–171). Boston, MA: Springer. doi:10.1007/978-1-4614-4142-7_7

Mohsin, M., & Sulaiman, R. (2013). A Study on e-Training Adoption for Higher Learning Institutions. *International Journal of Asian Social Science*, *3*(9), 2006–2018.

Moliner-Tena, M. A., Monferrer-Tirado, D., & Estrada-Guillén, M. (2019). Customer engagement, non-transactional behaviors and experience in services: A study in the bank sector. *International Journal of Bank Marketing*, *37*(3), 730–754. doi:10.1108/IJBM-04-2018-0107

Molla, A., & Licker, P. S. (2005). Perceived e-readiness factors in e-commerce adoption: An empirical investigation in a developing country. *International Journal of Electronic Commerce*, *10*(1), 83–110. doi:10.1080/10864415.2005.11043963

Mondy, R. W., & Mondy, J. B. (2012). *Human Resource Management*. London, UK: Pearson Education.

Monferrer-Tirado, D., Estrada-Guillén, M., Fandos-Roig, J. C., Moliner-Tena, M. Á., & Sanchez Garcia, J. (2016). Service quality in bank during an economic crisis. *International Journal of Bank Marketing*, *34*(2), 235–259. doi:10.1108/IJBM-01-2015-0013

Monsuwe, T. P., Dellaert, G. C., & Ruyter, K. D. (2004). What drives consumers to shop online? A literature review. *International Journal of Service Industry Management*, *15*(1), 102–121.

Montoya-Weiss, M. M., Voss, G. B., & Grewal, D. (2003). Determinants of online channel use and overall satisfaction with a relational, multichannel service provider. *Journal of the Academy of Marketing Science*, *31*(4), 448–458.

Moro, S., Cortez, P., & Rita, P. (2018). A divide-and-conquer strategy using feature relevance and expert knowledge for enhancing a data mining approach to bank telemarketing. *Expert Systems: International Journal of Knowledge Engineering and Neural Networks*, *35*(3), e12253. doi:10.1111/exsy.12253

Morris, M., Schindehutte, M., & Allen, J. (2005). The entrepreneur's business model: Toward a unified perspective. *Journal of Business Research*, *58*(6), 726–735. doi:10.1016/j.jbusres.2003.11.001

Morrison, A. J., & King, B. E. (2002). Small tourism businesses and e-commerce: Victorian tourism online. *Tourism and Hospitality Research*, *4*(2), 104–115.

Morrison, C., & Siegel, D. (1997). External capital factors and ıncreasing returns in USA manufacturing. *The Review of Economics and Statistics*, *79*(4), 647–654. doi:10.1162/003465397557051

Mostafa, M. M. (2013). More than words: Social networks' text mining for consumer brand sentiments. *Expert Systems with Applications*, *40*(10), 4241–4251. doi:10.1016/j.eswa.2013.01.019

Moustafa, M. (2011). *Evaluating the Potential of Mobile Technology in Tourism Destination Marketing.* (Doctoral dissertation, Cardiff Metropolitan University, UK).

MSG. (2019). *The 7 P's of Services Marketing*. Management Study Guide. Retrieved from https://www.managementstudyguide.com/seven-p-of-services-marketing.htmadresindenalındı

Mucuk, İ. (2012). *Pazarlama ilkeleri. 19. Basım.* İstanbul, Turkey: Türkmen.

Munoz-Leiva, F., Climent-Climent, S., & Liébana-Cabanillas, F. (2017). Determinants of intention to use the mobile banking apps: An extension of the classic TAM model. *Spanish Journal of Marketing-ESIC, 21*(1), 25-38.

Murray, K. B., & Schlacter, J. L. (1990). The impact of services versus goods on consumers' assessment of perceived risk and variability. *Journal of the Academy of Marketing Science*, *18*(1), 51–65.

Nemat, R. (2011). Taking a look at different types of e-commerce. *World Applied Programming*, *1*(2), 100–104.

Neuman, B. C., & Medvinsky, G. (1995). Requirements for Network Payment: Tthe Netcheque Perspective, *Proceedings of IEEE COMPCON'*95. 10.1109/CMPCON.1995.512360

Ngai, E. W., & Wat, F. K. T. (2002). A literature review and classification of electronic commerce research. *Information & Management*, *39*(5), 415–429. doi:10.1016/S0378-7206(01)00107-0

Nikolopoulos, K., Georgopoulos, N., & Karagiannopoulos, G. D. (2005). Fathoming Porter's five forces model in the Internet era. *Info, 7*(6), 66-76. doi:10.1108/14636690510628328

Nilsson, E. G. (2009). Design patterns for user interface for mobile applications. *Advances in Engineering Software*, *40*(12), 1318–1328. doi:10.1016/j.advengsoft.2009.01.017

Nilsson, J. (1999). Co-operative organisational models as reflections of the business environments. *The Finnish Journal of Business Economics*, *4*(99), 449–470.

Nivlouei, F. B. (2014). Electronic Human Resource Management System: The Main Element in Capacitating Globalization Paradigm. *International Journal of Business and Social Science*, *5*(2), 147–159.

Noulas, A., Salnikov, V., Hristova, D., Mascolo, C., & Lambiotte, R. (2018, October). Developing and deploying a taxi price comparison mobile app in the wild: Insights and challenges. In *2018 IEEE 5th International Conference on Data Science and Advanced Analytics (DSAA)* (pp. 424-433). IEEE.

O'Connor, P. (1999). *Electronics information distribution in tourism and hospitality*. Oxford, UK: CAB International.

O'Connor, P., & Frew, A. J. (2002). The future of hotel electronic distribution: Expert and industry perspectives. *The Cornell Hotel and Restaurant Administration Quarterly*, *43*(3), 33–45. doi:10.1016/S0010-8804(02)80016-7

O'Sullivan, D., Wilson, D., & Smyth, B. (2002, September). Improving case-based recommendation. In *Proceedings of European Conference on Case-Based Reasoning*, 278-291. 10.1007/3-540-46119-1_21

Obaidullah, M. (2015). Enhancing food security with Islamic microfinance: Insights from some recent experiments. *Agricultural Finance Review*, *75*(2), 142–168. doi:10.1108/AFR-11-2014-0033

Odabaşı, Y. (2014). *Post Modern Pazarlama Tüketim ve Tüketici*. İstanbul, Turkey: Mediacat Kitapları.

OECD. (2006). *Online Payment Systems for E-commerce*, OECD Digital Economy Papers, No:117.

OECD. (2019, Feb. 28). High-speed fibre makes up one quarter of fixed Internet in OECD countries. *OECD Broadband Statistics*. Retrieved from http://www.oecd.org/Internet/broadband-statistics-update.htm

Offutt, B. (2013). Travel Distribution 2018: A Look Ahead. *PhoCusWright's Analysis*. Retrieved from https://www.ithotelero.com/wp-content/uploads/2014/01/Analysis_TravelDistribution2018.pdf

Öğe, S. (2004). *Elektronik İnsan Kaynakları Yönetimi (E-HRM)'nde İnsan Kaynakları Enformasyon Sistemi (HRIS)'nin Önemi ve Temel Kullanım Alanları. 3* (pp. 109–117). Ulusal Bilgi, Ekonomi ve Yönetim Kongresi.

Ohsato, S., & Takahashi, M. (2015). Management efficiency in Japanese regional banks: A network DEA. *Procedia: Social and Behavioral Sciences*, *172*, 511–518. doi:10.1016/j.sbspro.2015.01.394

Okrent, M. D., & Vokurka, R. J. (2004). Process mapping in successful ERP implementations. *Industrial Management & Data Systems*, *104*(8), 637–643.

Olivas-Lujan, M. R., Ramirez, J., & Zapata-Cantu, L. (2007). e-HRM in Mexico: Adapting innovations for global competitiveness. *International Journal of Manpower*, *28*(5), 418–434.

Olmeda, I., & Sheldon, P. (2002). Data Mining Techniques and Applications for Tourism Internet Marketing. *Journal of Travel & Tourism Marketing*, *11*(2-3), 1–20. doi:10.1300/J073v11n02_01

Omran, K., & Anan, N. (2018). Studying the impact of using E-HRM on the effectiveness of HRM practices: An exploratory study for the internet service providers (ISP) in Egypt. *International Journal of Academic Research in Business and Social Sciences*, *8*(4), 458–492.

Onetti, A., Zucchella, A., Jones, M. V., & McDougall-Covin, P. P. (2012). Internationalization, innovation and entrepreneurship: Business models for new technology-based firms. *The Journal of Management and Governance*, *16*(3), 337–368. doi:10.100710997-010-9154-1

Öney, E., Öksüzoğlu, G. G., & Rizvi, W. H. (2017). The Determinants of Electronic Payment Systems Usage From Consumers' perspective. *Economic Research Journal*, *30*(1), 394–415.

Ong, K. S., Nguyen, B., & Syed Alwi, S. F. (2017). Consumer-based virtual brand personality (CBVBP), customer satisfaction and brand loyalty in the online banking industry. *International Journal of Bank Marketing*, *35*(3), 370–390. doi:10.1108/IJBM-04-2016-0054

Osterwalder, A., & Pigneur, Y. (2002). An eBusiness model ontology for modeling eBusiness. BLED 2002 Proceedings, 2.

Osterwalder, A., & Pigneur, Y. (2002). *An e-Business Model Ontology for Modeling e-Business.* In *Proceedings of the 15th BLED Electronic Commerce Conference e-Reality: Constructing the e-Economy,* Slovenia.

Osterwalder, A., Pigneur, Y., & Tucci, C. L. (2005). Clarifying business models: Origins, present, and future of the concept. *Communications of the Association for Information Systems, 16*(1), 1.

Ouma, S. (2016). From financialization to operations of capital: Historicizing and disentangling the finance–farmland-nexus. *Geoforum, 72,* 82–93. doi:10.1016/j.geoforum.2016.02.003

Oum, T. H., & Zhang, A. (2001). Key aspects of global strategic alliances and the impacts on the future of Canadian airline industry. *Journal of Air Transport Management, 7,* 287–301.

Ovans, A. (2015). What is a business model? *Harvard Business Review,* 1–7.

Ozatac, N., Saner, T., & Sen, Z. S. (2016). Customer satisfaction in the banking sector: The case of North Cyprus. *Procedia Economics and Finance, 39,* 870–878. doi:10.1016/S2212-5671(16)30247-7

Özbay, S., & Akyazı, S. (2004). Elektronik ticaret: e-ticaret.

Özcan, S. O. (2010). Internet pazarlama faaliyetlerinde tüketici satin alma karar süreci. *IUYD, 1*(2), 30–39.

Özdemir, Ö., & Taşkın, Ç. (2017). *Online itkisel satin alma davranişi: PLS-SEM ile bir model önerisi.* Bursa, Malaysia: Dora Basım Yayın.

Özgüven, N. (2013). *Mobil Pazarlama ve Mobil Reklam Tüketicilerin Mobil Reklamcılığa Karşı Tutumlarının Analizi.* İstanbul, Turkey: Babil Yayınları.

Özmen, Ş. (2013). *Ağ Ekonomisinde Yeni Ticaret Yolu – E-Ticaret.* İstanbul Bilgi Üniversitesi Yayınları.

Özsağır, A. (2014). *Yenilik ekonomisi.* Seçkin Yayıncılık.

Paranjape-Voditel, P., & Deshpande, U. (2013). A stock market portfolio recommender system based on association rule mining. *Applied Soft Computing, 13*(2), 1055–1063. doi:10.1016/j.asoc.2012.09.012

Parasuraman, A., Zeithaml, V. A., & Berry, L. L. (1988). Servqual: A multiple-item scale for measuring consumer perc. *Journal of Retailing, 64*(1), 12.

Park, C. H., & Kim, Y. G. (2003). Consumer purchase behavior in an online shopping context. *International Journal of Retail & Distribution Management, 31*(1), 16–29.

Park, H. P., & Ungson, G. R. (1997). The effect of national culture, organizational complementarities, and economic motivation on joint venture dissolution. *Academy of Management Journal, 40*(2), 279–307.

Parry, E. (2011). An examination of e-HRM as a means to increase the value of the HR function. *International Journal of Human Resource Management, 22*(5), 1146–1162.

Parry, E., & Tyson, S. (2011). Desired goals and actual outcomes of e-HRM. *Human Resource Management Journal, 21*(3), 335–354.

Pateli, A. (2003). A framework for understanding and analysing ebusiness models. *BLED 2003 Proceedings,* 4.

Paul, J., Mittal, A., & Srivastav, G. (2016). Impact of service quality on customer satisfaction in private and public sector banks. *International Journal of Bank Marketing, 34*(5), 606–622. doi:10.1108/IJBM-03-2015-0030

Pavic, S., Koh, S., Simpson, M., & Padmore, J. (2007). Could e-business create a competitive advantage in UK SMEs? Benchmarking. *International Journal (Toronto, Ont.)*, *14*(3), 320–351.

Pavitt, D. (1997). Retailing and the super high street: The future of the electronic home shopping industry. *International Journal of Retail & Distribution Management*, *25*(1), 38–43. doi:10.1108/09590559710156099

Payne, A., & Frow, P. (2005). A strategic framework for customer relationship management. *Journal of Marketing*, *69*(4), 167–176. doi:10.1509/jmkg.2005.69.4.167

Pedroni, P. (1999). Critical values for cointegration tests in heterogeneous panels with multiple regressors. *Oxford Bulletin of Economics and Statistics*, *61*(S1), 653–678. doi:10.1111/1468-0084.61.s1.14

Pedroni, P. (2004). Panel cointegration: Asymptotic and finite sample properties of pooled time series tests with an application to the ppp hypothesis. *Econometric Theory*, (20), 597–625.

Pender, L. (1999). *Marketing Management for Travel and Tourism*. Cheltenham, UK: Stanley Thornes.

Perry, P., Martai, B., & Stefano, P. (2013). Translating the need for touch to online fashion shopping via digital technology. *Proceedings of The First International Conference on Digital Technologies for the Textile Industries the University of Manchester*, 8.

Persson, A., & Stirna, J. (2001, June). Why enterprise modelling? an explorative study into current practice. In *International Conference on Advanced Information Systems Engineering* (pp. 465-468). Berlin, Germany: Springer. 10.1007/3-540-45341-5_31

Petre, A., Osoian, C., & Zaharie, M. (2016). Applicants' perceptions on online recruitment. *Managerial Challenges of the Contemporary Society*, *9*(1), 63–67.

Petrovic, O., Kittl, C., & Rappa, M. (2001). Managing the digital enterprise - Business models on the Web. North Carolina State University.

Pfeifer, P. E., & Carraway, R. L. (2000). Modeling Customer Relationships as Markov Chains. *Journal of Interactive Marketing*, *14*(2), 43–55. doi:10.1002/(SICI)1520-6653(200021)14:2<43::AID-DIR4>3.0.CO;2-H

Phan, D. D. (2003). E-business development for competitive advantages: A case study. *Information & Management*, *40*(6), 581–590. doi:10.1016/S0378-7206(02)00089-7

Philips, P. (2003). E-Business Strategy. New York, NY: McGraw Hill Education.

Pigneur, Y. (1996). A Framework for designing new information systems. In F. Bodart (Ed.), *Future of Information Systems – Challenge and Pitfalls* (pp. 61–102).

Pillai, K. (2010). Seven Ps Spectrum of Marketing in Tourism. *Indian Journal of Tourism & Hospitality Management*, *1*(2), 84–97.

Pınarbaşı, F., & Canbolat, Z. N. (2018). Evaluation of augmented reality mobile applications in turkey market: a data mining approach to consumer reviews. *Changing organizations,* 187.

Pinarbasi, F., & Türkyılmaz, C. A. (2017). Retro Marka Deneyiminin Yeniden Satın Alma Niyeti & Marka Bağlılığı Yaratmadaki Rolü. *International Journal of Research in Business and Social Science* (2147-4478), 6(2), 13-25.

Platanou, K., Mäkelä, K., Beletskiy, A., & Colicev, A. (2018). Using online data and network-based text analysis in HRM research. *Journal of Organizational Effectiveness: People and Performance*, *5*(1), 81–97.

Plutchik, R. (1980). *Emotion: A Psycho-evolutionary synthesis*. New York, NY: Harper and Row Publishing.

Pokharel, K. P., Regmi, M., Featherstone, A. M., & Archer, D. W. (2019). Examining the financial performance of agricultural cooperatives in the USA. *Agricultural Finance Review*, *79*(2), 271–282. doi:10.1108/AFR-11-2017-0103

Poorani, A. A., & Smith, D. R. (1995). Financial characteristics of bed and breakfast inns. *The Cornell Hotel and Restaurant Administration Quarterly*, *36*(5), 57–63.

Porter, M. E. (2002). Strateji ve İnternet. Stratejide İlerlemeler (11-59). İstanbul, Turkey: MESS Yayınları.

Porter, M. E. (2017, Oct. 3). *What Is Strategy?* Retrieved from https://hbr.org/1996/11/what-is-strategy

Porter, M. E., & Porter, M. (1985). Competitive Advantage: Creating and Sustaining Superior Performance. New York, NY: Free Press.

Porter, Q. (2005). Internet and Competitive advantage: an empirical study of UK retail banking sector (Doctoral dissertation, University of Warwick).

Porter, M. (2001). Strategy and the Internet. *Harvard Business Review*, *79*(3), 62–79. PMID:11246925

Porter, M. E. (1985). *Competitive Advantage: Creating and Sustaining Superior Performance*. New York, NY: The Free Press.

Porter, M. E. (2001). *Michael; ilustraciones Gibbs*. Strategy and the Internet.

Porter, M. E. (2008). *Competative Strategy. Çev. Gülen Ulubilgen*. İstanbul, Turkey: Sistem Yayıncılık.

Porth, L., & Tan, K. S. (2016). Introduction–2014 International Agricultural Risk, Finance, and Insurance Conference (IARFIC). *Agricultural Finance Review*, *76*(1). doi:10.1108/AFR-05-2016-0049

Power, G. J. (2016). Quantitative finance for agricultural commodities: Discussion and extension. *Agricultural Finance Review*, *76*(1), 27–41. doi:10.1108/AFR-02-2016-0013

Pradella, L. (2015). The working poor in Western Europe: Labour, poverty and global capitalism. *Comparative European Politics*, *13*(5), 596–613. doi:10.1057/cep.2015.17

Premchand, A., & Choudhry, A. (2015). Future of Payments – *E-Payments,* International Journal of Emerging Technology and Advanced Engineering, Website: www.ijetae.com (ISSN 2250-2459, ISO 9001:2008 Certified Journal, Volume 5, Issue 1, January 2015)

Priluck, R. (2001). The impact of Priceline. com on the grocery industry. *International Journal of Retail & Distribution Management*, *29*(3), 127–134. doi:10.1108/09590550110385883

Professional Academy. (2019). *MARKETING THEORIES – THE MARKETING MIX – FROM 4 PS TO 7 PS*. Retrieved from https://www.professionalacademy.com/blogs-and-advice/marketing-theories---the-marketing-mix---from-4-p-s-to-7-p-sadresindenalındı

Pui-Mun, L. (2002). Behavioral Model of Online Purchasers in E-Commerce Environment. *Electronic Commerce Research*, *2*(1-2), 75–86.

Qi, T., & Sun, R. (2017, July). An empirical study on the contribution of agricultural policy finance to agricultural economic growth in China. In *2017 3rd International Conference on Economics, Social Science, Arts, Education and Management Engineering (ESSAEME 2017)*. Atlantis Press. 10.2991/essaeme-17.2017.22

Qin, J., Liu, X., & Pedrycz, W. (2017). An extended TODIM multi-criteria group decision making method for green supplier selection in interval type-2 fuzzy environment. *European Journal of Operational Research*, *258*(2), 626–638. doi:10.1016/j.ejor.2016.09.059

Qin, Z. (2009). *Introduction to E-Commerce*. Springer.

Raghuwanshi, S., Pateria, R. K., & Singh, R. P. (2009). *A New Protocol Model for Verification of Payment Order Information Integrity in Online E-Payment System. World Congress on Nature & Biologically Inspired Computing, NABIC 2009*, 1665–1668. 10.1109/NABIC.2009.5393641

Rahman, S., Hussain, A., & Taqi, M. (2014). Impact of agricultural credit on agricultural productivity in Pakistan: An empirical analysis. *International Journal of Advanced Research in Management and Social Sciences*, *3*(4), 125–139.

Rajalakshmi, R., & Gomathi, S. (2016). A review on E-HRM: Electronic human resource management. *Indian Journal of Research*, *5*(8).

Ramanathan, R. (2010). E-commerce success criteria: Determining which criteria count most. *Electronic Commerce Research*, *10*(2), 191–208.

Ramezen, M., Nazari, Y., & Ahmadi, M. M. (2013). The effect of electronic human resources management on quality of services provided by human resources in the insurance industry (case study: Iran Insurance Company in Khorramabad City). *Journal of Social Issues & Humanities*, *1*(7), 223–232.

Rangaswamy, A., & Gupta, S. (1999). Innovation adoption and diffusion in the digital environment: Some research opportunities. *E-business Research Center Working Paper*, 02(1999), Penn State.

Rao, S., & Frazer, L. (2006). Australian franchisor websites: Moving towards network behaviour. *Journal of Theoretical and Applied Electronic Commerce Research*, *1*(1).

Rappa, M. (2003). Business models on the web. *Managing the Digital Enterprise website*. Available at http://digital-enterprise. org

Ray, A. (2017). *What are the different types of e-commerce payment systems?* https://services.amazon.in/resources/seller-blog/different-types-of-e-commerce-payment-systems.html

Read, R. J. (1989). *EFTPOS: Electronic Funds Transfer At Point Of Sale, Electronics & Communications Engineering Journal, I, 6* (pp. 17–25). Retrieved From; https://ieeexplore. ieee.org/ document/105349

Reichheld, F. F., & Schefter, P. (2000). E-loyalty: Your secret weapon on the web. *Harvard Business Review*, *78*(4), 105–113.

Rekabetdernegi (n.d.). Retrieved from http://www.rekabetdernegi.org/rekabethakkinda.htm

Řepková, I. (2015). Banking efficiency determinants in the Czech banking sector. *Procedia Economics and Finance*, *23*, 191–196. doi:10.1016/S2212-5671(15)00367-6

ReportW. P. (2018). Retrieved From https://worldpaymentsreport.com/wp-content/uploads/sites/5/2018/10/World-Payments-Report-2018.pdf

Rezaei, J., Kothadiya, O., Tavasszy, L., & Kroesen, M. (2018). Quality assessment of airline baggage handling systems using SERVQUAL and BWM. *Tourism Management*, *66*, 85–93. doi:10.1016/j.tourman.2017.11.009

Riahi, G. (2015). E-learning systems based on cloud computing: A review. *Procedia Computer Science*, *62*, 352–359.

Richins, M. L. (1997). Measuring emotions in the consumption experience. *The Journal of Consumer Research*, *24*, 127–146.

Riggins, F. J. (1999). A framework for identifying web-based electronic commerce opportunities. *Journal of Organizational Computing and Electronic Commerce*, *9*(4), 297–310.

Robson, L. S., Clarke, J. A., Cullen, K., Bielecky, A., Severin, C., Bigelow, P. L., ... Mahood, Q. (2007). The effectiveness of occupational health and safety management system interventions: A systematic review. *Safety Science*, *45*(3), 329–353. doi:10.1016/j.ssci.2006.07.003

Rodríguez, W. (2008). E-Business Method: A Cyclical-Model for Internet Commerce Development. *Journal of Internet Commerce*, *2*(3), 87–98. doi:10.1300/J179v02n03_07

Rogers, D. (2016). The Digital Transformation Playbook. New York, NY: Columbia University Press. doi:10.7312/roge17544

Rogers, J., Bennett, C., & Grewal, S. (2007). E-commerce for successful franchisors. *Franchising World*, *39*(8), 23.

Ron, D., & Shamir, A. (2013). *Quantitative Analysis of the Full Bitcoin Transaction Graph, in Financial Cryptography and Data Security*, 17th International, FC 2013,(Ahmad-Reza Sageghi ed., 2013), Retrieved From https://eprint.iacr.org/2012/584.pdf

Rothwell, W. J., Jackson, R. D., Knight, S., & Lindholm, J. (2005). *Career Planning and Succession Management: Developing Your Organization's Talent-for Today and Tomorrow*. Westport, CT: Greenwood Publishing Group.

Rowley, J. (2002). *E-business: Principles and practice*. Basingstoke, UK: Palgrave.

Rowley, J. (2007). The wisdom hierarchy: Representations of the DIKW hierarchy. *Journal of Information Science*, *33*(2), 163–180. doi:10.1177/0165551506070706

Ruël, H., Magalhães, R., & Chiemeke, C. C. (2011). Human Resource Information Systems: An Integrated Research Agenda. In Electronic HRM in Theory and Practice (pp. 21–39). Binkley, UK: Emerald Group Publishing Limited. doi:10.1108/S1877-6361(2011)0000008006

Ruel, H. J., Bondarouk, T. V., & Van der Velde, M. (2007). The contribution of e-HRM to HRM effectiveness. *Employee Relations*, *29*(3), 280–291. doi:10.1108/01425450710741757

Ruel, H. J., Bondarouk, T. V., & Van der Velde, M. (2007). The contribution of e-HRM to HRM effectiveness: Results from a quantitative study in a Dutch Ministry. *Employee Relations*, *29*(3), 280–291.

Ruël, H., Bondarouk, T., & Looise, J. K. (2004). E-HRM: Innovation or irritation. An explorative empirical study in five large companies on web-based HRM. *Management Review*, 364–380.

Ruël, H., Bondarouk, T., & Looise, J. K. (2004). E-HRM: Innovation or Irritation. *Management Review*, *15*(3), 364–381.

Ruël, H., & van der Kaap, H. (2012). E-HRM Usage and Value Creation: Does a Facilitating Context Matter? *Zeitschrift für Personalforschung*, *26*(3), 260–281.

Ruiz-Mercader, J., Merono-Cerdan, A., & Sabater-Sanchez, R. (2006). Information technology and learning: Their relationship and impact on organizational performance in small businesses. *International Journal of Information Management*, *26*(1), 16–29.

Russell, G. J., & Petersen, A. (2000). Analysis of cross category dependence in market basket selection. *Journal of Retailing*, *76*(3), 367–392. doi:10.1016/S0022-4359(00)00030-0

Rust, R. T., & Kannan, P. K. (2003). E-service: A new paradigm for business in the electronic environment. *Communications of the ACM*, *46*(6), 36–42.

Ryan, C. (2017). Gendering Palestinian dispossession: Evaluating land loss in the West bank. *Antipode*, *49*(2), 477–498. doi:10.1111/anti.12280

Rygielski, C., Wang, J. C., & Yen, D. C. (2002). Data mining techniques for customer relationship management. *Technology in society*, *24*(4), 483–502. doi:10.1016/S0160-791X(02)00038-6

Saarijärvi, H., Karjaluoto, H., & Kuusela, H. (2013). Customer relationship management: The evolving role of customer data. *Marketing Intelligence & Planning*, *31*(6), 584–600. doi:10.1108/MIP-05-2012-0055

Sadegh, T., Kohansal, M. A., & Haghshenas, M. (2016). E-HRM: From acceptance to value cretion. *Journal of Information Technology Management*, *27*(1), 18–27.

Sadowski, B. M., Maitland, C., & van Dongen, J. (2002). Strategic use of the Internet by small-and medium-sized companies: An exploratory study. *Information Economics and Policy*, *14*(1), 75–93. doi:10.1016/S0167-6245(01)00054-3

Sahar, S. (2009). Interestingness measures on determining what is interesting. In *Data mining and knowledge discovery handbook* (pp. 603–612). Boston, MA: Springer. doi:10.1007/978-0-387-09823-4_30

Şahbaz, U., Sökmen, A., & Aytaç, A. Türkiye' de E-İhracat: Fırsatlar ve Sorunlar, *Tepav,* 2014, Retrieved From https://www.tepav.org.tr/upload/files/haber/1415973180-5.Turkiyede _E_Ihracat _ Firsatlar_ve_Sorunlar.pdf

Sakarya Pehlivan, A. (2017, Feb. 28). *Getir tüm dünyada başarı hikayesi olacak*. Retrieved from https://www.ekonomist.com.tr/girisim-kobi/getir-tum-dunyada-basari-hikayesi-olacak.html

Salehan, M., & Kim, D. J. (2016). Predicting the performance of online consumer reviews: A sentiment mining approach to big data analytics. *Decision Support Systems*, *81*, 30–40. doi:10.1016/j.dss.2015.10.006

Salur, N. (2018, March 1). Talks2018: Nazım Salur. (A. E. Tamer, Interviewer)

Sánchez, D., Vila, M. A., Cerda, L., & Serrano, J. M. (2009). Association rules applied to credit card fraud detection. *Expert Systems with Applications*, *36*(2), 3630–3640. doi:10.1016/j.eswa.2008.02.001

Saqib, L., Zafar, M. A., Khan, K., Roberts, K. W., & Zafar, A. M. (2015). Local agricultural financing and Islamic banks: Is Qard-al-Hassan a possible solution? *Journal of Islamic Accounting and Business Research*, *6*(1), 122–147. doi:10.1108/JIABR-04-2012-0018

Sarkar, M. B., Butler, B., & Steinfield, C. (1995). Intermediaries and cybermediaries: A continuing role for mediating players in the electronic marketplace. *Journal of Computer-Mediated Communication*, *1*(3), 1–14.

Saxena, R. (2008). *Marketing Management* (3rd ed.). New York. NY: Tata McGraw-Hill.

Saygılı, Z. (2019, Jan. 22). Mobil Perakendecilik: Getir Uygulaması. (İ. Eken, & B. Gezmen, Interviewers)

Schafer, J. B., Konstan, J., & Riedl, J. (1999). Recommender systems in e-commerce. In *Proceedings of the 1st ACM conference on Electronic Commerce*, 158-166.

Schalk, R., Timmerman, V., & Van den Heuvel, S. (2013). How strategic considerations influence decision making on e-HRM applications. *Human Resource Management Review*, *23*(1), 84–92.

Schank, R. C. (2002). Designing world-class e-learning: How IBM, GE, Harvard Business School, and Columbia University are succeeding at e-learning.

Schaumann, P. (2004). *The Guide to Successful Destination Management*. Hoboken, NJ: John Wiley & Sons.

Schein, A. I., Popescul, A., Ungar, L. H., & Pennock, D. M. (2002). Methods and metrics for cold-start recommendations. In *Proceedings of the 25th annual international ACM SIGIR conference on Research and development in information retrieval*, 253-260.

Schibrowsky, J. A., Peltier, J. W., & Nill, A. (2007). The state of internet marketing research: A review of the literature and future research directions. *European Journal of Marketing*, *41*(7/8), 722–733. doi:10.1108/03090560710752366

Sebastianelli, R., Tamimi, N., & Rajan, M. (2008). Perceived quality of online shopping: Does gender make a difference? *Journal of Internet Commerce*, *7*(4), 445–469.

Seema, A., & Sujatha, S. (2013). Conceptual work on career management strategies from an organization perspective. *International Journal of Management, IT and Engineering*, *3*(7), 184.

Severini, S., Tantari, A., & Di Tommaso, G. (2017). Effect of agricultural policy on income and revenue risks in Italian farms: Implications for the use of risk management policies. *Agricultural Finance Review*, *77*(2), 295–311. doi:10.1108/AFR-07-2016-0067

Seviçin, A. (2006). Kaynaklara Dayalı Rekabet Stratejisi Geliştirme. Dumlupınar Üniversitesi Sosyal Bilimler Dergisi, (15).

Sezgin, A. G. (2013). Dünyada ve Türkiye de E-ticaret Sektörü. Türkiye İş bankası İktisadi Araştırmalar Bölümü.

Shafer, S. M., Smith, H. J., & Linder, J. C. (2005). The power of business models. *Business Horizons*, *48*(3), 199–207. doi:10.1016/j.bushor.2004.10.014

Shafiai, M. H. M., & Moi, M. R. (2015). Financial problems among farmers in Malaysia: Islamic agricultural finance as a possible solution. *Asian Social Science*, *11*(4), 1.

Shahbaz, M., Shahbaz Shabbir, M., & Sabihuddin Butt, M. (2013). Effect of financial development on agricultural growth in Pakistan: New extensions from bounds test to level relationships and Granger causality tests. *International Journal of Social Economics*, *40*(8), 707–728. doi:10.1108/IJSE-01-2012-0002

Sharma, Y. K., Mangla, S. K., Patil, P. P., & Uniyal, S. (2018). Sustainable Food Supply Chain Management Implementation Using DEMATEL Approach. In *Advances in Health and Environment Safety* (pp. 115–125). Singapore: Springer. doi:10.1007/978-981-10-7122-5_13

Shen, G. C. C. (2015). Users' adoption of mobile applications: Product type and message framing's moderating effect. *Journal of Business Research*, *68*(11), 2317–2321. doi:10.1016/j.jbusres.2015.06.018

Shilton, K., & Greene, D. (2017). Linking platforms, practices, and developer ethics: Levers for privacy discourse in mobile application development. *Journal of Business Ethics*, 1–16.

Shostack, L. (1977). Breaking Free from Product Marketing. *Journal of Marketing*, *41*(2), 73–80. doi:10.1177/002224297704100219

Şimşek, M. Ş., & Öğe, H. S. (2011). İnsan Kaynakları Yönetimi, *Eğitim Akademi Yayınları*. Baskı, Yayınevi Sertifika, (14824).

Singh, A., Shukla, N., & Mishra, N. (2018). Social media data analytics to improve supply chain management in food industries. *Transportation Research Part E, Logistics and Transportation Review*, *114*, 398–415. doi:10.1016/j.tre.2017.05.008

Singh, J. P., Irani, S., Rana, N. P., Dwivedi, Y. K., Saumya, S., & Roy, P. K. (2017). Predicting the "helpfulness" of online consumer reviews. *Journal of Business Research*, *70*, 346–355. doi:10.1016/j.jbusres.2016.08.008

Sirakaya, E., & Woodside, A. (2005). Building and testing theories of decision making by travellers. *Tourism Management*, *26*(6), 815–832. doi:10.1016/j.tourman.2004.05.004

Smith, K. T. (2011). Consumer perceptions regarding e-commerce and related risks, B>Quest, 1-20.

Snell, N. (1994). Virtual HR: Meeting New World Realities. *Compensation and Benefits Review*, *26*(12), 35–37. doi:10.1177/088636879402600606

Sola, H. B., Fernandez, J., Hagras, H., Herrera, F., Pagola, M., & Barrenechea, E. (2015). Interval type-2 fuzzy sets are generalization of interval-valued fuzzy sets: Toward a wider view on their relationship. *IEEE Transactions on Fuzzy Systems*, *23*(5), 1876–1882. doi:10.1109/TFUZZ.2014.2362149

Solomon, M., Bamossy, G., Askegaard, S., & Hogg, M. K. (2006). *Consumer behavior a European perspective*. UK: Prentice Hall.

Sparks, B. A., & Browning, V. (2011). The impact of online reviews on hotel booking intentions and perception of trust. *Tourism Management*, *32*(6), 1310–1323. doi:10.1016/j.tourman.2010.12.011

Spathis, C., & Constantinides, S. (2003). The usefulness of ERP systems for effective management. *Industrial Management & Data Systems*, *103*(9), 677–685.

Srinivasan, S. S., Anderson, R., & Ponnavolu, K. (2002). Customer loyalty in e-commerce: An exploration of its antecedents and consequences. *Journal of Retailing*, *78*(1), 41–50. doi:10.1016/S0022-4359(01)00065-3

Stafford, E. R. (1994). Using co-cooperative strategies to make alliances work. *Long Range Planning*, *27*(3), 69–70.

Standing, C., McManus, P., Standing, S., & Karjaluoto, H. (2007). Searching for value in researching the adoption and use of m-services. [IJeC]. *International Journal of e-Collaboration*, *3*(3), 16–30. doi:10.4018/jec.2007070102

StartupMarketBlog. (2018, Oct. 2). *Nazım Salur ile Girişimciliği ve Girişimlerinin Hikayesini Konuştuk*. Retrieved from https://blog.startupmarket.co/2018/10/02/nazim-salur-ile-girisimciligi-ve-girisimlerinin-hikayesini-konustuk/

Statistics Directorate, O. E. C. D. (n.d.). Electronic Commerce. Retrieved from https://stats.oecd.org/glossary/detail.asp?ID=4721

Stayman, D. M., & Aaker, D. A. (1988). Are all the effects of ad-induced feelings mediated by ad*? The Journal of Consumer Research*, *15*, 368–373.

Stayman, D. M., & Batra, R. (1991). Encoding and retrieval of ad affect in memory. *Journal of Marketing Research*, *28*, 232–239.

Steemit. (2018). *Bitcoin: E-Ticaret İçin 2 Saniyede Kripto Ödeme Çözümü*. Retrieved From https://steemit.com/ethereum/@ioseta/bitcoinus-e-ticaret-icin-2-saniyede-kripto-oedeme-coezuemue

Stefano, N. M., Casarotto Filho, N., Barichello, R., & Sohn, A. P. (2015). A fuzzy SERVQUAL based method for evaluated of service quality in the hotel industry. *Procedia CIRP*, *30*, 433–438. doi:10.1016/j.procir.2015.02.140

Stein, H., Maganga, F. P., Odgaard, R., Askew, K., & Cunningham, S. (2016). The formal divide: Customary rights and the allocation of credit to agriculture in Tanzania. *The Journal of Development Studies*, *52*(9), 1306–1319. doi:10.1080/00220388.2016.1146701

Stephen, A. T. (2016). The role of digital and social media marketing in consumer behavior. *Current Opinion in Psychology*, *10*, 17–21. doi:10.1016/j.copsyc.2015.10.016

Stewart, A. (2002). A Model of Web Use in Direct and Online Marketing Strategy. *Electronic Markets*, *12*(4), 262–269. doi:10.1080/101967802762553521

Stiles, J. (2001). Strategic alliances. In H. Volberda, & T. Elfi-ing (Eds.), *Rethinking strategy*. London, UK: Sage.

Stone, D. L., & Dulebohn, J. H. (2013). Emerging issues in theory and research on electronic human resource management (eHRM).

Stone, D. L., Stone-Romero, E. F., & Lukaszewski, K. (2003). The functional and dysfunctional consequences of human resource information technology for organizations and their employees. In Advances in human performance and cognitive engineering research (pp. 37–68). Binkley, UK: Emerald Group Publishing Limited.

Storey, V. C., & Song, I. Y. (2017). Big data technologies and management: What conceptual modeling can do. *Data & Knowledge Engineering*, *108*, 50–67. doi:10.1016/j.datak.2017.01.001

Strohmeier, S., & Piazza, F. (2011). "Web Mining" as a Novel Approaching e-HRM Research. In Electronic HRM in Theory and Practice (pp. 41–53). Binkley, UK: Emerald Group Publishing Limited. doi:10.1108/S1877-6361(2011)0000008007

Strohmeier, S. (2007). Research in e-HRM: Review and Implications. *Human Resource Management Review*, *17*(1), 19–37. doi:10.1016/j.hrmr.2006.11.002

Strohmeier, S., & Kabst, R. (2009). Organizational adoption of e-HRM in Europe: An empirical explanation of major adoption factors. *Journal of Managerial Psychology*, *24*(6), 482.

Suberg, W. (2018). South Korea E-Commerce Giant to Add 12 Cryptocurrencies With Bithumb, Cointelligence Research & Analysis For The Crypto Economy. Retrieved from https://www.cointelligence.com/content/south-korea-e-commerce-giant-add-12-cryptocurrencies-bithumb/

Sumanjeet, S. (2009). Emergence of Payment Systems in The Age of Electronic Commerce: The State of Art. *Global Journal of International Business Research*, *2*(2), 17–36.

Sumathi, S., & Sivanandam, S. D. (2006). *Introduction to Data Mining and its Applications*. Berlin, Germany: Springer-Verlag. doi:10.1007/978-3-540-34351-6

Su, Z., Guo, H., & Sun, W. (2017). Exploration and firm performance: The moderating impact of competitive strategy. *British Journal of Management*, *28*(3), 357–371.

Swaroop, K. R. (2012). E-HRM and how it will reduce the Cost in Organization. *Asia Pacific Journal of Marketing & Management Review*, *1*(4), 133–139.

Swift.com. (n.d.). Retrieved from https://www.swift.com/about-us/highlights-2017

Sylva, H., & Mol, S. T. (2009). E-Recruitment: A study into applicant perceptions of an online application system. *International Journal of Selection and Assessment*, *17*(3), 311–323. doi:10.1111/j.1468-2389.2009.00473.x

Sylvester, E. O., Bamidele, A. D., & Oluyemi, O. S. (2015). Implementing E-HRM System in Developing Countries: Challenges and Prospects. *International Journal of Applied Information Systems*, *9*(8), 38–41. doi:10.5120/ijais2015451452

Tajbakhsh, A., Rahmati, M., & Mirzaei, A. (2009). Intrusion detection using fuzzy association rules. *Applied Soft Computing*, *9*(2), 462–469. doi:10.1016/j.asoc.2008.06.001

Tan, Z., & Ouyang, W. (2002). Global and national factors affecting e-commerce diffusion in China.

Tanner, J. F. Jr, Ahearne, M., Leigh, T. W., Mason, C. H., & Moncrief, W. C. (2005). CRM in sales-intensive organizations: A review and future directions. *Journal of Personal Selling & Sales Management*, *25*(2), 169–180.

Tapscott, D. (2000). Digital capital: Harnessing the power of business webs. Brighton, MA: Harvard Business School Press.

Tapscott, D., Ticoll D., & Lowy, A. (1999). The rise of the business web. *Business 2.0,* November, 198-208.

Tatoğlu, F. Y. (2013). *İleri panel veri analizi: stata uygulamalı*. İstanbul, Turkey: Beta Yayıncılık.

Taylor, R. K. (2000). Marketing strategies: Gaining a competitive advantage through the use of emotion. *Competitiveness Review*, *10*(2), 146–152.

Tek, Ö. B. (1999). *Pazarlama İlkeleri Global Yönetimsel Yaklaşım Türkiye Uygulamaları*. İzmir, Turkey: Beta.

Tek, O. B., & Orel, F. D. (2008). *Perakende Pazarlama Yönetimi*. İzmir, Turkey: Birleşik Matbaacılık.

Tek, Ö. B., & Özgül, E. (2005). *Modern pazarlama ilkeleri*. İzmir, Turkey: Birleşik Matbaacılık.

Teksten, R. (2001). Developing Business Models for eBusiness. *Proceedings of the International Conference on Electronic Commerce*.

Teo, T. S. H., Lim, G. S., & Fedric, S. A. (2007). The adoption and diffusion of human resources information systems in Singapore. *Asia Pacific Journal of Human Resources*, *45*, 44–62.

Terzi, N. (2011). The impact of e-commerce on international trade and employment. *Procedia: Social and Behavioral Sciences*, *24*, 745–753. doi:10.1016/j.sbspro.2011.09.010

Tetteh, V. A. (2017). *Marketing Decision - Making*. Salem Basın Ansiklopedisi.

The Marketing Mix. (2019). *Marketing Mix Definition of the 4P's and 7P's*. Retrieved from https://marketingmix.co.uk/ adresindenalındı

Thite, M., & Kavanagh, M., & Johnson, R. D. (2009). Evolution of human resource management and human resource information systems: the role of information technology. In *M*. Thite, M. Kavanagh, & R. D. Johnson (Eds.), *Evolution of human resource management and human resource information systems*.

Thomas, D. (2018). *Managing online communications and feedback relating to the Welsh visitor attraction experience: apathy and inflexibility in tourism marketing practice?* (Doctor of Philosophy dissertation, University of Wales Trinity Saint David, UK).

Thota, C., Manogaran, G., Lopez, D., & Vijayakumar, V. (2017). Big data security framework for distributed cloud data centers. In Cybersecurity breaches and issues surrounding online threat protection (pp. 288–310). Hershey, PA: IGI Global. doi:10.4018/978-1-5225-1941-6.ch012

Tiago, M. T. P. M. B., & Veríssimo, J. M. C. (2014). Digital marketing and social media: Why bother? *Business Horizons*, *57*(6), 703–708. doi:10.1016/j.bushor.2014.07.002

Tian, Y., & Stewart, C. (2008). History of e-commerce. In A. Becker (Ed.), Electronic Commerce: Concepts, Methodologies, Tools, and Applications: Concepts, Methodologies, Tools, and Applications. Hershey, PA: IGI Global. doi:10.4018/978-1-59904-943-4.ch001

Timmers, P. (1998). Business models for electronic markets. *Electronic Markets*, *8*(2), 3–8. doi:10.1080/10196789800000016

Tinnila, M. (2002). Service processes in electronic travel services: A summary. *Information Technology & Tourism*, *4*, 203–214.

Toh, R., Raven, P., & DeKay, F. (2011). Satış odaları: Oteller vs. üçüncü taraf web siteleri. *Cornell Hospitality Üç Aylık*, *52*(2), 181–189. doi:10.1177/1938965511400409

Toivonen, H., Klemettinen, M., Ronkainen, P., Hätönen, K., & Mannila, H. (1995). Pruning and grouping discovered association rules. In *Workshop Notes of ECML Workshop on Statistics, Machine Learning, and Knowledge Discovery in Databases*, 47-52.

Torlak, O. (2018, Sept. 6). *2018 Türkiye Geneli Vakıf Üniversiteleri Lisans - Önlisans Doluluk Yerleşme ve Bursluluk Oranları*. Retrieved from https://univerlist.com/blog/2018-turkiye-geneli-vakif-universiteleri-lisans-onlisans-doluluk-yerlesme-ve-bursluluk-oranlari/

Trice, M. B. (2001). Managing Internet Issues Within the Franchise System: A Legal Perspective. *Franchising World, 33*(5), 37–38.

Tronvoll, B. (2010). Negative emotions and their effect on customer complaint behavior. *Journal of Service Management, 22*, 111–134.

Troshani, I., Jerram, C., & Rao, S. (2011). Exploring the Public Sector Adoption of HRIS. *Industrial Management & Data Systems, 111*(3), 470–488. doi:10.1108/02635571111118314

Trusov, M., Bucklin, R., & Pauwels, K. (2009). Effect of Word-of-Mouth Versus Traditional Marketing: Findings from an Internal Social Networking Site. *Journal of Marketing, 73*(5), 90–102. doi:10.1509/jmkg.73.5.90

Tsai, C. F., & Lu, Y. H. (2009). Customer churn prediction by hybrid neural networks. *Expert Systems with Applications, 36*(10), 12547–12553. doi:10.1016/j.eswa.2009.05.032

Tsai, S. B. (2018). Using the DEMATEL model to explore the job satisfaction of research and development professionals in China's photovoltaic cell industry. *Renewable & Sustainable Energy Reviews, 81*, 62–68. doi:10.1016/j.rser.2017.07.014

Tse, A. C. B. (2003). Disintermediation of travel agents in the hotel industry. *Journal of Hospitality Management, 22*(4), 453–460.

Tsiakis, T., & Sthephanides, G. (2005). The Concept of Security and Trust in Electronic Payments. *Computers & Security, 24*(1), 10–15. doi:10.1016/j.cose.2004.11.001

Tsiptsis, K. K., & Chorianopoulos, A. (2009). *Data mining techniques in CRM: Inside Customer Segmentation*. Hoboken, NJ: John Wiley & Sons.

TÜBİSAD. Deloitte, Etid, *Türkiye'de E-Ticaret 2017 Pazar Büyüklüğü,* Mayıs 2018, Retrieved From http://www.tubisad.org.tr/tr/images/pdf/tubisad_2018_e-ticaret_sunum_tr.pdf https://www2. deloitte. com/content/dam/Deloitte/tr/Documents/technology-media-telecommunications/turkiyede-2017-e-ticaret-pazar-buyuklugu.pdf

Tunay, N., Yüksel, S., & Tunay, K. B. (2019). The Effects of Technology on Bank Performance in Advanced and Emerging Economies: An Empirical Analysis. In Handbook of Research on Managerial Thinking in Global Business Economics (pp. 263–280). Hershey, PA: IGI Global. doi:10.4018/978-1-5225-7180-3.ch015

Tunçer, P. (2012). Değişen İnsan Kaynakları Yönetimi Anlayışında Kariyer Yönetimi. *Ondokuz Mayıs Üniversitesi Eğitim Fakültesi Dergisi, 31*(1).

Turban, E., Whiteside, J., King, D., & Outland, J. (2018). *Electronic Commerce 2018, A Managerial and Social Networks Perspective*. Springer. doi:10.1007/978-3-319-58715-8

Turvey, C. G. (2017). Historical developments in agricultural finance and the genesis of America's farm credit system. *Agricultural Finance Review, 77*(1), 4–21. doi:10.1108/AFR-09-2016-0076

TÜSİAD. (2014). *Dijital Pazarın Odak Noktası E-Ticaret: Dünyada ve Türkiye' nin Yeri, Mevcut Durum ve Geleceğe Yönelik Adımlar*, Yayın No: TÜSİAD-T/2014-06/553, İstanbul, Retrieved From https://tusiad.org/tr/yayinlar/raporlar/item/7891-dijital-pazarin-odak-noktasi-e-ticaret-dunyada-turkiyenin-yeri-mevcut-durum-ve-gelecege-yonelik-adimlar-raporu

TÜSİAD. (2017). *Dijitalleşen Dünyada Ekonominin İtici Gücü: E-Ticaret,* Yayın No: TÜSİAD-T/2017, 04-587, İstanbul, Retrieved From https://tusiad.org/tr/yayinlar/raporlar/item/9675-dijitallesen-dunyanin-itici-gucu-e-ticaret

TÜSİAD. (2017). *Dijitalleşen Dünyada Ekonominin İtici Gücü: E-Ticaret.* 04-587.

Twentyfy. (2018). Kripto Para Birimleri Algı & Güven Araştırması Türkiye'nin Sanal Cüzdanı, 2018, Retrieved From https://www.twentify.com/hubfs/Turkish_Reports/Twentify_Kripto-Para-Arastirmasi.pdf?hsCtaTracking=9c0%20cee2f-c64d-4d79-80cf-ce5a46cf46c3%7Ca4dbb8fe-29ab-4c7a-b1be-1536d9de794e

Twentyfy. (2018). *Türkiye'de E-ticaret: Çevrimiçi Alışverişte Tüketici Davranışları Araştırması ve Marka Karşılaştırması,* Retrieved From https://www.twentify.com/tr/raporlar/turkiyede-e-ticaret-cevrimici-alisveriste-tuketici-davranislari-arastirmasi-ve-marka-karsilastirmasi

Ülgen, H., & Mirze, S. K. (2010). *İşletmelerde Stratejik Yönetim (5. Baskı).* İstanbul, Turkey: Beta Basım Yayım Dağıtım.

Ulrich, D. (1996). Human resource champions: The next agenda for adding value and delivering results. Brighton, MA: Harvard Business Press.

Ulrich, D. (1998). A New Mandate For Human Resources. *Harvard Business Review, 76*(1), 128. PMID:10176915

Ulrich, D. L. (1990). *Organizational Capability: Competing From the Inside/Out* (pp. 78–94). New York, NY: John Wiley & Sons.

Ulugay, O. (2001). *Küreselleşme Korkusu.* İstanbul, Turkey: Timaş Yayınları.

UNWTO. (2019). *Understanding Tourism: Basic Glossary.* United Nations World Tourism Organization. Retrieved from http://cf.cdn.unwto.org/sites/all/files/docpdf/glossaryenrev.pdfadresindenalındı

UNWTO. (CTC). (2019). *Definitions Committee on Tourism and Competitiveness (CTC).* Available at http://cf.cdn.unwto.org/sites/all/files/pdf/unwto_tourism_definitions.pdfadresindenalındı

Urban, G. L., Sultan, F., & Qualls, W. J. (2000). Placing trust at the center of your Internet strategy. *Sloan Management Review, 42*(1), 39–48.

Ussahawanitchakit, P., & Intakhan, P. (2011). Internet strategy of e-commerce business in Thailand. *International Journal of Business Strategy, 11*(1), 1–15.

Üzün, C. (2000). *Stratejik Yönetim ve Halkla İlişkiler.* İzmir, Turkey: Eylül Yayınları.

Van Der Merwe, M. C. (2003). *Marketing communication methods used by tour operators in Guateng.* (Research Dissertation, University of South Africa, South Africa).

Van der Vorst, J. G., Van Dongen, S., Nouguier, S., & Hilhorst, R. (2002). E-business initiatives in food supply chains; definition and typology of electronic business models. *International Journal of Logistics, 5*(2), 119–138. doi:10.1080/13675560210148641

van Eijsden, G. A. I. (2000). *Banking in the Digital Economy* (Doctoral dissertation, Technical University Eindhoven, The Netherlands).

Van Hooft, F. P., & Stegwee, R. A. (2001). E-business strategy: How to benefit from a hype. *Logistics Information Management, 14*(1/2), 44–54.

Varfan, M. (2008). *Traditional Marketing vs. Internet Marketing A comparison.* (Bachelor thesis, Mälardalen University, Sweden).

Venkatesan, R., & Kumar, V. (2004). A customer lifetime value framework for customer selection and resource allocation strategy. *Journal of Marketing*, *68*(4), 106–125. doi:10.1509/jmkg.68.4.106.42728

Venkatraman, N., & Henderson, J. C. (1998). Real strategies for virtual organizing. *Sloan Management Review*, *40*(1), 33–49.

Venterink, J. H. (2017). *Practical Future Developments in e-HRM, HR SSC's and Employee Involvement.* (Master thesis, University of Twente).

Verkasalo, H., López-Nicolás, C., Molina-Castillo, F. J., & Bouwman, H. (2010). Analysis of users and non-users of smartphone applications. *Telematics and Informatics*, *27*(3), 242–255. doi:10.1016/j.tele.2009.11.001

Videla-Cavieres, I. F., & Rios, S. A. (2014). Extending market basket analysis with graph mining techniques: A real case. *Expert Systems with Applications*, *41*(4), 1928–1936. doi:10.1016/j.eswa.2013.08.088

Virilio, P. (2003). *Enformasyon Bombası.* İstanbul, Turkey: Metis Yayınları.

Vitiello, D., Grisso, J. A., Whiteside, K. L., & Fischman, R. (2015). From commodity surplus to food justice: Food banks and local agriculture in the United States. *Agriculture and Human Values*, *32*(3), 419–430. doi:10.100710460-014-9563-x

Voermans, M., & van Veldhoven, M. J. P. M. (2007). Attitude towards E-HRM: An empirical study at Philips. *Personnel Review*, *36*(6), 887–902.

Vural, Z., & Bat, M. (2010). Yeni bir iletişim ortamı olarak sosyal medya: Ege üniversitesi iletişim fakültesine yönelik bir araştırma. *Journal of Yaşar University*, *20*(5), 3348–3382.

Wade, M. R., & Nevo, S. (2005). Development and validation of a perceptual instrument to measure e-commerce performance. *International Journal of Electronic Commerce*, *10*(2), 123–146. doi:10.2753/JEC1086-4415100205

Wahyudi, E., & Park, S. M. (2014). Unveiling the value creation process of electronic human resource management: An indonesian case. *Public Personnel Management*, *43*(1), 83–117. doi:10.1177/0091026013517555

Wang, Y., Hahn, C., & Sutrave, K. (2016, February). Mobile payment security, threats, and challenges. In *2016 second international conference on mobile and secure services (MobiSecServ)* (pp. 1-5). IEEE. 10.1109/MOBISECSERV.2016.7440226

Wang, F., Head, M., & Archer, N. (2002). E-Tailing: An Analysis Of Web İmpacts On The Retail Market. *The Journal of Business Strategy*, *19*(1), 73.

Wang, F., Quach, T. T., Wheeler, J., Aimone, J. B., & James, C. D. (2018). Sparse Coding for N-Gram Feature Extraction and Training for File Fragment Classification. *IEEE Transactions on Information Forensics and Security*, *13*(10), 2553–2562. doi:10.1109/TIFS.2018.2823697

Wang, K. W., Zhou, S., Yang, Q., & Yeung, J. M. S. (2005). Mining customer value: From association rules to direct marketing. *Data Mining and Knowledge Discovery*, *11*(1), 57–79. doi:10.100710618-005-1355-x

Wang, W. M., Li, Z., Tian, Z. G., Wang, J. W., & Cheng, M. N. (2018). Extracting and summarizing affective features and responses from online product descriptions and reviews: A Kansei text mining approach. *Engineering Applications of Artificial Intelligence*, *73*, 149–162. doi:10.1016/j.engappai.2018.05.005

Weber, R.H. (2007). IT Markets, Asia's Chance for Revitalizing the WTO, 37 Hong Kong L. J. 185.

WEF. (2018). *Addressing E-Payment Challenges in Global E-Commerce, White Paper,* Retrieved From http://www3.weforum.org/docs/WEF_Addressing_E-Payment_Challenges_in_Global_E- Commerce _clean.pdf

Welsh, E. T., Wanberg, C. R., Brown, K. G., & Simmering, M. J. (2003). E-learning: Emerging uses, empirical results and future directions. *International Journal of Training and Development*, *7*(4), 245–258.

Wen, X. (2010). An E-Payment System Based on Quantum Group Signature. *Physica Scripta*, *82*(6), 065403. doi:10.1088/0031-8949/82/06/065403

Werthner, H., & Ricci, F. (2004). E-commerce and Tourism. *Communications of the ACM December, 47(12).*

Westbrook, R. A. (1987). Product-consumption-based affective responses and post purchase process. *Journal of Marketing Research*, *24*, 258–270.

White, C., & Yu, Y. T. (2005). Satisfaction emotions and consumer behavioral intentions. *Journal of Services Marketing*, *19*(6), 411–420.

Wigand, R. T. (1997). *Electronic commerce: definition, theory, and context. The Information Society. v13, n1.* January-March.

Wikipedia. (2019). *Subscription business model.* Retrieved from https://en.wikipedia.org/wiki/Subscription_business_modeladresindenalındı

Williams, A. P., & Palmer, A. J. (1999). Tourism destination brands and electronic commerce: Towards synergy. *Journal of Vacation Marketing*, *5*(3), 263–275. doi:10.1177/135676679900500306

Wirtz, B. W., Schilke, O., & Ullrich, S. (2010). Strategic development of business models: Implications of the Web 2.0 for creating value on the Internet. *Long Range Planning*, *43*(2-3), 272–290. doi:10.1016/j.lrp.2010.01.005

Wise, R., & Morrison, D. (2000). Beyond the exchange--the future of B2B. *Harvard Business Review*, *78*(6), 86–96. PMID:11184979

Wolfinbarger, M., & Gilly, M. C. (2003). eTailQ: Dimensionalizing, measuring and predicting etail quality. *Journal of Retailing*, *79*(3), 183–198. doi:10.1016/S0022-4359(03)00034-4

Wong, P. K. (2003). Global and national factors affecting e-commerce diffusion in Singapore. *The Information Society*, *19*(1), 19–32. doi:10.1080/01972240309471

Woodard, J. (2016). Big data and Ag-Analytics: An open source, open data platform for agricultural & environmental finance, insurance, and risk. *Agricultural Finance Review*, *76*(1), 15–26. doi:10.1108/AFR-03-2016-0018

Wood, C. M., Alford, B. L., Jackson, R. W., & Gilley, O. W. (2005). Can retailers get higher prices for "end-of-life" inventory through online auctions? *Journal of Retailing*, *81*(3), 181–190. doi:10.1016/j.jretai.2005.07.001

Worzala, E. M., McCarthy, A. M., Dixon, T., & Marston, A. (2002). E-commerce and retail property in the UK and USA. *Journal of Property Investment & Finance*, *20*(2), 142–158. doi:10.1108/14635780210420034

WTO. (n.d.) Retrieved from https://www.wto.org/english/rese/bookspe/ecombrochuree.pdf

Wu, Y. (2014). The ımpact of ınternet consumption on China's economic development.

Wu, T., Liu, X., & Liu, F. (2018). An interval type-2 fuzzy TOPSIS model for large scale group decision making problems with social network information. *Information Sciences*, *432*, 392–410. doi:10.1016/j.ins.2017.12.006

Wymer, S. A., & Regan, E. A. (2005). Factors influencing e-commerce adoption and use by small and medium businesses. *Electronic Markets*, *15*(4), 438–453. doi:10.1080/10196780500303151

Xie, F. T., & Johnston, W. J. (2004). Strategic alliances: Incorporating the impact of e-business technological innovations. *Journal of Business and Industrial Marketing, 19*(3), 208–222.

Yahuza, B. S. (2019). Viability of Muzara'ah Contract on Agro-financing in Alleviating Rural Poverty in Kano State, Nigeria. *Al-Muzara'ah, 6*(2), 91–102. doi:10.29244/jam.6.2.91-102

Yang, W. (2017). Analysis On Online Payment Systems of E-Commerce. *Bachelor's Thesis, Business Information Technology Oulu University of Applied Sciences*, Retrieved From https://www.theseus.fi/bitstream/handle/10024/139600/Yang_Wenjing.pdf?sequence=1&isAllowed=y

Yazıcı, S. (2004). *E-Öğrenme: İnsan Kaynakları Eğitiminde Stratejik Dönüşüm*. İstanbul, Turkey: Alfa Basım.

Ye, H., Hu, X., & Xie, M. (2019, February). Research on Supply Chain Finance Model based on Agricultural Logistics Park Information Platform. In *2018 International Symposium on Social Science and Management Innovation (SSMI 2018)*. Atlantis Press. 10.2991smi-18.2019.40

Yelkur, R., & Nêveda DaCosta, M. M. (2001). Differential pricing and segmentation on the Internet: The case of hotels. *Management Decision, 39*(4), 252–262. doi:10.1108/00251740110391411

Ye, Q., Law, R., & Gu, B. (2009). The impact of online user reviews on hotel room sales. *International Journal of Hospitality Management, 28*(1), 180–182. doi:10.1016/j.ijhm.2008.06.011

Ye, Q., Zhang, Z., & Law, R. (2009). Sentiment classification of online reviews to travel destinations by supervised machine learning approaches. *Expert Systems with Applications, 36*(3), 6527–6535. doi:10.1016/j.eswa.2008.07.035

Yeşil, A. (2008). E-Ticaret İnternet Ortamında Ticaret. İstanbul, Turkey: Kum Saati Yayın Dağıtım LTD. ŞTİ.

Yeşil, A. (2008). *E-ticaret-internet ortamında ticaret*. İstanbul, Turkey: Kum Saati Yayınları.

Yılmaz, Y., & Bititci, U. (2006). Performance measurement in tourism: A value chain model. *International Journal of Contemporary Hospitality Management, 18*(4), 341–349. doi:10.1108/09596110610665348

Yin, X., & Han, J. (2003). CPAR: Classification based on predictive association rules. In *Proceedings of the International SIAM Conference on Data Mining*, 331-335 10.1137/1.9781611972733.40

Yoganathan, D., Jebarajakirthy, C., & Thaichon, P. (2015). The influence of relationship marketing orientation on brand equity in banks. *Journal of Retailing and Consumer Services, 26*, 14–22. doi:10.1016/j.jretconser.2015.05.006

Yoon, C. (2010). Antecedents of customer satisfaction with online banking in China: The effects of experience. *Computers in Human Behavior, 26*(6), 1296–1304. doi:10.1016/j.chb.2010.04.001

Young, J. A., Clark, P. W., & McIntyre, F. S. (2006). The web as an e-commerce medium: An exploratory study of consumer perceptions in a restaurant setting. *Journal of Marketing Channels, 14*(1-2), 5–22. doi:10.1300/J049v14n01_02

Yrjola, H. (2001). Physical distribution considerations for electronic grocery shopping. *International Journal of Physical Distribution & Logistics Management, 31*(10), 746–761.

Yu, C. S. (2005). Causes influencing the effectiveness of the post-implementation ERP system. *Industrial Management & Data Systems, 105*(1), 115–132.

Yüce, A., Deniz, A., & Gödekmerdan, L. (2012). Tüketicilerin Mobil Pazarlama Faaliyetlerini Benimsemesi: Üniversite Öğrencileri Üzerine Bir Araştırma. *Süleyman Demirel Üniversitesi İktisadi ve İdari Bilimler Fakültesi Dergisi*, 183-184.

Yüksel, S., Dinçer, H., & Emir, Ş. (2017). Comparing the performance of Turkish deposit banks by using DEMATEL, Grey Relational Analysis (GRA) and MOORA approaches. *World Journal of Applied Economics*, *3*(2), 26–47. doi:10.22440/wjae.3.2.2

Yüksel, S., Dinçer, H., & Meral, Y. (2019). Financial Analysis of International Energy Trade: A Strategic Outlook for EU-15. *Energies*, *12*(3), 431. doi:10.3390/en12030431

Yumuşak, İ. G. (2001). Elektronik ticaretin gelişmekte olan ülkelere etkileri ve türkiye üzerine bir değerlendirme. (*Çevrimiçi http://128.118, 178.*)

Yunus, M., Moingeon, B., & Lehmann-Ortega, L. (2010). Building social business models: Lessons from the Grameen experience. *Long Range Planning*, *43*(2-3), 308–325.

Yu, X., Guo, S., Guo, J., & Huang, X. (2011). An extended support vector machine forecasting framework for customer churn in e-commerce. *Expert Systems with Applications*, *38*(3), 1425–1430. doi:10.1016/j.eswa.2010.07.049

Zahra, S. A., & George, G. (2002). The net-enabled business innovation cycle and the evolution of dynamic capabilities. *Information Systems Research*, *13*(2), 147–150.

Zainab, B., Awais Bhatti, M., & Alshagawi, M. (2017). Factors affecting e-training adoption: An examination of perceived cost, computer self-efficacy and the technology acceptance model. *Behaviour & Information Technology*, *36*(12), 1261–1273.

Zakariah, M. R., Zakariah, S., & Pyeman, J. (2016). IPA vs. SERVQUAL: Service quality measurement for higher education industry. In *Proceedings of the 1st AAGBS International Conference on Business Management 2014 (AiCoBM 2014)* (pp. 139-150). Singapore: Springer. 10.1007/978-981-287-426-9_12

Zerenler, M. (2013). *Dijital İş Yaşamı: Tüm Boyutlarıyla Elektronik Ticaret*. Ankara: Gazi Kitapevi.

Zhang, G., & Gai, J. (2005, August). Strategic choice for being e-business. In *Proceedings of the 7th international conference on Electronic commerce* (pp. 184-187). ACM.

Zhang, Z., Ye, Q., Law, R., & Li, Y. (2010). The impact of e-word-of-mouth on the online popularity of restaurants: A comparison of consumer reviews and editor reviews. *International Journal of Hospitality Management*, *29*(4), 694–700. doi:10.1016/j.ijhm.2010.02.002

Zhao, F. (2004). Management of information technology and business process re-engineering: A case study. *Industrial Management & Data Systems*, *104*(8), 674–680.

Zhuang, Y., & Lederer, A. L. (2003). An instrument for measuring the business benefits of e-commerce retailing. *International Journal of Electronic Commerce*, *7*(3), 65–99. doi:10.1080/10864415.2003.11044274

Zhu, K., & Kraemer, K. L. (2002). E-commerce metrics for net-enhanced organizations: Assessing the value of e-commerce to firm performance in the manufacturing sector. *Information Systems Research*, *13*(3), 275–295. doi:10.1287/isre.13.3.275.82

Zimmermann, H. D. (2000) Understanding the Digital Economy: Challenges for new Business Models. In: *Proceedings of the 2000 Americas Conference on Information Systems*. 10.2139srn.2566095

Zott, C., Amit, R., & Massa, L. (2010). The business model: Theoretical roots, recent developments, and future research. *IESE business school-University of Navarra*, 1-43.

Zott, C., Amit, R., & Massa, L. (2011). The business model: Recent developments and future research. *Journal of Management, 37*(4), 1019–1042. doi:10.1177/0149206311406265

Zrener, C. (2015). *Ausarbeitung eines Marketingkonzeptes für Radissimo Radreisen mit regionalem Schwerpunkt in Hinblick auf Kommunikations- und Distributions politik.* (Faculty of Media, Bachelor Thesis).

Zwass, V. (1996). Electronic commerce: Structure and issues. *International Journal of Electronic Commerce, 1*(1), 3–23.

Zwass, V. (2003). Electronic commerce and organizational innovation: Aspects and opportunities. *International Journal of Electronic Commerce, 7*(3), 7–37. doi:10.1080/10864415.2003.11044273

About the Contributors

Yurdagül Meral is currently working as Department Head of International Trade and Finance Department of Istanbul Medipol University and as Part Time in Boğaziçi University, International Trade Department. She has completed her PhD on 'Bank Mergers' and her master degree on 'Outsourcing' in Istanbul University. Prior to starting her career as an Assistant Professor at Medipol University, she pursued a 30 year career in the field of international trade finance (including 2,5 years in Frankfurt) in banking sector. She has started as management trainee in Interbank after having her Associate Degree from Boğaziçi University in Business Management. She worked as Vice President in International Trade and Finance Operations in Koçbank and Şekerbank covering import-export management, including letter of credits, counter guarantees, import, export, payments, SWIFT, credits, exim loans and has completed related system entegration projects of international trade. She is a documentary credit specialist, a CDCS (Certificate of Documentary Credit) certificate holder (http://cdcs.libf.ac.uk/). Married with two children.

* * *

Zafer Adıgüzel earned a Management and Organization Phd Degree at Gebze Technical University, a Business Administration Master Degree at Istanbul University, an MBA Degree at Cardiff Metropolitan University, and a Business Administration Bachelor Degree at Kocaeli University.

Habib Mehmet Akpınar is a Research Assistant at Istanbul Esenyurt University.

Rana Atabay Kuscu is an Associate Professor in Business School at Istanbul Medipol University where she has been a faculty member since 2015. She has been the Vocational School of Social Sciences' Director since 2016. Rana completed her Ph.D at Marmara University and her undergraduate studies also there. Her research areas are international trade and economic integrations. She started her academic career at Istanbul Commerce University in 2002. Rana is married and has three daughters.

Bersu Bahtiyar is serving as a lecturer in the Department of Economics at Bulent Ecevit University. She graduated from Ankara University. She completed PHD from Bulent Ecevit University. She has taught economics and politics, economic policy, and macroeconomics at Bulent Ecevit University. She has also published articles and papers on various economic issues, especially macroeconomics, energy economics, and social capital.

Ümit Bozoklu has been working in Istanbul Gedik University as a lecturer since 2012.

Yasemin Cicekcisoy, PhD., has been working at Halic University as a lecturer since 2008, and also currently works as an education consultant at OY Consultancy firm, Istanbul.

Dilaysu Cinar was born in 1986 in Bursa, Turkey. In 2008, she graduated from Muğla Sıtkı Koçman University, Faculty of Economics and Administrative Sciences, Department of Business Administration. Simultaneously, she also completed the Public Administration Department with the Double Major Program. In 2011, she received her master's degree from the Department of MBA at Dokuz Eylül University. In 2017, she completed her Ph.D. in Business Administration Program at Yıldız Technical University. Since 2012, Cinar has been working as an academician at Beykent University.

Ihsan Eken was born in 1986 in Istanbul. He studied Visual Communication Design at Istanbul Commerce University. Later on, he received his master's degree in Advertising and Brand Management at Bahcesehir University. He received his doctorate degree with his thesis on "Accessible Communication for Everyone, Mobile Accessibility of Visually Impaired Users: Analysis of Mobile Applications With Usability Approach" in Istanbul Commerce University Media and Communication Program. He is currently working as an assistant professor at Istanbul Medipol University Communication Faculty. He is Media and Visual Arts Program Vice Head of Department. He has won awards in national and international festivals. His work has been published in national and international scientific publications.

Başak Gezmen was born in 1978 in Izmir. She received her master's degree in Journalism at Marmara University. She received her doctorate degree with her thesis on "Technological developments in Journalism in Turkey" in Marmara University Journalism Program. She is working as an assistant professor at Istanbul Medipol University Communication Faculty. She has published in national and international scientific publications.

İnanç Kabasakal graduated from the Department of Computer Engineering of Bilkent University in 2001. He was involved in various projects as developer, team manager, and software development consultant from 2001 to 2012. He received his MBA degree (2009) from Hacettepe University, and PhD. degree (2017) in Department of Business Administration at Ege University. His research areas include Data Mining, Management Information Systems, Quantitative Methods in decision making, and Analytical CRM.

Asuman Koç Yurtkur is serving as a lecturer in the Department of Economics at Bulent Ecevit University. She graduated from Gazi University in 2002. In 2005, she completed her master's from Bulent Ecevit University. She received her PhD About the Authors 11 from İstanbul University in 2012. Since 2013, she has taught economics, monetary theory and politics, economic policy, and microeconomics at Bulent Ecevit University. She has also published articles and papers on various economic issues, especially macroeconomics, energy economics, and economics schools.

Fatih Pinarbasi is a Research Assistant at Istanbul Medipol University.

Nurten Polat Dede is working as an Assistant Professor in the field of Human Resource Management at the University of Medipol, Business School. She earned her PhD from İstanbul University, Faculty of Business Administration, Institute of Social Sciences, Human Resource Management, Istanbul University, 2007. She had her MBA, from İstanbul University, Institute of Social Sciences of Organizational Behavior, 2000. She earned her bachelor degree from İstanbul University, Faculty of Business Administration (English Programme), 1996. Her main research interests are how can line managers and HR managers collaborate to design and implement efficient HR systems, policies, and practices to achieve high organizational performance.

Duygu Toplu Yaşlıoğlu is a research and teaching assistant of management and organisation at Istanbul University, School of Business. She earned her PhD at Istanbul University Institute of Social Sciences in 2016. She was a visiting scholar at Ball State University Miller College of Business in Indiana. Her current focuses are on social and digital media management. She has written articles and book chapters about digital business strategy and digital business models.

Nihan Garipağaoğlu Uğur is writing her master thesis about 'Motivation's effect on Organizational Commitment' at İstanbul Medeniyet University, Tourism Management Department. She earned her BA from Anadolu University in Hospitality Management, and her Associate Degree from Bilkent University (in English) and Aydın University, Tourism Management Department. She has 22 years of tourism experience including working in front office, fast food (in London), cabin crew, Limousine and car rental services, travel agent, airline ticket sales, special tours, ingoing and outgoing tours. Research Areas include: Tourism, Bitcoin-Blockchain, Rental Services, Airline Ticketing, Motivation, Organizational Commitment.

Serhat Yüksel is Associate Professor of finance in İstanbul Medipol University. He previously worked as a senior internal auditor for seven years in Finansbank, Istanbul-Turkey and one year in Konya Food and Agriculture University as an assistant professor. Dr. Yüksel has a BS in Business Administration (in English) from Yeditepe University (2006) with full scholarship. He earned his master degree in economics at Boğaziçi University (2008). He also has a PhD in Banking from Marmara University (2015). His research interests are in banking, finance, and financial crisis. He has more than 70 publications (books, book chapters, scientific articles, etc.).

Index

Premier Reference Source
Emerging GIS Applications for Emergency and Disaster Management

Premier Reference Source
Managerial Strategies and Green Solutions for Project Sustainability

Premier Reference Source
Comparative Approaches to Using R and Python for Statistical Data Analysis

Premier Reference Source
Solutions for High-Touch Communications in a High-Tech World

www.ingramcontent.com/pod-product-compliance
Lightning Source LLC
LaVergne TN
LVHW062117300926
849161LV00010B/2479
* 9 7 8 1 7 9 9 8 0 0 3 5 4 *